Inside Excel 5
for Windows

Bruce Hallberg
with
Terry Carr
Michael Groh
Forrest Houlette
Tony Keller
Alan Neibauer
Mike Nemeth
Anne Poirson

NRP
NEW RIDERS PUBLISHING

New Riders Publishing, Indianapolis, Indiana

Inside Excel 5 for Windows

By Bruce Hallberg

Published by:
New Riders Publishing
201 West 103rd Street
Indianapolis, IN 46290 USA

Printed in the United States of America   3 4 5 6 7 8 9 0

Library of Congress Cataloging-in-Publication Data

```
Inside Excel 5 for Windows / Bruce Hallberg ... [et al.].
     p.   cm.
   Includes index.
   ISBN 1-56205-218-7 : $39.95
   1. Microsoft Excel for Windows.  2. Business—Computer programs.  3.
Electronic Spreadsheets.   I. Hallberg, Bruce A. 1964-  . II. Title: Inside
Excel Five for Windows.
HF5548.4.M523I57  1993
650'.0285'5369—dc20
93-41864


CIP
```

 The text in this book is printed on recycled paper.

Publisher
Lloyd J. Short

Associate Publisher
Tim Huddleston

Acquisitions Manager
Cheri Robinson

Managing Editor
Matthew Morrill

Marketing Manager
Gregg Bushyeager

Product Director
Rob Tidrow

Production Coordinator
Lisa D. Wagner

Senior Editor
Tad Ringo

Editors
Patrice Hartmann
Peter J. Kuhns
Mary Ann Larguier
Rob Lawson
Melinda Taylor
Angie Trzepacz
Steve Weiss
Lisa Wilson
Phil Worthington

Technical Editors
Bob Greenblatt, B&L Associates,
Lambertville, NJ
Ron Holmes

Acquisitions Coordinator
Stacey Beheler

Editorial Assistant
Karen Opal

Publisher's Assistant
Melissa Lynch

Production Manager
Kelli Widdifield

Book Design
Roger Morgan

Production Team Leader
Juli Pavey

Production Team
Nick Anderson
Stephanie Davis
Rich Evers
Dennis Clay Hager
Angela Pozdol Judy
Stephanie J. McComb
Jan Noller
Rochelle Palma
Kim Scott
Alyssa Yesh

Proofreading Coordinator
Joelynn Gifford

Proofreaders
Ayrika Bryant
Jamie Milazzo
Ryan Rader
Tonya R. Simpson
S.A. Springer
Dennis Wesner

Indexers
Rebecca Mayfield
Johnna Van Hoose

Production Analyst
Mary Beth Wakefield

About the Authors

Bruce Hallberg is the Director of Information Systems for a biotechnology company located in Redwood City, California. He has been heavily involved with PCs since 1980 and has specialized in accounting and business control systems for the past seven years. He has consulted with a large number of local and national companies in a variety of areas and has expertise in networking, programming, and system implementations. He works with a wide variety of PC computer platforms, including DOS, Windows, OS/2, UNIX, and Macintosh. Mr. Hallberg is the author or contributing author of numerous books from New Riders Publishing, including *OS/2 for Non-Nerds*, *WordPerfect for Wimps*, and *Inside OS/2*.

Over the last 15 years, **Michael Groh** has worked in a wide variety of situations such as programming in C and Pascal, selling expert systems, and designing user interfaces for Windows applications. His first personal computer was an Osborne I (circa 1982) with 64K of memory and two 180K floppy drives. Mr. Groh is the author of *DOS for Non-Nerds* and a contributing author to *Inside Windows 3.1*, *Windows 3.1 End-User Programming*, and *Inside Microsoft Access*, all by New Riders Publishing. He welcomes your questions and comments at (317) 581-3724 or via CompuServe at 70031,2231.

Forrest Houlette began programming in 1977, when he took a FORTRAN class in graduate school. He entered into the world of microcomputers when he began doing educational work on Apple II computers as a writing teacher. Since that time, he has shifted to the IBM-compatible platform, mastered Windows programming, and created a writing environment for the Windows operating system. Mr. Houlette's work in artificial intelligence has won two academic awards, the Zenith Data Systems Masters of Innovation award and the Ellen Nold Award sponsored by *Computers and Composition*. Forrest is author of *Windows 3.1 on Command* from New Riders Publishing, as well as a contributing author to several other New Riders' titles.

Alan Neibauer received a Masters of Public Administration from the Wharton School, University of Pennsylvania, and a BS in Journalism from Temple University. Mr. Neibauer has done doctoral work in Vocational Education and Communication at Temple University. Alan also has held various positions such as Assistant Professor, Adjunct Instructor, Teacher and Research Assistant, and President and owner of Eastham Printing Corporation. He currently is a freelance author and consultant. Alan is listed in *Who's Who in the East* and has won the *Silver Anvil Award*.

Michael Nemeth is an independent consultant living in Colorado Springs, Colorado. Mr. Nemeth first programmed in Word BASIC with Word for Windows and has since used Word for Windows to automate many templates and documentation tasks for various companies. He was the key author of the extensive editor contained in Softronics' Universal Help, which uses Word for Windows to automate Windows help file generation. Mr. Nemeth holds a BSEE and currently is employed at a semiconductor manufacturing firm.

Ann Poirson is a Microsoft Consulting Channel Partner in Excel. She owns Computer Synergy located in Cleveland, Ohio, a firm specializing in custom software development for Windows-based computers. Anne has been developing computer software for more than twenty years for firms, including General Electric, BP America, Newport News Shipbuilding, and Johnson Rubber. She holds a BS from the University of Dayton with a major in Computer Science and graduated from General Electric's Financial Management Program.

Acknowledgments

I would like to thank all of my friends at New Riders for continuing to put out great books and for tolerating me. In particular, Lisa Wagner, Rob Tidrow, and Rich Wagner all had much input into the excellent quality we achieved with *Inside Excel 5 for Windows*.

My appreciation to all of the superlative people at Genelabs, just because they deserve it.

The coauthors for this book, who worked their butts off to meet impossible deadlines but came through with style and grace.

Becky Campbell, who put up with far more than any human being should be asked for during the writing of this book.

A special thanks to the team at Expert DesignWare of Ann Arbor, Michigan, who compiled the Visual Basic Command Reference. Using their ReWord application, they generated and reformatted the extensive command summary in one week with marvelous results.

All of the hard working people on the *Inside Excel* team, who have worked together to produce the finest book about Excel 5 on the market.

Special thanks to Melissa Lynch, Stacey Beheler, and Karen Opal for their hard work on the On-Screen Advisor, and to the Prentice Hall Computer Publishing production team for their consistently excellent work.

Trademark Acknowledgments

Lotus 1-2-3 and VisiCalc are registered trademarks of Lotus Development Corporation.

Quattro and Quattro Pro are registered trademarks of Borland International, Inc.

ReWord is a registered trademark of Expert DesignWare, Inc.

Adobe Type Manager and PostScript are registered trademarks of Adobe Syustems Incorporated.

Macintosh is a registered trademark, and TrueType is a trademark of Apple Computer, Inc.

OS/2 is a registered trademark of International Business Machines Corporation.

Warning and Disclaimer

This book is designed to provide information about the Excel for Windows computer program. Every effort has been made to make this book as complete and as accurate as possible, but no warranty or fitness is implied.

The information is provided on an "as is" basis. The authors and New Riders Publishing shall have neither liability nor responsibility to any person or entity with respect to any loss or damages arising from the information contained in this book or from the use of the disks or programs that accompany it.

Dedication

For my brothers, Brian and Brad.

Contents at a Glance

Table of Contents

Part II: Databases   361

INTRODUCTION

Welcome to Inside Excel 5 for Windows!

This book is *the* most complete guide to Excel 5 available, with extensive information about using Excel, linking Excel to other applications, and developing your own applications by using Excel. When designing this book, we surveyed the marketplace of available Excel books and designed *Inside Excel 5 for Windows* to offer what no other publisher can: the single most comprehensive source of information about Microsoft Excel. We believe we have met that goal, and that *Inside Excel 5 for Windows* is truly the only book you will never outgrow.

This book also marks a new direction for the *Inside* series from New Riders Publishing. Previously, the best-selling *Inside* series has gained acclaim as the most comprehensive line of books on computer operating systems and networks available. *Inside Excel 5 for Windows* and its sister book, *Inside Word 6 for Windows,* are the first of a new breed of application-oriented New Riders books. Many more application-based versions of the *Inside* series are in the works; you'll see them appearing in your bookstores regularly, and can count on all of them to exhibit the quality that you have come to expect from New Riders Publishing.

Microsoft Excel 5 for Windows

Excel 5 for Windows is one of the most substantial upgrades to Excel in years. Normally, each upgrade to the Excel program incorporates nice changes and enhancements, but rarely are so many impressive features incorporated at once. The most notable enhancements to Excel 5 include the following:

✔ A new *workbook metaphor,* in which all your documents—worksheets, charts, programming sheets, and so forth—are part of a workbook. Workbooks can have one page or as many pages as you need (Microsoft recommends a maximum of 255 per workbook, but more are possible).

✔ More Wizards. Excel 4 included the ChartWizard, an easy-to-use tool for creating charts in Excel. Excel 5 now includes a number of new Wizards: the *Function Wizard,* which walks you through creating complex function-based formulas; the *TextWizard,* which makes loading text files into Excel easy; and the *PivotWizard,* which is used to help you analyze complex data in a table format using drag-and-drop data-pivoting features.

✔ The *TipWizard,* which helps you learn Excel. Whenever you do something in Excel that can be done in a more efficient way, the TipWizard icon in the standard toolbar (it's the small light bulb) lights up. Click on the icon to have Excel tell you about a feature or shortcut that can save you time. The TipWizard also remembers all the tips from your entire Excel session, so you can review it prior to quitting. This feature is somewhat revolutionary in that there really has been no software in the past which has *actively* taught you how to use it better. Most programs offer Help, but Help is a passive feature that requires you to seek it. Think of the TipWizard as a small Excel angel sitting on your shoulder, helping you whenever you want.

✔ The ability to *create objects on your worksheets or charts to control Excel* and make data entry easy. You can embed option buttons, drop-down menus, spinbuttons, and other Windows interface features directly onto your worksheet and actually use them to control Excel and gather input from the user of the worksheet.

✔ *More file input filters,* including the ability to read and write Quattro Pro for DOS files.

✔ *Microsoft Query,* a new tool included with Excel that enables you to access various types of database files and import the data directly into Excel. You can even query SQL databases with Query.

✔ *Substantial improvements to the charting function.* You now have much more flexibility for your charts, and the ability to add regression trend lines to your chart, with automatic placement on the chart of the regression formula and the R-Squared value. Microsoft has also added error bars and the ability to drag and drop data from a worksheet directly onto a chart.

✔ New *auditing features* for your worksheets.

✔ *Support for Object Linking and Embedding (OLE) version 2*, which makes building compound documents easier than ever.

✔ An entirely new programming model called *Visual Basic for Applications*. Excel 5 is the first Microsoft product to incorporate this new tool. It will eventually be added to all Microsoft applications, giving you a consistent programming language across all Microsoft applications.

✔ *Redesigned menus* that use the new Microsoft standard menu structure. You also can choose to use the older Excel 4 style of menus until its convenient for you to switch.

Inside Excel 5 for Windows shows you all these new features in detail, while also providing extensive coverage of every other Excel feature, complete with examples and step-by-step instructions.

How This Book is Organized

To keep the book well organized, *Inside Excel 5 for Windows* has been divided into eight main sections, each one detailing a particular area of Excel.

Part I: Worksheets

Chapter 1, "Introducing Excel," is for you if you are completely new to Excel. In this chapter, you walk through all of the steps necessary to create a simple worksheet, format the worksheet, create a chart from the worksheet data, and then save your work. Along the way, you learn about the key parts of the Excel screen, how to manipulate Excel, and so forth. If you have used Excel before, you can skip this chapter.

Chapter 2, "Working with Worksheet Data," is devoted to working with data on worksheets. This chapter shows you all the ways to enter and manage data on an Excel worksheet. You learn about data entry techniques, addressing cells in a variety of ways, moving data around the worksheet, working with named ranges on an Excel worksheet, and using Excel's AutoFill feature.

Chapter 3, "Worksheet Formatting," shows you ways to format your worksheets in an attractive fashion. You learn to format numbers, dates, times, and text. You also learn to apply fonts, underlining and shading, cell borders, format styles, and so forth.

Chapter 4, "Printing Documents," shows you all of the tricks to printing your worksheets and charts. You learn about previewing printouts, how different fonts work with Excel, how to get the most from your printer, and more.

Chapter 5, "Working with Multiple Windows," teaches you about working with all the different ways in which Excel can work with different views of your workbooks. You learn about 3D cell references that enable you to build workbooks, linking pictures between documents, and setting up workbook templates.

Chapter 6, "Advanced Worksheet Features," explains all the more advanced features in worksheets such as embedding sound objects, outlining, auditing tools, and the new PivotWizard.

Chapter 7, "Mastering Functions," teaches you to use Excel functions, which enable you to begin to really master Excel. You learn about entering functions, using parameters, and dealing with function error messages.

Chapter 8, "Complete Guide to Excel Functions," is a reference guide to all the Excel functions. Look here for detailed information about all the Excel functions.

Chapter 9, "Mastering Excel Analytical Tools," shows you how to use the more advanced analysis features in Excel that are part of the Analysis add-in. The Analysis add-in includes more technical tools that are not part of the base Excel package. These tools include functions for engineering and statistical analysis of your data.

Part II: Databases

The second part of *Inside Excel 5 for Windows* takes a detailed look at the database features in Excel.

Chapter 10, "Excel Database Basics," explains the process of creating databases, setting up fields, entering data, and editing data.

Chapter 11, "Using Microsoft Query," teaches you how to find query data in your Excel databases, how to use Microsoft Query to access other databases, and how to set up database reports.

Part III: Charts

Part III helps you learn about creating charts and graphics. It includes a complete guide to Excel charts, an advanced charting chapter, and a chapter on using the Excel drawing tools on worksheets and charts.

Chapter 12, "Complete Guide to Charts," takes you through all of the details about creating and changing charts. You learn to use the ChartWizard and to format and rearrange your charts. Chapter 12 also includes a guide to all of the Excel charts along with notes about each type of chart and how it best is used.

Chapter 13, "Drawing and Adding Graphics to Documents," educates you on using the drawing tools in Excel to annotate your worksheets and charts. The drawing tools in Excel are even good enough to use for general drawing purposes, and might just replace a dedicated drawing program that you might use. Chapter 13 also shows you how to import drawings from other programs and then use them in various ways in Excel.

Chapter 14, "Advanced Charts for Business and Science," covers more advanced charting needs. You learn about stock charts and technical charting features such as regression trend lines and error bars. You also learn about dual Y-axis charts and about adding new data to an existing chart as well as how to deal with missing data.

Part IV: Macros

Part IV marks the beginning of the part of the book devoted to automating Excel. Whether your needs are as simple as recording simple macros or learning the underlying techniques required to build complex applications using Excel, you can find the information you want in this section.

Chapter 15, "Understanding Macros," begins by exploring simple recorded macros. It continues with macro arguments and also discusses using Excel 4 macros in Excel 5.

Chapter 16, "Using the Excel Macro Language," shows you how to write your own macros from scratch. You learn to create new macro sheets, assign your macros to shortcut keys or to the menu, design macros, and test them.

Chapter 17, "Complete Macro Language Function Reference," is a guide to all the Excel macro commands, their arguments, syntax, and examples.

Part V: Building Applications

Chapter 18, "Linking Excel with Other Applications," details using Excel in harmony with other applications and covers such topics as importing and exporting files, creating and using DDE and OLE 2.0 links, and working with those links using macro commands.

Chapter 19, "Using Excel Visual Basic," takes you through using all that you have learned in the preceding chapters to build a complete Excel application using the Visual Basic tools built into Excel. The sample application is also included on the *Inside Excel 5 for Windows* disk so that you can view and modify the source code to your liking.

Chapter 20, "Creating Custom Menus and Dialog Boxes," details building your own dialog boxes for inclusion into your applications and creating menus for your application.

Part VI: Excel Tools

Chapter 21, "Using Excel Add-Ins," instructs you in the use of the Excel add-in programs—features not considered part of the main Excel program but included with Excel. These tools include an autosave feature that regularly saves your work, a report manager for generating recurring reports, a slide show add-in that lets you create Excel-based slide shows, and an advanced Solver, which finds optimal solutions to challenging problems, which would otherwise require programming to solve.

Part VII: Appendixes

Appendix A, "Installing Excel and Included Disk," shows you how to install or remove Excel from your computer and how to install and use the On-Screen Advisor, an exclusive New Riders Publishing program that contains many handy tips on using Excel.

Appendix B, "Getting Excel Help," details your choices when seeking additional help with Excel. From the built-in tutorials to Microsoft's technical support phone numbers to a complete guide to the CompuServe support areas for Excel, turn to this appendix when you are stumped with a problem and need further help.

Appendix C, "Keyboard Shortcuts," shows you, in one convenient place, all the shortcut keys in Excel that can make you more productive.

Visual Basic for Applications Command Reference

This comprehensive reference provides you with detailed information about each of Excel 5's new Visual Basic for Applications (VBA) Commands. The alphabetical entries describe the function, show the correct syntax form, and discuss the function's required and optional parameters and arguments.

Conventions Used in This Book

To make this book more readable, a number of type conventions have been established. Table A.1 explains these conventions.

Table A.1
Inside Excel Type Conventions

Example	Description
Bold	Boldface type represents something that you actually type. An example might be as follows: Type **=(A5*100)/2.34** and press Enter.
Italic	Italic type is used to draw your attention to new terms as they are defined. Occasionally, italic type is also used for *emphasis*.
<u>F</u>ile, <u>O</u>pen	Excel makes liberal use of shortcut keys. All the shortcut keys available in Excel have been marked out with bold underline type and are printed in blue so you can easily identify them.
Key1,Key2	When you are supposed to press two keys in succession, the keys are separated by a comma, as in this example: Press Alt,Tab and then press Enter.
Key1+Key2	When you are to press two keys at the same time, the keys are separated by the plus sign. When you see this, hold down the first key and then press the second key while the first key is still held down. Then release both keys. For example, you might see something like this: Press Ctrl+Enter to create a new line.

NOTE Excel 5 for Windows is a very flexible program. Don't worry if your program does not look exactly the same on the screen as those shown in the figures. The author might have used a customized setup or rearranged some of the elements on his or her machine.

Icons

Inside Excel 5 for Windows includes a number of different icon sections to cover material that isn't part of the normal text.

A *note* is an aside that contains information—sometimes background information—about the current subject. Notes are not critical to the discussion, but often contain helpful information.

Tips contain shortcuts that can speed your use of Excel. Tips also contains practical advice to make Excel easier to use.

If the book is covering material that might be dangerous to your data or your computer, a *stop* appears. Stops warn you to be especially careful about something. Pay very close attention to them.

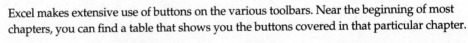

AUTHOR'S NOTE

Author's Notes generally are personal comments about the subject at hand. These notes might be witty or provide some additional information from the author's background that might be helpful for you to know.

Excel makes extensive use of buttons on the various toolbars. Near the beginning of most chapters, you can find a table that shows you the buttons covered in that particular chapter.

If you are an experienced Excel user and are mostly interested in reading about what's new to Excel 5, look for this icon. It usually points out places where new features are discussed.

Discussion that relates to exercises or files you can find on the *Inside Excel 5 for Windows* disk usually is noted by this icon. You can learn Excel more quickly by seeing the actual file or performing the exercise as it is discussed.

Publisher's Note

The staff of New Riders Publishing is committed to bringing you the very best in computer reference material. Each New Riders book is the result of months of hard work by the authors and staff, who research and refine the information contained within its covers.

As part of this commitment to you, New Riders invites your input. Please let us know if you enjoy this book, if you have trouble with the examples presented, or if you have a suggestion for the next edition.

If you have a comment or question about any New Riders book, please write to NRP at the following address. We will respond to as many readers as we can. Your name, address, or phone number will never become a part of a mailing list or be used for any purpose other than to help us continue to bring you the best books possible.

> New Riders Publishing
> Attn: Associate Publisher
> 201 West 103rd Street
> Indianapolis, Indiana 46290
>
> Fax: (317) 581-4670

New Riders also welcomes your electronic mail. You can reach us on CompuServe at {70031,2231}.

Please note that the New Riders staff cannot serve as a technical resource for Excel or Excel-related questions, including hardware- or software-related problems. Refer to the documentation that accompanies your hardware or software package for help with specific problems.

Author's Note

A lot of people—authors, developers, editors, technical editors, proofreaders, and production people—have worked very hard to bring *Inside Excel 5 for Windows* to you. I am extremely excited about the book and the impact it will have on the Excel community. If, however, you have any problems or suggestions about the book, I would love to hear from you directly, and would love to incorporate your comments into the next edition. Write to me in care of New Riders Publishing at the address given previously, or e-mail me directly on CompuServe at {76376,515}.

Enjoy the book!

Bruce Hallberg

Part I

Worksheets

Chapter Snapshot

In this chapter, you learn the basics of working with Microsoft Windows and Microsoft Excel 5 for Windows. Using what you learn here, you will be able to set up simple worksheets that contain numbers and formulas, create charts, and print your results. Chapter 1 teaches you the following:

✔ Starting Excel

✔ The parts of the Excel screen

✔ The parts of the worksheet

✔ Moving around the worksheet

✔ Creating a simple spreadsheet

✔ Creating a simple graph

✔ Printing the worksheet and graph

✔ Saving your work

✔ Quitting Excel

Although these operations are only the basics, you should get some idea of the programs ease of use, as well as just a touch of its power.

CHAPTER

Introducing Excel

With most software products, you use 10 percent of the features 90 percent of the time. Excel is no different in this regard. If you want to get going with Excel, learn to use the most fundamental features and functions, and achieve quick success with the product, then this chapter is for you. After learning these basics, you will be able to perform the most common tasks yourself and use the rest of this book as a guide to the more advanced features of Excel.

Excel 5 adds terrific new functionality to Excel. If you are an experienced Excel user, you can skim much of this chapter. Excel 5's key new features include the following:

- ✔ **Multidocument workbooks.** Workbooks enable you to keep all of the worksheets and charts for a particular project in a single workbook and also enable you to use true 3D worksheet features.

- ✔ **Function Wizard.** This helpful tool walks you through the process of using Excel functions.

- ✔ **TipWizard.** A revolutionary software tool that actively teaches you to use Excel more productively. Until now, almost all software help was passive in nature.

- ✔ **New auditing tools.**

- ✔ **PivotWizard.** The PivotWizard enables you to analyze scenarios of data quickly and easily.

✔ **Microsoft Query.** A powerful tool that can be used to query many databases, including SQL databases, then import the results of your queries into Excel.

✔ **Visual Basic for Applications.** An entirely new programming model, introduced for the first time in Excel 5 for Windows. Visual Basic for Applications is the new common macro language for all future Microsoft products and upgrades. (Of course, Excel 5 still supports all the macros written in the Excel 4 macro language.)

✔ **Powerful additions to the Charting module.** These features include automated regression trendlines, error bars, additional chart types, and more.

✔ **Support for OLE 2.** Excel 5 supports this Windows feature, which allows applications to seamlessly embed information from other applications.

✔ **Find File.** A new menu item that enables you to search your disk for workbooks.

Starting Excel

When you installed Excel, a program group was created in the Windows Program Manager for Excel and its associated programs, as shown in figure 1.1.

Figure 1.1
The Excel program
group.

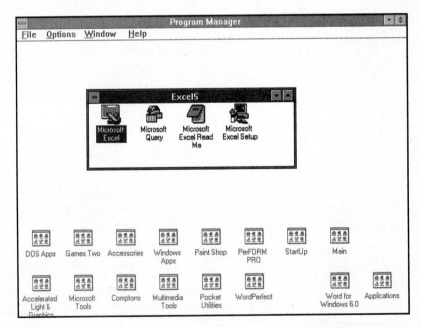

The following icons appear in the Excel program group:

- ✔ **Excel.** The Excel program

- ✔ **Microsoft Query.** A program that can be used to query a number of data sources and then move that data into Excel

- ✔ **Microsoft Excel Read Me.** Last-minute changes and tips about Excel

- ✔ **Microsoft Excel Setup.** Use the setup program to add or remove parts of Excel

To start Excel, double-click on the Excel icon. Excel opens and loads a blank worksheet, as shown in figure 1.2.

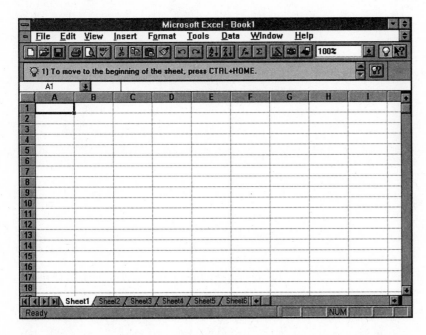

Figure 1.2
Excel opening screen.

Understanding the Excel Screen

Excel makes extensive use of graphical user interface features, such as menus, buttons, icons, and even different mouse pointers. The main elements of the Excel screen control the program itself, as shown in figure 1.3.

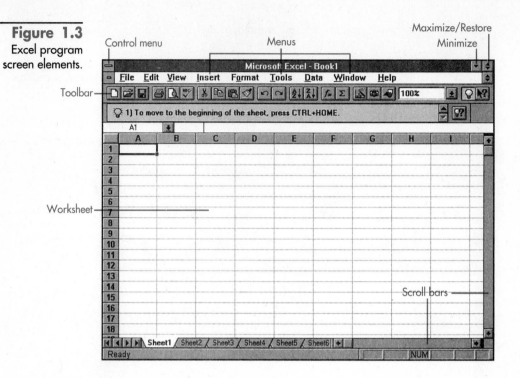

Figure 1.3
Excel program
screen elements.

Using Menus

Each menu in the menu bar contains many choices, most grouped logically. The File menu, for instance, shows commands that deal with files, Edit shows editing commands, and so on.

You can access menus in Excel (or any Windows program, for that matter) in two different ways using your mouse:

✔ Click on the menu to activate it, then position your pointer over the command you want in the menu and click on that command name to activate it.

✔ Move your mouse to the menu you want, click and *hold down the mouse button*, drag down to the command you want, then release the mouse button to select that menu command.

The second method is the same method that the Macintosh computer uses; the first is available only in Windows or OS/2 programs. Both procedures accomplish exactly the same thing, so use whichever one you prefer.

You also can access menus entirely using keyboard shortcuts. To pull down a menu by using only keystrokes, follow these steps:

1. Hold down the Alt key and press the letter on the keyboard that corresponds to the underlined letter in the menu. To activate the File menu, for example, hold down Alt and press the F key on your keyboard.

NOTE The underlined letter of a menu option is commonly called a "hot key."

2. After the menu appears, choose the option you want and press the letter on your keyboard that corresponds to the menu's hot key (you can just press the underlined letter to select a command within a menu).

Unlike the Macintosh, you can access every Windows or OS/2 menu option exclusively from the keyboard using this method. Many people find this method faster than constantly having to reach for the mouse.

Introducing the Toolbar

One of the more recent innovations in Windows programs is the wide use of *toolbars*, those rows of buttons that appear on your screen. These buttons typically show small icons; the icons represent the functions of pressing certain buttons. To print, for example, you simply click on the small button that looks like a printer.

The buttons in the toolbar are designed to provide you with quick access to the functions you use most often. Mastering the use of the Excel toolbars can dramatically increase the speed at which you can work with Excel.

When you open Excel for the first time, the Standard toolbar (the default), appears across the top of the window just below the menu bar, as shown in figure 1.4. The function of each button on the Standard toolbar is described in table 1.1.

Table 1.1
Standard Toolbar Icons

Icon	Name	Description
▢	New Workbook	Opens a new workbook.
📂	File Open	Opens an existing workbook on your disk.

continues

Table 1.1, Continued
Standard Toolbar Icons

Icon	Name	Description
	File Save	Saves the workbook document your disk.
	File Print	Prints the active document.
	Print Preview	Shows the document as it will look on the printed page.
	Cut	Cuts the currently selected area into the Windows Clipboard.
	Copy	Copies the contents of the active or marked cells into the Windows Clipboard.
	Paste	Pastes the contents of the Windows Clipboard beginning at the current cell location.
	Format Painter	Enables you to quickly copy the formatting of one cell to other cells.
	Undo	Reverses the last action you took.
	Redo	Repeats the last action you took.
	Sort Ascending	Sorts the contents of the selected cells in ascending order (lowest to highest).
	Sort Descending	Sorts the contents of the selected cells in descending order (highest to lowest).
	Function Wizard	Helps you use Excel functions and inserts the result into the current cell.
	AutoSum	Automatically determines which cells to sum, depending on the location of the active cell. Proposes a summation range that you can modify before you press Enter. When you press Enter, Excel automatically enters the SUM formula for you into the active cell.

5

Icon	Name	Description
	ChartWizard	Automatically walks you through the process of creating a chart.
	Camera	Enables you to insert graphic images into your worksheets.
	Graphics	Brings up the Graphics toolbar, which contains the tools you use to draw in your current document.
100%	Zoom Control	Enables you to quickly zoom in and out of your document.
	TipWizard	When selected, displays a bar under the main toolbar. The TipWizard automatically shows you shortcuts in Excel as you work.
	Region Help	Provides instant on-line help for any item on the screen. Select this button, then click on the area with which you want help.

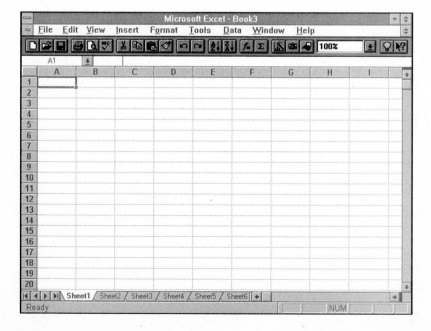

Figure 1.4
The Standard toolbar.

Using the Control Menu

The Control menu is the square button at the upper left corner of the Excel window. It functions the same in Excel as in most other Windows programs. The button has a bar through the middle of it to remind you that you can select it by holding down the Alt key and pressing the space bar. The Control menu is shown pulled down in figure 1.5.

Figure 1.5

The Control menu.

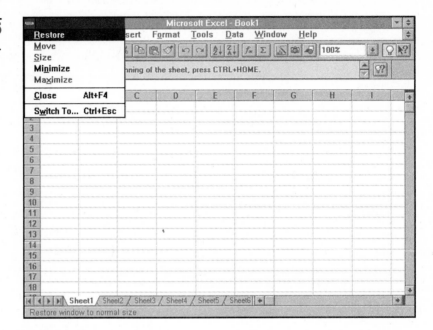

Table 1.2 explains the functions of each Control menu option. On your system, some options might be grayed (are not selectable), depending on whether they are appropriate options for the present context. See table 1.2 for notes about grayed options.

Table 1.2
Excel Control Menu

Menu Name	Description
Restore	Restores the Excel window to the size it was before the Maximize command was issued. This option is grayed when Excel is not maximized.
Move	When Excel is *windowed*, or not maximized to take over the entire screen, you can select the Move option then use the arrow keys to reposition the Excel window on the screen.

Menu Name	Description
Size	To resize the Excel screen using the keyboard, choose Size from the Control menu, then press the arrow key for the edge that you want to change (up arrow to adjust the upper edge of the Excel window, right arrow to adjust the right edge, and so on). After you select the edge you want to change, use the arrow keys to shrink or enlarge the Excel window.
Minimize	Choose Minimize to shrink Excel to an icon on the desktop. Excel continues to run and process data while it is minimized.
Maximize	Maximize causes Excel to grow to take up the entire screen area.
Close	Choose Close to exit Excel.
Switch To	Choose Switch To to open the Windows Task List. You then can use the Task List to choose another program already running in Windows.

Using Control Commands Shortcuts

Using the mouse or a keyboard shortcut is often a more convenient way to execute the Control menu commands. This section teaches you ways to accomplish similar tasks using a mouse or keyboard shortcut. See figure 1.6 for instructions on using these shortcuts.

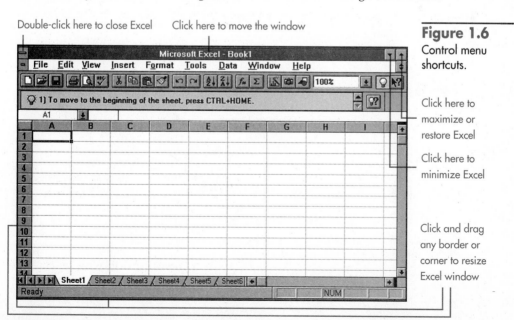

Double-click here to close Excel   Click here to move the window

Figure 1.6
Control menu shortcuts.

Click here to maximize or restore Excel

Click here to minimize Excel

Click and drag any border or corner to resize Excel window

Restore

To restore the Excel window to its windowed state so that it does not take up the entire screen, click once on the Restore button in the upper right corner of the Excel window. Also, when Excel is in its windowed state, this button changes to a single up arrow, which indicates that you can maximize Excel.

Move

To move the Excel window around on the desktop, click and hold on the Excel title bar, then drag your mouse to reposition the window.

Size

Resize the Excel window by carefully moving your mouse pointer to an edge of the Excel window. When the pointer is precisely over the edge, it changes shape and becomes a double-headed arrow. At this point, press the left mouse button and drag the mouse to resize that edge of the window.

Position the mouse pointer over the corner of the screen to control two dimensions at the same time. When your mouse is in the right place, the pointer changes to show two diagonal arrows.

Minimize

The Minimize button is located immediately to the left of the Maximize/Restore button. Click on it to immediately minimize Excel.

Maximize

The Maximize button is at the upper right corner of the Excel screen. When Excel is windowed, you can choose this button to cause Excel to take up the entire screen. When Excel is maximized, this button becomes the Restore button.

Close

Although you can use the Excel command to exit the program (File, Exit), you also can exit by double-clicking on the Control Menu. Another alternative is to press Alt-F4 on the keyboard.

Switch To

You can open the Control menu and then select S<u>w</u>itch To to bring up the Task List, or you can simply click on the window of another running program (you might need to minimize Excel down first to do this). You also can press Ctrl-Esc to bring up the Task List.

When the Task List appears, double-click on the program to which you want to switch, or use the arrow keys to move the pointer to the program you want and press the Enter key.

TIP

You can quickly switch between all your active programs running under Windows by holding down the Alt key and repeatedly pressing Tab. Each time you press Tab, a small window appears that shows the name and icon of a running program. Release the Alt key to switch to the program shown in the window.

Understanding the Workbook

Excel 5 introduces the metaphor of workbooks. A *workbook* is a collection of different documents, all grouped together. Some of the documents in the workbook might be worksheets, charts, macro sheets, and so on.

Excel has many different types of documents:

- ✔ **Worksheets.** Contain data and formulas. Worksheets also can contain other embedded objects, such as charts.

- ✔ **Charts.** Contain graphs that you create using Excel. A chart can be on its own document or embedded in a worksheet.

- ✔ **Modules.** Visual Basic modules for Excel. These modules contain program code for the programs you write using Excel's built-in programming language, Visual Basic for Applications.

- ✔ **Dialog sheets.** Contain dialog boxes you can use in your Excel application. You can draw dialog boxes using dialog sheets and attach program code for each button and field.

- ✔ **Excel 4 Macro Sheets.** Contain macros from version 4 of Excel.

Each workbook shares certain controls for managing the workbook itself. These controls are used to scroll around the current sheet of the workbook, minimize and maximize the workbook within the Excel window, and so on. This section discusses these workbook controls. Figure 1.7 shows the controls and key parts of a worksheet.

Figure 1.7
Excel document
controls.

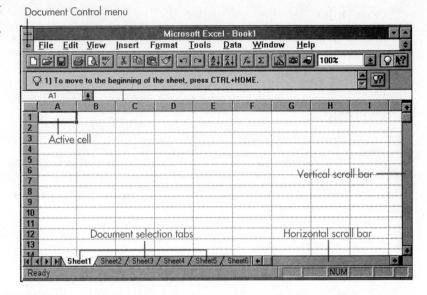

Understanding the Document Control Menu

The Document Control menu duplicates the functions of the Excel Control menu, but its commands affect only the current document itself, and not the overall Excel program. It contains the familiar commands Restore, Move, Size, Minimize, Maximize, and Close. This menu, however, also contains a command not found in the Excel Control menu: Next Window. The Document Control menu can also contain a command called Split, which you learn about momentarily.

Each time you select Next Window, Excel brings to the front each successive workbook until it reaches the last document you have open. Then it returns to the first document. It "circulates" between open Excel workbooks.

Split is available when you have a worksheet document open. This option enables you to split the worksheet into different sections so that you can work with and see different parts of the worksheet at the same time. This command is covered in detail in Chapter 5, "Working with Multiple Windows."

Exploring Other Document Controls

Excel offers several other document controls. You already learned to use these controls for the Excel program itself; this section shows you the way to use them in a workbook.

✔ Each workbook has its own Maximize/Restore and Minimize buttons, which are located at the upper right corner of the document. These buttons maximize or restore the workbook within the Excel window.

✔ Resize workbooks by positioning the mouse pointer over the edge of the workbook, then dragging the edge to resize the workbook. You can do this only when the workbook is not maximized.

✔ You can close the current workbook by double-clicking on the workbook's Control menu (as opposed to double-clicking on the Excel Control menu, which exits Excel).

✔ Reposition, or move, the workbook by clicking and holding your mouse while your pointer is on the workbook's title bar.

Double-click on the title bar of the workbook (or Excel itself) to maximize or restore it.

Identifying the Active Cell

The *active cell* is shown in figure 1.7. This cell is the one affected by whatever you type or whatever commands you execute (such as formatting commands).

Moving Around the Worksheet

During a typical Excel session, you move within one of the worksheets in your workbook, enter data in different places, view results in other places, and so on. Excel provides many ways to move around within the active workbook.

Some movements change the portion of the worksheet you are viewing without affecting the position of the active cell. This feature actually can be used to your advantage. If, for example, you want to view a different part of the spreadsheet before you enter some data, you can use the scroll bars to look at the information you want to see. Because using the scroll bars doesn't change the position of your active cell, you can just start entering data to immediately return to the active cell.

Using Scroll Bars

Very few worksheets can be viewed entirely on a single screen, and often take many, many screens of space to display. Given this fact, Excel enables you to scroll around the current document and view different parts of it at will.

Using the scroll bars does not move the position of the active cell. You can, however, move the active cell simply by clicking on a cell after you have scrolled to the desired place on the worksheet.

You can use scroll bars in a number of ways:

✔ Click on the scroll bar button and drag it to a different position to change the area you are viewing. If you drag the vertical scroll bar to the bottom or the horizontal scroll bar to the far right, you see the bottommost or rightmost part of your current worksheet.

In the upper left corner of the document, Excel shows you the row or column name that will appear after you release the scroll button. This "sneak preview" helps you avoid making guesses as to what will appear after you release the mouse button.

✔ Click on the arrows at either end of the scroll bar to move one cell in the direction of the arrow.

✔ Click on the blank area of the scroll bar (the area between the button and the arrow) to move an entire "screen full" at a time. You move in the direction away from the position of the scroll bar button. For example, if the vertical scroll bar button is in the middle of the vertical scroll bar, click once above the button to move your display up by one full screen.

Moving Around the Document Using the Keyboard

The keys and key combinations listed in table 1.3 provide alternative ways to move around within the worksheet.

Table 1.3
Keyboard Movement Keys

Key	Action
Arrow keys	Moves the active cell in the direction of the arrow key, one cell at a time.
PgUp/PgDn	Moves the display one full screen up or down. The active cell moves with the display, but stays in the same relative position on the screen.
Ctrl-arrow	Hold down the Ctrl key while you press an arrow key to move the active cell in that direction until it encounters a cell that contains data. If no cells contain data in that direction, Excel moves the active cell all the way to the boundary of the worksheet.
F5	Press F5 to open a dialog box in which you can enter the cell reference to which you want to jump. This dialog box also displays all your *named ranges* (areas of the worksheet to which you have assigned a name) so that you can just choose a named area. Otherwise, simply enter a cell reference (like AB255 or R3C4) and press Enter to immediately move the active cell there, and view that portion of the worksheet.

Creating a Worksheet

Now that you know the fundamentals of working with the Excel screen and of moving around the worksheet, it's time to set up a sample worksheet so that you can put these things into practice.

In the following sections, you create a worksheet that shows sales projections for the ACME Corporation. As you create the worksheet, you learn additional information about working with Excel.

Before you begin this exercise, start with a new workbook. Pull down the File menu and choose New. If you have defined multiple template documents, a dialog box appears that asks you what type of document you want to create. Click on Workbook and then click on the OK button.

Entering Text

The first order of business in creating your sample worksheet is to create the title and headings for the worksheet. Follow these steps:

1. Move your pointer to cell A1. (If you started a new worksheet, A1 should already be your active cell.) To quickly move to cell A1, press Ctrl-Home.

2. Type **ACME Corporation Sales Projections** and press the Enter key.

As you type, you see the text appear in the active cell on the worksheet and above the worksheet in the formula bar, as shown in figure 1.8.

Figure 1.8
The formula bar.

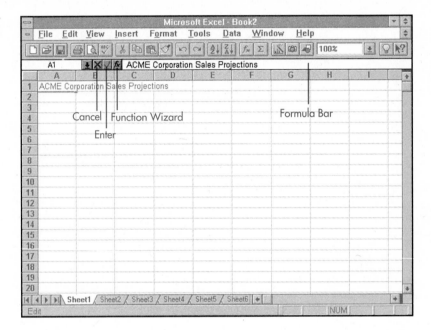

Formula Bar

The formula bar shows you the reference of the active cells, the data that you are typing, as well as the Cancel, Enter, and Function Wizard buttons (shown in figure 1.8).

When you are entering data in the formula bar, you can use the normal editing keys (arrow keys, Backspace, Del, and Ins) to change the data until you are satisfied with it. When you are finished editing the data, click on the Enter button (the check mark), or press the Enter key. To cancel your changes, click on the Cancel button (the X) or press Esc.

Centering Text

You can center text across a selection of cells by using the Format, Cells command:

1. Click on cell A1, hold down the mouse button, and drag the cursor to the right until the cells from A1 to I1 are highlighted. Release the mouse button.

2. Pull down the Format menu and click on Cells. This action brings up the Format Cells notebook, shown in figure 1.9. This notebook enables you to control the way in which the cells you select are formatted. Each "tab" of the notebook corresponds to a different formatting topic (or "page").

3. Because centering the title falls under the heading Alignment, click once on the tab marked Alignment.

4. On the Alignment page, click on the option button marked Center Across Selection.

5. To complete the change, click on the OK button.

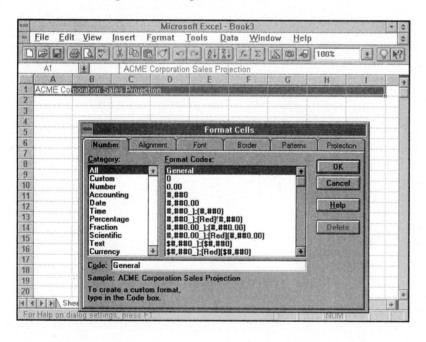

Figure 1.9
Cell Formatting
dialog box.

Continue entering the text labels for the exercise worksheet by entering the subtitle and two more labels:

1. Move to cell B1, enter **By Region**, and press Enter.

2. Center the text using the Center Across Selection method described earlier.

3. Move to cell B4, type **Region**, and press Enter.

4. Move to cell C4, type **Q1**, and press Enter.

AutoFill

Excel contains a powerful feature to automatically enter sequential labels. In the example you are creating, you want the labels Q2 through Q4 to appear in cells D4 through F4. You could type each label into each cell, or you can use the AutoFill feature.

In the lower right corner of your active cell, you see a small square. This square is the *fill handle*. You can use this feature to fill the rest of the titles:

1. Move to cell C4. Click on that cell or use the arrow keys to make it the active cell.

2. Position the mouse pointer immediately over the fill handle. When it is positioned correctly, the cursor changes to a small cross.

3. Press and hold down the left mouse button, then drag the mouse to the right to highlight the cells up to F4. When cells C4 through F4 are highlighted, release the mouse button.

If you drag the fill handle too far to the right, or not far enough, just grab it again and drag to the correct position. Excel refills the region correctly.

Voila! Excel intelligently interprets what you're trying to fill and correctly places each successive label into the correct cell. The AutoFill feature also works with month names or other types of labels.

Continue with the following steps to complete the entry of the labels for the worksheet.

1. Enter **Total** into cell G4.

2. Move to cell B5 and enter **North** and press Enter.

3. Repeat step 2 for the other three regions, as follows:

   ✔ Enter **East** into cell B6

   ✔ Enter **West** into cell B7

   ✔ Enter **South** into cell B8

4. In cell B9, enter **Total**.

At this point, you have entered all the labels for the worksheet. Your screen should look like figure 1.10.

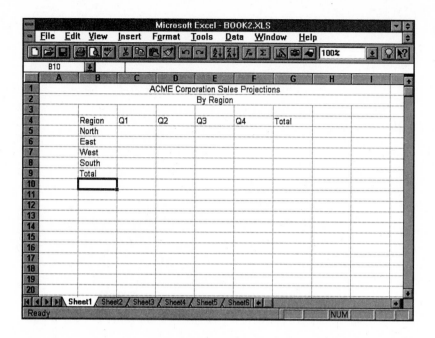

Figure 1.10
Sample worksheet
with labels.

Entering Numbers

For this example, assume that you already know the actual results for the first quarter, and you want to calculate the projections for the following three quarters, as well as the yearly total. Enter these values into each of the first quarter cells:

- ✔ **25292** in cell C5

- ✔ **13510** in cell C6

- ✔ **8900** in cell C7

- ✔ **43250** in cell C8

When you enter numbers into Excel, notice that they automatically appear aligned to the right edge of the cell. This alignment is the Excel default, because it is the most common way to format numbers, with their right edges aligned. It also serves as a useful way of knowing whether Excel is interpreting what you type as a number or text (sometimes it can fool you!).

Normally, Excel correctly determines if data is intended to be treated as a number or as text. Occasionally, however, you want a number to be treated as text. Perhaps you are preparing a table in which each line is labelled 1, 2, 3, and so on. In this case, to force Excel to treat those numbers as text, you must enter them in with a leading apostrophe. To force the number 145 to appear as text, for example, enter **'145** in the cell in question. The apostrophe does not appear in the cell, only the number.

Entering Formulas

Continuing with the sample worksheet, assume that each region is experiencing a 5 percent quarterly growth rate. You want Excel to calculate the remaining quarterly sales based on the sales of the first quarter, plus a 5 percent increase. Follow these steps:

1. Move to cell D5. Enter the formula **=C5*1.05** and press the Enter key. Excel immediately calculates the result and displays the answer.

> Excel, like most computer programs, uses the asterisk (*) to represent multiplication, and the forward slash (/) to represent division. Addition and subtraction are represented with plus (+) and a dash (–), respectively.

2. You now need to enter the formulas for the remaining calculated cells. You can enter the remaining formulas by hand, but why not let Excel's AutoFill feature do it for you? Grab the fill handle for cell D5, and drag it down so that the highlighted area extends from cell D5 to cell D8. Release the mouse button.

    Each cell now shows the correct amount: the cell to the left plus 5 percent of that amount. This calculation works correctly when you use AutoFill, because Excel automatically adjusts any cell references so that they are *relative* to the cell that contains the formula. You also can force Excel to look at a particular cell in a formula. No matter where you copy such a formula, it still works. This feature is called an *absolute reference*. Later in the book, you learn to control this reference and to use any combination of relative and absolute references that you want.

3. Finally, copy the entire column of formulas (cells D5 to D8) two columns to the right, so that all the quarterly sales are correct:

    Using the normal mouse pointer (the large plus symbol), select cells D5 to D8 (they should already be selected from the previous step). If not, move the pointer to cell D5, then click and drag the pointer down to cell D8. Release the mouse button after you have marked all the cells.

> You can use the keyboard to quickly select multiple cells. Use the arrow keys to move to the starting cell, hold down the Shift key, then use the arrow keys to move the ending cell. You also can click on the starting cell, hold down the Shift key, and click on the ending cell to select the entire range.

4. Grab the fill handle at the bottom of cell D8, and drag it two columns to the right. Excel now fills in all your formulas two columns to the right, and all the quarterly columns now show the correct sales figures. If everything has gone well for you, your screen should look like figure 1.11.

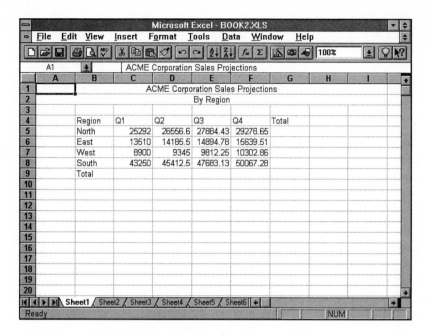

Figure 1.11
Completed sales
figures.

Worksheets

Using AutoSum

To finish building the data for the worksheet, you need to calculate the totals for both the columns and the rows. For example, to enter the total for cell G5, you have a couple of choices:

✔ You can enter the formula to add up all the cells. Using this method, you enter **=C5+D5+E5+F5** into cell G5 and then press Enter.

✔ You can use one of the Excel math functions. You can type the formula **=SUM(C5:F5)** and press Enter. Notice the way the range of cells is given in the formula. The first cell of the range to be summed is separated by the last cell from a colon. The colon tells Excel to work with all the cells in that range.

✔ You can use the Excel AutoSum tool, which is the fastest way to get totals of rows or columns of numbers. To use AutoSum, make G5 your active cell and click on the AutoSum button in the toolbar—the one that shows the Greek Sigma (Σ) icon. Excel automatically enters the SUM function, then determines which cells you most likely want to total and surrounds the suggested cells with a dotted line. If the range of cells that Excel guessed is correct, just press the Enter key. If the range isn't correct, use your mouse to select the correct cells and press Enter.

After you have entered the formula in cell G5 to total row 5, use the fill handle to copy the formula down to cell G9. When you are finished, move to cell C9 and use the AutoSum button again to total up the sales for the first quarter. Then, use the fill handle to copy that formula across to cell F9. When you are finished, your worksheet should look like figure 1.12.

Figure 1.12
The completed worksheet.

Microsoft Excel - BOOK2.XLS

File Edit View Insert Format Tools Data Window Help

A1   ACME Corporation Sales Projections

	A	B	C	D	E	F	G	H	I
1			ACME Corporation Sales Projections						
2			By Region						
3									
4		Region	Q1	Q2	Q3	Q4	Total		
5		North	25292	26556.6	27884.43	29278.65	109011.7		
6		East	13510	14185.5	14894.78	15639.51	58229.79		
7		West	8900	9345	9812.25	10302.86	38360.11		
8		South	43250	45412.5	47683.13	50067.28	186412.9		
9		Total	90952	95499.6	100274.6	105288.3	392014.5		
10									
11									
12									
13									
14									
15									
16									
17									
18									
19									
20									

Sheet1 / Sheet2 / Sheet3 / Sheet4 / Sheet5 / Sheet6

Ready   NUM

Using AutoFormat

Although all the numbers in your spreadsheet are correct, the document is not yet very presentable. Excel contains many commands that enable you to control the way your worksheet is formatted. One of the most convenient of these methods is the AutoFormat tool, which automatically applies one of a number of predesigned formats to a table.

To use AutoFormat, make sure that the active cell is anywhere within the table (for example, cell C5). Then, pull down the Format menu and choose AutoFormat. The AutoFormat dialog box appears as shown in figure 1.13.

The Table Format list box contains many different predefined table formats for you to choose from. For this example, choose Financial 1 and click on the OK button. The result is shown in figure 1.14.

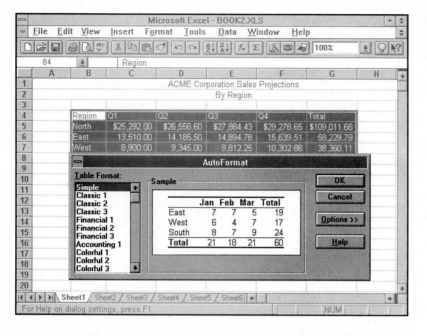

Figure 1.13
The AutoFormat
dialog box.

Worksheets

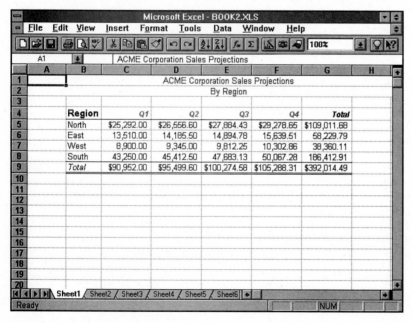

Figure 1.14
The formatted
worksheet.

Creating a Graph

Excel contains one of the most powerful graphing functions contained in any software product. Part of this power comes from the simple, easy-to-use tool called the ChartWizard.

In this example, you want to graph the sales data for each region for each quarter. Later in the book, you learn to do this manually. For this introduction to Excel, however, use the easy ChartWizard. Follow these steps:

1. Select B4 to F8 as the range to chart. You do not want to graph the totals for this chart.

2. Click on the ChartWizard button in the toolbar. Excel prompts you to indicate where you want to place the chart, and changes the mouse pointer to a small cross with narrow lines. You can embed charts right alongside your data in Excel, or you can place them in a separate sheet in your workbook. For this example, you place the chart right below your data.

3. Using the small cross, drag a rectangle in the area immediately below the table, so that you create the outline (sometimes called a *marquee*) from cell B11 to cell G18.

Excel now walks you through the five necessary steps required to create a chart. At any point, you can cancel the process by clicking on the Cancel button or by pressing Esc. You can also go backwards or forwards in the process by clicking on the Back or Next buttons.

1. The first step, shown in figure 1.15, verifies that you want to create the chart with the range that you selected. If the range was originally selected correctly, click on the Next button. If not, click on Cancel to go back and reselect it.

2. The second step, shown in figure 1.16, provides samples of different chart types and asks you to choose one. For this example, click on Column, which should already be selected. Click on the Next button to go to the next step.

3. The third step, (see fig.1.17), shows you a different set of pictures. These pictures represent all the different variations of the chart type you selected in the second step. Choose type 1 and click on the Next button.

4. The fourth step, shown in figure 1.18, asks you to select the way in which the data should be charted. These options are covered in detail later in the book. For now, the default choices are fine; click on the Next button.

5. The fifth and final step (figure 1.19) asks for information concerning labels on the chart. Everything is fine, except that you want to add a title to the chart. Click on the field under Chart Title, and type **ACME Sales Projections**. After you enter the title, wait a minute; the sample chart shows this text as it will appear. To complete the chart and place it into the worksheet, click on the Finish button.

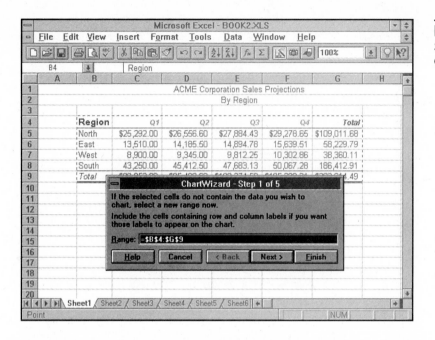

Figure 1.15
Step 1 of the
ChartWizard.

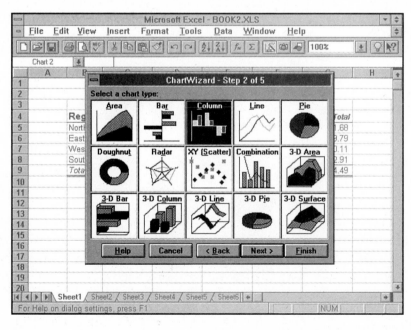

Figure 1.16
Step 2 of the
ChartWizard.

Figure 1.17
Step 3 of the
ChartWizard.

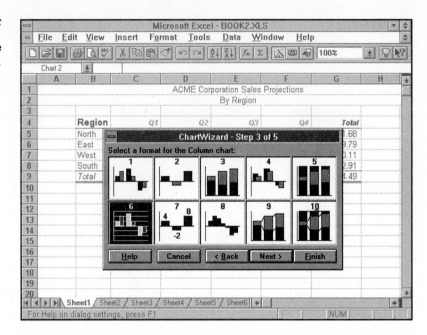

Figure 1.17
Step 3 of the
ChartWizard.

Figure 1.18
Step 4 of the
ChartWizard.

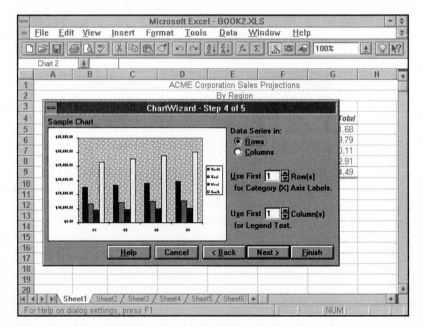

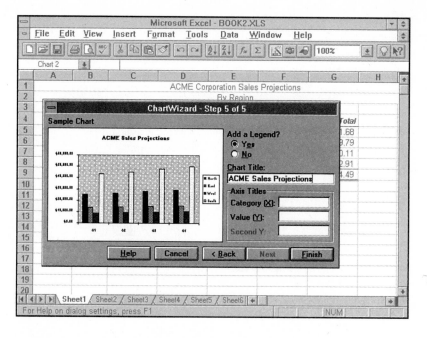

Figure 1.19
Step 5 of the
ChartWizard.

Worksheets

The completed chart is shown in figure 1.20.

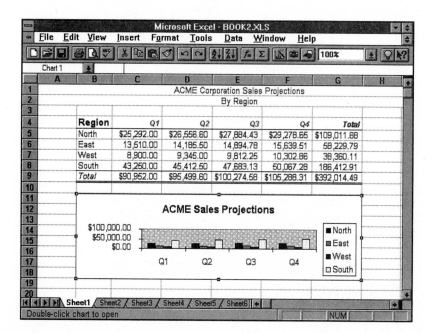

Figure 1.20
Completed chart
embedded in
worksheet.

The chart you see is *compressed*; you cannot see much detail because it is fairly small. To see the chart in more detail, click once on the chart to activate it, then drag up the upper handle (the small box in the middle of the top line). To return it to its original size, drag the handle back down.

When a chart is embedded into a worksheet, it is "floating" on top of the cells beneath it. If there was text in the cells behind the chart, that text is still there—it simply is covered by the chart.

Although charts are covered in detail elsewhere in this book, the following tips might help until you go through that information:

✔ If you need to delete a chart, click on the chart to select it. (You know it's selected when the small squares, called *handles,* appear at the corners and edges of the chart.) When the chart is selected, press Del to get rid of it.

✔ You can move the chart within the worksheet by selecting the chart and dragging it to a new location.

✔ You can resize the chart. To do this, select it, then drag one of the small handles at the perimeter of the chart.

Printing

To print the worksheet, select the area from cell A1 to cell H20, then pull down the File menu and choose Print. This step brings up the Print dialog box, shown in figure 1.21.

In the dialog box, click on the option button marked Selection. This option tells Excel to print only the selected area of the worksheet rather than the entire document. Finally, click on the button marked OK to print the document.

Saving Your Workbook

To save the completed workbook, pull down the File menu and choose Save As. This action opens the dialog box shown in figure 1.22.

Enter the name of your workbook in the File Name field and click on the OK button to save the workbook. If you need to change the directory in which the workbook is saved, use the Drives and Directories list boxes to navigate to the location where you want your file stored.

After you have assigned a name to a workbook, you can save more quickly by choosing Save from the File menu.

Worksheets

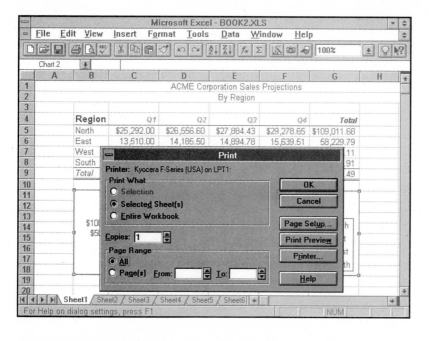

Figure 1.21
Print dialog box.

Figure 1.21
Print dialog box.

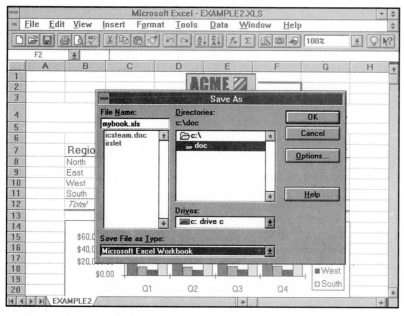

Figure 1.22
Save As dialog box.

Saving frequently is very important. Many people lose lots of time by forgetting to save their work. Then, when they lose power or their computer crashes, they lose all the work they have done since the last time they saved the file. Excel also includes an AutoSave feature. You learn about AutoSave in Chapter 21, "Using Excel Add-ins."

Chapter Snapshot

Nearly all your time working with Excel will include manipulating the data in your worksheets. Entering data, moving it, cutting and pasting it, and even transforming it are all functions you will spend significant amounts of time doing. This chapter teaches you the following tasks:

- ✔ Entering different types of data into an Excel worksheet

- ✔ Taking advantage of some large scale data-entry shortcuts

- ✔ Building simple formulas

- ✔ Referencing other cells—including combinations of cells—in your formulas

- ✔ Taking advantage of absolute versus relative cell addresses

- ✔ Understanding the difference between R1C1 cell addressing and A1 cell addressing

- ✔ Naming portions of your spreadsheet for better control and accountability

- ✔ Including detailed notes in individual cells

- ✔ Rearranging the data in your worksheet

By mastering the techniques presented in this chapter, you learn to work with your worksheet data and use Excel as efficiently as possible.

CHAPTER 2

Working with Worksheet Data

T his chapter covers the basics of working with data—text, numbers, and formulas—on the Excel worksheet. You need to be able to enter and manipulate data in Excel to be productive with the program.

Entering Data

The first thing you have to do when you build a spreadsheet usually is data entry. You must know how to enter labels for different parts of your worksheet, and you really need to know how to enter numbers and dates for calculations, as well as other information.

This section discusses entering text and numbers and how to make Excel accept a number and treat it as text when you need to do so. Through examples in the chapter, you learn how to enter and manipulate text so you can do an inventory spreadsheet in Excel. You enter different inventory items and the quantity and price of each. Then, you use Excel to calculate the inventory value.

Entering Text

To enter text, position the active cell where you want the text to appear, then begin typing. When you type the first letter, the text appears in the active cell *and* in the formula bar.

The following steps tell you how to enter a title and headings for the different parts of the inventory spreadsheet:

1. Type **ACME Company** Inventory in cell C2. Then click once on the Checkmark button next to the formula bar, or simply press Enter to store your entry. If you want to cancel what you have typed, click on the X button in the formula bar, or press Esc.

If the active cell moves down a row when you press Enter, you might want to turn off the feature that controls this action. Pull down the Tools menu and choose Options. Click on the Edit tab, then select or clear the option marked Move Selection after Enter.

2. In cell A4, type **Quantity** and press Tab.

The Tab key moves you one cell to the right. When you are editing a cell and press the Tab key, the contents of the cell you just entered is saved before the active cell is moved. Similarly, press Shift+Tab to move one cell to the left.

3. In cell B4, type **Description** and press Tab.

   Description spans two cells, and the last part of the word covers part of cell C4. When no text or numbers are in an adjacent cell, Excel allows the text of one cell to continue to the right.

4. In cell C4, type **Model #** and press Enter.

   When you enter the text, the final part of the word Description is obscured. Because of the text in C4, Excel cannot display the complete word, so it shows the contents of cell C4 rather than the final portion of the preceding cell.

5. In cell D4, type **Price** and press Enter.

Compare your spreadsheet to figure 2.1.

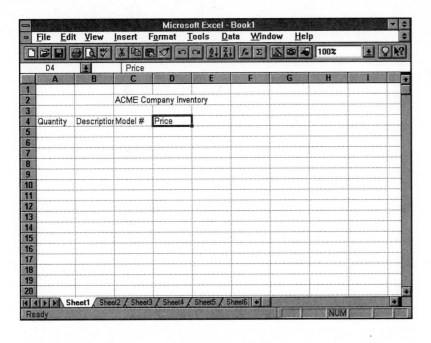

Figure 2.1
The spreadsheet with title and labels.

Before you continue, you should widen column B in the spreadsheet. Not only does text Description not fit, but the actual inventory descriptions you will enter are unlikely to fit, either. Use the following procedure to widen column B:

1. Position your pointer directly on top of the line that separates B and C at the top of the spreadsheet. When positioned correctly, the pointer changes to a vertical bar with two horizontal arrows.

2. When this vertical bar appears, click and hold the left mouse button and drag the mouse to the right until the column is close to twice the original size.

3. Release the mouse button to finish the change (see fig. 2.2).

Figure 2.2
The spreadsheet
with column B
widened.

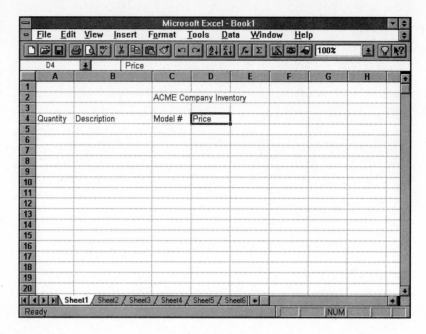

Entering Numbers

Move to cell A5, type **5** and press Enter. The number immediately springs to the right of the cell after you press Enter instead of aligning to the left of the cell. Excel's default setting assumes that you want text to be left-aligned and numbers to be right-aligned.

Move to cell B5, and type the following description entry: **Paper Clips**.

Entering Numbers as Text

You should type the model number **00587** for this item in cell C5 and press Enter. Excel displays 587, rather than 00587.

Normally, Excel correctly anticipates whether you want an entry to be treated as text or as a number. In this case, it interprets your entry as a number and eliminates the unnecessary leading zeros. You want this entry to be treated as text, however, for two reasons: you need to preserve the leading zeros for the model number to be accurate, and you want all the model numbers to be similarly aligned. Some are pure text. If you mix numbers and text, some entries are right-aligned, while others are left-aligned.

To make Excel treat a number as text, you need to enter the number differently. In cell C5, type **'00587** (note the leading single quote mark) and press Enter. Voilà ! Excel knows you want the entry to be treated as text, and displays it accordingly. The single quote mark is all it takes.

To finish the first line of data, move to the Price column and enter **.75** to represent 75 cents.

Entering Times and Dates

Before you continue with the exercise, you should learn to enter times and dates into Excel.

Excel stores times and dates differently from the way it displays them. When you enter a time, Excel records two things: a number that represents a decimal fraction of a 24-hour day and a formatting command that tells Excel to display that number as a time, rather than as a simple number. In Excel, you can enter times in the following formats:

- ✔ 21:45
- ✔ 21:45:50 (hours, minutes, seconds)
- ✔ 9:45 PM
- ✔ 9:45:50 PM
- ✔ 5/6/95 9:45 PM

In the last example, you also can combine dates and times in the same cell entry. You actually can use any of the valid date combinations that follow with any of the valid time combinations.

You also can enter dates in a variety of ways:

- ✔ 5/6/95
- ✔ 5-6
- ✔ 6-May-93
- ✔ 6/May/93
- ✔ May-93 (uses your computer's day)
- ✔ May 6 (uses your computer's year)

You can use /, -, or a space to separate the elements of a date. If Excel does not recognize your entry as a date, it treats it as a normal text entry and displays it accordingly.

NOTE

No matter how the date appears in the spreadsheet, it always appears with the format mm/dd/yyyy in the formula bar. For example, if you enter **5 May** into a cell, you see 5/6/1994 in the formula bar. Seeing the way the date appears lets you know whether Excel correctly recognized your entry as a date or displayed it as normal text.

Excel stores a special number, called a *serial number,* when you enter a date. The serial number counts the number of days from the beginning of the century up to the date entered in the cell. For example, if you view the serial number for the date 1/1/2000, you see the number 36526. This number represents 365 days per year multiplied by 100 years (36500), plus the number of days added by leap years (25), plus one additional day (the first of January).

TIP

To see the serial number for a particular date, enter the date and press Ctrl+Shift+~, the shortcut key to force a cell to assume a numeric format (also called Normal formatting).

To return the cell to a date format, press Ctrl+Shift+#, which is the shortcut key for the standard date format.

Performing Data Entry

Entering large amounts of data is extremely boring, rife with the potential for error. By using some of Excel's data-entry shortcuts, however, you can reduce the chance of error and complete the task more easily and quickly.

Selecting the Data-Entry Range

Normally, you need many extra keystrokes to move from the end of one line to the beginning of the next when you enter several records. Fortunately, you can automate this process with Excel.

If you use the mouse to select the range of cells into which to enter data before you type the data, Excel moves between cells for you automatically. After you choose your data-entry area, use the keys listed in table 2.1 to move your active cell in an efficient manner for data entry.

Table 2.1
Data-Entry Key Actions

Key	Movement
Tab	Stores your entry and moves one cell right in the selected area. If you are at the right border of the area when you press Tab, the active cell moves to the beginning of the next row down.
Shift+Tab	Stores your entry and moves one cell left in the selected area. If you are at the left border, the active cell moves to the right end of the next row up.

Key	Movement
Enter	Stores your entry and moves one cell down in the selected area. If you are at the bottom row, the active cell moves to the top row, one column to the right.
Shift+Enter	Stores your entry and moves one cell up in the selected area. If you are at the top row, the active cell moves to the bottom row, one column to the left.

Using the Numeric Keypad

If you are used to entering numbers with a 10-key calculator that automatically places the decimal point in the number, you will be pleased to know that Excel can emulate that capability. To activate this feature, follow these steps:

1. Pull down the Tools menu, then select Options.

2. The Options notebook appears, which enables you to change many global characteristics of Excel. In this notebook, first click on the Edit tab. The Edit notebook page appears. Click on the Fixed Decimal checkbox. The field below the checkbox should already have 2 in it, which indicates that two decimal points are entered automatically.

3. Click on the OK button to close the notebook.

After you activate this option, all numbers have a decimal point automatically inserted two places from the right. So, if you enter **12345**, Excel stores it as text 123.45. If you enter the number **5**, Excel stores it as .05, and so on. You can override this format in an individual cell by entering the decimal point by hand (for example, if you enter **5.**, you get 5). Excel uses the automatic decimal places until you uncheck the Fixed Decimal checkbox.

Special Data-Entry Keys

Often when you enter a large amount of data, certain parts of each line are repeated in the following line. For example, if you enter inventory locations in your inventory spreadsheet, many adjacent records share the same location. And then, sometimes you want to copy the formula in a cell, or automatically enter the date or the time into a cell.

The keys in table 2.2 perform such actions.

Table 2.2
Special Data-Entry Key Actions

Key	Effect
Ctrl+; (Semi-colon)	Enters the present date
Ctrl+: (Colon)	Enters the present time
Ctrl+' (Apostrophe)	Copies the formula from the cell above without adjusting the cell references
Ctrl+" (Quotation mark)	Copies the value (text or number) from the cell above

Completing Data Entry

Using the preceding tools, enter the remainder of the inventory information into your spreadsheet. Table 2.3 shows all the records, including the one you already entered. As you enter the data, remember the following points:

✔ Select cells A5 through D9 before you begin. Then, use the Tab key to move between cells.

✔ When you enter model numbers, remember to enter the number-only entries as **'nnn**, where *nnn* is the number you want to enter. The single quote mark forces the numbers to be treated as text.

✔ If you use the Fixed Decimal feature, remember to enter the numbers correctly. For example, to enter the number 31, you can enter **3100** or **31.** (with a decimal).

Table 2.3
Inventory Records

Qty	Description	Model #	Price
5	Paper clips	00587	.75
31	Faber #2 Pencils	2002	.05
12	Office Calendars	OCTZAB	12.95
93	Cs. Manilla Folders	12MAN	6.95
12	Rm. #20 Copy Paper	20#500	5.35

After you finish entering the data from table 2.3, your screen should look like figure 2.3.

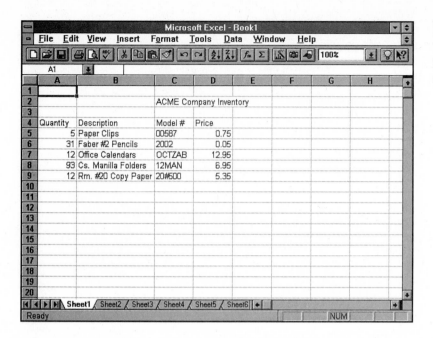

Figure 2.3
The completed inventory spreadsheet.

Working with Formulas

To add to your inventory spreadsheet, you might want to add a column that shows the value of the goods on hand, as well as a total amount for all of the inventory items. You can do this work by using a few simple formulas.

To begin, create a new column called Value in column E. Move to cell E4, type **Value** and press Enter.

Using Cell References

Now, you must enter the formula. In this case, all you want to do is take the price in column D and multiply it by the quantity in column A—far from difficult, you shall soon discover.

Keyboard

You can enter this formula in two ways, using only the keyboard. Both methods are depicted in the following two examples. Use E5 as your active cell.

The first method is merely a matter of typing in the formula. In cell E5, type **=D5*A5** and press Enter. The result appears in your active cell. Notice, however, that the formula appears in the formula bar when a cell is selected. This display lets you see the basis for the result as you work in your spreadsheets.

The second method involves "pointing" with the arrow keys. Follow these steps:

1. Type an equal sign.

2. Press the left arrow once. The cell reference D5 appears in the formula bar, and a dashed line appears in cell D5 (showing the cell to which you point).

3. Type an asterisk (*) for multiplication. The dashed box (called a *marquee*) disappears, and =D5* appears in the formula bar.

4. Press the left arrow four times. The marquee moves one cell at a time to the left, until it rests on cell A5.

5. Press Enter.

Both methods produce the same result. The method you use is up to you. Sometimes the pointing method works better because your spreadsheet is too big for you to know which cell you want. In that case, you can arrow quickly to the cell you want as you build your formula without having to know the cell reference. In a small worksheet, however, like the one used in this example, you might find it faster to use the first method and directly type the formula.

Mouse

You also can enter the formula using the mouse by following these steps:

1. In cell E5, type an equal sign.

2. Move the mouse pointer to cell D5 and click once. The marquee appears, and D5 appears in the formula.

3. Enter an asterisk (*).

4. Move the mouse pointer to cell A5 and click once. A5 appears in the formula bar. You can press Enter to store the formula.

Another variation of this procedure is to use the scroll bars to locate the cell to which you want to point with the mouse. After you find the cell you want, click on it with the left mouse button. Then, enter an appropriate math symbol and your display automatically returns to the cell into which you are entering the formula. In a small worksheet, however, like the one used in this example, you might find it faster to use the first method and directly type the formula.

Working with Ranges of Cells

Finish the column of formulas. If you want to practice the methods you just learned, do so until each row has the inventory value in column E. If, however, you see that as drudgery and would prefer to circumvent it, copy the formula to the other cells automatically by using the following steps:

1. Select the range of cells from E5 to E9 by moving your mouse pointer to cell E5, clicking and holding the left mouse button, and dragging down to cell E9. After the cells are highlighted, release the mouse button.

2. Pull down the Edit menu, and select Fill, then Down.

NOTE If you pay attention to Excel's menu, you can see that most of Excel's shortcut keys are listed next to their respective menu options. In step 2, for example, Ctrl+D also performs the Fill Down operation.

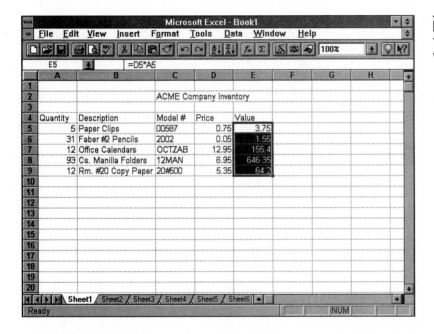

Figure 2.4
The completed Value column.

After you select the Fill Down command, the formula you entered is copied automatically to all the cells below E5. Those cells should all display the correct result, as shown in figure 2.4.

Referring to Multiple Ranges

Next, you want to total the Value column. You already know how to total it by entering a formula, **=E5+E6+E7+E8+E9**, in cell E10. If you have a spreadsheet that has a large table (one that contains hundreds or thousands of rows), however, entering that formula takes much too long. Furthermore, Excel cells are limited to 255 characters, which is hardly enough if you enter formulas after such a manner.

Fortunately, Excel includes a function called SUM that can add a range of cells and display the result. To use SUM, enter **=SUM(E5:E9)** in cell E10 and press Enter.

TIP   You can enter the SUM function in several ways. You can type =**SUM**(and use the keyboard arrow keys to indicate the range. (When you use the keyboard, you move the marquee to the first cell, hold down Shift, and then arrow to the last cell). After you indicate the range, enter the closing parenthesis to complete the formula.

You can also use the mouse. Enter =**SUM**(and select a range of cells, then enter) and press Enter to complete the formula.

Lastly, you can use the Sum tool on the Standard toolbar as discussed in Chapter 1.

The shorthand notation in the preceding SUM command is important. In Excel, you can refer to a range of cells by indicating only the beginning and ending cells, separated by a colon. If the range covers multiple rows and columns, you refer to the range by indicating the top left cell and the bottom right cell.

Also, for some formulas you might want to refer to many ranges of cells. For instance, you might want to total two columns with a column of text between them. In that case, you can separate each range of cells with a comma. For example, if you want to sum all of range C5 through C9 and E5 through E9, enter the formula =**SUM(C5:C9,E5:E9)**.

Understanding Relative and Absolute References

By default, the cells you refer to in your formulas are treated as though they refer to cells that are relative to your current cell. For this reason, you can copy the formula in cell E5 to cells E6 through E9 and still get the correct answers for each different row. This type of referencing is called *relative cell referencing* and means that the cells you enter in your formulas are relative references. Most formulas use this relative method.

Excel also can use *absolute cell referencing*, meaning that your formulas always refer to a particular cell, no matter where you copy the formula.

Using Absolute References

To enter a formula in Excel using absolute cell referencing, add a dollar sign ($) before the row and the column. For example, in cell E5 enter =$D$5*A5$. If you copy this formula to a different cell, it still refers to cell D5 and A5.

Using Mixed References

Excel enables you to mix absolute and relative cell references. For example, you can enter the formula in cell E5 as =$D5*$A5; in essence, telling Excel that you want the column letters to be absolute, but that the row numbers can be relative. This formula still yields the correct answers in each cell, because only the row number actually needs to change. If you copy the formula to the right, it still works, because this formula always refers to the values found in columns A and D of the current row.

TIP

After you enter a cell reference, you can use the F4 key to toggle between the different combinations of relative and absolute cell references. For an example of these combinations, select a blank cell and enter =**D8**. Then, before you continue, press F4 to cycle through D8, D8$, and D$8, which are the different combinations available. You also can use this method when editing a formula. Move to the formula you want to edit and press F2 to begin editing. Use the arrow keys to move the cursor so that it is in the cell reference you want to change, then press F4 to cycle through the changes.

Understanding A1 and R1C1 Cell Addressing

By default, Excel refers to cells using what is called the *A1 reference method*, which uses the alphabet to represent columns and numbers to represent rows. Columns are lettered from A through IV (A to Z, AA to AZ, BA to BZ, and so on, up to IV, which is the 256th column). Rows are numbered from 1 to 16384—a heck of a lot of rows!

Excel also can use a different reference method, called the *R1C1 reference method*, in which the rows *and* columns are numbered.

In the R1C1 method, cells are referenced by using a combination of their row and column number. The equivalent of cell A1 is R1C1 (meaning Row #1, Column #1). Cell E5, for example, would be R5C5, and so on.

Toggling between A1 and R1C1 Addressing

To toggle Excel between the A1 and the R1C1 methods, pull down the Options, select Options, then click on the General tab in the Options notebook that appears. Select the checkbox marked R1C1, then click on the OK button. To toggle Excel back to the A1 method, choose the same menu item and check the A1 option.

After you follow those steps, your formulas and cells are referenced using this different method. Table 2.4 shows two examples of the differences you observe.

Table 2.4
A1 versus R1C1 Formula Changes

A1 Cell	R1C1 Cell	A1 Formula	R1C1 Formula
E5	R5C5	=D5*A5	=RC[-1]*RC[-4]
E10	R10C5	=SUM(E5:E9)	=SUM(R[-5]C:R[-1]C)

If you look at the first example, the R1C1 formula =RC[-1]*RC[-4], translated into English, reads:

> "Take the value in the current row, one column to the left, and multiply it by the value in the current row, four columns to the left."

The second example, =SUM(R[-5]C:R[-1]C), translates to the following:

> "Sum the values starting form the cell five rows up in the current column to the cell one row up in the current column."

These formulas refer to cell positions that are *relative* to the current cell. The formulas in cells R5C5, R6C5, R7C5, R8C5, and R9C5 are all *exactly* the same formula. When a number is not given after the 'R' or the 'C' in the R1C1 addressing method, Excel assumes you are referring to the current row or column. Because of this assumption, it is easy to understand how formulas copied to different locations in the spreadsheet refer to cells in the same positions, relative to the cell that contains the formula. So, for example, if you copy the formula =SUM(R[-S]C:R[-1]C) to cell R19C34, it sums the values found in cells R14C34, R15C34, R16C34, R17C34, and R18C34.

Using the A1 or the R1C1 method changes only the *appearance* of your worksheet. Nothing internal is any different about your spreadsheet. If you give a copy of your spreadsheet to someone using a different method, they see the formulas in the method they are using, and the worksheet functions exactly the same as it did using the other method.

If you use the R1C1 method, you also can enter formulas that are not relative to the current cell but are absolute. If for example, you enter the formula **=R5C1*R5C4**, the formula always refers to those two cells, no matter where in the worksheet you copy the formula.

Understanding the Importance of Names

One of the most useful, but least used, features of Excel is ability to assign names to parts of the worksheet. In Excel, you can name ranges of cells, constant values, and formulas. Possibly, names are not used by many people, because the normal cell references work just fine and they don't want to take the time to learn something new. Or, perhaps, people think their worksheets won't grow large enough to benefit from using names, but then their worksheets do grow! In any case, consider the following advantages and features of using names in Excel:

✔ If you name cells or ranges of cells, you can then use those names in your formulas. It is far easier to remember to type **=Amount*Quantity** than to know to type **=D5*A5**.

✔ Using names improves the ability to audit your worksheets. When you use names in your formulas, you can see easily that the formula **=Amount*Quantity** is correct, but it is not as apparent that **=D5*A5** is correct.

✔ In Excel, you can assign a constant value to a name. For instance, if you work with many financial statements from many different companies, you can assign the name *Number_of_Periods* the value 12 or 13, depending on how many accounting periods the company uses. Then, use the *Number_of_Periods* name in your formulas in place of the number 12 or 13. When you need to use the same worksheet for a company with a different number of accounting periods, just change the value of the *Number_of_Periods* constant, and then all the formulas that use the name automatically are based on the new value.

✔ When you need to jump around a large worksheet, it is easier to use the name to which you want to jump with the Goto command (F5), as opposed to using, for example, cell BZ157. You can press F5 for the Go to command, then just enter **SALES** to jump to the cells name SALES.

✔ Using names can reduce the potential for errors. If you type in a formula with the column or the row even slightly wrong, Excel can give you the answer based on what is in the wrong cell, and you might think that the answer is correct. If you use a name incorrectly, however, Excel gives you a **#NAME?** error, instead of using an erroneous cell and possibly giving you an incorrect answer.

✔ The preceding advantage is even more important when you consolidate multiple worksheets. It is far easier to validate the formula =AUGSUM.XLS!Units than to validate =AUGSUM.XLS!AR214.

Creating Names

As you create and work with names, remember the following rules:

✔ **Names cannot contain spaces.** Instead, use the underscore (_) or the period (.) to separate words. For example, use West_Sales, West.Sales, or even WestSales rather than West Sales.

✔ **Use short names.** Excel allows names as long as 256 characters, but no cell can have an entry that exceeds 256 characters. Also, long names make it difficult to find the name you want when you search through a list of names in a list box.

You can name parts of your worksheet in two ways. The method you use depends on the way your data is structured and the way you want to use the names. Try both of the following exercises so you can understand the differences between the two methods.

Manually

To manually name a range, follow these steps:

1. Select the range of cells A4 through A9.

2. Pull down the Insert menu, select Name, then Define. The Define Name dialog box appears, as in figure 2.5.

3. Click on the OK button.

Because you preselected the range you wanted to name, the dialog box already has filled in the range you want to name, as well as the name you want to use. (Excel uses the text found in the top row or far left column that you selected in order to "guess" the name.) If you don't select the range before you issue the Insert Name Define command, you have to type the name you want in the Names in Workbook field and the range of cells in the Refers to field. Excel has also used absolute cell references in the Refers To field, which is correct.

Figure 2.5
The Define Name
dialog box.

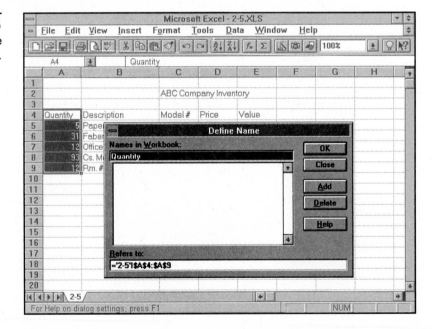

Automatically

In Excel, you also can create names for multiple ranges at the same time, which is most useful for tables, not unlike the inventory table you have created. To use this method, follow these steps:

1. Select ranges A4:A9, D4:D9, and E4:E9. Remember to hold down the Ctrl key when you select the second and third ranges. If you select all three ranges properly, your screen will look like figure 2.6.

2. Pull down the Insert menu, select Name, then Create Names. The Create Names dialog box appears (see fig. 2.7).

In the Create Names dialog box, you can tell Excel where to look for the names you want to apply automatically to the ranges. Here, you want Excel to automatically use the titles in the top row for each range, so you need to make sure that the Top Row checkbox is selected.

If you are working in a table that has labels in both the top and left rows, you can select both of those checkboxes (Top Row and Left Column), which creates a name for each range. **Important:** You can have many names that all refer to the same cell. For instance, you might have vertical ranges named Q1_Sales, and Q2_Sales and horizontal ranges named West_Region and East_Region. In this example, each cell will be referenced by two different names, and you can use those two names appropriately in formulas. If you are creating a new row that adds West_Region and East_Region, you can enter those names. If you are creating a column that totals Q1_Sales and Q2_Sales to the right of your table, you also can use those names.

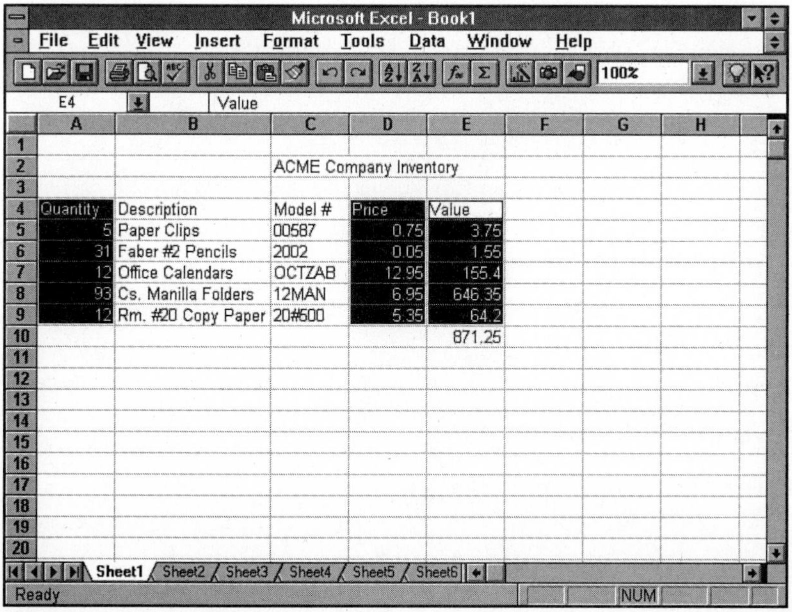

Figure 2.6
Multiple ranges selected.

Worksheets

Figure 2.7
The Create
Names dialog
box.

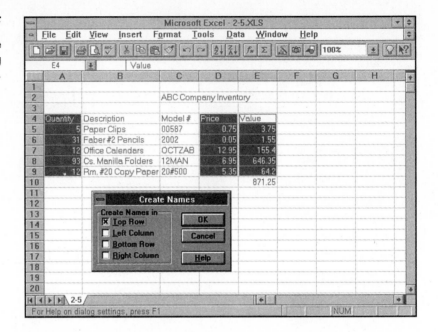

3. With the Top Row checkbox selected, click on the OK button.

After you click on the OK button, Excel opens a dialog box that asks if you want to replace any existing names (in this example, Quantity was defined earlier). Click on the OK or Cancel button in that dialog box. If your worksheet has no preexisting named ranges in the area in which you are working, nothing happens when the new names are created. You can , however, test these new named ranges. To test them, follow these steps:

1. Move to cell E5.

2. Enter the formula **=Quantity*Price** and press Enter.

If you created the named ranges correctly, you see the same result that previously existed in cell E5, but the formula bar shows your new formula. If the names did not exist, or if you mistyped them in the formula, you get a #NAME? error in that cell.

Applying Names

If you are working with an existing worksheet, it is hardly worth it to manually re-enter all your formulas the way you did for cell E5. Fortunately, in Excel you can take your new named ranges and automatically change all the applicable formulas to use those names. To do this with the inventory worksheet, follow these steps:

1. Select the ranges A4:A9, D4:D9, and E4:E10 (make sure to include the total at the bottom of the Value column). Press and hold down Ctrl while you use your mouse to select the second and third ranges.

2. Pull down the Insert menu, select Name, then select Apply. The Apply Names dialog box appears, as in figure 2.8.

3. Click on the OK button.

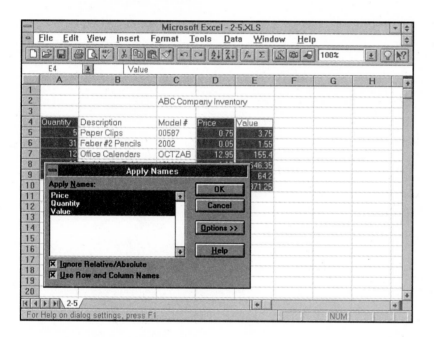

Figure 2.8
The Apply Names dialog box.

Before you use it, make sure that the names you want to apply are selected in the list box, which they are by default if you completed the range selection process in step 1. If the names are not selected, you need to select them using the mouse, holding down Ctrl if you want to apply more than one name.

The Apply Names dialog box has several options:

✔ **Ignore Relative/Absolute.** Controls the way Excel substitutes names for relative and absolute references. If this box is not checked, Excel applies only names that match the absolute or relative reference found in the original formula. You usually want to have this box checked.

✔ **Use Row and Column Names.** Controls how liberally Excel applies names. If this box is not checked, Excel applies only names that refer to the individual cells used in the formula rather than names that might refer to an entire column or row. If this box is checked (the default), Excel uses the name for the entire row or column. Normally, you want to leave this box checked.

Check around the worksheet. All the formulas have been replaced with the simpler, name-based formulas. Even the =SUM formula reads =SUM(Value), which is far easier to read and remember (and understand!) than =SUM(E4:E9).

Creating Named Constants

An oft-overlooked feature in Excel is being able to create named constants. If you use Excel's name feature, constants don't even have to take up cell space.

Use a constant when parts of your worksheet depend on a single number. One example is a sales projection worksheet that uses a single value for sales growth assumptions. Or, perhaps, a profit and loss statement that has an assumption about your gross margin. In either case, you can handle the numerical assumption in one of two ways:

✔ You can enter the assumption in a single cell on the worksheet, and then have your other formulas refer to that cell (using an absolute cell reference).

✔ You can define a named constant that contains the number.

Using the named constant keeps your worksheet a little neater and also makes it easier to see the ways your formulas work.

 TIP
When you create named constants, use something consistent in the name to distinguish it as a constant rather than a named range of cells. For example, you could use only uppercase letters for the names of your constants. Or, you could begin the name of each constant with C_. For example, you might create a constant named C_GROWTH. Using this kind of visual clue helps you see quickly which names in your formulas are constants and which are named cells.

To create and work with named constants, use the following steps. You add a new column to the example worksheet that shows the retail value of the inventory in stock. As part of the exercise, you create a named constant called C_MARKUP that you use to calculate the retail value.

1. Move to cell F4, type **Retail Value**, and press Enter.

2. Pull down the Insert menu, select Name, then Define.

3. In the Define Names dialog box that appears, move to the field called Names in <u>W</u>orkbook and type **C_MARKUP**.

4. Move to the <u>R</u>efers to field and type **1.40**—a 40 percent markup after you use it in the formula to multiply against the Value.

5. Click on OK to return to the worksheet.

6. Move to cell F5 and type the formula **=Value*C_MARKUP** and press Enter. Cell F5 now shows you the retail value of the inventory in row 5.

7. Select the range F5:F9. While those cells are selected, pull down the <u>E</u>dit menu, select <u>F</u>ill, then <u>D</u>own.

TIP You also can press Ctrl+D instead of choosing <u>F</u>ill, <u>D</u>own from the <u>E</u>dit menu.

8. While the range still is selected, pull down the <u>I</u>nsert menu, select <u>N</u>ame, then <u>D</u>efine.

9. The Define Name dialog box already has the name—Retail_Value—and the range of cells entered. So just click on the OK button.

10. Move to cell F10, enter the formula **=SUM(Retail_Value)**, and press Enter.

Your worksheet now has the new column, along with the total retail value in cell F10. To change the assumption contained in the constant value C_MARKUP, (your retail markup assumption), follow these steps:

1. Pull down the <u>I</u>nsert menu, select <u>N</u>ame, then <u>D</u>efine.

2. In the Names in <u>S</u>heet list box, select C_MARKUP. Then, click in the <u>R</u>efers to field and change the value from 1.40 to 1.5.

3. Click on the OK button for your changes to take effect. The results are shown in figure 2.9.

Immediately after you click on the OK button, the retail value of each item changes to reflect the new markup in the constant C_MARKUP. The total at the bottom of the column also changes to reflect the new assumption.

Figure 2.9
The retail value column after changing the constant C_MARKUP.

		Microsoft Excel - Book1					
	A	B	C	D	E	F	G	H

F11

	A	B	C	D	E	F	G	H
1								
2			ACME Company Inventory					
3								
4	Quantity	Description	Model #	Price	Value	Retail Value		
5	5	Paper Clips	00587	0.75	3.75	5.625		
6	31	Faber #2 Pencils	2002	0.05	1.55	2.325		
7	12	Office Calendars	OCTZAB	12.95	155.4	233.1		
8	93	Cs. Manilla Folders	12MAN	6.95	646.35	969.525		
9	12	Rm. #20 Copy Paper	20#500	5.35	64.2	96.3		
10					871.25	1306.875		
11								
12								
13								
14								
15								
16								
17								
18								
19								
20								

Sheet1 / Sheet2 / Sheet3 / Sheet4 / Sheet5 / Sheet6

Ready   NUM

Creating Named Formulas

Even as you can define a named constant, so too can you define a named formula. While named formulas have fewer uses, they can come in handy. One example in which named formulas are useful might be if your worksheet uses a single formula in many places. If you use a named formula, you can simply change the named formula, rather than finding and changing the formula in every cell in which it occurs.

To see how this works, create a named formula called Calc.Retail.Value. This named formula has the formula necessary to calculate the retail value. Follow these steps:

1. Pull down the Insert menu, select Name, then Define.

2. In the Define Name dialog box, move to the Name field and type **Calc.Retail.Value**.

TIP

For the same reason you want your named constants to have a distinct naming style from named ranges, you also want named formulas to have a distinct naming style. In this example, the named formula uses periods to separate the words and also has the word Calc at the beginning of the name, which helps you see that this name refers to a named formula.

3. Move to the <u>R</u>efers to field, type **=(E5*C_MARKUP)** and press Enter to create the name and click on the OK button to close the Define Name dialog box.

4. Move to cell F5, type **=Calc.Retail.Value**, and press Enter.

   Cell F5 now contains a reference to Calc.Retail.Value that contains the formula that does the calculation. To complete this change, copy the new formula down to the other cells.

5. To copy the named formula to the rest of the column, select the cells F5:F9 and press Ctrl+D (the shortcut for <u>E</u>dit, Fi<u>l</u>l <u>D</u>own).

Deleting Names

Sometimes you have to delete names from a workbook. For example, if the name in question is no longer in use, you might want to remove it from the list to reduce clutter. To remove a name, use the following procedure.

1. Pull down the <u>I</u>nsert menu, select <u>N</u>ame, then <u>D</u>efine.

2. Click on the name you want to delete in the Names in <u>W</u>orkbook list box.

3. Click on the <u>D</u>elete button, then the OK button.

STOP

If you delete a name that is being used in other formulas, Excel doesn't warn you. What happens is, after you click on the OK button, a #NAME? error message appears in all the cells that have formulas using that name, as well as in any cells that refer to the cells using that deleted name. For example, if you delete the Price name from the example worksheet, all the cells in columns E and F show the #NAME? error, because those cells depend on the Price name. To rectify such a mistake, you must re-create the name or edit the formulas in the affected cells.

Working with Notes in Cells

Naming parts of your workbook is only the beginning of documenting it. Often, you still have to explain *why* certain calculations were made or provide other information pertinent to the workbook. Here are a couple of reasons why notes make sense:

✔ If you need to look at the workbook again in several months, you might not re-member why you made certain choices.

✔ If others work with your workbooks, they might not understand why you did certain things or the way in which you did them.

In Excel, you can attach notes to individual cells—notes that you can use to explain the worksheet. In essence, you can annotate your worksheet.

Figure 2.10
The ACME sales
projections
worksheet.

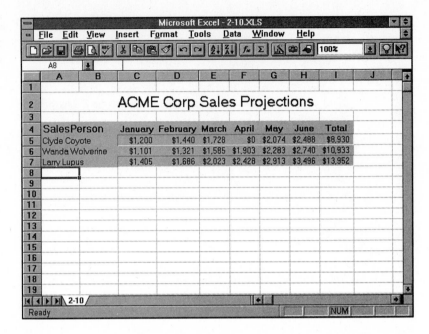

Adding Notes

In the worksheet in figure 2.10, the sales for Clyde Coyote are at zero for the month of April, but why the sales go to zero that month is totally inexplicable.

Any proper documentation must certainly explain that "zero" entry—a perfect occasion for Excel's note feature. To add a note that explains the lack of sales during April, follow these steps:

1. Move to cell F5.

2. Pull down the Insert menu and select Note. The Cell Note dialog box appears, as shown in figure 2.11.

TIP   Press Shift+F2 to pull up the Cell Note dialog box.

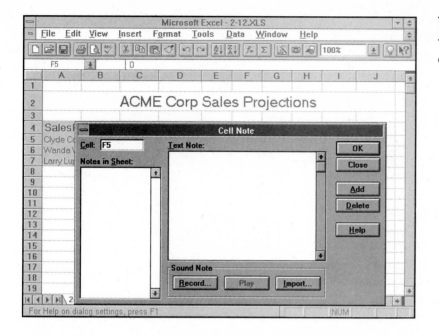

Figure 2.11
The Cell Note
dialog box.

The Cell Note dialog box has many fields and buttons, which are described in the following list:

✔ **Cell.** Indicates the cell to which this note is to be attached. You can attach notes only to single cells and not to ranges of cells.

✔ **Notes in Sheet.** Displays all notes that the worksheet contains. The notes are listed in order of cell location. Only the first 10 or so characters of the note appear in the list.

✔ **Text Note.** You type the complete note in this field. Also, if you browse in the Cell Note dialog box, you can see the complete note if you select it from the Notes in Sheet list box.

✔ **Sound Note.** If your computer contains a sound board and a microphone, you can record a note and attach it to the cell. You also can import a sound clip and attach it to the cell. Double-click on the individual cells that contain the sound note to play the sound notes.

For this example, move to the Text Note field and type **Clyde is on vacation this month**. To store the note, press Enter or click on the OK button.

A small red dot in the upper-right corner of a cell indicates the presence of a note (see fig. 2.12).

Figure 2.12
The note indicator.

Small red dot—
indicates note
attached to cell

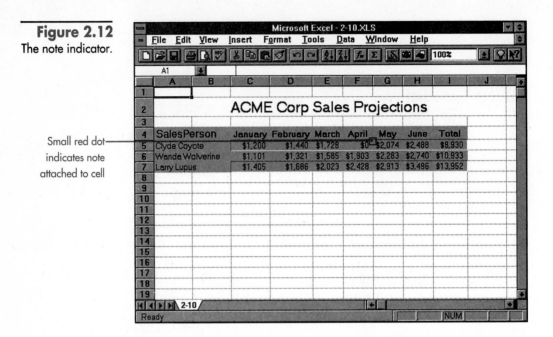

Showing Notes

If a note is indicated by the small red dot, press Shift+F2 after you select the cell to play the note or bring up the note dialog box.

You can turn off the appearance of the small red dot by following these steps:

1. Pull down the Tools menu, select Options, then click on the View tab.

2. On the View notebook page, find the checkbox marked Note Indicator and click on it to deselect the checkbox.

3. Click on the OK button.

Finding Notes

To search the spreadsheet for a specific note, follow these steps:

1. Pull down the Edit menu and select Find (or press Shift+F5). The Find dialog box appears.

2. In the Find What field, type the word you want to find.

3. In the Look In drop box, select Notes.

4. Click on the OK button.

Excel searches all the notes in the worksheet for the word you typed, and the cell that contains the note becomes the active cell. To bring up the note, press Shift+F2 when you are on that cell.

Editing Notes

To edit a note, pull down the Insert menu, select Note, then select the note from the Notes in Sheet list box. After you select the note, you can edit it in the Text Note field.

Also, after you select a note, you can click on the Delete button to remove the note from the worksheet.

Rearranging Data

One of the most powerful notions behind worksheets is that they allow you to to work through an idea or analysis progressively. It is vital to know how to rearrange the data you enter into the worksheet as you decide to try new approaches, consider new information, and so on. Whether you want to analyze the data in a different way, rearrange the data the better to graph it, or accomplish some other task, manipulating data and rearranging it are important skills. This section covers the following:

- ✔ Cutting data from one location and paste it to another

- ✔ Copying data in your document

- ✔ Moving data in a single mouse movement

- ✔ Moving not only ranges, but entire rows or columns

- ✔ Filling ranges of cells automatically with numbers or text

- ✔ Utilizing the AutoFill feature to complete various numeric and date progressions

Cut and Paste

The basic method for moving and duplicating data in a worksheet is to Cut and Paste or Copy and Paste—similar, but not duplicate, activities. You can cut or copy data into the "Clipboard," then paste it from the Clipboard to a new location.

All Windows-based programs have access to the Windows Clipboard, a place that temporarily stores data that you cut, copy, and paste.

For these examples, you use the inventory worksheet that you created at the beginning of this chapter.

1. Begin by selecting range B4:B9.

2. Pull down the Edit menu and select Cut. A marquee surrounds the area you have cut, but it doesn't disappear right away (in many programs, your data disappears immediately after choosing Cut, but not in Excel).

3. Move your active cell to location B12.

4. Pull down the Edit menu and select Paste.

When you cut and paste cells on which other cells are dependent, Excel automatically adjusts the references so that the formulas still work properly with the data in the new location.

Immediately, the data vanishes from its original location and reappears in the new location (see fig. 2.13). The pasted data starts in the active cell (B12) and fills the cells downwards. The destination you select is always the upper-left corner of the area you want to paste.

Figure 2.13
The pasted data in new location.

	A	B	C	D	E	F	G	H
1								
2			ACME Company Inventory					
3								
4	Quantity		Model #	Price	Value	Retail Value		
5	5		00587	0.75	3.75	5.625		
6	31		2002	0.05	1.55	2.325		
7	12		OCTZAB	12.95	155.4	233.1		
8	93		12MAN	6.95	646.35	969.525		
9	12		20#500	5.35	64.2	96.3		
10					871.25	1306.875		
11								
12		Description						
13		Paper Clips						
14		Faber #2 Pencils						
15		Office Calendars						
16		Cs. Manilla Folders						
17		Rm. #20 Copy Paper						
18								
19								
20								

Microsoft Excel - 2-1.XLS
File Edit View Insert Format Tools Data Window Help
B12   Description

Sheet1 / Sheet2 / Sheet3 / Sheet4 / Sheet5 / Sheet6

Ready   NUM

To reverse the process, select the data from cells B12:B17, then choose Cut from the Edit menu. Move your active cell to cell B4, then select Paste from the Edit menu.

NOTE   Of course, if you wanted to undo the cut and paste operation, you simply choose Undo from the Edit menu.

You cut, copy and paste frequently in Excel, so you can save a great deal of time by learning to use the cut, copy, and paste shortcut keys. These keys are shown in table 2.5, which follows.

Table 2.5
Cut, Copy, and Paste Shortcut Keys

Function	Shortcut Key	Memory Cues
Cut	Ctrl+X	Think of 'X' as similar to a pair of scissors, or think of crossing something out on a paper document with a big X.
Copy	Ctrl+C	'C' stands for Copy
Paste	Ctrl+V	Think of the 'V' as an insertion point that you would make hand-editing a document.

AUTHOR'S NOTE

All these keys are on the keyboard in the order shown. Cut, Copy, and Paste are in the same order, from left to right, as X, C, and V on your keyboard. Excel is one of the few Windows programs that uses Ctrl+X, Ctrl+C, and Ctrl+V for these functions. Most Windows-based programs use Shift+Delete for Cut, Ctrl+Insert for Copy, and Shift+Insert for Paste.

These easier key combinations originated on the Macintosh, for which they have been standards ever since the Mac was developed more than 10 years ago.

Copying Data

Copying data works just like cutting and pasting. Instead of cutting from one location and pasting onto another, you copy the data from the selected range onto the Clipboard and then paste it onto the new location. The original data is unaffected.

For an example of how copying works, select the range B4:B9 and press Ctrl+C (for copy). Move your active cell to B12 and press Ctrl+V (for paste). You should see a copy of the data appear in the new location.

Also, because the data is still in the Windows Clipboard, you can paste the copied data into an unlimited number of new locations, until you cut or copy something else, which overwrites the old data in the Clipboard. To see the way this works, move to cell C12 and press Ctrl+V again.

Deleting Data

To delete data from your worksheet, select a range such as C12:C17 in the example, pull down the Edit menu, and choose Clear, then All.

You will see the cascading menu shown in figure 2.14, which follows.

TIP   Pressing the Del key does the same thing as selecting Clear, All from the Edit menu.

Figure 2.14
The Clear
cascading
menu.

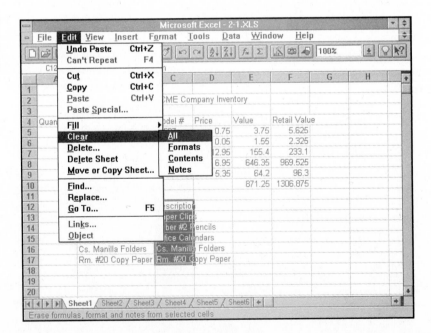

The Clear cascading menu has four options:

✔ **All.** Removes the data in the selected range, as well as any formatting applied to the cell and any notes attached to the cell. When formatting is removed, the cell reverts to General—the default format.

✔ **Formats.** Causes the formatting for the cell to be removed. The cell reverts to the General format.

✔ **Contents.** Removes any cell contents, including formulas, numbers, and text labels, but does not affect the cell format or any notes attached to the cell. This is the default.

✔ **Notes.** Removes only the note attached to the selected cells. The cell contents and formatting remain.

In this example, you want to remove the entire range contents. Because the menu already is set to <u>A</u>ll, click on <u>A</u>ll.

TIP

To remove all cell contents quickly, select the range you want to clear and press Ctrl+Del. Pressing Del only removes cell contents, whereas Ctrl+Del clears everything from the selected cells.

Entire Rows and Columns

You can cut, copy, paste, or clear entire rows and columns. As an example, move column E to column G by using the following steps:

1. At the top of the worksheet, click once on the column marker labeled E. The entire column becomes highlighted.

2. Press Ctrl+X to cut the data from column E.

3. Click on the column marker for column G.

4. Press Ctrl+V to paste the data into the new location. Depending on your computer's available memory, you might see a dialog box that warns you that the section is too large to undo. If you are sure you want to proceed, click on the OK button.

You can perform the same operation on rows by selecting the numbered row label.

You also can perform the operation on multiple rows or columns. Hold down Ctrl as you select each row or column. If, by chance, you select an operation (such as <u>E</u>dit, <u>D</u>elete) that Excel cannot perform on multiple rows or columns, an error box appears.

Dragging

Cutting and pasting with Ctrl+X and Ctrl+V are quick methods, but Excel includes one other shortcut that lets you move data with a simple drag of the mouse. To see how shortcuts work, move the cells D4:D9 to G4:G9:

1. Select the range D4:D9.

2. Very carefully move your pointer to the outside border of the selected cells. When your pointer is in precisely the right place, it changes to a white arrow.

3. With your pointer in the arrow shape, click and hold down the left mouse button. With the button held down, move your mouse to the right. As you move it, a thick marquee moves.

4. Position the thick marquee so that it encloses cells G4:G9, and then release the mouse button.

This procedure works with both single cells and ranges. You even can use it with entire rows and columns!

When you move sections of your worksheet that contain formulas or numbers used by formulas in other cells, be careful. Moving cells can mess up the formulas they contain or formulas in other cells that use the moved data. Often these problems appear as #REF! or #VALUE! errors in the affected cells.

Filling Ranges of Cells

Often, you need to copy the contents of one cell into many cells. You can copy the data into the Clipboard, then paste it into the new cells, but there are yet faster ways available to duplicate cell contents into many cells.

For these examples, begin a new worksheet. Pull down the File menu and select New. A dialog box prompts you for the type of document that you want to create. Select Workbook and click on the OK button.

Menu Commands

Follow these steps to see how to fill ranges of cells with menu commands:

1. Move to cell D6, type **Example**, and press Enter.

2. Select the range D6:D10.

3. Pull down the Edit menu and select Fill, then Down.

The word Example is copied into each of the selected cells. You also can do this to fill cells to the right by selecting a horizontal range and selecting Edit, Fill, Right.

TIP You can fill down faster by pressing Ctrl+D. Filling right can be done using Ctrl+R.

Fill Handle

Using the Fill handle is far easier than using the menu commands to fill ranges. The Fill handle also has some neat tricks! For these examples, delete anything on the worksheet left over from the previous example. Select a range that includes all the worksheet contents and press Ctrl+Delete to clear the worksheet contents.

Use table 2.6 to set up several cells to use to explore the different ways in which the Fill handle works. After you set up the worksheet, it should look like figure 2.15.

Table 2.6
Fill Handle Example Setup

Cell	Contents
B3	1
B4	1
C4	3
B5	January
B6	Jan
C6	Apr
B7	Quarter 1
B8	1/1/95
B9	1/1/95
C9	2/1/95

Figure 2.15

The worksheet for Fill handle examples.

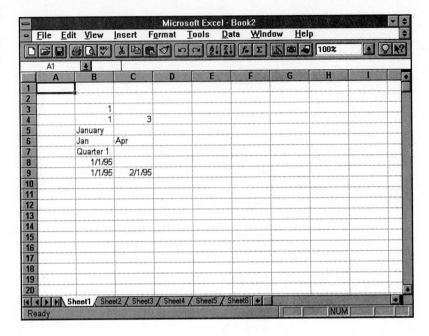

Follow these steps to start using the Fill handle:

1. Make sure that cell B3 is your active cell.

2. Locate the Fill handle. It is the small box at the lower right corner of the active cell. See figure 2.16.

3. Carefully move your pointer until it is immediately on top of the Fill handle. When positioned correctly, the pointer changes to a small cross.

4. Hold down the left mouse button and drag the mouse to the right until the thick marquee surrounds the cells from B3 to H3.

5. When the marquee is positioned correctly, release the mouse button.

The number 1 is automatically copied into each of the selected cells. You also can use the Fill handle to fill on each of the other four directions.

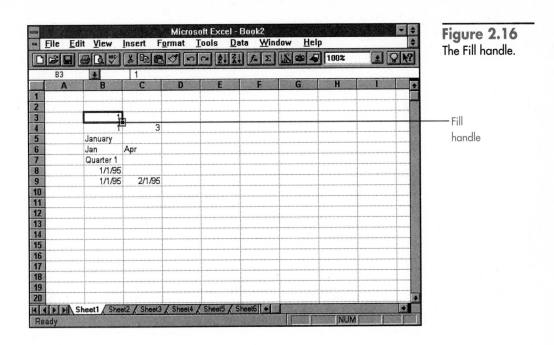

Figure 2.16
The Fill handle.

AutoFill

If you use the Fill handle with a single number or a text label, Excel simply copies the data. Similarly, if you use the Fill handle with a formula, Excel copies it, adjusting any relative cell references as it fills the formula.

Sometimes, however, the Fill handle activates a feature called *AutoFill*. Follow these examples to see some of the ways in which AutoFill works.

Numeric Progression

1. Select the cells B4:C4

2. Drag the Fill handle in the lower right hand corner of cell C4 until the thick marquee extends to H3 and release the mouse button. The results are shown in figure 2.17.

Excel determined that you had marked out two cells that contained a numeric progression. Excel assumed that you wanted to continue the numeric progression and filled the cells accordingly.

Figure 2.17
Numeric
progression
with the Fill
handle.

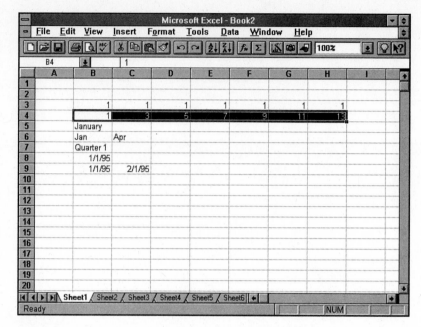

Date Progressions

AutoFill also is very intelligent about filling dates into cells. For each of the remaining lines in the example worksheet, use the Fill handle to copy the contents to column H. In the two cases where two initial examples are provided (when column C has a value), remember to select both examples before dragging the Fill handle to the right. The results are shown in figure 2.18.

Table 2.7 contains some comments on each of these examples.

Table 2.7
Comments on AutoFill Examples

Row	Starting Data	Comments
5	January	Excel recognizes the word "January" as a valid month name. It automatically fills the remaining months into the filled cells.
6	Jan, Apr	Excel also recognizes Jan and Apr as valid month titles. Because you used two month names that are three months apart, Excel continues the series, even starting over again at Jan when it finishes the first year.

Row	Starting Data	Comments
7	Quarter 1	Excel recognizes Quarter 1 as a common financial heading. It correctly fills the remaining three quarters, and then starts over again at Quarter 1. Excel also recognizes 'Qtr1', and 'Q1' as quarterly titles.
8	1/1/93	AutoFilling this range produces dates each one day apart. If you AutoFill many cells, you find that Excel knows the day on which each month ends and that it even takes into account leap years!
9	1/1/93,2/1/93	As you observed in previous progressions, Excel is fairly intelligent about assuming your desires. In this case, it automatically fills each cell with the first day of each month.

As you can see, Excel's AutoFill feature is very intelligent and saves you a tremendous amount of time.

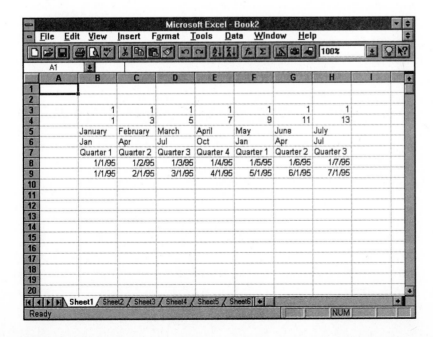

Figure 2.18
Completed examples of AutoFill.

Worksheets

Inserting and Deleting Data

Aside from cut, copy, paste, and clear operations, Excel also offers insertion and deletion areas on the worksheet. Using the Edit, Insert and Edit, Delete commands, you can accomplish the following tasks:

✔ Insert new rows or columns, pushing the existing rows or columns down or to the right to make room.

✔ Insert blocks of data, pushing the existing data to the right or down.

✔ Delete entire rows or columns, moving the remaining data up or to the left.

✔ Delete ranges of data, moving the remaining data up or to the left.

Inserting Blank Space

To insert new blank space in your worksheet, select the area in which you want the new cells to appear, pull down the Insert menu, then select Cells.

As an example, select the range C4:F7, pull down the Insert menu and then select Cells. The Insert dialog box appears, as in figure 2.19.

Figure 2.19
The Insert dialog box.

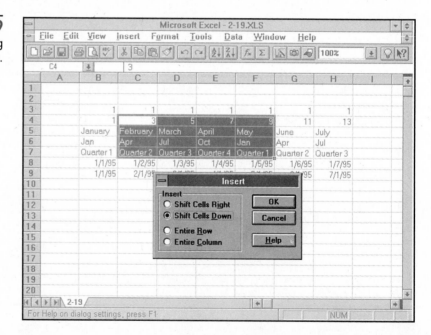

The Insert dialog box lets you choose from the following four options:

- ✔ **Shift Cells** **R**ight. Makes new space by forcing the existing cells to the right of the new area.

- ✔ **Shift Cells** **D**own. Pushes the existing cells downward.

- ✔ **Entire** **R**ow. Inserts entire rows in the selected range, pushing the existing rows down.

- ✔ **Entire** **C**olumn. Inserts entire columns, pushing the existing columns to the right.

For this example, select Shift Cells **D**own. The results are shown in figure 2.20.

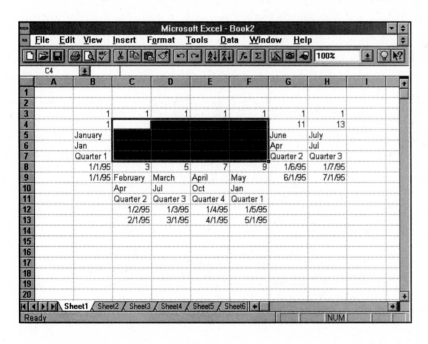

Figure 2.20
The inserted blank range.

Inserting Data

You also can copy data from one location and insert it into a new location by selecting the range you want to copy, pressing Ctrl+C to copy it to the Clipboard, positioning the active cell where you want the data to be inserted, pulling down the **I**nsert menu, and selecting **C**ell. The Insert dialog box appears, which enables you to shift the existing cells to the right or down. After you make your decision in the dialog box, Excel performs the insert operation, moving the existing cells in the direction you specify.

Deleting Ranges

Deleting entire ranges is accomplished in a similar way. Select the range of cells to delete, pull down the Edit menu, and select Delete. You will be shown a Delete dialog box, which enables you to choose to shift the cells up, to the left, or to delete entire rows and columns. Select the appropriate choice and click on the OK button.

Inserting and Deleting Entire Rows and Columns

Finally, you can insert and delete entire rows and columns by selecting the row or column. Click on the row or column label, then choose Insert Row, Insert Column, or Edit Delete.

You also can select multiple rows and columns. Just hold down the mouse on the first row or column, then drag the mouse in the appropriate direction to select the desired rows or columns.

Special Paste Tricks within Excel

Excel has a few other tricks up its sleeve concerning the rearrangement of data. Under the Edit menu is a command called Paste Special. Paste Special enables you to accomplish the following tricks:

- ✔ Selectively paste only cell values, formulas, formatting, or notes.

- ✔ Automatically take the originating range and perform a mathematical function with its cells on the destination cells.

- ✔ Transpose a series of cells, which has the effect of rotating the data 90 degrees.

To understand the way these features work, set up the worksheet as follows:

1. In cell B2, enter **1**.

2. In cell C2, enter **3**.

3. Use the Fill handle to AutoFill the numeric series to column G (select B2:C2 and drag the Fill handle to cell G2).

4. In cell B3, enter **2**.

5. In cell C3, enter **4**.

6. Use the Fill handle to AutoFill the numeric series to column G.

7. In cell B4, enter the formula **=B2*B3** and press Enter.

8. Use the Fill handle to copy the formula in cell B4 to all of the cells over to cell G4.

Your worksheet should look like figure 2.21.

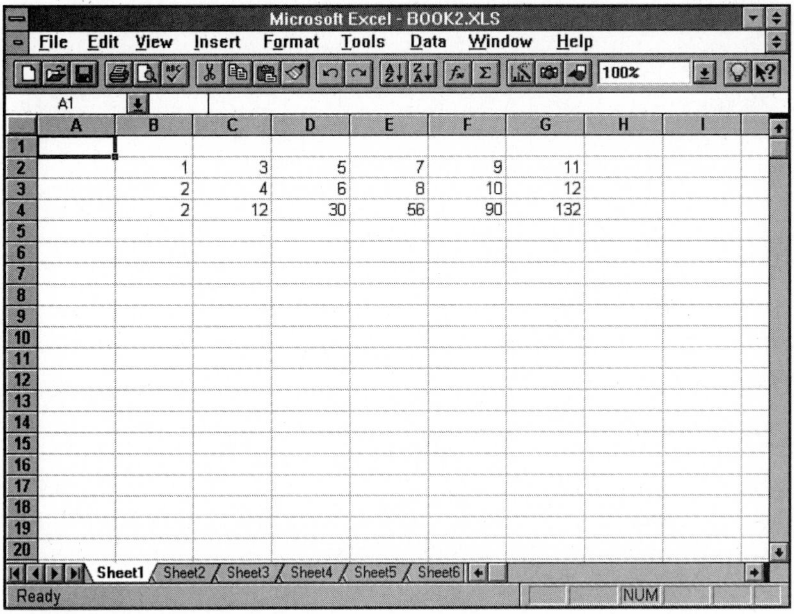

Figure 2.21
The sample worksheet for Paste **S**pecial examples.

Pasting Values

Excel enables you to copy a series of formulas and paste only their results. You can, for example, select a series of formulas which result in numeric values and copy those formulas into the clipboard. Then you can move to the destination cell, use Paste **S**pecial, and select **V**alues from the dialog box. Click on OK to complete the operation. The destination cells contain the results, not the formulas of the originating cells.

To perform this operation:

1. Select the cells B4:G4 and press Ctrl+C to copy them into the Clipboard.

2. Move to cell B6.

3. Pull down the **E**dit Menu and select Paste **S**pecial.

4. On the Paste Special dialog box, select **V**alues, and click the OK button.

If you look at the cell contents of the original cells (B4:G4) you can see that they contain formulas. The destination cells, however, contain only the resulting values. It is as if Excel took the values and simply typed the results for you in the new location.

Performing Math Operations

Excel enables you to copy one series of numbers (either from a formula or simple, entered numbers), and then add, subtract, multiply, or divide those values against a different range.

To see how this operation works, follow these steps:

1. Select the series of cells B3:G3.

2. Press Ctrl+C to copy the cells into the Clipboard.

3. Move to cell B6, where the results of the previous example start.

4. Pull down the Edit menu and select Paste Special.

5. In the Paste Special dialog box, select Divide and click on the OK button.

Excel takes the numbers in the destination cells and divides them by the contents of the Clipboard. Using the same method, you also can add, subtract, or multiply two ranges of numbers against one another.

Transposing Data

You also can change the orientation of your data quickly using the Paste Special command. For example, if you have some data for which you want the rows to become columns and the columns to become rows, Paste Special enables you to "rotate" the data 90 degrees. This capability is separate from the new Pivot Table feature, which is discussed in a later chapter.

When you transpose cells that contain formulas, you change any formulas in the transposed cells. To deal with this potential problen, select the Values option button when performing the Paste Special command. This option converts any formulas to pure numbers.

To see how the transpose feature in Paste Special works, follow these steps:

1. Select the range of cells B2:G4.

2. Press Ctrl+C to copy the cells to the Clipboard.

3. Move to cell B6.

4. Pull down the Edit menu and select Paste Special.

5. In the Paste Special dialog box, click on the Transpose checkbox, then click on the OK button.

The results are shown in figure 2.22.

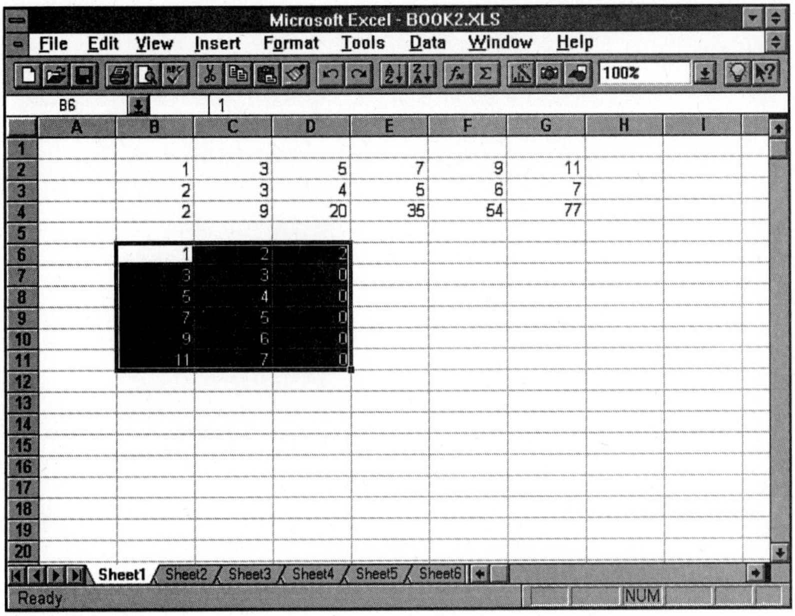

Figure 2.22
The results of Transpos**e**.

Excel rearranges the data 90 degrees from its original arrangement in the source cells. Also, notice that the far right column now shows primarily zeroes. This rightmost column originally was the formula in row 4. Now that the data is rearranged, those formulas no longer refer to meaningful cells. To avoid this problem, select the **V**alues option when you select Transpos**e** if you have any formulas in the copied area that are dependent on other data or on data structure.

Chapter Snapshot

Now that you understand the basics of working with data in Excel, you need to know how to make the worksheet look more professional and appealing. In this chapter, you learn to use Excel's formatting tools to do the following:

✔ Formatting numbers for different display styles

✔ Changing fonts in your worksheet

✔ Changing the height of your rows and the width of your columns

✔ Dressing up your worksheet with border lines and shading

✔ Controlling the alignment of the data in your worksheet, including how to center a title across the worksheet quickly

✔ Using Excel's styles to format your worksheets quickly

✔ Using Excel's AutoFormat feature to format a table quickly and easily

✔ Zooming in and out of your worksheet to see more area or more detail

A nicely formatted document helps you present your information much more effectively.

3 CHAPTER

Worksheet Formatting

Setting up a worksheet, entering the data, getting all the formulas to work, and structuring the worksheet in a useful way are usually only half the battle. Before you can use Excel to share information with others, you must be able to format the worksheet so you can communicate quickly and effectively.

Excel provides many tools that help you control the way your worksheet appears and prints. This chapter teaches you how to produce professional, eye-catching reports and worksheets.

Activating the Formatting Toolbar

This chapter shows you how to use the Style toolbar for faster and easier formatting. To open the Style toolbar, follow these steps:

1. Pull down the <u>V</u>iew menu and choose <u>T</u>oolbars. The Toolbars dialog box appears, as shown in figure 3.1.

Figure 3.1
The Toolbars
dialog box.

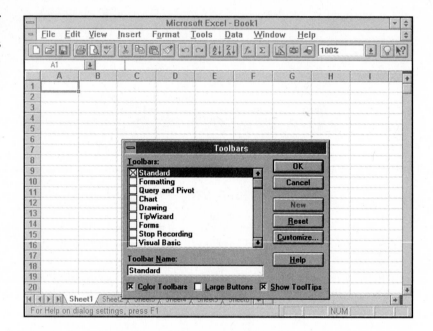

2. Click on the checkbox to the left of the word Formatting.

3. Click on the OK button. You see the Formatting toolbar beneath the standard toolbar.

Figure 3.2 shows all the buttons in the Formatting toolbar. The function of each button is described in table 3.1.

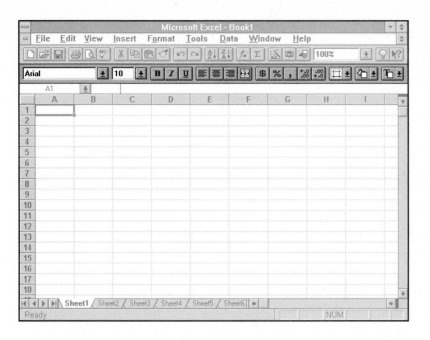

Figure 3.2
The Formatting toolbar.

Table 3.1
Formatting Toolbar Buttons

Icon	Name	Description
Arial ↓	Font	Chooses font name for selected range
10 ↓	Font Size	Chooses font size for selected range
B	Bold	Makes selected range bold
I	Italic	Makes selected range italic
U	Underline	Underlines selected range
☰	Align Left	Makes selected range left-justified

continues

Table 3.1, Continued
Formatting Toolbar Buttons

Icon	Name	Description
	Align Center	Makes selected range centered
	Align Right	Makes selected range right-justified
	Center Across Selection	Centers the text across selected range
	Currency Style	Applies the currency style to numbers in selected range
	Percent Style	Applies the percentage style to numbers in selected range
	Comma Style	Applies the comma style to numbers in selected range
	Increase Decimal	Increases the number of digits after the decimal point for numbers in selected range
	Decrease Decimal	Decreases the number of digits after the decimal point for numbers in selected range
	Color	Chooses the color for selected cells
	Borders	Chooses the border style for selected cells
	Font Color	Chooses the color for text in selected cells

Formatting Numbers

The first step when you format a worksheet is to control the way numeric information appears in the individual cells. Many choices are available:

- ✔ Use commas for the thousands separator?
- ✔ Display negative numbers in red?
- ✔ Use brackets for negative numbers, and if so, what characters to use for the brackets?

✔ How many decimal positions to show?

✔ What format to use to display dates and times?

Because you can create your own numeric and date formats, the possibilities for using different numeric formats are virtually endless.

Using Built-In Formats

Excel uses format codes to control the way numbers are formatted in your worksheets. *Format codes* are collections of special formatting characters that Excel interprets in order to know how to format the numbers in the worksheet. Although these format codes can be a bit cryptic, you learn in the following sections to read and create them quickly.

Table 3.2 shows the different format codes included with Excel, along with examples of how each number appears when that code is used.

Table 3.2
Built-In Excel Formats

Format Section	Format Setting	Examples Positive	Negative
All	General	12345.67	–12345.67
Custom	(Shows formats that you create)		
Number	0	12346	–12346
	0.00	12345.67	–12345.67
	#,##0	12,346	–12,346
	#,##0.00	12,345.67	–12,345.67
	#,##0_);(#,##0)	12,346	(12,346)
	#,##0_);[Red](#,##0)	12,346	**(12,346)**
	#,##0.00_);(#,##0.00)	12,345.67	(12,345.67)
	#,##0.00_);[Red](#,##0.00)	12,345.67	**(12,345.67)**
Accounting	_(*#,##0_);_(#,##0);_(*"-"_);_(@_)	12,345	(12,345)
	_(*#,##0.00_);_(*(#,##0.00);_(*"-"??_);_(@_)	12,345.67	(12,345.67)
	_($*#,##0_);_($*(#,##0);_($*"-"_);_(@_)	$12,345	$(12,345)

continues

Table 3.2, Continued
Built-In Excel Formats

Format Section	Format Setting	Examples Positive	Negative
	_($*#,##0.00_);_($*(#,##0.00);_($*"-"??_);_(@_)	$12,345.67	$(12,345.67)
Date	m/d/y	4/15/95	
	d–mmm–yy	15–Apr–95	
	d–mmm	15–Apr	
	mmm–d	Apr–95	
	m/d/y h:mm	4/15/95 6:31	
Time	h:mm AM/PM	6:31 AM	
	h:mm:ss AM/PM	6:31:00 AM	
	h:mm	6:31	
	h:mm:ss	6:31:00	
	m/d/yy h:mm	4/15/95 6:31	
	mm:ss	31:00	
	mm:ss.0	31:00.0	
	[h]:mm:ss	6:31:00	
Percentage	0%	12%	–12%
	0.00%	12.35%	–12.35%
Fraction	# ?/?	12345 2/3	–12345 2/3
	# ??/??	12345 65/97	–12345 65/97
Scientific	0.00E+00	1.23E+04	–1.23E+04
Text	@ (Text placeholder)		
Currency	$#,##0_);($#,##0)	$12,346	($12,346)
	$#,##0_);[Red]($#,##0)	$12,346	**($12,346)**
	$#,##0.00_);($#,##0.00)	$12,345.67	($12,345.67)
	$#,##0.00_);[Red]($#,##0.00)	$12,345.67	**($12,345.67)**

NOTE Numbers that appear in bold in the preceding table appear in red on a color monitor.

See file CHAP3-1.XLS for examples of all the built-in numeric formats.

Applying Built-In Formats

You can apply different numeric formats to your cells in two ways. The first way, using menu commands, is the most flexible. The second way is to use some shortcut keys that are available for the most common formatting needs.

To apply a format using menu commands, use the following procedure:

1. Select the cell or range that you want to format.

2. Pull down the F<u>o</u>rmat menu and select C<u>e</u>lls.

TIP As a shortcut, after you select the cell or range to format, you can click on the selected range using the right mouse button to bring up the pop-up menu for the selection. From the pop-up menu, choose **N**umber to access the Number dialog box.

3. Step 2 causes the Cell formatting notebook to appear. If it is not selected already, click on the Number tab. You see the Number page, shown in figure 3.3.

4. Click on the appropriate category in the <u>C</u>ategory list box.

5. Click on the desired format in the <u>F</u>ormat Codes list box. Use the small sample at the bottom of the dialog box to help you determine which format you want.

6. Click on the OK button.

Excel also includes some key combinations that format the cells you select instantly with a number of commonly used formats. Table 3.3 shows a list of these shortcut keys.

Figure 3.3
The Number
Format notebook
page.

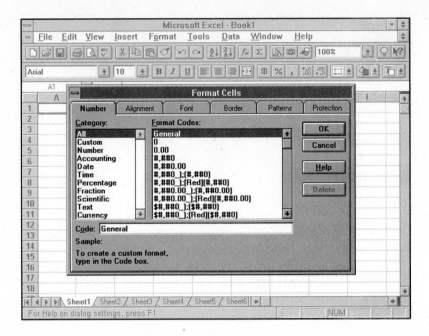

Table 3.3
Excel Format Shortcut Keys

Key Combination	Format Code	Example
Ctrl+Shift+~	General	12345.67
Ctrl+Shift+!	0.00	12345.67
Ctrl+Shift+@	h.mm	6:31
Ctrl+Shift+#	d-mmm-yy	15-Apr-95
Ctrl+Shift+$	$#,##0.00);($#,##0.00)	$12,345.67
Ctrl+Shift+%	0%	12%
Ctrl+Shift+^	0.00E+00	1.23E+04

Creating New Formats

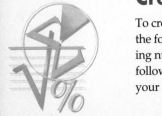

To create your own custom number formats, you need to understand how Excel interprets the format code and learn the various available codes. Excel is extremely flexible for displaying numbers, times and dates, or text. This flexibility creates some complexity, but the following section clearly explains how these formatting codes work. You can begin writing your own formats in no time!

When you create a new format using the symbols that follow, Excel automatically stores the new format in its list of formats. The formats you create, however, are stored only as part of the workbook for which you create them. Other workbooks have only the default Excel formats in the Format dialog box.

Format Code Structure

Each format code is divided into four parts:

```
Positive_Section;Negative_Section;Zero_Section;Text_Section
```

Codes that appear in the positive section format positive numbers; the negative section contains the format codes for negative numbers; the zero section formats zero values; and the text section formats any text entries. Each section is separated from the others with a semicolon. Only the first section, the positive section, is required. If the remaining sections are not specified, Excel provides default formatting for numbers that match those characteristics.

Consider the following format:

```
#,###;[Red]#,###;0;[RED]/"@/" "is not allowed. Entry must be a number!!"
```

The preceding format specifies that positive numbers appear with a thousands separator, that negative numbers are red, that a zero appears as "0", and that if text is entered into this cell, the message *x* is not allowed. Entry must be a number!!, where *x* is whatever you typed, appears in red instead of the text you enter. The preceding format uses several tricks. "Format Codes," later in this chapter, explains how the format works.

Format Code Conditions

You can define the conditions that Excel uses for each section of the format. By default, the first section applies to numbers greater than 0, the second section to numbers less than 0, and the third section for all other numbers (generally 0).

If you use a conditional operator surrounded by square brackets at the beginning of the code section, you can specify the conditions for each of the three format code sections that Excel uses, rather than the default number ranges. Consider the following format code:

```
[>100][Blue]#,##0;[<-100][Yellow]#,##0;[Green]0
```

This code specifies that numbers greater than 100 are blue and that numbers less than 100 are yellow. Zeroes and numbers less than zero are green. The reason that the third position applies to zeros and numbers less than zero is that the third section must format everything the first two formats don't control. Usually, only zero values are involved, because the first section typically formats all positive numbers, and the second section typically formats all negative numbers. When you change the numeric conditions of the first two sections, however, the third section has to take care of everything else.

Format Codes

You can use a variety of different codes in each format code. Table 3.4 lists each code symbol, along with an explanation of its function.

Table 3.4
Format Symbols

Symbol	Explanation
General	The word "General" is actually one of the format symbols. For example, you might have a specific format for positive numbers, but specify General format for negative numbers. An example follows: `$#,###;General`. The general format symbol displays numbers exactly as they were entered. The symbol 0 acts as a placeholder for a number. The 0 placeholder indicates that if the number being formatted does not have as many digits as the number of 0s in the format, a zero is to appear. For example, if the number 123 is formatted with the code 0.000; the result is 123.000. As another example, if the number 23.12 is formatted with 0000.000, the result is 0023.120; note that zeros appear in place of the missing digits.
#	The pound sign acts similarly to the 0 symbol, except that it does not force a digit to appear if the digit doesn't exist in the underlying number. For example, the number 123 formatted with `#,###.##` simply appears as 123.
?	The question mark functions like the pound sign (#), except that it inserts a space for the missing digits. This function is useful when you need to make decimal points align with numbers for which the number of digits that follow the decimal point varies. The question mark is also used for fraction displays, as in the format # ???/???, which displays the fractional portion of the number with up to three-digit accuracy.
.	The period enables you to define the number of digits that are to appear following the decimal point. If your format code specifies a decimal point, a decimal point always appears, even if no digits follow the decimal point. If the format code has one or more #s before the period, Excel displays numbers less than one as starting with a decimal point. To force Excel to always display at least one zero before the decimal point, use 0 before the period, as in the format 0.0#

Worksheets

Symbol	Explanation
%	If you use a percentage mark in your format code, Excel multiplies the number by 100 and then appends the % symbol to the number that appears.
,	The comma tells Excel to include commas as a thousands separator. Also, if you put the comma after a single placeholder, Excel divides the number by 1000 before displaying it. Following a placeholder with two commas divides the number by one million before displaying it. #, displays the number 145000 as 145, and #,, displays the number 12000000 as 12. This trick is very useful for financial statements displayed in thousands (000s) or millions.
e+,e–,E+,E–	The E symbol followed by a plus or minus causes the number to appear in scientific notation, along with the letter "E" in the appropriate place on the display. See table 3.2 for an example of this format symbol.
–+/()$:(space)	Including any of these characters in your format code causes them to appear. If you need to display a character other than one of these, use the backslash followed by the character you want to display. For example, \" causes a double-quotation mark to appear—particularly useful when you want your format to display a character otherwise used as a formatting symbol. \# displays the pound sign, which is otherwise interpreted as a formatting symbol.
\	The backslash character is a special character that is not displayed in the format. Use it to tell Excel to display the character that follows it. For example, \? displays a question mark, which Excel normally interprets as a special format code symbol. If you need to display a backslash in your format, use two backslashes.
*	The asterisk is similar to the backslash, except that it causes the following character to repeat often enough to fill up the cell. The format code #,###;#,###;*! displays positive and negative numbers, but if a zero is entered, it fills the entire cell with exclamation points.

continues

Table 3.4, Continued
Format Symbols

Symbol	Explanation
_	The underline is used to tell Excel to insert a space in its location. For example, in a format that surrounds negative numbers with parentheses, the decimal points of positive numbers do not align, because the negative number takes more space to the right of the decimal point to display the closing parenthesis. In this case, you use an underline at the end of the positive section of the format to tell Excel to save a space in that location for any possible parentheses.
"Text"	If you want Excel to display a text string, you should enclose it in quotation marks. The following example displays "DR" or "CR" (abbreviations for debit and credit) after positive and negative numbers, respectively: `#,###"DR";[Red]#,###"CR";0`
@	The at symbol represents any text that is entered into the cell. In the example given above, the @ is used to show what was entered, followed by a message that indicates the entry is not correct.
m	Displays the month number (1-12).
mm	Displays the month number, but with leading zeroes for months 1-9.
mmm	Displays the month name using its three letter abbreviation (Jan, Feb, Mar, and so on).
mmmm	Displays the full name of the month (January, February, March, and so on).
d	Displays the day of the month without leading zeroes.
dd	Displays the day of the month with leading zeroes.
ddd	Displays the three letter abbreviation of the day of the week (Mon, Tue, Wed, and so on).
dddd	Displays the full name of the day of the week (Monday, Tuesday, Wednesday, and so on).
yy	Displays the last two digits of the year (00-99).

Symbol	Explanation
yyyy	Displays all the digits of the year (1900-2078).
h	Displays the hour without leading zeroes. If the format contains an AM or PM, Excel uses the 12-hour clock; otherwise it uses the 24-hour clock.
hh	Displays the hour with leading zeroes, if necessary. If the format contains an AM or PM, Excel bases the number on a 12-hour clock; otherwise it uses the 24-hour clock.
m	Displays the minutes without leading zeroes, but must be preceded by an h or hh or Excel interprets them as a request for the month.
mm	Displays the minutes with leading zeroes, if necessary. Note that the mm must be preceded by an h or hh or Excel treats it as a month code.
s	Displays the seconds without leading zeroes.
ss	Displays the seconds with leading zeroes, if necessary.
AM/PM	Forces Excel to use a 12-hour clock for the time display, and displays AM or PM in the location specified. You also can use am/pm (lowercase letters), A/P, or a/p to tell Excel to use those indicators.
[color]	If you place a color name in square brackets at the beginning of the appropriate section of the formatting code, Excel displays the matching number in that color. Valid colors are Black, Blue, Cyan, Green, Magenta, Red, White, or Yellow.
[condition]	As you saw in an earlier section, you can tell Excel which condition to use for each different section of the format code. Valid operators include <, <=, >, >=, =, and <> (not equal).

As an exercise, use the preceding format code explanations to examine what the standard Excel formatting codes do.

Changing Row Height

When you use different font sizes in your worksheets, the rows in which the text appears might need to be taller to accommodate the taller font. On the other hand, you might be designing a form in Excel and need taller rows to give your form the appearance you desire.

If you change the font in a given cell, Excel automatically heightens the column to accommodate taller letters.

You can alter the height of a row using the mouse or menu commands.

To use the mouse, follow these steps:

1. Move your mouse pointer over to the row labels. Carefully maneuver the pointer so that it is directly on top of the line at the bottom of the row you want to adjust. When you have positioned the pointer correctly, you see a horizontal line with two vertical arrows, one pointing up and one pointing down.

2. Press and hold the left mouse button and drag your mouse up or down to shorten or heighten the row as you see fit. Release the mouse button.

While you are dragging the mouse up and down, the row height appears in the upper left corner of the Excel screen in the cell indicator box to the left of the formula bar.

As an alternative to this method, you can select multiple rows before you adjust the height of one. When you finish sizing one row, all the other selected rows use the new row height.

If a row doesn't display the full height of any text in the row, you can command Excel to set the row height automatically to display all text. To make that command, move your mouse so that it is on top of the line at the bottom of the row label you want to change and double-click your mouse. Excel uses a "best fit" method to determine the row size. This method also works if you select multiple rows before double-clicking on one of the rows' adjustment lines.

To change the height of a row using menu commands, follow these steps:

1. Pull down the Format menu and select Row. You see the cascading menu shown in figure 3.4. The Row menu offers the following choices:

    ✔ **Height.** Brings up a dialog box in which you can enter the desired row height for the selected rows or the current row manually.

    ✔ **AutoFit.** Sets the row height to the tallest characters in the entire row.

    ✔ **Hide.** Hides the selected rows.

    ✔ **Unhide.** Reveals the hidden rows.

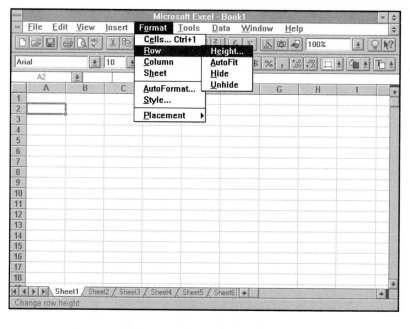

Figure 3.4
The Row menu
selected from the
Format menu.

2. Select Height from the Row menu. The Row Height dialog box appears, as
shown in figure 3.5.

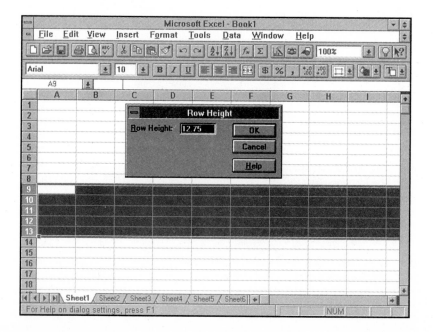

Figure 3.5
The Row Height
dialog box.

3. Enter the height you want for your row in the Row Height field. Enter the value as a decimal figure in points.

4. Click on the OK button.

Hiding a Row

You hide a row the same way you change height. You can drag the height adjustment line for the row until the row height is zero, or you can use the Hide command. To use the Hide command, select the row or rows you want to hide, pull down the Format menu, select Row, then select Hide.

When you have a row or rows selected, you can press Ctrl+9 to hide them.

Unhiding a Row

You unhide a row the same way you hide a row. Select the rows that include the hidden rows. For example, if row 10 is hidden, select rows 9 and 11. Then, pull down the Format menu, select Row and then select Unhide.

When you have selected the rows, including the hidden rows, press Ctrl+Shift+(to unhide the row.

Changing Column Width

Changing column widths is similar to adjusting row heights. The main difference is that you drag the line to the right of the column label to adjust a given column. You also can double-click on that column heading to have Excel examine all the entries in that column and adjust the column width so that all entries fit within the column's borders.

Column Width Menu

To see the column width menu, pull down the Format menu and select Column (see fig 3.6).

As you can see, the Column menu is much the same as the Row menu, and it functions in the same way. The only difference is the addition of the Standard Width option. Selecting Standard Width opens a dialog box that enables you to change the default width for all columns in the worksheet to appear (see fig. 3.7).

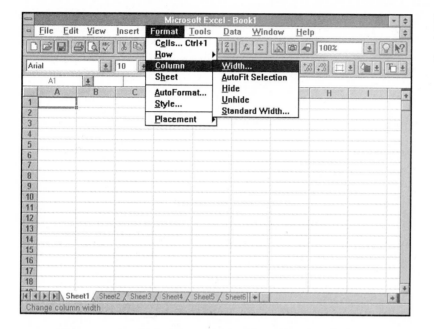

Figure 3.6
The Column Width menu.

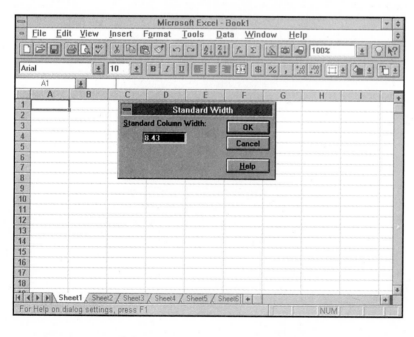

Figure 3.7
The Standard Width dialog box.

Changing Worksheet Display Characteristics

You can change many of the characteristics of the Excel display to suit your tastes. Pull down the Tools menu and select Options.

The Options notebook appears. Click on the View tab to see the view settings, shown in figure 3.8.

Figure 3.8
The View notebook page.

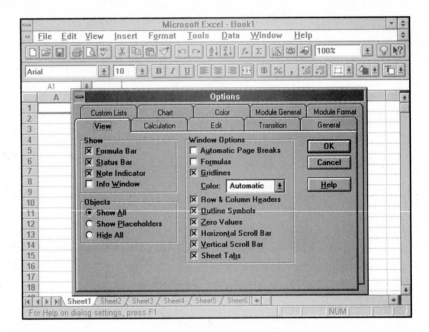

The notebook page has settings as shown in table 3.5:

Table 3.5
View Settings

Section	Setting	Explanation
Show	Formula Bar	Controls the presence of the formula bar. If this box is not selected, the formula bar is not shown.
	Status Bar	The status bar is the area at the bottom of the screen that shows you the status of various options in Excel. Deselect this checkbox to hide the status bar.

Section	Setting	Explanation
	Note Indicator	When you attach notes to cells, a small, red dot appears in that cell's upper right corner. If this option is not selected, the note indicator is not shown.
	Info Window	If this checkbox is selected, a new window is created that shows you all the details about the current cell. Use the Window menu to move between the Info Window and the workbook. Deselect this checkbox to hide the Info Window.
Objects	Show All	If this option button is selected, all graphic objects in the workbook (buttons, graphics, etc.) are displayed.
	Show Placeholders	If this option button is selected, a gray rectangle appears on your screen in place of any graphic objects. This option can help you scroll through the worksheet more quickly.
	Hide All	This option button causes all graphic objects to be hidden. They are not printed.
Window Options	Automatic Page Breaks	This checkbox causes Excel's automatically determined page breaks to appear.
	Formulas	Choose this checkbox to show the formulas in the cells instead of the results. At the same time, it doubles the width of the cells (so that they are likely to be capable of displaying the formula), and it left-justifies all the displayed formulas. This option is useful for checking the validity of the formulas in your worksheet or for documenting your work.
	Gridlines	Deselect this option to turn off the gridline display in the worksheet.
	Color	This option is a drop-down list that enables you to choose the color of the gridlines in the worksheet.
	Row and Column Headers	Deselect this choice to turn off the labels for rows and columns. If you are developing worksheet-based forms, this option can be useful when you distribute the worksheet, because the people who are completing the form should have little need for the row and column markers.

continues

Table 3.5, Continued
View Settings

Section	Setting	Explanation
Window Options	Outline Symbols	This checkbox controls whether Excel displays the symbols used when you are using the outline feature in Excel.
	Zero Values	If this option is unchecked, cells that have a zero value and are formatted using the General format are displayed as blank. Cells formatted with a specific format calling for zeroes still display the zeroes.
	Horizontal Scroll Bar	This checkbox hides or unhides the horizontal scroll bar.
	Vertical Scroll Bar	This checkbox hides or unhides the vertical scroll bar.
	Sheet Tabs	This checkbox controls the display of the workbook sheet tabs at the bottom of the screen.

TIP Press Ctrl+', the left single quote, beneath the tilde (~) on most keyboards, to switch quickly between the normal worksheet and formulas.

NOTE See Chapter 6, "Advanced Worksheet Features," to learn more about Excel's Outlining features.

Changing Fonts

Excel has many tools that enable you to format the fonts—typefaces, sizes, and styles—that your worksheet uses.

Understanding Different Font Types

Depending on the font tools you have installed on your system, a wide variety of fonts are available with Excel. Each type of font appears differently on your screen and prints differently on your printer. The most popular types of fonts include the following:

✔ **Screen Fonts.** Windows has several screen fonts that approximate the fonts your printer uses. For these fonts to print correctly, your printer must have similar fonts built into it. Examples of screen fonts on a standard Windows system are Roman, Helvetica, Modern, Script, and Symbol. These fonts are available only in the sizes installed in your system: if you choose a size that your system doesn't have, Windows tries to approximate it on the screen, but the results usually are poor.

✔ **TrueType Fonts.** TrueType fonts were introduced in Windows 3.1. They include both *display fonts,* which you can see on your worksheet, and equivalent *printer fonts,* which Windows can generate for your printer when you print. Even if your printer does not contain that font, Windows (and therefore Excel) can make your printer use them. TrueType fonts can be scaled to different sizes, and the underlying Windows TrueType software generates the appropriate display and printer fonts automatically so that what you see on the screen is as close as possible to what you see when you print. Examples of TrueType fonts include Arial, Courier New, and Symbol. TrueType fonts have a 'TT' symbol before their names in the Excel font dialog box.

✔ **PostScript Fonts.** PostScript fonts are the most professional available, although the untrained eye often cannot distinguish between TrueType fonts and PostScript fonts. PostScript fonts can be printed in any size desired, from 1 point up to 999 points (which fits about one letter per page!). If you have a PostScript printer, Excel can print these fonts, and has screen fonts that are roughly the same as what you see on paper. Examples of PostScript fonts are Courier, Times Roman, and Helvetica.

✔ **ATM (PostScript) Fonts.** Many Windows-based applications include a program called *Adobe Type Manager* (ATM), which gives the capabilities of TrueType fonts. You also can purchase ATM separately. If you have ATM installed, you can view and print PostScript fonts, even if your printer doesn't normally support PostScript fonts. ATM fonts include Courier, Times New Roman, and GillSans (similar to Helvetica).

You should know that when you use ATM, PostScript, or TrueType fonts and your printer does not include TrueType or PostScript fonts, your printouts take longer, because Windows has to draw the letters for your printer. In other words, rather than instruct the printer to print the letter 't' in a certain location and at a certain size, Windows must download the letter to the printer as a graphic image. This procedure slows printing.

Changing Fonts

Excel includes several tools to change the current font quickly. You can make the current font bold, italic, or underlined. You can change fonts, and you can change the size of the selected font.

Many of these functions can be accomplished using the toolbar. Figure 3.9 shows the toolbar buttons for these fonts styles.

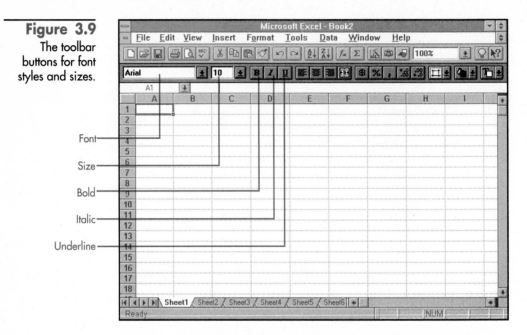

Figure 3.9
The toolbar buttons for font styles and sizes.

Font
Size
Bold
Italic
Underline

To use these buttons, select the cells you want to format and click on the appropriate button.

You also can change fonts and font styles by using the Font dialog box and following these steps:

1. Pull down the Format menu, select Cell, then click on the Font tab in the Cell formatting notebook. You see the Font notebook page, shown in figure 3.10.

TIP

To access the Cell formatting notebook quickly, select the cells you want to format and then click your right mouse button in the selected region. This procedure causes a pop-up menu to appear. From the pop-up menu, select Cells from the Format menu.

2. In the Font box, select or enter the typeface you want to use. When you select the font, Excel shows an example of the font in the Preview window.

3. In the Font Style list box, select the display style of the font (Bold, Bold Italic, Italic, and so on).

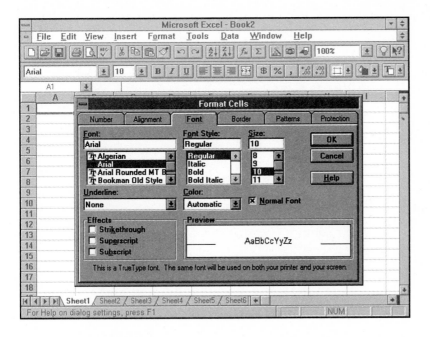

Figure 3.10
The Font page.

4. You also can use the Underline list box to select from a variety of underline styles.

5. Use the Strikethrough, Superscript, and Subscript list boxes for those effects.

6. Finally, select the size you want from the Size list box.

7. After you finish making the font choices you want, click on the OK button.

AUTHOR'S NOTE

Here is a bit of typography trivia: The term *font* is often used incorrectly. A set of letters in a particular style (like Courier, Times Roman, or Helvetica) is actually a *typeface*. When you take a typeface and define the size and attributes (bold, italic, and so on), you end up with a *font*. Many incorrectly call a typeface a font. The Excel dialog box makes this mistake, for example. Many programs do!

Excel also has some shortcut keys for many of the font attributes. Table 3.6 shows these shortcut keys.

Table 3.6
Font Style Shortcut Keys

Function	Shortcut Key
Bold	Ctrl+B
Italic	Ctrl+I
Underline	Ctrl+U
Strikethrough	Ctrl+5
Normal Font	Ctrl+1 (Uses the font in the Normal Style)

Using Borders

You can spice up your worksheets by using borders. By drawing lines around certain portions of your worksheets, you can make the worksheets prettier and separate them into different sections. Borders make your work more presentable and easier for others to understand.

You can make a border around a cell or group of cells quickly using the toolbar. You can find an example of the Border button in figure 3.2 near the beginning of this chapter.

To use the Border button to create a border quickly, follow these steps:

1. Select the cell or group of cells that you want the border to surround.

2. Click on the down arrow next to the Border button, which causes the border list to appear, as you can see in figure 3.11.

3. Examine the border list to find the border style you want. After you find the border style you want, click on that box to select it for the selected cells.

After you choose a particular border, the Border button changes to show the most recently used border. You simply can click on that button to choose immediately the most recently used border.

TIP

If you do a lot of work with borders, the border list accessed from the toolbar can be "torn off" and left right on top of your worksheet. To "tear off" the border list, pull down the list by clicking on the down arrow to the right of the border button. Then, click and hold the mouse button within the border list, and drag your mouse down out of the border list box. When your mouse leaves the region of the list, the border list is torn off and can be left on your worksheet to more quickly access it.

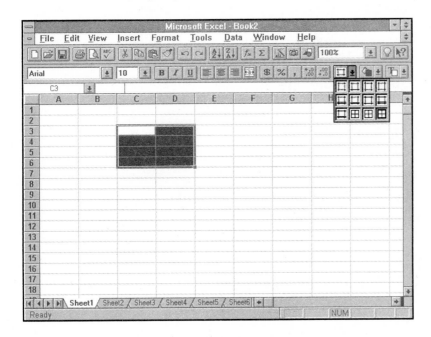

Figure 3.11
The Border list.

You can achieve even more control over the borders you create by using the Border page in the Cell format notebook. To use this page, pull down the Format menu and select Cell. When you see the Cell notebook, click on the tab marked Border. The Border page is shown in figure 3.12, which follows.

Use the following fields to control the way the border lines are drawn.

- ✔ **Outline.** The outside edges of the selected cell or cells. If you have selected many cells before pulling up the Border dialog box, only the outline of the selected cells is given a border.

- ✔ **Left.** All selected cells have a border line drawn on their left edges.

- ✔ **Right.** All selected cells have a border line drawn on their right edges.

- ✔ **Top.** The tops of the selected cells get a border.

- ✔ **Bottom.** The bottoms of the selected cells get a border.

- ✔ **Style.** This section presents a number of different border styles, from double lines to dashed lines.

- ✔ **Color.** This drop box lists the various color choices for the border lines.

Figure 3.12
The Border page.

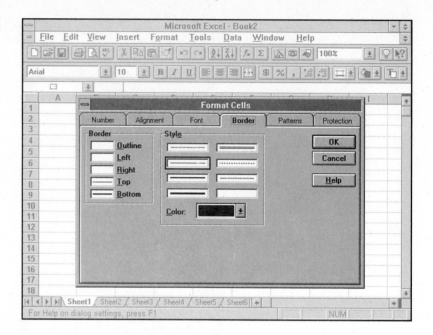

Shading and Coloring Cells

You also have many choices about changing the color and shading of cells in your worksheet, just as you did with the Border command. You can color cells and text with the Color and Font Color buttons on the Formatting toolbar. These buttons are shown near the beginning of the chapter in figure 3.2.

To change the color of specific cells, follow these steps:

1. Select the cells you want to color.

2. Click on the down arrow to the right of the Color button to show the colors available. This color list is shown in figure 3.13.

3. Click on the color you want for the selected cells.

You also can control the color and further the background pattern in selected cells by using the Format Cell notebook by following these steps:

1. Select the cells you want to format.

2. Pull down the Format menu and select Cells. Then, click on the Patterns tab in the formatting notebook. You see the page shown in figure 3.14.

3. Choose the color you want from the selection of colors available.

4. Open the drop-down box labeled Pattern to see a variety of patterns that you can use. Click on the pattern you want.

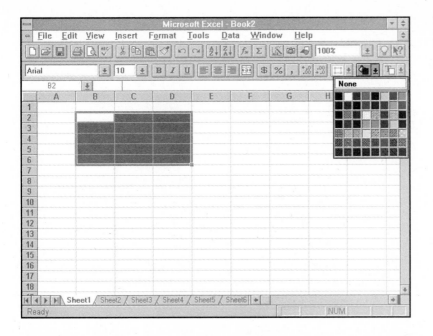

Figure 3.13
The color list.

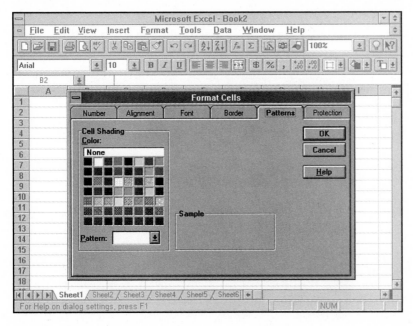

Figure 3.14
The Pattern page.

After you choose a color and pattern, you can see an example of the way they look in the Sample box on the Pattern page.

The final coloring option comes from the Font Color button on the Formatting toolbar. You can change the color of the text in cells. Select the cells you want to affect and then click on the down arrow to the right of the Font Color button. You see a list of colors that you can use. Choose one to change the text color for the cells you selected.

Aligning Text

By default, Excel aligns text to the left edges of cells and numbers to the right. You can override these default alignments.

The Formatting toolbar contains three buttons to control text alignment within cells. Figure 3.2, at the beginning of this chapter, shows these buttons.

To use the Toolbar alignment buttons, select the cells you want to realign and click on the desired alignment button.

Excel has some other text alignment tricks up its sleeve. You can align text vertically, and you can arrange text so that the words appear vertically. To access these options:

1. Select the cells you want to change.

2. Pull down the Format menu and select Cells to cause the Format Cell notebook to appear.

3. Click on the Alignment tab. You see the page shown in figure 3.15, which follows.

Figure 3.15
The Alignment page.

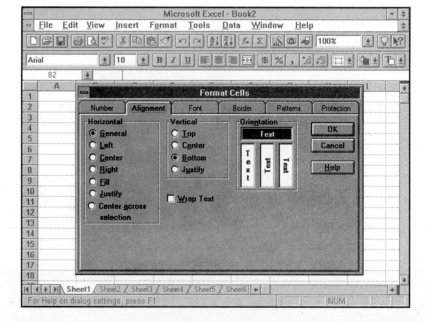

The page is grouped into three sections: Horizontal, Vertical, and Orientation. Table 3.7 describes some of these choices.

Table 3.7
Alignment Dialog Choices

Section	Button	Function
Horizontal	General	Aligns text using the default Excel alignments. Numbers are right-aligned and text is left-aligned.
	Left	Aligns cell contents to the left side of the cells.
	Center	Centers cell contents within the cells.
	Right	Aligns cell contents to the right side of the cells.
	Fill	Repeats the text as many times as necessary to completely fill the cell with whatever is entered.
	Justify	Attempts to spread the text so that it uses the entire width of the cell.
	Center across Selections	When you select a range of cells that begins with a cell that contains text and choose this option, Excel takes the text contents of the first cell and centers it across all the cells you selected.
Vertical	Top	Aligns cell contents against the top of the cells.
	Center	Aligns cell contents vertically between the top and bottom boundaries.
	Bottom	Aligns cell contents against the bottom boundary of the cells.
	Justify	Causes the text, when wrapped, to align against the top and bottom of the cell.

You also can choose one of four different orientations to display the text, choosing among the displayed options for vertically arranging the text so that it reads from top to bottom or bottom to top. Finally, if you select the Word Wrap checkbox, Excel causes text that is longer than an individual cell to wrap downward.

Worksheets

5

Centering Text across a Range

Often, you want centered titles at the tops of your worksheets. Achieving a perfectly centered title can be difficult, however, given the number of columns in your worksheet, the width of each column, and the width of your title.

AUTHOR'S NOTE

In the early days of spreadsheets with VisiCalc, Lotus 1-2-3, Multiplan, and the like, the only way to center text across the page was to manually insert spaces in the title. With the advent of proportional typefaces, even that trick became impossible, because each letter takes up a different amount of space.

Fortunately, Excel can center text across a range automatically. To center text within a range, follow these steps:

1. Type the title in the far left column of the range in which you want the text to appear centered. For example, if you want the text centered between columns A and I, enter the text into column A.

2. Select the range of cells starting from the cell that contains your title, and extending to the right to the full width of your worksheet (or print range).

3. Click on the Center within Selection button on the Formatting Toolbar. Alternately, pull down the F<u>o</u>rmat menu, choose <u>C</u>ell, click on the Alignment tab, and then choose the Center <u>W</u>ithin Selection option button. Then, click on OK.

Filling a Range with Text

Excel also can take a piece of text—a single letter, word, or sentence— and fill that text across a range. To do this, follow these steps:

1. Type the text to be repeated in far left cell of the range you want to fill.

2. Select the range of cells starting with the cell that contains the text to be repeated and extending as far right as you want to repeat it.

3. Pull down the F<u>o</u>rmat menu, select <u>C</u>ell, then click on the Alignment tab.

4. Choose the <u>F</u>ill option button and click on the OK button.

Figure 3.16 shows the effect of filling an asterisk across the visible worksheet in Row 2.

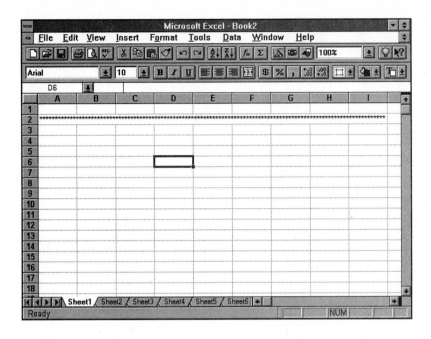

Figure 3.16
The filled range.

Protecting and Hiding Cells

When you develop worksheets for others to use, it is wise to restrict their choices. Certain cells should be unmodifiable, others should hide their formulas. This makes your worksheet easier for them to use and protects your work from being modified in such a way that it stops working properly.

By default, cells you create already are marked as being *locked*. After the entire document is protected, locked cells cannot be modified. You also can designate certain other cells as *hidden*, which doesn't mean that the cell itself is hidden, only that the underlying formulas are hidden.

To change the protection characteristics of a cell or group of cells, follow these steps:

1. Select the cell or group of cells you want to protect.

2. Pull down the Format menu and choose Cells. Click on the Protection tab to display the protection page. You see the page shown in figure 3.17.

3. In the dialog box, click on the Locked or Hidden checkboxes. Then, click on the OK button.

After you finish your worksheet, you need to protect the document so that these settings take effect. Follow these steps:

Figure 3.17
The cell protection
page.

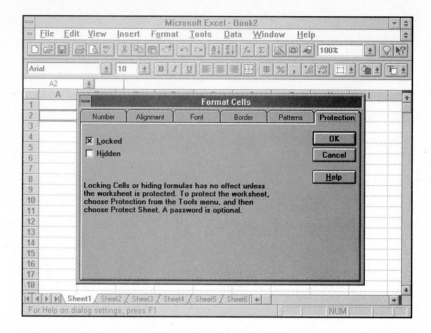

1. Pull down the Tools menu and select Protection to display a cascading menu, from which you can select Protect Sheet or Protect Workbook. Selecting either option displays the dialog box shown in figure 3.18.

Figure 3.18
The Protect dialog
box.

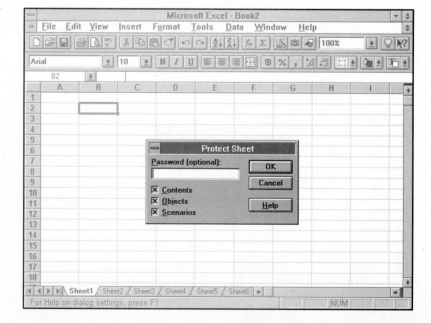

2. If necessary, enter a password in the Password field. (Passwords are optional.)

 STOP

Passwords in Excel are case-sensitive. In other words, they depend on exact capitalization. Also, when you use a password in a document, be sure to use one that you can remember. If the document you work on is important to your company, make sure someone else knows your password. Your computer department may have stringent policies regarding the use of application-specific passwords. Follow them!

3. Choose from the remaining three checkboxes:

   ✔ **Contents.** Causes the cells you mark as hidden to hide their formulas, or the cells you mark as locked to be unchangable.

   ✔ **Objects.** Causes graphic objects in your worksheet to be made unmodifiable.

   ✔ **Scenarios.** Makes the scenarios in a workbook unmovable and unsizable.

4. With the appropriate options selected, click on the OK button to protect the document.

To unprotect the document. pull down the Tools menu, select Protection and then select either Unprotect Document or Unprotect Workbook. If a password was used to protect the document, you need to enter it before the document becomes unprotected. If no password was used, the document or workbook is unprotected instantly.

Using Styles

Styles enable you to predefine collections of formatting settings and quickly apply those settings to selected cells. Rather than choose a range and then tediously select the typeface, font style, size, alignment, shading, and so on, you can define entire styles that you commonly use and then apply them to a cell or collection of cells quickly and easily.

Styles enable you to define the follow properties:

   ✔ Typeface (Font)

   ✔ Number format

   ✔ Cell alignment

   ✔ Borders

   ✔ Cell patterns

   ✔ Cell protection

Applying a Style

For styles that already exist, apply them by following these steps:

1. Select the cells you want to format.

2. Pull down the Format menu and select Styles. You see the dialog box shown in figure 3.19.

Figure 3.19
The Style dialog box.

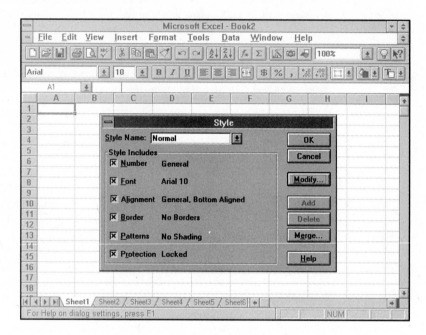

3. Pull down the Style Name drop-down list and choose the style you want.

4. Click on the OK button to close the Style dialog box.

Creating a Style

To create a new style, use the Style dialog box that you saw in figure 3.19.

The first thing you probably notice on the dialog box is a series of checkboxes: Number, Font, Alignment, Border, Patterns, and Protection. These checkboxes define which formatting aspects the style contains. If you want a style that controls only the font, for example, deselect all of checkboxes except for Font.

To begin creating your new style, click on the Style Name box and type in the name for your new style. Then, using the checkboxes, choose the formatting elements that you want your new style to affect and click on the Modify button. This procedure brings up the Format Cell notebook. Any changes you make to it now, however, impact only the style you are creating.

Worksheets

Use the notebook to change all the aspects of the style until they are satisfactory. After you are finished, click on the OK button to return to the Style dialog box.

You also see a button marked M<u>e</u>rge. Click on this button to import styles that you have created in other workbooks. The other workbooks must be open in a different Excel window before the styles in those workbooks can be available.

NOTE Styles that you create appear only in the workbook in which you create them. To move them to other workbooks, use the preceding merge procedure.

After you finish changing the style attributes, click on the <u>A</u>dd button to create the new style. The new style can then be applied just like any other style in the list. Similarly, if you want to delete an existing style, select it in the <u>S</u>tyle Name list box and click on the <u>D</u>el button.

To finish working with the Style dialog box, click on the OK button.

Using AutoFormats

Examine the worksheet in figure 3.20. You could spend a lot of time reformatting the table to give it a polished, professional appearance. Fortunately, instead of spending much time on reformatting, you can use the Excel AutoFormat feature to format a table quickly in one of many predefined, professionally designed formats.

Figure 3.20
The sample sales table.

	A	B	C	D	E	F	G	H
1								
2			ACME Corporation					
3			Sales by Product by Region					
4			(in 000's)					
5								
6								
7	Product	North US	East US	West US	South US	Europe	Asia	Total
8	Paper Clips	$123	$160	$80	$160	$213	$85	$823
9	Faber #2 Pencils	$93	$120	$60	$120	$160	$64	$617
10	Office Calendars	$67	$87	$43	$87	$115	$46	$445
11	Cs. Manilla Folders	$111	$144	$72	$144	$192	$77	$741
12	Rm. #20 Copy Paper	$247	$321	$160	$321	$427	$171	$1,646
13	Total	$640	$833	$416	$833	$1,107	$443	$4,272
14								
15								
16								
17								

Microsoft Excel - 3-18.XLS

File Edit View Insert Format Tools Data Window Help

MS Sans Serif 10 B I U

A8 Paper Clips

3-18

Ready NUM

Before you use AutoFormat, make sure that your active cell is within a table, and that the table elements are contiguous. If blank columns or rows are in the table, then select the entire range of cells that contains the table; otherwise Excel does not know where your table begins and ends. After you select the table, follow these steps:

1. Pull down the Format menu and choose AutoFormat. The AutoFormat dialog box appears, as shown in figure 3.21.

Figure 3.21

AutoFormat dialog box.

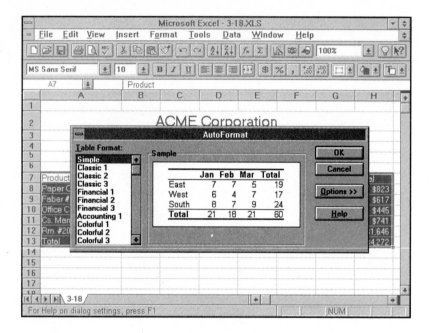

2. Scroll through the list of formats. If you click on a format, you can preview the results of a particular AutoFormat in the Sample window.

3. After you find a format you like, click on the OK button to apply it.

When using the AutoFormat dialog box, you also can control which parts of the format to apply by clicking on the Options button, which expands the dialog box, as shown in figure 3.22.

The expanded AutoFormat dialog box enables you to select the aspects of the format you want to apply by using the various checkboxes.

Figure 3.23 shows the example table with the List 1 table format applied.

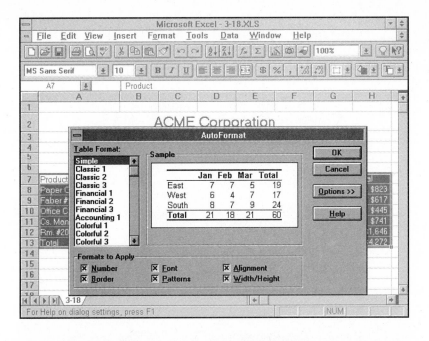

Worksheets

Figure 3.22
The expanded AutoFormat dialog box.

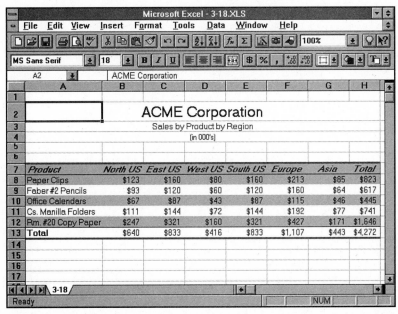

Figure 3.23
The formatted table.

Chapter Snapshot

Putting your work on paper typically is your final goal when using Excel. Whether you are printing to proofread your work, to get a better look at the overall picture your work represents, or to distribute your worksheets and charts to others, you need to master Excel's printing tools. In this chapter, you learn the following:

- ✔ Using different types of printers
- ✔ Using different types of fonts
- ✔ Printing with Excel
- ✔ Adjusting Excel's printing
- ✔ Creating and editing headers and footers
- ✔ Using Print Titles
- ✔ Using the Excel Report Manager

The tasks and tips you learn in this chapter help you produce high-quality, professional-looking worksheets every time.

CHAPTER 4

Printing Documents

Printing is usually easy: you select the area to print, click on a given print button, and that's it, you're done. In Excel, however, you can do a variety of printing tricks. This chapter covers these features.

Understanding Your Printer's Capabilities

Before you can understand your printer, you need to know what type of printer it is and which fonts are built into it. This section discusses different types of printers, built-in fonts, and print quality.

Dot-Matrix Printers

Dot-matrix printers fire little pins into an inked printer ribbon. The resulting pattern of the dots form the letters and images that appear on the paper. Dot-matrix printers are relatively slow, and the output quality varies considerably depending on the model. They are inexpensive, often right around $200 to $400.

Some dot-matrix printers use 9 pins to form characters; these offer poor print quality. Some use 24 pins and perform better than their 9-pin counterparts, but still not as well as laser printers.

Dot-matrix printers typically have a limited number of fonts preinstalled, often at fixed sizes. If your printer supports graphics printing, as many do, Excel can use TrueType fonts to create different typefaces, sizes, and styles on the printer.

Impact Printers

Few impact printers are in use today. *Impact* printers form characters just like a typewriter: they hammer individually formed metal or plastic letters into an inked printer ribbon, which then hits the page. These printers are really slow compared to other types of printers. Although text quality is very high, you are limited to the one font installed in the printer and have no graphics capabilities.

Inkjet Printers

Inkjet printers shoot small amounts of ink directly onto the paper. Inkjet printers are very quiet, form near-laser quality text and graphics, and are relatively inexpensive, typically costing between $300 to $700. The main drawbacks to inkjet printers are that they are fairly slow compared to laser printers, and they don't offer the same sharpness of printing as laser printers.

Most inkjet printers have a limited number of typefaces and sizes preinstalled. Due to the fairly high resolution (generally about 360 dots per inch) of these printers, however, you often can get good print quality by using TrueType fonts, which Windows prints on the inkjet printer as a graphic image. Printing this way is slower than using the printer's built-in fonts, but offers flexibility you don't otherwise have, because an inkjet printer's built-in fonts rarely handle multiple sizes beyond the sizes of type built into the printer.

One advantage of inkjet printers over laser printers is that many good color inkjet printers are available. With a color inkjet printer, you can produce color charts and overhead transparencies. Equivalent color capabilities on laser-type printers still cost $7000 or more, but color inkjet printers can be purchased for as little as $500 to $600.

Laser Printers

Laser printers set the standard for high-quality output in today's business world. They are fast, quiet, and have become fairly inexpensive in recent years, with some selling for $1000 or less.

Laser printers shoot a laser beam onto a drum. The drum picks up an electrical charge in the areas that the laser hits. The drum then is rolled through powdered ink, known as *toner*, which sticks to the charged places on the drum. The drum then rolls onto the paper, depositing the toner particles. Finally, the paper is rolled through a very hot roller called a *fuser*, which fuses the toner particles onto the paper.

Two major standards exist in the world of laser printers: PostScript and Printer Control Language (PCL). PostScript laser printers are the most expensive, but give you the greatest capabilities for accurate graphics and text. PCL printers have somewhat less capability, but more recent versions of PCL (version 5 and up) can scale the printer's built-in typefaces to different sizes. Hewlett-Packard sets the standard in the PCL world, although almost all laser printers are "PCL-Compatible" and can emulate HP LaserJet printers. PostScript printers also are available from a number of different printer manufacturers. PCL-based laser printers are available starting at about $700, while PostScript printers begin at around $1200.

Graphics

By default, Excel prints graphics at the highest resolution allowed by your printer. You can also change the resolution used if you use the Printer Setup dialog box to select a different resolution.

Fonts

Font support is one of the more complex areas of effective printing, because so many fonts are available, and each one has its own limitations and abilities. Windows (and, therefore, Excel) offers four major font types, as noted and described in the following list. Knowing which types of fonts are best for different tasks and which fonts work best with your printer can make your job of turning out attractive output much easier.

✔ **Screen Fonts.** Windows has a number of screen fonts that approximate the fonts your printer uses. For a screen font to print correctly, similar fonts must be built into your printer. Examples of screen fonts on a standard Windows system are Roman, Helvetica, Modern, Script, and Symbol. These fonts are available only in the sizes installed in your system. If you choose a size your system doesn't have, Windows tries to approximate it on the screen, but with poor results.

✔ **TrueType Fonts.** TrueType fonts are new in Windows 3.1. They include display fonts that you can see on your Excel screen and equivalent printer fonts that Windows can generate for your printer. Even if your printer doesn't have a particular TrueType font or its equivalent, Windows can make your printer use them by printing each letter as a graphic image. TrueType fonts can be scaled to different sizes, and the underlying Windows software generates the appropriate display and printer fonts automatically so that what you see on the screen is as close as possible to what you print. Examples of TrueType fonts include Arial, Courier New, and Symbol. TrueType fonts have a 'TT' symbol before their name in the Excel font list.

TrueType fonts work with any printer that can print graphics. The TrueType software in Windows prints these fonts at the highest resolution your printer allows. You also can adjust the resolution with which Windows prints TrueType fonts by accessing the Page Setup command in the File menu, then closing the Options button.

Professionals consider TrueType fonts to be inferior to PostScript fonts, but TrueType fonts are far cheaper, often only 1/100 the price of PostScript fonts (primarily due to the fact that Adobe charges dearly for its fonts). TrueType fonts are a better value because the quality versus PostScript fonts is generally detected only by professionals and because those differences are not very pronounced on most laser printers.

As a general rule, you should use PostScript fonts if you are doing graphics work that a professional printing company will print for you.

✔ **PostScript Fonts.** PostScript fonts are the most professional available, although the untrained eye cannot often distinguish between TrueType and PostScript fonts. You can print PostScript fonts in any size you want, from 1 point up to 999 points (which fits about one letter on each page!). If you have a PostScript printer, Excel is capable of printing these fonts, and displays screen fonts that approximate what prints on paper. Examples of PostScript fonts are Courier, Times Roman, and Helvetica.

To use PostScript fonts, you must have a PostScript-based printer or Adobe Type Manager, a special software that emulates a PostScript printer and prints the graphic images to a non-PostScript printer rather than the actual fonts.

✔ **ATM (PostScript) Fonts.** Many Windows-based applications include a program called *Adobe Type Manager* (ATM), which provides capabilities equal to TrueType fonts. You also can purchase ATM separately. If you install ATM, you can view and print PostScript fonts, even if your printer does not normally support PostScript fonts. ATM fonts include Courier, Times New Roman, and GillSans (similar to Helvetica).

ATM functions like TrueType. If your printer can print graphic images, then ATM can print the PostScript fonts at the highest resolution your printer supports.

Printing Worksheets

Excel prints your entire worksheet automatically when you select the Print command. To print your entire worksheet, use the following procedure:

1. Pull down the File menu and select Print. The Print dialog box appears, as shown in figure 4.1.

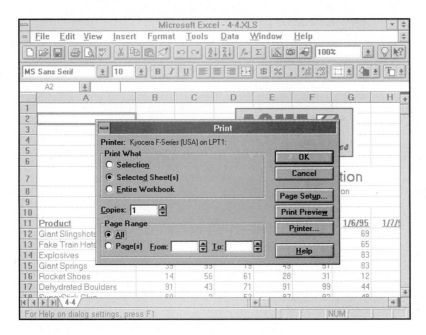

Figure 4.1

The Print dialog box.

Table 4.1 shows your options:

Table 4.1
Print Dialog Box Choices

Option	Description
Page Range	Here you choose whether to print All pages of the worksheet, or a range of pages by selecting Pages, then a starting page (From) and an ending page (To).
Selection	If you select a range of cells prior to selecting the Print menu, then click on the Selection option button, only the preselected range of cells is printed.

continues

Table 4.1, Continued
Print Dialog Box Choices

Option	Description
Selected Sheet(s)	Excel enables you to print multiple worksheets from your workbook simultaneously. You must click on the first sheet you want to print, then click on the remaining sheets while holding the Ctrl key. When you print, use the Selected Sheet(s) option button to print only those sheets.
Entire Workbook	Choose this option button to print all sheets in your workbook.
Copies	The number you enter in this field is the number of copies of the worksheet Excel prints. In most office environments, it is easier, cheaper, and faster to use the photocopier than printing multiple copies of your documents on the laser printer.
Print Preview	If you click on this button, Excel displays a rough representation of how the printed output should appear. You can use this option to resolve problems with different fonts, graphic positioning, and any other problems, without having to print each time. Because you usually need to print many times to resolve printing problems with your worksheet, using the Print Preview option can greatly speed up this process.
Page Setup	Selecting this button brings up a new dialog box that enables you to control many aspects of your printouts, including headers, footers, and so on. This dialog box is explored completely in a later section of this chapter.
Printer	Click on this button to choose which printer to use if you have more than one printer.

After you select the options you want to use, click on the OK button to print your document.

Selecting Areas to Print

Often, you don't want to print the entire worksheet. Sometimes you do not need parts of the worksheet, or parts of the worksheet contain only support information used to generate the actual worksheet. For example, you might have detailed sales records in your worksheet, but you only use them to generate the totals you are using for a sales report.

In such cases, follow these steps:

1. Select the range of cells you want to print.

2. Pull down the File menu and select Print.

3. When the Print dialog box appears, click on the Selection option button to print only the selected area.

Excel shows you where the pages of your worksheet will break onto multiple pages with dashed lines. If these locations are not acceptable, you have several choices:

✔ You can reformat your worksheet to fit in the number of pages you want, usually by choosing smaller fonts and reducing the width of columns and the height of rows. You might also rearrange your data to print the way you want, inserting or deleting rows and columns in order to fit everything on the pages.

✔ You can insert page breaks to force Excel to break the pages earlier.

✔ You can use Excel's Print-To-Fit feature, which automatically shrinks the entire selected print area to fit on a single page. You also can choose varying levels of reduction or enlargement.

Working with Page Breaks

In Excel, you can print certain parts of your worksheet on certain pages by inserting page breaks into the document. To insert page breaks, use the following procedure:

1. Decide where you want to begin a new page.

2. Move your active cell to immediately below and to the right of where you want the page break. The page break is created at the upper left corner of the active cell.

3. Pull down the Insert menu and select Page Break.

The page break indicator lines show the new page layout. Excel automatically adjusts the other page breaks accordingly. To remove an inserted page break, use the following procedure:

1. Move your active cell to immediately below and to the right of the page break.

2. Pull down the Insert menu and select Remove Page Break.

The Remove Page Break menu option is in the same place on the menu as the Set Page Break command, but appears in place of Set Page Break when your active cell is next to an inserted page break. If you see the Set Page Break command instead of the Remove Page Break command, then your active cell is in the wrong location, or you are trying to remove a page break that Excel has inserted because no room is available on the page. You cannot remove Excel's automatic page breaks. You can, however, insert new page breaks before the Excel-inserted page breaks and let Excel reformat the rest of the document accordingly.

Using Print-To-Fit

You can instruct Excel to take a print area and reduce it automatically so that the entire area fits on one page. Of course, it might be reduced so much you can't read it, so this option doesn't prove useful if you ingeniously try to cram a twenty-page printout on a single page. The reduction in size is accomplished by Excel choosing exactly the right font shrinkage.   To use the print-to-fit feature, use the following procedure:

1. Select the range of cells you want to print.

2. Pull down the File menu and choose Page Setup. The Page Setup notebook appears. Click on the Page tab. The Page notebook page in figure 4.2 appears.

Figure 4.2
The Page Setup
page.

Fit to option button ———

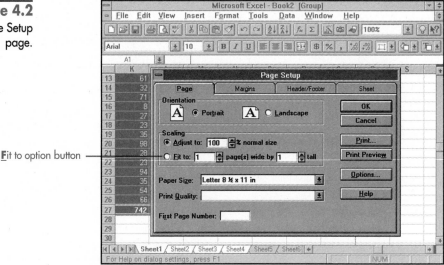

3. Click on the Fit to option button (refer to fig. 4.2).

4. If you need to modify the number of pages into which Excel fits your selected area, change each field appropriately.

If you follow the preceding instructions, Excel automatically calculates the necessary percentage reduction, which you can see in the Reduce/Enlarge field.

You also can manually adjust the percentage reduction or enlargement by selecting the Reduce/Enlarge button and entering a percentage amount.

NOTE

If your printer doesn't support scalable typefaces, or you use fixed-size typefaces in your document, you might be unable to reduce or enlarge the page exactly as you want. To avoid this problem, try to use scalable typefaces (such as PostScript or TrueType fonts) often as possible.

Using Headers and Footers

By default, Excel prints the name of your worksheet in a print header, and the page number in the footer. You can remove these and create your own headers and footers. Some uses for headers and footers include confidentiality notices, specially formatted page numbers, dates and times, or author name.

Headers and footers are managed in the Page Setup dialog box, shown in figure 4.2. Clicking on the Header/Footer brings up the Header/Footer notebook page, shown in figure 4.3.

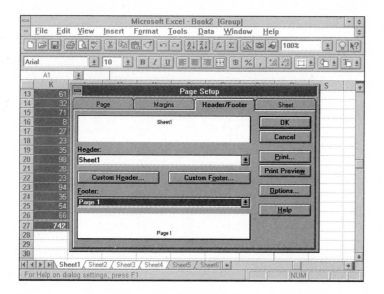

Figure 4.3
The Header/Footer notebook page.

Headers and footers are printed in a 1/2-inch border at the top and bottom of the page. If you use headers or footers that exceed this amount of space, your worksheet contents will probably print on top of the header or footer. To avoid this problem, change the top or bottom margins by using the Page Setup command in the File menu.

One of the thoughtful touches included in Excel 5 is predefined headers and footers. To use these, pull down Header or Footer drop-down list and select from the list. Figure 4.4 shows the predefined header list.

In the Header/Footer page you can see two windows. The top window shows you what the header will look like; the bottom window shows the footer. You cannot edit these two windows directly, because they are preview windows. To change the header or footer, you must choose from Excel's predefined headers and footers or create your own.

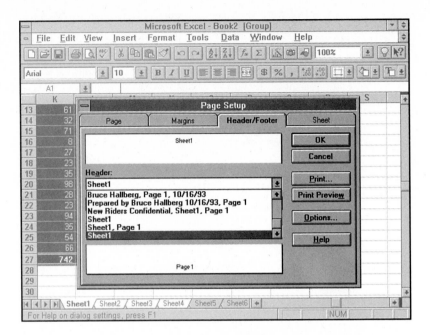

Figure 4.4
The predefined headers.

Creating headers and footers works the same way. The following example shows you the screens for creating a header, but the steps shown work identically for footers. Click on the Custom Header button. The Header dialog box appears (see fig. 4.5).

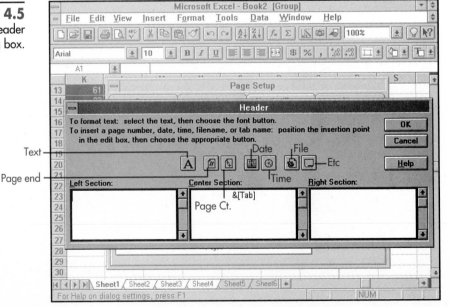

Figure 4.5
The Header dialog box.

The Header dialog box has three windows—the Left Section, Center Section, and Right Section—which are used to enter information that should be left-aligned, centered, or right-aligned, respectively. In each window you can enter text information or special codes. You use the special codes to insert things like the system date and time, the name of the worksheet, or formatting commands to select a particular font and type style.

To enter text in any window, simply click in that window and type the text you want. To insert a code, click on one of the buttons shown in table 4.2.

Table 4.2
Header and Footer Codes

Icon	Code	Result
A	None	Use this icon to format the header or footer text. After you select the text to be formatted, click on this icon to bring up the Font dialog box. Code-based equivalents exist, but using this button and the Font dialog box is easier.
None	&"*fontname*"	Text that follows this code uses the font specified in *fontname*. The name used in *fontname* must be exactly as spelled in the Font dialog box, and the surrounding quote marks are required.
None	&*xx*	Replace *xx* with the point size of the font desired. Be sure to use two-digit point sizes, as in 06, 08, 12, and so on. Also, be sure to leave a space after the numbers for the font size.
None	&B	Makes the following text bold. The next &B turns bold printing off, then the next turns it back on, and so forth.
None	&I	Makes the following text italic. The second &I turns italic printing off, and so on.
None	&S	Causes the following text to be printed with strikethrough emphasis. The second &S turns strikethrough printing off.
None	&U	Underlines the following text. The second &U turns underline off, and so forth.
(icon)	&D	Prints the system date.

continues

Table 4.2, Continued
Header and Footer Codes

Icon	Code	Result
📄	&F	Prints the name of the worksheet.
📄	&T	Prints the system time.
📄	&P	Prints the current page number.
📄	&N	Prints the total number of pages. Useful for footers that read Page 1 of 12, which would be accomplished with this entry: Page &P of &N.
None	&P+x	
None	&P-x	These two header or footer code forms instruct Excel to print the page number plus or minus the number specified by *x* and are useful when your worksheet is part of a larger report. Use this code to have Excel print the correct page numbers for your report instead if its own page numbers. For example, if you have several sheets that need to be numbered from page 10 to page 15, you can use this code to start the page numbers at 10 instead of 1.
None	&&	Prints an ampersand. Because Excel normally interprets an ampersand as part of a header or footer code, the double-ampersand code is provided if you need to print an ampersand rather than have Excel try to interpret it as a code.

Figure 4.6 shows an example header using some of these codes.

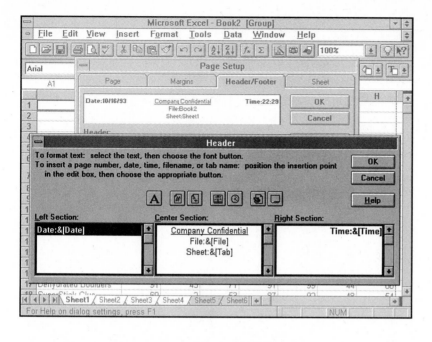

Figure 4.6
The sample
Custom Header.

Setting Up Repeating Titles

Multipage tables that span many pages can make finding specific data difficult, because the labels that define the data are often on a different page. You can avoid this problem in two ways:

- ✔ Use tape and scissors to combine all the pages into one large document (not very practical!).

- ✔ Use an Excel feature called Print Titles to automatically print the labels for the data on each page.

Consider the worksheet in figure 4.7.

When you print your worksheet using a normal font, the results appear as shown in figures 4.8 and 4.9.

This example illustrates the problems that exist in a strictly horizontal format. In reality, you must work in both dimensions, sometimes crossing many pages. The cure is Print Titles, which causes part of your worksheet to repeat automatically on each page. You can select the rows or columns that contain the header information you want repeated so that it prints on each page.

Figure 4.7
The large
worksheet.

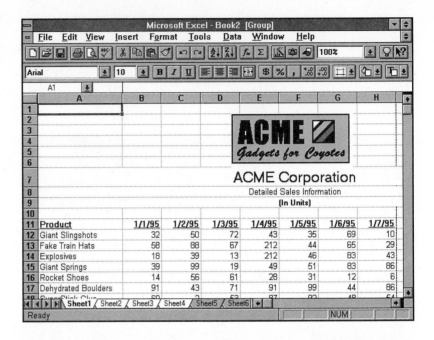

Figure 4.8
The first page
looks fine.

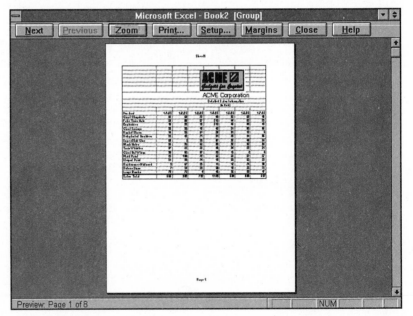

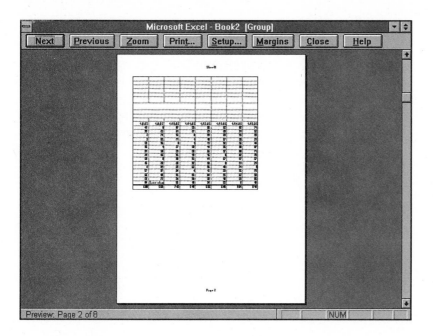

Figure 4.9
The second page is difficult to interpret.

In this example, you want to make the row titles (the product names) into print titles. To make print titles, use the following procedure:

1. Pull down the File menu and select Print Setup. The Page Setup notebook appears.

2. Click on the Sheet tab to display the Sheet page, as shown in figure 4.10.

   On the Sheet page, click on the Rows to Repeat at Top or Columns to Repeat at Left field. Then, use your mouse to select the rows or columns you want to repeat. The rows or columns you select must be contiguous.

3. Click on the Columns to Repeat at Left field.

4. Click on the A column label at the top of the worksheet. The column range is entered into the field automatically.

You might need to move the dialog box in order to select the rows or columns you want to use. Also, either field will accept a named range of columns or rows rather than column letters or row numbers.

5. Click on OK to close the Page Setup notebook.

Figure 4.11 shows the new page 2 of the example printout, complete with titles.

Figure 4.10
The Set Print titles
page

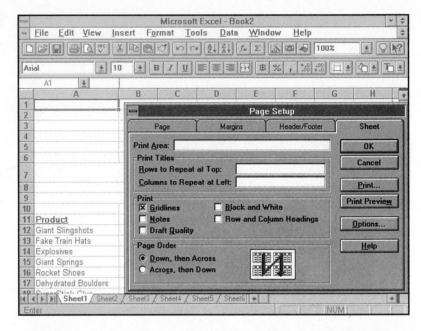

Figure 4.11
Page 2 with titles.

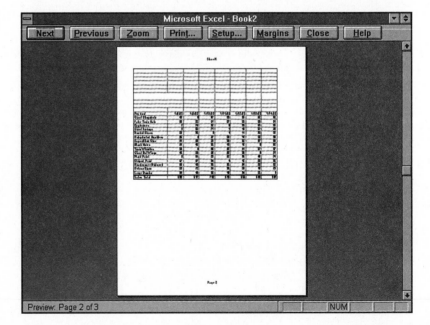

Previewing Your Printout

In earlier versions of Excel, every time you made a change to your worksheet, you had to print it, look for problems in layout or presentation quality, fix the problems, and print again. With complex worksheets using many different fonts, it often took many printouts to achieve the desired result. Aside from being a tremendous waste of paper, this process consumed a great deal of time.

With Excel 5, you can preview your printouts. Excel shows you, as closely as possible, exactly what you will see when you print out to paper. You also can adjust certain print characteristics when you view the print preview, until you are happy with the results. When you are satisfied, you can print the final document quickly and easily.

To preview a document, pull down the File menu and select Print Preview. Alternately, click on the Print Preview button on the Standard toolbar. The preview appears, as shown in figure 4.12.

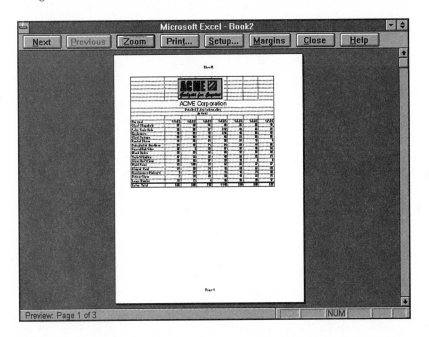

Figure 4.12
The Print Preview screen.

Along the top of the screen are a number of buttons, listed in table 4.3.

Table 4.3
Print Preview Buttons

Button Name	Function
<u>N</u>ext	In a multipage document, click on this button to move to the next page. If no more pages remain, this button is grayed out.
<u>P</u>revious	In a multipage document, click on this button to move to the previous page. If you are on the first page, this button is grayed out.
<u>Z</u>oom	This button acts as a toggle switch. Click on it once to zoom in for a closer view of your document. Click on it again to view the entire page. You also can simply point to a particular region of the screen with the magnifying glass pointer. A zoomed view of that particular area then appears. Click again with the magnifying glass pointer to return to viewing the full page.
<u>P</u>rint	Clicking on this button closes the preview window and returns you to the document, automatically bringing up the Print dialog box.
<u>S</u>etup	Click on this button to bring up the Page Setup dialog box. You can make any changes you want. When you click on the OK button, the preview window reflects your changes.
<u>M</u>argins	Clicking on this button brings up control handles that enable you visually to set the margins and column widths (see the next section).
<u>C</u>lose	This button closes the preview window and returns you to your worksheet.

In this example, the document might benefit from a number of changes. Clicking on the <u>S</u>etup button allows you to make the following changes:

- ✔ Switch from Por<u>t</u>rait to <u>L</u>andscape Orientation on the Page page.

- ✔ Remove the gridlines. Use the Sheet page and deselect the <u>G</u>ridlines checkbox.

- ✔ Remove the header and footer. Use the Header/Footer page. Pull down the <u>H</u>eader and <u>F</u>ooter list box and choose (none). The (none) entry can be found at the top of the list box.

- ✔ Automatically center the document vertically and horizontally. Use the Margin page and select the Hori<u>z</u>ontally and <u>V</u>ertically checkboxes in the Center on Page section of the page.

After these changes are made in the Page Setup dialog and the OK button is selected, the results appear (see fig. 4.13).

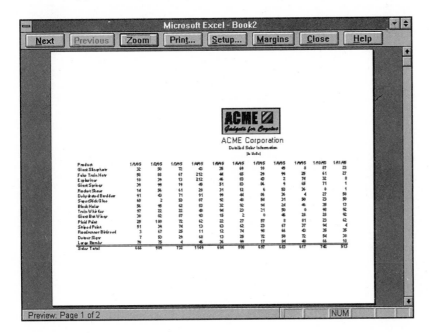

Figure 4.13
The Preview example after changes.

Adjusting Margins and Column Widths in Print Preview

When you are in the preview window, you can adjust the margin and column widths visually by clicking on the Margins button. Control handles to appear, as shown in figure 4.14.

To adjust the margins or the column widths, position your pointer on top of the relevant control handle and drag it to the new position. The results appear instantly.

After you make adjustments to the preview, click on the Print button to print the document.

Figure 4.14
The Margin and
Column control
handles.

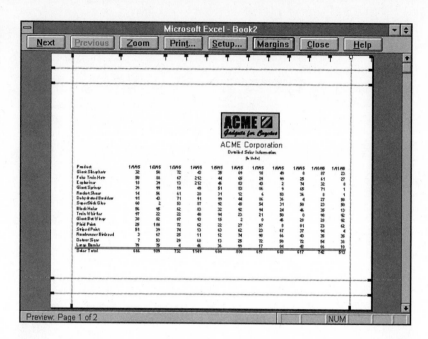

Chapter Snapshot

One of the real strengths of Excel is its ability to help you manage complex data. You can view and work with large amounts of data fairly effortlessly, using the built-in tools designed for that purpose. You can view one or more documents in multiple windows or views and easily consilidate information from different worksheets — even when they are in different workbooks. You also can set up titles and different scrollable areas of a single worksheet to make them easier to work with. In this chapter, you learn about these tools, including the following:

✔ Viewing and working with multiple windows in the Excel work area

✔ Managing sheets within the workbook: inserting new sheets, deleting sheets, and renaming sheets

✔ Managing and switching between multiple workbooks

✔ Using three-dimensional references in your workbooks

✔ Linking data between multiple worksheets or workbooks

✔ Setting up and using Excel templates

By learning to manipulate multiple windows and views, you learn to work more efficiently. The features discussed in this chapter can help you put more of Excel's power to work for you.

Working with Multiple Windows

One of Excel's most valuable aspects is its capability to help you to consolidate and analyze data that would otherwise be very cumbersome. Particularly with the new workbooks in Excel 5, this task becomes even easier. The new workbook organizing metaphor makes it easier to keep similar types of data together, with different sheets for different parts of your data, for charts, or even for Excel programming instructions.

This chapter discusses ways to view different parts of a single sheet simultaneously, shows you how to work with multiple workbooks on your screen, teaches you to work with data across different sheets or from entirely different workbooks, and discusses linked graphics and Excel templates.

AUTHOR'S NOTE

Much of what happens in a computer is represented by metaphor. Complex programming details are masked by ideas like notebooks, workbooks, buttons, and the like. These constructions are said to be *metaphors,* because they are abstractions designed to mask the underlying complexity, much like a story that illustrates a point but ignores many details. Metaphors like these make it easier to work with the computer.

Splitting the Worksheet

In many cases, you might want to view different parts of a single sheet at the same time. You might, for example, want to keep the labels of a table visible, or to view multiple parts of the worksheet to better understand the way a complex formula works, while you scroll across it.

Creating Multiple Viewing Areas

To split the worksheet into multiple *panes* (different scrollable portions of the same sheet) by using the mouse, drag the horizontal split bar down or the vertical split bar to the left. Figure 5.1 shows you the location of the two split bars. When you put your mouse pointer on top of the split bar, the pointer changes to two vertical or horizontal bars with arrows to indicate that you can move the bar. When your pointer is in the right place, click and drag the bar to the position you want.

Figure 5.2 shows the effect of dragging the vertical split bar to the middle of the worksheet.

You also can split the worksheet into four parts instantly with the menu command provided by using the following procedure:

1. Pull down the <u>W</u>indow menu.

2. Choose <u>S</u>plit from the menu.

You can move between panes simply by clicking your mouse in the pane with which you want to work. Each pane area can scroll independently of the other panes. As you see in figure 5.2, each pane gets its own scroll bars for this purpose.

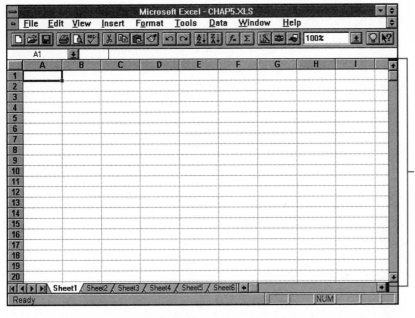

Figure 5.1
Split bar locations.

—Split bars

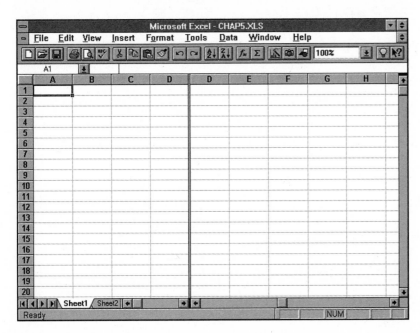

Figure 5.2
The vertical split bar.

Freezing Panes

You also can "freeze" the window panes in a single position. Freezing is useful when you are working with large tables. Look at the sales worksheet shown in figure 5.3, for example.

Figure 5.3
The table example.

	J	K	L	M	N	O	P	Q	R
10									
11	1/9/95	1/10/95	1/11/95	1/12/95	1/13/95	1/14/95	1/15/95		
12	8	87	23	95	62	82	71		
13	25	61	27	23	28	91	52		
14	74	32	8	99	63	95	93		
15	65	71	1	18	67	28	21		
16	36	8	1	11	32	56	44		
17	4	27	58	14	56	30	87		
18	50	23	50	66	37	80	71		
19	46	35	13	16	0	82	70		
20	0	98	92	41	67	97	57		
21	28	28	92	58	0	51	21		
22	81	23	62	36	48	74	3		
23	37	94	4	12	59	35	79		
24	43	35	35	84	95	62	50		
25	72	54	38	58	10	29	85		
26	18	66	10	34	25	8	10		
27	587	742	513	665	649	901	814		
28									
29									

Microsoft Excel - 4-10.XLS — A27: Sales Total — Select destination and press ENTER or choose Paste — NUM

When you look at the data to the right of the table, you really can't tell what each line represents, because the labels in column A are not visible (they are far to the left of the visible portion of the worksheet). This example shows the problem in only one dimension. If the table extended down further, you would have similar problems with the dates at the top of the table — they would not be visible while looking at the lower parts of the table. To deal with this problem, Excel enables you to create independently scrollable portions of the worksheet. You then can continue to view one part of the worksheet (the labels, for example), while you scroll the other portion to see data located elsewhere in the worksheet. To see the way this command works, follow these steps:

1. Move to cell A1.

TIP   Ctrl-Home quickly takes you to cell A1.

2. Pull down the **W**indow menu and choose **S**plit.

3. Position your mouse pointer directly over the intersection of the two panes. Drag the panes so that the two lines intersect at cell A11, as shown in figure 5.4.

TIP

Excel normally creates the split above or to the left of the active cell. For the preceding example, you could position the active cell to B12 before using the **S**plit command to automatically create the split in the correct position.

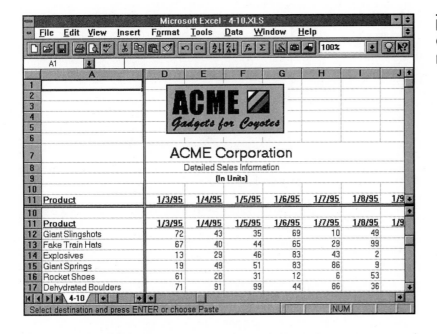

Figure 5.4
Correctly positioned panes.

4. Pull down the **W**indow menu again and choose **F**reeze Panes. The result is shown in figure 5.5.

Notice that several things have happened. First, the pane indicators are made up of fine lines rather than the thicker lines shown in figure 5.4. Second, the worksheet only has a single set of scroll bars, because you no longer can scroll the frozen portions independently as you could before you chose the **F**reeze Panes command. Now when you scroll the worksheet, you scroll everything *except* the frozen panes (in this case, rows 1 through 11 and column A). If, for example, the worksheet is scrolled down and to the right, the frozen pane areas still are visible, as in figure 5.6.

Figure 5.5
Frozen panes.

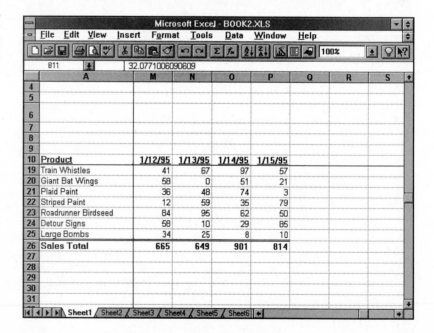

Figure 5.6
Scrolled
worksheet with
frozen panes.

Removing Frozen Panes

To unfreeze the existing panes, pull down the Window menu and choose Unfreeze Panes. You also can remove the panes without unfreezing them first by pulling down the Window menu and choosing Remove Split.

Using Multiple Views of a Single Workbook

Another useful trick is to work with multiple views of a single workbook, which enables you to have different pages of a single workbook on the screen at one time. Using a related feature, you also can show multiple workbooks on the screen at one time with this feature.

To open a second view of a single workbook:

1. Pull down the Window menu.

2. Choose New Window.

This procedure creates a second *instance* of the workbook, so you can switch using the Window menu, as shown in figure 5.7.

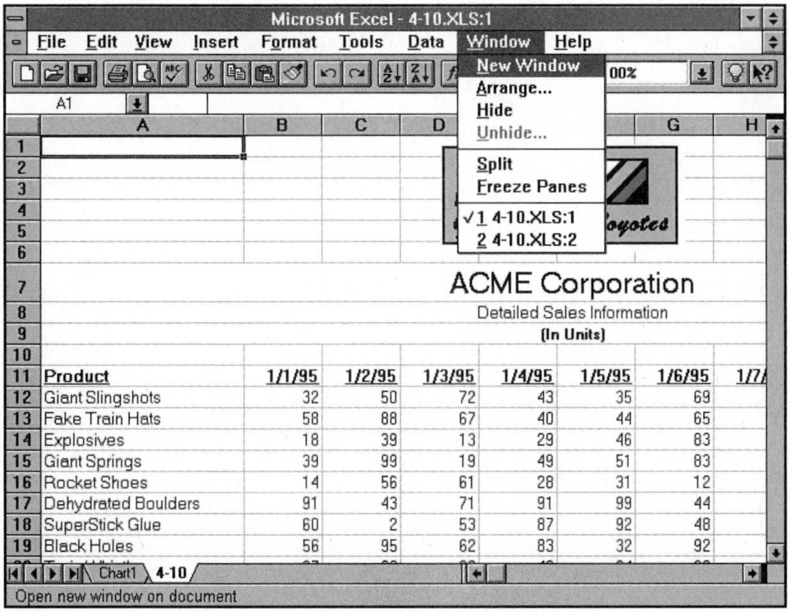

Figure 5.7
The Window menu.

Choosing either window from the list takes you to that copy of the workbook. Notice each workbook has a colon following its name, with a number after the colon, indicating these are different windows of the same workbook. Changes to one window are shown instantly in the other.

Arranging Windows

You also can arrange the windows on your screen so that you can view them all simultaneously. To make this arrangement using the mouse, first click on the Restore button. This button reduces the current view to a window that can be moved and resized on the Excel work area. Figure 5.8 shows what this view looks like after you click on the document restore button.

After the current view is windowed, you can drag the borders of the worksheet to change its size. You also can drag on the title bars of a window to reposition it.

Figure 5.8
The windowed view.

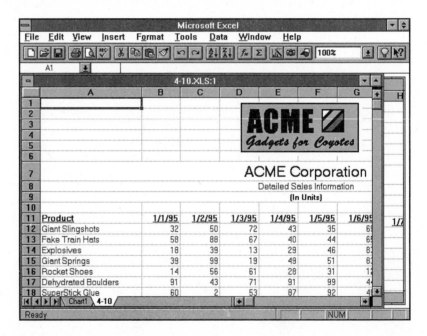

Arranging Automatically

Some Excel commands rearrange multiple windows automatically. You can follow these steps:

1. Pull down the <u>W</u>indow menu.

2. Choose <u>A</u>rrange. The Arrange Windows dialog box appears, as shown in figure 5.9.

The Arrange Windows dialog box offers several options:

✔ **Tiled.** Arranges windows so that they each use an equal portion of the screen, as in figure 5.10.

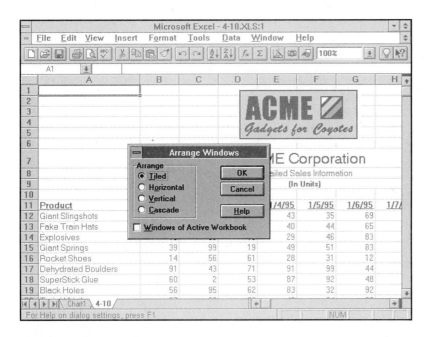

Figure 5.9

The Arrange Windows dialog box.

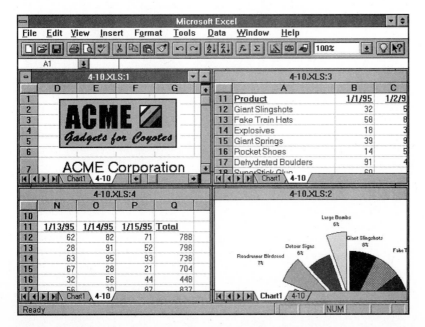

Figure 5.10

The Tiled option.

✔ **Horizontal.** Arranges windows so that they span the entire screen and are arrayed vertically, as in figure 5.11.

Figure 5.11
The Horizontal
option.

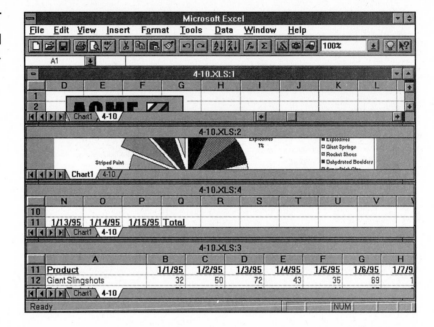

✔ **Vertical.** Arranges windows so that they stretch from the top of the screen to the bottom and are arranged next to each other, as in figure 5.12.

✔ **Cascade.** Arranges the windows vertically, as you can see in figure 5.13. The Cascade option gives each window the most space possible, while still enabling you to click on any of the windows at any time to bring it to the front.

The Arrange Windows dialog box also has a checkbox called Windows of Active Workbook. If this option is selected before you click on the OK button in the dialog box, Excel only includes different views of the workbook currently selected in the arrange operation.

You can close any of the views by double-clicking on that window's Control menu. The remaining views are renumbered accordingly.

TIP

Normally, you switch between windows by using the Window menu. You also can switch between all open windows by pressing Ctrl+Tab.

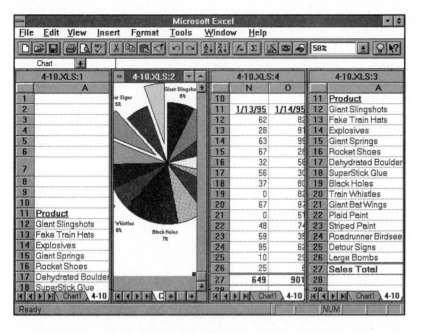

Figure 5.12
The **V**ertical option.

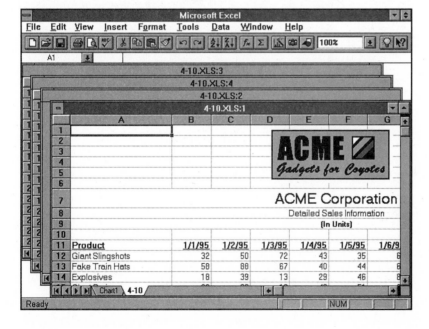

Figure 5.13
The **C**ascade option.

Hiding and Showing Windows

You can easily hide any of the open windows by using the Window menu's Hide command. Make sure the window you want to hide is active, then select Hide. The window vanishes and does not appear in the Window menu as it normally would. This option is valuable for worksheets that you distribute to others. You can hide the underlying details of the worksheet, if necessary.

To unhide a hidden window, pull down the Window menu and choose Unhide. The Unhide dialog box, shown in figure 5.14, lists all currently hidden windows.

Figure 5.14
The Unhide dialog box.

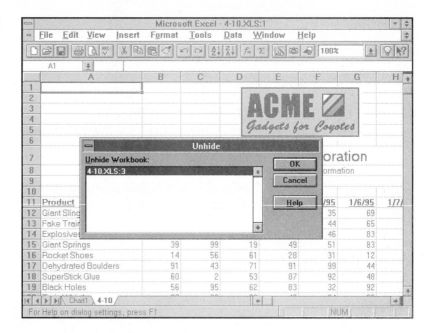

Select the window you want to unhide from the list and click on OK.

Locking Down Windows

When you are developing workbooks for others to use, you might want to take away the user's ability to rearrange the windows. For example, perhaps your workbooks might be used by novice Excel users who might become confused and disoriented if they mistakenly closed a window in the workbook. Prevent this possibility by locking the windows of the workbook into your assigned positions.

To lock windows, follow these steps:

1. Arrange the windows in exactly the way you wish them to remain.

2. Pull down the <u>T</u>ools menu, choose <u>P</u>rotection, and then choose Protect <u>W</u>orkbook. You see the Protect Workbook dialog shown in figure 5.15.

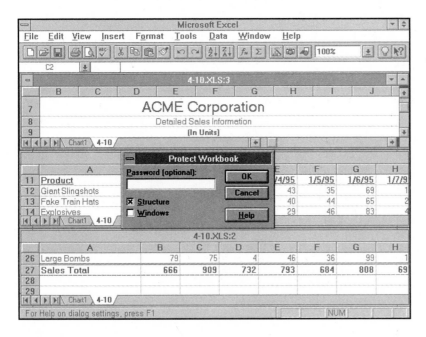

Figure 5.15
The Protect Workbook dialog box.

Before protecting the workbook, make sure that the <u>W</u>indows checkbox is selected. This step ensures that the border around each window that normally enables you to resize it is hidden. Also, attempts to use the <u>A</u>rrange option on the <u>W</u>indow menu are ignored.

To restore Excel's capability to arrange the windows, simply unprotect the workbook. Pull down the <u>T</u>ools menu, choose <u>P</u>rotection, and then choose Unprotect <u>W</u>orkbook.

Using Excel Workbooks

Among Excel 5's exciting new features, the most important one is the new workbook feature. A *workbook* enables you to work easily with many worksheets, all containing different data, switch easily between them, and consolidate the information on each sheet. This section teaches you about this feature, which is new to Excel 5.

Controlling Sheets

You can move easily between different worksheets in your workbook by clicking on the tabs found at the bottom of the workbook.

You also can switch between your active sheets using a keyboard combination. Ctrl+PgDn moves you to the next sheet in the workbook; Ctrl+PgUp moves you to the previous sheet.

Rearranging Sheets

To rearrange sheets in your workbook, click on the sheet you want to move, hold down the left mouse button, and drag to the right or left. A small arrow indicates where the sheet will be "dropped" when you release the mouse button.

You also can use the object menu to move or copy sheets in your workbook by using the following method:

1. Click the right mouse button on the sheet you want to copy or move.

2. From the menu, choose Move or Copy. You see the dialog box shown in figure 5.16.

Figure 5.16
The Move or Copy
dialog box.

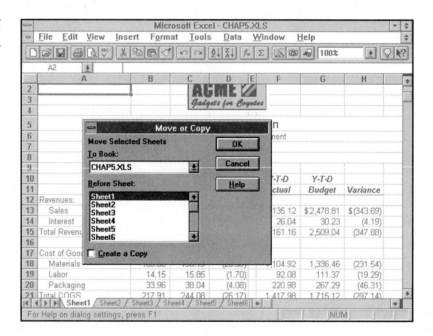

This dialog box offers many options:

✔ **To Book.** Enables you to choose any other open workbook to which to move the sheet.

✔ **Before Sheet.** Enables you to choose where to position the moved sheet in the target workbook. Choose the sheet before which you want the moved or copied sheet to be inserted.

✔ **Create a Copy.** Tells Excel to make a copy of the sheet rather than moving it.

3. After you have selected the options you want, click on the OK button.

Creating Sheets

The easiest way to create new sheets in an existing workbook is to use the pop-up menu. Follow these steps:

1. Right-click on one of the sheet tabs.

2. Choose Insert from the pop-up menu. You see the dialog box shown in figure 5.17.

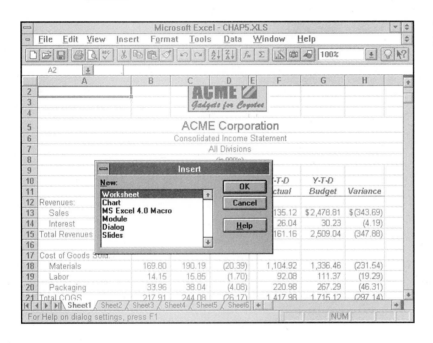

Figure 5.17
The Insert dialog.

As you can see from the dialog box, Excel supports many types of sheets:

✔ **Worksheet.** A worksheet is an Excel spreadsheet. The sheet in the background of figure 5.17, for instance, is a worksheet.

✔ **Chart.** Excel supports charts embedded in worksheets or that exist as separate sheets in the workbook. If you want to create a chart on a separate sheet in the workbook, choose this option.

✔ **MS Excel 4.0 Macro.** The old macro language that was used in Excel 4 has been replaced with the new Visual Basic Application tools. Excel 5 still contains support for the Excel 4 macros, however. To use a macro from Excel 4, include it in an MS Excel 4.0 Macro sheet in your workbook.

✔ **Module.** Module sheets are Visual Basic Application modules. These sheets contain the programming code that defines your Excel application.

✔ **Dialog.** For use with Modules, Dialog sheets contain dialog boxes that accept input and choices from the user of the VBA application.

✔ **Slides.** A slide sheet coordinates a presentation based in Excel. These sheets contain commands designed to enable you to prepare a sequence of charts and worksheets for a presentation.

3. After you choose the type of sheet you want to insert, click on the OK button.

You also can insert new sheets by using the Insert menu:

✔ To create a new worksheet, access the Insert Worksheet command.

✔ To create a new chart, access the Insert Chart command. Then, from the cascading menu, choose either On This Sheet or As New Sheet to tell Excel where to create the new chart.

✔ To create a module, pull down the Insert menu and choose Macro. You then can choose, from the cascading menu, either Module, Dialog, or MS Excel 4.0 Macro.

Deleting Sheets

To delete a sheet or sheets in Excel, follow these steps:

1. Select the sheet you want to delete. If you want to delete more than one sheet, Ctrl-click to select additional sheets.

2. Pull down the Edit menu and choose Delete Sheet. Alternately, you can access the pop-up menu from here by clicking your right mouse button on the sheet tab. From the pop-up menu, choose Delete.

Renaming Sheet Tabs

You probably will find it difficult to manage your sheets with the default names of Sheet1, Sheet2, Sheet3, and so on. Fortunately, Excel enables you to rename the tabs for each sheet so that each sheet has a more meaningful name. To rename tabs using the menus, follow these steps:

1. Select the sheet you wish to rename.

2. Pull down the Format menu and choose Sheet. Choose Rename from the cascading menu.

3. Type the new sheet name in the dialog box that appears.

As with almost all Excel commands, you also can rename tabs using the pop-up menus. Right-click on the sheet tab and choose Rename from the pop-up menu.

Figure 5.18 shows the sample worksheet for this chapter with new tab names.

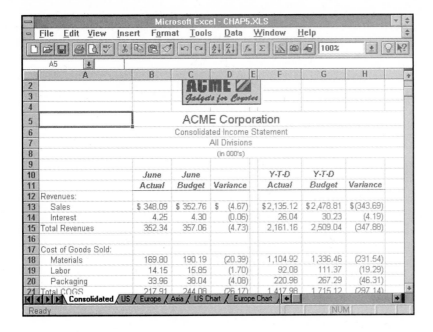

Figure 5.18
The renamed tabs.

Worksheets

Adding an Existing Worksheet to a Notebook

To take an existing Excel 4 worksheet and add it to a workbook, follow these steps:

1. Open the workbook of which you want the existing worksheet to be a part.

2. Open the existing worksheet. It opens into a single-sheet workbook, with the file name where you normally see the tab name.

3. With the existing worksheet active, pull down the Edit menu and then choose Move or Copy Sheet from the menu.

4. In the Move or Copy dialog box, select the name of the workbook in the To Book drop box.

5. In the list labeled Before Sheet, select the sheet in the workbook before which you want the existing worksheet to appear.

6. Click on the OK button.

Linking Data Between Sheets

The workbook is one of Excel's most powerful features. It enables you to organize your worksheets more logically, with major sections of your project each contained in a single worksheet. Thus, you spend less time worrying about organizing your data and more time actually getting answers and analyzing your data. Also, workbooks make developing more complicated worksheets, such as multicompany spreadsheets, much easier.

The following sections discuss various ways to link data between different sheets, whether they are in the same workbook or different workbooks. Table 5.1 defines many terms you need to know in order to understand these sections.

Table 5.1
Linked Data Terms

Term	Definition
3-D Reference	A reference to another sheet in the current workbook. These references are updated automatically when Excel recalculates the workbook.
Source Document	When linking different files, this document contains the source data.
Dependent Document	When linking different files, the dependent document is the one that relies on data in other documents.
External Reference	A cell reference that refers to cells in a different workbook.
Remote Reference	A remote reference refers to data in a file that was created by an application other than Excel. This data might be graphic data from a drawing program or word processing data from a word processor.

To access the full power of the workbook, however, you must learn to link data between the different sheets of the workbook. From these examples, you can learn to create a simple income statement, with individual sheets for each major division in the company and a sheet that combines all divisions into a consolidated total. The consolidated sheet is made of formulas that automatically total each of the other sheets in the workbook. After the consolidated sheet is completed, changes in any of the divisional sheets are reflected there automatically. Consider figure 5.19, which shows all four sheets in the same workbook.

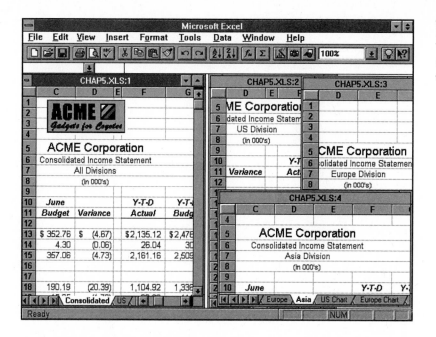

Figure 5.19
The ACME consolidating 3-D workbook.

Worksheets

Creating 3-D References

The easiest way to link cells from different sheets into a formula is to use the mouse. This section shows you how to perform mouse references and tells you what to type when you want to enter 3-D references manually.

To see the way a 3-D reference works, follow these steps:

1. Move to the cell in which you want the total placed from another sheet.

2. Type the equal sign to begin the formula.

3. Click on the tab of the sheet that contains the data you want.

4. Click on the cell you want to reference.

5. Press Enter to complete the formula.

After you press Enter, Excel returns to the sheet that contained the formula, and the data from the other sheet now appears in the cell. This data is said to be *dynamic*. In other words, if you change the source cell, the destination cell (which contains the formula) instantly changes to reflect the new number.

Also, as you can see, Excel entered the formula in the format:

```
=SheetName!CellName
```

Sheet names in a 3-D reference always are absolute. Individual cells or ranges in the 3-D reference can be absolute or relative.

This method is the general way in which references to other sheets are entered. The only exception is when you have spaces in the sheet name, in which case Excel surrounds the sheet name with single quote marks, as in the following example:

```
='Sheet with a Space'!CellName
```

When you enter references to other sheets using the mouse, Excel automatically uses the single quote marks, if needed.

The next step in entering multisheet references with the mouse is to perform some arithmetic. In figure 5.20, the formula bar shows one way to add cells from three sheets into a total in the consolidating sheet.

Figure 5.20
3-D arithmetic.

Microsoft Excel - CHAP5.XLS

File   Edit   View   Insert   Format   Tools   Data   Window   Help

B13   =US!B13+Europe!B13+Asia!B13

	A	B	C	D	E	F	G	H
1								
2			ACME					
3			Gadgets for Coyotes					
4								
5			ACME Corporation					
6			Consolidated Income Statement					
7			All Divisions					
8			(in 000's)					
9								
10		*June*	*June*			*Y-T-D*	*Y-T-D*	
11		*Actual*	*Budget*	*Variance*		*Actual*	*Budget*	*Variance*
12	Revenues:							
13	Sales	$ 348.09						
14	Interest							
15	Total Revenues							
16								
17	Cost of Goods Sold:							
18	Materials							
19	Labor							
20	Packaging							
21	Total COGS							

Consolidated / US / Europe / Asia / US Chart / Europe Chart

Working with Sheet Ranges

Excel also enables you to use references that refer to many sheets all in one reference. The example in figure 5.20 is not very practical if you are consolidating tens or hundreds of worksheets (and Excel *can* handle hundreds of worksheets!). In these cases, you want to use the SUM function and enter the sheet names as a range. This operation can be done entirely with mouse commands:

1. Move to the cell that contains the formula.

2. Start the formula by entering **=SUM(**.

3. Switch to the first sheet in the range and then click on the cell you want to total, or select the range you want to use.

4. Shift-click on the last sheet in the range.

5. Press Enter to complete the formula.

Figure 5.21 shows the range of sheets with the completed formula.

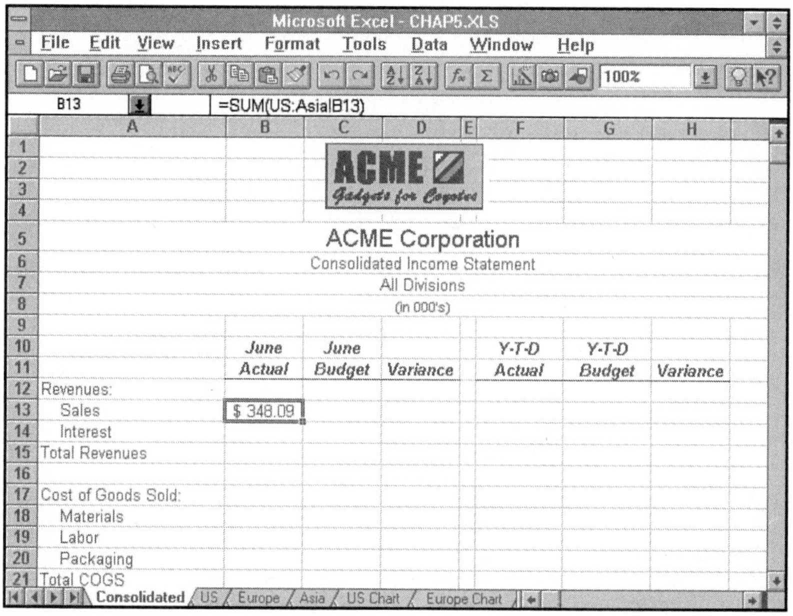

Figure 5.21
The range of sheets.

As you can see, multisheet references are given in the following form:

```
FirstSheet:LastSheet!Cell_Or_Range
```

Figure 5.22 shows this form using a range of cells in each sheet, with the resulting formula
=SUM(Sheet2:Sheet3!A6:D6).

Figure 5.22
The 3-D reference
with range.

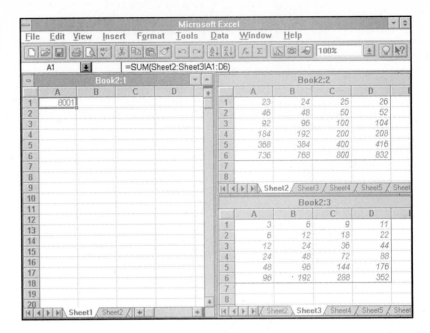

If you rearrange the order of the sheets in your workbook, you might change the way sheet ranges are calculated. In the range Sheet4:Sheet8, for instance, if you move Sheet6 somewhere outside of the range in the formula, its cells are no longer part of the solution. Similarly, if you insert a new sheet in a range of sheets, the new sheet's data become part of the answer.

If you move the first or last sheet to an area outside of the original range, the formula adjusts to exclude that sheet. In the preceding example, if Sheet4 is moved to follow Sheet8, then the formula changes to Sheet5:Sheet8.

For this reason, be careful when you rearrange sheets in a workbook that contains 3-D references.

Using References to Other Workbooks

Linking between different workbooks (and not just different sheets within a workbook) has many possible uses, including the following:

✔ **Look at different analyses of your data.** You can create new workbooks from your source workbooks to present key data in different ways without changing the structure of the original data. This procedure helps you look at your data differently.

✔ **Simplify complex workbooks.** Often, in very large workbooks, you can simplify the organization of your data by breaking it down into different workbooks.

✔ **Conserve memory.** You can conserve your computer's memory by breaking large workbooks into smaller pieces. In fact, if you are working with a workbook that includes many sheets, and you start getting `out of memory` error messages, break the large workbook into smaller workbooks.

✔ **Create a hierarchy of different workbooks for very large projects.** You can create multiple levels of linked workbooks, if necessary. In other words, workbook #1 can refer to workbook #2, which references workbooks #3 and #4 (or any other hierchial organization that makes sense for your project).

✔ **Coordinate large projects.** For example, you can use Excel to do your company's budgeting. Prepare and distribute workbooks for budgeting managers. When the managers complete and return the workbooks, consolidate them into a single, company-wide budget workbook.

To link workbooks, you can use all the same tools about which you just learned. You can use the mouse, as you saw earlier, to create the links between the different workbooks. The only exception is that you should open the workbook you want to link, and use the <u>W</u>indow menu to switch between the workbooks instead of just clicking on the workbook tabs.

References to other workbooks that are open in Excel take the following form:

```
=[Workbook_Filename]Sheet_Name!Cell_Or_Range
```

When the workbook you want to reference is not open in Excel, the full path name of the workbook is added to the beginning of the reference, as in the following example:

```
='C:\EXCEL\DATA\[WORKBOOK.XLS]Sheet_Name'!Cell_Or_Range
```

NOTE

Make sure that the entire sequence of path name, workbook file name, and sheet name is enclosed with single quote marks before the exclamation point.

Also, if the workbook you are linking is located in the same directory as the dependent workbook, you do not need to type the path name.

When opening a workbook that contains links to other Excel workbooks stored on your computer's disk, you see the message shown in figure 5.23.

If you click on <u>Y</u>es, Excel automatically goes into the referenced workbooks to find the most recent data and updates all the formulas that access that data.

If you select <u>N</u>o, Excel simply shows you the most recent answer that was stored the last time you saved the dependent workbook. The links to the other workbook are still present, but are not necessarily accurate if the other workbooks are updated. You might want to choose the <u>N</u>o button when you are working with a very large workbook that contains many links to many different workbooks. If you do not need the most current data, you can save time by telling Excel to skip the update process.

Figure 5.23
The Update
Reference
message box.

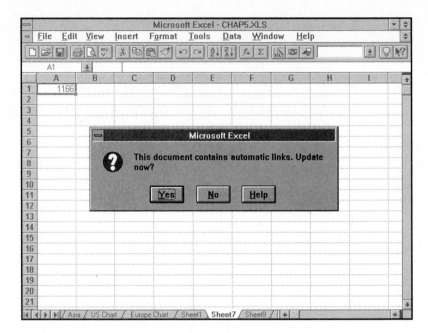

Figure 5.23
The Update
Reference
message box.

Managing Workbook Links

You can manage the links between your workbooks to do the following tasks:

✔ Update the dependent workbook at any time

✔ Redirect a workbook link from one workbook to another

✔ Open the source workbooks

NOTE

A *dependent document* is one that contains a formula that uses data from another document. The document that contains the original data is the *source document.*

To manage your document links, pull down the Edit menu and choose Links. You see the dialog box shown in figure 5.24.

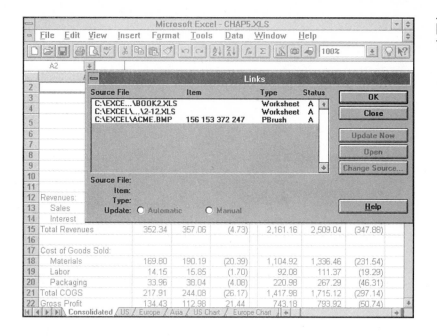

Figure 5.24
The Links dialog.

The Links dialog box shows you all active links in the current document. You can select the link with which you want to work by clicking on it. After you have selected a link, you can perform the following functions:

✔ Click on the **U**pdate Now button to update the links immediately with any new information in the source document.

✔ Click on the **O**pen button to open the source document.

✔ Click on the **C**hange Source button to tell Excel to link to a different workbook. You are shown the Change Links dialog box (much like the File Open dialog box), as you can see in figure 5.25. Use the Change Links dialog box to find and open the new document to which you want to link. The links automatically use the same ranges in the new source document that you select.

> The Links dialog box shows all the links available to control. Links are not limited to other Excel workbooks. Excel allows linked graphics, word processing files, and so on. The Links dialog box shows all these links for your current workbook.

Save the source workbook first when you are saving linked workbooks. This precaution ensures that the data is calculated properly before the dependent workbook is closed.

Be careful when renaming or moving workbooks. If you rename a source workbook, do two things to make sure that all the dependent references are properly updated:

1. Check to see that the source and dependent workbooks are open so Excel can automatically correct any dependent references to the renamed workbook.

2. Use the Excel Save As command to rename the workbook

Figure 5.25
The Change Links
dialog box.

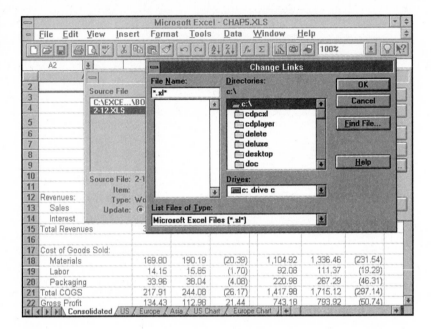

If a source workbook is renamed or moved using the File Manager, you must update the links in the dependent workbook manually, because Excel does not know what you did with the source workbook. When you open the dependent workbook, it automatically notes that the source workbook is no longer present and automatically brings up a File Not Found dialog box, shown in figure 5.26. Use this dialog box to relocate the file that contains the source data.

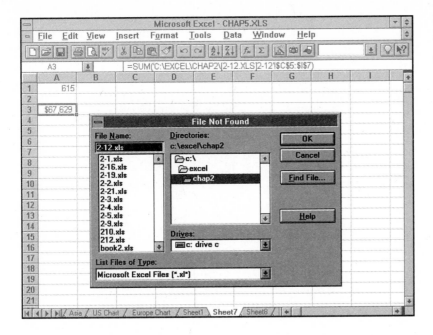

Figure 5.26
The File Not Found
dialog box.

Worksheets

Using Paste Special

Often, you want to share data in different sheets, but when you use the normal copy and paste between worksheets, you do not create a link between those sheets. Instead, you have to use Paste Special to copy data to a new sheet that still is linked back to the original sheet. To use Paste Special, follow these steps:

1. Select the source range of cells.

2. Pull down the Edit menu and choose Copy.

3. Move to the destination workbook, and click on the cell in which you want the data to be copied.

4. Pull down the Edit menu and choose Paste Special. You see the dialog box shown in figure 5.27.

5. Click on the Paste Link button.

The data is placed in your destination cells, with an automatic link back to the source document.

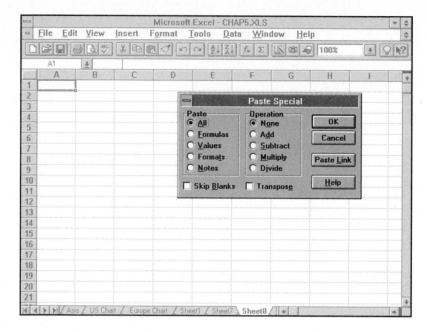

Figure 5.27
The Paste **S**pecial
dialog box.

Removing Links

To remove a link but retain the results, follow these steps:

1. Select the range you want to retain.

2. Pull down the **E**dit menu and choose **C**opy.

3. Pull down the **E**dit menu again and choose Paste **S**pecial. In the Paste Special dialog box, click on the button marked **V**alues and then click on the OK button.

When you follow the preceding steps, the links are removed, but the results that were present are converted to regular data, as if you simply retyped them.

Pasting Pictures from a Workbook

Excel enables you to take "pictures" of a series of cells and paste them into another worksheet or workbook so they appear as graphic images. These images can be resized, reshaped, and so on. Use the following procedure:

1. Select the range of cells of which you want to take a picture.

2. Pull down the **E**dit menu and choose **C**opy, or click on the Camera button on the toolbar.

3. Move to the destination worksheet.

Worksheets

4. If you copied the cells using the Camera button on the toolbar, simply click in the destination area to create the linked picture. If you used the Copy command, then hold down the Shift key while you pull down the Edit menu and choose Paste Picture Link.

Although Paste Picture Link creates a linked picture that changes if the source cells change, you also can create a simple picture that has no links and does not update if the source cells change. Simply hold down the Shift key while you pull down the Edit menu and choose Paste Picture, instead of Paste Picture Link.

Linking to Other Applications

Many business and science documents are really *compound documents*. They are composed of information from a variety of sources: spreadsheets, charting programs, drawing programs, word processors, and so on. Instead of cutting or pasting information from all of these sources, you can use a Windows technology called *Object Linking and Embedding* (OLE, pronounced like a bullfighter saying "Olé!") to make the creation of compound documents much easier.

Earlier versions of Excel used OLE 1.0, which enabled you to link data between different Windows-based applications. You could, for instance, take an Excel chart and link it to a Microsoft Word or WordPerfect for Windows document. The linked chart would be updated automatically if it was changed in Excel, so the word processor automatically showed the most current version of the chart. Also, if you were to double-click on the chart in the word processing program, Excel would be launched automatically with the chart loaded and ready for changes. Many Windows applications support OLE 1.0 and can perform these tricks.

New to Microsoft Excel version 5 is an updated version of OLE called *OLE 2.0*. Excel is one of the first applications to feature version 2 of OLE. Currently, all Microsoft products are being updated to use OLE 2.0, including Word 6 for Windows, Microsoft Project, Microsoft Publisher, and Microsoft Mail. Many other application developers also are working to include OLE 2.0 capabilities in their programs.

OLE 2.0 adds two key capabilities to OLE 1.0:

✔ **In-place editing of embedded (linked) objects.** If you double-click on an Excel chart embedded in a word processor that supports OLE 2.0, you are able to edit the chart without leaving your word processing document. The word processor's menus become Excel menus, and you have full access to Excel's power, almost as if Excel is built into the word processor!

✔ **Dragging and dropping of objects.** This capability enables you to grab data in one application and simply "drop" it into another application.

Using OLE

You can take information from one Windows application and link it to another application in two ways. You can take the source data and drag it to the destination, or you can use the Copy command in the Edit menu of the source program and then use some form of Paste Special in the destination program.

Although Microsoft programs generally use a command called Paste Special, other programs might call this command something else. For example, WordPerfect for Windows calls it Paste Link. When in doubt, consult the documentation for the program with which you are linking Excel.

Using Drag and Drop

Drag and drop might function differently, depending on the application you are using. Some applications, for instance, might interpret a drag-and-drop operation as a command to move data from the source application to the destination application. Other applications might assume you are attempting a link creation. The interpretation depends on the application you are using, and also on the specific data you are trying to drag and drop.

For Drag and Drop to work with Excel, you must enable a checkbox in the Options notebook. Pull down the Tools menu and choose Options. Then click on the Edit tab in the options notebook. Make sure that the checkbox labeled Allow Cell Drag and Drop is checked.

Figure 5.28 shows a chart that was dragged from Excel to Microsoft Word 6.0.

To perform the drag-and-drop function, follow these steps:

1. Arrange the applications on the screen so you can see them both at the same time.

2. Select the graphic object (such as a chart) or range of cells you want to drag and drop.

3. If you are selecting a graphic object, click on the object and hold down the left mouse button. Then drag the mouse to the destination application. If you are copying a range of cells, then select the border of the selected range before dragging.

4. Position the cursor in the destination application and release the left mouse button.

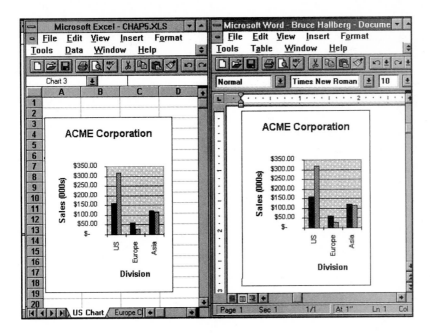

Figure 5.28
Drag and drop.

TIP

To force the drag and drop to insert the new data, hold down the Shift key while you perform the operation. To remove the data from Excel and place it in the destination application, hold down Ctrl during the drag-and-drop operation.

After the chart is dragged to the destination application, you can edit the data simply by double-clicking on it. This operation brings up Excel with the data ready for editing, or if Excel was not running when you double-clicked on the data, Word uses Excel's capabilities to help you edit the data. Excel is started in the background and "inserts" itself into Word so it still appears that you are working with Word, even though you have full access to all of the power of Excel (the menu commands appear in place of the Word menu commands, and so forth). This capability is called *in-place editing*.

AUTHOR'S NOTE

Microsoft is changing all its applications' menus so they are as standardized as possible. One reason for this change is to make the in-place editing process more "seamless."

Some applications do not support in-place editing of Excel objects. In those cases, when you double-click on the Excel data in the destination application, Excel is launched with the data loaded in it. Edit the data in Excel and exit Excel to update the data in the destination application.

Controlling Link Requests

While Excel is running, it services any requests for link updates from other applications. You can control whether Excel responds to these requests by following these steps:

1. Pull down the Tools menu and choose Options.

2. Click on the Calculation tab in the notebook.

3. Select or deselect the checkbox labeled Update Remote References.

Using the Camera

You probably have wondered about the function of the Camera button on the Standard toolbar. It is used to prepare a "snapshot" of part of an Excel document that can be placed easily in another program (or another sheet in Excel, for that matter). If, for example, you use the Copy and Paste commands to move part of a worksheet into a Word document, you actually paste only the data; you do not place the data so that it appears with all of its formatting intact. Instead, use the Camera tool to prepare a snapshot of part of your worksheet (which includes all formatting), then place the resulting image into the other application. Follow these steps:

1. Select the part of your worksheet you want to present in a different application (in this example, Microsoft Word).

2. Click on the Camera button. A marquee appears around the selected cells, and your pointer changes to a small cross.

3. Click on another area of the worksheet to create the image. Figure 5.29 shows the resulting image on top of the worksheet.

The image created is dynamic. Even though you expect it to be a fixed image, you discover that if you change the data in the area you used for the image, the image changes.

After you have the image, you can drag it to another Windows application that supports OLE 2.0, or you can copy it to the clipboard, then paste the object into the destination application so that the image is linked to Excel.

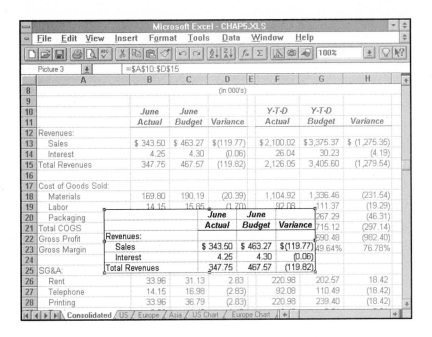

Figure 5.29
The worksheet image.

Setting Up Templates

One useful Excel application is setting up template workbooks that can be completed by people with whom you work. To set up template workbooks, follow these steps:

1. Prepare the workbook you want to make into a template.

2. Pull down the File menu and choose Save As.

3. In the Save As dialog box, click on the button to the right of the Save File as Type field to see a list of the different types of files you can save from Excel.

4. Choose Template from the list, enter a file name, then click on the OK button to save the document, which is given an XLT extension.

After you create the template and it is opened, a copy of the document is loaded and given a temporary name to preserve the original template file from changes.

To edit a template file, follow these steps:

1. Pull down the File menu and choose Open.

2. Select the template file.

3. Hold down the Shift key while you click on the OK button.

This procedure opens the template file. Make any necessary changes and resave the template.

Chapter Snapshot

Excel has some advanced features that the typical user does not use on a day-to-day basis. When you do need these features, however, they can be real time-savers. In this chapter, you learn about the following advanced features:

- ✔ Embedding sound objects into your workbooks

- ✔ Using the Excel outlining feature

- ✔ Creating different scenarios using the Scenario Manager

- ✔ Using the PivotTable Wizard, which enables you to look at information in a table by rotating data categories to show new relationships

- ✔ Importing text files using the TextWizard

By taking advantage of Excel's powerful worksheet tools, you can go far beyond the basics and become an Excel "power user."

6 CHAPTER

Advanced Worksheet Features

Excel includes many advanced features that are available to you when needed. This chapter discusses a number of these features—some of them new to version 5 of Excel. The features discussed in this chapter are not needed by everyone who wants to benefit from using Excel; for those who need them, however, they can be incredible timesavers.

Using Sound with Excel

In Excel, you can annotate your worksheets and charts with sound. These *sound objects* can be prerecorded sounds you use to emphasize a point or recorded voice annotations that explain certain features of the worksheet.

You must have certain sound hardware to play or record sounds in Excel. You also have to set up Windows so that it can access the sound hardware. For more information on using sound with your computer, consult *Crank It Up!* from New Riders Publishing.

Creating Sound Notes

Just as you can attach text notes to cells, you also can attach or record sound in addition to or in place of the written note. To record a sound note, follow these steps:

1. Click on the cell to which you want to attach the sound note.

2. Open the Cell Note dialog box by selecting Note from the Insert menu or pressing Shift+F2. The Cell Note dialog box appears in figure 6.1.

Figure 6.1
The Cell Note dialog box.

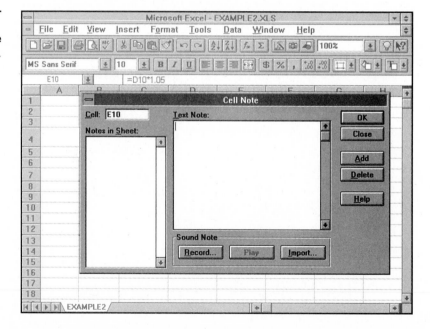

3. To record a sound using a microphone connected to your sound hardware, click on the Record button in the Cell Note dialog box. The Record dialog box appears, as shown in figure 6.2.

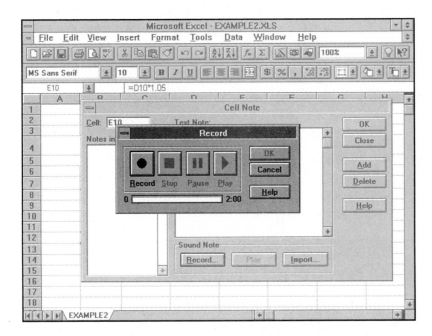

Figure 6.2
The Record dialog box.

4. Click on the Record button in the Record dialog box and begin speaking. After you finish your sound note, click on Stop.

5. To check your sound note before you save it, click on the Play button. If you don't like your sound note, click on the Record button again and rerecord it.

6. After you are satisfied with your sound note, click on OK to save the sound note.

You also can use prerecorded sound notes that are stored on your disk as WAV files. To use prerecorded sound notes, follow these steps:

1. Select the cell to which you want to attach the sound note.

2. Open the Cell Note dialog box by selecting Note from the Insert menu or by pressing Shift+F2.

3. Click on the Import button. You see the Import Sound dialog box, which functions like the standard File, Open dialog box.

4. Find the WAV file on your disk by using the Import Sound dialog box. Select the file, then click on OK.

To play a sound note on the worksheet, select the cell that has the sound note and press Shift+F2 to call up the Cell Note dialog box. Then click on <u>P</u>lay to hear the sound note.

Importing Sounds into Excel

In Excel, you can import sound objects stored on your disk and embed them directly on the worksheet. After you embed the sound object, you can simply double-click on the icon shown in the worksheet to play the sound. To create an embedded sound object, follow these steps:

1. Select <u>O</u>bject from the <u>I</u>nsert menu. The Object dialog box appears (see fig. 6.3).

2. Select Sound from the <u>O</u>bject Type list box and click on OK. This step creates the sound icon on your worksheet and starts the Windows Sound Recorder (see fig. 6.4).

3. To record a sound, click on the button in the Sound Recorder that looks like a microphone. After you finish speaking, click on Stop.

Figure 6.3
The Object dialog box.

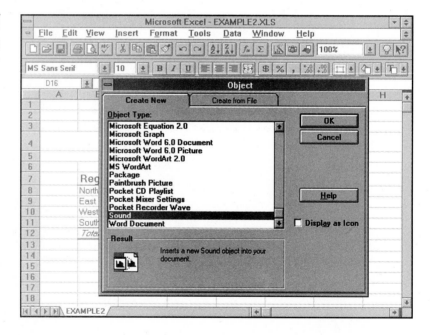

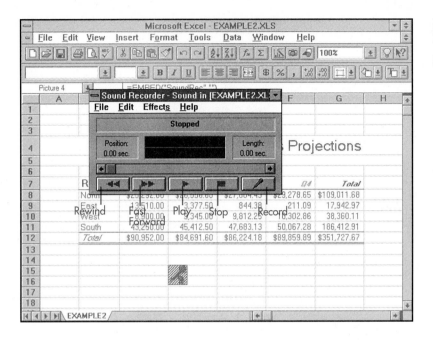

Figure 6.4
The Windows
Sound Recorder.

You also can use an existing sound file stored on your disk in WAV format. To use an existing sound file, select Insert File from the Sound Recorder's Edit menu. The Insert File dialog box appears, which you can use to find the WAV file on your disk, and then click on the OK button.

4. When you have finished recording or inserting the sound you want, select the File menu in the Sound Recorder and choose Update to update Excel with your changes. After you have chosen Update, close the Sound Recorder by double-clicking on its control menu or by choosing Exit from the File menu.

After you complete the preceding steps, you have an icon in your worksheet (see fig. 6.5).

AUTHOR'S NOTE

In the example I prepared for this book, I embedded a sound file taken from the old TV show "Lost in Space." The recording is of the robot saying "Warning! Warning! Warning!" Given the East region's sales trend, this sound seemed completely appropriate.

Figure 6.5
An embedded
sound object.

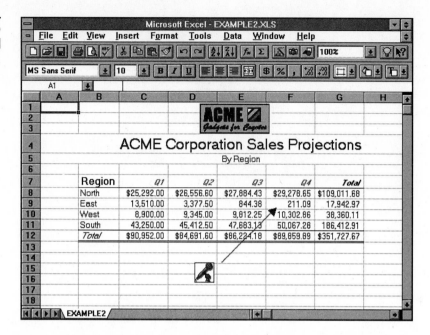

To play an embedded sound object, double-click on the icon in the worksheet. To edit a sound object, select the sound object and then select Edit menu. From the Edit menu, select Sound Object, then Edit, which brings up the Sound Recorder with the sound automatically loaded and ready to edit. To delete a sound object, select it and press the Del key.

Mastering Excel's Outlining Feature

Excel enables you to hide and show detail in your worksheets by using outlining. You can designate ranges of rows or columns and group them so that you can quickly hide or show their detail. You also can create *nested outline groups* (groups within groups) so that you can achieve exactly the level of detail you want.

Examine the worksheet shown in figure 6.6 and again in figure 6.7. This worksheet shows a detailed income statement (organized by quarter) that has been outlined.

Click here to collapse monthly detail

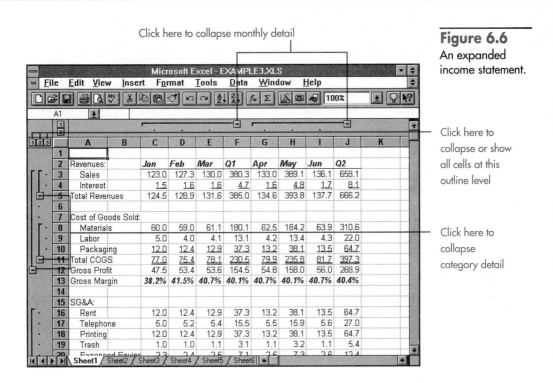

Figure 6.6
An expanded
income statement.

Click here to
collapse or show
all cells at this
outline level

Click here to
collapse
category detail

By using the outlining that has been added to the worksheet shown in the figures 6.6 and 6.7, you can switch quickly to any level of detail you want. In a large, complex worksheet, you can navigate faster with collapsed groups. When you get to the area in the worksheet in which you want to work with the detail, just click on the appropriate outline button to reveal the detailed information.

Creating an Outline Range Manually

To manually create an outline range, follow these steps:

1. Select a range of rows or columns. Be sure to select the rows or columns them-selves rather than cells within the worksheet.

2. Pull down the Data menu and choose Group and Outline. Then choose Group from the cascading menu that appears.

TIP

After you select a range of rows or columns, you can quickly group or ungroup them for the outline by pressing Alt+Shift+right arrow to group or Alt+Shift+left arrow to ungroup.

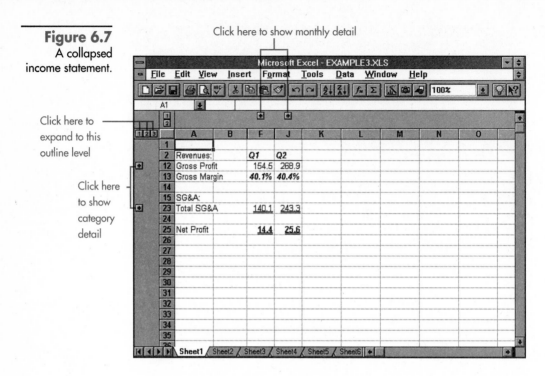

Figure 6.7
A collapsed
income statement.

Click here to show monthly detail

Click here to
expand to this
outline level

Click here
to show
category
detail

You don't always have to select whole rows or columns as you did in the previous example. You also can select a range of cells on the worksheet before you select the Group command. When you select a range of cells and then Group them, the Group dialog box appears, asking whether you want to group the rows or columns for the selected range of cells (see fig. 6.8). Select Rows to group the rows that contain the selected cells, or Columns to group the columns in the selected cell range.

Creating an Outline Automatically

With most worksheets, Excel can examine the structure of the worksheet and generate all the appropriate outlining levels automatically. Excel bases its decisions on factors such as location of formulas compared to actual data, location of SUM formulas, and so forth. Excel then creates an outline level for each consistent structure in the worksheet.

You can control how Excel looks for this consistency before you create the automatic outline by pulling down the Data menu and selecting Group and Outline. When you choose Settings from the cascading menu, the Outline dialog box appears (see fig. 6.9).

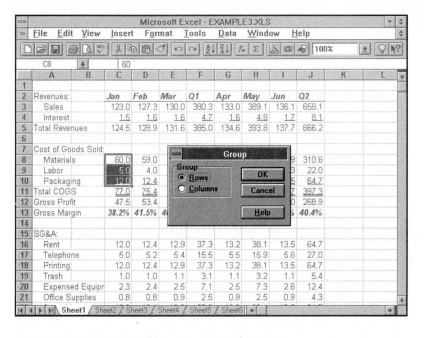

Worksheets

Figure 6.8
The Group
dialog box.

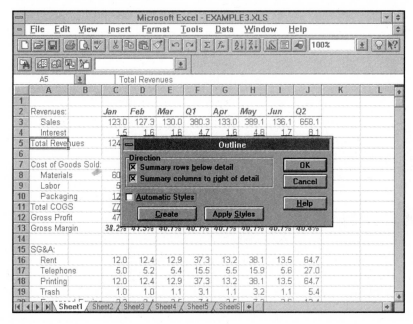

Figure 6.9
The Outline
dialog box.

In the Outline dialog box, select the Summary rows below detail checkbox marked if your data summarize downward (in other words, the totals are at the bottom of the worksheet). If your summary formulas are above the detail they represent, deselect this checkbox. Also, if your column summaries are to the right of the detail they represent, select the Summary columns to right of detail checkbox.

If you select the Automatic Styles checkbox, Excel formats your document with boldface in the summary cell locations, to help you distinguish summary information from detailed information.

If you want to create the outline from the Outline dialog box, click on the Create button. Otherwise, pull down the Data menu, select Group and Outline, and then select Auto Outline. Excel then applies the rules you set in the Outline dialog box and automatically creates all the appropriate outline levels for your worksheet.

TIP

To restrict the area that Excel outlines with the Auto Outline feature, select the cells you want to outline before executing the command. Otherwise, Excel will outline the entire document.

If you restructure your data, you can select the Auto Outline command again to restructure the outline.

Deleting Outlines

Excel offers two ways to delete outlines. You can either delete individual outlines or you can delete all outlines in the worksheet with a single action.

To delete individual outlines, select the rows or columns in the outline level you want to remove. Then pull down the Data menu, select Group and Outline, then select Ungroup. You also can press Alt+Shift+left arrow instead of using the menu command.

To delete all outlines on your worksheet, begin with no rows or columns selected. Then pull down the Data menu, select Group and Outline, then select Clear Outline.

Using the Scenario Manager

Excel has a tool called the Scenario Manager that you can use to help track multiple scenarios of your data in a single workbook. The Scenario Manager enables you to define *changing cells* for a single worksheet. You then define different scenarios based on those changing cells. Using this feature, you can store multiple scenarios of your data in a single worksheet

Worksheets

without having to maintain multiple copies of your data. This method is a fundamentally better way to accomplish multiple scenarios, because if you change the formulas that make up your worksheet and are not using the Scenario Manager, you might forget to update all of the copies of your worksheet. When you use the Scenario Manager to model many scenarios, you need to make structural changes to your worksheet in only one place.

When you create different scenarios, you can use the Scenario Manager to switch quickly between the different sets of data, which lets you quickly examine and compare the different scenarios. As an example, you might have a budgeting worksheet for which you want to examine three budget "cases:" Projected (or expected), Best Case, and Worst Case. Or, you might define scenarios such as "Best case if the Johnson deal goes through" or "Projected profits if we freeze salaries."

For even more complex analysis, use the Scenario Manager together with PivotTables. PivotTables are discussed in the next section of this chapter.

Examine the worksheet shown in figure 6.10. This worksheet shows a sales budget for four different regions in the company. Each region has a projected sales growth target, which is defined below in the Sales Growth cells.

The easiest way to access the Scenario Manager is through the Workgroup toolbar, although you also can select the S̲cenarios command from the T̲ools menu. You activate the Workgroup toolbar by using the T̲oolbars command in the V̲iew menu.

One way to use the Scenario Manager might be to look at the total company sales if the regions experience different sales growth rates. This example defines simple Projected, Best Case, and Worst Case scenarios, but you could also define scenarios that examine different events in each of the individual regions (such as Projected: West Loses Sales Manager, or Best Case: New Product Introduction in East).

Creating a Scenario

To create a scenario, pull down the T̲ools menu and select S̲cenarios. The Scenario Manager dialog box appears, as shown in figure 6.11.

You begin to define the new scenario by clicking on the A̲dd button in the Scenario Manager dialog box, which brings up the Add Scenario dialog box, shown in figure 6.12.

Figure 6.10
Scenario sample
worksheet.

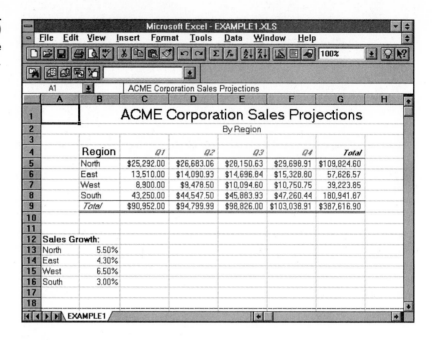

Figure 6.11
The Scenario
Manager dialog
box.

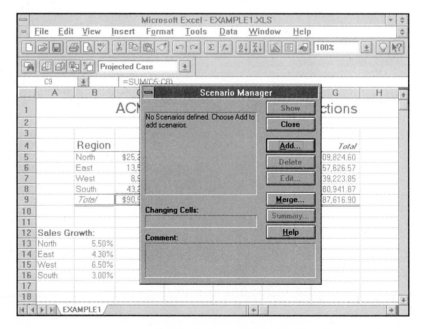

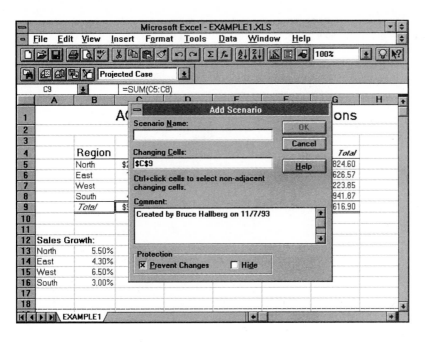

Figure 6.12
The Add Scenario dialog box.

Type the name of your scenario in the Scenario Name field. Define the changing cells by clicking in the Changing Cells field, and then select the cells in the worksheet. Excel automatically generates your name and the date you created the scenario in the Comment field, although you can easily edit it. The Add Scenario dialog box also has two checkboxes: Prevent Changes and Hide. Select the Prevent Changes checkbox to prevent other users from being able to modify your scenario. Select the Hide checkbox to prevent the new scenario from appearing in the Scenario Manager dialog box.

After you select the changing cells (in this case, cells B13:B16), click on OK. The Scenario Values dialog box then appears (see fig. 6.13).

Use the Scenario Values dialog box to define the values in the changing cells for the new scenario. You are limited to 32 changing cells per scenario. Each cell has a *field*, in which you input the value for the cell. After you enter the values for the new scenario, click on OK.

TIP

If you need to define a scenario that uses more than 32 changing cells, create multiple scenarios — each of which changes a different range of cells. For example, you can define scenario #1 to change cells A1:A32, scenario #2 to change cells B1:B32, and so forth.

Figure 6.13
The Scenario
Values dialog
box.

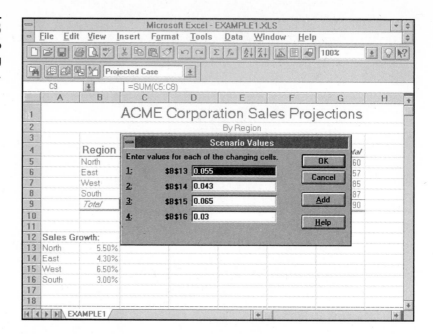

Creating a Scenario with the Toolbar

If you have the Workgroup toolbar visible, you can quickly create a scenario by following these steps:

1. Manually change the values in the changing cells in the worksheet for the new scenario.

2. Select the range of changing cells. If necessary, use Ctrl+click to select multiple noncontiguous ranges.

3. Click in the Scenarios field on the Workgroup toolbar, type the new name of the scenario, and press Enter.

Switching between Scenarios

You can quickly switch between scenarios by using the Scenario Manager dialog box or the Scenarios drop-down list on the Workgroup toolbar.

To display different scenarios using the Scenario Manager dialog box, follow these steps:

1. Access the Scenario Manager dialog box by using the Scenarios command in the Tools menu.

2. Click on the desired scenario in the Scenarios field.

3. Click on the Show button.

After you click on the Show button, the scenario you selected appears. When you finish viewing scenarios, or have the scenario you want to work with, click on the Close button to return to the worksheet.

To display different scenarios using the Scenario drop-down list in the Workgroup toolbar, simply click on the drop-down arrow and choose the scenario name from the list. After you click on the name, the selected scenario appears.

Creating a Scenario Summary Report

You can create a summary report of your different scenarios that shows the different assumptions and the results you want to view based on each scenario. To create a scenario summary report, follow these steps:

1. Access the Scenario Manager dialog box by pulling down the Tools menu and selecting Scenarios.

2. Click on the Summary button in the Scenario Manager dialog box. The Scenario Summary dialog box appears, as shown in figure 6.14.

3. In the Report Type box, choose Scenario Summary.

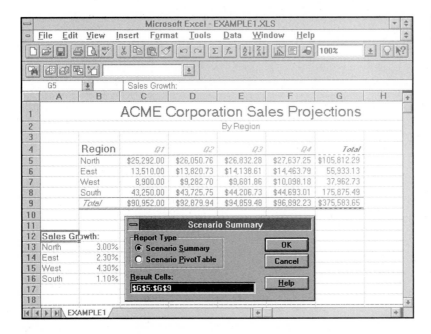

Figure 6.14

The Scenario Summary dialog box.

4. Click on the <u>R</u>esult Cells field, and then select the cells in your worksheet that have the results you want to see in your scenario summary report. In this example, select the range G5:G9. Remember, you can hold down the Ctrl key to select multiple ranges to view.

5. Click on the OK button to create the scenario summary report.

The preceding steps create the scenario summary report in a new sheet in your workbook (see fig. 6.15).

Figure 6.15
A scenario
summary report.

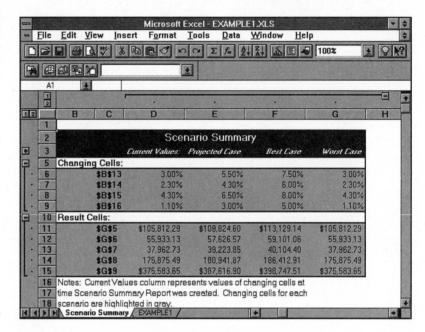

Note the following features of the scenario summary report:

✔ Excel automatically creates the formatting you see in figure 6.15.

✔ Excel automatically outlines the report for you.

✔ You can view the comments (creation date and creator) for each summary by clicking on the Outline button to the left of row 3 to expand the row 3 outline.

✔ The scenario summary report is somewhat difficult to understand with only cell references for the categories in the report. You can correct this problem by using named ranges in your worksheet. Figure 6.16 shows a scenario summary report with named ranges.

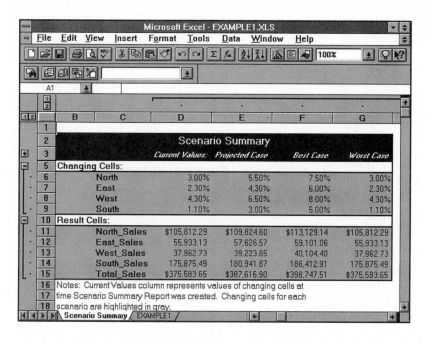

Figure 6.16

A scenario summary report with named ranges.

Creating a Scenario PivotTable

You can create a scenario PivotTable to view your scenarios by following these steps:

1. Access the Scenario Manager dialog box by pulling down the Tools menu and choosing Scenarios.

2. Click on the Summary button in the Scenario Manager dialog box. The Scenario Summary dialog box shown in figure 6.14 appears.

3. Select Scenario PivotTable from the Report Type box.

4. Click in the Result Cells field, then select the cells in your worksheet that contain the results you want to view in the summary report. In this example, you select the range G5:G9.

5. Click on the OK button to create the scenario PivotTable shown in figure 6.17.

Figure 6.17
A scenario
PivotTable.

	A	B	C	D	E	F	G
1							
2	$B$13:$B$16 by	(All)					
3							
4		Result Cells					
5	$B$13:$B$16	North_Sales	East_Sales	West_Sales	South_Sales	Total_Sales	
6	Best Case	$ 113,129	$ 59,101	$ 40,104	$ 186,413	$ 398,748	
7	Projected Case	$ 109,825	$ 57,627	$ 39,224	$ 180,942	$ 387,617	
8	Worst Case	$ 105,812	$ 55,933	$ 37,963	$ 175,875	$ 375,584	
9							
10							

Using PivotTables

One of the most powerful additions to Excel 5 is the PivotTable feature. PivotTables enable you to summarize detailed information for easier analysis. You can use PivotTables to analyze the following:

✔ Detailed sales records

✔ Shipping cost statistics

✔ Purchase order details

✔ Engineering safety records

PivotTables have many other potential applications as well. You can summarize a detailed list or database records (such as the preceding list) into PivotTables, which show summary information only. You can then *rotate* the data with your mouse to analyze it in different ways.

This section teaches you about Excel's PivotTable feature by using sample call records from a call accounting system. Figure 6.18 shows the top of the worksheet that contains the detailed records.

A *call accounting system* is software that runs on a computer connected to your telephone system. A call accounting system captures telephone statistics so you can manage your telephone costs. Most such systems can output their data into text files that Excel can read.

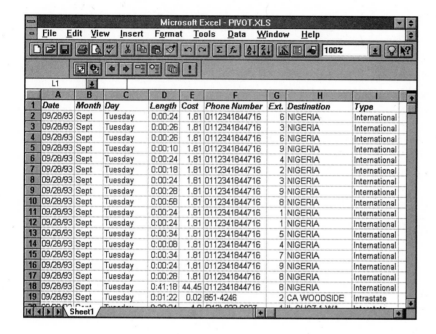

Figure 6.18
Call records.

Approximately 500 call records have been imported into Excel for this example (although you can use thousands without any trouble). Table 6.1 shows the fields in the sample worksheet.

Table 6.1
Worksheet Fields

Field Name	Description
Date	The date the call was placed
Month	The month in which the call was placed
Day	The day of the week when the call was placed
Length	The length of the call in minutes

continues

Table 6.1, Continued
Worksheet Fields

Field Name	Description
Cost	The estimated cost of the call (generated by the call accounting system)
Phone Number	The phone number dialed
Extension	The extension number from which the call was placed
Destination	The name of the geographic destination
Type	The type of call: International, Interstate, or Intrastate

If you were the telecommunication manager at your company, you might want to ask certain types of questions about the telephone data, such as the following:

✔ **What were the total dollars spent by each telephone extension?** Because you know who is assigned to each extension, you can figure out the amount each person spends from the data. You might even provide the data to accounting so that each person's department can be charged for its calls.

✔ **How much is spent on different call types?** In other words, how much is spent on international, interstate, and intrastate calls? This information might help you justify a different telephone carrier who has cheaper rates for the most common types of calls.

✔ **What are the most expensive destinations called?** If you can identify a couple of frequently called and expensive destinations, you can use that data to negotiate targeted discounts with your telephone carrier.

✔ **What are the traffic patterns by day of week or by time of day?** This data can help you look at different carriers rates for different time periods. Also, if you make the assumption that outgoing call volume has a rough relationship to incoming calls, this information can help you schedule your telephone operators better.

✔ **What is the average time spent on each call for each extension?** These statistics can indicate, for example, that you need to work with a couple of people to try to make their expensive international calls briefer.

The preceding questions are only a few of the valid questions you can ask with the data shown in the sample worksheet. You also can use Excel's capability to manipulate the records to ask even more questions. You might use the MID() function, for example, to strip out the area code called in the telephone number field and then get summaries by area code.

Use Excel's extensive list of functions to massage your data into different categories, so you can ask different questions about the data. These questions, and many more, cannot be easily answered by looking through hundreds or thousands of data records. PivotTables work well with this type of application.

Figure 6.19 shows an example of a PivotTable created from the sample data. This PivotTable shows the total dollar amount of calls made by type of call (International, Intrastate, or Interstate) for each extension, and also has a Page field that enables you to look at all calls or just the totals for a given month.

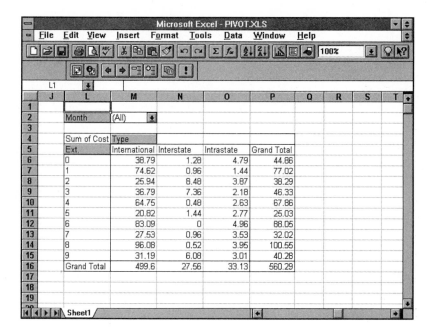

Figure 6.19
A sample PivotTable.

Using the PivotTable Wizard

You use the PivotTable Wizard to generate the sample PivotTable shown in figure 6.19. To begin creating a PivotTable, pull down the Data menu and select PivotTable. The first page in the PivotTable Wizard appears (see fig. 6.20).

In step 1 of the PivotTable Wizard, you select from the four choices explained in table 6.2.

Figure 6.20
PivotTable
Wizard: step 1.

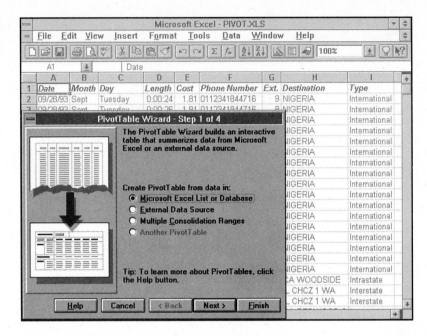

Table 6.2
PivotTable Wizard: Step 1 Options

Option	Description
Microsoft Excel List or Database	Choose this option to use data in a single worksheet in your workbook.
External Data Source	Choose this option to automatically start Microsoft Query, a tool that comes with Excel and is used to query other database files or sources.
Multiple Consolidation Ranges	Choose this option to build the PivotTable from multiple worksheets in your workbook.
Another PivotTable	If your workbook contains other PivotTables, choose this option to incorporate one of them in the new PivotTable.

For this example, select Microsoft Excel List or Database, and then click on the Next button (or press Enter) to proceed to step 2 of the PivotTable Wizard (see fig. 6.21).

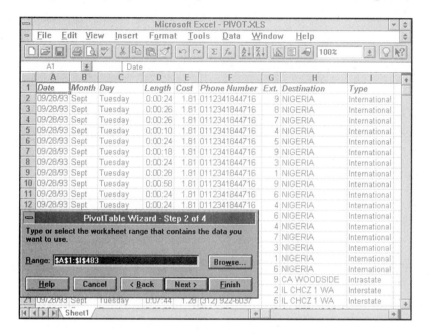

Figure 6.21
PivotTable
Wizard: step 2.

In step 2 of the PivotTable Wizard, you select the range of data on which you want to report. If the range Excel guesses for you is incorrect (Excel assumes you want to create the PivotTable using all cells contiguous with your active cell), use your mouse to select the range that contains the data. You also can click on the Browse button to select a file on the disk that has the data, if the data is in a different worksheet. After you select the range of data for the PivotTable, click on the Next button to go to step 3 of the PivotTable Wizard (see fig. 6.22).

Step 3 of the PivotTable Wizard is the most important step. To the right a number of buttons are arrayed, one for each category of data. In the center of the page is the layout area divided into four different sections (described in table 6.3).

Figure 6.22
PivotTable
Wizard: step 3.

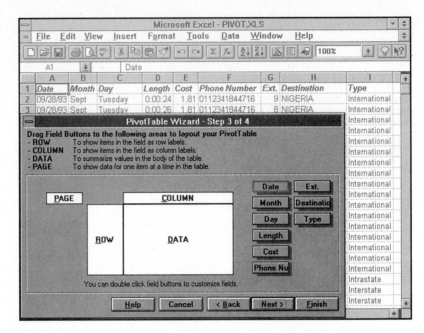

Table 6.3
PivotTable Wizard Layout Sections

Section	Description
Page	Defines a section of the PivotTable in which you can select the records shown in the table. For example, you could drag the Type field to the Page section to enable you to show only international calls.
Row	Enables you to choose which categories are shown in rows.
Column	Controls which categories appear along the horizontal axis of the table.
Data	Can be summarized in different ways. You can show totals, counts, or averages of the category in the Data section.

After you drag the categories you want to report on into the layout area, click on the Next button to display the fourth and final step of the PivotTable Wizard (see fig. 6.23).

Figure 6.23
PivotTable
Wizard: step 4.

Worksheets

Table 6.4 shows the settings available in the fourth step of the PivotTable Wizard.

Table 6.4
PivotTable Wizard: Step 4 Settings

Setting	Description
PivotTable Starting Cell	Use this field to tell the PivotTable Wizard which cell to use for the upper left corner of the PivotTable. After you select this field, you can click on your worksheet in the location you want.
PivotTable Name	Some other functions in Excel (for example, the Scenario Manager) use the name of the PivotTable for certain features. Indicate the name here, or accept the default name.
Grand Totals For Columns	If this checkbox is selected, the PivotTable Wizard automatically creates grand totals for all the columns in your PivotTable.
Grand Totals For Rows	If this checkbox is selected, the PivotTable Wizard automatically creates grand totals for all the rows in your PivotTable.

continues

Table 6.4, Continued
PivotTable Wizard: Step 4 Settings

Setting	Description
Save Data With Table Layout	Normally the PivotTable contains a copy of the source data in a hidden area. If you are having memory-constraint problems, you can clear this checkbox to avoid creating duplicate data.
AutoFormat Table	Select this checkbox to automatically format the PivotTable with the default table AutoFormat.

Click on the Finish button to complete the creation of the PivotTable. Figure 6.24 shows the completed PivotTable.

Figure 6.24
Completed
PivotTable.

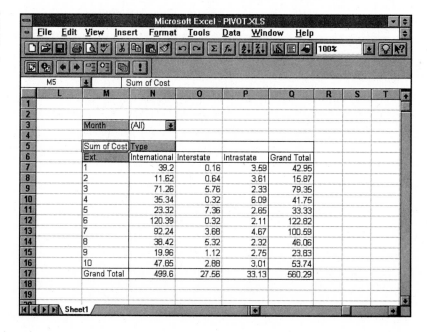

Changing the PivotTable

Not only can you use the PivotTable Wizard to create PivotTables, you also can use it to determine which categories to include in the PivotTable. To change categories, place your active cell in the PivotTable, then access the PivotTable Wizard command in the Data menu. The layout page of the PivotTable Wizard immediately appears. Then you can drag categories and drop them in different locations. Just as you can drag new categories from the right into the layout area, you can delete categories by dragging them from one of the layout sections to a blank part of the screen.

Manipulating the PivotTable

Figure 6.25 shows a new PivotTable created from the sample data. This PivotTable shows the call totals by looking at the mix of calls placed on different days of the week. This PivotTable also has two Page fields: Month and Extension.

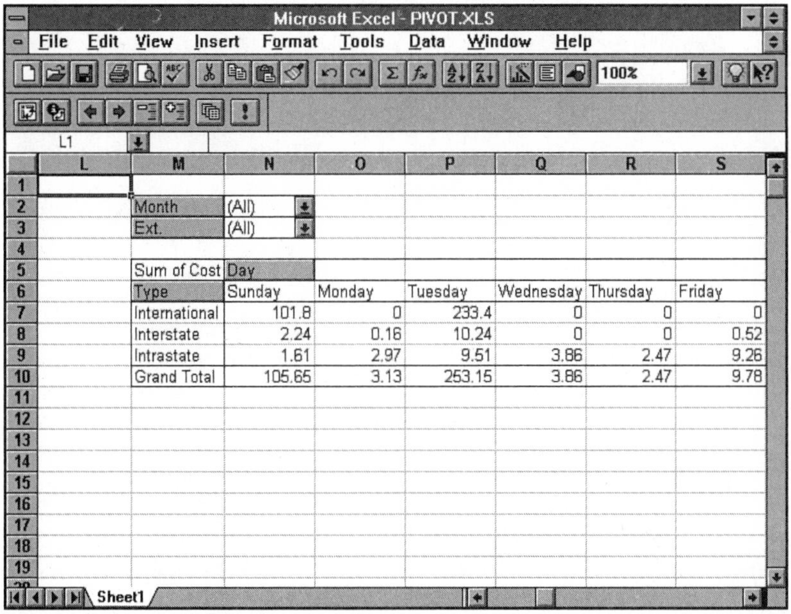

Figure 6.25

A sample PivotTable.

You use the Page fields to restrict the data being looked at. To use the Page fields, click on the drop-down arrow to display the valid choices. When you make a selection, your PivotTable shows only that category. On the sample PivotTable shown in figure 6.25, it is easy to show the information for only one extension by using the Extension Page field. You also can look at one extension in a given month or all extensions for a given month by using the appropriate combination of choices in the Page fields.

You can drag and drop the categories used in the PivotTable. Figure 6.26 shows the result of dragging the Extension field to the vertical axis of the table. You then see what the breakdown is in call type by extension. You can see, for example, that whoever uses Ext. 1 does most of his or her calls on Tuesday, and these calls are mostly international (at least in terms of dollars).

Figure 6.26

Comparing mix of type per extension.

			Sunday	Monday	Tuesday	Wednesday	Thursday
Month	(All)						
Sum of Cost		Day					
Ext.	Type	Sunday	Monday	Tuesday	Wednesday	Thursday
1	International	4.8	0	24.8	0	0
	Interstate	0.16	0	0	0	0
	Intrastate	0.41	0.04	1.87	0.28	0
1 Total		5.37	0.04	26.67	0.28	0
2	International	0	0	8.75	0	0
	Interstate	0.32	0	0.32	0	0
	Intrastate	0.06	0.18	1.18	0.12	0.65
2 Total		0.38	0.18	10.25	0.12	0.65
3	International	3.68	0	63.68	0	0
	Interstate	0	0.16	0	0	0
	Intrastate	0.22	0.04	0.33	0.23	0.26
3 Total		3.9	0.2	64.01	0.23	0.26
4	International	12.16	0	19.86	0	0

The new format is not useful if you want to compare the mix of calls made by each extension. For example, you now know that Ext. 1 makes many international calls, but does Ext. 1 make the most international calls? To change the PivotTable to show that information, drag the Ext. field to the right of the Type field so that the Ext. field becomes a subcategory of Type, as shown in figure 6.27.

On the new PivotTable, you can easily see that Exts. 3 and 6 make more international calls than Ext. 1. When you scroll the PivotTable to the right to view the Grand Totals, you discover that Ext. 6 is the international call leader.

Figure 6.28 shows a new configuration of the fields in the PivotTable. The new arrangement shows only international calls and also shows that most international calls are made on Tuesday.

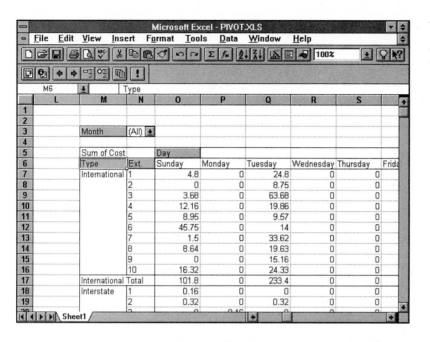

Worksheets

Figure 6.27
Comparing type for extensions.

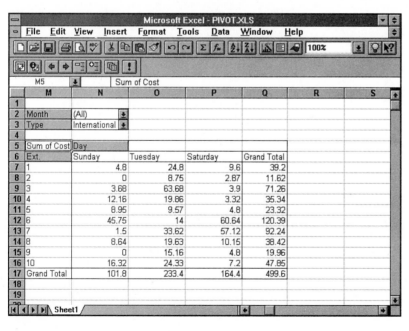

Figure 6.28
International call totals.

In figure 6.28, only three days are listed (Sunday, Tuesday, and Saturday). The PivotTable lists only these three days, because no international calls were made by any extension in the database on the other days of the week. PivotTables automatically filter out completely blank categories.

Controlling Fields

You can control the treatment of different categories by using the PivotTable Field command in the Data menu. Before you select the PivotTable Field command, select the category you want to reformat. If you select an axis field, such as Extension, the PivotTable Field dialog box appears, as shown in figure 6.29.

Figure 6.29
The PivotTable
Field dialog box.

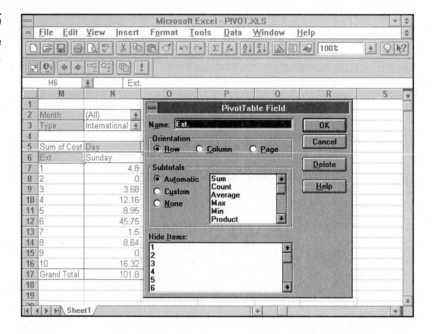

You can change the name of the category by typing a new name in the Name field. If you want to reposition the category without dragging and dropping, select the Row, Column, or Page option button. If the category you format is divided into subcategories, select the different summarization options in the Subtotals box. Choose from the various methods listed, such as Sum, Average, Count, and so on. You can select as many subtotals as you want by clicking on each one individually. Finally, you can choose to hide parts of the data by selecting from the list in the Hide Items list box.

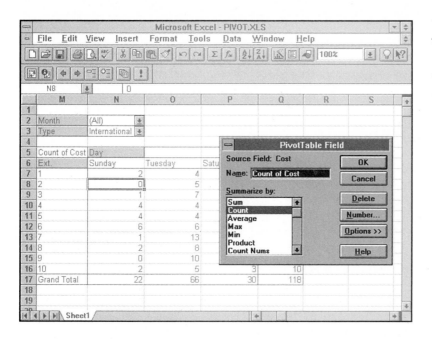

Worksheets

Figure 6.30
The PivotTable
Field dialog box
with the data area
selected.

You also can reformat the data portion of the PivotTable. For example, if you want to show
the number of calls rather than total dollars spent, reformat the data area accordingly. Place
the active cell in the data area of the PivotTable, then select the PivotTable Field command in
the Data menu. A somewhat different version of the PivotTable Field dialog box appears, as
shown in figure 6.30.

Use the Name field to change the name of the subtotal. Select the type of subtotal from the
Summarize by list box in the PivotTable Field dialog box. Click on the Number button to
choose what number format to use to format the subtotals.

Refreshing Data

PivotTables do not automatically update data when the data in the worksheet changes. You
have to use the Refresh Data command. Select the Refresh Data command from the Data
menu, or click on the Refresh Data button in the Query and Pivot toolbar (if the toolbar is
displayed).

Removing Categories

You can remove categories by dragging them out of the PivotTable area. When you do this,
your pointer changes to a category button that has a large X in it. If the X is displayed and
you drop the category (by releasing the mouse button), you effectively remove the category
from the table.

Instead of removing categories from the PivotTable that you might want to use again later, you can drag the category to the Page area of the PivotTable and set it to display all records. You get the same result as far as the data shown in the table is concerned, and you can drag the category back into the PivotTable later without having to call up the PivotTable Wizard again.

Grouping Data in a PivotTable

Sometimes groups you might want to view in a PivotTable do not exist within the data you are using. In these cases, you can group together similar types of records. As an example, you could group interstate and intrastate call types together to compare international call and noninternational call costs.

To group data together, select the records you want to group in the PivotTable, then click on the Group button in the Query and Pivot toolbar or select the Data menu, choose Group and Outline, and then choose Group. Figure 6.31 shows a PivotTable with the interstate and intrastate calls grouped.

Figure 6.31
Grouped records.

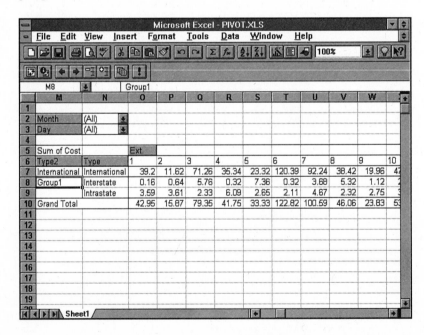

After you create a group using the Group command, you can then rename the group to make more sense for your data (here, noninternational would be a good name). You can then hide the subgroups by selecting the Type2 category, selecting the Data menu, selecting Group and Outline, then Hide detail. To show hidden detail, select the Data menu, select Group and Outline, and then choose Show detail.

Charting PivotTables

You can create charts from your PivotTables using all the charting tools covered Part III of this book. When you change your PivotTable, the chart is updated with the changes automatically.

Importing Text Files

Although Excel can read and write many different file formats, sometimes you have to import text files into Excel. Some examples of cases where you would want to import text files into Excel include the following:

✔ Downloading stock data from an on-line service such as CompuServe and then importing the stock data into Excel.

✔ Taking the output of another program and importing it into Excel; for instance, you might want to import detailed measurements from a piece of test equipment. Most automated test devices have interface software that can export the test data into text files, which can then be used in Excel.

✔ Importing accounting data from your accounting system into Excel. Very few accounting systems can create Excel files for analysis, but almost all accounting systems can create a text file that can be used in Excel. After you load the detailed accounting data (General Ledger transactions, for example), you can use the PivotTable feature to analyze the data.

Any time you open a text file in Excel, the TextWizard starts automatically. The *TextWizard* is a tool that enables you to import almost any format of text data into Excel, and you have far more control over the data's eventual format than has ever been possible in previous versions of Excel.

Using the TextWizard

To use the TextWizard, simply open a text file by accessing the Open command in the File menu. If the file you open has an extension other than the normal Excel file extension (which it probably does), make sure that List Files of Type is set to All Files (*.*). Select your file in the File Open dialog box, then click on the OK button.

Excel recognizes the file as a text file and starts the TextWizard, as shown in figure 6.32.

The TextWizard examines the data in the text file and guesses whether the fields are delimited in some way or the file is composed of fixed-width fields. *Delimited data* generally separates each field with a comma, but you can choose spaces, tabs, or other characters. Fixed-width records are set up in such a way that each field is at exactly the same horizontal position within each line. If Excel guesses incorrectly about your data, select the appropriate option button before proceeding.

Figure 6.32

TextWizard:
step 1.

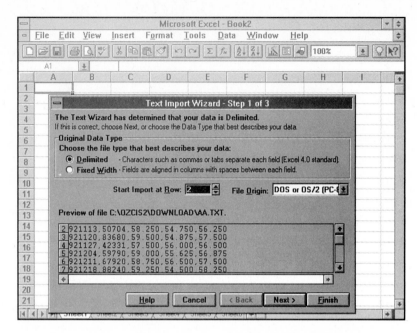

The Step 1 page also has two other fields. The first field, Start Import at **R**ow, enables you to choose from which row in the data to begin reading. Often the first row or rows have header information for the file that you might not want or need. In those cases, set Start Import at **R**ow to the appropriate value. You can use the Preview window to help determine from which row the import should start. The second field is labeled File **O**rigin. You can choose from three file origins: DOS or OS/2 (PC-8), Windows (ANSI), and Macintosh. The File **O**rigin field determines the way certain control characters in the file should be interpreted. Usually, DOS or OS/2 (PC-8) is the most correct choice, although Windows (ANSI) works with almost all files as well. If the data you see in the Preview window is garbled, try another type of file origin. If the data appears garbled using any of the file origin choices, then the file is not a text file; you need to go back to the originating application and reexport the data into a text-based format.

Importing a Delimited File

Assuming your file is delimited, select the **D**elimited option button before you click on the Next button to move to step 2, as shown in figure 6.33.

If your file is fixed width, see the following section. Fixed-width files go through different steps in the TextWizard.

The second step for importing delimited files is to tell Excel what character was used to delimit the fields in each record. Examine the Preview window of this screen to see what the delimiter character is. In most cases, Excel correctly guesses what the delimiter character is, but you may need to change the checkboxes shown if Excel guesses wrong.

In addition to the Delimiters section of this dialog box, you can set two other choices: Treat consecutive delimiters as one, and Text Qualifier. Selecting Treat consecutive delimiters as one has the effect of making the import records vary in length, so this option is not normally set. If, however, you want to discard blank records rather than just leave them blank in the Excel worksheet, select this checkbox.

You use the Text Qualifier field to indicate which character has been used in the text file to indicate textual data as opposed to numeric or date information. Most delimited text files surround purely textual data with quotation marks ("). Because you want to import text data as text, and because you probably don't want the text qualifier character to be imported along with the text, this field is important to set.

To finish the TextWizard import of a delimited file, skip the following section.

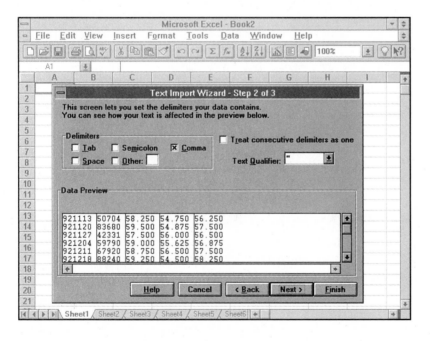

Figure 6.33
TextWizard:
Delimited step 2.

Importing a Fixed-Width File

If you select Fixed Width in step 1 of the TextWizard, you see a different step 2 screen (see fig. 6.34) than if you choose Delimited.

Figure 6.34
TextWizard: Fixed
Width step 2.

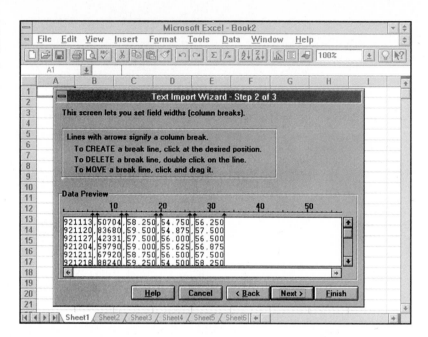

In step 2 of a fixed-width file import, you see a preview of the data with a ruler above it, as shown in figure 6.34. For fixed-width files, Excel does not have the capability to recognize where each field is separated; you need to indicate where each field starts and ends by clicking at the ruler position for each field. Each time you click in the Preview window, a new vertical line is created that shows where Excel will break the field. You can move these lines by clicking and dragging them to a new position, and you can delete these lines by double-clicking on them. After you place all the field markers, click on the Next button to proceed to step 3.

Using the TextWizard: Step 3

In the final step of using the TextWizard (see fig. 6.35), you tell Excel what type of data each field should contain.

Each field has a button above it that has the type of data listed inside the button. By default, all fields are marked as General data type, which causes them to be created in Excel with the General cell format. To change the field format, click on the button for the field you want to change and then select the appropriate option button in the Column Data Format box. The Column Data Format box enables you to choose from the options listed in table 6.5.

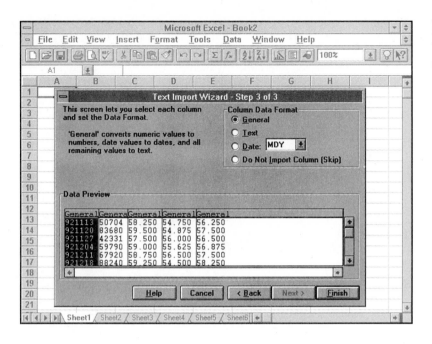

Figure 6.35
TextWizard:
step 3.

Table 6.5
Field Format Options

Option	Description
General	This option uses the Excel General cell format when the data is imported.
Text	This option forces the field to be treated as text, even if it contains only numbers. It can be important to force some numeric fields to be treated as text, particularly if you want to retain any leading zeros.
Date	Select this option if the field contains dates. Further, choose the format the dates are in by using the drop-down list to the right of the Date option button.
Do Not Import	Select this option to avoid loading the selected field. Column (Skip)

After you finish designating the fields in step 3, click on the Finish button to complete the operation and import the data into Excel, as shown in figure 6.36.

Figure 6.36
Completed
TextWizard
import.

	A	B	C	D	E	F	G	H	I
1	921113	50704	58.25	54.75	56.25				
2	921120	83680	59.5	54.875	57.5				
3	921127	42331	57.5	56	56.5				
4	921204	59790	59	55.625	56.875				
5	921211	67920	58.75	56.5	57.5				
6	921218	88240	59.25	54.5	58.25				
7	921225	61990	61.25	58	59				
8	930101	33888	60.75	58.75	59.75				
9	930108	106250	63	57.25	62.25				
10	930115	186610	65.25	60	60.25				
11	930122	97970	60.5	58	59.5				
12	930129	103980	62	58.75	59.5				
13	930205	112760	61.5	56.25	57.25				
14	930212	109970	57.5	53.75	53.875				
15	930219	99580	55.5	51.5	55				
16	930226	93010	56	52.125	53				
17	930305	68730	55.75	52.75	55				
18	930312	65682	57.5	55	56.25				
19	930319	60139	57.75	53.5	53.75				
20	930326	65444	54.75	52.5	53.25				
21	930402	99180	52.75	49.5	50.125				

Microsoft Excel - AA.TXT

File Edit View Insert Format Tools Data Window Help

A1 : 921113

Sheet1

Chapter Snapshot

This chapter covers the functions included in Excel.
Knowing how to use these functions can help you create
worksheets that solve what-if questions, assist with special
analysis, and much more. Functions constitute the backbone
of Excel's power. Chapter 7 shows you how to utilize
Excel's power by including the following:

✔ Understanding what a function is

✔ Understanding the parts of a function

✔ Understanding how to create a function

✔ Using Function Wizard

✔ Using functions to select prize winners

✔ Using functions to answer refinancing questions

✔ Troubleshooting functions

7

CHAPTER

Mastering Functions

In this chapter you will see how easy it is to use and master functions in Excel. Even if you feel that functions are complicated and you avoid them, you can learn about tools like Function Wizard and Help, which make using functions easy. Learn about functions and use Excel to its full potential and make your life loads easier.

Understanding Functions

How often do you have to repeat a certain task or calculation when you wish you could just snap your fingers and be done with it automatically? With the aid of functions in Excel 5, you can come quite close to just that. You can make your life significantly simpler: just automate procedures by using some of the methods covered in this chapter.

A *function* is a precoded formula that can automatically calculate results, perform worksheet actions, or assist with decision-making based on information you provide. You can use functions that Microsoft built into Excel 5 for Windows, or you can write your own. This chapter discusses the functions provided with Excel, called *worksheet functions*.

User-defined functions, those that you write, can be used in your worksheet just like normal worksheet functions. These functions, called *macros,* are discussed in Chapter 15.

Functions most commonly are used to generate calculated results. You might, for example, want to find out your monthly payment if you refinance your house. Or, you might need to track revenues and expenses to calculate your profit margin. Maybe you are developing a marketing survey and want a statistical analysis. To answer these kinds of questions and more, Microsoft has included a wide variety of functions with Excel.

Function Groups and Forms

Excel categorizes functions into the following groups:

- ✔ **Financial.** Calculates interest, depreciation, return on investment, and other types of financial information.

- ✔ **Date & Time.** Calculates the number of days between two dates based on a 360-day year, translate dates to serial numbers, and so on.

- ✔ **Math & Trigonometry.** Useful with basic engineering and math problems, such as calculating the cosine or tangent of a number.

- ✔ **Statistical.** Helps with statistical problems, like calculating the binomial distribution probability.

- ✔ **Lookup & Reference.** Provides information about your worksheet, such as returning the column number of a reference or the number of areas in a reference.

- ✔ **Database.** Helps with database information, like selecting the minimum or maximum value from database entries.

- ✔ **Text.** Helps you manipulate text data.

✔ **Logical.** Calculates results based on certain conditions in your worksheet.

✔ **Information.** Returns general information about your worksheet, such as formatting, or the contents of a cell.

✔ **Engineering.** Useful for engineering analysis.

No matter which type of function you use, you always express the function in the same way. You can see an example of a function in figure 7.1. The worksheet in that figure is a template for Computers R Us sales. As data is entered for different quarters, column G automatically reflects the YTD totals and row 11 reflects Total Country totals because formulas have been previously defined. The formula appears in the formula bar when you select a cell in the worksheet that contains a function. The formula bar shows an equal sign followed by the function name, then a set of parentheses enclosing the information that is used to calculate the result.

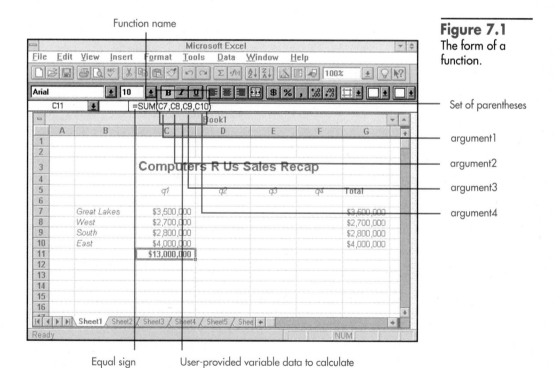

Figure 7.1
The form of a function.

Using Arguments

The information you provide to a function is called an *argument*. A function can include more than one argument, because different kinds of information might be needed to calculate the desired answer. Each function includes a predetermined set of arguments, always separated by commas. This format is defined by *syntax*, the rules or "model" you must follow to describe the information you want to use in the function. The syntax for each function is different. Thus, you must pay attention to the way Excel looks for information, or you might get some very strange results.

TIP Particular function syntax and arguments are documented in the Excel documentation. You also can use the Function Wizard or the On-Line Help, both discussed later in the chapter, to help you with your functions and argument lists.

In the example illustrated in figure 7.1, you need to calculate the total of first quarter sales for each territory in the United States. The function name, SUM, is followed by the information you want to sum enclosed in parentheses. Total first quarter sales for the first territory, Great Lakes, is located at cell C7; this is *argument1*. Total first quarter sales for West, South and East territories are located in cells C8, C9, and C10; these amounts represent *argument2*, *argument3* and *argument4*. Simply put, arguments in a function tell the function what information to use when the function is calculated.

You can describe function arguments in several ways. The preceding example uses *cell references*. You told the Excel function SUM which cells to reference to find the information to calculate the sum. A better way to describe what we want to sum, however, is to use a *cell range*, or a group of cells. In the next example (see fig. 7.2), you use a *cell range* to calculate the second quarter sales, because you anticipate a realignment of the West territory and think another territory might be added.

Figure 7.2
The SUM function using a range as an argument.

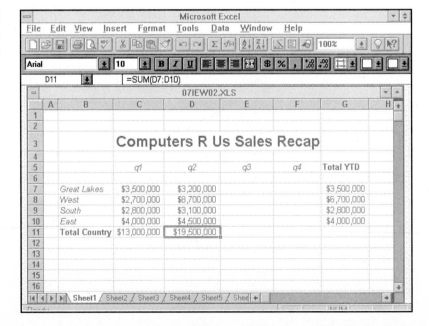

This example contains only one argument, the range D7:D10. This range includes cells D7 through D10 and all cells in between. One good reason to use a cell range and not individual cell references is because if you insert or delete rows or columns within a cell range, Excel automatically adjusts all references to reflect the new range. Excel does not adjust individual cell references to include a new row or column, because it doesn't know it is part of a range. You can also build this function by dragging across D7 through D10 after you insert the left parenthesis.

Look at Total first-quarter sales, now located at C12 (see fig. 7.3). Notice that after you insert a row to add a new Central territory, Excel changes the last two arguments in that SUM function to reflect the new location of South and East first-quarter sales, C10 and C11. It does not change the first two arguments, C7 and C8, because the location of first-quarter sales for Great Lakes and West territories did not change. If you add a number to show Central first-quarter sales, C9, it would not be included in the total at C12.

Now look at Total second-quarter sales in D12, as shown in figure 7.4. The argument for the SUM function, cell range D7:D10, changed to D7:D11 after we added the Central territory.

In this case, any second-quarter sales for Central territory shown in D9 would be included in the sum at D12. Figure 7.5 illustrates these last two points.

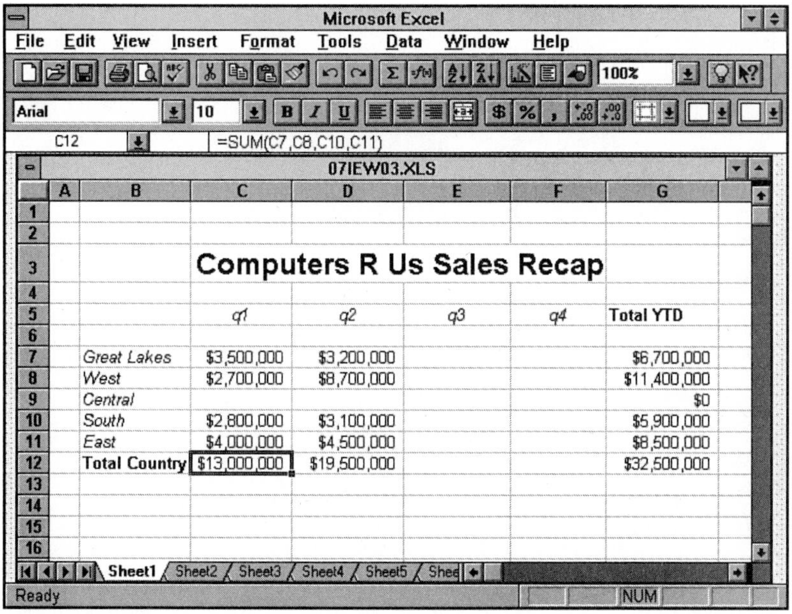

Figure 7.3

Individual cell references not adjusted to include added row.

Figure 7.4
Cell range automatically adjusts to include added row.

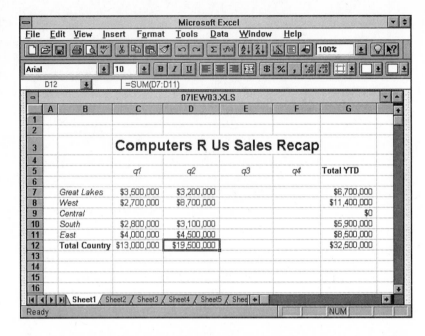

Figure 7.5
C12 value is incorrect, but D12 value is correct when Central territory sales are added.

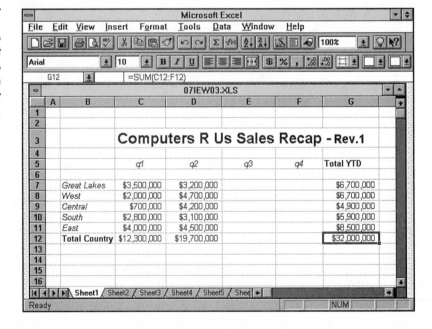

Keep in mind that, although the formula for grand total YTD in G12 is correct, the value calculated is incorrect. G12 sums the range C12 through F12, but total first quarter, C12, is in error. This common problem emphasizes why you should use care when constructing formulas: a simple error in one cell can throw off the accuracy of the entire spreadsheet.

TIP

Cell references and ranges are most commonly used as arguments in functions. You also can use formulas, constants, and other functions (nested up to seven times), however.

Function Wizard

5

Mastering function construction is one of the most difficult steps to becoming a proficient Excel user. Fortunately, Microsoft has made it easier in version 5. To assist you in choosing functions and determining the information Excel needs to calculate them, Excel 5 provides the *Function Wizard*, a step-by-step tool that helps you choose and build functions in your worksheet.

Activate the Function Wizard by choosing Insert, Function or by clicking the Function Wizard tool on the Standard toolbar (see fig. 7.6).

To understand the way the Function Wizard works, the next demonstration adds a logical function to the worksheet. In the following exercise, you need to know which territories met their sales quotas because those salespeople win a trip to Bora Bora.

Open file EX07.XLS located on the disk provided with *Inside Excel 5 for Windows*. Your excel worksheet should look like figure 7.7.

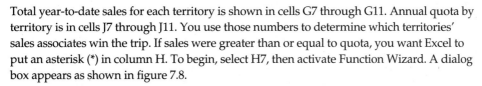

Total year-to-date sales for each territory is shown in cells G7 through G11. Annual quota by territory is in cells J7 through J11. You use those numbers to determine which territories' sales associates win the trip. If sales were greater than or equal to quota, you want Excel to put an asterisk (*) in column H. To begin, select H7, then activate Function Wizard. A dialog box appears as shown in figure 7.8.

The first dialog box of Function Wizard shows the function categories on the left and specific function names on the right. As you select different categories, the function list changes. Below the list boxes, Excel provides a description of the currently highlighted function and its syntax.

Figure 7.6
The Function
Wizard Tool.

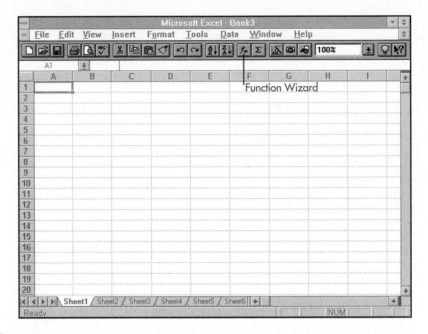

Figure 7.7
The EX07.XLS
spreadsheet.

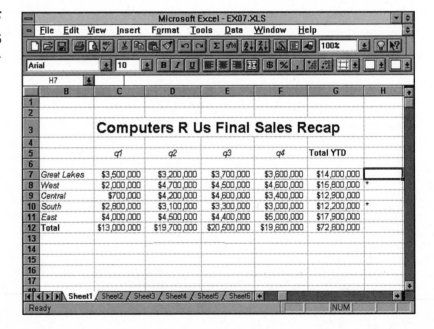

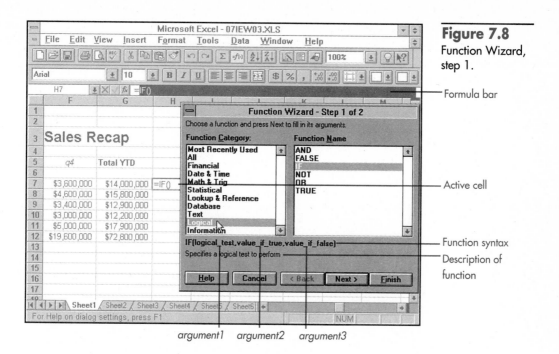

Figure 7.8
Function Wizard, step 1.

For this example, click on the category Logical. Then select the IF function by clicking on the function name or by pressing the Tab key and then the arrow keys. Function Wizard tells you that *argument1* for this function is *logical_test*, *argument2* is *value_if_true*, and *argument3* is *value_if_false*. Also notice that the formula bar is highlighted, and Function Wizard automatically constructs the IF function in the active cell, H7.

TIP

This information might be enough for you to complete your function. If you need more guidance, click on **H**elp or press F1, then select **S**earch and enter or select the function name. Select Show Topics and Go To. To exit Help, select E**x**it from the **F**ile menu (see fig. 7.9).

Now click on the Next button in Function Wizard dialog box. You see the second step dialog box as shown in figure 7.10.

The Function Wizard gives you three edit boxes in which you can provide the three arguments for the IF function. Notice the first argument, *logical_test*, is bold, which means it is required. You must enter a value or expression that can be evaluated to TRUE or FALSE. In the example, you want to know if Total YTD Sales for the Great Lakes Territory, cell G7, is greater than or equal to Great Lakes' Annual Quota, cell J7.

Enter the expression **G7>=J7** into the *logical_test* box. Because this expression can be evaluated to true or false, it is a legitimate logical test. In this case, the expression evaluates to TRUE. Notice that the expression also appears in the formula bar, because Function Wizard builds the function as you proceed.

When an argument is in bold type, it is required. If it is in regular type, it is optional. If you omit the optional arguments, Excel applies an assumed value. This assumption is documented in the Help file and also in the Excel documentation.

Figure 7.9
Help for the IF
function.

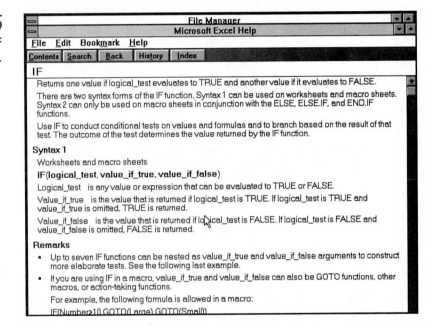

To enter *argument2, value_if_true*, click on the second box or press Tab. You want H7 to show an asterisk if sales met the quota, so enter * in the second edit box (see fig. 7.11). Because *value_if_true* is optional, you can omit this argument, and Excel assumes the value TRUE, as you learned from reading the Help screen in figure 7.9.

To enter the third argument, *value_if_false*, click on the third edit box or press Tab. If sales did not meet quota, you want H7 to be blank, so you press the space bar (see fig. 7.12). (This argument also is optional, so you can omit this argument and Excel assumes the value FALSE.)

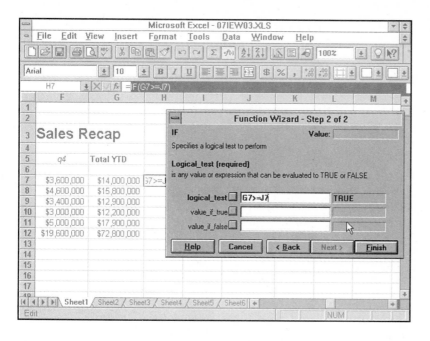

Figure 7.10
Function Wizard,
step 2.

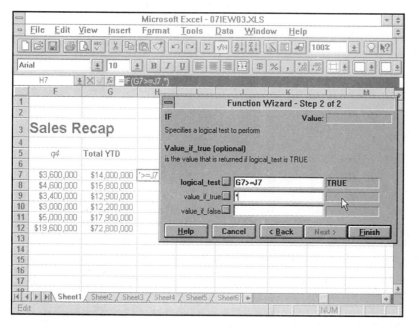

Figure 7.11
Enter argument2.

Figure 7.12
Enter argument3.

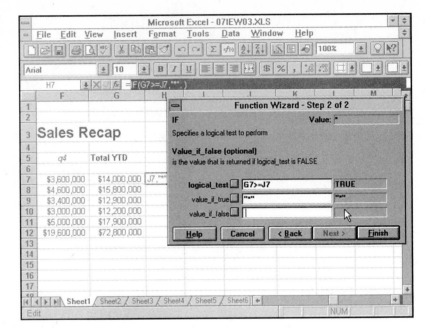

You now are finished building your function. Click on the Finish button or press F. Pressing F puts the function in the edit box. Figure 7.13 shows the completed IF function in the formula bar and the * at H7 to show that Great Lakes sales met quota. The Formula Wizard puts quotation marks around the asterisk in *argument2* and the space in *argument3*. Formula Wizard understands you want these entries to be treated as text values (all text values must be enclosed in quotation marks).

Select H7 through H11 and choose Down under the Fill option from the Edit menu. Now cells H8 through H11 contain similar IF functions to show what other territories win the trip. Your analysis shows that West and South sales people also will be going to Bora Bora.

Nesting Functions

Excel enables you to include functions inside other functions. This process is called *nesting* functions. You can use functions and nested functions as arguments. Suppose, for example, the vice president of sales gets to accompany her sales team to Bora Bora if Total National YTD sales is greater than or equal to the sum of all quotas. One way to construct the IF function might be as follows:

```
=IF(SUM(G7:G11)>=SUM(J7:J11),"*****"," ")
```

The SUM function is nested within the IF function.

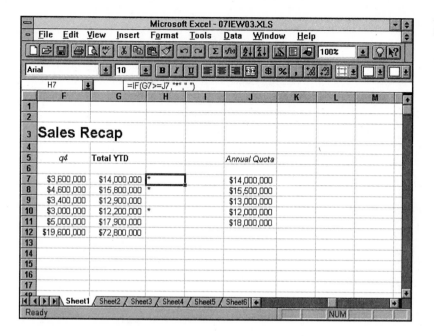

Figure 7.13
Completed IF function.

Worksheets

Entering Functions

Now take a look at a worksheet that is designed to calculate mortgage payments based on mortgage amount, points, interest and term. Open file EX7A.XLS from the disk provided with *Inside Excel 5 for Windows*. It should look like figure 7.14.

For this analysis, you want to finance the fees and points along with the mortgage. To calculate the total amount financed, you again use the SUM function. Select cell C10 and enter **=sum(c6:c8)** so that your worksheet looks like the one illustrated in figure 7.15.

Notice the function appears in C10 as well as in the formula bar. When you press Enter, Excel calculates the equation, and the $82,900 appears in cell C10. Also notice SUM is in capital letters in the formula bar, telling you that Excel recognizes the function and can calculate the formula based on the argument you specified (the range C6:C8), as shown in figure 7.16.

Figure 7.14
Refinance Analysis
worksheet.

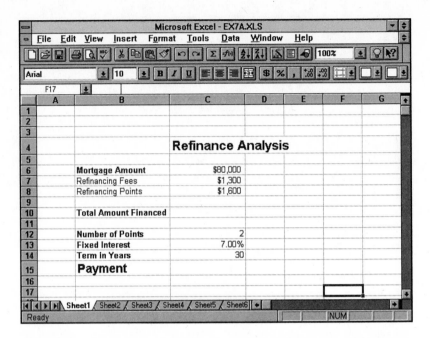

Figure 7.14
Refinance Analysis
worksheet.

Figure 7.15
SUM function
keyed from the
keyboard.

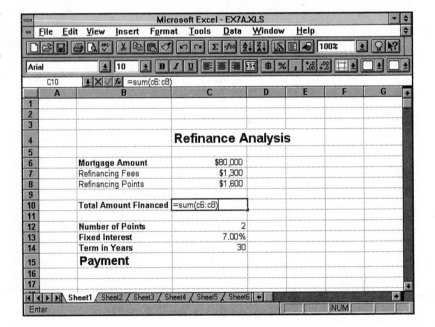

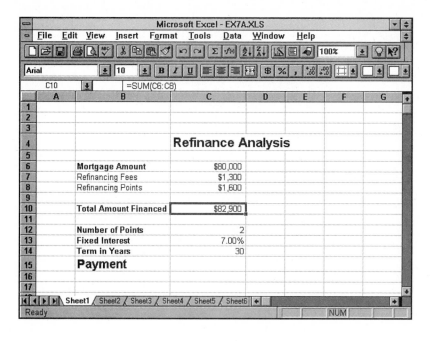

Figure 7.16
SUM function calculated.

The next step is to construct the payment function. You can enter it from the keyboard as you did in C10, use the Function Wizard step by step as you did in your sales recap worksheet, or use a combination of methods. For this function, use the Function Wizard to get the syntax of the PMT function, paste information from the worksheet for part of the arguments, then edit the formula bar to get the final result. Use the following steps:

1. Select cell C15.

2. Activate Formula Wizard.

3. Select the Financial Category and Function Name PMT. Your screen should look like figure 7.17.

Click on Finish or press Alt+F (see fig. 7.18). Bypass step 2 of the Function Wizard to get the syntax of the PMT function into the formula bar. If you were to continue with Function Wizard, you would enter argument information into the dialog box. Instead, you want to get information from the worksheet, then edit it (see fig. 7.18).

Notice *rate*, the first argument of the PMT function, is highlighted in the formula bar. Click on cell C13 to paste that cell reference into *argument1* (see fig. 7.19).

The next step is to edit the rest of the arguments: *nper*, *pv*, *fv*, and *type*. If you want help with this part of the function construction, activate the Help screen. Press F1 or choose Help, Search for Help on, then enter **PMT,** press Enter, and choose Go To. The PMT function help screen shows as in figure 7.20.

Figure 7.17
PMT function activated by Function Wizard.

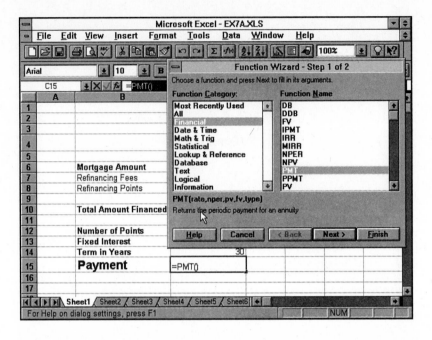

Figure 7.18
PMT function syntax put into the formula bar by Function Wizard.

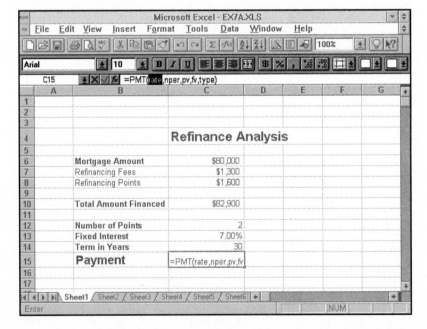

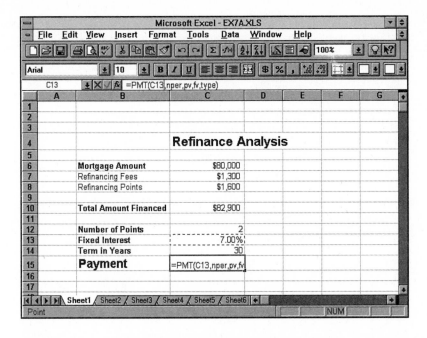

Figure 7.19
Cell reference for *rate* pasted into the PMT function.

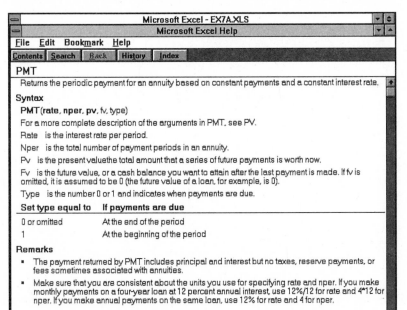

Figure 7.20
PMT function help screen.

Notice that *rate*, *nper* and *pv* are in bold because they are required arguments. The *fv* and *type* variables are optional arguments. As discussed in Help, *rate* is the interest rate per period; *nper* is the total number of payment periods in an annuity; *pv* represents the total payments' present value; *fv* is the future value, or cash balance after the last payment is made; and *type* indicates when payments are due.

> **NOTE** Note the second remark: You must be consistent about the units you use for specifying *rate* and *nper*. If you use monthly payments on a four-year loan at 12 percent annual interest, use 12%/12 for *rate* and 4*12 for *nper*.

To put this into simpler terms: you are making monthly payments, so your units must be in monthly terms. Our annual interest rate of 7% must be divided by 12 to get the monthly interest rate; the period for the loan (30 years) must be multiplied by 12 to determine the number of monthly payments throughout the life of the loan. *pv* is the total amount financed, because that is what the future payments are worth now. The value of *fv* is zero, because the mortgage balance will be zero after all payments are made. *type* tells when the payments are due, assumed to be the end of the period.

So, for the example, *rate* is C13/12. *nper* is C14*12, and *pv* is C10. You can omit *fv* and *type*, because they are assumed to be zero, as desired. To place these arguments into the PMT function, first complete *rate* to show C13/12.

Select E\ufff0xit from the File menu to exit the Help screen.

1. The I-beam is to the right of C13 in the formula bar. Enter **/12**. The first argument now is complete.

2. Select *argument2*, nper, by dragging the mouse across it, or by double-clicking on it.

3. Click on C14 to paste it into the argument list.

4. The I-beam is to the right of C14 in the formula bar. Enter ***12** to complete *argument2*.

5. Select *argument3*, pv, by dragging the mouse across it, or by double-clicking on it.

6. Click on C10 to paste it into the argument list. This step completes *argument3*.

7. Select ,fv,type in the formula bar by dragging the mouse across it. Press Del. This step removes the optional arguments.

8. Press Enter to calculate the monthly payment at C15. Your worksheet should look like the one in figure 7.21.

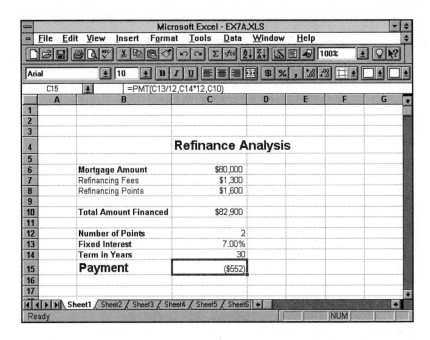

Figure 7.21
PMT function
complete.

Note that the payment appears as ($552). The parentheses mean it is a negative number—money paid out.

You can use the Function Wizard in the following ways:

✔ When you enter a function from the keyboard, press Ctrl+A to display Function Wizard Step 2, then use it to assist you when you enter arguments.

✔ When you select a cell that contains a function and then activate Function Wizard, Function Wizard Edit mode opens so that you can make changes to arguments.

✔ Use the same order of precedence for Excel functions as you do for other Excel formulas. Excel performs operations in the following order:

()	parentheses
:	range
Space	intersection
,	union
–	negation (single operand)
%	percent

^	exponentiation
*	multiplication
/	division
+	addition
–	subtraction
&	text joining
=	equals
<	less than
>	greater than
<=	less than or equal
>=	greater than or equal
<>	not equal

Troubleshooting Function and Syntax Messages

If a function name remains in lowercase after you complete the formula and press Enter, check for spelling errors in the function name.

TIP Get into the habit of using lowercase so that Excel can help you spot spelling errors.

When Excel displays an error message rather than a calculated result from the worksheet function, check these things:

✔ Check for typing errors.

✔ Make sure all your parentheses match.

✔ Make sure all the required arguments are defined and in the order that Excel expects to see them.

✔ Make sure all data types are valid for the argument.

✔ Make sure you leave out commas in numbers, or Excel will think you are separating arguments. (1,000 should be entered as **1000**, for example.)

✔ When you omit an optional argument, and you want to define another argument later in the list, make sure you place a comma (,) as a place holder for the omitted argument.

Excel also displays formula errors instead of function results when you make an error in a formula that serves as an argument. These errors include #DIV/0, #N/A, #NAME?, #NULL!, #NUM!, #REF!, and #VALUE!.

Chapter Snapshot

This chapter picks up where the last chapter left off, showing in more detail the functions available in Excel 5 for Windows. This reference details the following information about each function:

✔ The function's group or category, as defined by the Function Wizard

✔ The purpose of the function

✔ The correct syntax of the function

✔ The function's available arguments or variables

Keep this function reference in mind as you use functions in your daily Excel life.

8

CHAPTER

Complete Guide to Excel Functions

The last chapter discussed ways to use functions in your Excel spreadsheets. This chapter provides you with a complete guide to the functions available in Excel. The functions are divided into the groups you see in the Function Wizard for easy reference, as shown in the following list:

- ✔ Database
- ✔ Date and Time
- ✔ Engineering
- ✔ Financial
- ✔ Information
- ✔ Logical
- ✔ Look-Up and Reference
- ✔ Mathematical and Trigonometric
- ✔ Statistical
- ✔ Text

Within each category, functions are listed alphabetically. An explanation of what each function does is provided, as well as its correct syntax and options.

To see examples of each function in use, consult the Help file that accompanies Excel 5. From the Help Contents, click on Reference Information, and then click on Worksheet Functions. You can use the Worksheet Function help screen to access examples of the functions alphabetically by function name or alphabetically by category.

In addition, you can open the worksheet SAMPLES.XLS, which you can find in the \EXCEL\EXAMPLES directory. This worksheet contains examples of almost all the Excel worksheet functions correctly formatted and operating. Several of the other example spreadsheets in this directory also help to illustrate using worksheet function.

Database Functions

Database and list management functions in Excel enable you to extract information from a database or list and to perform operations on information you have extracted. With these functions, you can access databases you have defined within Excel and databases you maintain with database software external to Excel. If you are working with an external database, you should bring your data in with SQLREQUEST and then manipulate the data using functions that work on databases internal to Excel. All database function examples refer to figure 8.1, which shows a sample database defined by the range A1:E10.

Figure 8.1
A sample Excel spreadsheet used with database functions.

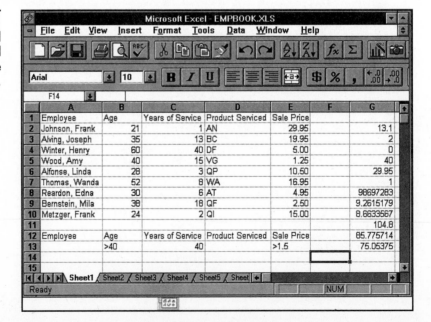

	A	B	C	D	E	F	G
1	Employee	Age	Years of Service	Product Serviced	Sale Price		
2	Johnson, Frank	21	1	AN	29.95		13.1
3	Alving, Joseph	35	13	BC	19.95		2
4	Winter, Henry	60	40	DF	5.00		0
5	Wood, Amy	40	15	VG	1.25		40
6	Alfonse, Linda	28	3	QP	10.50		29.95
7	Thomas, Wanda	52	8	WA	16.95		1
8	Reardon, Edna	30	6	AT	4.95		98697283
9	Bernstein, Mila	38	18	QF	2.50		9.2615179
10	Metzger, Frank	24	2	QI	15.00		8.8633567
11							104.8
12	Employee	Age	Years of Service	Product Serviced	Sale Price		85.775714
13		>40	40		>1.5		75.05375
14							
15							

NOTE When you enter a function into a spreadsheet cell, remember to include an equal sign (=) before the function name.

DAVERAGE

Purpose: Arithmetically averages the database entries you have selected.

Syntax: DAVERAGE*(database, field, criteria)*

Arguments: *Database* is the range of cells that define the database. *Field* is the named field or range of cells representing the column to average. *Criteria* is the named field or range of cells containing any criteria that define which values of field to include in the average.

DCOUNT

Purpose: Counts the number of cells matching the criteria defined in the last argument that contain numbers.

Syntax: DCOUNT*(database, field, criteria)*

Arguments: *Database* is the range of cells that define the database. *Field* is the named field or range of cells representing the column in which to count. (The field argument is optional. If it is absent, the count applies to the entire database.) *Criteria* is the named field or range of cells containing any criteria that define which fields containing numbers to include in the count.

DCOUNTA

Purpose: Counts the number of cells matching the criteria defined in the last argument that are not blank.

Syntax: DCOUNTA*(database, field, criteria)*

Arguments: *Database* is the range of cells that define the database. *Field* is the named field or range of cells representing the column in which to count. *Criteria* is the named field or range of cells containing any criteria that define which nonblank fields to include in the count.

DGET

Purpose: Gets a single value from a database that matches the criteria identified in the third argument.

Syntax: DGET*(database, field, criteria)*

Arguments: *Database* is the range of cells that define the database. *Field* is the named field or range of cells representing the column from which to extract the value. *Criteria* is the named field or range of cells containing any criteria that define which record to extract. This function returns the #VALUE! error value if no match is found. It returns the #NUM! error value if more than one match is found.

DMAX

Purpose: Gets the largest number in a column of data records.

Syntax: DMAX*(database, field, criteria)*

Arguments: *Database* is the range of cells that define the database. *Field* is the named field or range of cells representing the column in which to find the maximum value. *Criteria* is the named field or range of cells containing any criteria that define any constraints on the search for a maximum value (such as within all the employees whose name begins with "J" represented in the "Years with Company" column).

DMIN

Purpose: Gets the smallest number in a column of data records.

Syntax: DMIN*(database, field, criteria)*

Arguments: *Database* is the range of cells that define the database. *Field* is the named field or range of cells representing the column in which to find the minimum value. *Criteria* is the named field or range of cells containing any criteria that define any constraints on the search for a minimum value (such as within all the employees whose name begins with "J" represented in the "Years with Company" column).

DPRODUCT

Purpose: Multiplies (takes the product of) the numbers in the column identified by the field parameter that match the stated criteria.

Syntax: DPRODUCT*(database, field, criteria)*

Arguments: *Database* is the range of cells that define the database. *Field* is the named field or range of cells representing the column in which to multiply. *Criteria* is the named field or range of cells containing any criteria that define which fields to include in the product.

DSTDEV

Purpose: Calculates the standard deviation for a sample of cells in the column named in the field parameter. The criteria parameter defines the way in which the sample is selected.

Syntax: DSTDEV*(database, field, criteria)*

Arguments: *Database* is the range of cells that define the database. *Field* is the named field or range of cells representing the column for which to calculate the standard deviation.

Criteria is the named field or range of cells containing any criteria that define which fields to include in the calculation.

DSTDEVP

Purpose: Calculates the standard deviation for a sample of cells in the column named in the field parameter as if the cells defined were the entire population. The criteria parameter defines the way in which the sample is selected.

Syntax: DSTDEVP*(database, field, criteria)*

Arguments: *Database* is the range of cells that define the database. *Field* is the named field or range of cells representing the column for which to calculate the standard deviation. *Criteria* is the named field or range of cells containing any criteria that define which fields to include in the calculation.

DSUM

Purpose: Sums the numbers in the column named by the field parameter that meet the criteria defined in the criteria parameter.

Syntax: DSUM*(database, field, criteria)*

Arguments: *Database* is the range of cells that define the database. *Field* is the named field or range of cells representing the column of numbers to sum. *Criteria* is the named field or range of cells containing any criteria that define which fields to include in the calculation.

DVAR

Purpose: Estimates the variance for a sample of cells in the column named in the field parameter. The criteria parameter defines the way in which the sample is selected.

Syntax: DVAR*(database, field, criteria)*

Arguments: *Database* is the range of cells that define the database. *Field* is the named field or range of cells representing the column for which to calculate the variance. *Criteria* is the named field or range of cells containing any criteria that define which fields to include in the calculation.

DVARP

Purpose: Calculates the variance for a sample of cells in the column named in the field parameter as if the cells defined were the entire population. The criteria parameter defines the way in which the sample is selected.

Syntax: DVARP*(database, field, criteria)*

Arguments: *Database* is the range of cells that define the database. *Field* is the named field or range of cells representing the column for which to calculate the variance. *Criteria* is the named field or range of cells containing any criteria that define which fields to include in the calculation.

SQLREQUEST

Purpose: Uses the Excel add-in XLODBC.XLA to connect to an external database and collect information. The information enters Excel as an array.

Syntax: SQLREQUEST*(connection_string, output_ref, driver_prompt, query_text, column_names_logical)*

Arguments: *Connection_string* supplies information required by the external database in its own format. Sample formats for three databases appear in table 8.1.

Table 8.1
Sample Connection Strings for Three Databases

Database	Connection_string
dBASE	DSN=STind;PWD=woof
SQL Server	DSN=Server;UID=fhoulet; PWE=123;Database=Pubs
ORACLE	DNS=My Oracle Data Source;DBQ=MYSER VER; UID=ForrH;PWD=Quack

Output_ref is the cell in your Excel spreadsheet in which you want the completed connection string placed. *Driver_prompt* is a number that defines the way in which the dialog box for the external database driver is displayed. Its values are shown in table 8.2.

Table 8.2
Driver_prompt Values

Driver_prompt	Description
1	Dialog box always displayed.
2	Dialog box displayed only if there is not enough information in the function parameters to complete the connection to the external database and all options are available.
3	Dialog box displayed only if there is not enough information in the function parameters to complete the connection to the external database and only necessary options are available.
4	Dialog box is not displayed. If no connection is made, the function returns an error.

Query_text is the text of the actual query statement you are sending to the external database. *Column_names_logical* takes a value of TRUE if you want column names returned as the first row of results and FALSE if you do not. This function returns an array of data if it is successful, and the #N/A error if it is not.

> To install add-in functions and toolpacks, run Excel Setup and select the **A**dd/ Remove option. Select the Add-ins option in the **O**ptions list box, and click on Chan**g**e Option. You then can select the add-ins to install from the **O**ptions list box that appears in the Add-ins dialog box and click on OK.

Date and Time Functions

Date and time functions enable you to look up dates and times and to perform mathematical calculations on dates and times with ease. Excel for Windows uses a serial number system to work with dates. Although this system might seem strange at first, it provides efficient calculation of dates and times.

Each date between January 1, 1900, and December 31, 2078, is assigned a serial number between 0 and 63,918. Times also are assigned serial numbers as well, so you can represent a date and time string with a decimal number. The number to the left of the decimal is the date serial number, while the number to the right is the time serial number. The number 367.5, for instance, represents 12:00 noon on January 1, 1901.

Many of the date and time functions work with serial numbers. Their use is demonstrated by the spreadsheet shown in figure 8.2.

DATE

Purpose: Returns a date's serial number.

Syntax: DATE*(year, month, day)*

Arguments: Each argument is a number representing the year, month, and day for which a serial number is desired. If the *day* value is larger than the number of days in the month indicated, the *month* value is incremented and the extra days are added to the *day* value for the incremented month. DATE(91,1,35) gives the same serial number as DATE(91,2,4), for example.

Figure 8.2
A spreadsheet showing the use of date and time functions.

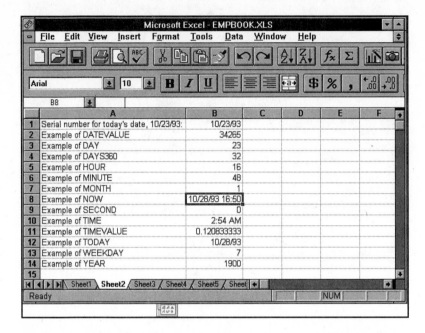

	A	B	C	D	E	F
1	Serial number for today's date, 10/23/93:	10/23/93				
2	Example of DATEVALUE	34265				
3	Example of DAY	23				
4	Example of DAYS360	32				
5	Example of HOUR	16				
6	Example of MINUTE	48				
7	Example of MONTH	1				
8	Example of NOW	10/28/93 16:50				
9	Example of SECOND	0				
10	Example of TIME	2:54 AM				
11	Example of TIMEVALUE	0.120833333				
12	Example of TODAY	10/28/93				
13	Example of WEEKDAY	7				
14	Example of YEAR	1900				
15						

DATEVALUE

Purpose: Returns a serial number for a date written as text, as long as the date falls between January 1, 1900, and December 31, 2078.

Syntax: DATEVALUE*(date_text)*

Arguments: The only argument is a date written as text. If the year is not present, Excel assumes the date refers to the year set on the system clock.

DAY

Purpose: Converts a serial number to a day of the month.

Syntax: DAY*(serial_number)*

Arguments: *Serial_number* is a number you want to convert to a date.

DAYS360

Purpose: Calculates the number of days between two dates based on a 360-day year (twelve thirty-day months). This function is used when an accounting system is based on twelve thirty-day months.

Syntax: DAYS360*(start_date, end_date, method)*

Arguments: *Start_date* and *end_date* can be text strings or serial numbers. *Method* takes a value of 1 if you are using the US (NASD) method. *Method* is 2 if you are using the European method of calculating a 360-day year. If you omit *method*, Excel assumes the US convention.

EDATE

Purpose: Gives the serial number for a date the indicated number of months afterward or before.

Syntax: EDATE*(start_date, number_of_months)*

Arguments: *Start_date* is serial number for the date in question. *Number_of_months* is the number of months after *start_date*. You can use a negative number to calculate the number of months before a date.

EOMONTH

Purpose: Gives the serial number for a date at the end of the month the indicated number of months afterward or before.

Syntax: EOMONTH*(start_date, number_of_months)*

Arguments: *Start_date* is serial number for the date in question. *Number_of_months* is the number of months after *start_date*. You can use a negative number to calculate the number of months before a date.

HOUR

Purpose: Converts a serial number for a date into an hour.

Syntax: HOUR*(serial_number)*

Arguments: *Serial_number* is a serial number that represents a date-time code. You also can include the time string as text.

MINUTE

Purpose: Converts a serial number for a date into a minute.

Syntax: MINUTE*(serial_number)*

Arguments: *Serial_number* is a serial number that represents a date-time code. You also can include the time string as text.

MONTH

Purpose: Converts a serial number for a date into a month.

Syntax: MONTH*(serial_number)*

Arguments: *Serial_number* is a serial number that represents a date-time code. You also can include the time string as text.

NETWORKDAYS

Purpose: Calculates the number of working days, excluding weekends and identified holidays, between two dates.

Syntax: NETWORKDAYS*(start_date, end_date, holidays)*

Arguments: *Start_date* and *end_date* are serial numbers representing the dates in question. *Holidays* is an optional list of serial numbers to exclude from the count as holidays.

NOW

Purpose: Gives the serial number for the current date and time.

Syntax: NOW*( )*

Arguments: None.

SECOND

Purpose: Converts a serial number for a time into a second.

Syntax: SECOND*(serial_number)*

Arguments: *Serial_number* is a serial number that represents a date-time code. You also can include the time string as text.

TIME

Purpose: Gives the serial number for the time indicated. A time serial number is reported as a decimal fraction (for example, .9999999).

Syntax: TIME*(hour, minute, second)*

Arguments: *Hour* is a number (0-23) indicating the hour, *minute* a number (0-59) indicating the minute, and *second* a number (0-59) indicating the second.

TIMEVALUE

Purpose: Gives the serial number (0-0.99999999) for a time represented as text.

Syntax: TIMEVALUE*(time_text)*

Arguments: *Time_text* is a text string that represents the time in question.

TODAY

Purpose: Gives the serial number for the current date.

Syntax: TODAY*()*

Arguments: None.

WEEKDAY

Purpose: Converts a serial number to a day of the week.

Syntax: WEEKDAY*(serial_number, return_type)*

Arguments: *Serial_number* is the serial number to be converted or a text representing the date. *Return_type* takes values from table 8.3.

Table 8.3
Return Types for WEEKDAY

Return_type	Range for Number Returned
1 (or omitted)	1 (Sunday) - 7 (Saturday)
2	1 (Monday) - 7 (Sunday)
3	0 (Monday) - 6 (Sunday)

YEAR

Purpose: Gives the year (1900-2078) associated with a serial number.

Syntax: YEAR*(serial_number)*

Arguments: *Serial_number* is the serial number to be converted. You also can use a text string to represent this date.

YEARFRAC

Purpose: Gives the fraction of the year represented by the number of whole days between two dates.

Syntax: YEARFRAC*(start_date, end_date, basis)*

Arguments: *Start_date* and *end_date* are the serial numbers representing the two dates. *Basis* is a value from table 8.4.

Table 8.4
Values of Basis for YEARFRAC

Basis	Description
0 (or omitted)	30/360 (US/NASD)
1	Actual/Actual
2	Actual/360
3	Actual/365
4	30/360 (European)

Engineering Functions

Excel's engineering functions enable engineers to include specialized calculations and conversions in their worksheets. To use these functions, however, you must have installed the Analysis Add-in toolpak.

BESSELI, BESSELJ, BESSELK, BESSELY

Purpose: These four functions return the values of different forms of the Bessel function. BESSELI returns the modified Bessel function $In(x)$, BESSELJ the Bessel function $Jn(x)$, BESSELK the modified Bessel function $Kn(x)$, and BESSELY the Bessel function $Yn(x)$.

Syntax: BESSELI*(x,n)*, BESSELJ*(x,n)*, BESSELK*(x,n)*, or BESSELY*(x,n)*

Arguments: *X* represents the value at which the function evaluates. *N* is the function's order.

BIN2DEC, BIN2HEX, BIN2OCT

Purpose: These three functions convert binary numbers to other bases. BIN2DEC converts from binary to decimal, BIN2HEX from binary to hexadecimal, and BIN2OCT from binary to octal.

Syntax: BIN2DEC*(number)*, BIN2HEX*(number, places)*, or BIN2OCT*(number, places)*

Arguments: *Number* is the binary number for conversion. *Places* is the number of characters to use in the conversion. (If omitted, Excel uses the minimum number of characters necessary. If you specify extra characters, Excel pads with leading zeros.)

COMPLEX

Purpose: Combines real and imaginary coefficients and converts them to a complex number.

Syntax: COMPLEX(*real_num, i_num, suffix*)

Arguments: *Real_num* is the real coefficient, *i_num* is the imaginary coefficient, and *suffix* is the suffix to be used to identify the imaginary component of the converted complex number. (If *suffix* is omitted as an argument, the suffix "i" is used.)

CONVERT

Purpose: Converts numbers among several units of measurement.

Syntax: CONVERT(*number, from_unit, to_unit*)

Arguments: *Number* is the number to be converted from one unit to another. It is a value expressed in *from_units*. *From_unit* is a text string denoting the measurement system to convert from. *To_unit* is a text string denoting the measurement system to which you want to convert. Table 8.5 shows the text strings you can use in CONVERT.

Table 8.5
Text Strings for Use as From_unit or To_unit

Unit	Text String
Angstrom	"ang"
Atmosphere	"atm"
BTU	"BTU"
Cup	"cup"
Day	"day"
Degree Celsius	"C"
Degree Fahrenheit	"F"
Degree Kelvin	"K"
Dyne	"dyn"
Electron volt	"eV"
Erg	"e"
Fluid ounce	"oz"

continues

Table 8.5, Continued
Text Strings for Use as From_unit or To_unit

Unit	Text String
Foot	"ft"
Foot-pound	"flb"
Gallon	"gal"
Gauss	"ga"
Gram	"g"
Horsepower	"HP"
Horsepower-hour	"HPh"
Hour	"hr"
Inch	"in"
IT calorie	"cal"
Joule	"J"
Liter	"l"
Meter	"m"
Minute	"mn"
mm of Mercury	"mmHg"
Nautical mile	"Nmi"
Newton	"N"
Ounce mass (avoirdupois)	"ozm"
Pascal	"Pa"
Pica (1/72 in.)	"Pica"
Pint	"pt"
Pound force	"lbf"
Pound mass (avoirdupois)	"lbm"
Quart	"qt"
Second	"sec"

Unit	Text String
Slug	"sg"
Statute mile	"mi"
Tablespoon	"tbs"
Teaspoon	"tsp"
Tesla	"T"
Thermodynamic calorie	"c"
U (atomic mass unit)	"u"
Watt	"W"
Watt-hour	"Wh"
Yard	"yd"
Year	"yr"

Table 8.6 shows the set of prefixes that can be added to the text strings for metric measurements.

Table 8.6
Prefixes for Use with Metric Measurements

Common Metric Prefix	Multiplier for Measurement Unit	Text String Prefix to Add in CONVERT
atto	1E-18	"a"
centi	1E-02	"c"
deci	1E-01	"d"
dekao	1E+01	"e"
exa	1E+18	"E"
femto	1E-15	"f"
giga	1E+09	"G"
hecto	1E+02	"h"

continues

Table 8.6, Continued
Prefixes for Use with Metric Measurements

Common Metric Prefix	Multiplier for Measurement Unit	Text String Prefix to Add in CONVERT
kilo	1E+03	"k"
mega	1E+06	"M"
micro	1E-06	"u"
milli	1E-03	"m"
nano	1E-09	"n"
peta	1E+15	"P"
pico	1E-12	"p"
tera	1E+12	"T"

If a conversion is not possible for some reason, the function returns the #N/A error value.

DEC2BIN, DEC2HEX, DEC2OCT

Purpose: These three functions convert decimal numbers to other bases. DEC2BIN converts from decimal to binary, DEC2HEX from decimal to hexadecimal, and DEC2OCT from decimal to octal.

Syntax: DEC2BIN*(number, places)*, DEC2HEX*(number, places)*, or DEC2OCT*(number, places)*

Arguments: *Number* is the decimal number for conversion. *Places* is the number of characters to use in the conversion. (If omitted, Excel uses the minimum number of characters necessary. If you specify extra characters, Excel pads with leading zeros.)

DELTA

Purpose: Verifies that two numbers are equal, returning a value of 1 if so and 0 if not.

Syntax: DELTA*(number1, number2)*

Arguments: *Number1* and *number2* are the two numbers whose equality are verified.

ERF

Purpose: Integrates the error function between the specified lower and upper limits.

Syntax: ERF*(lower_limit, upper_limit)*

Arguments: The two arguments are the lower and upper limits for integration. If *upper_limit* is omitted, the function integrates between *lower_limit* and 0.

ERFC

Purpose: Evaluates the complementary ERF function between the value specified and 0.

Syntax: ERFC*(x)*

Arguments: *X* is the lower bound for the ERF function involved in the calculation.

GESTEP

Purpose: Determines whether a number is greater than the specified threshold value. This function returns the value 1 if number>=step, and 0 otherwise.

Syntax: GESTEP*(number, step)*

Arguments: *Number* is the number to be tested. *Step* is the threshold value. If *step* is omitted, the threshold of 0 is used.

HEX2BIN, HEX2DEC, HEX2OCT

Purpose: These three functions convert hexadecimal numbers to other bases. HEX2BIN converts from hexadecimal to binary, HEX2DEC from hexadecimal to decimal, and HEX2OCT from hexadecimal to octal.

Syntax: HEX2BIN*(number, places)*, HEX2DEC*(number)*, or HEX2OCT*(number, places)*

Arguments: *Number* is the hexadecimal number for conversion. *Places* is the number of characters to use in the conversion. (If omitted, Excel uses the minimum number of characters necessary. If you specify extra characters, Excel pads with leading zeros.)

IMABS

Purpose: Gives the absolute value in modulus form of a complex number.

Syntax: IMABS*(inumber)*

Arguments: *Inumber* is that complex number in x+yi or x+yj format for which you want the absolute value.

IMAGINARY

Purpose: Gives the imaginary coefficient of a complex number.

Syntax: IMAGINARY*(inumber)*

Arguments: *Inumber* is a complex number in x+yi or x+ji form for which you want the imaginary coefficient.

IMARGUMENT

Purpose: Calculates the argument of a complex number, and returns it as an angle measured in radians.

Syntax: IMARGUMENT*(inumber)*

Arguments: *Inumber* is the complex number whose argument you want.

IMCONJUGATE

Purpose: Calculates and returns the complex conjugate of a complex number.

Syntax: IMCONJUGATE*(inumber)*

Arguments: *Inumber* is the complex number in x+yi or x+yj form for which you want the conjugate.

IMCOS

Purpose: Calculates and returns the cosine of a complex number.

Syntax: IMCOS*(inumber)*

Arguments: *Inumber* is the complex number in x+yi or x+yj form for which you want the cosine. *Inumber* is in text format.

IMDIV

Purpose: Divides two complex numbers in text format and returns the quotient.

Syntax: IMDIV*(number1, number2)*

Arguments: *Number1* and *number2* are complex numbers in x+yi or x+yj form. *Number1* is the numerator or dividend. *Number2* is the denominator or divisor.

IMEXP

Purpose: Calculates and returns the exponential for a complex number.

Syntax: IMEXP*(inumber)*

Arguments: *Inumber* is the complex number in x+yi or x+yj form for which you want the exponential.

IMLN

Purpose: Calculates and returns the natural logarithm for a complex number.

Syntax: IMLN*(inumber)*

Arguments: *Inumber* is the complex number in x+yi or x+yj form for which you want the natural logarithm.

IMLOG10

Purpose: Calculates and returns the common logarithm (base 10) for a complex number.

Syntax: IMLOG10*(inumber)*

Arguments: *Inumber* is the complex number in x+yi or x+yj form for which you want the common logarithm.

IMLOG2

Purpose: Calculates and returns the base-2 logarithm for a complex number.

Syntax: IMLOG2*(inumber)*

Arguments: *Inumber* is the complex number in x+yi or x+yj form for which you want the base-2 logarithm.

IMPOWER

Purpose: Calculates a complex number raised to an integer power.

Syntax: IMPOWER*(inumber, power)*

Arguments: *Inumber* is the complex number in x+yi or x+yj form that you want to raise to an integer power. *Power* is the integer.

IMPRODUCT

Purpose: Calculates the product of from 2 to 29 complex numbers.

Syntax: IMPRODUCT*(inumber1, inumber2, ..., inumber29)*

Arguments: *Inumber1* and so on are the complex numbers in x+yi or x+yj form that you want to multiply together.

IMREAL

Purpose: Returns the real coefficient for the complex number specified.

Syntax: IMREAL*(inumber)*

Arguments: *Inumber* is the complex number in x+yi or x+yj form for which you want the real coefficient.

IMSIN

Purpose: Calculates the sine of a complex number.

Syntax: IMSIN*(inumber)*

Arguments: *Inumber* is the complex number in x+yi or x+yj form for which you want the sine.

IMSQRT

Purpose: Calculates the square root of a complex number.

Syntax: IMSQRT*(inumber)*

Arguments: *Inumber* is the complex number in x+yi or x+yj form for which you want the square root.

IMSUB

Purpose: Subtracts one complex number from another.

Syntax: IMSUB*(inumber1, inumber2)*

Arguments: *Inumber1* and *inumber2* are the complex numbers in x+yi or x+yj form that you want to subtract. *Inumber2* is subtracted from *inumber1*.

IMSUM

Purpose: Calculates the sum of from 2 to 29 complex numbers.

Syntax: IMSUM*(inumber1, inumber2, ..., inumber29)*

Arguments: *Inumber1* and so on are the complex numbers in x+yi or x+yj form that you want to add together.

OCT2BIN, OCT2DEC, OCT2HEX

Purpose: These three functions convert octal numbers to other bases. OCT2BIN converts from octal to binary, OCT2DEC from octal to decimal, and OCT2HEX from octal to hexadecimal.

Syntax: OCT2BIN*(number, places)*, OCT2DEC*(number)*, or OCT2HEX*(number, places)*

Arguments: *Number* is the octal number for conversion. *Places* is the number of characters to use in the conversion. (If omitted, Excel uses the minimum number of characters necessary. If you specify extra characters, Excel pads with leading zeros.)

SQRTPI

Purpose: Calculates the square root of a the expression (number*pi).

Syntax: SQRTPI*(number)*

Arguments: *Number* is the number to be multiplied by pi before the square root is taken.

External Functions

Excel's external functions enable you to call routines in *dynamic link libraries (DLLs)*, which are files of executable functions external to Excel. Using this feature, you can execute code that belongs to other applications or that you have programmed yourself and stored in a dynamic link library. External routines are the ultimate in customization. You can make Excel do anything you want it to, as long as you can program the function that will execute the activity. The catch is that you have to have a fairly sophisticated knowledge of Windows programming to create a DLL.

CALL

Purpose: Calls a function in a dynamic link library or other type of code resource.

Syntax: CALL*(register_id, argument1, ...)* or CALL*(module_text, procedure, type_text, argument1, ...)*

Arguments: Use the first form of the function to call a DLL or code resource previously registered using the REGISTER.ID function. Use the second form to simultaneously register and call a DLL or code resource.

In the first form, *register_id* is a value returned from a call of the REGISTER.ID function. *Argument1* and subsequent arguments are the arguments to be passed to the function called.

In the second form, *module_text* is a text string enclosed in quotes identifying the name of the DLL or other code resource. *Procedure* is a text string specifying the name of the function you are calling. *Type_text* is a text string specifying the name of the Windows data type returned by the function. (See the Excel Development Kit documentation and the Windows Software Development Kit documentation for more information about Windows data types.) *Argument1* and subsequent arguments are the arguments passed to the function.

Worksheets

REGISTER.ID

Purpose: Collects the register ID of a function in a dynamic link library. The register ID is a unique number that identifies the function to Excel.

Syntax: REGISTER.ID(*module_text, procedure, type_text*)

Arguments: *Module_text* is a text string that gives the name of the DLL or other code resource containing the function. *Procedure* is a text string that specifies the name of the function. *Type_text* is a text string specifying the name of the Windows data type returned by the function. (See the Excel Development Kit documentation and the Windows Software Development Kit documentation for more information about Windows data types.) If the function has already been registered somewhere else on a worksheet, you can omit *type_text*.

Financial Functions

The financial functions provided by Excel enable you to make financial calculations a part of your worksheets. You can calculate principal and interest for loans and make several related calculations. You also can calculate depreciation and yields for a variety of assets. Examples of using many of the financial functions are provided in the spreadsheet shown in figure 8.3.

Many financial functions require the use of a code indicating the day count basis to be used. Table 8.7 gives the codes used by the financial functions for this purpose.

Figure 8.3
A sample spreadsheet showing the use of financial functions.

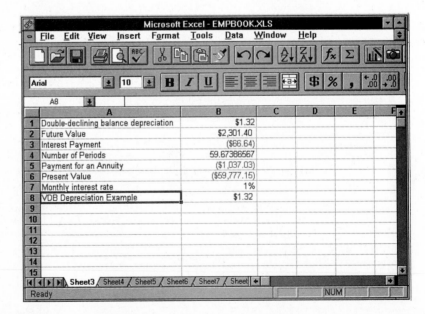

Table 8.7
Codes for Day Count Basis

Code	Basis
0 or omitted	US (NASD) 30/360
1	Actual/actual
2	Actual/360
3	Actual/365
4	European 30/360

Financial functions also use codes for different year bases. Table 8.8 shows the codes used for year basis.

Table 8.8
Year Basis Codes for Financial Functions

Code	Year Basis
0	360 days (NASD method)
1	Actual
3	365 days in a year
4	360 days in a year (European method)

In addition, certain financial functions need codes that represent the timing of payments. Table 8.9 shows the codes used for this purpose.

Table 8.9
Payment Timing Codes for Financial Functions

Code	Timing of Payments
0	Payment at the end of the period
1	Payment at the beginning of the period

ACCRINT

Purpose: Calculates accrued interest for a security paying periodic interest.

Syntax: ACCRINT(*issue, first_interest, settlement, rate, par, frequency, basis*)

Arguments: *Issue* is the security's issue date. *First_interest is the first date the security paid interest. Settlement* is the settlement date for the security (entered as a serial date number). *Rate* is the annual coupon rate. *Par* is the par value for the security. If you omit par, Excel assumes a par value of $1,000. *Frequency* is an integer representing the number of coupon payments in one year. Basis is day count basis code from table 8.7 in the introduction to the financial functions.

ACCRINTM

Purpose: Calculates the accrued interest for a security that pays interest at maturity.

Syntax: ACCRUINTM(*issue, maturity, rate, par basis*)

Arguments: *Issue* is the issue date of the security (entered as a serial date number). *Maturity* is the maturity date (entered as a serial date number). *Rate* is the coupon rate. *Par* is the par value. If you omit *par*, Excel assumes a value of $1,000. *Basis* is the day count basis from table 8.7.

AMORDEGRC

Purpose: Calculates the depreciation for each accounting period. (This function is provided for those using the French accounting system.)

Syntax: AMORDEGRC(*cost, purchase, first_period, salvage, period, rate, year_basis*)

Arguments: *Cost* is that amount the asset cost. *Purchase* is the purchase date for the asset. *First_period* is that date that ends the first period. *Salvage* is that value of the asset at the end of its life. *Period* is the period. *Rate* is the depreciation rate. *Year_basis* is the year basis to be used from table 8.8.

AMORLINC

Purpose: Calculates the depreciation for each accounting period. (This function is provided for those using the French accounting system.)

Syntax: AMORLINC(*cost, purchase, first_period, salvage, period, rate, year_basis*)

Arguments: *Cost* is that amount the asset cost. Purchase is the purchase date for the asset. *First_period* is the date that ends the first period. *Salvage* is that value of the asset at the end of its life. *Period* is the period. *Rate* is the depreciation rate. *Year_basis* is the year basis to be used from table 8.8.

COUPDAYBS

Purpose: Calculates the number of days from the beginning of the coupon period to the settlement date.

Syntax: COUPDAYBS*(settlement, maturity, frequency, basis)*

Arguments: *Settlement* is a serial date number for the settlement date. *Maturity* is a serial date number for the maturity date. *Frequency* is the number of coupon payments annually. *Basis* is the day count basis from table 8.7 in the introduction to the financial functions.

COUPDAYS

Purpose: Calculates the number of days in the coupon period containing the settlement date.

Syntax: COUPDAYS*(settlement, maturity, frequency, basis)*

Arguments: *Settlement* is a serial date number for the settlement date. *Maturity* is a serial date number for the maturity date. *Frequency* is the number of coupon payments annually. *Basis* is the day count basis from table 8.7 in the introduction to the financial functions.

COUPDAYSNC

Purpose: Calculates the number of days from the settlement date to the next coupon date.

Syntax: COUPDAYSNC*(settlement, maturity, frequency, basis)*

Arguments: *Settlement* is a serial date number for the settlement date. *Maturity* is a serial date number for the maturity date. *Frequency* is the number of coupon payments annually. *Basis* is the day count basis from table 8.7 in the introduction to the financial functions.

COUPNCD

Purpose: Calculates the next coupon date after the settlement date.

Syntax: COUPNCD*(settlement, maturity, frequency, basis)*

Arguments: *Settlement* is a serial date number for the settlement date. *Maturity* is a serial date number for the maturity date. *Frequency* is the number of coupon payments annually. *Basis* is the day count basis from table 8.7 in the introduction to the financial functions.

COUPNUM

Purpose: Calculates the number of coupons payable between settlement and maturity dates.

Syntax: COUPNUM*(settlement, maturity, frequency, basis)*

Arguments: *Settlement* is a serial date number for the settlement date. *Maturity* is a serial date number for the maturity date. *Frequency* is the number of coupon payments annually. *Basis* is the day count basis from table 8.7 in the introduction to the financial functions.

COUPPCD

Purpose: Calculates the previous coupon date before the settlement date.

Syntax: COUPPCD(*settlement, maturity, frequency, basis*)

Arguments: *Settlement* is a serial date number for the settlement date. *Maturity* is a serial date number for the maturity date. *Frequency* is the number of coupon payments annually. *Basis* is the day count basis from table 8.7 in the introduction to the financial functions.

COMIPMT

Purpose: Calculates the cumulative interest paid between the starting period and ending period of a loan.

Syntax: CUMIPMT(*rate, nper, pv, start_period, end_period, type*)

Arguments: *Rate* is the interest rate, *nper* the number of payment periods, and *pv* the present value. *Start_period* is the first period for the purposes of the calculation, and *end_period* the last period for the calculation. *Type* is the payment timing, as shown in table 8.9 in the introduction to the financial functions.

CUMPRINC

Purpose: Calculates the cumulative principal paid between the starting period and ending period of a loan.

Syntax: CUMPRINC(*rate, nper, pv, start_period, end_period, type*)

Arguments: *Rate* is the interest rate, *nper* the number of payment periods, and *pv* the present value. *Start_period* is the first period for the purposes of the calculation, and *end_period* the last period for the calculation. *Type* is the payment timing, as shown in table 8.9 in the introduction to the financial functions.

DB

Purpose: Calculates depreciation for an asset using the fixed-declining balance method for a specified period.

Syntax: DB(*cost, salvage, life, period, month*)

Arguments: *Cost* is what you paid for the asset, *salvage* its value after depreciation, *life* the number of periods in the useful life of the asset, *period* the period over which to calculate depreciation, and *month* the number of months in the first year. (If *month* is omitted, Excel assumes a value of 12.)

DDB

Purpose: Calculates depreciation for an asset using the double-declining balance method, or another method you specify.

Syntax: DDB(*cost, salvage, life, period, factor*)

Arguments: *Cost* is what you paid for the asset, *salvage* its value after depreciation, *life* the number of periods in the useful life of the asset, *period* the period over which to calculate depreciation, and *factor* the rate at which the balance declines. (If *month* is omitted, Excel assumes a value of 12.)

DISC

Purpose: Calculates a security's discount rate.

Syntax: DISC(*settlement, maturity, pr, redemption, basis*)

Arguments: *Settlement* is a serial date number representing the settlement date. *Maturity* is the serial date number representing the maturity date. *Pr* is the price per $100 of face value of the security. *Redemption* is the redemption value per $100 of face value. *Basis* is the day count basis, given in table 8.7 in the introduction to the financial functions.

DOLLARDE

Purpose: Converts a dollar price written as a fraction to a dollar price written as a decimal.

Syntax: DOLLARDE(*fractional_dollar, fraction*)

Arguments: *Fractional_dollar* is the number of dollars expressed as a fraction. *Fraction* is the integer used as the denominator of the fraction.

DOLLARFR

Purpose: Converts a dollar price written as a decimal number to a dollar price written as a fraction.

Syntax: DOLLARFR(*decimal_dollar, fraction*)

Arguments: *Decimal_dollar* is the dollar price as a decimal number. *Fraction* is the denominator for the fraction you wish to use in the conversion.

DURATION

Purpose: Calculates the annual duration with periodic interest payments for a security.

Syntax: DURATION(*settlement, maturity, coupon, yld, frequency, basis*)

Arguments: *Settlement* is the serial date number representing the security's settlement date. *Maturity* is a serial date number representing the security's maturity date. *Coupon* is the annual coupon rate, *yld* the annual yield, and *frequency* the number of payments in a given year. *Basis* is the day count basis given in table 8.7 of the introduction to the financial functions.

EFFECT

Purpose: Calculates the effective annual interest rate.

Syntax: EFFECT(*nominal_rate, npery*)

Arguments: *Nominal_rate* is the nominal interest rate involved. *Npery* is the number of periods for compounding the interest in a given year.

FV

Purpose: Calculates the future value of an investment that has constant periodic payments and a constant interest rate.

Syntax: FV(*rate, nper, pmt, pv, type*)

Arguments: *Rate* is the interest rate expressed as a per period value. *Nper* is the total number of payment periods. *Pmt* is the payment made each period. *Pv* is the present value. *Type* is the payment timing code shown in table 8.9 in the introduction to the financial functions.

FVSCHEDULE

Purpose: Calculates the future value of an investment with variable or adjustable interest rates.

Syntax: FVSCHEDULE(*principal, schedule*)

Arguments: *Principal* is the present value of the investment. *Schedule* is an array of interest rates that apply.

INTRATE

Purpose: Calculates the interest rate for a security that is fully invested.

Syntax: INTRATE(*settlement, maturity, investment, redemption, basis*)

Arguments: *Settlement* is a serial date number that represents the settlement date, and *maturity* is a serial date number that represents the maturity date. *Investment* is the amount invested, *redemption* the amount received at maturity, and *basis* the day count basis given in table 8.7 in the introduction to the financial functions.

IPMT

Purpose: Calculates the interest payment over a given period of time for an investment based on constant periodic payments and a fixed interest rate.

Syntax: IPMT(*rate, per, nper, pv, fv, type*)

Arguments: *Rate* is the constant interest rate, *per* the period over which you want to calculate the interest rate, and *nper* the total number of periods in the investment. *Pv* is the

present value. *Fv* is the future value you wish to attain. (If omitted, Excel assumes the future value of a loan, or 0.) *Type* is the payment timing code shown in table 8.9 in the introduction to the financial functions.

IRR

Purpose: Calculates the internal rate of return based on a series of cash flows.

Syntax: IRR(*values, guess*)

Arguments: *Values* is an array or reference containing the numbers representing the cash flows. *Guess* is a number representing your estimate of the result of the calculation. (The *guess* parameter is optional.)

NOTE For the purposes of this function, your initial investment should be entered as a negative number, such as –$70,000.

MDURATION

Purpose: Calculates the modified Macauley duration for a security. The function assumes a par value of $100.00.

Syntax: MDURATION(*settlement, maturity, coupon, yld, frequency, basis*)

Arguments: *Settlement* is a serial date number representing the settlement date. *Maturity* is a serial date number representing the maturity date. *Coupon* is the annual coupon rate. *Yld* is the annual yield. *Frequency* is the number of coupon payments annually. *Basis* is the day count basis from table 8.7 in the introduction to the financial functions.

MIRR

Purpose: Calculates the modified internal rate of return for a series of cash flows. The function includes the cost of investment and interest on reinvestment of cash.

Syntax: MIRR(*values, finance_rate, reinvest_rate*)

Arguments: *Values* is an array or reference of numbers that represent the cash flows. *Finance_rate* is the interest rate paid on the money used for the cash flows. *Reinvest_rate* is the interest the reinvested cash flows generate.

NOMINAL

Purpose: Calculates the nominal annual interest rate.

Syntax: NOMINAL(*effect_rate, npery*)

Arguments: *Effect_rate* is the effective interest rate, and *npery* the number of compounding periods in one year.

NPER

Purpose: Calculates the number of periods necessary for an investment.

Syntax: NPER(*rate, pmt, pv, fv, type*)

Arguments: *Rate* is one period's rate of interest, *pmt* the payment made during each period, *pv* the present value, *fv* the future value, and *type* the payment timing code given in Table 8.9 in the introduction to the financial functions.

NPV

Purpose: Calculates the net present value for an investment, assuming a discount rate and a series of periodic cash flows representing future payments and income.

Syntax: NPV(*rate, value1, value2,...*)

Arguments: *Rate* is one period's discount rate. The values are up to 29 values that represent the future payments (negative values) and income (positive values).

ODDFPRICE

Purpose: Calculates the price per $100.00 face value for a security with an odd first period.

Syntax: ODDFPRICE(*settlement, maturity, issue, first_coupon, rate, yld, redemption, frequency, basis*)

Arguments: *Settlement* is a serial date number representing the settlement date. *Maturity* is a serial date number representing the maturity date. *Issue* is a serial date number representing the issue date. *First_coupon* is a serial date number representing the first coupon date. *Rate* is the interest rate, *yld* is the annual yield, *redemption* the redemption value per $100 of face value, *frequency* the number of coupon payments per year, and *basis* the day count basis given in table 8.7 in the introduction to the financial functions.

ODDFYIELD

Purpose: Calculates the yield of a security with an odd first period.

Syntax: ODDFYIELD(*settlement, maturity, issue, first_coupon, rate, pr, redemption, frequency, basis*)

Arguments: *Settlement* is a serial date number representing the settlement date. *Maturity* is a serial date number representing the maturity date. *Issue* is a serial date number representing the issue date. *First_coupon* is a serial date number representing the first coupon date. *Rate* is the interest rate, *pr* the security's price, *redemption* the redemption value per $100 of face value, *frequency* the number of coupon payments per year, and *basis* the day count basis given in table 8.7 in the introduction to the financial functions.

ODDLPRICE

Purpose: Calculates the price per $100.00 of face value for a security with an odd last period.

Syntax: ODDLPRICE(*settlement, maturity, last_interest, rate, yld, redemption, frequency, basis*)

Arguments: *Settlement* is a serial date number representing the settlement date. *Maturity* is a serial date number representing the maturity date. *Last_interest* is a serial date number representing the last coupon date. *Rate* is the interest rate, *yld* is the annual yield, *redemption* the redemption value per $100 of face value, *frequency* the number of coupon payments per year, and *basis* the day count basis given in table 8.7 in the introduction to the financial functions.

ODDLYIELD

Purpose: Calculates the yield for a security with an odd last period.

Syntax: ODDLYIELD(*settlement, maturity, last_interest, rate, pr, redemption, frequency, basis*)

Arguments: *Settlement* is a serial date number representing the settlement date. *Maturity* is a serial date number representing the maturity date. *Last_interest* is a serial date number representing the last coupon date. *Rate* is the interest rate, *pr* the security's price, *redemption* the redemption value per $100 of face value, *frequency* the number of coupon payments per year, and *basis* the day count basis given in table 8.7 in the introduction to the financial functions.

PMT

Purpose: Calculates the payment for an annuity built on fixed payments and a fixed interest rate.

Syntax: PMT(*rate, nper, pv, fv, type*)

Arguments: *Rate* is the interest rate per period, *nper* the number of periods in an annuity, *pv* the present value, *fv* the future value, and *type* the payment timing code given in table 8.9 in the introduction to the financial functions.

PPMT

Purpose: Calculates the payment on the principal in a given period for an investment built on fixed payments and fixed interest.

Syntax: PPMT(*rate, per, nper, pv, fv, type*)

Arguments: *Rate* is the interest rate per period, *per* identifies the period, *nper* is the number of payment periods, *pv* the present value, *fv* the future value, and *type* the payment timing code given in table 8.9 in the introduction to the financial functions.

PRICE

Purpose: Calculates the price per $100.00 of face value for a security paying periodic interest.

Syntax: PRICE(*settlement, maturity, rate, yld, redemption, frequency, basis*)

Arguments: *Settlement* is a serial date number representing the settlement date. *Maturity* is a serial date number representing the maturity date. *Rate* is the annual coupon rate, *yld* the annual yield, *redemption* the redemption value per $100 of face value, *frequency* the number of payments annually, and *basis* the day count basis given in table 8.7 in the introduction to the financial functions.

PRICEDISC

Purpose: Calculates the price per $100.00 of face value for a discounted security.

Syntax: PRICEDISC(*settlement, maturity, discount, redemption, basis*)

Arguments: *Settlement* is a serial date number representing the settlement date. *Maturity* is a serial date number representing that maturity date. *Discount* is the discount rate, *redemption* the redemption value per $100 of face value, and *basis* the day count basis given in table 8.7 in the introduction to the financial functions.

PRICEMAT

Purpose: Calculates the price per $100.00 of face value for a security that pays its interest at maturity.

Syntax: PRICEMAT(*settlement, maturity, issue, rate, yld, basis*)

Arguments: *Settlement* is a serial date number representing the settlement date. *Maturity* is a serial date number representing the maturity date. *Issue* is a serial date number representing the issue date. *Rate* is the interest rate at date of issue, *yld* the annual yield, and *basis* the day count basis given in table 8.7 in the introduction to the financial functions.

PV

Purpose: Calculates the present value for an investment.

Syntax: PV(*rate, nper, pmt, fv, type*)

Arguments: *Rate* is the interest rate per period, *nper* the number of payment periods in an annuity, *pmt* the payment for each period, *fv* the future value, and *type* the payment timing code given in table 8.9 in the introduction to the financial functions.

RATE

Purpose: Calculates the interest rate per period for an annuity.

Syntax: RATE(*nper, pmt, pv, fv, type, guess*)

Arguments: *Nper* is the number of payment periods in an annuity, *pmt* the payment for each period, *pv* the present value, *fv* the future value, *type* the payment timing code given in table 8.9 in the introduction to the financial functions, and *guess* your estimate of what the rate will be. If you do not give a guess, Excel assumes a guess of 10 percent.

RECEIVED

Purpose: Calculates the amount received at maturity for a security that is fully invested.

Syntax: RECEIVED(*settlement, maturity, investment, discount, basis*)

Arguments: *Settlement* is a serial date number representing the settlement date. *Maturity* is a serial date number representing the maturity date. *Investment* is the amount invested, *discount* the discount rate, and *basis* the day count basis given in table 8.7 in the introduction to the financial functions.

SLN

Purpose: Calculates straight-line depreciation for an asset over one period.

Syntax: SLN(*cost, salvage, life*)

Arguments: *Cost* is the initial cost of the asset, *salvage* the value of the asset after the depreciation period (salvage value), and *life* the number of periods over which you depreciate the asset (useful life of the asset).

SYD

Purpose: Calculates the sum-of-years' digits depreciation for an asset over one period.

Syntax: SYD(*cost, salvage, life, per*)

Arguments: *Cost* is the initial cost of the asset, *salvage* the value of the asset after the depreciation period (salvage value), and *life* the number of periods over which you depreciate the asset (useful life of the asset). *Per* is the period in question.

TBILLEQ

Purpose: Calculates a Treasury bill's bond-equivalent yield.

Syntax: TBILLEQ(*settlement, maturity, discount*)

Arguments: *Settlement* is a serial date number representing the settlement date. *Maturity* is a serial date number representing the maturity date, and *discount* is the discount rate.

TBILLPRICE

Purpose: Calculates a Treasury bill's price per $100.00 of face value.

Syntax: TBILLPRICE(*settlement, maturity, discount*)

Arguments: *Settlement* is a serial date number representing the settlement date. *Maturity* is a serial date number representing the maturity date, and *discount* is the discount rate.

TBILLYIELD

Purpose: Calculates a Treasury bill's yield.

Syntax: TBILLYIELD(*settlement, maturity, pr*)

Arguments: *Settlement* is a serial date number representing the settlement date. *Maturity* is a serial date number representing the maturity date, and *pr* is the price per $100 of face value.

VDB

Purpose: Calculates the depreciation of an asset over a specified period using the depreciation method you specify.

Syntax: VDB(*cost, salvage, life, start_period, end_period, factor, no_switch*)

Arguments: *Cost* is the initial cost of the asset, *salvage* the value of the asset after the depreciation period (salvage value), and *life* the number of periods over which you depreciate the asset (useful life of the asset). *Start_period* is the starting period for the depreciation calculation. *End_period* is the ending period for the calculation. *Factor* is the rate of decline for the balance (assumed as 2 if *factor* is omitted). *No_switch* is a logical value that causes the calculation to switch to straight-line depreciation if depreciation is greater using this method. (TRUE enables the switch, and FALSE disables it. Excel assumes FALSE if you omit this argument.)

XIRR

Purpose: Calculates the internal rate of return for a nonperiodic schedule of cash flows.

Syntax: XIRR(*values, dates, guess*)

Arguments: *Values* is an array of cash flows. *Dates* is an array of payment dates corresponding to the cash flows. *Guess* is your estimate of the result of the function.

XNPV

Purpose: Calculates net present value for a nonperiodic schedule of cash flows.

Syntax: XNPV(*rate, values, dates*)

Arguments: *Rate* is the discount rate. *Values* is an array of cash flows. *Dates* is an array of payment dates corresponding to the cash flows.

YIELD

Purpose: Calculates yield for a security that pays periodic interest.

Syntax: YIELD(*settlement, maturity, rate, pr, redemption, frequency, basis*)

Arguments: *Settlement* is a serial date number representing the settlement date. *Maturity* is a serial date number representing the maturity date. *Rate* is the annual coupon rate. *Pr* is the price per $100 of face value, *redemption* the redemption value per $100, *frequency* the number of coupon payments per year, and *basis* the day count basis given by table 8.7 in the introduction to the financial functions.

YIELDDISC

Purpose: Calculates the annual yield of a discounted security.

Syntax: YIELDDISC(*settlement, maturity, pr, redemption, basis*)

Arguments: *Settlement* is a serial date number representing the settlement date. *Maturity* is a serial date number representing the maturity date. *Pr* is the price per $100 of face value, *redemption* the redemption value per $100 of face value, and *basis* the day count basis given by table 8.7 in the introduction to the financial functions.

YIELDMAT

Purpose: Calculates the annual yield for a security paying interest at maturity.

Syntax: YIELDMAT(*settlement, maturity, issue, rate, pr, basis*)

Arguments: *Settlement* is a serial date number representing the settlement date. *Maturity* is a serial date number representing the maturity date. *Issue* is a serial date number representing the issue date. *Rate* is the interest rate at date of issue. *Pr* is the price per $100 of face value, and *basis* the day count basis given by table 8.7 in the introduction to the financial functions.

Information Functions

Excel's information functions enable you to collect information about the cells on your worksheets. You can determine the nature of information stored in any cell. You also can collect information about error types. Relevant examples of using these functions are shown in the sample spreadsheet in figure 8.4.

Figure 8.4
A sample
spreadsheet
showing the
use of
information
functions.

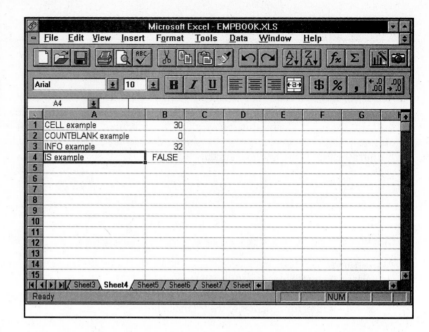

CELL

Purpose: Gets information regarding formatting, location, or contents for the upper left cell in a reference.

Syntax: CELL(*info_type*, *reference*)

Arguments: *Info_type* is a text string that identifies the type of information requested. Appropriate text strings are shown in table 8.10.

Table 8.10
Text Strings for Info_type

Info_type	Returns
"address"	First cell's reference.
"col"	First cell's column number.
"color"	1 if the cell is formatted in color, 0 if not.
"contents"	Upper left cell's contents.
"filename"	File name containing the reference ("" if the worksheet has not been saved).

Info_type	Returns
"format"	Text expressing the number format of the cell. "–" appended if cell is in color. "()" appended if parentheses for positive values or all values.
"parentheses"	1 if the cell uses parentheses for either positive or all values, 0 if not.
"prefix"	Text expressing the label prefix of the cell. "'" if text is left-aligned. """ if the text is right-aligned. "^" if text is centered. "\" if text is fill-aligned. "" if the cell contains anything else.
"protect"	0 if cell is unlocked, and 1 if cell is locked.
"row"	Row number for the first cell.
"type"	Text expressing the type of data in the cell. "b" if the cell is empty. "l" if the cell contains text. "v" if the cell contains anything else.
"width"	Cell's column width rounded to the nearest integer. Units of column width equal one character in the current font.

When *info_type* is "format," this function returns one of the codes shown in table 8.11.

Table 8.11
Return Codes for Info_type "Format"

Format	Code Returned
General	"G"
0	"F0"
#,##0	",0"
0.00	"F2"
#,##0.00	",2"
$#,##0_);($#,##0)	"C0'
$#,##0_);[Red]($#,##0)	"C0–"
$#,##0.00_);($#,##0.00)	"C2"
$#,##0.00_);[Red]($#,##0.00)	"C2–"

continues

Table 8.11, Continued
Return Codes for Info_type "Format"

Format	Code Returned
0%	"P0"
0.00%	"P2"
0.00E+00	"S2"
# ?/? or # ??/??	"G"
m/d/yy or m/d/yy h:mm or mm/dd/yy.	"D4"
d–mmm–yy or dd–mmm–yy	"D1"
d–mmm or dd–mmm	"D2"
mmm–yy	"D3"
mm/dd	"D5"
h:mm AM/PM	"D7"
h:mm:ss AM/PM	"D6"
h:mm	"D9"
h:mm:ss	"D8"

Reference is the reference for any cell in the worksheet.

COUNTBLANK

Purpose: Gets the number of blank cells in a range.

Syntax: COUNTBLANK(*range*)

Arguments: *Range* is the range of cells in which you want to count the blank cells.

ERROR.TYPE

Purpose: Gets a number that corresponds to an Excel error value.

Syntax: ERROR.TYPE(*error_val*)

Arguments: *Error_val* is the error value whose number you want to have. Numbers associated with error values are shown in table 8.12.

Table 8.12
Error Values and Associated Error Numbers

Error Value	Error Number Returned
#NULL!	1
#DIV/0!	2
#VALUE!	3
#REF!	4
#NAME?	5
#NUM!	6
#N/A	7
Other values	#N/A

INFO

Purpose: Gets information about the current operating environment.

Syntax: INFO(*type_text*)

Arguments: *Type_text* is a text string that determines what information is collected. Valid values for *type_string* appear in table 8.13.

Table 8.13
Values for Type_string

Type_string	Value Returned
"directory"	Current directory or folder path
"memavail"	Memory available, expressed in bytes
"memused"	Memory used to store data
"numfile"	Number of worksheets loaded
"origin"	Absolute A1-style reference, as text, prepended with "$A:" for Lotus 1-2-3 release 3.*x* compatibility. Returns the cell reference of the top left cell visible in the window based on the current scrolling position.

continues

Table 8.13, Continued
Values for Type_string

Type_string	Value Returned
"osversion"	Operating system version
"recalc"	Recalculation mode that is current, either "Automatic" or "Manual"
"release"	Text expressing Excel version
"system"	Operating environment, either "mac" for Macintosh or "pcdos" for Windows
"totmem"	Memory available for use, including memory currently in use, expressed in bytes

ISBLANK, ISERR, ISERROR, ISEVEN, ISLOGICAL, ISNA, ISNONTEXT, ISNUMBER, ISODD, ISREF, ISTEXT

Purpose: These nine functions test the type of a value or reference. They return TRUE if the value is of the correct type, FALSE if not.

Syntax:

```
ISBLANK(value)
ISERR(value)
ISERROR(value)
ISLOGICAL(value)
ISNA(value)
ISNONTEXT(value)
ISNUMBER(value)
ISREF(value)
ISTEXT(value)
```

Arguments: *Value* is the value to be tested. These functions perform the tests indicated in table 8.14.

Table 8.14
Tests Performed by the Nine IS Functions

Function	TRUE If:
ISBLANK	The cell is empty
ISERR	Refers to an error code except #N/A
ISERROR	Refers to any error value, including #N/A
ISLOGICAL	Is a logical value
ISNA	Is the #N/A error code
ISNONTEXT	Is any value, including a blank cell, that is not text
ISNUMBER	Is a number
ISREF	Is a reference
ISTEXT	Is text

N

Purpose: Converts a value to a number.

Syntax: N(*value*)

Arguments: *Value* is the value to convert. A number is, of course, converted to that number. Dates are converted to serial date numbers. TRUE is converted to 1. All other values are converted to 0.

NA

Purpose: Returns the "no value is available" (#N/A) error value.

Syntax: NA()

Arguments: None.

TYPE

Purpose: Gets the type of a value.

Syntax: TYPE(*value*)

Arguments: *Value* is the value whose type you want to know. TYPE returns the values shown in table 8.15.

Table 8.15
Return Types for the TYPE Function

Type	Return Code
Number	1
Text	2
Logical value	4
Formula	8
Error value	16
Array	64

Logical Functions

Excel's logical functions enable you to make decisions about information in various cells on your worksheets. You can check to see whether certain conditions are true. If they are, you can take appropriate action with another function. The logical functions enable you to take complex actions using Excel's simple functions. Examples of their use appear in the sample worksheet shown in figure 8.5.

Figure 8.5
A sample spreadsheet showing the use of the logical functions.

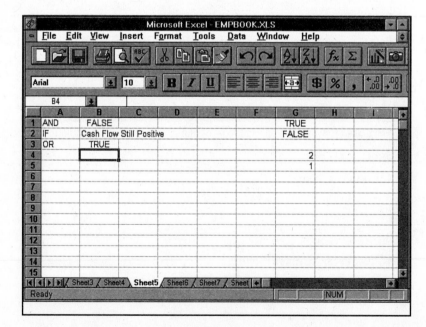

Worksheets

AND

Purpose: Evaluates to TRUE if all the arguments are TRUE, FALSE if one or more arguments are FALSE.

Syntax: AND(*logical1, logical2,...*)

Arguments: Each logical represents a condition that can evaluate to TRUE or FALSE. You can include up to 30 conditions.

FALSE

Purpose: Returns the value FALSE.

Syntax: FALSE()

Arguments: None.

IF

Purpose: Returns a value if the logical test evaluates as TRUE and some other value if the test evaluates as FALSE.

Syntax: IF(*logical_test, value_if_true, value_if_false*)

Arguments: *Logical_test* is an expression or value that can evaluate to TRUE or FALSE. *Value_if_true* is the value returned if *logical_test* evaluates to TRUE. *Value_if_false* is the value returned if *logical_test* evaluates to FALSE.

NOT

Purpose: Converts the value of the argument to its reverse.

Syntax: NOT(*logical*)

Arguments: *Logical* is any value or expression that can evaluate to TRUE or FALSE.

OR

Purpose: Returns a value of TRUE if any argument evaluates to TRUE, and a value of FALSE if all arguments evaluate to FALSE.

Syntax: OR(*logical1, logical2,...*)

Arguments: Each logical is a condition that can evaluate to TRUE or FALSE. You can include up to 30 logicals.

TRUE

Purpose: Returns the value TRUE.

Syntax: TRUE()

Arguments: None.

Look-Up and Reference Functions

The look-up and reference functions provided in Excel enable you to access cells on your worksheet by address, row, and column. You can use these functions to convert row-column addresses to row numbers and column numbers. Using these functions, you easily can navigate your worksheet. Examples of their use appear in the sample worksheet shown in figure 8.6.

Figure 8.6
A sample spreadsheet showing the use of the look-up and reference functions.

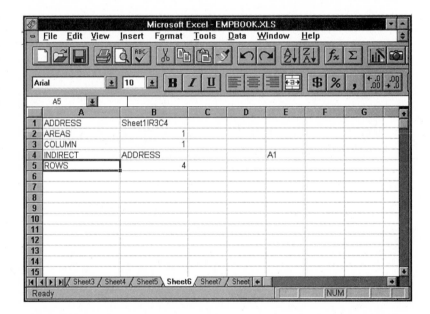

ADDRESS

Purpose: Converts a cell address to text, given specified row and column positions.

Syntax: ADDRESS(*row_num, column_num, abs_num, a1, sheet_text*)

Arguments: *Row_num* is the row number. *Column_num* is the column number. *Abs_num* is 1 (or omitted) for an absolute reference, 2 for an absolute row but relative column reference, 3 for a relative row but absolute column reference, or 4 for a relative reference. *A1* is TRUE (or omitted) for an A1 style reference, or FALSE for an R1C1 style reference. *Sheet_text* is a text

string that names the worksheet or macro sheet to be used as external reference. (If omitted, no such name is used.)

AREAS

Purpose: Gets the number of areas, ranges of contiguous cells, or single cells in a given reference.

Syntax: AREAS(*reference*)

Arguments: *Reference* is a cell or a range of cells. You can refer to multiple areas.

CHOOSE

Purpose: Selects a value from the list provided using an index number.

Syntax: CHOOSE(*index_num, value1,value2,...*)

Arguments: *Index_num* is the index number indicating the position in the list to choose. The values represent the values in the list. You can include up to 29 values.

COLUMN

Purpose: Gets the column number for the specified reference.

Syntax: COLUMN(*reference*)

Arguments: *Reference* is a cell or a range of cells for which you need a column number.

COLUMNS

Purpose: Gets the number of columns in an array or a reference.

Syntax: COLUMNS(*array*)

Arguments: *Array* is an array, array formula, or range of cells for which you want to count the number of columns used.

HLOOKUP

Purpose: Searches the top row of an array for value and returns the value in the cell indicated.

Syntax: HLOOKUP(*lookup_value, table_array, row_index_num, range_lookup*)

Arguments: *Lookup_value* is the value you are searching for in the first row of the array. *Table_array* is the reference to the table of information. *Row_index_num* is the row number in the table from which you want the data returned. (It serves as the offset from the first row for selecting the cell from which to return information.) *Range_lookup* is TRUE (or omitted) if you want an approximate match or FALSE if you want an exact match.

Worksheets

INDEX

Purpose: Gets the reference to a cell or set of cells, or value of a cell in an array, or an array of values from an array.

Syntax: This function has two forms:

```
INDEX(reference, row_num, column_num, area_num)
INDEX(array, row_num, column_num)
```

The first form returns a reference to a cell or cells. The second form returns the value of a cell or array of cells in an array.

Arguments: *Reference* is a reference to cells in the worksheet. *Array* identifies an array. *Row_num* is the row number, *column_num* is the column number, and *area_num* identifies the area in a reference for use.

INDIRECT

Purpose: Gets the reference of a reference stored in a cell.

Syntax: INDIRECT(*ref_text, a1*)

Arguments: *Ref_text* is a reference to a cell containing a reference. The reference stored in the cell may be expressed in A1 style, R1C1 style, or as a name. *A1* is TRUE (or omitted) if the style of *ref_text* is A1, or FALSE if the style is R1C1.

LOOKUP

Purpose: Looks up and returns values in a vector or array.

Syntax: The function has two forms, the first for vectors, the second for arrays.

```
LOOKUP(lookup_value, lookup_vector, result_vector)
LOOKUP(lookup_value, array)
```

Arguments: *Lookup_value* is the value you search for. *Lookup_vector* is a reference to one row or column, and its values must be in ascending order. *Result_vector* is a reference to a single row or column and must be the same size as *lookup_vector*. *Array* is a range of cells containing values, which can be text, numbers, or logical values and must be in ascending order. If the function cannot match the specified value, it does an approximate match.

MATCH

Purpose: Gets the relative position of an array element that matches a specified value and in a specified way.

Syntax: MATCH(*lookup_value, lookup_array, match_type*)

Arguments: *Lookup_value* is the value to find. *Lookup_array* is a reference to the array to search. *Match_type* is 1 if you want to match the largest value less than or equal to

lookup_value, 0 if you want an exactly equal match, or –1 if you want to match the smallest value greater than or equal to *lookup_value*. If *match_type* is 1, the *array* must be in ascending order. If *match_type* is –1, the *array* must be in descending order. If *match_type* is 0, the *array* can be in any order. If you omit *match_type*, Excel assumes a value of 1.

OFFSET

Purpose: Gets a reference of a specified row and column height offset from another reference of a given number of rows and columns.

Syntax: OFFSET(*reference, rows, cols, height, width*)

Arguments: *Reference* is a reference to the region serving as the basis for the offset. *Rows* is the number of rows up (negative) or down (positive) specifying the upper left cell of the new region. *Cols* is the number of columns right (positive) or left (negative) specifying the upper left cell of the new region. *Height* is the number of rows high the new region will be. *Width* is the number of columns wide the new region will be. If you omit either *height* or *width*, the height or width for reference is used.

ROW

Purpose: Gets the row number of a reference.

Syntax: ROW(*reference*)

Arguments: *Reference* is a reference to the cell or cells for which you want the row number.

ROWS

Purpose: Gets the number of rows in a reference or array.

Syntax: ROWS(*array*)

Arguments: *Array* is an array, an array formula, or a reference to cells that defines the array.

TRANSPOSE

Purpose: Shifts the vertical and horizontal orientation of an array, returning the array's transpose.

Syntax: TRANSPOSE(*array*)

Arguments: *Array* is a reference to the array that you want to transpose.

VLOOKUP

Purpose: Looks up a value in the far left column of an array, and returns the value of the cell indicated.

Syntax: VLOOKUP(*lookup_value, table_array, col_index_num, range_lookup*)

Arguments: *Lookup_value* is the value to find in the first column. *Table_array* is a reference to the table to be searched. *Col_index_number* is the column number from which the value should be returned. *Range_lookup* is TRUE (or omitted) if you want an approximate match, or FALSE if you want an exact match.

Mathematical and Trigonometric Functions

Excel's math and trig functions, of course, perform a variety of calculations. They form the core of Excel's mathematical capabilities. Examples of their use appear in the spreadsheet shown in figure 8.7.

Figure 8.7
A spreadsheet showing the use of math and trig functions.

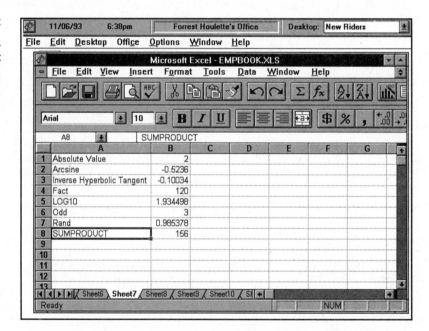

ABS

Purpose: Gets the absolute value of a number.

Syntax: ABS(*number*)

Arguments: *Number* is a real number for which you want the absolute value.

ACOS

Purpose: Calculates a number's arccosine.

Syntax: ACOS(*number*)

Arguments: *Number* is the cosine of the angle in question. It must range between 1 and –1.

ACOSH

Purpose: Calculates a number's inverse hyperbolic cosine.

Syntax: ACOSH(*number*)

Arguments: *Number* is a real number greater than or equal to 1.

ASIN

Purpose: Calculates a number's arcsine.

Syntax: ASIN(*number*)

Arguments: *Number* is the sine of the angle in question. It must range between 1 and –1.

ASINH

Purpose: Calculates a number's inverse hyperbolic sine.

Syntax: ASINH(*number*)

Arguments: *Number* is a real number.

ATAN

Purpose: Calculates a number's arctangent.

Syntax: ATAN(*number*)

Arguments: *Number* is the tangent of the angle in question.

ATAN2

Purpose: Calculates the arctangent from x/y coordinates.

Syntax: ATAN2(*x_num, y_num*)

Arguments: *X_num* is the x-coordinate and *y_num* is the y-coordinate of the point in question.

ATANH

Purpose: Calculates a number's inverse hyperbolic tangent.

Syntax: ATANH*(number)*

Arguments: *Number* is a real number ranging from 1 to –1.

CEILING

Purpose: Rounds numbers up to the nearest integer or multiple of significance.

Syntax: CEILING*(number, significance)*

Arguments: *Number* is the value to round, *significance* the multiple to which you want to round.

COMBIN

Purpose: Calculates the number of combinations for a number of objects.

Syntax: COMBIN*(number, number_chosen)*

Arguments: *Number* is the number of objects in the set from which to choose. *Number_chosen* is the number of objects selected in each combination.

COS

Purpose: Calculates a number's cosine.

Syntax: COS*(number)*

Arguments: *Number* is the angle in question, measured in radians.

COSH

Purpose: Calculates a number's hyperbolic cosine.

Syntax: COSH*(number)*

Arguments: *Number* is the number for which you want the hyperbolic cosine.

COUNTIF

Purpose: Counts the number of non-blank cells meeting the given criteria.

Syntax: COUNTIF*(range, criteria)*

Arguments: *Range* is the set of cells in which you want to count. *Criteria* is a number, expression, or text that defines whether a cell is counted.

DEGREES

Purpose: Converts from radians to degrees.

Syntax: DEGREES*(angle)*

Arguments: *Angle* is an angle measured in radians.

EVEN

Purpose: Rounds a number up to the nearest even integer.

Syntax: EVEN*(number)*

Arguments: *Number* is the number to round.

EXP

Purpose: Calculates e raised to a given power.

Syntax: EXP*(number)*

Arguments: *Number* is the value to be used as the exponent.

FACT

Purpose: Calculates the factorial of a number.

Syntax: FACT*(number)*

Arguments: *Number* is a positive number or 0 for which you want the factorial.

FACTDOUBLE

Purpose: Calculates the double factorial of a given number.

Syntax: FACTDOUBLE*(number)*

Arguments: *Number* is the number for which you want a double factorial.

FLOOR

Purpose: Rounds a number down to the nearest multiple of significance.

Syntax: FLOOR*(number, significance)*

Arguments: *Number* is the number to round, *significance* is the multiple to round to.

GCD

Purpose: Calculates the greatest common divisor of two or more integers.

Syntax: GCD*(number1, number2, ...)*

Arguments: *Number* is up to 29 values to include in the calculation.

INT

Purpose: Rounds a number down to the nearest integer.

Syntax: INT*(number)*

Arguments: *Number* is a real number.

LCM

Purpose: Calculates the least common multiple for a set of integers.

Syntax: LCM*(number1, number2, ...)*

Arguments: *Number* is up to 29 values to include in the calculation.

LN

Purpose: Calculates the natural logarithm for a number.

Syntax: LN*(number)*

Arguments: *Number* is a positive real number.

LOG

Purpose: Calculates the logarithm of a number in a specified base.

Syntax: LOG*(number, base)*

Arguments: *Number* is a positive real number. *Base* is the value to be used as the base of the logarithm. If *base* is not present, Excel assumes the base is 10.

LOG10

Purpose: Calculates the logarithm of a number in base 10.

Syntax: LOG10*(number)*

Arguments: *Number* is a positive real number.

MDETERM

Purpose: Calculates the matrix determinant of an array.

Syntax: MDETERM`(array)`

Arguments: `Array` is an array of numbers with the same number of rows as columns.

MINVERSE

Purpose: Calculates the inverse matrix of a matrix stored in an array.

Syntax: MINVERSE`(array)`

Arguments: `Array` is an array of numbers with the same number of rows as columns.

MMULT

Purpose: Calculates the matrix product of two arrays.

Syntax: MMULT`(array, array2)`

Arguments: `Array1` and `array2` are the two arrays.

MOD

Purpose: Gets the remainder in a division problem.

Syntax: MOD`(number, divisor)`

Arguments: `Number` is the number for the numerator. `Divisor` is the number by which you want to divide.

MROUND

Purpose: Rounds a number to the specified multiple.

Syntax: MROUND`(number, multiple)`

Arguments: `Number` is the number to round. `Multiple` is the multiple to which you want to round.

MULTINOMIAL

Purpose: Calculates the ratio of the factorial of a sum of values to the product of the factorials.

Syntax: MULTINOMIAL`(number1, number2, ...)`

Arguments: `Number` is up to 29 values to include in the calculation.

ODD

Purpose: Rounds a number up to the nearest odd integer.

Syntax: ODD(*number*)

Arguments: *Number* is the number to round.

PI

Purpose: Returns the value of Pi calculated to 15 digits.

Syntax: PI()

Arguments: None.

POWER

Purpose: Raises the given number to the specified power.

Syntax: POWER(*number, power*)

Arguments: *Number* is the base. *Power* is the exponent.

PRODUCT

Purpose: Multiples the specified numbers.

Syntax: PRODUCT(*number1, number2, ...*)

Arguments: *Number* is up to 30 values to multiply. You can use cell references.

QUOTIENT

Purpose: Calculates the integer portion of a division problem.

Syntax: QUOTIENT(*numerator, denominator*)

Arguments: *Numerator* is the number for the numerator, *denominator* the number for the denominator.

RADIANS

Purpose: Converts from degrees to radians.

Syntax: RADIANS(*angle*)

Arguments: *Angle* is an angle measured in degrees.

RAND

Purpose: Gets an evenly distributed random number between 0 and 1. This function gets a new number each time the worksheet is recalculated.

Syntax: RAND()

Arguments: None.

RANDBETWEEN

Purpose: Gets a random number between the specified numbers. This function gets a new random number each time the worksheet is recalculated.

Syntax: RANDBETWEEN*(bottom, top)*

Arguments: *Bottom* is the smallest integer to return, *top* the largest.

ROMAN

Purpose: Converts an Arabic numeral to text representing a Roman numeral.

Syntax: ROMAN*(number, form)*

Arguments: *Number* is an Arabic numeral. *Form* is 0 (or omitted) for a Classic Roman numeral. The values 1, 2, 3, and 4 specify increasingly concise (shorter) numerals. If *form* is TRUE, the number is classical, if FALSE it is a simplified form.

ROUND

Purpose: Rounds a number to the number of digits indicated.

Syntax: ROUND*(number, num_digits)*

Arguments: *Number* is the real number to round. *Num_digits* gives the number of digits to which you want to round.

ROUNDDOWN

Purpose: Rounds a number down to the specified number of digits.

Syntax: ROUNDDOWN*(number, num_digits)*

Arguments: *Number* is the real number to round. *Num_digits* gives the number of digits to which you want to round.

ROUNDUP

Purpose: Rounds a number up to the specified number of digits.

Syntax: ROUNDUP*(number, num_digits)*

Arguments: *Number* is the real number to round. *Num_digits* gives the number of digits to which you want to round.

SERIESSUM

Purpose: Calculates the sum of a power series.

Syntax: SERIESSUM*(x, n, m, coefficients)*

Arguments: *X* is the input value. *N* is the initial power to raise which you want to raise *x*. *M* is the step by which to increase *n*. *Coefficients* is a set of coefficients for multiplying each successive power of *x*.

SIGN

Purpose: Gets the sign of a number, returning 1 if the number is positive, 0 if the number is 0, and –1 if the number is negative.

Syntax: SIGN*(number)*

Arguments: *Number* is a real number.

SIN

Purpose: Calculates an angle's sine.

Syntax: SIN*(number)*

Arguments: *Number* is an angle measured in radians.

SINH

Purpose: Calculates a number's hyperbolic sine.

Syntax: SINH*(number)*

Arguments: *Number* is a real number.

SQRT

Purpose: Calculates the positive square root of a number.

Syntax: SQRT*(number)*

Arguments: *Number* is any number greater than 0.

SQRTPI

Purpose: Calculates the square root of a number multiplied by Pi.

Syntax: SQRTPI*(number)*

Arguments: *Number* is any number greater than 0.

SUM

Purpose: Adds the numbers listed as its arguments.

Syntax: SUM*(number1, number2, ...)*

Arguments: *Number* is up to 30 numbers you want to add together.

SUMIF

Purpose: Adds the cells that match the criteria specified.

Syntax: SUMIF*(range, criteria, sum_range)*

Arguments: *Range* is a reference to a set of cells that contain the values tested by criteria. *Criteria* is a number, expression, or text string that determines which cells to sum. *Sum_range* is a reference to cells paired with *range* that are the cells containing the values to be summed.

SUMPRODUCT

Purpose: Multiplies the corresponding cells in two arrays and adds the products calculated.

Syntax: SUMPRODUCT*(array1, array2, array3, ...)*

Arguments: *Array* is from 2 to 30 arrays to include in the operation.

SUMSQ

Purpose: Squares its arguments, then adds the squares.

Syntax: SUMSQ*(number1, number2, ...)*

Arguments: *Number* is up to 30 numbers to include in the operation.

SUMX2MY2

Purpose: Squares the corresponding values in two arrays, determines the difference between the corresponding squared values, and adds the resulting differences.

Syntax: SUMX2MY2*(array_x, array_y)*

Arguments: *Array_x* and *array_y* are two arrays containing the x and y values for the calculation.

SUMX2PY2

Purpose: Squares the corresponding values in two arrays and then sums the squared values.

Syntax: SUMX2PY2*(array_x, array_y)*

Arguments: *Array_x* and *array_y* are two arrays containing the x and y values for the calculation.

SUMXMY2

Purpose: Determines the difference between corresponding values in two arrays, squares the differences, then sums the squared differences.

Syntax: SUMXMY2*(array_x, array_y)*

Arguments: *Array_x* and *array_y* are two arrays containing the x and y values for the calculation.

TAN

Purpose: Calculates the tangent of an angle.

Syntax: TAN*(number)*

Arguments: *Number* is the measure of an angle in radians.

TANH

Purpose: Calculates a number's hyperbolic tangent.

Syntax: TANH*(number)*

Arguments: *Number* is a real number.

TRUNC

Purpose: Truncates a number to an integer according to the precision you specify.

Syntax: TRUNC*(number, num_digits)*

Arguments: *Number* is the number to truncate. *Num_digits* is the precision of truncation. (If *num_digits* is omitted, Excel assumes a value of 0.)

Statistical Functions

Excel's statistical functions enable you to analyze the data you have stored in your spreadsheets. They form Excel's core analytical engine. You can use them to determine trends and make statistical decisions. Examples of their use appear in the example spreadsheet shown in figure 8.8.

AVEDEV

Purpose: Averages the absolute deviation of data points from the mean.

Syntax: AVEDEV*(number1, number2, ...)*

Arguments: *Number* is up to 30 numbers to include in the operation.

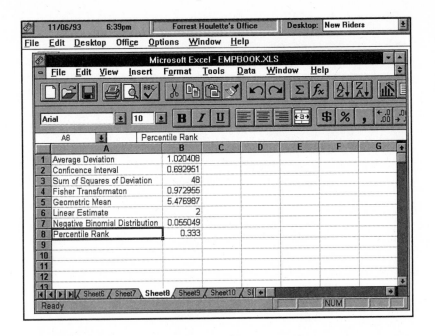

Worksheets

AVERAGE

Purpose: Calculates the arithmetic mean of its arguments.

Syntax: AVERAGE*(number1, number2, ...)*

Arguments: *Number* is up to 30 numbers to include in the operation.

BETADIST

Purpose: Calculates the cumulative beta probability density function. This function is used to study variation in a percentage across samples, as in the percentage of the day Americans spend driving automobiles.

Syntax: BETADIST*(x, alpha, beta, A, B)*

Arguments: *X* is the value at which to evaluate the function and is a value between A and B. *Alpha* and *beta* are parameters for the distribution. *A* and *B* are optional and represent the lower and upper bounds for the interval of x.

BETAINV

Purpose: Calculates the inverse of the cumulative beta probability density function. This distribution often is used to model the probable completion time of a project when you know the expected completion time and variability.

Syntax: BETAINV*(probability, alpha, beta, A, B)*

Arguments: *Probability* is the probability value for the beta distribution. *Alpha* and *beta* are the parameters for the distribution. *A* and *B* are the optional lower and upper bounds for the interval of x, the value that is the result of applying this function.

BINOMDIST

Purpose: Calculates the individual term binomial distribution probability. The binomial distribution is used to study problems consisting of a fixed number of trials with only two possible outcomes. A common example is predicting the outcome of a coin toss.

Syntax: BINOMDIST*(number_s, trials, probability_s, cumulative)*

Arguments: *Number_s* is the number of successes. *Trials* is the number of trials. *Probability_s* is the probability of success in a trial. *Cumulative* is TRUE for calculating the cumulative distribution function, the probability that there are at most *number_s* successes, and FALSE for calculating the probability mass function, the probability that there are *number_s* successes.

CHIDIST

Purpose: Calculates the one-tailed probability of the chi-squared distribution. This distribution is used when comparing observed and expected values in relation to contingency tables.

Syntax: CHIDIST*(x, degrees_freedom)*

Arguments: *X* is the value at which to evaluate the function. *Degrees_freedom* is the degrees of freedom associated with x.

CHIINV

Purpose: Calculates the inverse of the one-tailed probability of the chi-squared distribution. This function is used to compare observed results with expected results.

Syntax: CHIINV*(probability, degrees_freedom)*

Arguments: *Probability* is the probability associated with the distribution. *Degrees_freedom* is the degrees of freedom associated with the distribution.

CHITEST

Purpose: Calculates the chi-squared test for independence.

Syntax: CHITEST*(actual_range, expected_range)*

Arguments: *Actual_range* is a reference to the cells containing the observations to test against expected values. *Expected_range* is a reference to the cells containing the expected values.

CONFIDENCE

Purpose: Calculates a confidence interval for a population mean.

Syntax: CONFIDENCE*(alpha, standard_dev, size)*

Arguments: *Alpha* is the significance level. *Standard_dev* is the population standard deviation for the data. *Size* is the sample size.

CORREL

Purpose: Calculates the correlation coefficient for the values stored in two arrays. You use this value to study the relationship between two properties.

Syntax: CORREL*(array1, array2)*

Arguments: *Array1* and *array2* represent the two arrays to be correlated.

COUNT

Purpose: Determines how many numbers are in a list of arguments.

Syntax: COUNT*(value1, value2, ...)*

Arguments: *Value* is a reference to up to 30 spreadsheet regions that can contain any kind of data. Only numbers are counted, however.

COUNTA

Purpose: Determines how many nonblank values are in a list of arguments.

Syntax: COUNTA*(value1, value2, ...)*

Arguments: *Value* is up to 30 references to spreadsheet regions containing information of any type. Only nonblank cells, including cells containing "", are counted.

COVAR

Purpose: Calculates the covariance for data points stored in two arrays. Covariance can be used to study the relationship between two data sets.

Syntax: COVAR*(array1, array2)*

Arguments: *Array1* and *array2* are references to the arrays containing the two data sets.

CRITBINOM

Purpose: Determines the smallest value for which the cumulative binomial distribution is less than or equal to the criterion you set. This value is often used to determine the maximum number of defective products allowed off an assembly line before rejecting the entire lot.

Syntax: CRITBINOM*(trials, probability_s, alpha)*

Arguments: *Trials* is the number of Bernoulli trials. *Probability_s* is the probability of success of a trial. *Alpha* is the criterion.

DEVSQ

Purpose: Calculates the sum of squares of deviation of data points from the mean.

Syntax: DEVSQ*(number1, number2, ...)*

Arguments: *Number* is up to 30 values to include in the calculation.

EXPONDIST

Purpose: Calculates the exponential distribution, used to study problems in which the time between events is of interest.

Syntax: EXPONDIST*(x, lambda, cumulative)*

Arguments: *X* is the value at which to evaluate the function. *Lambda* is the parameter for the distribution. *Cumulative* is TRUE to calculate the cumulative distribution function, FALSE to calculate the probability density function.

FDIST

Purpose: Calculates the F probability distribution, used to study whether different data sets possess different degrees of diversity.

Syntax: FDIST*(x, degrees_freedom1, degrees_freedom2)*

Arguments: *X* is the value at which the function will evaluate. *Degrees_freedom1* is the degrees of freedom for the numerator. *Degrees_freedom2* is the degrees of freedom for the denominator.

FINV

Purpose: Calculates the inverse of the F probability distribution. You can use this function to compare the variation in two data sets.

Syntax: FINV*(probability, degrees_freedom1,degrees_freedom2)*

Arguments: *Probability* is the probability associated with the cumulative distribution. *Degrees_freedom1* is the degrees of freedom for the numerator. *Degrees_freedom2* is the degrees of freedom for the denominator.

FISHER

Purpose: Calculates the Fisher transformation at a given value. This function is used in hypothesis testing regarding the correlation coefficient.

Syntax: FISHER*(x)*

Arguments: *X* is the value for which to calculate the transformation.

FISHERINV

Purpose: Calculates the inverse of the Fisher transformation. This function can be used to analyze the correlations between data sets.

Syntax: FISHERINV*(y)*

Arguments: *Y* is the value for which to calculate the inverse transformation.

FORECAST

Purpose: Calculates predicted values for the x and y terms of a linear regression model. This function is used to predict unknown values, like future sales, in a correlation study.

Syntax: FORECAST*(x, known_y's, known_x's)*

Arguments: *X* is the value for which to predict a y value. *Known_x's* and *known_y's* are references to cells containing known x and y values.

FREQUENCY

Purpose: Calculates a frequency distribution as a vertical array of cells. This function sorts the data values into a set of intervals so that you know how many values occur within each interval.

Syntax: FREQUENCY*(data_array, bins_array)*

Arguments: *Data_array* is an array or reference to an array of values within which you wish to count the frequencies. *Bins_array* is an array or reference to an array that contains values defining the intervals over which to count the frequencies. The numbers in *bins_array* represent the endpoints of the frequency intervals. The array {10,20,30} defines intervals of 0-10, 11-20, and 30 to the endpoint of the data.

FTEST

Purpose: Calculates the one-tailed F test, the one-tailed probability that the variances of two arrays of values are not significantly different. You can use this test, for instance, to compare the test scores of students entering public and private universities.

Syntax: FTEST*(array1, array2)*

Arguments: *Array1* and *array2* are references to the two sets of data to be compared.

GAMMADIST

Purpose: Calculates the gamma distribution, used to study variables whose distribution might be skewed, as in queuing analysis.

Syntax: GAMMADIST*(x, alpha, beta, cumulative)*

Arguments: *X* is the value at which to evaluate the distribution. *Alpha* and *beta* are the parameters of the distribution. *Cumulative* is TRUE to calculate the cumulative distribution function, FALSE to calculate the probability mass function.

GAMMAINV

Purpose: Calculates the inverse of the gamma cumulative distribution, used in studying variables whose distribution might be skewed.

Syntax: GAMMAINV*(probability, alpha, beta)*

Arguments: *Probability* is the probability associated with the distribution. *Alpha* and *beta* are parameters for the distribution.

GAMMALN

Purpose: Calculates the gamma function's natural logarithm.

Syntax: GAMMALN*(x)*

Arguments: *X* is the value for which you want the natural log of the gamma function.

GEOMEAN

Purpose: Calculates the geometric mean of positive data points. This function often is used in calculating issues like growth rates that invlolve compound interest with variable rates.

Syntax: GEOMEAN*(number1, number2, ...)*

Arguments: *Number* is up to 30 numbers to include in the calculation. You can substitute a single array or reference to an array instead of listing the numbers as arguments.

GROWTH

Purpose: Calculates an exponential curve to fit known data points and calculates predicted y values for x values you supply.

Syntax: GROWTH*(known_y's, known_x's, new_x's, const)*

Arguments: *Known_y's* and *known_x's* are arrays of known values. (*Known_x's* are optional). *New_x's* are x values for which you want corresponding y values. *Const* is TRUE (or omitted) to calculate the constant b normally, FALSE to force b equal to 1.

HARMEAN

Purpose: Calculates a data set's harmonic mean, the reciprocal of the arithmetic mean of reciprocals.

Syntax: HARMEAN*(number1, number2, ...)*

Arguments: *Number* is up to 30 values to include in the calculation. You can use a reference to an array.

HYPGEOMDIST

Purpose: Calculates the hypergeometric distribution, used to study problems within a finite population, in which observations are either successes or failures, and from which each subset is chosen with equal likelihood.

Syntax: HYPGEOMDIST*(sample_s, number_sample, population_s, number_population)*

Arguments: *Sample_s* is the number of successes appearing in the sample. *Number_sample* is the sample size. *Population_s* is the number of successes appearing in the population. *Number_population* is the size of the population.

INTERCEPT

Purpose: Calculates the y intercept for a regression line.

Syntax: INTERCEPT*(known_y's, known_x's)*

Arguments: *Known_y's* and *known_x's* are sets of data that represent the x and y values defining the regression line.

KURT

Purpose: Calculates the kurtosis, the relative peakedness or flatness of the curve describing the data distribution, for a data set.

Syntax: KURT*(number1, number2, ...)*

Arguments: *Number* is up to 30 values to include in the calculation. You can use a reference to an array.

LARGE

Purpose: Gets the k-th largest value in the data set.

Syntax: LARGE*(array, k)*

Arguments: *Array* is the array of data from which to select the value. *K* is the position from the largest value to return.

LINEST

Purpose: Fits a straight line to describe a data set using the least squares method.

Syntax: LINEST*(known_y's, known_x's, const, stats)*

Arguments: *Known_y's* and *known_x's* are the set of known data points that will define the line. (*Known_x's* is optional.) *Const* is TRUE if the constant b is to be calculated normally, FALSE if b is to be forced to 0. *Stats* is TRUE to return regression statistics, FALSE (or omitted) to return only the m coefficients and the constant b.

LOGEST

Purpose: Fits an exponential curve that best describes a data set.

Syntax: LOGEST*(known_y's, known_x's, const, stats)*

Arguments: *Known_y's* and *known_x's* are the set of known data points that will define the curve. (*Known_x's* is optional.) *Const* is TRUE if the constant b is to be calculated normally, FALSE is b is to be forced to 1. *Stats* is TRUE to return regression statistics, FALSE (or omitted) to return only the m coefficients and the constant b.

LOGINV

Purpose: Calculates the inverse of the lognormal cumulative distribution, used for analyzing logarithmically transformed data.

Syntax: LOGINV*(probability, mean, standard_dev)*

Arguments: *Probability* is the probability associated with the distribution. *Mean* is the mean and *standard_dev* the standard deviation of ln(x).

LOGNORMDIST

Purpose: Calculates the cumulative lognormal distribution for a given value. This function is used to analyze logarithmically transformed data.

Syntax: LOGNORMDIST*(x, mean, standard_dev)*

Arguments: *X* is the value at which the function is to be evaluated. *Mean* is the mean and *standard_dev* is the standard deviation of ln(x).

MAX

Purpose: Gets the maximum value from its argument list.

Syntax: MAX*(number1, number2, ...)*

Arguments: *Number* is up to 30 numbers from which you want to select the maximum value.

MEDIAN

Purpose: Calculates the median for a set of numbers.

Syntax: MEDIAN*(number1, number2, ...)*

Arguments: *Number* is up to 30 numbers to include in the calculation.

MIN

Purpose: Gets the smallest number from the list of arguments.

Syntax: MIN*(number1, number2, ...)*

Arguments: *Number* is up to 30 numbers from which you want to select the minimum value.

MODE

Purpose: Gets the most frequent value in a data set.

Syntax: MODE*(number1, number2, ...)*

Arguments: *Number* is up to 30 numbers for which you want the mode.

NEGBINOMDIST

Purpose: Calculates the negative binomial distribution, the probability that there will be a given number of failures before a given success.

Syntax: NEGBINOMDIST*(number_f, number_s, probability_s)*

Arguments: *Number_f* is the number of failures, *number_s* the threshold number of successes, and *probability_s* the probability of a success.

NORMDIST

Purpose: Calculates the normal cumulative distribution with a given mean and standard deviation.

Syntax: NORMDIST*(x, mean, standard_dev, cumulative)*

Arguments: *X* is the number for which to evaluate the function, *mean* is the mean for the distribution, *standard_dev* is the standard deviation for the distribution. *Cumulative* is TRUE to calculate the cumulative distribution function, FALSE to calculate the probability mass function.

NORMINV

Purpose: Calculates the inverse of the normal cumulative distribution with a given mean and standard deviation.

Syntax: NORMINV*(probability, mean, standard_dev)*

Arguments: *Probability* is the probability associated with the distribution, *mean* the mean for the distribution, and *standard_dev* the standard deviation for the distribution.

NORMSDIST

Purpose: Calculates the standard normal cumulative distribution function, which has a mean of 0 and standard deviation of 1.

Syntax: NORMSDIST*(z)*

Arguments: *Z* is the value for which to calculate the distribution.

NORMSINV

Purpose: Calculates the inverse of the standard normal cumulative distribution.

Syntax: NORMSINV*(probability)*

Arguments: *Probability* is the probability associated with the distribution.

PEARSON

Purpose: Calculates the Pearson product moment correlation coefficient (r) for two data sets.

Syntax: PEARSON*(array1, array2)*

Arguments: *Array1* is the set of independent values, and *array2* the set of dependent values, for the calculation.

PERCENTILE

Purpose: Calculates the k-th percentile for a range of values. This function is often used to calculate thresholds, as when deciding to examine only job candidates who score above the 90th percentile on an evaluation criterion.

Syntax: PERCENTILE*(array, k)*

Arguments: *Array* is the range of data defining relative standing, and *k* is the percentile value desired.

PERCENTRANK

Purpose: Calculates the percentile rank for a given value in a set of data.

Syntax: PERCENTRANK*(array, x, significance)*

Arguments: *Array* is a reference to an array of numeric values defining relative standing. *X* is the value to be ranked. *Significance* is an optional value expressing the number of significant digits to include in the percentage value returned. (Three significant digits are included by default.)

PERMUT

Purpose: Calculates the number of permutations for a set of objects to be selected from a larger set of objects.

Syntax: PERMUT*(number, number_chosen)*

Arguments: *Number* is an integer expressing the number of objects, and *number_chosen* is an integer expressing the number of objects in each permutation.

POISSON

Purpose: Calculates the Poisson distribution, used for predicting the number of events in a fixed period of time.

Syntax: POISSON*(x, mean, cumulative)*

Arguments: *X* is the number of events, *mean* the expected numeric value. *Cumulative* is TRUE to calculate the cumulative probability function, FALSE to calculate the probability mass function.

PROB

Purpose: Calculates the probability that a set of values are between two limits.

Syntax: PROB*(x_range, prob_range, lower_limit, upper_limit)*

Arguments: *X_range* is the range of values for x with associated probabilities. *Prob_range* is the probabilities associated with *x_range*. *Lower_limit* and *upper_limit* represent the lower and upper bounds of the value for which you calculate the probability.

QUARTILE

Purpose: Calculates the quartiles for a data set.

Syntax: QUARTILE*(array, quart)*

Arguments: *Array* is a reference to the values to be split into quartiles. *Quart* is which quartile to return.

RANK

Purpose: Determines the rank of a number in a given list of numbers.

Syntax: RANK*(number, ref, order)*

Arguments: *Number* is the number to be ranked, *ref* is an array or list of numbers, and *order* is 0 (or omitted) if reference is to be sorted in descending order of a non-zero value if reference is to be sorted in ascending order.

RSQ

Purpose: Calculates the square of the Pearson product moment correlation coefficient, a value that gives the percentage of the variance in one factor y attributable to the variance in another factor x.

Syntax: RSQ*(known_y's, known_x's)*

Arguments: *Known_y's* and *known_x's* are the set of data points for which you want the squared correlation coefficient.

SKEW

Purpose: Calculates the skewness, the degree of asymmetry in a distribution's curve, for a set of data.

Syntax: SKEW*(number1, number2, ...)*

Arguments: *Number* is up to 30 numbers to include in the calculation. You can use a reference to cells.

SLOPE

Purpose: Calculates the slope of a linear regression line.

Syntax: SLOPE*(known_y's, known_x's)*

Arguments: *Known_y's* is an array of dependent data points, and *known_x's* an array of independent data points.

SMALL

Purpose: Gets the k-th smallest value in a set of data.

Syntax: SMALL*(array, k)*

Arguments: *Array* is an array of data from which to select the value. *K* is the position from the smallest value to make the selection.

STANDARDIZE

Purpose: Normalizes a value from a distribution with a given mean and standard deviation, transforming it to a value on a scale with a mean of 0 and a standard deviation of 1.

Syntax: STANDARDIZE*(x, mean, standard_dev)*

Arguments: *X* is the value to normalize, *mean* the mean of the distribution, and *standard_dev* is the distribution's standard deviation.

STDEV

Purpose: Estimates the standard deviation based on a sample.

Syntax: STDEV*(number1,number2,...)*

Arguments: *Number* is up to 30 values to be included in the calculation. You can use a reference to a range of cells.

STDEVP

Purpose: Calculates a standard deviation based on an entire population.

Syntax: STDEVP*(number1,number2,...)*

Arguments: *Number* is up to 30 values to include in the calculation. You can use a reference to cells.

STEYX

Purpose: Calculates the standard error of predicted y values for the x values in a regression problem.

Syntax: STEYX*(known_y's, known_x's)*

Arguments: *Known_y's* and *known_x's* are arrays of dependent and independent data points, respectively.

TDIST

Purpose: Calculates the T distribution, used for hypothesis testing in small data sets.

Syntax: TDIST*(x, degrees_freedom, tails)*

Arguments: *X* is the value for which to evaluate the function, *degrees_freedom* is the number of degrees of freedom, and *tails* is the number of tails (1 or 2).

TINV

Purpose: Calculates the inverse of the T distribution with given degrees of freedom.

Syntax: TINV*(probability, degrees_freedom)*

Arguments: *Probability* is the probability associated with a two-tailed text, and *degrees_freedom* is the number of degrees of freedom.

TREND

Purpose: Calculates values along a linear trend.

Syntax: TREND*(known_y's, known_x's, new_x's, const)*

Arguments: *Known_y's* and *known_x's* are arrays of known values. (*Known_x's* are optional). *New_x's* are x values for which you want corresponding y values. *Const* is TRUE (or omitted) to calculate the constant b normally, FALSE to force b equal to 0.

TRIMMEAN

Purpose: Calculates the mean of an interior data set. You use this function to exclude spurious outliers from your data analysis.

Syntax: TRIMMEAN*(array, percent)*

Arguments: *Array* is the range of values to use, and *percent* is the fractional number of data points to trim from the data set.

TTEST

Purpose: Calculates the probability value associated with the t-test, which determines whether two samples come from the same or different underlying populations.

Syntax: TTEST*(array1, array2, tails, type)*

Arguments: *Array1* and *array2* are the two data sets. *Tails* is the number of tails in the test (1 or 2). *Type* is the kind of t-test to perform (1=paired, 2=two-sample equal variance, 3=two-sample unequal variance).

VAR

Purpose: Calculates the variance of a sample.

Syntax: VAR*(number1, number2, ...)*

Arguments: *Number* is up to 30 values to be included in the calculation. You can use a reference to cells.

VARP

Purpose: Calculates the variance for an entire population.

Syntax: VARP*(number1, number2, ...)*

Arguments: *Number* is up to 30 values to be included in the calculation. You can use a reference to cells.

WEIBULL

Purpose: Calculates the Weibull distribution, used in reliability analysis.

Syntax: WEIBULL*(x, alpha, beta, cumulative)*

Arguments: *X* is the value at which the function will evaluate, *alpha* and *beta* are parameters for the distribution, and *cumulative* determines the form of the function (TRUE for the cumulative distribution, FALSE for the probability mass function).

ZTEST

Purpose: Calculates the two-tailed probability value associated with the z-test, used to determine whether data was drawn from the same or different populations.

Syntax: ZTEST*(array, x, sigma)*

Arguments: *Array* is the data set to test. *X* is the value to test for the likelihood it was drawn from the population. *Sigma* is the population standard deviation. (If omitted, the sample standard deviation substitutes.)

Text Functions

Excel's text functions enable you to manipulate text in your worksheets. You can format text, search for text, substitute text, and perform other such operations outlined for each function. Examples for functions described in this section appear in the example spreadsheet in figure 8.9.

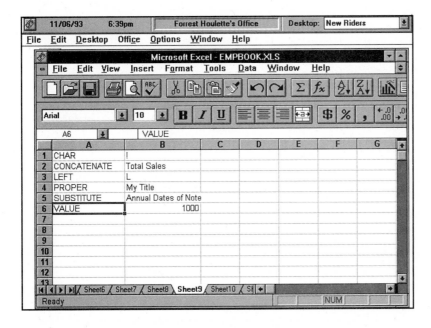

Figure 8.9

An example spreadsheet showing the use of text functions.

CHAR

Purpose: Gets the character associated with a code number.

Syntax: CHAR*(number)*

Arguments: *Number* is the number that represents the ASCII code for the character you want.

CLEAN

Purpose: Strips nonprintable characters from text.

Syntax: CLEAN*(text)*

Arguments: *Text* is the worksheet information you wish to clean of nonprinting characters.

CODE

Purpose: Gets the numeric code associated with the first character in a text string.

Syntax: CODE*(text)*

Arguments: *Text* is the text string for which the function returns the code of the first character.

CONCATENATE

Purpose: Links several text strings into a single text string.

Syntax: CONCATENATE *(text1, text2, ...)*

Arguments: *Text* is up to 30 text strings that you want to concatenate into a single text string. You can use references to cells containing text as arguments.

DOLLAR

Purpose: Converts a number to text in an appropriate currency format.

Syntax: DOLLAR*(number, decimals)*

Arguments: *Number* is a numeric value, a formula that evaluates as a numeric value, or a reference to a cell holding a numeric value. *Decimals* is the number of decimal places to include. (If decimals is omitted, Excel assumes a value of 2.)

EXACT

Purpose: Returns TRUE if the text strings in the argument list are exactly the same.

Syntax: EXACT*(text1, text2)*

Arguments: *Text1* and *text2* are the two text strings to compare.

FIND

Purpose: Searches for a string of text within another string of text. The return value is the position of the first character in the found string. This function is case-sensitive and will not accept wild-card characters.

Syntax: FIND*(find_text, within_text, start_num)*

Arguments: *Find_text* is the text to find. *Within_text* is the text to search in. *Start_num* is the position in the string at which to start the search.

FIXED

Purpose: Rounds a number to the given number of decimal places and converts the number to text with the appropriate use of periods and commas.

Syntax: FIXED*(number, decimals, no_commas)*

Arguments: *Number* is the number to round and convert. *Decimals* is the number of decimal places. *No_commas* is a logical value. If TRUE, no commas appear in the text returned. If FALSE or omitted, the text returned includes commas.

LEFT

Purpose: Returns the far left number of characters specified from a text string.

Syntax: LEFT*(text, num_chars)*

Arguments: *Text* is the text string from which to get characters. *Num_chars* is the number of characters to get. (If omitted, Excel assumes a value of 1 for *num_chars*.)

LEN

Purpose: Gets the number of characters that make up a text string. This function counts spaces as characters.

Syntax: LEN*(text)*

Arguments: *Text* is the text whose length is determined.

LOWER

Purpose: Converts a text string to all lower case.

Syntax: LOWER*(text)*

Arguments: *Text* is the text to convert.

MID

Purpose: Gets the specified number of characters from a text string, starting at the position you indicate.

Syntax: MID*(text, start_num, num_chars)*

Arguments: *Text* is the string from which to get characters. *Start_num* is the position at which to begin selection. *Num_chars* is the number of characters to get.

PROPER

Purpose: Capitalizes the first letter in a text string, as well as any letters that come after characters that are not letters, like spaces and punctuation marks. All other characters are converted to lower case. This function can be used to capitalize all words in a title.

Syntax: PROPER*(text)*

Arguments: *Text* is the text to convert.

REPLACE

Purpose: Replaces a given number of characters starting at a given position with a new set of characters.

Syntax: REPLACE*(old_text, start_num, num_chars, new_text)*

Arguments: *Old_text* is the text in which characters are replaced. *Start_num* is the position of the character to be replaced. *Num_chars* is the number of characters to replace. *New_text* is the text that replaces characters in *old_text*.

REPT

Purpose: Repeats a text string a specified number of times. This function can fill a cell with a fixed number of instances of the same text string.

Syntax: REPT*(text, number_times)*

Arguments: *Text* is the text to repeat. *Number_times* is the number of times to repeat.

RIGHT

Purpose: Gets the far right number of characters specified in a text string.

Syntax: RIGHT*(text, num_chars)*

Arguments: *Text* is the text string or reference to a cell containing text from which to get characters. *Num_chars* is the number of characters to get. (If omitted, Excel assumes a value of 1 for *num_chars*.)

SEARCH

Purpose: Gets the number of the character at which the specified text is found, going from left to right, in a text string. This function accepts wild-card characters.

Syntax: SEARCH*(find_text, within_text, start_num)*

Arguments: *Find_text* is the text to find. *Within_text* is the text to search within. *Start_num* is the position within *within_text* at which to start the search.

SUBSTITUTE

Purpose: In a text string, substitutes the new text you specify for the old text you specify.

Syntax: SUBSTITUTE*(text, old_text, new_text, instance_num)*

Arguments: *Text* is the text string or reference to a cell holding text in which to substitute characters. *Old_text* is the text to replace. *New_text* is the text to substitute in place of the *old_text*.

T

Purpose: Gets the text referred to by a value. (Generally, you do not need to use this function because Excel automatically performs this action for you.)

Syntax: T*(value)*

Arguments: *Value* is the value to test. *Value* can be a reference to a cell, a text string, or any other value. If *value* refers to text, the text is returned. Otherwise "" is returned.

TEXT

Purpose: Converts a numeric value to text in the numeric format you specify.

Syntax: TEXT*(value, format_text)*

Arguments: *Value* is a number, a formula that evaluates a number, or a reference to a cell containing a number. *Format_text* is the number format in text form that you want to use.

TRIM

Purpose: Standardizes the spacing in a text string by removing all spaces but the single spaces between words.

Syntax: TRIM*(text)*

Arguments: *Text* is the text string or reference to a cell holding text from which you want the spaces removed.

UPPER

Purpose: Converts a text string to uppercase.

Syntax: UPPER*(text)*

Arguments: *Text* is the string or reference to a cell holding text that you want to convert.

VALUE

Purpose: Converts the text to number.

Syntax: VALUE*(text)*

Arguments: *Text* is the text string or reference to a cell holding text that you want to convert.

Chapter Snapshot

In this chapter, you learn about using the Analysis ToolPak provided with Excel. This bonus package of software applications enables the user to apply statistical analysis in an easy-to-use fashion. Statistics have always been frightening for most people, but after you complete this chapter and work a few of the examples—and some of your own—you'll work numbers like a pro. Chapter 9 leads you through the following:

✔ Installing the Analysis ToolPak

✔ Understanding the Analysis Tools

✔ Using Business Tools

✔ Using Engineering Tools

✔ Using Statistical Tools

The examples given in this chapter should help you get started. Feel free to use and experiment with them as you want. If you can't quite master a tool or two right away, don't worry. Find some that you want to work with, and after you have mastered those, you can go back and try one of the others. The more you use these tools, the easier it becomes, and you will soon wonder how you ever managed without them!

Mastering Excel Analytical Tools

Excel 5, along with the Analysis ToolPak, can rival—and even rise above—other software packages that are designed solely as statistical analysis packages. Using the data analysis tools in the Analysis ToolPak, you easily can perform simple or complex statistics with any amount of data. The results of the analysis then can be used as the basis of further calculations, graphed in a variety of ways, or both. Excel 5's robust features add an extra dimension to statistical analysis by enabling you to merge statistics into spreadsheet calculations or database operations. You can organize your data in separate workbooks or on separate worksheets of the same workbook, and still have access to it all from the data analysis tools in the Analysis ToolPak.

Installing the Analysis ToolPak

If the Data Analysis entry already appears in your Tools menu, skip this section—the Analysis ToolPak has already been installed in your copy of Excel. If not, use the steps that follow to install the Analysis ToolPak.

NOTE   Be sure to close Excel before you run Setup. If you do not, Setup first asks you to close Excel. You might as well save time by doing it now.

Installing the Analysis ToolPak Add-In

To install the Analysis ToolPak, follow these steps:

1. In the Windows File Manager, change to your Excel directory, then double-click on SETUP.EXE to run the Microsoft Excel Setup program. You also can run SETUP.EXE from the Control menu's Run command.

2. Click on the Add/Remove button. A series of checkboxes for the available options appear (see fig. 9.1).

STOP   The items currently installed are already checked; do not uncheck those items unless you are sure you want to remove them from your system.

3. Double-click anywhere on the word Add-ins or its checkbox. The Microsoft Excel 5.0 — Add-ins dialog box appears, showing a list of add-ins with checkboxes (see fig. 9.2).

4. If not already checked, click on Analysis ToolPak to select it, then click on OK and proceed with the rest of the Excel Setup, inserting the appropriate disk(s) as prompted.

NOTE   If Analysis ToolPak is already checked, the Analysis ToolPak is already present in your system. You can exit Setup (click on Cancel) and go on to the next section.

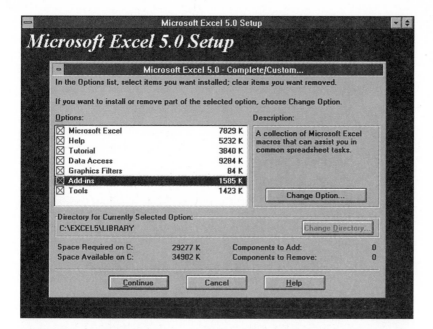

Figure 9.1
Complete/Custom
installation
options.

Figure 9.2
Excel 5's optional
add-ins.

Adding the Analysis ToolPak to an Excel Menu

After you install the add-in tools, you must let Excel know they now are available. Use the following steps:

1. Select the Tools menu, then select Add-ins. After a moment, the Add-ins dialog box appears, displaying all the available add-ins, as shown in figure 9.3.

2. Click on the Analysis checkbox and select OK. Click on OK in the Adding Analysis .XLL dialog box. Data Analysis then appears in the Tools menu.

Figure 9.3
The available
add-ins.

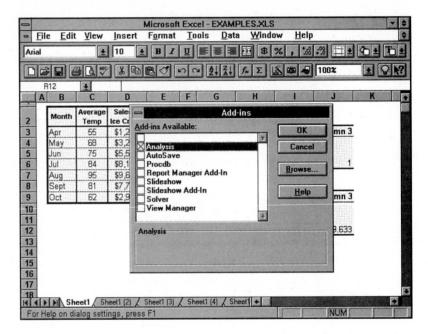

Understanding the Analysis Tools

For clarity, this discussion is split into three tool types: business tools, engineering tools, and pure statistical tools. Although all these tools are statistical in nature, they are grouped into their most commonly used fields. Their uses, however, are not restricted to any one field. Histograms, for example, are discussed in the "Business Tools" section, but also are used by engineers and statisticians.

Each section explains the use of a particular tool and provides an example of each. Many sections in this chapter contain an introductory paragraph that assumes little or no prior knowledge of statistics. These paragraphs are not intended as complete discussions of each statistical operator, but rather, are simple explanations intended to bridge the gap for the uninitiated into a more full explanation of each statistical tool in the ToolPak. Tools that

require more prior knowledge of statistical terms than an introductory paragraph can dutifully perform do not include such a paragraph.

To use any tool in the ToolPak, select Data Analysis from the Tools menu. The Data Analysis dialog box appears, as shown in figure 9.4. Scroll through the list until you find the tool you want to use, and either double-click on it or click on it and then choose OK. You also can use the up- or down-arrow keys to scroll through the list.

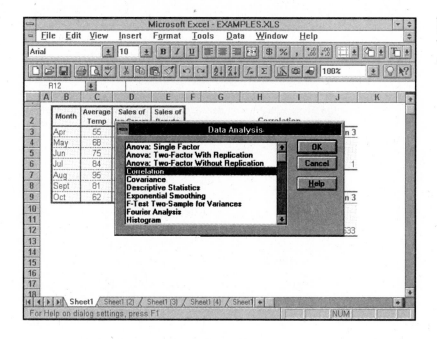

Figure 9.4
The Data Analysis dialog box.

Using Business Tools

The tools discussed in this section are statistical tools used more often in business applications than anywhere else. The tools covered in this section are:

- ✔ Correlation

- ✔ Covariance

- ✔ Exponential Smoothing

- ✔ Histogram

- ✔ Moving Average

- ✔ Random Number

- ✔ Rank and Percentile

These tools are not only used in business applications. Generally, the tools explained in this section are the most basic and easiest to use of the statistical tools in the Analysis ToolPak. It pays to know what each one of them does, regardless of how you might plan to use them.

Most of the dialog boxes for the tools in this section have some common features, including the following:

- ✔ **Input Range.** In the Input Range field, enter the range of cells in a spreadsheet where the source data resides. You can enter the range in A1 or R1C1 format—depending on Excel's setting, and you can include external references.

- ✔ **Grouped By.** If the source data is oriented in columns, select the Grouped By Column option button. For data that is oriented in row(s), select the Grouped by Rows option button.

- ✔ **Labels in First Row.** If the Input Range includes labels for each column in the first row of the range, check Labels in First Row to indicate that the row does not contain data. If you have labels in the first row of data, but did not select this box, Excel assumes that the first row contains data that it can use, and Excel tries to compute the first row with the rest of the data. This mistake can either throw off your result, or generate an error message.

- ✔ **Output Range.** The result of the tool appears in the cell location that you indicate in the Output Range. Single-cell reference can be used for an output range, to indicate the upper left corner of the resultant data; Excel automatically expands the range to include as many cells as necessary.

- ✔ **New Worksheet Ply.** Selecting this option enables you to send the tool's results to a new worksheet in the same workbook. To do this, you need to check the box and supply Excel with a name for the new sheet.

- ✔ **New Workbook.** If you want to send the tool's results to an entirely new workbook, check this box.

Correlations

A *correlation* can indicate whether a particular set of data might be related by cause-and-effect to another set of data. The Correlation tool checks each data point against its corresponding data point in the other data set. It returns a positive number if both sets of numbers move in the same direction (positive or negative) throughout the data. Likewise, it returns a negative number if the sets of numbers move in opposite directions (positive or negative). The more closely the sets of values move together, the higher the correlation value. A correlation value of 1 indicates that the values move exactly together, and a value of -1 indicates that they move exactly opposite.

If more than two sets of data are given, correlation values are returned for each set of data to every other set of data. The data to be analyzed must be located in adjacent rows or columns.

The example shows three columns from which correlation is drawn: column 1 is Average

Temp, Column 2 is Sales of Ice Cream, and Column 3 is Sales of Donuts. You can see that a high correlation exists between Average Temp and Sales of Ice Cream, and very little for donut sales.

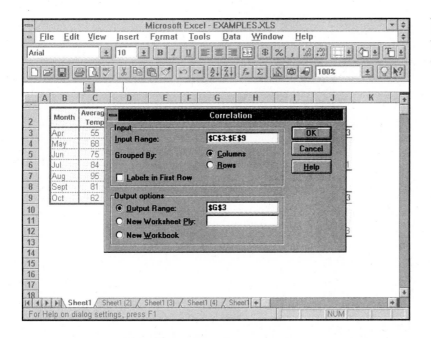

Figure 9.5

The Correlation dialog box.

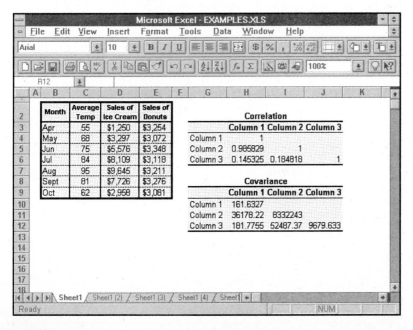

Figure 9.6

Example of correlation and covariance.

Covariances

Covariance is much like correlation, except covariances aren't restricted to numbers between -1 and +1. Thus, results from covariance can be misleading if different units or widely different data set values are compared. You might want to use covariance under special circumstances, such as when dealing with sets of closely similar data or for more in-depth statistical analysis; but correlation is useful far more often.

In the example, you can see how covariance can be misleading. The covariance of Column (Average Temp to Column 2 (Sales of Ice Cream) is 36178, but the covariance of Column 2 to Column 3 (Sales of Donuts) is 52487, or greater than that of Column 1 to 2. This fact suggests that the sales of ice cream and sales of donuts are closely related, but a look at the correlations for these columns tells you that they are not related. The correlation values are, in this case, the correct numbers, and say that only as the temperature goes up, so do ice cream sales.

Covariances can be useful in comparing, for example, two years of sales data for ice cream. The data in this case would be about the same, but would more closely show relationships because of the larger resulting numbers. For in-depth statistical analysis, the covariance results can be more useful when using them in succeeding calculations because they have not been "normalized" to 1.

You use the Covariance dialog box (see fig. 9.7) in much the same way you use the Correlation dialog box. The results of both the correlation and covariance examples are shown in figure 9.6 to better show the relationship between the two tools.

Figure 9.7
The Covariance
dialog box.

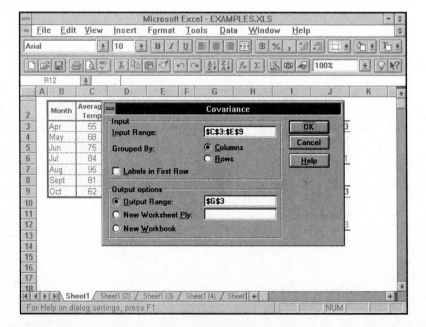

Exponential Smoothing

Exponential smoothing is most commonly used to forecast trends—a forecast is generated that shows the current trend of existing data. You then can tailor a forecast using a "Damping Factor" to smooth out random variations in the data or to detect trends in the data that are delayed from their stimulus.

A good example is plotting mortgage applications to determine housing sales. The actual housing sales are delayed from their loan applications because of the time it takes for the lender to process the loan. This results in about a one month or so delay between mortgage applications and the desired housing sales trend. The mortgage applications suddenly stop, housing sales will still continue for about a month; if applications suddenly abound, however, sales will not start booming for about a month.

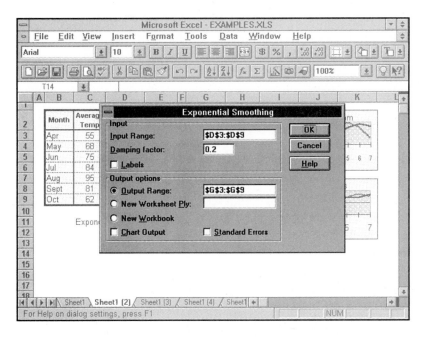

Figure 9.8
The Exponential Smoothing dialog box.

The Damping factor field enables you to tune the sensitivity of the smoothed output to any variability of the input data. A larger damping factor provides smoother data. A good damping factor to use is between 0.2 and 0.3—these numbers are a good balance between highly smoothed output data (greater than 0.5) and an output that is sensitive to changes in the input data (less than 0.1).

In the example in figure 9.9, if you had data for many years of ice cream sales—and you wanted to know in general if your business was improving or receding, you would want to choose a large damping factor (for example, 0.8) to mask the seasonal variation in sales and show you the "big picture." If, however, you wanted to see how your business varied from week to week, you would probably want a small damping factor (for example, 0.1) to show those weekly fluctuations in sales. These damping factors are not given as fixed numbers, but as general starting points for analysis. You will probably need to use different damping factors a few times until you get just the results you want.

If you select the Chart Output option, Excel automatically generates a chart for the output data. The charts presented in this chapter, however, were generated manually for better appearance in this book. Automatic charts are quick, however, and usually work well for interactively displaying "pictures" of the numerical results.

If you select the Standard Errors checkbox, Excel includes standard errors for each data point in the output data. *Errors* are how much the smoothed output data is different from the raw input data.

Notice the charted result for the Donut Sales data in figure 9.9. The smoothed data makes the sales trend more obvious than does the raw data. The raw data tends to fluctuate up and down, and it is difficult to see just from that line whether sales are growing, declining, or holding steady. The smoothed line shows clearly that sales are on the rise.

Figure 9.9
Examples of exponential smoothing.

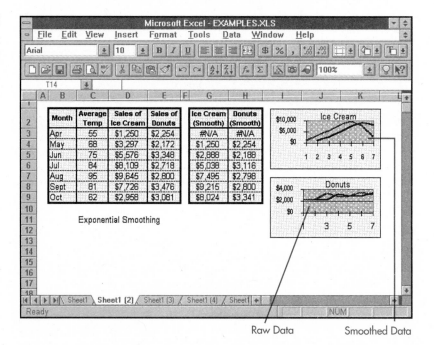

Raw Data   Smoothed Data

Histograms

A *histogram* counts the number of occurrences of a unique piece of information within a set of data. Each unique piece of information is called a *bin*, and the number of times each bin is repeated in a set of data is called the *frequency*.

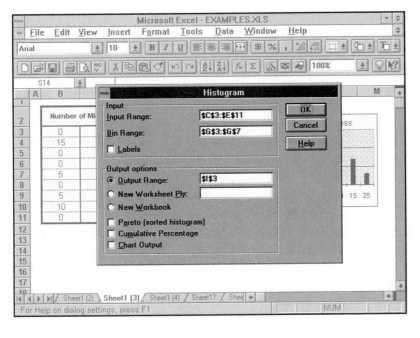

Figure 9.10
The Histogram
dialog box.

Worksheets

Excel 5 generates bins by default if you do not enter anything in the Bin Range field. But if you want to show only certain bins, or explicitly declare bins, enter the bin you want to show in a specific row or column, then indicate that range in the Bin Range field.

You can get a Pareto histogram (not shown) by selecting the Pareto checkbox under Output options. A *Pareto histogram* uses the same data as a standard histogram, but the bins are presented in descending order of frequency, rather than simply in order of bin numbers. The first (leftmost) bar in a Pareto chart would always be the tallest bar, and the chart would proceed in order from left to right, concluding with the rightmost bar as the shortest.

If the Cumulative Percentage checkbox is selected, cumulative percentages are included in the output data. *Cumulative percentage* is the percentage of data covered from the first bin to the current bin. Cumulative percentage is most useful with Pareto histograms, because it indicates the percentage of the total that the largest bins occupy. In the example, a cumulative percentage of the 10 minute bin would equal the number of times the employee was 10 minutes late for work, or 14+6+6=26 times.

Check the Chart Output checkbox if you want Excel to automatically generate charts for the output data. The chart presented in this example was, however, generated manually.

Moving Averages

A *moving average* is the average of a range of data taken from within a set of data. Moving averages are typically used in forecasting in this example, as we want to see the trend in donut sales and make some guesses from it about future sales. The input data points, which are used to generate the output data points, overlap. If, for example, three input data points are used to generate one output data point (an *interval* of 3), output data point #2 is generated from input data points #2, #3, and #4. Output data point #3 is generated from input data points #3, #4, and #5, and so on.

Figure 9.11
Histogram example.

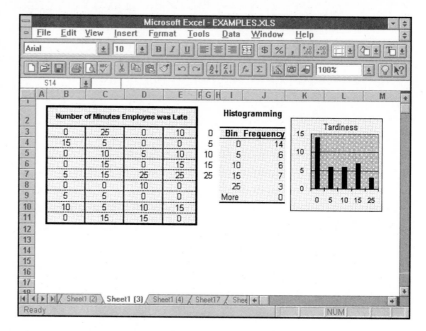

In our donut sales example, you can see how variations in sales are averaged into one generally increasing line. Notice how the average flattens out around the fifth and sixth months. This is the result of averaging the previous three months' sales—two of which were somewhat sluggish.

Another explanation of moving averages can be made by taking a year-long set of data, using only three months worth of data for each data point in a forecast. The total set of data fell significantly, but then returned to its original value. A total average in such a case indicates a zero trend, because the beginning and the end are at the same point—a flat trend. A moving average, however, shows a true upward trend, because only the most recent data points are used for the last few output data points.

The Moving Average dialog box is shown in figure 9.12.

The Interval field indicates the number of data points from the input data Excel should use to create each data point in the output data.

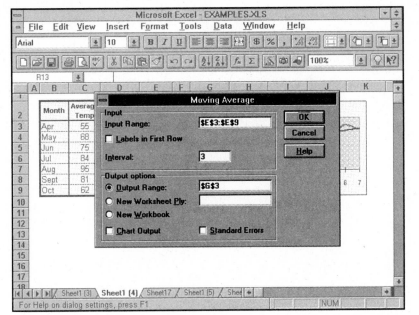

Figure 9.12
The Moving Average dialog box.

NOTE The total number of output data points is determined by the following formula:

(Number of input points — Interval + 1)

Check the Chart Output checkbox if you want Excel to automatically generate a chart for the output data.

Use the Standard Errors checkbox to include standard errors for each data point in the output data. These errors are the result of the differences between the raw input data and the averaged output data.

Random Numbers

Excel can generate a set of random numbers that fit certain criteria you specify in the Random Number Generation dialog box (see fig. 9.14). The most important of these criteria is *distribution*, or the chance that any random number will fall within certain limits. If you are unfamiliar with distributions, you might want to use the Uniform Distribution option at first, then experiment later with others. A *uniform distribution* simply generates random numbers between given upper and lower limits. There is not as much tailoring of the data available inside of those limits as there is in other distributions.

Figure 9.13
Moving Average
examples.

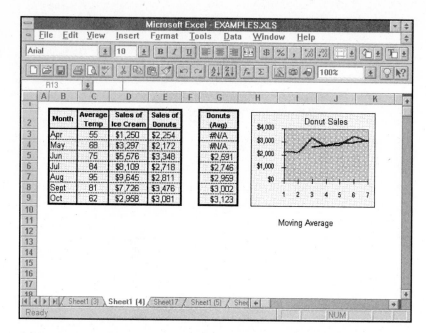

AUTHOR'S NOTE

More accurately, these numbers should be called *pseudorandom*, because the numbers are not truly random (instead, they are generated mathematically), but their distributions can be somewhat tailored for a specific use.

The Number of Variables field enables you to tailor the distribution of the random data by using more than one random variable to generate the random numbers. If you have this box blank, Excel assumes one variable.

The Number of Random Numbers field is where you indicate how many random numbers to generate.

In the Parameters box, your entry varies depending on the selected Distribution. If you use Uniform distribution, however, numbers can be given for the upper and lower limits (see Between and and) of the output data; all random numbers generated fall between the limits you specify.

Use Random Seed for any set of random numbers. Random Seed is the number Excel uses to initiate the mathematical process of generating pseudorandom numbers. Normally, Excel uses its own seed number, but you can enter a different number. Because the numbers are

generated mathematically and are not truly random, the numbers on rare occasions can follow a pattern. The pattern, if any does exist, might not be obvious, and certainly defeats the purpose of using "random" numbers. Entering your own seed number can sometimes ward off unwanted repetition of certain numbers or sequences of numbers.

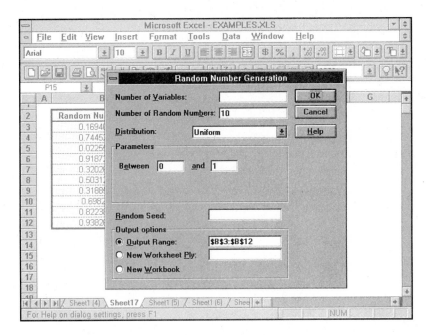

Figure 9.14
The Random Number Generation dialog box.

Two separate columns of random numbers are presented in the example to illustrate the use of the Parameters in the Uniform distribution (see fig. 9.15). The first list is a Uniform distribution set between 0 and 1; the second is a Uniform distribution set between 0 and 10.

Ranks and Percentiles

Rank and Percentile generates a list of all values within a set of data, assigns each a rank from greatest to least, and generates the percentile of each data point to the top data point in the data set. This tool is most commonly used in schools and universities to calculate each student's class rank (like, 8th out of 92 in the class) and the student's percentile in the class (84 percent, or in the top 16 percent of the class). See the Rank and Percentile dialog box in figure 9.16.

In the example in figure 9.17, a Rank and Percentile are performed on the Donut sales column. The sales figures are ranked from highest to lowest sales volume so you can see at a quick glance how high and how low sales became during the plotted period of time. Each point is also ranked in order and assigned a percent value from the current, highest value.

Figure 9.15
Two sets of random numbers with different parameters.

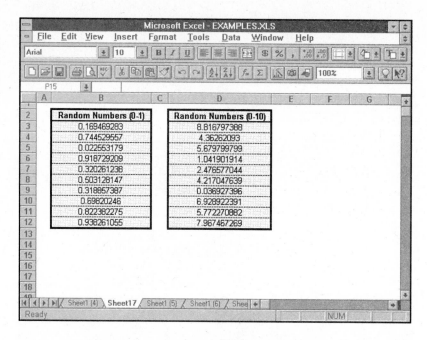

Figure 9.16
The Rank and Percentile dialog box.

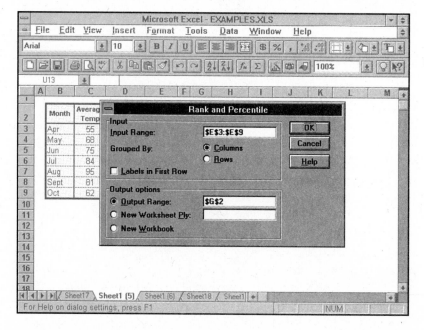

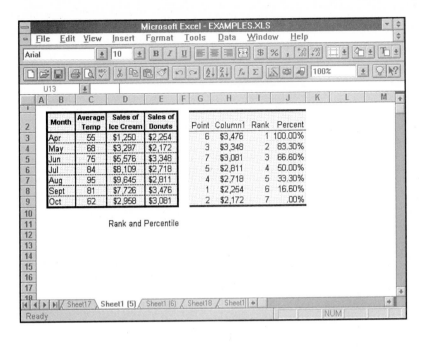

Figure 9.17
Rank and
Percentile
example.

Using Engineering Tools

The tools discussed in this section are statistical tools used most often in engineering applications. These tools include the following:

✔ Fourier Analysis

✔ Sampling

As in the previous section, these tools are not dedicated to engineering use only. Although Fourier Analysis is rarely used outside of engineering circles, Sampling is a useful tool in many areas, especially where a great deal of data is analyzed.

The dialog boxes for these tools have some common features, including the following:

✔ **Input Range.** In the Input Range field, enter the range of cells in a spreadsheet where the source data resides. You can enter the range in either A1 or R1C1 format—depending on Excel's setting—and you can include external references.

✔ **Grouped By.** If the source data is oriented in columns, select the Grouped By Column option button. For data that is oriented in row(s), select the Grouped by Rows option button.

✔ **Labels in First Row.** If the Input Range entered above includes labels for each column in the first row of the range, check Labels in First Row to indicate that the row does not contain data. If you have labels in the first row of data, but did not select this box, Excel assumes that the first row contains data that it can use, and Excel tries to compute the first row with the rest of the data. This can either throw off your result, or generate an error message.

- ✔ **Output Range.** The result of the tool appears in the cell location that you indicate in the Output Range. Single-cell reference can be used for an output range, to indicate the upper left corner of the resultant data; Excel automatically expands the range to include as many cells as necessary.

- ✔ **New Worksheet Ply.** Selecting this option enables you to send the tool's results to a new worksheet in the same workbook. To do this, you need to check the box and supply Excel with a name for the new sheet.

- ✔ **New Workbook.** If you want to send the tool's results to an entirely new workbook, check this box.

Fourier Analysis

Fourier analysis is most often used by engineers to translate a set of time-dependent (*time-domain*) data into a set of complex constants (*frequency-domain*) that more clearly show the frequencies of certain data. See the Fourier Analysis dialog box in figure 9.18.

Figure 9.18

The Fourier Analysis dialog box.

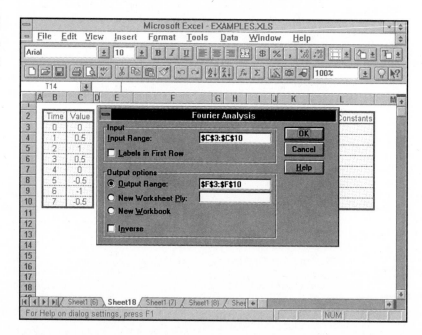

Excel requires that the number of input data points be a factor of 2 (2, 4, 8, 16, and so on).

An *inverse fourier* transform is available by selecting the I<u>n</u>verse check box. This procedure converts frequency-domain data into time-domain data.

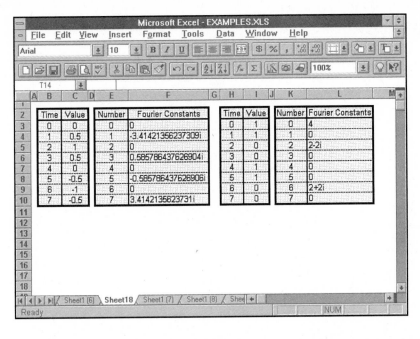

Figure 9.19
Two separate examples of Fourier Analysis.

Two different sets of time-domain data are presented in the example (see fig. 9.19) to illustrate different frequency-domain outputs produced by Excel 5's fourier transform.

Two standard wave forms are shown in the preceding figure. The first is a triangle wave of amplitude Vpk=2v and period t=8 milliseconds.

The "Number" column is the harmonic number of the frequency output. Harmonic 0 is DC, harmonic 1 is the fundamental frequency (in this case, 125hz), harmonic 2 is the second harmonic (250hz), and so on. The Fourier Constants column is the amplitude of the given harmonic, presented as a complex number.

Sampling

Sampling extracts a selected number of values from a set of data. Sampling helps to reduce the size of a large set of data, while changing its overall qualities as little as possible.

Two sampling methods are available in Excel 5. The first method, periodic, moves down the data in order and returns every *interval* number of input data points as an output data point. You specify the interval in the Period edit box. An interval of 3, for instance, samples every third data point. The second method is termed Random. Use it to generate a specified number of output data points randomly chosen from the input data.

Both sampling methods are shown in this figure 9.21. The ice cream sales data was periodically sampled, and the donut sales data was randomly sampled.

Figure 9.20
The Sampling
dialog box.

Figure 9.20
The Sampling
dialog box.

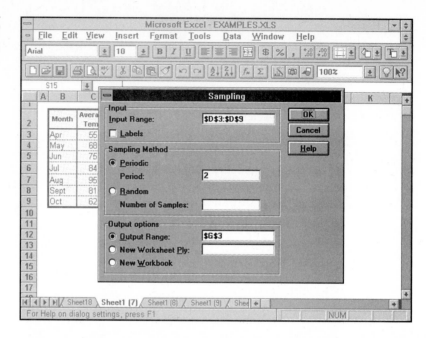

Figure 9.21
The results of the
different types of
sampling.

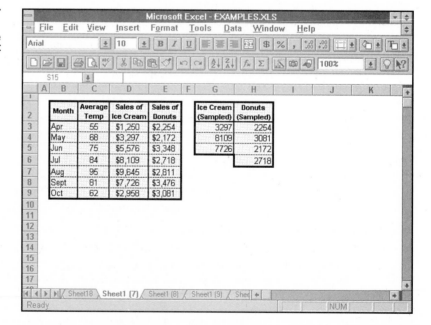

Notice that periodic samples ("Ice Cream Sales") might not include the true peak and low sales, even with a large volume of data. This fact can be especially true if the sample interval is high and only a few data points are taken for a lot of data. The data order is retained, however, and you can draw a general trend from the sampled data.

Random samples ("Donut Sales") can include the peak sales and low sales values, even if only a few samples are taken. Data order is lost, however; you have no way to track back and find out at what time each of the data points occurred. Thus, you cannot draw general trends from this sampled data. Random sampling, however, is more effective than periodic when used with distribution and average statistics.

Using Statistical Tools

The tools discussed in this final section are purely statistical tools. The tools in this group include the following:

- ✔ Anova
- ✔ Descriptive Statistics
- ✔ Regression Analysis
- ✔ Sampling Tests

The tools in this section are not necessarily useful just to statisticians. Some, however (like the Sampling Tests), are better suited for those who are somewhat experienced in statistics. Descriptive statistics, however, can be very useful in many areas as they can give you easy access to such basic calculations as means (averages) and standard deviations.

The dialog boxes for these tools have some common features, including the following:

- ✔ **Input Range.** In the Input Range field, enter the range of cells in a spreadsheet where the source data resides. You can enter the range in either A1 or R1C1 format—depending on Excel's setting—and you can include external references.

- ✔ **Grouped By.** If the source data is oriented in columns, select the Grouped By Column option button. For data that is oriented in row(s), select the Grouped by Rows option button.

- ✔ **Labels in First Row.** If the Input Range entered above includes labels for each column in the first row of the range, check Labels in First Row to indicate that the row does not contain data. If you have labels in the first row of data, but did not select this box, Excel assumes that the first row contains data that it can use, and Excel tries to compute the first row with the rest of the data. This can either throw off your result, or generate an error message.

- ✔ **Output Range.** The result of the tool appears in the cell location that you indicate in the Output Range. Single-cell reference can be used for an output range, to indicate the upper left corner of the resultant data; Excel automatically expands the range to include as many cells as necessary.

✔ **New Worksheet Ply.** Selecting this options enables you to send the tool's results to a new worksheet in the same workbook. To do this, you need to check the box and supply Excel with a name for the new sheet.

✔ **New Workbook.** If you want to send the tool's results to an entirely new workbook, check this box.

Anova: Analysis of Variance

In general, an *analysis of variance*, or *Anova*, examines the mean values of multiple sets of data (assuming all means are equal) to determine if the mean values of samples taken from these sets also are equal. Three types of anova tools are available in Excel 5:

✔ **Anova: Single-Factor.** Performs a single factor analysis of variance. Data sets of different sizes can be used with this tool. A single-factor analysis of variance tests the effect of a single factor (one column on the sample).

✔ **Anova: Two-Factor With Replication.** Performs a two-factor anova, including more than one sample for each group of data. Data sets must be the same size.

A two-factor anova classifies input data by two different factors. The total variation is partitioned into the part which can be attributed to each factor (each row), and the interaction of each factor.

✔ **Anova: Two-Factor Without Replication.** Performs a two-factor anova, but does not include more than one sampling per group.

Figure 9.22
The Anova:
Single-Factor
dialog box.

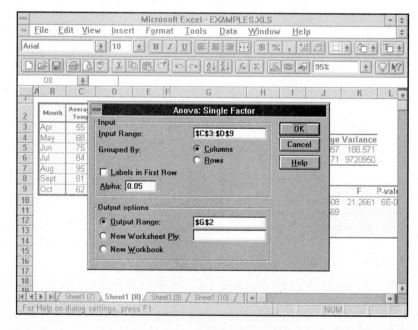

Enter the anova alpha factor in the <u>A</u>lpha box. The *alpha factor* is the significance of the fit as a whole. It is the significance level of the ration of the regression mean square value to the residual (error) mean square value.

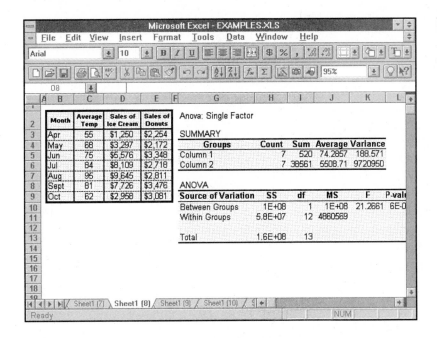

Figure 9.23

Single-factor anova results.

Worksheets

The Anova: Two-Factor With Replication dialog box is shown in figure 9.24. It is very similar to the Anova: Single Factor dialog box. You can use data from multiple rows as a single data point by indicating the number of rows to use in the Rows Per Sample box.

Figure 9.25 illustrates the results of the sample data.

Figure 9.26 shows the Anova: Two-Factor Without Replication dialog box, which works in much the same way as the other two anova dialog boxes. The results of figure 9.26 are illustrated in figure 9.27.

Descriptive Statistics

Descriptive statistics generate various numbers that describe properties of a data set, such as mean, standard deviation, and so on. The Descriptive Statistics dialog box is shown in figure 9.28.

Figure 9.24
The Anova: Two Factor With Replication dialog box.

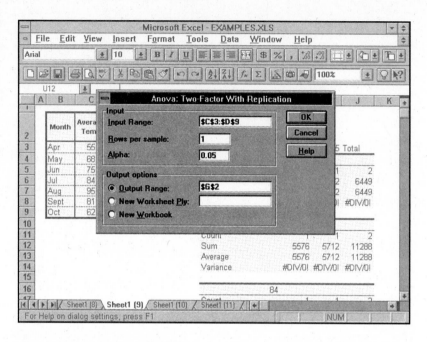

Figure 9.25
Two-factor with replication results.

Month	Average Temp	Sales of Ice Cream, Year 1	Sales of Ice Cream, Year 2
Apr	55	$1,250	$1,325
May	68	$3,297	$3,152
Jun	75	$5,576	$5,712
Jul	84	$8,109	$8,094
Aug	95	$9,645	$9,922
Sept	81	$7,726	$7,518
Oct	62	$2,958	$3,008

Anova: Two-Factor With Replication

SUMMARY	1250	1325	Total
68			
Count	1	1	2
Sum	3297	3152	6449
Average	3297	3152	6449
Variance	#DIV/0!	#DIV/0!	#DIV/0!
75			
Count	1	1	2
Sum	5576	5712	11288
Average	5576	5712	11288
Variance	#DIV/0!	#DIV/0!	#DIV/0!

	Total	
Count	6	6
Sum	37311	37406
Average	37311	37406
Variance	3E-164	3E-164

ANOVA

Source of Variation	SS	df	MS	F	P-value	F crit
Sample	8E+07	5	1.5E+07	65535	#NUM!	#NUM!
Columns	752.08	1	752.083	65535	#NUM!	#NUM!
Interaction	80367	5	16073.5	65535	#NUM!	#NUM!
Within	0	0	65535			
Total	8E+07	11				

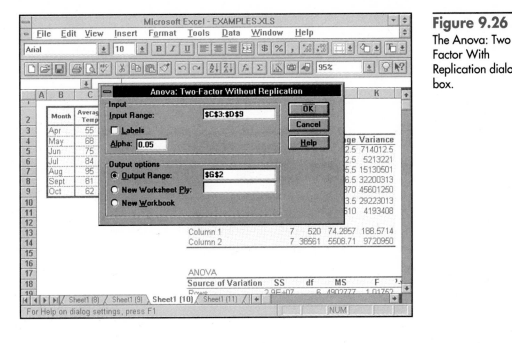

Figure 9.26
The Anova: Two Factor With Replication dialog box.

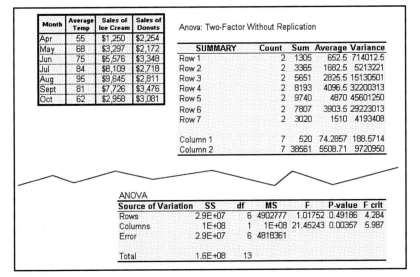

Figure 9.27
Two-factor without replication results.

Anova: Two-Factor Without Replication

SUMMARY	Count	Sum	Average	Variance
Row 1	2	1305	652.5	714012.5
Row 2	2	3365	1682.5	5213221
Row 3	2	5651	2825.5	15130501
Row 4	2	8193	4096.5	32200313
Row 5	2	9740	4870	45601250
Row 6	2	7807	3903.5	29223013
Row 7	2	3020	1510	4193408
Column 1	7	520	74.2857	188.5714
Column 2	7	38561	5508.71	9720950

ANOVA

Source of Variation	SS	df	MS	F	P-value	F crit
Rows	2.9E+07	6	4902777	1.01752	0.49186	4.284
Columns	1E+08	1	1E+08	21.45243	0.00357	5.987
Error	2.9E+07	6	4818361			
Total	1.6E+08	13				

Figure 9.28
The Descriptive Statistics dialog box.

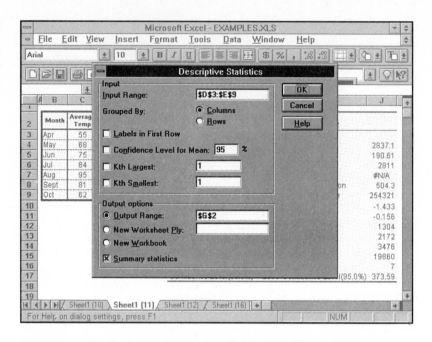

Enter the desired confidence level in the Confidence Level for Mean box. The confidence level, 95 percent in this example, means that 95 percent of the time a given data point will be contained within a certain range (interval) about the mean value.

The Kth largest and the Kth smallest boxes enable you to exclude a number of data points from either the largest of the data points, or the smallest—or both. Often, in large amounts of data, a few data points can be wildly different than the rest, and this difference can introduce error into your descriptive statistics. If you want to exclude, for example, the largest two values from your analysis, enter a 3 in the Kth largest box; the analysis will then start with the third-largest data point and proceed to the smallest. If then, you wanted to exclude the smallest value as well, enter 2 in the Kth smallest box. The analysis then ranges from the third-largest to the second smallest data values.

You also can ask Excel to provide **S**ummary statistics, which are shown in figure 9.29.

The descriptive statistics produced are as follows:

1. **Mean.** The average between the Kth largest and the Kth smallest values.

2. **Standard Error.** The standard error of the data.

3. **Median.** The middle value.

4. **Mode.** The mode of the data.

5. **Standard Deviation.** A measure of the data spread.

6. **Sample Variance.** Another measure of the data spread.

7. **Kurtosis.** A measure of the "tails" of a distribution, or how much of the data is far away from the mean.

8. **Skewness.** A measure of how the distribution of the data is "balanced" around the mean.

9. **Range.** The largest valued used minus the smallest value used.

10. **Minimum.** The smallest value used.

11. **Maximum.** The largest value used.

12. **Sum.** The total of all data points.

13. **Count.** The number of data points used.

14. **Confidence Level.** The interval (range) within which 95 percent of the time a given data point can be found.

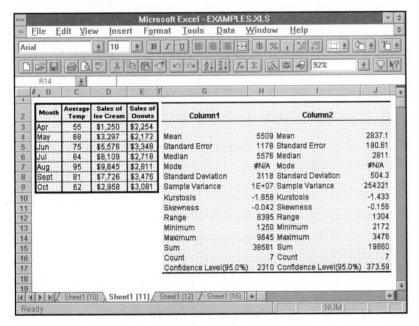

Figure 9.29
Examples of descriptive statistics for both columns.

Regression Analysis

Regression fits a smooth line (not necessarily a straight line) to a set of otherwise jagged data. This statistical tool is most often used graphically, where a straight or line is superimposed on rough data. Regression allows you to more easily see a trend where the trend may not be obvious from the raw data. Statistical data is also given for each data point. Regression is also useful in reducing raw data into a mathematically simple function.

The Regression dialog box is shown in figure 9.30. Use the Input X̲ and Y̲ Range fields to indicate where the X and Y data resides within the spreadsheet.

Figure 9.30
The Regression
dialog box.

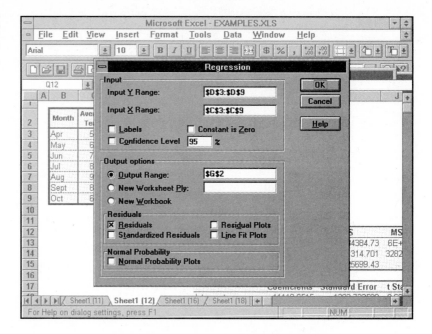

Regression uses a series of x-y values—coordinates of each data point—to calculate its results, then both the Input Y Range and the Input X Range must be entered.

The confidence level is the same as that described in the Descriptive Statistics section.

You have a variety of options for results to be displayed, in addition to the standard expression results. You can display the Residuals (errors), the Standardized Residuals, or both. You can choose to have the Residuals Plotted for each independent variable. A plot of the central data with the regression line also drawn on the same graph is available by selecting "Line Fit Plots." You also can specify a Normal Probability Plot to be displayed as well.

The statistic result is placed in the range indicated (the single reference points to the upper left corner of the result table). You also can select S̲ummary statistics.

The results of the example are partially shown in figure 9.31.

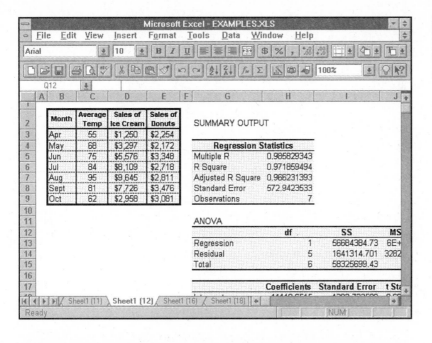

Figure 9.31
Portions of the Regression summary results.

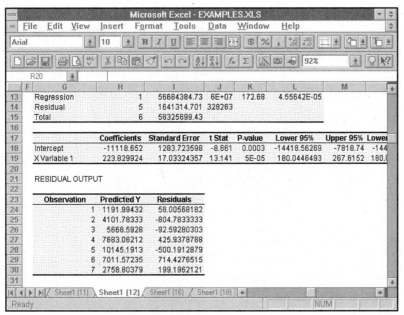

Sampling Tests

The *sampling tests* compare certain properties of two sets of data. Five varieties of this tool are available:

- ✔ **Two-Sample For Variances F-Test.** Compares the variances between two sets of data.

- ✔ **Paired Two-Sample for Means t-Test.** Compares the means between two paired sets of data. The data should show a natural pairing of data points, such as running the same experiment twice, and must contain the same number of data points. The variances between the two sets of data are not assumed to be equal.

- ✔ **Two-Sample Assuming Equal Variances t-Test.** Determines whether the means of two samples are equal, based upon the assumption that the variances of the two samples are equal.

- ✔ **Two-Sample Assuming Unequal Variances t-Test.** Determines whether the means of two samples are equal, based upon the assumption that the variances of the two samples are not equal.

- ✔ **Two-Sample For Means z-Test.** Tests the probability that a sample was drawn from a certain population.

The F-Test: Two-Sample For Variances dialog box appears in figure 9.32. Enter the data range in the Input Variable 1 and 2 Range fields. Enter the alpha factor in the Alpha edit box. The Output options section is identical to those discussed earlier in this chapter.

Figure 9.32
F-Test Two-Sample for Variances dialog box.

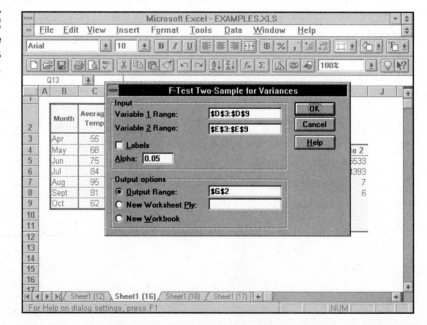

The dialog boxes for the remaining sampling test tools are all very similar and are used in the much same way. By studying figures 9.33 through 9.37, you can see the difference results returned by each of these tests.

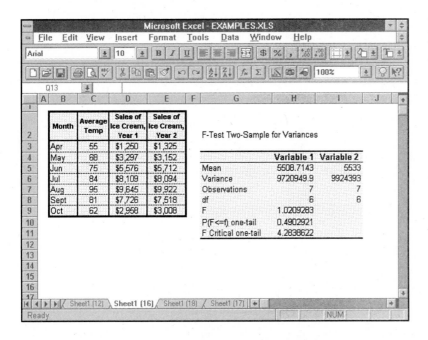

Figure 9.33
Two-sample for variances F-test results.

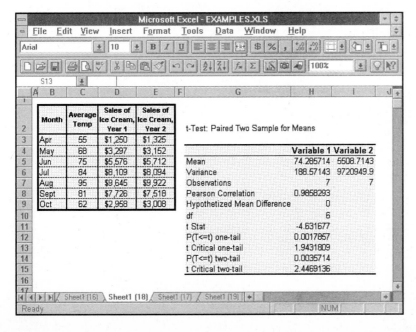

Figure 9.34
Paired two-sample for means t-test results.

Figure 9.35
Two-sample assuming equal variances t-test results.

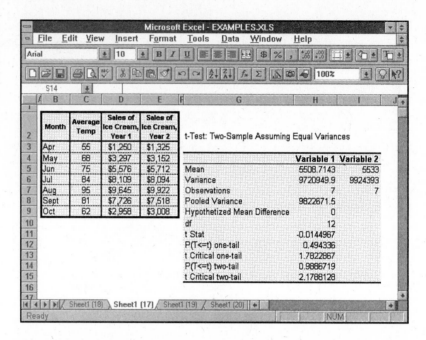

t-Test: Two-Sample Assuming Equal Variances

	Variable 1	Variable 2
Mean	5508.7143	5533
Variance	9720949.9	9924393
Observations	7	7
Pooled Variance	9822671.5	
Hypothetized Mean Difference	0	
df	12	
t Stat	-0.0144967	
P(T<=t) one-tail	0.494336	
t Critical one-tail	1.7822867	
P(T<=t) two-tail	0.9886719	
t Critical two-tail	2.1788128	

Month	Average Temp	Sales of Ice Cream, Year 1	Sales of Ice Cream, Year 2
Apr	55	$1,250	$1,325
May	68	$3,297	$3,152
Jun	75	$5,576	$5,712
Jul	84	$8,109	$8,094
Aug	95	$9,645	$9,922
Sept	81	$7,726	$7,518
Oct	62	$2,958	$3,008

Figure 9.36
Two-sample assuming unequal variances t-test results.

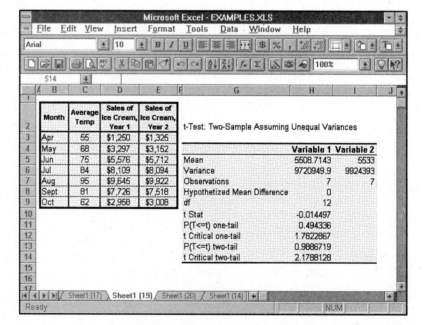

t-Test: Two-Sample Assuming Unequal Variances

	Variable 1	Variable 2
Mean	5508.7143	5533
Variance	9720949.9	9924393
Observations	7	7
Hypothetized Mean Difference	0	
df	12	
t Stat	-0.014497	
P(T<=t) one-tail	0.494336	
t Critical one-tail	1.7822867	
P(T<=t) two-tail	0.9886719	
t Critical two-tail	2.1788128	

Month	Average Temp	Sales of Ice Cream, Year 1	Sales of Ice Cream, Year 2
Apr	55	$1,250	$1,325
May	68	$3,297	$3,152
Jun	75	$5,576	$5,712
Jul	84	$8,109	$8,094
Aug	95	$9,645	$9,922
Sept	81	$7,726	$7,518
Oct	62	$2,958	$3,008

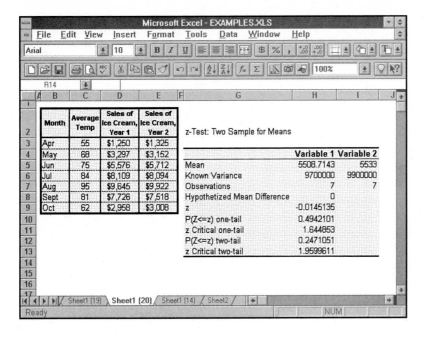

Figure 9.37
Two-sample for means z-test results.

Part II

Databases

Chapter Snapshot

Among Excel's more powerful capabilities are its excellent data-management features. Although Excel worksheets are most often used to manipulate numeric data, with a little work, your worksheets can be used as a database to store and retrieve text and other nonnumeric information. Chapter 10 presents the following information:

✔ Introducing database terminology

✔ Using spreadsheets as database tables

✔ Designing a database list in Excel

✔ Using Excel's data filters

✔ Sorting data in a list

✔ Knowing when to use a "real" database system

As you will see, Excel 5 provides interactive, visual methods for sorting, filtering, and searching the data stored in Excel worksheets. This chapter shows you the basic technology you must master to use Excel spreadsheets as databases.

10 CHAPTER

Excel Database Basics

usinesses run on data. Customer lists, inventory control, employee records, and sales histories all are examples of common business data-management needs.

In many ways, Microsoft Excel is the ideal data-management tool for small to medium businesses and many personal data-management needs. You can use Excel spreadsheets to store and retrieve data, just like more sophisticated, specialized database management systems. Excel also is more forgiving and easier to learn than most database systems, such as Microsoft FoxPro or Borland's dBASE.

Excel has many functions specifically designed to help you sort and filter data stored in worksheets. This chapter covers sorting and filtering, as well as general database design considerations for the novice database user.

Database Terminology

The first step to learning databases is to become familiar with the specialized database terminology database experts use. The following list is by no means complete and might be Excel-specific, but is intended to provide a basic understanding of common Excel database terms.

✔ **Database.** The term database is used in several different ways, depending on what database system is being used. In Microsoft FoxPro and Borland dBASE, for instance, a *database* is a single table that is part of a database application. A Microsoft Access database includes all of the tables, forms, and other objects that make up the application.

✔ **Table.** A database *table* is just like an Excel worksheet. An Excel database table contains rows and columns of data contained in the worksheet cells (which might be empty). A table is usually referred to as a *list* in Excel.

✔ **List.** In Excel terms, *list* is another name for a database table. Based on certain design elements (discussed later in this chapter) and the way in which it is used, Excel automatically recognizes a list on a worksheet.

✔ **Field.** A *field* is a column of data in a database table. A field contains a specific type of data, which might be alphanumeric or numeric. The fields in a table might include "Name," "Address," and "Phone Number." All fields in a database table are of the same type.

✔ **Record.** A *record* is a set of related data that corresponds to a row in the database table. A record in a database table might be a person's name, address, and phone number.

✔ **Query.** A *query* is a request to a database to retrieve data. Normally, a query only retrieves specific information from the database table.

In Excel terms, a *query definition* is all the information needed by Microsoft Query (an Excel add-in discussed in Chapter 11) to extract data from a source of data (like an external database). This information includes the table name(s), field name(s), and specific search criteria needed to complete the database search.

✔ **Query criteria or search criteria.** Because a *query* returns specific information from a database table or Excel list, some way must exist for specifying which data to extract from the table. The expressions *query criteria* and *search criteria* both apply to the set of information that specifies the data to be retrieved from the Excel list.

✔ **Query design.** When using Microsoft Query, *query design* refers to the tables, relationships between tables, and other elements included in the query criteria used to extract data from an external database.

Using Spreadsheets as Database Tables

Whatever the underlying database system, a table (or list, in Excel) consists of rows and columns of data. A Microsoft Excel worksheet is perfectly analogous to a database table in FoxPro, Access, or dBASE.

However, because Excel is designed primarily to handle financial or other numeric data, certain principles apply differently to Excel than to most other database systems.

Guidelines

Because many Excel features can be applied to only one list on a worksheet at a time, it is generally a good idea to put only one list on a worksheet. It also is a good idea to dedicate a worksheet to maintaining a single list of data.

Surround the list with blank rows above and below and blank columns to the left and right. This arrangement makes it easy for Excel to distinguish your list from other things on the worksheet.

As you soon learn, *filtering* a list hides rows that are excluded from the list, leaving only those fields meeting the selection criteria. If you have important information on the left or right of your list, it might be hidden when you filter the list.

Using the Data List

An Excel data list can be used interactively or through macros and other automation techniques. Excel provides a number of menu options that enable you to quickly and easily filter the data contained in lists. A number of macro functions greatly enhance your ability to utilize data in Excel lists and external databases. These techniques are discussed later in this chapter.

Databases

Basic Design Elements

As already mentioned, when you build Excel data lists, worksheet columns become fields and worksheet rows serve as database records. However, several other important concepts should be kept in mind as you design and build Excel data lists.

Designing a Database Worksheet

As an example of a common database, consider the address and phone directory you carry in your briefcase. This phone directory is correctly thought of as a *database* of contact information. Most often, these directories are pre-printed with areas for a person's name, an address, and phone numbers.

Columns Become Fields

Each of these areas is a *field* in the directory database. If you are designing an Excel worksheet to use as a phone directory, you should add *columns* for the name, address, and phone number information.

Rows Become Records

Each row in the worksheet will serve as a database *record* and will contain all of the contact information for a person.

Allow Enough Columns

Very often, people design databases without enough fields. You'll want columns for each different type of information you might want to access. As you will soon see, it would be much easier to search for a person's last name if it appears in a column of its own, rather than being included with the first name in the "Name" column. Most databases function more efficiently if only one type of data (like the first or last name) is stored in a field.

Figure 10.1 shows an Excel worksheet containing a data list that serves as a simple address book. In figure 10.1 the data list covers the entire worksheet.

Figure 10.1
A data list on an
Excel worksheet.

Microsoft Excel - ADDRESS.XLS

	First Name	Last Name	Address 1	Address 2	City	State	Zip	Phone
1								
2	Paul	Helms	7840 Southbay Drive		Carmel	IN	46032	317-555-2387
3	Richard	Lyons	9039 Fall Creek Rd		Carmel	IN	46032	317-555-9067
4	Pam	Fields						317-844-7261
5	Stuart	Wagner						813-555-1939
6	Karen	McGraw	8442 Doral Drive		Indy	IN	46180	317-555-6769
7	Mike	Lewis	7681 E. Davenport		Iowa City	IA	52240	319-555-9110
8	Steve	Miller	11326 Rolling Rock Drive		Orlando	FL	33936	813-555-4104
9	Lee	Perkins	9551 Vest Mill Road		Winston-Salem	NC	27103	919-555-2085
10	Brad	Pease	8854 Sunblest Lane		Hingham	MA	02186	617-555-9639
11	Harry	Slabosky	11918 College Drive		Indianapolis	IN	46110	317-555-0805
12	David	Allen	1350 Pennsylvania Ave		Indianapolis	IN	46130	317-555-8712
13	Tim	Murray	1473 Stormy Ridge		Galesburg	FL	33936	813-555-5287
14	Linda	Matthews	8713 Woodstock Ct.		Hingham	MA	01287	617-555-2279
15	Tom	Reid	6244 Dover Court		Marlboro	MA	02173	508-555-0381
16	Darryl	Ryan	680 West Piper		Erie	PA	16506	814-555-1162
17	Cliff	Flanders	861 Gulfview Terrace	#136	Ft. Meyers	FL	33935	813-555-5952
18	Sheila	Miller	7127 Plaza Lane	#23	Carmel	IN	46032	317-555-2521
	David	Lovett	8415 Deer Ridge Rd	#12	Speedway	IN	46810	317-555-9353

Sheet1 / Sheet2 / Sheet3 / Sheet4 / Sheet5

Ready

Use Column Labels

It is generally a good idea to use column labels on the list. Excel uses column labels when finding data in the list and for creating reports from the data.

Column labels should appear in a different font or typeface than the data stored in the column. Most often, column labels will appear in a bold typeface. It's enough to use a pattern or cell border to distinguish the column labels from the data in the columns.

If you want to separate the column labels from the data in the column, use a border along the bottom of the labels, rather than empty cells. If the column labels aren't contiguous with the data in the columns, Excel won't know that the column labels belong to the list.

Entering Data into Cells

When entering data into the cells of an Excel data list, don't put blanks at the beginning of a cell. The extra blanks will be used by Excel when sorting the list and might cause unexpected results.

Some Windows fonts (for instance, Arial) are *proportionally spaced*, which means that blanks take up less room than wide characters like "m" or "w." The extra blanks at the front of cells displayed in a proportionally spaced font can be difficult to see.

Formatting Cells

Use the same font characteristics (bold, size, and so on) for all of the cells in a column. Arbitrarily mixing typefaces can lead to some unnecessary confusion.

Name the List and its Major Elements

After you have the basic list in place, assign a name to the entire list. If you plan to use the worksheet only to hold the data list, assign the list name by highlighting all of the columns in the list, and selecting the Name option from the Insert menu. The cascading menu shown in figure 10.2 will appear.

When you select Define from the cascading menu, the Define Name dialog box (see fig. 10.3) appears. Enter the name you want to assign to your data list in the Names in Workbook text field.

In figure 10.3, names have already been applied to the Address, First Name, and Last Name columns. Each of these columns was named by highlighting the column, and entering appropriate names in the Define Name dialog box. Later, these columns and the list can be referenced by the names assigned to them.

II

Databases

Figure 10.2
The Name
cascading menu.

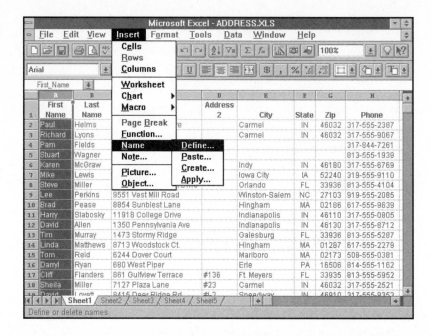

Figure 10.3
The Define Name
dialog box.

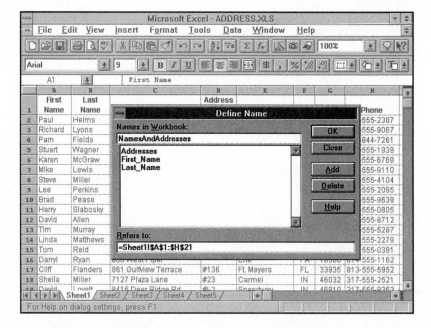

It's easy to find the names assigned to the list or parts of the list. Click on the down arrow next to the names box on the Formatting toolbar to reveal the list of named items in the list (see fig. 10.4).

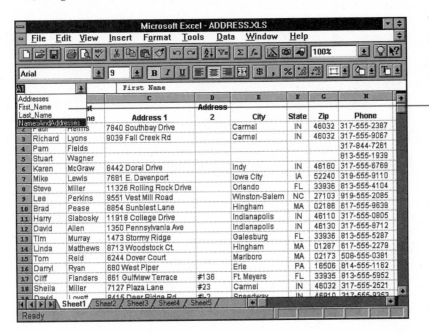

Figure 10.4
The names of elements of the data list.

Name list

Although it isn't necessary to name the items in the list, you can use the appropriate element name any time Excel requires a reference to data in the list. For instance, when sorting the list by the values in the "Last Name" column, you can use the name assigned to that column ("Last_Name") rather than a range or other reference.

Designing a Database: A Case Study

Designing a database table is a rather straightforward exercise. A little advance planning can make it much easier when it comes time to lay out the list in an Excel worksheet.

Determining the Structure

The first step is to decide what data you want the database list to manage. Expanding somewhat on the address book analogy, consider the case of Sarah Wood, the manager of a busy shoe store, who is building an Excel database to manage the commissions paid to her salespeople.

Sarah's data management needs are similar to those of most businesses. Dissimilar information (employee names, sales figures, and commission rates) will all be contained within the

Excel data list. Calculations will be applied to the data in the worksheet to determine sales commissions and bonuses (Sarah's shoe store pays a monthly bonus to the top-grossing salesperson). Finally, summary reports can be used to determine which salespeople are showing the most improvement in their sales figures.

Sarah Wood's Data List

Sarah's first iteration of her worksheet is shown in figure 10.5. The names of the 10 sales-people are listed in the column labeled "Employee Name," and the gross sales by each employee for the first six months of 1994 are in the six columns to the right of the Employee Name column. (For clarity, the figures in this section are being shown with gridlines turned off.)

Figure 10.5
Sarah Wood's worksheet.

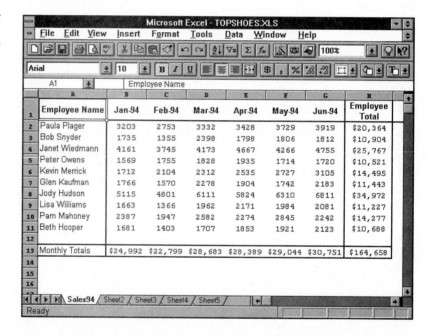

Employee Name	Jan-94	Feb-94	Mar-94	Apr-94	May-94	Jun-94	Employee Total
Paula Plager	3203	2753	3332	3428	3729	3919	$20,364
Bob Snyder	1735	1355	2398	1798	1806	1812	$10,904
Janet Wiedmann	4161	3745	4173	4667	4266	4755	$25,767
Peter Owens	1569	1755	1828	1935	1714	1720	$10,521
Kevin Merrick	1712	2104	2312	2535	2727	3105	$14,495
Glen Kaufman	1766	1570	2278	1904	1742	2183	$11,443
Jody Hudson	5115	4801	6111	5824	6310	6811	$34,972
Lisa Williams	1663	1366	1962	2171	1984	2081	$11,227
Pam Mahoney	2387	1947	2582	2274	2845	2242	$14,277
Beth Hooper	1681	1403	1707	1853	1921	2123	$10,688
Monthly Totals	$24,992	$22,799	$28,683	$28,389	$29,044	$30,751	$164,658

The wide disparity in gross sales is because most of the Top Shoes employees are employed only part time. The full-time employees have much higher gross sales figures than the part-time employees.

Sarah is interested in the monthly sales totals for each month, so she added a simple formula (=SUM(B2:B11)) in column B, a couple of rows below the last row of data. It is easy to copy this formula into row 13, below each column of monthly data. She also adds a column to the right of the list containing the total sales of each employee over the six-month period.

Being new to Excel, Sarah isn't sure what to do next. The data in the worksheet in figure 10.5 is somewhat difficult to work with. The rows and columns are in no particular order, so not much information can be derived.

Sarah does understand, however, that her worksheet qualifies as an Excel database list. In any column, all the cells contain the same type of data. Each row is the sales record for one employee, so each cell in a row is related to the other cells in the same row. Sarah assigns the name "Sales94" to the range of cells from A1 to H11. Excel recognizes the column labels at the top of each column because Sarah has set their typefaces to Bold and put a thick single-line border at the bottom of each cell in the top row.

Sorting the List Alphabetically

First, Sarah wants to sort the list alphabetically. This arrangement would make it easier when entering data in the store's ledger or calculating withholding taxes.

Sorting the list by the Employee Name column is easy. All she needs to do is to click on any cell within the "Sales94" area (she chose the Employee Name column label) to inform Excel that she intends to work with the "Sales94" data list.

Next, she selects the Sort option from the Data menu. The Sort dialog box (fig. 10.6) appears. Notice that the Sales94 list is highlighted while the Sort dialog box is open to let you know that Excel understands what area is about to be sorted.

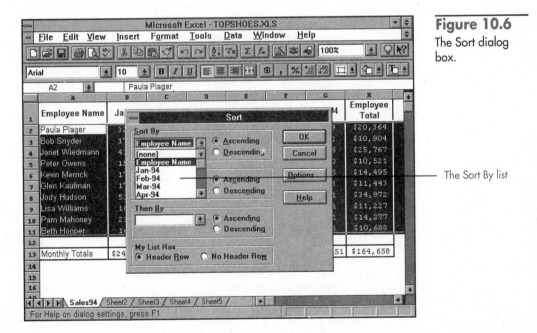

Figure 10.6
The Sort dialog box.

The Sort By list

Sarah opens the combo box in the <u>S</u>ort By area of the Sort dialog box by clicking on the down arrow and selects "Employee Name" from the list of names. Because Excel recognizes "Sales94" as a data list, each column label is automatically added to this list.

What Ascending and Descending Mean

Notice that there are selections for <u>A</u>scending and <u>D</u>escending for each sort option. An *ascending* sort (the default) reorders the list from the smallest number (including negative numbers) to the largest number on numeric columns. If the column is alphabetic, an ascending sort follows alphabetic order (A to Z). Columns containing date or time data are sorted from earliest date or time to latest. Remember, because all of the data within a column is of the same type (numeric, alphabetic, or date/time), Excel won't become confused by changing data types during a sort. *Ascending* sort reorders the list from largest to smallest, and so on.

Using Column Headings during Sorting

At the bottom of the Sort dialog box in figure 10.6 is an area (labeled My List Has) in which you can tell Excel if it has found the correct column labels. If, for some reason, your list has column labels, but Excel didn't find them (most likely because you did not use a different typeface for the column labels), the "No Header Ro<u>w</u>" option button will be selected. If you click on the "<u>H</u>eader Row" option button, Excel will use the top row of the list as column labels.

If Excel thinks your list does *not* have column headings, the top row of your list will be included in the sort. This can lead to unexpected changes to the list order. Always check the results of a sort. If the column headings (also called the *column labels*) have been included in the sort, undo the sort by selecting the <u>U</u>ndo option in the <u>E</u>dit menu, then check to make sure the column headings have a different appearance than the items in the list.

When Sarah clicks on the OK button, the Sales94 list is instantly sorted alphabetically, as shown in figure 10.7. If Sarah wanted the list to be sorted by the employees' last names, she probably should have put the names into the list as "Last Name, First Name." As it is, the list is nicely sorted by the employees' first names.

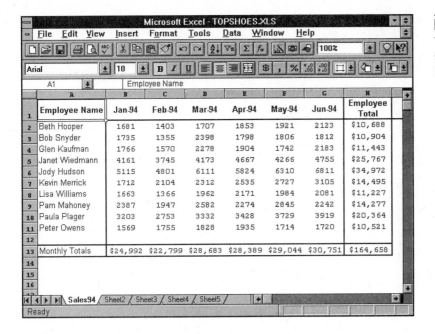

Figure 10.7
The list sorted by
the Employee
Name column.

Sorting the List Numerically

Working with a sorted list is easier than dealing with rough, unorganized data. Although the alphabetically sorted list is easier to use, it still doesn't give Sarah any direct indication of which employees are her top performers. Sarah sorts the list once more, this time choosing "Employee Total" as the Sort By column. She also clicks on the Descending button. The results of this sort are shown in figure 10.8.

From this list, it is easy to see that Jody Hudson was, by far, the highest-grossing employee for the first half of 1994 (although a case could be presented that, in such a small list, it is easy to pick out the highest number from the Employee Total column). Consider for a moment how different the situation would be if there were several hundred rows and dozens of columns in the data list. It is very difficult to pick out the highest (or lowest) number if the list spans across many screens.

More advanced sorting options are discussed later in this chapter.

Figure 10.8
The list sorted by
Employee Total.

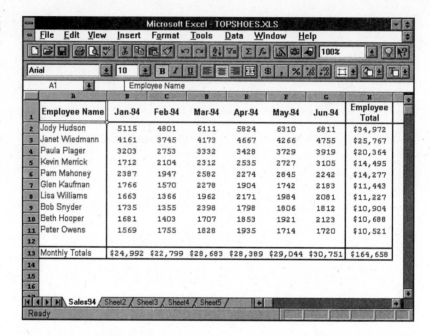

Filtering Data in a List

So far, Sarah Wood has sorted her list by both alphabetic and numeric data. Excel's built-in sorting routines made these tasks quick and easy.

Her next step is to experiment *filtering* the data in the list. Bonuses in the Top Shoes store were only paid to employees exceeding certain monthly quotas. Any full-time employee bringing in more than an average of $3,000 in sales was eligible for a tidy bonus every six months. Sarah wants to *filter out* employees who didn't make their quota.

Using AutoFilter

Obviously, Sarah wants to exclude any employees with gross sales of less than $18,000 for the six-month period covered in her list. Excel makes simple filters like this easy to do. Again, Sarah's first step is to click on a cell in the Sales94 data list. She then selects the Filter option in the Data menu to reveal the Filter cascading menu (see fig. 10.9).

Initially, Sarah just wants a quick and easy filter, so she selects the AutoFilter option. AutoFilter places drop-down arrows on each column in the data list (see fig. 10.10).

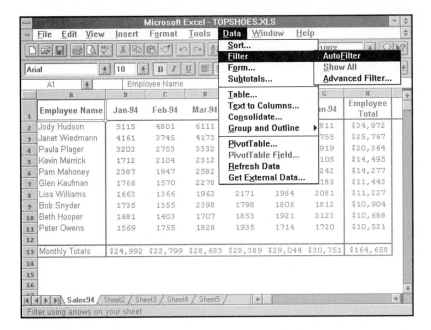

II

Databases

Figure 10.9
The Filter
cascading menu.

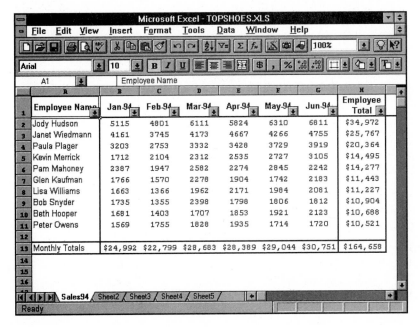

Figure 10.10
The AutoFilter
drop-down arrows
on the data list.

Specifying AutoFilter Criteria

When you click on the down arrows, a list of filter criteria is revealed, as shown in figure 10.11. This drop-down list contains all of the unique value in the column.

By clicking on a value in this list, Sarah could quickly exclude all rows except for those that contain the value she selected.

Figure 10.11

The filter criteria list.

Filter criteria list ——

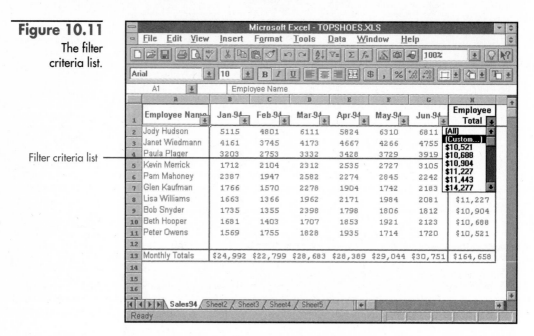

This approach, however, does not help her determine which employees have met their quota. Instead, she selects the Custom option from the list, which opens the Custom AutoFilter dialog box (see fig. 10.12). This dialog box contains fields for specifying which data should be included in the filtered data.

Because she wants all employees who brought in more than $18,000 in gross sales, Sarah enters 18000 in the text box in the Custom AutoFilter dialog box and clicks on the OK button. The list instantly changes to what is shown in figure 10.13.

Although at first glance it appears that a lot of rows have been deleted from the list, look at the row numbers at the far left of this figure. The row numbers indicate that all of the rows from 5 through 11 have been hidden rather than deleted. When you filter data in an Excel database list, the rows excluded by the filter are simply hidden from view.

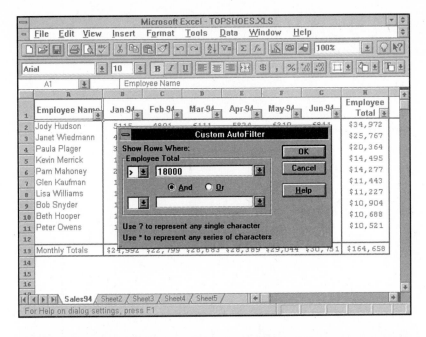

Figure 10.12
The Custom
AutoFilter dialog
box.

II

Databases

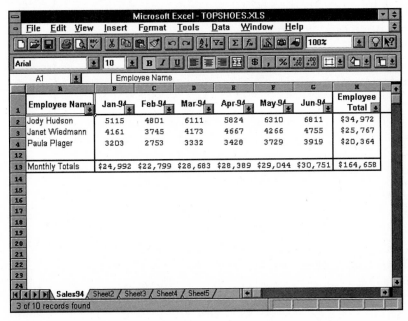

Figure 10.13
The result of the
custom AutoFilter.

How Filters Affect List Operations

Many list operations like printing, copying, and charting work only on displayed data. The fields hidden by a filter will not be printed or copied along with the displayed fields.

NOTE To leave AutoFormat, select Filter in the Data menu and click on AutoFilter. When you return to the worksheet, all the drop-down arrows disappear.

Summing across Hidden Rows

A couple of things are worth noting here. For instance, notice that the grand total in the lower right corner of figure 10.13 is the same as when all data was displayed (see fig. 10.10). The formula for the grand total is =SUM(H2:H11), which includes rows that are hidden from view.

Even when rows are hidden from view, Excel continues to correctly display summary data based on the hidden values.

Advanced Filters

January and February were particularly difficult months for Top Shoes. Bad weather kept away many customers and a few employees called in sick several days during this period. Sarah is interested in knowing which employees had been able to make their quotas during the bad weather, indicating a willingness to tough it out when things got bad.

Although AutoFilter is easy to use, Sarah cannot get AutoFilter to show all rows with values above $3,000 in either January or February. This more complex filter criteria required Excel's Advanced Filter capabilities.

The advanced filter feature requires a certain amount of setup before selecting the Advanced Filter menu option. First, Sarah must specify the criteria she wishes to use for the filter. The criteria was quite simple: for the months of January and February, she needs all rows with values greater than 3000.

The advanced filter option requires Sarah to build an area on the worksheet with this information (figure 10.14). Just below the data list, Sarah puts exact duplicates of the column labels for the January and February data, and, below each label, the value for which she wants to search. The column labels and criteria make up the *criteria range* for the advanced filter.

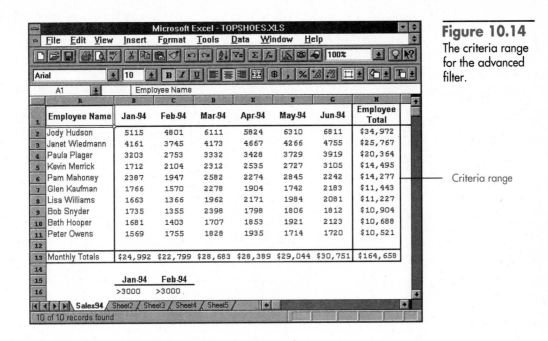

Figure 10.14
The criteria range for the advanced filter.

Criteria range

NOTE The labels for the criteria range must be exactly like the labels on the columns you want to filter. The best way to get exact duplicates of the column labels is to copy and paste them into the criteria range.

Next, Sarah selects the **A**dvanced Filter option from the Filter cascaded menu (figure 10.15). It is important to note that you must have the criteria range established before invoking the **A**dvanced Filter option.

The Advanced Filter dialog box (see fig. 10.16) then opens. The **L**ist Range box is automatically filled in by Excel with the range for the Sales94 data list. Sarah has to fill in the **C**riteria Range box herself, however.

When Sarah clicks on the OK button, the data in her list is instantly filtered according to the information specified in the criteria range (see fig. 10.17). Only those rows with values above 3000 in January or February appear.

NOTE To remove the advanced filter, select the **S**how All option in the **F**ilter cascade menu under the **D**ata main menu. The **S**how All option is available only when a filter has been applied to a data list.

Figure 10.15
The **A**dvanced Filter option in the filter cascaded menu.

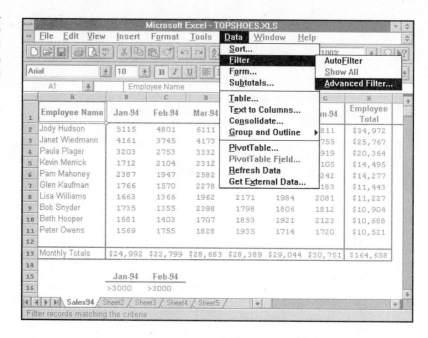

Figure 10.16
The Advanced Filter dialog box.

Criteria Range box

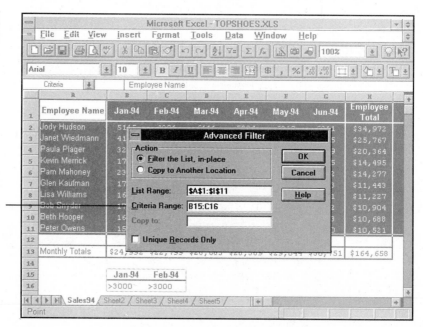

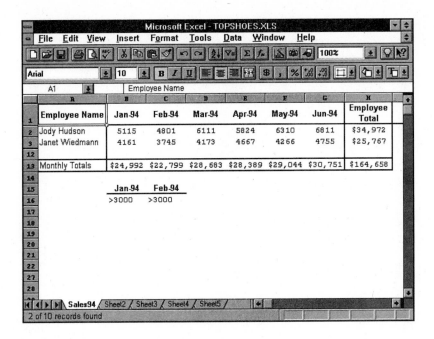

Figure 10.17
The result of the advanced filter.

II

Databases

Advanced Sorting and Filtering Features

In addition to the basic sorting and filtering operations described earlier in this chapter, Excel 5 provides a number of advanced features that extend your ability to manage lists used as databases.

Custom Sort Order

The default, sort orders are simply "ascending" and "descending." When Sarah Wood wanted to see who was the highest-selling employee, she simply sorted the list by the "Employee Total" column. As you read this chapter, it might have occurred to you that it was not entirely fair to her part-time employees to include them along with the full-time employees during this sort.

Since part-time salespeople have less opportunity to sell shoes, their sales figures are naturally lower than those of full-time workers. With the current Sales94 list design, it is not possible to easily include information indicating employment status in a sort or filter.

Even a column added to the list indicating FT (for full-time) and PT (for part-time) does not provide a full solution. "PT" will always fall after "FT," because it comes after "FT" when sorted in alphabetical order. Sarah Wood wants to be able to sort by more than just FT and

PT, however. She'd like to be able to use FT (full-time), TQ (three-quarter time, or 30 hours a week), and HT (half-time, 20 hours or less a week). Sorting this column alphabetically puts the half-time people at the top of the sorted list.

What Sarah needs is a "custom sort order" that appropriately sorts or filters FT, TQ, and HT columns. She first adds a new column to the list to contain the employment status, as shown in figure 10.18.

Figure 10.18
The Sales94 list with the new column added.

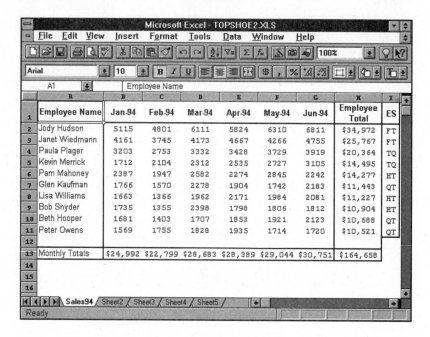

Next, Sarah needs to add the custom sort order to her Excel 5 installation. She simply opens the Options notebook by selecting Options in the Tools menu and clicks on the Custom Lists tab (figure 10.19).

The left half of the Custom Lists page displays the current set of custom lists. Excel is pre-installed with lists for sorting by months of the year and days of the week.

To add a list, simply enter it in the List Entries box to the right of the Custom Lists area. Figure 10.20 shows the Custom Lists page after Sarah enters the employment status items. When Sarah clicks on the OK button, she is returned to the Sales94 list.

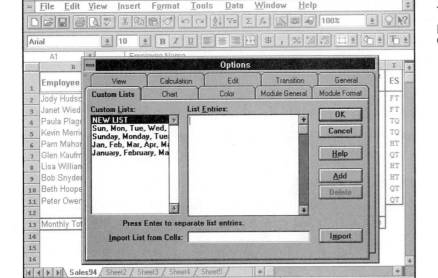

Figure 10.19
The Custom Lists page in the Options notebook.

II

Databases

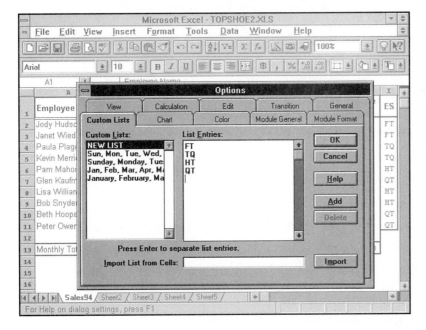

Figure 10.20
The new custom list.

Sorting the list by the Employee Total and ES columns is easy. When she selects the **S**ort option in the **D**ata menu, the Sort dialog box appears as shown in figure 10.21.

Figure 10.21
The Sort
dialog box.

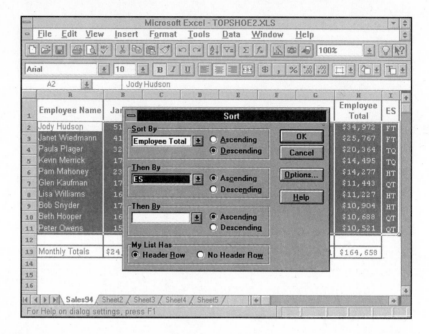

Sarah enters the Employee Total column in the **S**ort By box and the new ES in the **T**hen By box. This sequence means that employees will be grouped together by their employment status, then, within the employment status group, by the Employee Total column.

To make sure the new custom list is used to sort the ES column, with the **T**hen By box highlighted, Sarah clicks on the **O**ptions button in the Sort dialog box to open the Sort Options (fig. 10.22).

When open, the **F**irst Key Sort Order combo box shows the list of custom lists known to Excel (fig. 10.23). Sarah selected her custom list (FT, TQ, HT, QT) from this list and clicked on the OK button.

After she sorts her list, the results are shown in figure 10.24.

A quick look at the Employee Total column shows Sarah that she has one quarter-time employee (Glen Kaufman) who has out-performed two half-time people (Bob Snyder and Lisa Williams). Either Glen Kaufman is an exceptional salesperson or Bob Snyder and Lisa Williams need a little training!

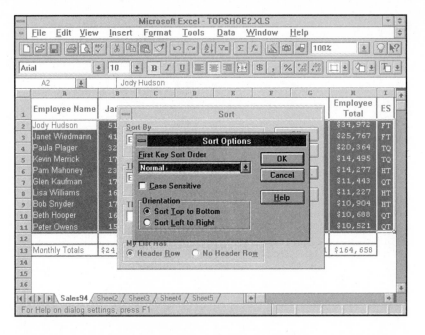

Figure 10.22
The Sort Options
dialog box.

II

Databases

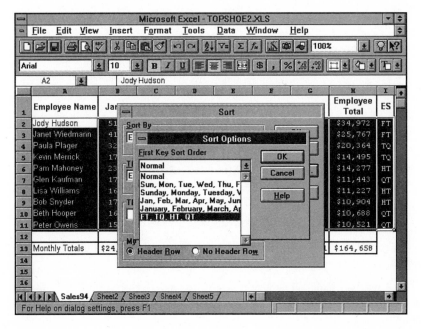

Figure 10.23
The custom orders
that can be used
for sorting.

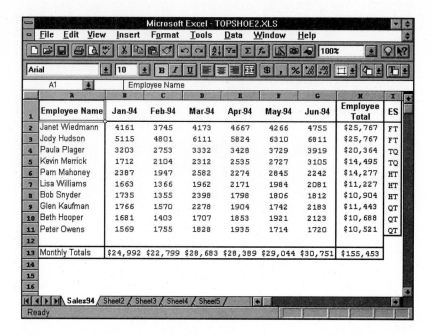

Sorting More Than Three Columns

Only three columns can be sorted at a time. If you need to sort by four or more columns, perform the sort in stages. Sorting rearranges the rows in the list; unlike filtering, this rearrangement is permanent (unless you immediately undo the sort, of course). Therefore, you should sort by the least important columns in the first pass and by the more important columns in the last pass. Sorting by the most important columns last allows those columns to wield the most influence on the arrangement on the rows in the list.

Sorting multiple columns makes sense when one of the columns is likely to contain multiple entries with the same value. The Top Shoes example is not a good candidate for a multiple-column sort, because each column contains unique values.

Sorting Selected Rows or Columns

It is possible to sort only certain rows or columns in the list. Simply highlight the rows or columns you wish to sort, then proceed as if you were sorting the entire list.

Figure 10.25 shows the Sales94 list with the middle six rows marked for sorting. Rows from 4 through 9 were highlighted by clicking the mouse on the row heading for row 4 and dragging the mouse down to row 9.

Figure 10.25
The Sales94 list prepared for a partial sort.

```
┌─────────────────────────────────────────────────────────────────────────┐
│ ─        Microsoft Excel - TOPSHOE2.XLS                          ▼ ◆      │
│ ═  File  Edit  View  Insert  Format  Tools  Data  Window  Help      ◆     │
│ ┌──┬──┬──┬──┬──┬──┬──┬──┬──┬──┬──┬──┬──┬──┬──┬──┬──┬──┬──────┬──┬───┐      │
│ │  │  │  │  │  │  │  │  │  │  │  │  │  │  │  │ 100%│ ± │ ♀ │N?│      │
│ ┌──────────┬──┬──┬──┬──┬──┬──┬──┬──┬──┬──┬──┬──┬──┬──┬──┬──┬──┬──┐         │
│ │Arial     │± │10│± │B │I │U │≡ │≡ │≡ │⊞ │$ │, │% │⋮ │.00│□│◇│□│          │
│ ┌──────┬──┐        ┌───────────────┐                                      │
│ │  A4  │± │        │ Paula Plager  │                                      │
│ ├──────┴──┼────┬────┬────┬────┬────┬────┬─────────┬──┬                    │
│ │    A     │ B  │ C  │ D  │ E  │ F  │ G  │   H    │I │                    │
│ │Employee  │Jan-│Feb-│Mar-│Apr-│May-│Jun-│Employee│ES│                    │
│1│  Name    │ 94 │ 94 │ 94 │ 94 │ 94 │ 94 │ Total  │  │                    │
│2│Janet Wiedmann│4161│3745│4173│4667│4266│4755│$25,767│FT│                 │
│3│Jody Hudson│5115│4801│6111│5824│6310│6811│$25,767│FT│                    │
│4│Paula Plager│3203│2753│3332│3428│3729│3919│$20,364│TQ│                   │
│5│Kevin Merrick│1712│2104│2312│2535│2727│3105│$14,495│TQ│                  │
│6│Pam Mahoney│2387│1947│2582│2274│2845│2242│$14,277│HT│                    │
│7│Lisa Williams│1663│1366│1962│2171│1984│2081│$11,227│HT│                  │
│8│Bob Snyder│1735│1355│2398│1798│1806│1812│$10,904│HT│                     │
│9│Glen Kaufman│1766│1570│2278│1904│1742│2183│$11,443│QT│                   │
│10│Beth Hooper│1681│1403│1707│1853│1921│2123│$10,688│QT│                   │
│11│Peter Owens│1569│1755│1828│1935│1714│1720│$10,521│QT│                   │
│12│                                                                        │
│13│Monthly Totals│$24,992│$22,799│$28,683│$28,389│$29,044│$30,751│$155,453││
│14│                                                                        │
│15│                                                                        │
│16│                                                                        │
│ ◄│◄│►│►│ Sales94 / Sheet2 / Sheet3 / Sheet4 / Sheet5 /   │◄│             │
│ Ready                                                                      │
└─────────────────────────────────────────────────────────────────────────┘
```

Figure 10.26 shows the Sales94 list after alphabetically sorting the list by the Employee Name column. As you can see, Bob Snyder has been moved to row 4, the top of the area marked in figure 10.25.

Figure 10.26
The Sales94 list after sorting rows 4 through 9.

```
┌─────────────────────────────────────────────────────────────────────────┐
│ ─        Microsoft Excel - TOPSHOE2.XLS                          ▼ ◆      │
│ ═  File  Edit  View  Insert  Format  Tools  Data  Window  Help      ◆     │
│ ┌──┬──┬──┬──┬──┬──┬──┬──┬──┬──┬──┬──┬──┬──┬──┬──┬──┬──┬──────┬──┬───┐      │
│ │  │  │  │  │  │  │  │  │  │  │  │  │  │  │  │ 100%│ ± │ ♀ │N?│      │
│ ┌──────────┬──┬──┬──┬──┬──┬──┬──┬──┬──┬──┬──┬──┬──┬──┬──┬──┬──┬──┐         │
│ │Arial     │± │10│± │B │I │U │≡ │≡ │≡ │⊞ │$ │, │% │⋮ │.00│□│◇│□│          │
│ ┌──────┬──┐        ┌───────────────┐                                      │
│ │  A1  │± │        │ Employee Name │                                      │
│ ├──────┴──┼────┬────┬────┬────┬────┬────┬─────────┬──┬                    │
│ │    A     │ B  │ C  │ D  │ E  │ F  │ G  │   H    │I │                    │
│ │Employee  │Jan-│Feb-│Mar-│Apr-│May-│Jun-│Employee│ES│                    │
│1│  Name    │ 94 │ 94 │ 94 │ 94 │ 94 │ 94 │ Total  │  │                    │
│2│Janet Wiedmann│4161│3745│4173│4667│4266│4755│$25,767│FT│                 │
│3│Jody Hudson│5115│4801│6111│5824│6310│6811│$25,767│FT│                    │
│4│Bob Snyder│1735│1355│2398│1798│1806│1812│$10,904│HT│                     │
│5│Glen Kaufman│1766│1570│2278│1904│1742│2183│$11,443│QT│                   │
│6│Kevin Merrick│1712│2104│2312│2535│2727│3105│$11,443│TQ│                  │
│7│Lisa Williams│1663│1366│1962│2171│1984│2081│$11,227│HT│                  │
│8│Pam Mahoney│2387│1947│2582│2274│2845│2242│$14,277│HT│                    │
│9│Paula Plager│3203│2753│3332│3428│3729│3919│$20,364│TQ│                   │
│10│Beth Hooper│1681│1403│1707│1853│1921│2123│$10,688│QT│                   │
│11│Peter Owens│1569│1755│1828│1935│1714│1720│$10,521│QT│                   │
│12│                                                                        │
│13│Monthly Totals│$24,992│$22,799│$28,683│$28,389│$29,044│$30,751│$152,401││
│14│                                                                        │
│15│                                                                        │
│16│                                                                        │
│ ◄│◄│►│►│ Sales94 / Sheet2 / Sheet3 / Sheet4 / Sheet5 /   │◄│             │
│ Ready                                                                      │
└─────────────────────────────────────────────────────────────────────────┘
```

II

Databases

Figure 10.27 shows the Sales94 list with the Jan-94 and Feb-94 columns sorted numerically in the ascending order of the Jan-94 column (the other columns in the list are sorted in descending order). The data in both the Jan-94 and Feb-94 columns were highlighted, but only the Jan-94 column was selected in the Sort dialog box.

Figure 10.27

The Sales94 list with columns Jan-94 and Feb-94 resorted.

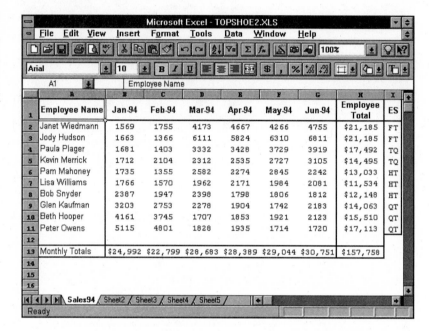

Obviously, a word of caution is in order here. Notice that the data in the Sales94 list is hopelessly scrambled after sorting the Jan-94 and Feb-94 columns. The data in each row is completely different than it was before sorting. Arbitrary sorting of rows and columns can invalidate an Excel list as a reliable database.

Sorting Columns Rather Than Rows

You also can sort columns of data rather than rows. Clicking on the Options button in the Sort dialog box (which, itself, was opened by selecting the Sort option in the Data menu) opens the Sort Options dialog box (figure 10.28).

In the lower left corner of the Sort Options dialog box is an area labeled Orientation. By default, the Sort Top to Bottom option button is selected, meaning that sorts will rearrange the order of the rows in the list. When the Sort Left to Right is pressed, the *columns* of data are sorted instead.

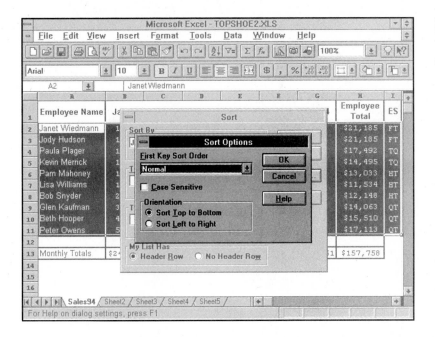

Figure 10.28
The Sort Options
dialog box.

Copying Filtered Data to Another Location

Occasionally, you want to copy filtered data to another worksheet location. By default, an advanced filter occurs "in place." The rows that are filtered out of the data by the information in the criteria range are hidden from view, leaving only the selected rows displayed.

If you want to leave the original data list intact and want to make a copy of the filtered data somewhere else, click the Copy to Another Location option button in the Advanced Filter dialog box (fig. 10.29).

When this button is selected, the Copy to text box becomes active (it normally is grayed). All Excel needs is the worksheet cell in which you want the upper left corner of the filter results to appear. In figure 10.29, this location is cell A18. When you click on the OK button, Excel immediately copies the filter results to the location specified in the Copy to box.

Figure 10.30 shows the results of the advanced filter set up in figure 10.29. The Excel toolbars have been turned off in figure 10.30 to permit more vertical viewing space, and the overall dimensions have been scaled to 90 percent. The filtered data has been copied to the area beginning with cell A18.

Figure 10.29
The Copy to
Another Location
option button.

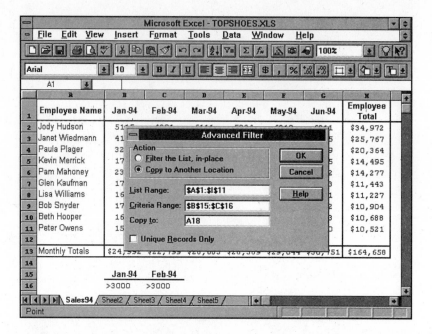

Figure 10.30
Copying the result
set to a different
location.

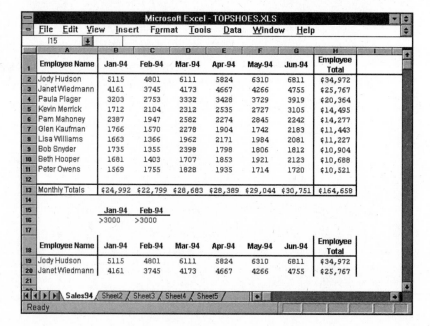

Be careful when using the advanced filter Copy to option. Any data already in the area specified in the Copy to will be overwritten without warning!

It is even possible to copy the results set to another worksheet. Simply include a reference to the worksheet in the Copy to box on the Advanced Filter dialog box. For instance, to copy the filter results set to the upper left corner of a worksheet named Q1-94, the entry in the Copy to box should read **Q1-94!A1**.

The destination worksheet specified in the Copy to box must already exist in the current workbook. Excel does not create a new worksheet to serve as the destination for the copy to action.

Copying Filtered Data to Another Application

If you want to copy filtered data to another Windows application, be sure to leave the filter criteria in place before the copy operation. Because the records excluded by the filter criteria are hidden, they are not copied.

When you copy a list from Excel to Word for Windows, the list becomes a table in Word.

Using the Excel Data Form

Excel provides an incredibly easy-to-use tool for entering new data into lists. The Excel data form displays the data from one record in a list and enables you to add, delete, or otherwise modify the field information in the list.

To open the data form for a list, put the cursor anywhere inside the list and select the Form option in the Data menu. The data form opens with the first record of the data list already displayed (figure 10.31).

Figure 10.31
The Excel Data
Form.

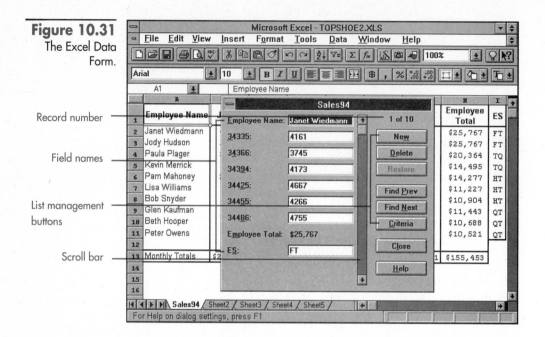

The data form contains all the fields in the record, arranged vertically. In figure 10.31, the column labels containing dates are expressed as the numbers that Excel uses internally to store dates.

The data form also contains all the items needed to add, delete, or modify records in the data list. The data form can also be used to search for a particular record based on specific criteria entered in the form.

Notice that the Employee Total field cannot be changed in the data form. The information in this field is calculated—it is the sum of all of the "month" fields in the record. Therefore, its value is dependent on other fields in the record, and it cannot be changed directly by the user.

Adding New Records Using the Data Form

A new record can be added to the list by clicking on the New button. All the fields in the form are blanked (see fig. 10.32) and "New Record" appears in the upper right corner of the data form. Any data filled in the fields on the data form are added to the data list when the Close button is selected.

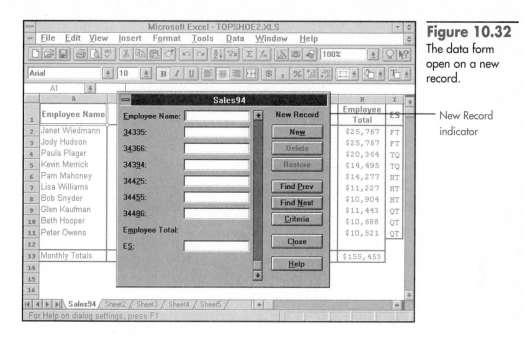

Figure 10.32
The data form
open on a new
record.

New Record
indicator

Deleting a Record Using the Data Form

The record that appears on the form will be deleted when the Delete button is pressed. The record deletion is permanent and cannot be undone.

If any data in an existing record displayed in the form is changed, the Restore button becomes active (by default, the Restore button is grayed as it appears in figure 10.32). When pressed, the Restore button reverts all changes to the original condition of the record. After you move on to another record, however, the changes become permanent, and you cannot restore the record or undo changes to it.

Navigating Records Using the Data Form

The Find Prev and Find Next buttons simply move up and down the data list, displaying records one at a time. As you move through the records, you can make changes to the displayed record or delete it using the list management buttons.

Searching for Records Using the Data Form

The Criteria button enables you to search for a particular record based on information you enter in the fields on the data form. After the Criteria button is pressed, the form clears and the scroll bar becomes inactive (figure 10.33). The word "Criteria" appears in the upper right corner of the form to indicate the form is ready to accept search criteria.

Figure 10.33
The Excel data form prepared to receive criteria.

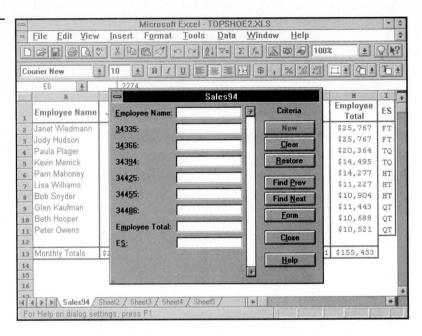

To perform a search, enter search criteria in the appropriate field and click the Find Next or Find Prev buttons to find the next or previous record (respectively) meeting the criteria entered in the field.

Figure 10.34 illustrates a search using the Criteria button.

In figure 10.34, <15000 has been entered in the Employee Total field. When the Find Prev or Find Next buttons are pressed, Excel finds the previous or next record (respectively) with a value of less than 15,000 in the Employee Total field (as shown in figure 10.35).

Criteria can be entered in more than one field, if desired. Complex criteria can be built to narrow or broaden the search. An AND condition is implied between the criteria in multiple fields (for example, < 15000 AND > 10000).

If no records meet the search criteria, no error message is generated. Instead, the form simply displays the current field. Always check the results of the searches you conduct through the data form to be sure you've retrieved the information you intended.

 The data form can display as many us 32 fields. If the form contains more than 32 fields (Excel worksheets can contain as many as 256 columns) the leftmost 32 fields are shown.

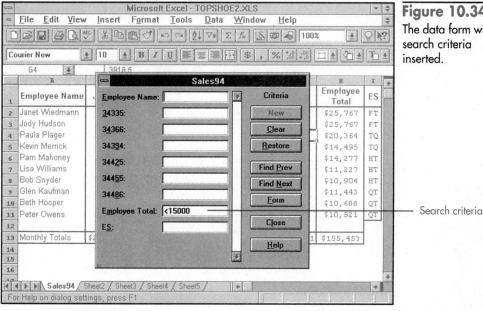

Figure 10.34

The data form with search criteria inserted.

Search criteria

II

Databases

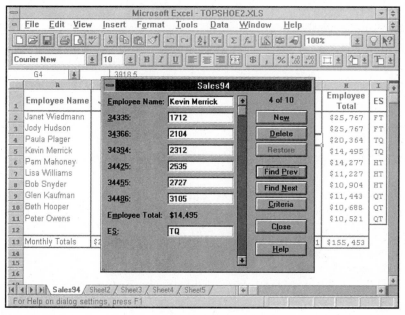

Figure 10.35

The next record with Employee Total < 15000.

Knowing When To Use a Real Database Program

Although Excel offers some very powerful list management options, it does not qualify as a full-fledged database management system. If your data management needs are complex, or if you are working with large data sets, a full-fledged database system like Microsoft Access, Microsoft FoxPro for Windows, Borland Paradox, or Borland dBASE for Windows might be more appropriate for your needs.

The Advantages of Relational Databases

First and foremost, Excel does not offer *relational* database capabilities. In a relational database system like FoxPro or Access, items in a table can be "tied" to items in another table through a *relationship* maintained and managed by the database system.

In other words, a table that contains employee names and addresses and other employment information can be related to another table that contains payroll information. Each record in the employee table has many connections to the payroll table (one connection for each paycheck that has been issued to the employee). After the employee name or other identifier has been determined, a lookup in the payroll table is very fast and efficient.

The same example in Excel would require a very large table of employee data. Each record would contain all the employment information plus payroll data for an employee. Each time a payroll check is issued, a new record would be added to the table for each employee. The new record would contain all of the employee data plus the new payroll information.

Alternatively, a new field could be added onto the end of the table to hold the new payroll information.

In either case, a simple table approach to managing complex data quickly becomes unmanageable. Relational database systems like FoxPro, Access, Paradox, and dBASE contain all the features and utilities necessary to efficiently manage the links between tables.

Databases Provide Powerful Query Capabilities

The query capabilities of relational database systems are formidable and permit rapid performance of very complex queries on large data sets. A database system built of a number of Excel tables just cannot compete with the vast capabilities of modern relational database systems.

You Can Build Powerful Forms Using a Database

Although the Excel data form (discussed earlier in this chapter) is extremely easy to use, it lacks many of the features of a true forms-oriented database system like Microsoft Access or Borland Paradox for Windows.

Forms produced by Access, Paradox for Windows, and other Windows database applications can contain routines for validating input. If, for instance, a field is expecting numeric data, and the user tries to input text in the field, the *form* notices the error and informs the user. The Excel data form cannot perform data validation.

Windows database forms can contain a wide variety of objects like text input fields, option buttons (often called *radio buttons*, because they provide selection between *mutually exclusive* options, much like the buttons on a radio), check boxes, combo boxes, selection lists, and so on.

True database forms are flexible. Because of the wealth of different objects and designs that can be used to construct forms in Access, Paradox for Windows, or FoxPro, the developer is not limited to a fixed size and shape or appearance of the form. The Excel data form is designed for a few specific tasks and cannot be modified for more complex functions.

Should You Use a Database Rather Than Excel?

There is no simple answer to the question of whether a true database is better suited to managing your data than Excel 5. The list management tools in Excel are easy to learn and use. In contrast, a product like Access or Paradox for Windows can take months (or even years) to master completely.

Generally speaking, however, Excel lists are well-suited for managing reasonably small sets (less than 1,000 records) of data or data with fewer than 20 or 30 fields. After you exceed the practical limits of Excel's list management tools (for instance, a simple sort or filter does not yield the information you need), it is time to consider a true database.

The good news is that *all* contemporary Windows database systems like Access, Paradox for Windows, and FoxPro for Windows can read and write Excel worksheets. If you discover you have outgrown Excel's list management capabilities after investing a considerable amount of time and effort building Excel worksheets to contain your data, you can always migrate to a Windows database system.

Microsoft Access is bundled in the Microsoft Office Professional package. If you own Microsoft Office Professional or another Windows database, you might want to import a worksheet or two in a true database table and experiment. Obviously, however, you should carefully back up your Excel worksheets before experimenting with another data management system.

CHAPTER SNAPSHOT

In this chapter, you learn the power built into Microsoft Query, an add-in built into Excel 5. The information in this chapter enables you to directly access data stored in database tables produced by Microsoft Access and FoxPro, Borland dBASE and Paradox, and other database systems. Chapter 11 explains the following:

- ✔ Understanding Microsoft Query

- ✔ Installing and starting Microsoft Query

- ✔ Mastering the Microsoft Query environment

- ✔ Retrieving data with Microsoft Query

- ✔ Building query criteria

- ✔ Sorting data in Microsoft Query

- ✔ Saving and reusing queries

- ✔ Transferring data from Microsoft Query to Excel

A little practice using Microsoft Query can greatly extend the data access capabilities of Excel 5.

CHAPTER

Using Microsoft Query

Microsoft Excel 5 provides several different ways to access data stored in external database files. Because, as you learned in Chapter 10, an Excel worksheet is comparable to a database table, you might find it very useful to extract data directly from database files to use within Excel.

Virtually any database can be used to supply information to Excel. Even if Excel does not contain a driver specifically designed for your database (for example, no drivers exist in Excel for Alpha Four or Lotus Approach), it is very likely your database uses a standard database format (like dBASE or Paradox) or can export its tables in one of the common formats like dBASE or Paradox or as delimited text.

Although not an "official" abbreviation, this chapter uses the expression *MSQuery* to indicate the Excel add-in application named Microsoft Query.

What Is Microsoft Query?

Microsoft Query (MSQuery) is a complete, stand-alone application that enables you to retrieve data from a number of external data sources. MSQuery is added to your system when you install Excel 5 and resides in the MSAPPS\MSQUERY subdirectory under the Windows directory (which is almost always C:\WINDOWS). Microsoft MSQuery can be used as a stand-alone application or run from within Excel through an add-in macro.

MSQuery provides you with ways to perform many common database tasks: extract data from database tables, delete or modify data in databases tables, or add new data to database tables.

Understanding What Microsoft Query Does

When used within Excel, data retrieved from external database sources (like Microsoft Access and FoxPro or Borland Paradox and dBASE) can be added to Excel worksheets. Using Microsoft Query, data can be piped into Excel worksheets directly from database tables.

MSQuery is designed to build complex database queries without the aid of the entire database engine. These queries draw data from database tables and provide a mechanism for adding that data to Excel worksheets.

As this chapter shows, when you start MSQuery (whether from Program Manager or from within Excel) you find yourself inside a complete Windows application. Microsoft Query has its own menu, toolbar, and other controls. You are able to create, save, and reuse database queries from within MSQuery.

This chapter explains Microsoft Query and describes the learning that is required to put MSQuery to work for you.

Installing MSQuery

During the Excel 5 installation process, you are asked to specify which options you want to install (see fig. 11.1) along with the basic features of Excel 5.

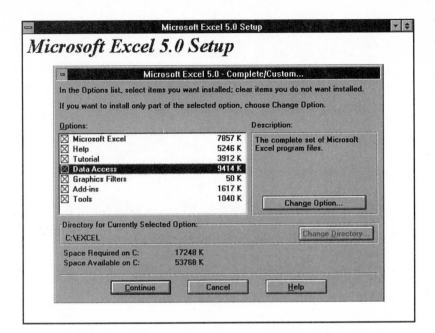

Figure 11.1
The Excel
installation options
dialog box.

If the Data Access check box is marked, Microsoft Query and its support files are installed in the MSAPPS\MSQUERY and WINDOWS\SYSTEM directory under the Windows main directory.

Data Access Installation Options

You might wonder why the data access option requires so much disk space (almost 9.5M more than Excel itself). MSQuery has a separate driver for each type of database that it can access. Most of these drivers are installed in the WINDOWS\SYSTEM directory.

If you want to view the drivers that are installed as part of the Data Access options during the Excel 5 installation process, click on the Change Option button in the installation options screen (you saw this screen in figure 11.1) to reveal the Data Access options dialog box (figure 11.2).

MSQuery comes with a fairly large number of database drivers. By default, all drivers (which are actually custom dynamically linked libraries or *DLLs*) are installed into the WINDOWS\SYSTEM directory when Excel is installed. If you are sure you do not need to use a specific driver or two (for instance, your company has no plans to ever use Btrieve-format database files), deselect the corresponding box in the Options list in the Data Access dialog box.

Figure 11.2
The Data Access
options dialog
box.

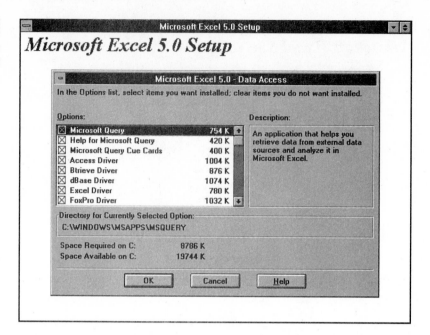

NOTE   At least *one* driver must be checked. Otherwise, Microsoft Query is not installed.

If you change your mind, you can reinstall the data access options easily by re-running the Excel 5 setup.

TIP   If you are not sure which drivers to specify, install the dBASE, Paradox, Access, and FoxPro drivers—these database systems are extremely popular. And, of course, the Excel driver should be installed to give you access to Excel 3, 4, and 5 worksheets.

If you obtained Excel as part of the Microsoft Office Professional package, be sure to leave the Access Driver box checked.

Which Installation Options Should You Choose?

No hard and fast rules exist about installing the optional database drivers. Generally speaking, you should install more drivers than you expect to use. It is impossible to predict all the database file formats that may eventually be used in your working environment.

Even though you can always add drivers later by running the Excel 5 setup program (its icon is located in the Excel 5 program group), Murphy's law clearly states that, when it is time to reinstall Excel drivers, finding the original disks which came in the Excel 5 package is impossible . The drivers do not take up much disk space (the Access, FoxPro, Paradox, dBASE, and SQL server drivers combined require a few megabytes in the Windows system directory), so there is little reason not to install them all.

Starting Microsoft Query

You can start Microsoft Query a number of different ways. The start-up method you choose depends on the way you want to use MSQuery.

Starting MSQuery as a Windows Application

From time to time, you might want to view or use a database from the Windows desktop, rather than from within Excel or another Windows application. When you installed Excel 5, the Microsoft Query icon was added to the program group (see fig. 11.3).

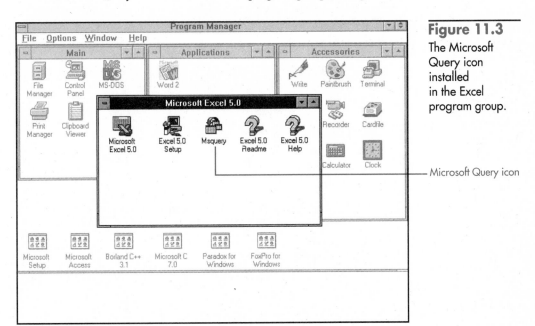

Figure 11.3

The Microsoft Query icon installed in the Excel program group.

When you double-click the Microsoft Query icon, the application starts up. With the exception of its toolbar, the Microsoft Query environment (figure 11.4) is quite featureless.

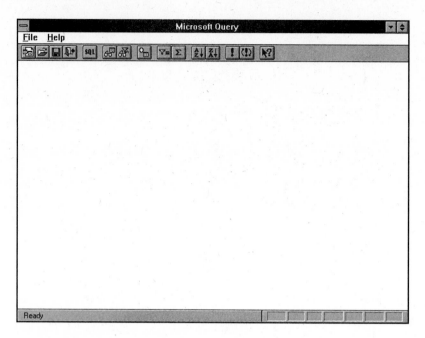

Figure 11.4
The Microsoft
Query
environment is
quite featureless.

Exactly the same capabilities and options are available when using MSQuery as a stand-alone application as when starting MSQuery from within Excel.

Starting MSQuery from Inside Excel

Although Microsoft Query can function as a stand-alone Windows application, you normally start MSQuery as an add-in from within Excel.

The MSQuery add-in is located in the Data menu. When you click on the Get External Data option (figure 11.5) Microsoft Query starts up.

Excel still is running after the MSQuery environment appears—just behind the MSQuery window. When started as an Excel add-in, MSQuery is able to transfer data directly from database files into Excel. Because MSQuery includes the tools and options necessary to extract only the data you are interested in, MSQuery is much more efficient to use than importing the same files directly into Excel.

Although Excel can directly open only dBASE database files, most database systems like Access, FoxPro, and Paradox are able to convert their native table formats to dBASE. Opening a Paradox table inside Excel, therefore, would require two steps: using Paradox to save the table in dBASE format, and opening the dBASE format file in Excel. MSQuery enables you to work directly with the Paradox, dBASE, FoxPro, or other database file from within Excel.

If you cannot find a Get External Data option in the Data menu, the Microsoft Query add-in has not been installed on your computer.

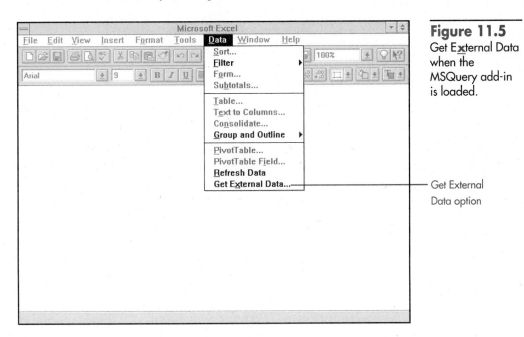

Figure 11.5
Get External Data when the MSQuery add-in is loaded.

Get External Data option

Installing the Microsoft Query Add-In

It is possible that the Microsoft Query add-in was not installed when Excel 5 was initially installed on your computer. A quick check of the Data menu tells you whether the MSQuery add-in is installed. If you see a Get External Data option in the Data menu (figure 11.5), MSQuery can be started from within Excel 5 easily.

If you do not see a Get External Data option, you must install the MSQuery add-in. Select Add-Ins from the Tools menu to open the Add-Ins dialog box (figure 11.6).

The Add-Ins dialog box contains a list of all add-ins currently installed in Excel 5. Scrolling the list, you should notice "XLQuery" near the bottom of the list. Even if the box to the left of "XLQuery" is checked, the Microsoft Query add-in might not be installed.

Usually, all that is necessary to load the Microsoft Query add-in is to click on the box next to the XLQuery entry in the add-in list and click on the OK button. After Excel locates and installs XLQUERY.XLA, the Microsoft Query add-in library, you are returned to your worksheet. Check the Data menu again to verify that you now have a Get External Data option.

If, for some reason, Excel was not able to find the MSQuery add-in library, you should locate XLQUERY.XLA manually. It is possible, for instance, that the directory holding

XLQUERY.XLA has been moved or renamed. In any case, use the Browse button in the Add-Ins dialog box to open the Browse dialog box (figure 11.7).

Figure 11.6

The Add-Ins dialog box.

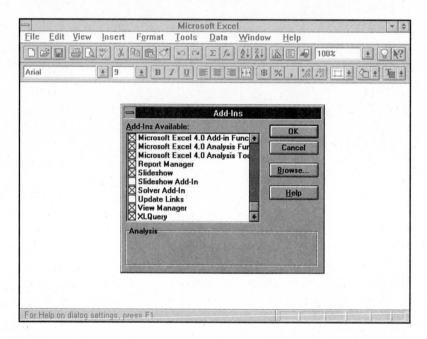

Figure 11.6

The Add-Ins dialog box.

Figure 11.7

The Browse dialog box.

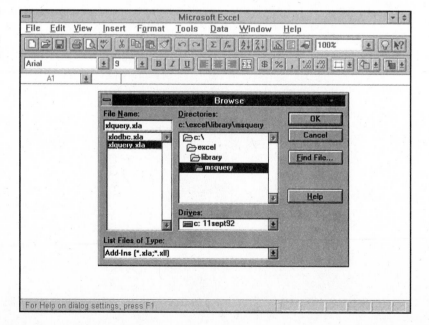

Figure 11.7

The Browse dialog box.

XLQUERY.XLA should be found in the MSQUERY directory under the LIBRARY directory. The MSQUERY directory was created during the Excel 5 installation procedure if you checked the Microsoft Query box in the Data Access screen during installation (this process was described earlier in this chapter).

When you locate XLQUERY.XLA, double-click on it or highlight it and click the OK button in the Browse dialog box. Excel automatically installs the Microsoft Query add-in, adding the Get E_xternal Data option to Excel's _Data menu.

If you cannot locate XLQUERY.XLA on your computer's file system, you might have to run the Excel Setup program (its icon is found in the Excel 5 program group). You can install or remove specific components of Excel 5 using the Excel Setup program. You need the original Excel 5 disks, so make sure you locate them.

Removing the Microsoft Query Add-In

Removing the Microsoft Query add-in is easy. Simply uncheck the box next to XLQuery in the _Add-Ins Available list in the Add-Ins dialog box (found under the _Data menu, of course). The next time you start Excel 5, there is no Get E_xternal Data option in the _Data menu.

Normally, you want to leave the MSQuery add-in installed in Excel. Excel starts up a little fast, however, if you remove it from the _Add-Ins Available list. After XLQUERY.XLA is located on your computer, you can always reinstall the MSQuery add-in.

The Microsoft Query Toolbar

All of your interaction with Microsoft Query takes place through the toolbar and menu options in the MSQuery environment. Although a complete description of the Microsoft Query environment is not necessary at this point, it might be useful to become familiar with the icons on the toolbar. Figure 11.8 shows the entire MSQuery toolbar. These tools are explained in table 11.1.

Table 11.1
Microsoft Query Toolbar Icons

Icon	Name	Description
🔲	New Query	Begins the process of building an entirely new database query.
📂	Open Query	Opens an existing query.

continues

Table 11.1, Continued
Microsoft Query Toolbar Icons

Icon	Name	Description
	Save File	Saves the current query for future use.
	Return Data to Excel	Returns you to Excel when your query activity is complete. This button is not on the toolbar when Microsoft Query is started as a stand-alone application.
SQL	View SQL	Queries generated by Microsoft Query are converted to SQL (structured query language) by Microsoft Query, even when the database does not require SQL. You might want to use this button to view the SQL statement during your work.
	Show/Hide Tables	Hides the "Table pane" in Microsoft Query to provide more room for the Query pane.
	Show/Hide Criteria	Hides the "Query pane" in Microsoft Query to provide more room for the Table pane.
	Add Tables	Opens the Add Tables dialog box so that you can add another table to the query.
	Add Criteria	Automatically adds criteria to the query.
Σ	Cycle Through Totals	Provides access to a number of basic statistics for data retrieved from databases (discussed later in this chapter).
	Sort Ascending	Quickly sorts columns of data in ascending order.
	Sort Descending	Quickly sorts columns of data in descending order.
	Query Now	Activates the query.
	Auto Query	Runs the query when the query criterion is complete.
	Help	Provides specific help for the objects you see in the MSQuery window.

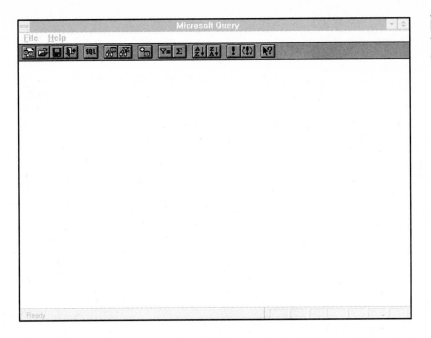

Figure 11.8
The Microsoft
Query toolbar.

Databases

Although most of your work with MSQuery involves little more than opening a database source, specifying which tables to examine, and building the query criteria, this chapter details each of the options available to you as you use Microsoft Query.

It is not necessary to memorize the purpose of each toolbar button. As you move the mouse cursor across the buttons, the MSQuery status bar shows you each button's function.

The rest of this chapter deals with using MSQuery to extract data from database tables. Although a Microsoft Access database is used as the example, the principles are the same for essentially any database source.

Using MSQuery To Retrieve Data

The first thing you see when you open Microsoft Query with the MSQuery add-in in Excel is the Select Data Source dialog box (figure 11.9). This dialog box also appears when you click on the New Query button or select New Query in the File menu of stand-alone Microsoft Query.

Selecting the Data Source

Microsoft Query needs to know the data source from which you want to get data. The first time MSQuery is opened, the Select Data Source dialog box is empty.

Microsoft Query needs to know what kind of data source you want to use. Clicking on the Other button opens the ODBC Data Sources dialog box (figure 11.10).

Figure 11.9
The empty Select
Data Source
dialog box.

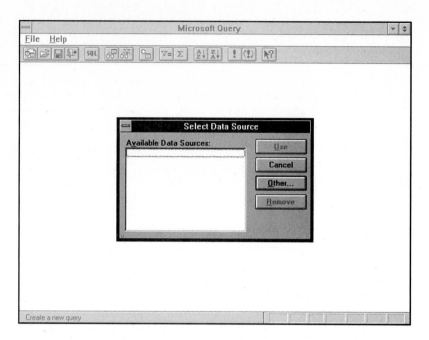

Figure 11.9
The empty Select
Data Source
dialog box.

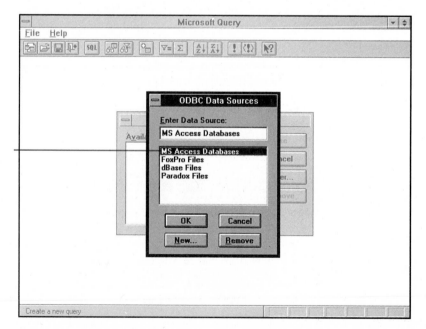

Figure 11.10
The installed
ODBC drivers.

Selected ODBC
driver

Your system might have more or fewer ODBC drivers than shown in figure 11.10.

What is ODBC? Microsoft has established the Open Database Connectivity for Windows applications in an attempt to provide a standard application interface to the bewildering variety of database file formats that exist in the world today. Any application (like Microsoft Query) that understands ODBC can use ODBC drivers to connect to a wide variety of database files.

An ODBC driver usually is written by the database vendor and is distributed as a particular type of dynamically linked library (DLL). DLLs usually are stored in the Windows system directory.

When Microsoft Query is started, it checks for ODBC drivers that have been installed on the computer system. When you ask MSQuery to open a particular type database (like Access, FoxPro, or Paradox), MSQuery uses the ODBC driver DLL to find out how to interpret the data stored in the database tables.

Figure 11.10 shows "MS Access Databases" selected as the data source for this example.

Adding ODBC Drivers

New ODBC drivers can be added to your system by clicking on the New button in the ODBC Data Sources dialog box. The Add Data Source dialog box (figure 11.11) enables you to notify Microsoft Query of any new ODBC drivers located on your system.

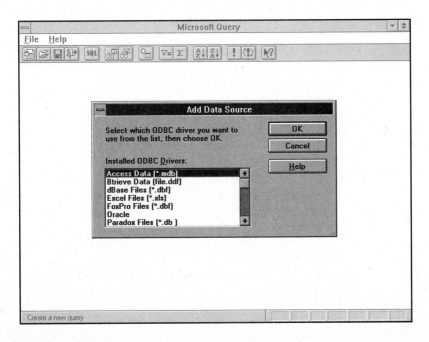

Figure 11.11
All ODBC drivers installed on the system.

Simply click on the ODBC driver you wish to install in MSQuery and press the OK button. This action informs MSQuery that the ODBC driver is available and should be added to the list of drivers in the ODBC Data Source dialog box.

Entirely new ODBC drivers, those not yet located on your system are installed through the ODBC icon in Windows Control Panel.

Deleting ODBC Drivers

If you do not need to use Microsoft Query with one of the data sources shown in the list in the ODBC Data Sources dialog box, highlight it by clicking on its name one time and press the Remove button. This action does not remove the ODBC DLL from the Windows system directory, so the ODBC driver still is available to other Windows applications.

Opening the Data Source

After the data source has been selected in the ODBC Data Source dialog box and the OK button is pressed, Microsoft Query immediately searches for candidate database files in the active directory.

The Select Database dialog box (figure 11.12) shows all candidate databases in the active directory. Because we selected "MS Access Databases" in the ODBC Data Sources dialog box (figure 11.10), only Microsoft Access databases appear in the Database Name list.

Figure 11.12
All databases available in the current directory.

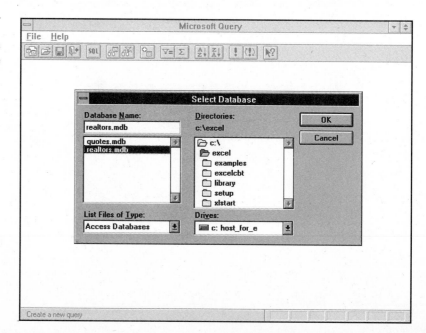

The REALTORS.MDB database is found on the *Inside Excel 5 for Windows* disk.

For this example, we use the REALTORS.MDB database.

Do not be misled by the List Files of <u>T</u>ype combo box in the lower left corner of the Open Database dialog box. Although it might appear that this list enables you to select a different type of database file, it is there only in case your database file has a different extension than the default for the type of database selected in the ODBC Data Sources dialog box.

For instance, the default extension for Microsoft Access database is MDB. If, for some reason, the Access database had a different extension, its name would not appear in the Database <u>N</u>ame list. The List Files of <u>T</u>ype combo box enables you to see either the Access Databases with the MDB extension or All Files in the current directory. It does not permit you to select a different type of database file.

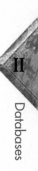

Adding More Database Types to the Query

Oddly enough, when the Microsoft Access database is selected, instead of being returned to the MSQuery environment to proceed with the query, you are returned to the Select Data Source dialog box. The only difference this time is that MSQuery already knows that you intend to use the MS Access Database type in your query (figure 11.13).

This design permits you to add another type of database to your query. Because our example involves only the Microsoft Access database, the <u>U</u>se button returns to the MSQuery environment.

Opening a Database Source

After the <u>U</u>se button is clicked in the Select Data Source dialog box, MSQuery opens the Microsoft Access database previously selected in the Select Database dialog box (figure 11.12) and examines the tables found within it.

In the case of REALTORS.MDB, six different tables (named "AGENTS", "AGENCIES", and so on) are in the database. The Add Tables dialog box (figure 11.14), which opened automatically upon return to the MSQuery environment, shows the tables in the REALTORS.MDB database.

Figure 11.13
The Select
Data Source
dialog box.

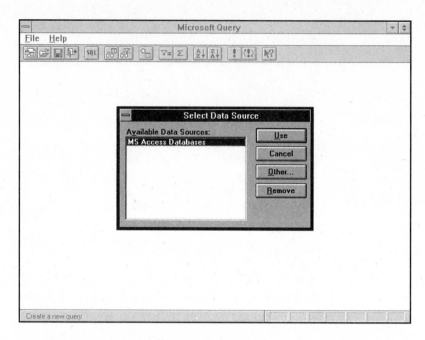

Figure 11.13
The Select
Data Source
dialog box.

Figure 11.14
The
REALTORS.MDB
database contains
six tables.

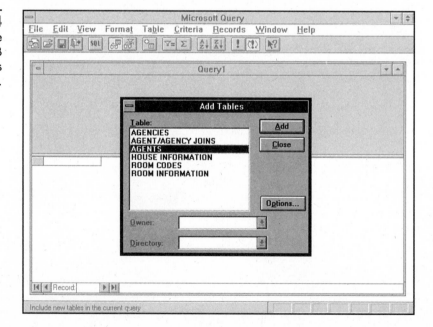

The data contained in the REALTORS database includes the names and contact information for a number of different realtors and the real estate agencies for which they work, plus the selling information for several different homes.

The AGENTS table is part of the REALTORS.MDB database on the *Inside Excel 5 for Windows* disk.

When you click on the Add button is clicked, the AGENTS table is added to the current query (figure 11.15).

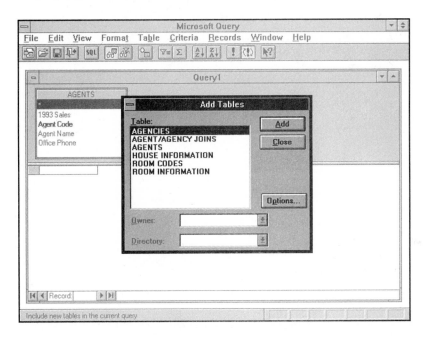

Figure 11.15
The AGENTS table has been added to the query.

The large window on the MSQuery screen is called the *Query window*. MSQuery features a multiple document interface, which means that more than one Query window can be placed within the MSQuery environment at one time. Normally, however, you work with only one query at a time.

Displaying Data

The fields in the AGENTS table appear in the upper pane of the Query window. To display the data stored in the database fields, click on the field names (one at a time) in the table window in the upper portion of the Query window and drag them to the data display area in the bottom half of the Query window. Figure 11.16 shows the Query window after the "Agent Name" and "1993 Sales" fields from the AGENTS table have been added to the data area.

Figure 11.16
The Query window.

Fields are dragged to the Data pane

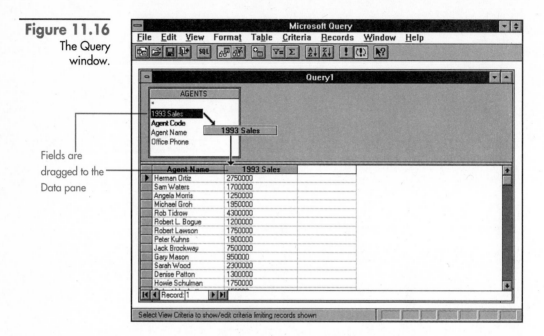

Notice that no query criteria have been applied to extract the data in figure 11.16. All the data in the Agent Name and 1993 Sales fields are displayed. None of the records in the AGENTS table have been excluded. This query is similar to the situation in which a database table is imported directly into Excel.

TIP   Instead of dragging fields to the Data pane, you can move them by double-clicking on them in the table field list.

Understanding the Query Window

The Query window is rather complicated. It contains all of the information necessary to build complicated database queries, and although it is quite straightforward to use, it can be confusing to understand. Before we proceed with building complicated queries, a quick overview of the Query window's components is necessary.

Initially, the Query window is divided into upper and lower portions. The upper portion contains all the tables involved in the query, while the lower area contains the data retrieved by the query.

Figure 11.17 explains the default components of the Query window.

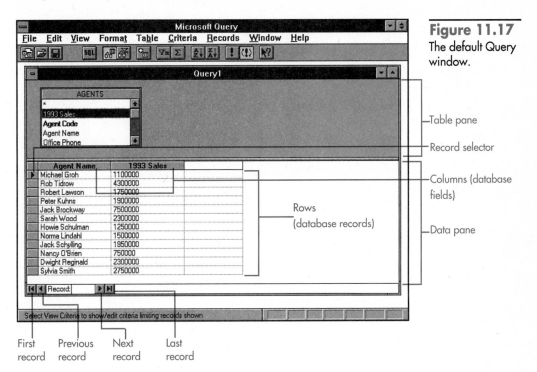

Figure 11.17
The default Query window.

✔ **Table pane.** The Table pane contains all of the tables included in the query. Each table window shows the database fields within the table. In the case of the QUOTES table, the fields are named "1993 Sales," "Agent Code," "Agent Name," and so on.

✔ **Data pane.** Although currently empty, the data pane displays the data extracted from the QUOTES table by MSQuery. The data extracted from the database source is called the *results set*.

✔ **Record selector.** The small triangle at the extreme left of each record in the Data pane can be used to highlight (or "select") the entire record.

✔ **Navigation ("VCR") buttons.** In the lower left corner of the Data pane are a number of highly specialized buttons that provide navigational functions to move through the records in the Data pane. Large data sets might have hundreds or even thousands of records. The VCR buttons (so named for their similarity to the control buttons on most VCRs) provide a way to quickly move through the records in the Data pane.

✔ **Columns (database fields).** Each column in the Data pane holds data from a field in the database table.

✔ **Rows (database records).** Each row in the Data pane contains the data for the selected fields for one record in the database table.

As you work your way through this chapter, you should become familiar with the various components of the Query window.

Be aware of the difference between the words *field* and *column*. A *field* is the name of a specific part of a database table. Database fields normally are displayed as *columns* of data. In this chapter, the words *field* and *column* are used almost (but not quite) interchangeably.

Similarly, a *record* is a component of a database table. Database records normally are displayed as *rows* of data. All of the data items in a record are related to each other—for instance, your name, address, and phone number might make up a record in a database and can be displayed on the screen in a row of a table.

This chapter strives to use the word *field* when referring to the structure of the database table, and *column* to the way in which database fields are displayed. Similarly, a *record* is a specific unit of data stored in a database that appears on the screen as a row of a table.

Selecting Individual Fields

A field is selected for display in the Data pane by clicking on its name in the table window on the Table pane and dragging it to the Data pane. If you release the field anywhere in the unoccupied area of the Data pane, the column displaying the new field's data is added to the right of the far right column currently displayed in the Data pane.

If you release the new field on top of an existing column in the Data pane, the new column is inserted in the existing column's location and the existing column is pushed to the right.

Selecting All Fields

Notice in figure 11.17 that an asterisk (*) appears at the very top of the list of fields in the AGENTS table. If you drag the asterisk to the Data pane, all fields in the AGENTS table are added to the Data pane in the order in which they were created in the AGENTS database table.

If you want to add all the fields to the Data pane in alphabetical order, double-click on the field list's title bar (in figure 11.17, the field list title bar says "AGENTS") to highlight all the fields in the list, and drag any of the fields to the Data pane. All fields are automatically added to the Data pane in alphabetical order.

Specifying Query Criteria

So far, the examples have involved working with the complete set of records from the AGENTS database table. In most cases, however, you do not really want to work with the complete set. Most often, you want to select only certain records from the database for display or manipulation.

A thorough understanding of constructing and using *query criteria* is essential to success using Microsoft Query.

What Is Query Criteria?

Before you can extract specific records for a database table, you must specify the *query criteria* that MSQuery should use during its search of the database table.

Perhaps the simplest form of query criteria is something similar to "Show me the names of all real estate agents who sold more than $2,000,000 of property in 1993." Intuitively, we know that somewhere along the way, the mathematical expression "> 2,000,000" must figure into the query criteria.

Furthermore, we must be able to tell MSQuery that we want the criteria to be applied to the "1993 Sales" field and that we want to see only those records whose "1993 Sales" fields contain values greater than 2,000,000.

Query criteria are not restricted to a single field, as in this simple example. You might, for instance, want to see the real estate listings of all four-bedroom (or larger) houses in the database with offering prices between $100,000 and $150,000 that have attached two-car garages and have at least two full bathrooms. This query involves no fewer than four different fields: "Number of Bedrooms," "List Price," "Garage," and "Number of Bathrooms."

It should come as no surprise that MSQuery is carefully designed to help you construct query criteria exactly like these examples.

The Add Criteria Button

So far in this chapter, we have not used the Show/Hide Criteria button on the MSQuery toolbar. By default, the Show/Hide Criteria button is not pressed, meaning that the Criteria pane of the Query window is hidden from view.

When you click on the Show/Hide Criteria button, the Query window changes, as shown in figure 11.18, to reveal the Criteria pane. The Criteria pane normally is kept hidden between the Table and Data panes.

II

Databases

Figure 11.18
The criteria pane.

Criteria grid

Criteria pane

Criteria field

Criteria value

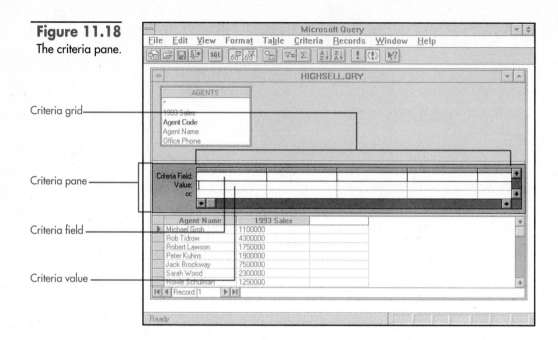

Notice that when the Criteria pane is revealed, the Data pane shrinks to accommodate the space required by the Criteria pane.

Using the Criteria Pane

The query criteria area in the Criteria pane appears as a grid, usually called the *query grid*. Each column in the query grid represents one field that is involved in the criteria. The row labeled "Value" is where you enter the *expression* you want MSQuery to apply to the data in the field when searching for records to display in the Data pane.

To add a field to the Criteria field row of the Criteria grid, click on the name of a field in the Table pane and drag it down to the Criteria field row, as shown in figure 11.19.

Next, enter the mathematical expression that completes the query criteria. In this case ">2000000" yields the records of all real estate agents who sold more than $2,000,000 of real estate in 1993. The expression ">2000000" is entered into the Value row under the name of the field in the Criteria pane. The completed query criteria is shown in figure 11.20.

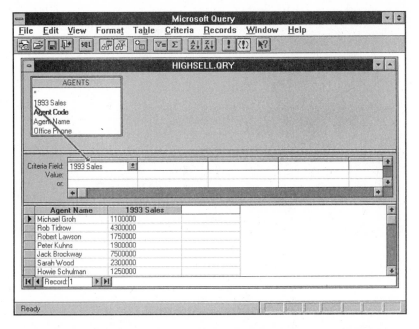

Figure 11.19
Drag fields from
the table field list
to the Query grid.

II

Databases

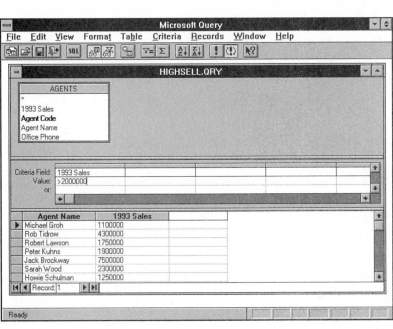

Figure 11.20
The completed
query criteria in
the query grid.

By default, the query is triggered as soon as you complete the query criteria and move the insertion point someplace else on the Query window. To test the autoquery capability of MSQuery after the ">2000000" is filled in, click the mouse on the table field list in the Table pane or use the Tab key to move to the next column in the query grid. You see the screen change, as shown in figure 11.21.

Figure 11.21
By default, the query runs automatically after the criteria is complete.

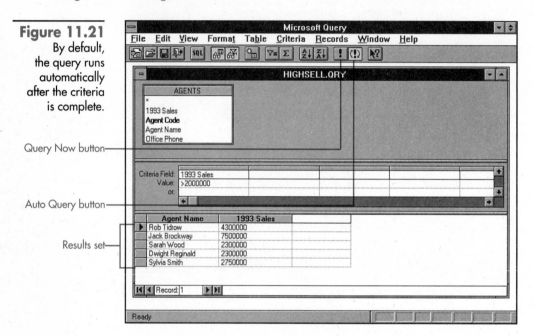

If you do not like the autoquery behavior, which can cause significant delays when the data set is very large and can hinder building complex queries (discussed later in this chapter), you can turn off the function by clicking on the Auto Query button.

The Auto Query button remains depressed after it has been clicked. The Query Now button, however, is a "momentary contact" button—it works only when you click it.

After the Auto query button is released, you must explicitly trigger the query by clicking on the Query Now button on the toolbar (the Query Now button looks like an exclamation mark).

NOTE Notice that MSQuery does not accept commas in the expression, although you can have a space between the ">" and "2000000."

Adding Criteria to the Query Grid

Usually, a successful query requires more than simple criteria built from a single field. Most real-world exercises involve multiple fields and even multiple tables.

Adding a field to the query criteria is simple. Notice that the query grid has space for more than one field. Figure 11.22 shows the effect of adding fields to the query grid. In this case, both the List Price and Number of Bedrooms fields are examined, apparently because the user wants to see the MLS numbers and addresses of all houses with three or more bedrooms at list prices less than $150,000. The results set has been sorted in descending order of the items in the List Price column.

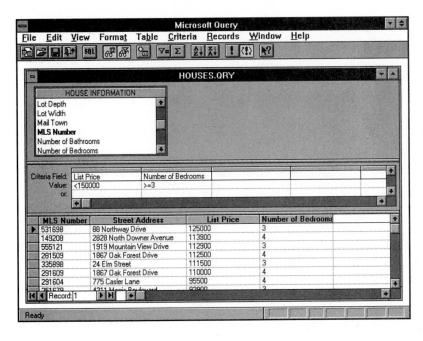

Figure 11.22
A query with two fields in the query grid.

When adding fields to the query grid, you might find that the Auto Query feature of MSQuery gets in the way. Because Auto Query runs the query every time a criteria set (field and query criteria) is completed (for instance, List Price < 150,000), you might find that Auto Query interrupts your work. After you enter the information for the query on one field and move to another field, Auto Query runs before you can enter the information for the next field.

In all of the cases illustrated in this chapter, the data sets involved are so small that queries run pretty quickly. On larger data sets, particularly if the data source is located on a server or another node on a network, you might find that the pause while queries run is intolerable.

Be sure to disable Auto Query if the delay becomes too intrusive.

Saving the Query

After you build a query and are satisfied that you are retrieving the data you want from the database table, you might want to save the query for reuse at a later time.

When you click on the Save Query button, the Save As dialog box (figure 11.23) opens. Notice that the default extension for MSQuery files is QRY.

Figure 11.23
Saving
the query for
future use.

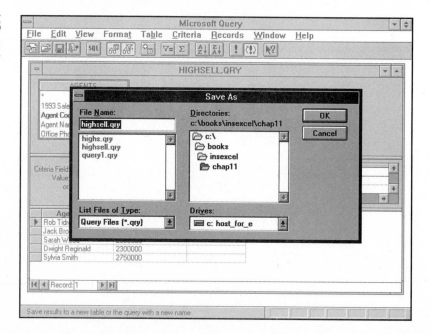

All the information necessary for MSQuery to rebuild the query conditions are saved in the query file: the database type and name, the table name, and the SQL statement.

You can open the query later and run or modify it as needed.

Understanding Expressions

Microsoft Query recognizes a wide variety of different expressions. Simple expressions like ">" (greater than) are easy to understand, but MSQuery can work with much more complicated expressions.

Using Comparison Operators in Query Criteria

The "greater than" sign (">") is an example of a comparison operator. When you use ">" in the query criteria, you are telling MSQuery that you want to *compare* the data in a field with the value to the right of the ">". For instance, ">2000000" means, "show me all of the records with values higher than 2000000."

MSQuery understands a number of other comparison operators as well:

<   *Value* **less than.** Returns all records with field data less than *value*. "< 2000000" returns records with numbers like 1,500,000 and 1,900,000.

<= *Value* **less than or equal to.** Returns all records with field data larger than or equal to *value*. "<= 2000000" returns 1,500,000 and 1,900,000, as well as 2,000,000.

>   *Value* **greater than.** You saw this comparison operator in action. Returns all records with field values greater than *value*.

>= *Value* **greater than or equal to.** Returns all records with field data smaller than or equal to *value*. ">= 2000000" returns 2,350,000 and 4,300,000, as well as 2,000,000.

=   *Value* **equal to.** Returns only those records with field data equal to *value*. Be careful with this one, because often you might not find any records meeting this criteria. This operator often is used with text that you want to find in the database. For instance, ='Sarah Wood' in the Agent Name field returns all the records in which the agent's name is Sarah Wood.

Notice that single quotes are used around the text in expressions. Spaces within the quotes are permissible. Also, MSQuery is not case-sensitive. ='Sarah Wood' and ='sarah wood' return the same records.

<> *Value* **not equal to.** Returns all records with field data that are not equal to *value*.

Most of the mathematical comparison operators look like the algebraic symbols you learned in high school. A little practice is all that is necessary to master the use of these symbols in MSQuery expressions.

> **NOTE** Always remember that mathematical expressions cannot contain commas. ">2,000,000" is an illegal MSQuery expression.

Using Logical Operators in Expressions

Another category of operator uses multiple conditions when performing the search. These expressions combine the expressions or use them separately when building the query criteria.

- ✔ **Value1 AND** *value2*. *Value1* and *value2* are combined for the search to narrow the results set to only those records which match both conditions. Only those records meeting both criteria are returned. Figure 11.24 illustrates an example using the And operator.

- ✔ **Value1 OR** *value2*. The Or operator expands the search somewhat by returning records that match either *value1* or *value2*. In figure 11.25, The query criteria has returned all houses with list prices less than $75,000 or more than $150,000. (The results set also was sorted in ascending order on the List Price column.)

- ✔ **NOT** *value*. Returns all records that *do not* have value in the field. Figure 11.26 illustrates a query that returns all houses with list prices not less than $150,000 (which is almost silly, since it is the same as saying "Show me all houses with list prices *more than* $150,000).

Figure 11.24
This query criteria returns only those houses with list prices between $120,0000 and $150,000.

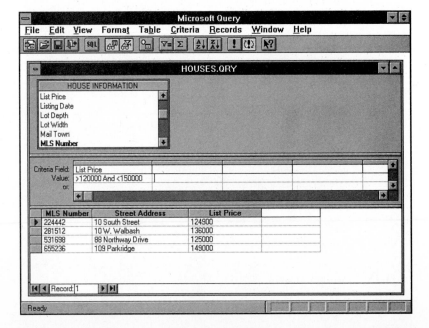

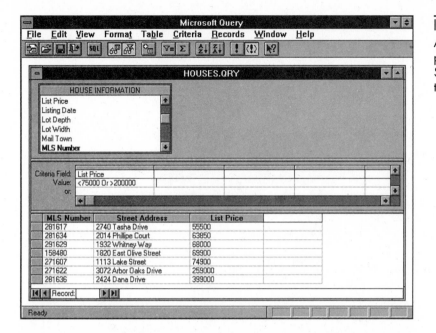

Figure 11.25
All houses with list
prices less than
$75,000 or more
than $150,000.

II

Databases

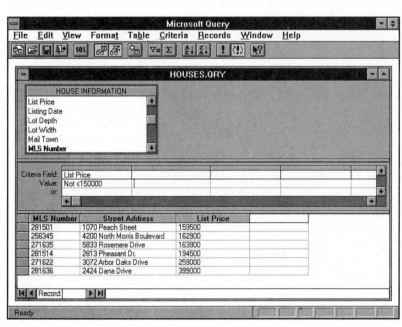

Figure 11.26
All houses with
prices not less than
$150,000.

Esoteric Operators

A few operators are not often used in expressions. For the most part, these operators are equivalent to other, more commonly used operators in expressions.

✔ **Between** *value1* **and** *value2*. Returns all records with data in the field between *value1* and *value2*. You might want to see all houses with list prices between $120,000 and $150,000, for instance. This operator is easily replaced with the And operator, as described earlier in this chapter.

✔ **In (*value1, value2, ...*).** Returns records with values found in a list of values. The list of values must be enclosed in parentheses. An example might be finding the records with Agent Names In('Sarah Wood', 'Rob Lawson', 'Rob Tidrow').

✔ **Is Null, Is Not Null.** Determines whether the value in the field is null (has no value) or not null (has a value). When used with Null, this operator returns all records with empty values in the field.

✔ **Like '*value*'.** Returns values matching value, where *value* contains the wildcard character ("%"). In fact, *value* must contain the wildcard character. Figure 11.27 shows how the Like operator works. All records with Agent Name fields that begin with "Rob" have been returned in the results set.

Figure 11.27
Using the Like operator to get fields with agent names beginning with "Rob."

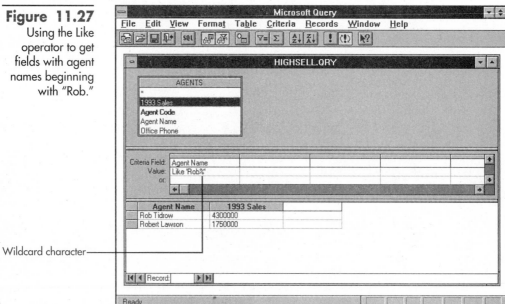

Wildcard character

The Like operator is very powerful and can be used to return records from fairly ambiguous query criteria.

Sorting the Results Set

The data displayed in the Data pane is difficult to use in its current condition. The records in the results set are in no order; the records appear in the order in which they were entered into the AGENTS database table.

Sorting the Results Set in Ascending Order

You can understand the results of a query more easily if the data is sorted in alphabetical or numeric order. Perhaps the objective of this query is to determine the best-selling real estate agent in the database. It is, therefore, useful to sort the 1993 Sales data in ascending order so that the top agent appears at the bottom of the list.

It is not necessary to highlight the entire column before sorting. Simply position the insertion point somewhere within the 1993 Sales column and click on the Sort ascending button. Figure 11.28 shows the result of an ascending sort on the 1993 Sales column.

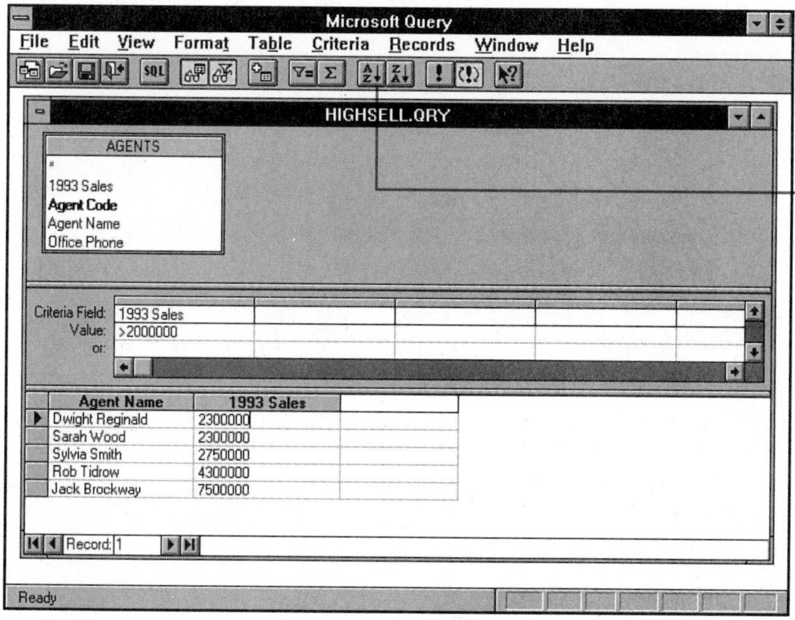

Microsoft Query
File Edit View Format Table Criteria Records Window Help

HIGHSELL.QRY

AGENTS

#
1993 Sales
Agent Code
Agent Name
Office Phone

Criteria Field:	1993 Sales			
Value:	>2000000			
or:				

Agent Name	1993 Sales	
Dwight Reginald	2300000	
Sarah Wood	2300000	
Sylvia Smith	2750000	
Rob Tidrow	4300000	
Jack Brockway	7500000	

Record: 1

Ready

Figure 11.28
The 1993 Sales column sorted in ascending order.

Sort ascending button

NOTE Sorting the data in the results set does not modify the data in the underlying database tables.

Sorting the Results Set in Descending Order

It looks a bit odd, however, to have the top sales agent at the bottom of the list. To reverse the sort order, click on the Sort descending button (figure 11.29).

Figure 11.29

The 1993 Sales column sorted in descending order.

Sort descending button

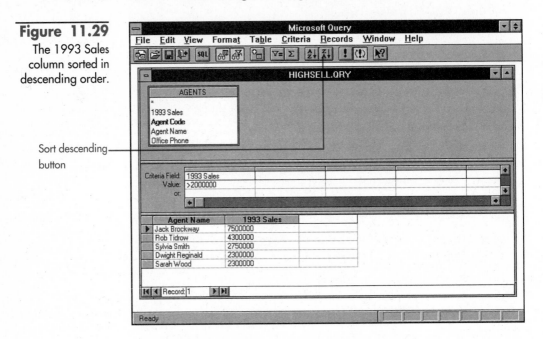

Sorting on Multiple Columns

Although it does not make sense in this example, you can sort on multiple columns. Maybe the results set is so large that, even when sorted on one column in the Data pane, it still is difficult to pick out the individual data item that is important.

Two basic methods are available for sorting multiple columns. The first method involves sorting columns sequentially. Start with the data that is most important and sort it first. Then, while holding down the Ctrl key, sort each column in the order of decreasing importance, so that the least important column is sorted last.

For instance, maybe the results set includes the names of agents and all the houses each agent has listed for sale. You might sort the houses by their Agent Code first, then sort the column of MLS numbers next. The results set are sorted with all houses being sold by each agent grouped together.

The HOUSE INFORMATION table is part of the REALTORS.MDB database on the *Inside Excel 5 for Windows* disk.

Figure 11.30 illustrates this principle. Rather than the AGENTS table, the HOUSE INFOR-MATION table was used for this query. The Agent Code column was sorted first; then, while holding down the Ctrl key, the MLS number column was sorted.

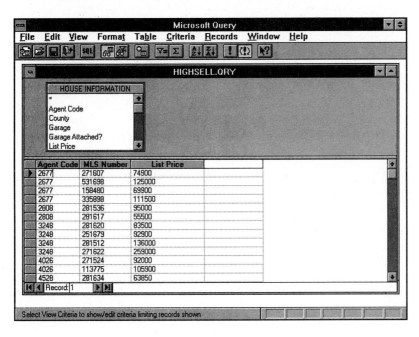

Figure 11.30
The HOUSE INFORMATION table.

II

Databases

Notice that, for each agent code, the MLS numbers assigned to that agent are sorted in ascending order.

NOTE Be sure to hold down the Ctrl key when sorting subsequent columns. Otherwise, the entire results set is sorted according to the last column sorted.

Queries on More than One Database Table

Very often, you need to use more than one table in a query. So far in this chapter, the examples have used only one table in the Table pane, and all queries have been directed to that one table. More complex queries require two, three, or more tables to provide data. In fact, multiple table queries often are used to consolidate and filter data before adding it to Excel worksheets.

Adding Tables to the Query

For the moment, return to the HIGHSELL built earlier in this chapter. This was the simple query that extracted all records from the AGENTS table for agents who had sold more than $2,000,000 of property in 1993.

Suppose you want to see listing information on the houses these agents currently have listed. The only fields in the AGENTS table are Agent Code, Agent Name, Office Phone, and 1993 Sales. Nothing in the AGENTS table tells you about the houses in the database. How can you determine which houses each of these agents has listed?

The HOUSE INFORMATION table in the REALTOR.MDB database contains all the information relating to house listings, including the MLS number, list price, address, and other data. Obviously, the HOUSE INFORMATION table contains the information you want to see.

Ideally, there ought to be some way to *join* the AGENTS table to the HOUSE INFORMA-TION so that you can see just which houses each agent has listed.

Relational databases like Microsoft Access, FoxPro, and Paradox, are the answer. Each table contains one or more *key fields,* which serves as a "connector" to tie the table to the other tables in the database.

The REALTORS.MDB database described in this section can be found on the disk accompanying *Inside Excel 5 for Windows.*

Joining Tables

To begin the process of joining the AGENTS and HOUSE INFORMATION tables, a new query is created by clicking on the New Query button. Microsoft Query "remembers" the database sources that have been used in the past and presents them in the Select Data Sources dialog box (figure 11.31).

Because the AGENTS and HOUSE INFORMATION tables are part of REALTORS.MDB, a Microsoft Access database, select the MS Access Databases option and click on the Use button.

Next, the Select Database dialog box (figure 11.32) opens, enabling you to select REALTORS.MDB from the list of Access databases in the current directory.

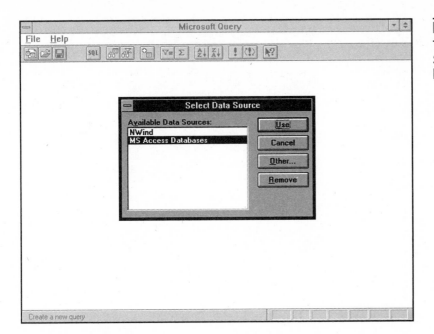

Figure 11.31
The Select Data Sources dialog box.

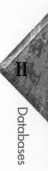

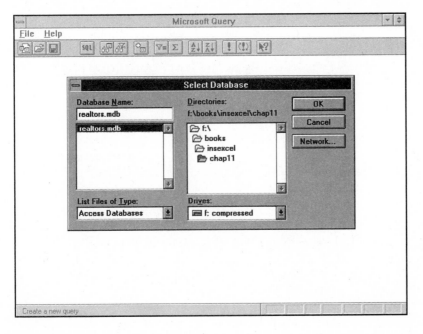

Figure 11.32
Selecting REALTORS.MDB.

Next, the Add Tables dialog box opens (figure 11.33). This time, instead of selecting only the AGENTS table, the HOUSE INFORMATION table is added to the Table pane, as well.

Figure 11.33
The Select Tables dialog box.

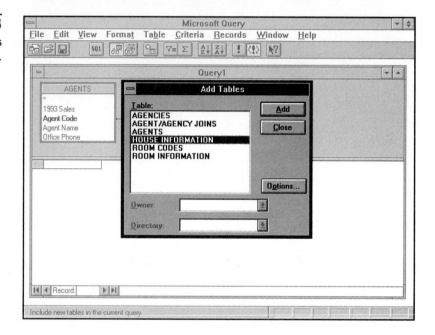

When the Select Tables dialog box is closed, the AGENTS and HOUSE INFORMATION tables appear in the Tables pane (figure 11.34). Notice that Microsoft Query has drawn a line connecting these tables.

To be more specific, the line joining the AGENTS and HOUSE INFORMATION tables is drawn from the Agent Code field in the AGENTS table to the Agent Code field in the HOUSE INFORMATION table. In the AGENTS table, Agent Code appears in bold-face type to indicate that it is a key field for the AGENTS table. The Agent Code in the HOUSE INFORMATION is just another bit of data contained in this table.

The line drawn between these tables, however, represents a *relational join* between the AGENTS and HOUSE INFORMATION tables. Microsoft Query draws lines between fields in the field lists that the tables share. This relational join means that the Agent Code in the AGENTS table can be used to find all of the corresponding Agent Code fields in the HOUSE INFORMATION table. You can, therefore, determine which houses an agent has listed by looking for the agent's code in the HOUSE INFORMATION table.

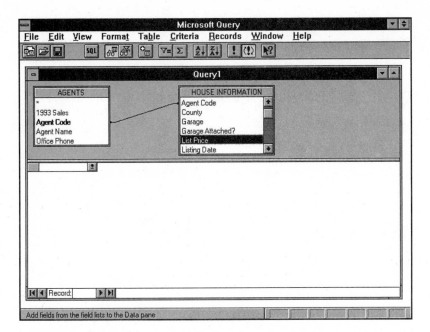

II

Databases

Figure 11.34
The AGENTS and HOUSE INFORMATION tables in the Tables pane.

Using Joined Tables in Queries

Microsoft Query makes it easy to use joined tables in queries. Start by dragging the Agent Name field from the AGENTS table to the Data pane. Next, drag the MLS Number, Street Address, and List Price fields from the HOUSE INFORMATION table to the Data pane. The result looks like figure 11.35.

Each row of data in the Data pane represents a real-estate agent's name and some information on one house that the agent has listed.

Notice that you do not need to add the Agent Code to the Data pane. MSQuery understands the relationship between these tables and brings the related data to the Data pane.

The data displayed in the Data pane is a little difficult to understand. You have a hunch that each agent has more than one house listing in the database, but at first glance, it looks as though only one house is listed for each agent. If you look more closely at the Agent Name column, you notice that Sarah Wood and Norma Lindahl appear twice, indicating that each agent has more than one house listed.

It is easy to clarify the data displayed in the Data pane. An ascending sort is applied to the Agent Name column, resulting in figure 11.36.

Mission accomplished! Now you easily can see that Dwight Reginald has only one house listed, while Howie Schulman has a total of three different houses in the database.

Figure 11.35
Adding fields from
multiple tables to
the Data pane.

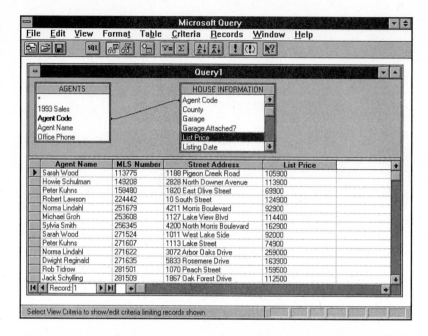

Figure 11.36
After sorting on
the Agent Name
column.

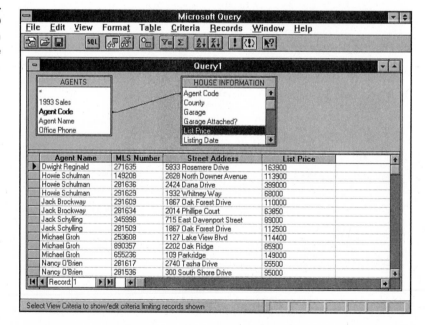

Although much more complicated multiple-table queries are possible, the principles involved are the same as presented in this example: open the database source, add the tables to the Table pane, and drag the desired fields to the Data pane. Often, sorting or other manipulation is required to make sense of the data as it is drawn from the database tables.

Automatic Joins

Microsoft Query calls the lines drawn between related tables *automatic joins* to indicate that it automatically recognizes the relationship between the tables. Sometimes MSQuery needs you to perform a *manual join* to give it a little help understanding relationships between tables.

Manual Joins

From time to time, no automatic relationship exists between tables in the Table pane. In the example described earlier in the section, the Agent Code field in the AGENTS and HOUSE INFORMATION tables defined a relationship between these tables. The relationship was formed in Microsoft Access at the time the tables were created.

Consider the situation in which one table comes from an Access database and another from a dBASE application. Although the data in the tables might be related (for instance, the Access application contains customer names and addresses and the dBASE table contains invoice information), no direct link exists between the tables, because they came from different applications.

Microsoft Query enables you to specify relationships between tables manually. You can create manual joins only if the tables share common fields, even if the tables were created in different applications.

Add the tables to the Table pane using the techniques discussed earlier in this chapter. Then, use the mouse to drag a common field from one of the tables to the field list of the other table. Microsoft Query understands the relationship between the table and builds the relational join between them.

II

Databases

Part III

Charts

Chapter Snapshot

One of the most valuable parts of Excel is its charting function. By using this feature, you can prepare a wide variety of charts that help you communicate or analyze the information contained in your worksheets. Whether your need is based on analyzing data or presenting information, Excel's charting function will most likely suit your needs. In this chapter, you learn the following:

✔ Charting terminology

✔ Creating charts using the ChartWizard

✔ Editing and changing charts

✔ Embellishing your charts using legends, text, arrows, and graphics

✔ Determining which types of charts are better for presenting or analyzing your data

Despite the wide variety of choices available in generating your charts, Excel makes creating and formatting charts easy. Use this chapter to understand all the fundamentals involved in using charts.

12 CHAPTER

Complete Guide to Charts

Excel 5 for Windows has one of the most complete charting functions of any spread sheet. In fact, it's so good that there is little need for dedicated charting programs— even for difficult technical charts. It can produce not only standard charts like bar charts and line charts, but also attractive charts with a three-dimensional appearance.

Excel also contains many tools for embellishing your charts, including the capability to add legends, text, arrows, and graphics images to your charts. You also have full control over the symbols and colors that Excel uses on your charts, and you can even use a graphics image rather than colors in certain types of charts. (For example, a chart showing auto sales might have stacked cars, as you see in many newspapers and magazines.)

Microsoft also has made creating attractive, effective charts in Excel 5 fairly easy. A function called the ChartWizard walks you through all the steps required to quickly create a chart, previewing the eventual results at each step.

The tools you learn about in this chapter are shown in table 12.1.

Table 12.1
Charting Toolbar Buttons

Tool	Name	Description
	ChartWizard	Starts the ChartWizard
	Grid toggle	Turns on and off the grid
	Legend tool	Turns on and off the legend
	Arrow tool	Draws a line with an arrowhead
	Text tool	Creates a box that can contain text and can be positioned anywhere in your chart

Understanding Charts

Before you begin, you need to understand the terminology used to describe the different parts of each chart. Please examine figure 12.1.

Data Points

The *data points* are the individual points on the chart. You can control the way the data points are represented by using different symbols (squares, circles, triangles, and so on) to make your chart more readable. This idea is particularly important when you are presenting black-and-white charts, as opposed to color ones.

As you learn in this chapter, certain types of charts enable you to move data points manually. When you are finished, Excel actually changes the worksheet data to match your changes to the chart. A marketing person's dream!

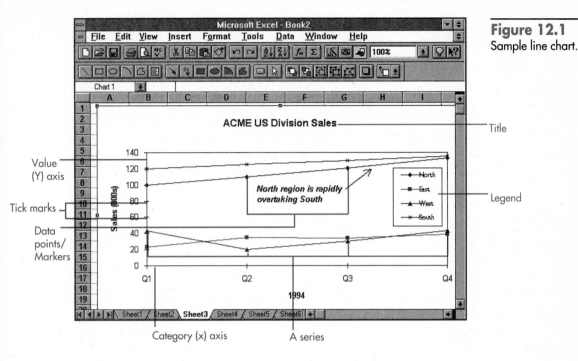

III

Charts

Figure 12.1
Sample line chart.

Series

A *series* is a group of data that forms one part of the data shown on a chart. In the sample chart in figure 12.1, each line represents a series of data. Each series of data is made up of a formula that you can see when you click on the series. If, for example, you click on the North line, you see the series formula appear in the formula bar. The series formula in this case is as follows:

```
=SERIES('12-1'!$B$4,'12-1'!$C$3:$F$3,'12-1'!$C$4:$F$4,1)
```

Understanding and editing series formulas is covered in Chapter 14, "Advanced Charts for Business and Science."

Axes

The *axes* are the vertical and horizontal lines that show what is being charted. Excel offers many features to control these axes, including formatting, manual control of the scale shown, and double y-axes (the vertical axis).

Most charts have two axes: the *X-axis*, also known as the *Category* axis, and the *Y-axis*, typically called the *Value* axis. Some charts also can contain a second Value (Y) axis. Certain 3D charts can be formatted to contain a Z-axis (a 3D chart can show categories along two dimensions, with the Z-axis normally showing the categories or values from the front of the 3D chart to back).

NOTE See Chapter 14 for more information on creating dual Value (Y) axis charts.

Legend

The *legend* defines what each series represents. In figure 12.1, the boxed legend explains that North is represented by diamonds, East by squares, West by triangles, and South by Xs. Legends can be formatted in many different ways, and you can place them anywhere in your chart.

Markers

The *markers* are the symbols (squares, diamonds, and so on) used at each intersection of the plotted data on a line chart. The markers show what the actual data is; the lines between each marker are generated by Excel simply to "connect the dots." You can control the color, type, and style of markers in Excel.

Tick Marks

Tick marks are the incremental marks that appear along each axis to measure or designate the data. The chart shown in figure 12.1 shows four tick marks along the X-axis that mark where each quarter's sales are plotted, and six tick marks along the value axis to show exactly where each value falls. Excel enables you to control the degree of detail the tick marks show, or if they are shown at all. You could, for example, show a tick mark for each month of the year. Because the chart only deals with quarterly data, however, these extra tick marks serve no purpose.

Grid

Figure 12.2 shows the same sample chart as figure 12.1, but a grid has been added. *Grids* help the reader see more easily where the chart markers line up with the axis references.

AUTHOR'S NOTE

Be careful when using gridlines. Sometimes they don't really add anything to the chart, and they can actually make it more difficult to read. The sample chart with gridlines shown in figure 12.2 is a good example. The gridlines make the chart too busy and don't really help the reader of the chart. It was easy to see where the data markers lined up with the sales figures and categories without the gridlines.

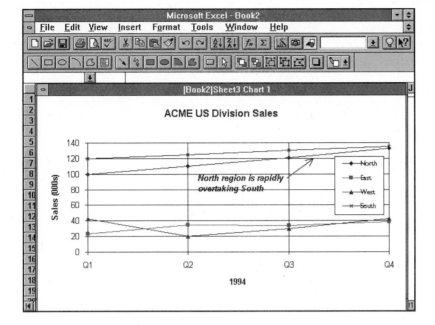

Figure 12.2
Sample chart with grid.

III

Charts

Titles

Titles are lines of text you use to label or identify elements of a chart (or the chart itself). The sample chart has a main title at the top ("ACME US Division Sales") as well as titles attached to each axis ("1994" and "Sales (000s)").

Introducing the ChartWizard

Excel includes a powerful utility that walks you through each step of the chart creation process. This utility is called the *ChartWizard*, and it makes creating charts in Excel a snap. Not only can you use the ChartWizard to create new charts, but you also can use it to change existing charts.

Selecting Chart Data

To use the ChartWizard, you begin by selecting the data you want to plot.

1. Click or Shift-click on the cells you want to include. Select noncontiguous ranges by holding down the Ctrl key as you select each range.

2. Click on the ChartWizard button in the toolbar (see table 12.1). Your pointer changes to a small cross.

3. Use the cross to select the area in the workbook in which you want Excel to

create the chart. Move the pointer to the upper left corner of that area, then drag down and to the right. When the chart area is what you want, release the mouse button.

TIP

Hold down the Alt key as you drag to force Excel to align the chart box with cell borders. Hold down the Shift key as you drag to force Excel to create a perfectly square chart area.

After you have selected the area in which to place the chart, the first ChartWizard dialog box appears, shown in figure 12.3.

Figure 12.3
Step 1 of the
ChartWizard.

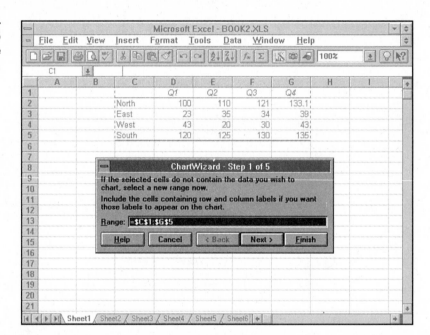

Using ChartWizard Dialog Boxes

Each ChartWizard dialog box uses the buttons described in table 12.2.

Table 12.2
ChartWizard Dialog Box Buttons

Button	Function
Help	Get help on the current step in the ChartWizard
Cancel	Cancel the chart
Back	Go back to the previous steps to change your choices
Next	Move to the next step in the ChartWizard
Finish	Complete the chart creation process using Excel's standard chart and default chart settings

Confirming Plot Data

The first step of the ChartWizard shows you the range of cells you have selected to create the chart. You can edit the cell ranges shown in the first dialog box, although it's typically easier just to cancel the chart and reselect the data you want to plot, reactivating the ChartWizard after you have chosen the correct ranges.

Selecting the Chart Type

The second dialog box in the ChartWizard (see figure 12.4) shows you the various Excel chart types, with the default column chart already selected for you. Choose the chart you want by clicking on it and then clicking on the Next button or by double-clicking on the desired type.

Selecting the Chart Format

After you select the Next button, you see the third dialog box, which shows you the different ways in which the selected chart type can be formatted. Figure 12.5 shows this dialog box for three-dimensional line charts.

III

Charts

Figure 12.4
Step 2 of the
ChartWizard.

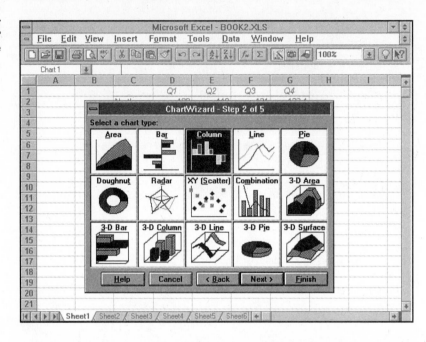

Figure 12.5
Step 3 of the
ChartWizard.

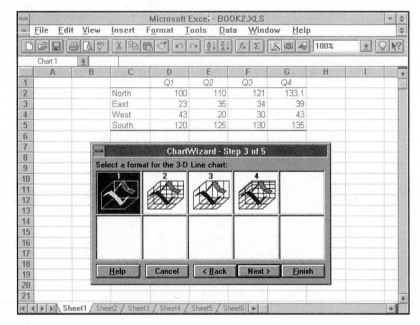

Choosing Chart Options

Depending on the type of chart you selected in step 2, Excel asks you for various settings that control the way it presents the chart.

The Step 4 dialog box, shown in figure 12.6, offers the following options:

✔ **Data Series in Rows or Columns.** These two option buttons control whether Excel assumes that each chart series should originate from columns in your data or from rows. If you choose Rows, for example, each series of the chart is created from a row in your worksheet data. When you select one of these buttons, Excel shows you a sample of that option.

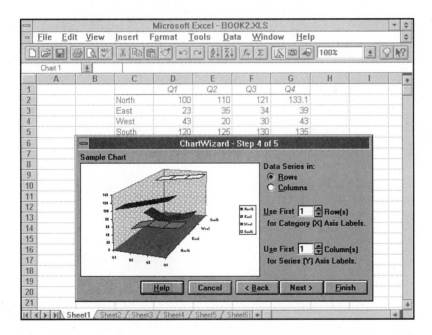

Figure 12.6
Step 4 of the ChartWizard.

Excel uses the "shape" of your data range to assume whether you want the data series plotted in rows or columns. If the data is wider than it is tall, for example, Excel assumes that you want the series to be plotted in the rows. If Excel guesses incorrectly, you easily can change the option button setting.

✔ **Use First *x* Row(s) for Category (X) Axis Labels.** Change the value of *x* in this setting to control the number of data rows to use to label the Category axis of the chart. If your data has no labels in the first row, set this number to 0.

✔ U<u>s</u>e First *x* Column(s) for Value (Y) Axis Labels. Change the value of *x* in this setting to control the number of data columns to use to label the Value axis of your chart. If the first column has no labels, set this number to 0.

Adding Legends and Titles

The fifth step in the ChartWizard enables you to add titles and a legend to your chart. Enter each label in the field provided. Figure 12.7 shows this dialog box.

TIP

You can force Excel to update or *refresh* the Sample Chart view immediately by pressing the Tab key.

Figure 12.7
Step 5 of the
ChartWizard.

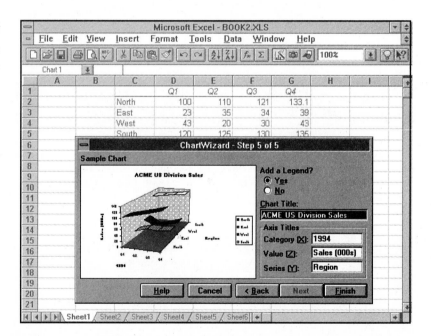

After you click on the <u>F</u>inish button in the final ChartWizard dialog box, your chart is created, as shown in figure 12.8.

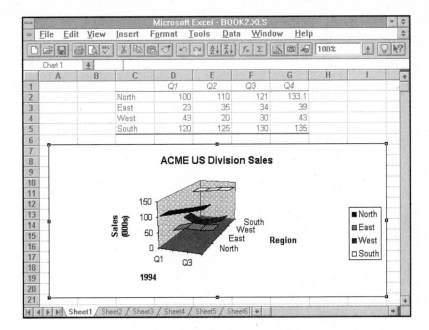

Figure 12.8
The finished chart.

Using the ChartWizard to Create a Chart Sheet

You also can use the ChartWizard to create an entire sheet in your workbook devoted to your chart. This method creates a full-page chart, as opposed to an embedded chart that coexists on the same page as the rest of your worksheet.

To create a chart page with the ChartWizard, follow these steps:

1. Select the data to be charted.

2. Click your right mouse button on the sheet tab for the current sheet. From the pop-up menu, choose Insert. This selection brings up the Insert dialog box, shown in figure 12.9.

3. Choose Chart in the dialog box and click on the OK button.

As an alternative to steps 2 and 3, pull down the Insert menu and choose Chart. This step activates a cascading menu from which you select As New Sheet to begin the ChartWizard with your selected data. Figure 12.10 shows a chart created as a separate page in your workbook.

Figure 12.9
Insert
dialog box.

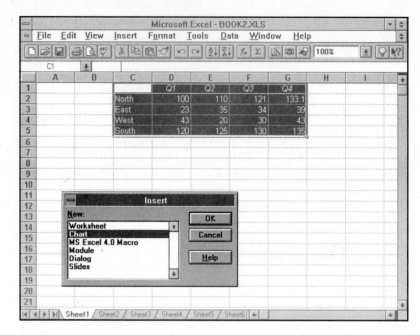

Figure 12.10
Full-page chart
in workbook.

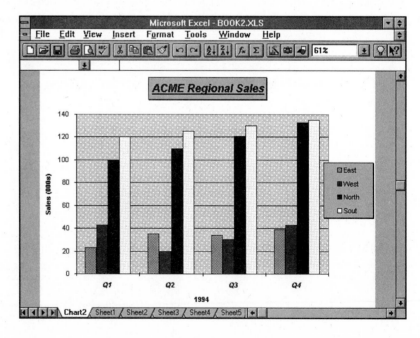

TIP If you simply want a chart of your data using the Excel chart defaults, select the data you want to chart and press the F11 key to instantly create the chart.

Changing Charts

Creating charts is only half the battle. Even with the ChartWizard, you often have to format and reformat charts until you achieve the exact results you want. This section teaches you to format all of the elements of your charts.

Selecting Areas of the Chart

You can select each element of a chart simply by clicking on it. Alternatively, you can press the right arrow key repeatedly to cycle through all the selectable chart elements. You might want to try this on a couple of charts to see which parts of the chart you can select individually.

TIP To select an individual data point, click once on the point to select the entire series. Click a second time on the point to select just that data point. Alternatively, click on the series to select it, and then press the right arrow key to cycle through each data point.

Adding a New Series to a Chart

Figure 12.11 shows a chart that was created before the Europe data line was added to the table.

To add the new line of data to the chart, follow these steps:

1. Select the new data to be added.

2. Grab the border of the new data selection and drag it to the chart. When you move the mouse to the chart, the chart is enclosed in a gray line.

3. Release the mouse button. The Paste Special dialog box appears as shown in figure 12.12.

III

Charts

Figure 12.11
Column chart before adding series.

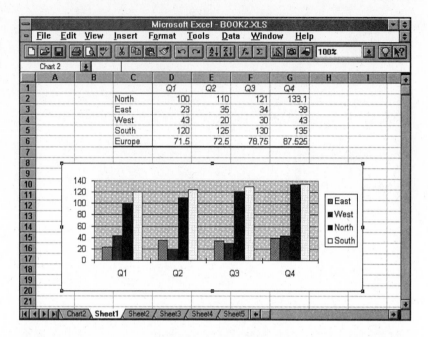

Figure 12.12
Paste Special dialog box for charts.

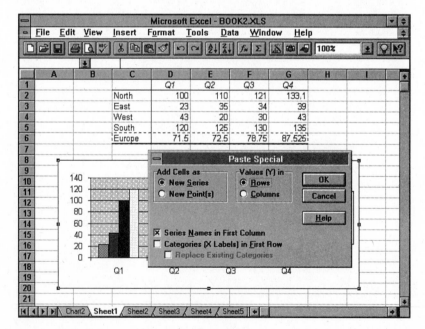

The Paste Special dialog box for charts has the following choices:

- ✔ **Add Cells as.** Choose between New Series or New Point(s). Select New Series to insert the data as a separate data series. New Points creates a new category with the inserted data. In this example, New Series is the appropriate choice.

- ✔ **Values (Y) in.** Here you can choose between your pasted data being contained in Rows or Columns. Although the data in this example obviously is in a row, you also can paste larger selections of data where this choice is not so obvious.

- ✔ **Series Names in First Column.** If selected, Excel uses the first column of the pasted data for the series labels.

- ✔ **Categories (X Labels) in First Row.** If the data you are pasting has its labels in the top row, select this checkbox.

- ✔ **Replace Existing Categories.** This option is available only if the previous selection also is checked. It specifies that the new labels should replace the existing labels in the chart.

After you click on OK, Excel shows you the updated version of your chart (see fig. 12.13).

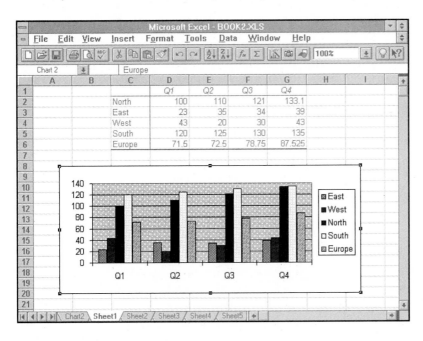

Figure 12.13
Chart with
added data.

III

Charts

Removing a Series from a Chart

To remove a data series from a chart, follow these steps:

1. If you are working with an embedded chart, open the chart you want to edit by double-clicking on it. If the chart is on its own chart sheet, this step is not necessary, although you might need to click on the tab for the page which contains the chart.

Figure 12.14
Selected series.

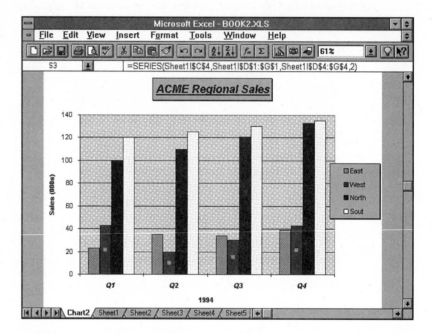

2. Click on the series you want to remove. You should see all the parts of the series selected with small boxes visible, as in figure 12.14.

3. To remove the series, perform one of these operations:

   ✔ Click the right mouse button on the series you want to remove, then choose Clear from the pop-up menu.

   ✔ Select the series and then pull down the Edit menu and choose Clear. This displays a cascading menu from which you can choose All (clear all series), Series (clear only the selected series), or Formats (which removes any formatting you have applied). Select Series.

Moving and Sizing Chart Elements

Many elements of the chart can be moved, including text and legends. To move a chart element, just select it and drag it to its new location. In the case of text objects in the chart, select the text object, then grab the border of the text box and drag it to a new location.

You also can resize many parts of a chart, such as the plot area or text boxes. To do so, select the object. Grab one of the small boxes in the corner, which are called *handles*. You then can drag the handle to a new position. When resizing an element by dragging one of the handles, hold down the Shift key to force the element to retain its original proportions.

Changing the Appearance of Chart Elements

Excel provides you with virtually unlimited capabilities to format your chart so that it is as pleasing and effective as possible. To format any chart element, select that chart element and click the right mouse button on the selected element. From the pop-up menu, choose Format *x*, where *x* is the name of the element you want to format. Also, rather than using the pop-up menu, you can pull down the Format menu and choose Selected Object. The actual name of the menu item changes depending on which object you have selected when you access the Format menu.

TIP To instantly pull up the formatting notebook, press Ctrl+1 after selecting the object you want to format.

Each type of object presents a different formatting notebook depending on what can be formatted for the selected object. For example, if you pull up the formatting notebook with an axis selected, you see a page to change the axis scale.

The following sections show you each notebook page and explain which types of objects apply to the notebook page.

Patterns

Depending on what type of element you are formatting, the Patterns page has different choices available. Sometimes the different choices are subtle, like adding a checkbox called Smoothed line if you are formatting a series in a line chart. Other times the differences might be obvious, such as a section on the page for choosing tick mark styles when you are formatting an axis.

The Patterns page of the formatting notebook is used to control the following formatting tasks:

✔ **Borders.** You can control the style, color, and weight of the line used to border the object. With some objects, you also can choose a *drop shadow,* which gives the box the appearance of depth.

✔ **Area fill.** Some objects enable you to control their fill colors and patterns. You can, for example, control the color and pattern of each bar in a bar chart or each slice of a pie chart. Also, with some charts, you can select a checkbox called Invert if Negative, which tells Excel to reverse the color for any parts of the series that represent negative numbers.

✔ **Lines.** Some objects—notably gridlines and axes—enable you to control the style of the line with which they are drawn. You can control the color, style, and weight of these lines. Also, if you are formatting a series in a line chart, the Patterns page has a checkbox that enables you to select smoothed lines. On a line chart, you can use the Patterns notebook to select the style of the markers used for each plot point.

One example of the Patterns notebook page is shown in figure 12.15.

Figure 12.15
Patterns page.

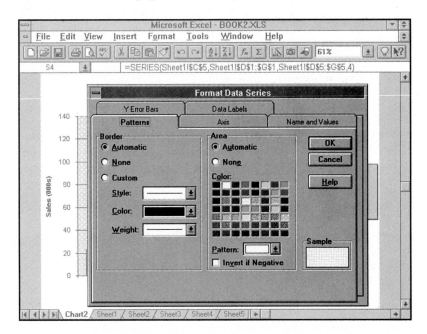

Font

If the object you are formatting is a text box or has text associated with it (such as an axis), you can use the Font page in the formatting notebook to change the characteristics of the font used. Figure 12.16 shows the Font page.

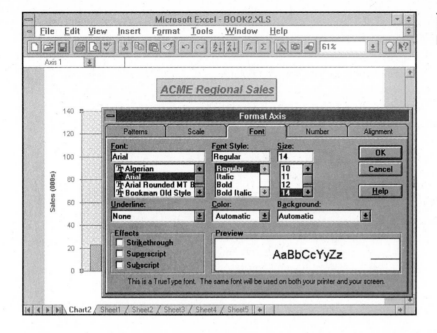

Figure 12.16
Font page.

Using AutoFormat

After you have found a chart format that you like and that you might want to use again, Excel enables you to store your formatting choices as an AutoFormat template. You then can apply these templates to a new chart and escape the drudgery of constantly reformatting your charts. AutoFormat also helps reduce error in cases where you constantly produce charts you want to format the same way.

To add to the AutoFormat table, follow these steps:

1. Start with a chart selected that contains all the formatting you want to store.

2. Pull down the Format menu and choose AutoFormat. The AutoFormat dialog box appears (see fig. 12.17).

    The AutoFormat dialog box initially shows you the different types of charts in the list on the left called Galleries. After you click on each different chart type in the Galleries list, you can select from the subtypes shown in the windows to the right.

3. To access the user-defined charts, click on the option button marked User-Defined. You now see the dialog box changed, as in figure 12.18.

    The AutoFormat dialog box already has a user-defined chart format called MS Excel 4.0. This format was the default chart in Excel 4. If you want to use it, click on the OK button.

Figure 12.17
AutoFormat
dialog box.

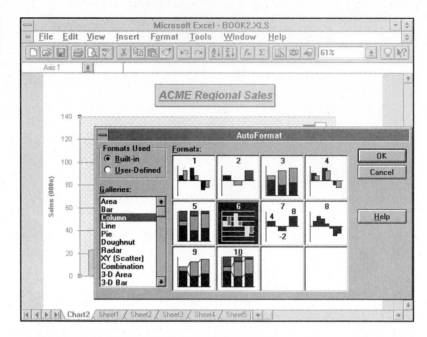

Figure 12.17
AutoFormat
dialog box.

Figure 12.18
AutoFormat dialog
box with user-
defined styles.

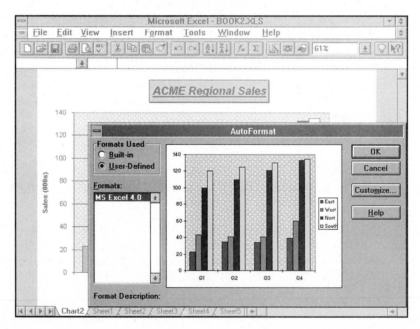

4. Click on the Customize button. The AutoFormat dialog box changes again, as shown in figure 12.19.

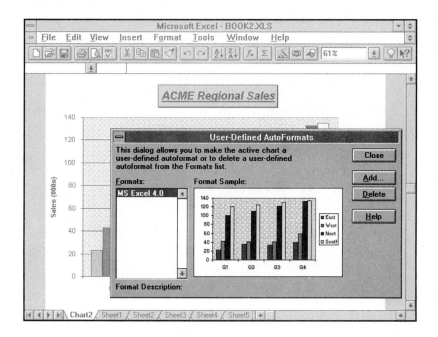

Figure 12.19
AutoFormat dialog box in Customize mode.

5. Click on the Add button to add the current chart format to the AutoFormat system. The AutoFormat system prompts you for the name of your chart format with the dialog box shown in figure 12.20.

You also can select an existing format in the Formats list and delete it using the Delete button.

6. Type a name and a description for the chart in the fields provided and click on the OK button. The User-Defined AutoFormat dialog box reappears. To close it, click on the Close button.

After you have defined a chart in AutoFormat, it is available for all your Excel workbooks. You can apply your automatically formatted charts by accessing Format, AutoFormat. In the AutoFormat dialog box, click on the User-Defined button, then click on the name of your format in the Formats list. Finally, click on the OK button to apply the AutoFormat to the currently selected chart.

Figure 12.20
Add Custom
AutoFormat
dialog box.

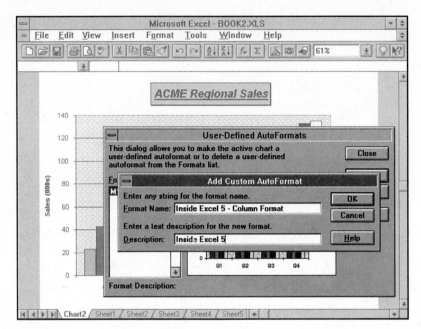

Adding Text

Excel charts have several types of text available: axis labels, attached labels, attached text, and unattached text. *Axis labels* indicate what each point on the axis labels represents; this type of text cannot be moved. *Attached labels* are titles, axis titles, and data labels. *Attached text*, although it is created in certain predefined locations, can be moved freely around the chart. Finally, you can create *unattached text* that you also can place anywhere you want in the chart.

Creating Unattached Text

To create unattached text in an Excel chart, deselect any selected chart elements and simply start typing. Your text appears in the center of the chart area. After you press Enter, you can click on the text to select it, format it, and move it.

Creating Data Labels

Data labels are attached to each data point of the chart. For example, numbers next to each bar in a bar chart are data labels. Depending on the type of chart you are working with, several different types of labels are available.

NOTE A label is text attached to a chart element, but a title is text attached to the title position at the top of the chart or to the axes.

To control data labels, pull down the Insert menu and choose Data Labels. You see the dialog box shown in figure 12.21.

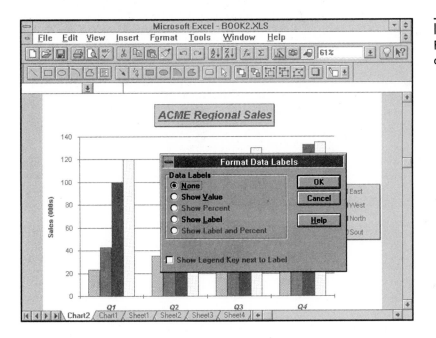

Figure 12.21
Format Data Labels dialog box.

The Format Data Labels dialog box has these choices:

✔ **None.** Suppresses all data labels

✔ **Show Value.** Places the appropriate number next to each data point

✔ **Show Percent.** Places the percentage of the total next to each data point for pie charts

✔ **Show Label.** Shows the category label next to each data point

✔ **Show Label and Percent.** Shows the category label and the percent of the total next to each data point on pie charts

Figure 12.22 shows a column chart with value data labels attached to each bar.

Figure 12.22
Column chart
with value labels.

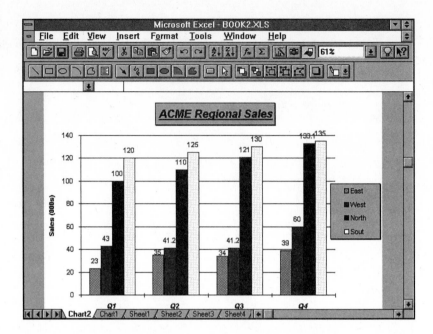

Figure 12.22
Column chart
with value labels.

Creating Titles

To create a title, select Insert, Titles. You see the dialog box shown in figure 12.23.

Figure 12.23
Titles dialog box.

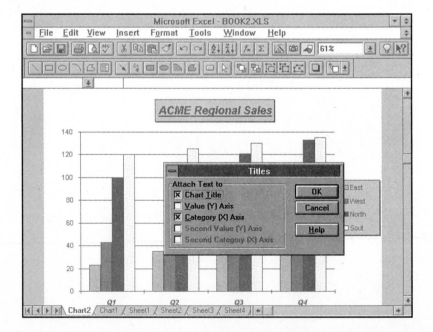

The Titles dialog box has a selectable checkbox for each type of title your chart can accept. In the example in figure 12.23, you see that the chart has no Value (Y) Axis title. To create one, select the checkbox and click on the OK button. A new text area is created next to the Value axis, ready to accept your input. Type in the text for the title and press Enter.

Changing Text Alignment

Most of the text on the Excel chart, with the exception of legend text, can be realigned or rotated so that you can fit more data on the page at very little cost in readability. To try these options, select the text you want to align and press Ctrl+1 to bring up the formatting notebook for that text. Click on the Alignment page, which is shown in figure 12.24. These options are self-explanatory.

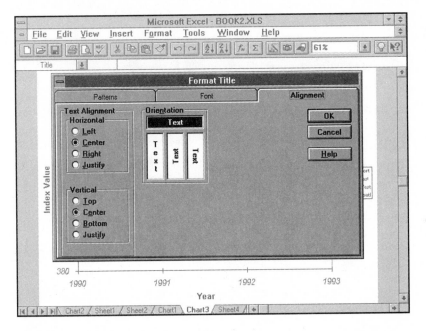

Figure 12.24
Alignment formatting page.

III

Charts

Controlling Legends

You can decide whether to include a legend on your Excel charts. To delete an existing legend, select the legend and press Del or click on the Legend button in the Chart Toolbar. To create a new legend, pull down the Insert menu and choose Legend. A default legend is created, which you can then format as you want using the formatting techniques covered earlier in this chapter.

You also can change the way a legend is arranged by dragging its lower right handle. As you drag the handle, an outline previews the way your legend will be arranged, from a straight vertical arrangement of legend items, to multicolumn legends, to a straight horizontal arrangement.

Controlling Axes

Controlling the axes of your charts can play a powerful role in the impact of the information you convey. For example, consider figure 12.25, which shows a line chart of an imaginary index (sort of like the Consumer Price Index). Notice that it is virtually impossible to tell what the chart is saying with all the lines grouped together so closely at the top of the chart. Because Excel defaults to showing zero as the bottom value axis entry, this problem is a common one.

Figure 12.25
Imaginary index chart.

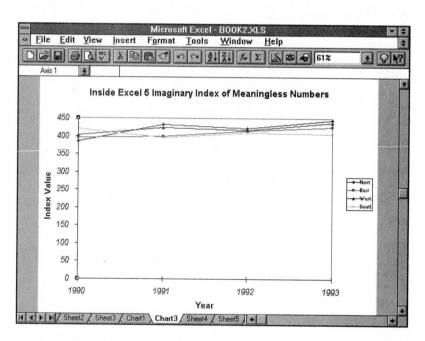

You can solve this problem by changing the Value axis scale:

1. Select the Value axis by using your mouse.

2. Pull down the Format menu and choose Selected Axis. The axis formatting notebook appears.

TIP

After you have selected the object you want to format, press Ctrl+1 to instantly pull up the formatting notebook for that object.

3. Click on the notebook tab labeled Scale. The Scale notebook page is shown in figure 12.26.

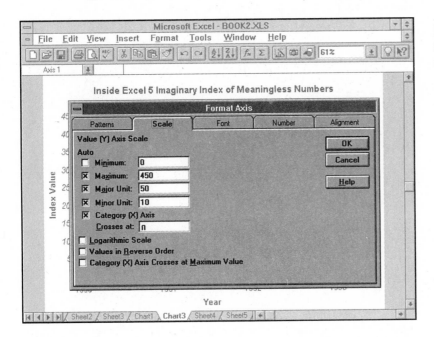

Figure 12.26
Scale
notebook page.

III

Charts

Table 12.3 shows the different settings available on the Scale notebook page.

Table 12.3
Scale Notebook Page

Setting	Purpose
Minimum	Defines the minimum point on the scale. If the checkbox in this field is selected, Excel uses the default value (0 or the lowest data point on the chart, whichever is lowest). Entering in a minimum value automatically deselects the checkbox.
Maximum	Defines the maximum point on the scale. If the checkbox is selected, Excel automatically uses the highest data point on the chart, rounded up to the next highest major axis number.

continues

Table 12.3, Continued
Scale Notebook Page

Setting	Purpose
Major Unit	Defines the Major Unit used for gridline control. You can choose to have gridlines display at each major unit on the axis. You also can control the tick marks used to denote the major unit. See the following section on controlling tick marks for information about the way this page and the tick marks relate.
Minor Unit	Defines the Minor Unit used for gridline control. You can choose to have gridlines displayed at each minor unit on the axis. You also can control the tick marks used to indicate each minor unit on the axis.
Category (X) Axis Crosses at	Enables you to tell Excel where on the Value axis you want the Category axis to intersect. You could, for example, enter the number used in the Maximum field, which would cause Excel to place the Category axis along the top of the chart.
Logarithmic Scale	Causes Excel to use a logarithmic scale for the axis.
Values in Reverse Order	Forces Excel to reverse the default order for the Value axis, so that the lower numbers are at the top of the axis, and the higher numbers are at the bottom of the axis.
Category (X) Axis Crosses Maximum Value	If you select this checkbox, Excel places the Category axis wherever the maximum value of the Value axis is. In the example chart, this would cause the Category axis to be displayed at the top of the chart.

Figure 12.27 shows the sample line chart with the Minimum value set to 380. As you can see, the chart is now much more readable, and you now can see how each region is doing with respect to the other regions. You also can discern an overall upward trend in the numbers. Although the trend is somewhat difficult to see, you can see it far easier than before when all the lines were grouped very tightly together.

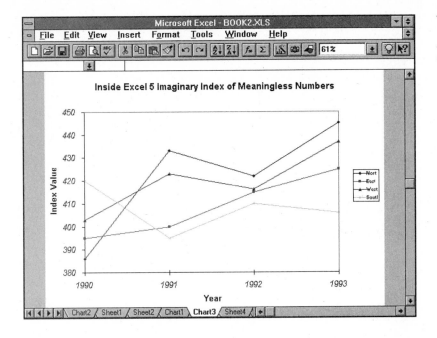

Figure 12.27
Adjusted Value
axis.

AUTHOR'S NOTE

Although being able to adjust the axis measurements on your charts is a valuable tool for analysis and presentation, I have to admit that I really dislike it when newspapers make economic data more alarming than it really is by making it unclear that they are playing with the Value axis in the charts they show. Some charts that purport to show steep economic increases or declines actually say very little (or show only very small changes) after the values used in the Value axis are considered.

Changing Axis Tick Marks

You can control the tick marks used for your charts with the Patterns page of the formatting notebook for the selected axis. Select the axis and press Ctrl+1 to pull up the formatting notebook, then click on the Patterns tab. The Patterns page is shown in figure 12.28.

The Patterns page enables you to control whether tick marks appear for your minor and major axis numbers, what type of tick marks to use (None, Inside, Outside, or Cross), and the way the labels next to the tick marks appear. Select the options you want for the axis and click on the OK button.

Figure 12.28

Pattern notebook page for axis.

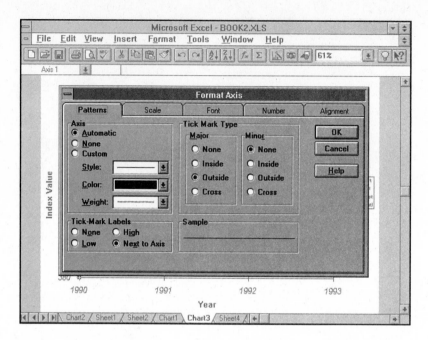

Changing 3D Perspective

Excel contains six different types of 3D charts. Using a 3D chart, however, presupposes that you can change your viewing perspective. Fortunately, Microsoft did not forget to include this capability. Being able to rotate 3D charts can be critical in showing information that might otherwise be hidden, and it can also be used to change the impact that a chart has. For instance, all else being equal, viewing a chart as if you are looking up at it can have a profoundly different impact than viewing it from above looking down.

Figure 12.29 shows a 3D bar chart with the hindmost series being somewhat obscured by the other bars. You can fix this problem simply by rotating your viewpoint of the chart to the left about 1/8 turn. You can accomplish this feat using a dialog box or the nifty wire frame feature.

To change the perspective of the chart using the dialog box, follow these steps:

1. Pull down the Format menu and choose 3D View. You see the dialog box shown in figure 12.30.

2. Adjust the Elevation, Rotation, and Perspective to the new viewpoint.

    The viewpoint fields are accompanied by convenient buttons that help indicate their functions. See table 12.4 for a breakdown of all the choices on the Format 3-D View dialog box.

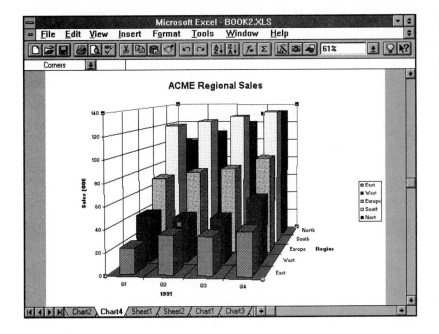

Figure 12.29
A 3D chart with
an obscured
series.

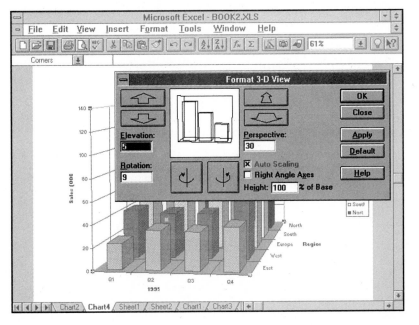

Figure 12.30
Format
3-D View
dialog box.

Table 12.4
Format 3-D View Dialog Box Settings

Field	Function
Elevation	This field controls the height of your viewpoint and is expressed in degrees (from –90 degrees, looking up at the chart, to 90 degrees, which is looking down onto the chart). Pie charts and bar charts have different limits. The elevation for pie charts is limited to 10-80 degrees; bar charts are limited to 0-40 degrees.
Rotation	Rotation also is given in degrees, from 0-360 degrees. Bar charts are restricted from 0-44 degrees.
Perspective	Perspective controls the perceived depth of the chart. This value controls the ratio of the size of the front of the chart to the size of the rear of the chart. Perspective can range from 0 to 100.
Right Angle Axes	When this checkbox is selected, the axes always are displayed at right angles (90 degrees, 180 degrees, 270 degrees, and 0 degrees). Otherwise, the axes are free to be displayed at varying angles called for by the chart perspective.
Auto Scaling	This choice is available only if Right Angle Axes is selected. When Auto Scaling is selected, the chart is scaled proportionally to take up as much of the chart area as possible.
Height % of base	This field controls the percentage of the height of the chart in relationship to the Category axis. If you set this number to 300, for example, the chart will be three times taller than the Category axis is wide.
Apply	This button applies your changes without exiting the dialog box, so that you can see your changes before you commit to them. You might need to move the dialog box off to the side to see the chart, however. Note that when you apply your changes, they are not cancelled by exiting the dialog box. Instead, the Apply button enables you to adjust and view your changes, allowing you to quickly readjust and view until the chart view is to your liking.
Default	When clicked on, this button returns the chart to the Excel default settings for 3D view.

3. Click on the Apply button to look at your changes. If you are not happy with the result, continue to adjust the values in the dialog box and click on the Apply button until you see what you want.

4. Click on the OK button to finalize your changes and exit the dialog box.

Excel also enables you to change the 3D view more directly by dragging handles on the chart itself.

1. Select one of the chart corners. Handles appear at each corner of the chart. Click on one of these handles and hold down the mouse button to begin dragging. As you drag, you see a *wireframe* (three-dimensional outline) image of your chart, as shown in figure 12.31.

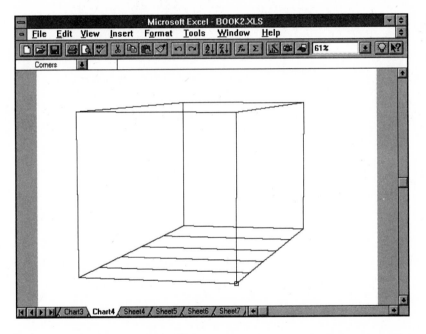

Figure 12.31
Wireframe of
a 3D chart.

2. When the wireframe indicates the view you want, release the mouse button to have Excel redraw the chart based on the new perspective.

Changing Data from the Chart

In most Excel charts, you can change the value of a particular data marker directly by simply dragging it. When you do this, Excel automatically adjusts the values in the original worksheet data so that they correspond to the new data marker position.

If you are going to be adjusting a chart in this way, you should consider making a copy of the worksheet data on which the chart is based before manipulating the chart and changing the data.

Consider the chart and worksheet example in figure 12.32. You see a simple line chart graphing two data series. The second data series is based on the first, with 40 percent added to it.

Figure 12.32
Sample line chart.

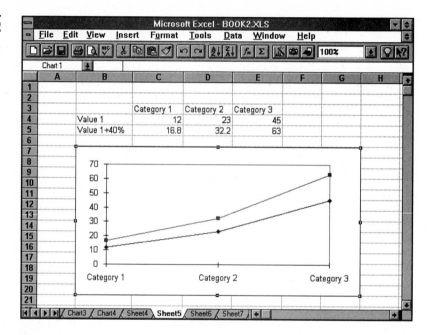

To directly change the middle data point in the first series, follow these steps:

1. Click on the center data marker of the lower series once to select the series, then again to select the individual data point. After the individual data point is selected, your pointer changes to a small double-headed arrow that points up and down.

2. Drag the data point to a new position and release the mouse button to complete the change. You see as you are dragging the data marker that a small cross appears in the Value axis to help you select the new value more accurately.

When the change is finished, the sample chart looks something like figure 12.33. As you can see, the data in the worksheet was changed automatically to be consistent with the chart data.

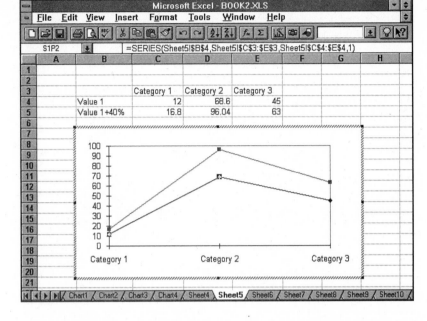

Figure 12.33
Moved
data marker.

If you move a data marker that represents the result of a calculation, Excel automatically updates the data. In this example, moving one of the markers in the top data series would also have to change the number in the lower data series, because the top data series is dependent on the lower data series.

When you move a dependent data marker, Excel automatically invokes its Goal Seek feature so that it can reverse the change to the cells that make up the formula. Figure 12.34 shows the Goal Seek Status dialog box after you move one of the dependent data markers.

The Goal Seek Status dialog box has three fields. The Set Cell field shows the cell on the worksheet that you have changed with the data marker. The To Value field shows the new value for the cell associated with the moved data marker. The final field, By Changing Cell, prompts you for the cell that should be changed in order for all the calculations on the worksheet to remain consistent. This field must be set to a cell that provides a constant value (in this case, cell D4 is the cell that must be changed in order for cell D5 to remain consistent). If the cell being changed is based on many constant values, the Goal Seek Status dialog box enables you to choose which one to manipulate to reverse the calculations. Select the appropriate cell by making the By Changing Cell field active and clicking on the cell to change. Click on the OK button to initiate the Goal Seek process.

If Goal Seek is not able to find a solution that fits all the formulas involved, it displays an error message and the Goal Seek fails. If it finds a solution, it shows you the message in figure 12.35.

III

Charts

Figure 12.34
Goal Seek
dialog box.

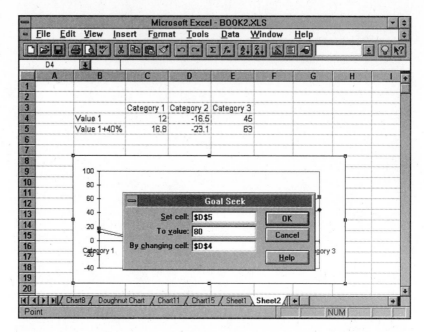

Figure 12.35
Goal Seek
Status dialog
box.

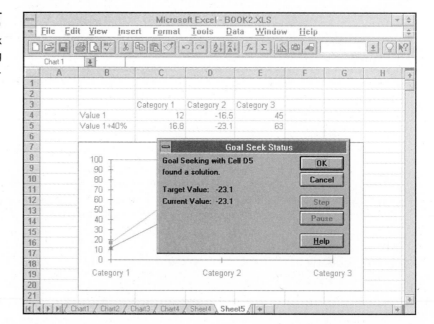

The Goal Seek function works by trying many different values in the target cell, zeroing in on a solution until it finds one that works perfectly. Note that you might not be able to solve some formulas with the Goal Seek function. Also, if more than one possible solution exists, Excel might not choose the solution you want. Examine the results carefully before you accept the change.

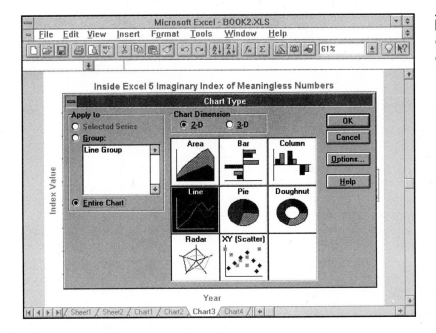

Figure 12.36
Chart Type
dialog box.

Changing Chart Type

You easily can change the type of chart used to plot your data. To do this, select the chart, pull down the Format menu, and choose Chart Type. Figure 12.35 shows the Chart Type dialog box.

The Chart Type dialog box is divided into two main sections—Apply To and the display of chart types. To display available two-dimensional chart types, click on the 2-D button. The 3-D button shows you available three-dimensional charts.

To select a new chart type, click on the chart you want in the display, then click on the OK button, or simply double-click on the chart type you want.

You also can choose to change the chart type for only selected series in the chart. Select the series you want to change before invoking the Chart Type dialog box. Then click on the Selected Series button before choosing a chart type. This capability enables you to form combination charts. For example, you could have some of the series plotted with lines and others plotted with bars. You can even take a single series of a line chart and plot it as a pie chart, superimposed on top of the line chart (if you want to get really wild, that is).

Guided Tour of Excel Charts

The remainder of this chapter shows you examples of each major type of chart in Excel, along with suggestions about how best to use each chart and notes about special features particular to that chart.

The different charts in Excel are not built in for aesthetic reasons. Rather, each chart specializes in showing different types of information.

AUTHOR'S NOTE

The chart you choose to present your data can have a subtle but profound impact on your audience. Different charts prompt different questions about the information and can influence your audience to come to different conclusions. Take some care in choosing the right chart for the job and in anticipating the questions that your chart might prompt.

Area Charts

Area charts work best when you want to show the relationship of different series of numbers and the way each series contributes to the total of all series. If figure 12.36 were done with a line chart, you would have to add a line to represent total sales in order to easily see the sum of all series in a given category, and even then it would be difficult to see how each one contributed to the whole.

Area charts emphasize change across the categories, particularly relative change between different series.

Area charts can show error bars and standard deviations. Access these features by selecting a particular series, pulling up its formatting notebook (double-clicking on the series), and using the Y Error Bars page in the notebook.

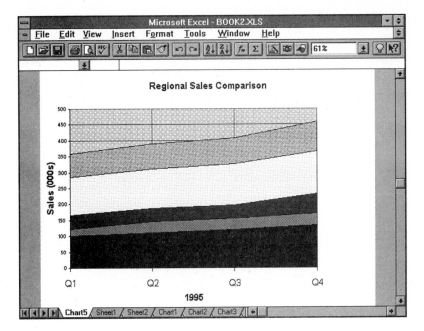

Figure 12.37
Sample area
chart.

Bar Charts

Bar charts emphasize comparison of the different categories rather than emphasizing comparison across time, as column charts do. Several different subgroups of bar charts exist, including the stacked bar and 100-percent stacked bar. The *stacked bar* shows the relationships between the different series more accurately, whereas the *100-percent stacked bar* shows the percentage of the whole for each series. Figure 12.38 shows a sample bar chart.

NOTE

Bar charts, along with column charts, are an excellent place to use error bars. Typically, *error bars* are used to show the standard deviation on technical charts. To add error bars to a bar chart, select the series to which you want to add the error bars, pull down the **I**nsert menu, and choose **E**rror bars. On the notebook page that appears, choose the style of error bars you want and define the amount of error to be shown in the Error section of the page. See Chapter 14, "Advanced Charts for Business and Science," for more information.

III

Charts

Figure 12.38
Sample bar chart.

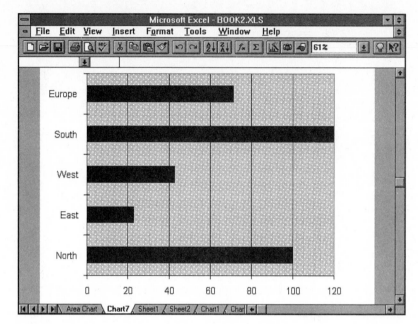

Column Charts

Column charts are best at illustrating the way values change over time, and they also help the reader compare different values side by side. Because time is on the horizontal access, column charts emphasize change over time. Column charts, like bar charts, can use error bars and can also be produced in a stacked column format and a 100-percent stacked format. Figure 12.39 shows a simple column chart.

One key difference between a column chart and a line or area chart is that the column chart shows only discrete values across time. Line and area charts, on the other hand, presuppose activity between each data point because of the line drawn between each point.

Line Charts

Line charts emphasize trends in your data. Although line and area charts have some similarities, they also have some big differences. Area charts, for example, easily express the total of all series, but line charts do not (unless you add that as a separate series). Line charts are designed to show a trend over time, and the Category axis is almost always time-based (months, quarters, years, and so on).

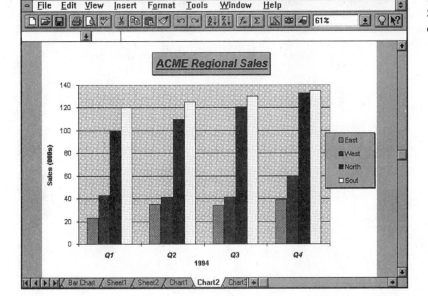

Figure 12.39
Sample column chart.

If you need to show a trend using a measurement other than time on the Category axis, use a scatter chart with the data points connected by lines (one of the scatter subtypes; see the following section on scatter charts). Because line charts are designed to use time on their Category axis, you cannot have a logarithmic scale on the Category axis, as you can with scatter charts.

You also can add trend lines to your charts. See Chapter 14, "Advanced Charts for Business and Science," to learn more.

Pie Charts

Pie charts always show percentages of a whole and emphasize a particular part of your data, as the emphasized Europe slice shows in figure 12.41.

You can rotate the pie chart by selecting the chart, pulling down the Format menu, and selecting Pie Group from the menu. On the notebook that appears, click on the Options tab. On this page, you can change the Angle of First Slice field, which specifies the degrees at which the first pie slice appears.

Figure 12.40
Sample line chart.

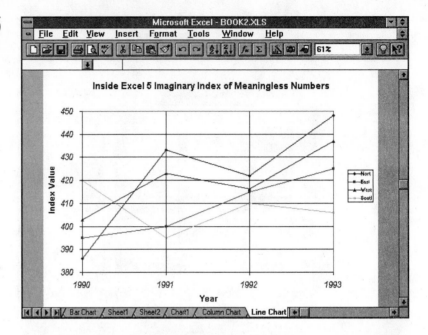

Figure 12.41
Sample pie chart.

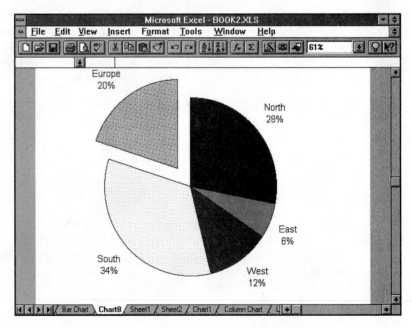

Doughnut Charts

Doughnut charts are very similar to pie charts, because they show proportion of a whole. The main advantage of a doughnut chart, however, is that it enables you to compare multiple series of data, as shown in figure 12.42.

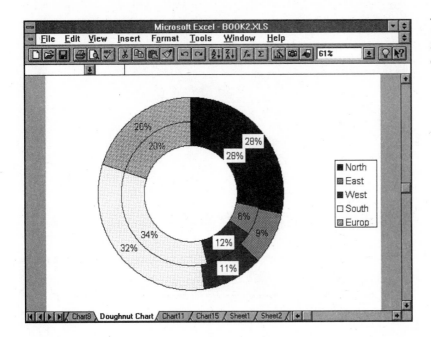

Figure 12.42
Sample doughnut chart.

III

Charts

Radar Charts

Radar charts (see fig. 12.43) show changes between categories. Each radiating axis from the center represents a category, and each line is a series. As you can see in category 1 (the vertical category at the top of the chart), radar charts also can be formatted to use a logarithmic scale to represent their data. Radar charts are most commonly used in Asia and Europe.

Scatter (XY) Charts

Scatter (XY) charts show the relationship between two (or more) scales. Generally, both scales are numeric measurements. In fact, the scatter chart is not really designed to show a time series, although it can if needed. A scatter chart often is used for scientific plots, and they are often seen with logarithmic scales, as shown in figure 12.44.

Figure 12.43
Sample
radar chart.

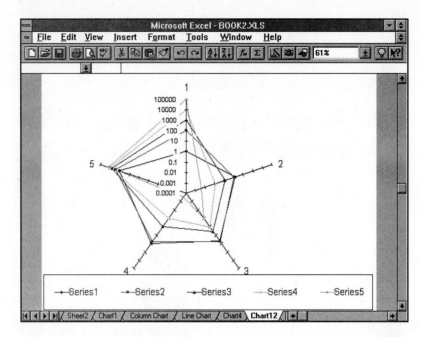

Figure 12.44
Sample
scatter (XY) chart.

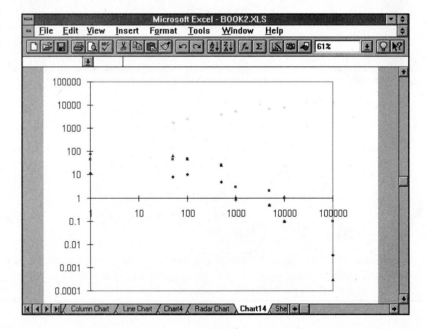

If you need to show the relationship between two number-based axes, but want connecting lines between the data points, you can use the scatter chart, but choose the subtype of scatter chart that connects the dots.

For more information about Scatter (XY) charts, see Chapter 14, "Advanced Charts for Business and Science."

3D Charts

The pie, bar, column, and line charts also are available in a 3D format. The 3D variants are provided for aesthetic reasons; the preceding notes for bar, column, and line charts also apply to the 3D versions of these charts. See figures 12.45–12.48 for examples of these charts.

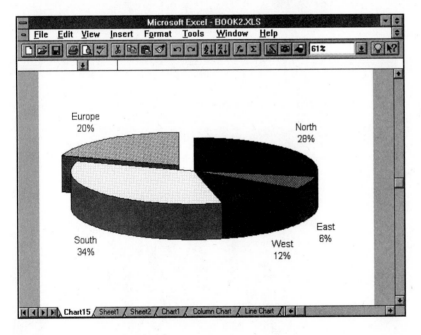

Figure 12.45
3D pie chart.

III

Charts

Figure 12.46
3D bar chart.

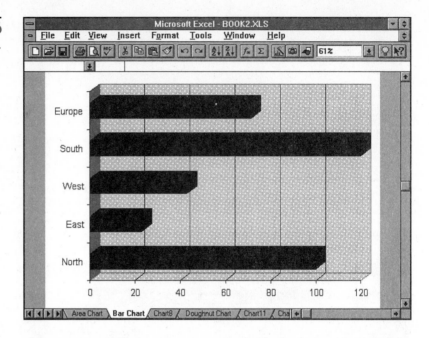

Figure 12.47
3D column chart.

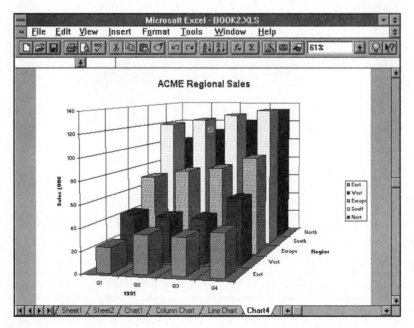

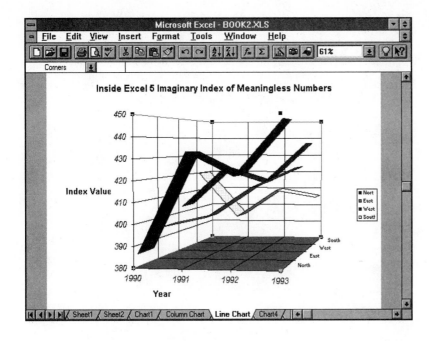

Figure 12.48
3D line chart.

3D Surface Charts

The *3D surface chart*, as shown in figure 12.49, is used to help you find the best combination of two sets of data. Using the surface chart can make large sets of data easier to interpret.

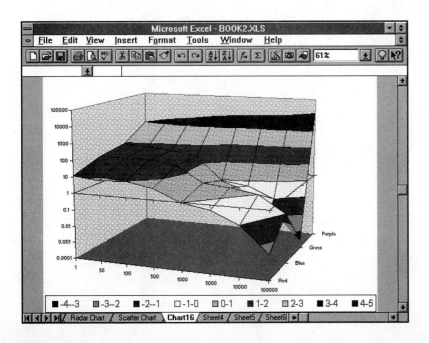

Figure 12.49
3D surface chart.

The colors on the 3D surface chart show different axis ranges rather than different series.

Chapter Snapshot

Not only can you use the graphics capabilities of Excel 5 to annotate your worksheets and charts, you also can use the graphics tools to create more complex drawings, such as organizational charts, freehand drawings, and flow charts. In this chapter, you learn the following tasks:

- ✔ Drawing and controlling graphics on your Excel documents

- ✔ Linking an Excel macro to a graphics object

- ✔ Incorporating pictures from other programs into your worksheets and charts

- ✔ Using a graphics image as your charting symbol

Even aside from the ability to annotate your charts and worksheets with graphics, the drawing tools in Excel 5 are almost as good as many dedicated drawing packages. Unless you have complex needs, you will find that most drawing tasks can be accomplished easily and quickly in Excel.

CHAPTER

Drawing and Adding Graphics to Documents

Now more than ever before, spreadsheet programs are being used not only as analysis and automation tools for numbers, but also as presentation tools. Some people might feel that graphics capabilities are more toys than serious business tools, but you can make a strong case for their use.

In addition to preparing complete presentations with spreadsheet programs such as Excel, you can use graphics capabilities to make a spreadsheet clearer for the people who need to read it. Pointing out a particular number with an arrow, placing borders around parts of the spreadsheet, or even illustrating a point graphically are all functions that have a very serious purpose—not only to show results, but to help communicate them. This capability to communicate more effectively is, in one sense, the very purpose of spreadsheets.

Spreadsheet programs such as Excel can be thought of as *decision support tools* rather than tools to crunch numbers together. Because Excel plays a role in helping people make decisions, you also must consider the ability to communicate the information as an integral part of the tool.

As you discover in this chapter, Excel 5 for Windows has a wealth of capabilities that you can put to work immediately to help convey your information more concisely, accurately, and most important, compellingly.

Enhancing Your Documents Using the Drawing Tools

This chapter makes extensive use of the Drawing toolbar. To see the Drawing toolbar on-screen, pull down the <u>V</u>iew menu and choose <u>T</u>oolbars. In the dialog box that appears, select the checkbox next to Drawing and then click on OK. Alternatively, click on the Drawing tool icon on the Standard toolbar to display or hide the Drawing toolbar. Yet another way to access the Drawing toolbar is to right-click anywhere on the visible toolbars, then select Drawing from the pop-up menu.

The Drawing toolbar automatically opens in floating mode. To make it part of the toolbar area, drag it left, right, or down until it is positioned along one of the screen borders (such as below the Standard toolbar), and then release the mouse button.

The following sections show you ways to use the tools built into Excel to add drawings to your charts and worksheets.

The drawing tools work the same way on both charts and worksheets. Although this chapter shows most of the drawing tools on a worksheet, they work equally well on a chart and function identically.

Although each drawing tool has some differences, they have many common characteristics. To use any of the drawing tools, simply click on the tool you want to use and drag it to the document to begin drawing with it.

Normally, when you click on a drawing tool and then draw something with it, the tool immediately becomes deselected as soon as you have finished drawing the object. To make a tool "stick" on so that you can draw several items of the same object type, double-click on the tool. It remains selected until you click on it again to deselect it, or click on another drawing tool.

Drawing Tools Summary

Table 13.1 shows you each of the drawing tools and discusses features specific to each tool.

Table 13.1
Drawing Toolbar Icons

Icon	Name	Description
	Line	The Line tool draws straight lines. You can take a line drawn with the line tool and make it into an arrow by bringing up the formatting notebook and changing the <u>S</u>tyle on the Patterns page.
	Rectangle	Use the Rectangle tool to draw rectangles and boxes. The Patterns page of the rectangle's formatting notebook has two checkboxes: Sha<u>d</u>ow, which gives the rectangle a drop shadow, and <u>R</u>ound Corners, which rounds the corners of the rectangle. When you give a rectangle a drop shadow, Excel automatically assigns the rectangle a white color fill. Figure 13.1 shows a normal rectangle alongside one with rounded corners and a drop shadow.

TIP   After selecting the object, click on the Shadow button in the Drawing toolbar to turn the shadow on and off.

Icon	Name	Description
	Ellipse	The Ellipse tool draws ovals and circles. The Patterns page of an ellipse's formatting notebook has a checkbox called <u>S</u>hadow, which gives the ellipse a drop shadow.
	Arc	The Arc tool draws arcs that begin and end at 90 degree angles, although the arc does not have to have perfect proportions in height and width. Hold down the Shift key as you draw an arc to force it to have equal height and width measurements (in other words, 90 degrees of a circle). Figure 13.2 shows three different arcs.
	Freeform	The Freeform tool is very powerful. You can use it in two modes: a connect mode and a freehand mode. To use connect mode, select the tool and click where you want the first line to start. Move to the ending location for the line and click again. Keep repeating this point-and-click operation until you have drawn your shape. In connect mode, you can hold down the Shift key to constrain the

continues

III

Charts

Table 13.1, Continued
Drawing Toolbar Icons

Icon	Name	Description
		lines to 45 degree angles. Hold down the mouse button and drag to draw in freehand mode. You can use both modes in a single object drawing. Double-click the mouse to finish drawing the object. After your object is drawn, you can use the Patterns page of the formatting notebook to give the entire object a drop shadow by selecting the Shadow checkbox.
	Text Box	The Text Box tool enables you to draw rectangles that contain text. After the rectangle is drawn, a cursor automatically appears within the rectangle, ready for you to begin typing the text. The Text Box object has two extra pages in its formatting notebook: Alignment, which controls the alignment of the text in the box, and Font, which controls the font used. You also can mix fonts and styles within the box by selecting only the text you want to format before you open the notebook. Also, the Protection page has a Lock Text checkbox that controls the locking property of text in the box when the workbook is protected.
	Arrow	The Arrow tool enables you to draw lines with arrowheads at either end. By default, the arrowhead is automatically placed at the end of the line. Control the format of the arrowheads using the Patterns page of the formatting notebook, which is shown in figure 13.3. In the Arrow Patterns page, you can control the Style of the arrow (no arrowhead, open arrowhead, filled arrowhead, and double-ended arrowheads), the Width of the arrowhead (the amount of space between the end of the tines), and the Length of the arrowhead (the distance from the tip to the back of the arrowhead).
	Freehand	Using the Freehand tool, you can draw in a pure freehand mode, as opposed to the Freeform tool, which also lets you draw straight lines. Stop drawing the freehand line by releasing the mouse button after the object is drawn.

Icon	Name	Description
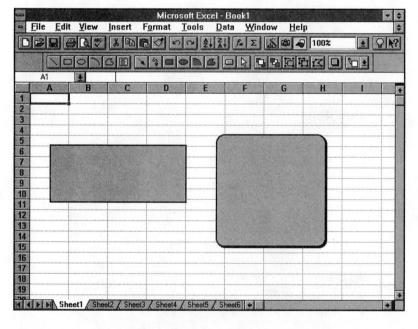	Button	The button tool draws objects on your worksheet or chart that look just like dialog box buttons. After you have drawn the button object, a dialog box appears that enables you to specify a macro that you want to run when the button is clicked on. See the section in this chapter called "Linking Actions to Objects" for more information.
	Drop Shadow	Use this tool to add a drop shadow to an object without opening the formatting notebook.
	Pattern	Use this tool to change the fill or line style of an object without opening the formatting notebook.

Figure 13.1
Two rectangles.

Charts

Each of the area drawing tools (Rectangle, Ellipse, Arc, and Freeform) also have filled counterparts, which automatically fill the area of the drawing with a fill color. When you use a filled drawing tool, Excel fills the shape with a white color fill. To change the color, use the object's Patterns formatting page and select a color from the Area section of the page. You also can choose a pattern to draw the color by using the Pattern drop-down tool. Figure 13.4 shows a drawing created using various filled objects with different colors and patterns. The filled object drawing tools are shown in table 13.2.

Figure 13.2
Three arcs.

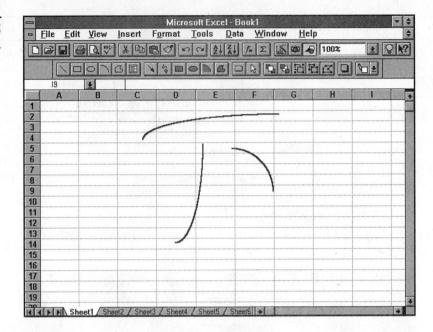

Figure 13.3
Arrow and
Patterns notebook
page.

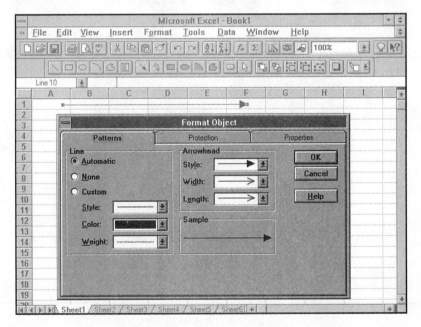

Table 13.2
Filled Object Drawing Tools

Icon	Tool Name
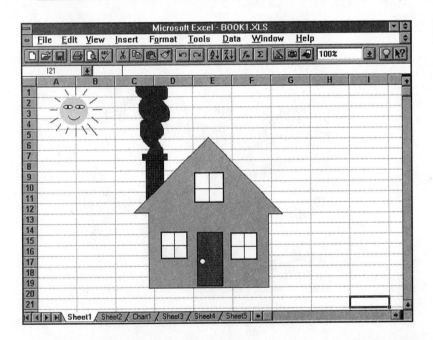	Filled Rectangle
	Filled Ellipse
	Filled Arc
	Filled Freeform

III

Charts

Figure 13.4
The house that
Excel built.

AUTHOR'S NOTE

I prefer to be called "artistically challenged."

Understanding Constrained Drawing

Most of the drawing tools support a feature called *constrained drawing*. This feature is activated when you hold down the Shift key as you draw the object. Constrained drawing is used to ensure that a line is at a perfect 45 degree angle, that a rectangle is perfectly square, or that an ellipse is perfectly round.

TIP

When you resize a drawing with the Shift key held down, Excel ensures that the drawing retains its original proportions. Also, you can select multiple objects by holding down the Shift key when you click on each object. Then, after they all are selected, hold down the Shift key while you resize one object. All objects are resized proportionately.

Formatting Graphics Objects

Figure 13.5
Format Object notebook for a line object.

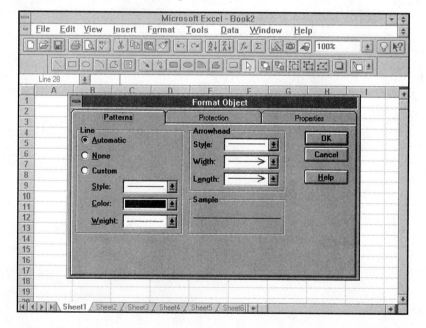

To format an object that you have drawn, select the object, pull down the Format menu and choose Object. You also can select the object and press Ctrl+1 to bring up the Format Object notebook. The notebook for a simple line object is shown in figure 13.5.

The Patterns page of the notebook controls the fill pattern and line style for the object. In addition, some objects have some special effects or attributes; these, too, are found on the Patterns page. You can, for example, choose to give a rectangle rounded corners.

TIP You can change the fill pattern of an object by selecting the object and clicking on the Pattern button in the Drawing toolbar. You also can double-click on the object to bring up the formatting notebook for that object.

The Protection page has a single checkbox called Locked. If the Locked checkbox is selected, the graphics object is frozen in place when the document is protected.

The Properties page (shown in figure 13.6) has some very important settings that control the way an object interacts with a worksheet as the worksheet is reformatted.

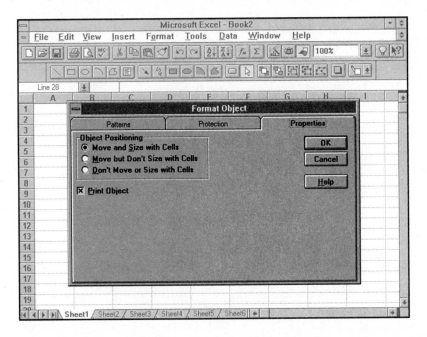

Figure 13.6
Properties page.

Charts

III

✔ **Move and Size with Cells.** This selection automatically adjusts the object when the cells it is on top of are resized. Suppose, for example, you have drawn a circle that spans several columns. If you later delete a column in the area of the circle, Excel makes the circle into an ellipse to compensate for the deleted area. Similarly, when cells are resized within the area of the graphics object, the object changes shape and size so that its borders are still in the same cells.

✔ **Move but Don't Size with Cells.** Choose this option to cause the graphics object to move along with the cell in its upper left corner but not to be resized if cells are added or deleted within the boundaries of the object.

✔ **Don't Move or Size with Cells.** Objects that have this option button selected are not affected by any cell insertions or deletions.

✔ **Print Object.** You can control whether graphics objects print. All objects are set to print by default, with the exception of button objects. This feature can be useful to shorten the printing time when you do not need final output (printing graphic images takes longer on most printers).

Linking Actions to Objects

Any objects you draw can be linked to macros so that they can perform actions when clicked on. To edit an object with an attached macro, you must right-click or Ctrl-click on the object to select it, because a left-click executes the macro.

Macros normally are linked to button objects you create using the Button tool, although they can be attached to any graphic object on your worksheet or chart.

To attach an existing macro to a graphics object, follow these steps:

1. Draw the object to which you want to attach the macro.

2. Click the right mouse button on the object to bring up the pop-up menu. From the pop-up menu, choose Assign Macro to access the Assign Macro dialog box, shown in figure 13.7.

Figure 13.7
Assign Macro
dialog box.

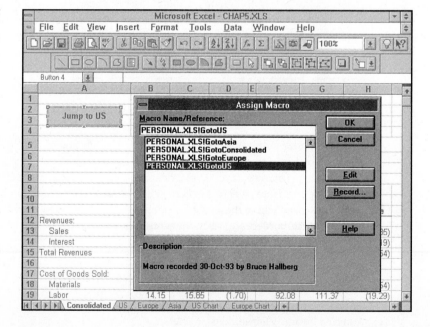

Step 2 is unnecessary when you draw a button object. The Assign Macro dialog box appears automatically as soon as you finish drawing the button.

3. Choose the macro you want to assign by clicking on it in the list box. Click on the OK button to store your choice.

You also can edit or record a macro from the Assign Macro dialog box. Click on the **E**dit or **R**ecord button.

To detach a macro from a graphics object, bring up the Assign Macro dialog box, clear the field titled **M**acro Name/Reference, and click on the OK button.

Controlling Graphics Objects

Excel provides six buttons to assist in the management and arrangement of your graphics objects, as detailed in table 13.3.

Table 13.3
Graphics Management Tools

Icon	Name	Description
![Drawing Selection icon]	Drawing Selection	The Drawing Selection tool is used to select multiple graphics objects. You can accomplish this task in two ways. Select the tool, then drag it over the objects you want to select. As you drag, a marquee appears around the area you are selecting. After all the objects are contained within the marquee, release the mouse button to select them all. Alternatively, you can select multiple objects by holding down the Shift key as you select each object.
![Bring to Front icon]	Bring to Front	Click on the Bring to Front button after you have selected an object to make the object appear on top of any overlapping objects.

continues

Table 13.3, Continued
Graphics Management Tools

Icon	Name	Description
	Send to Back	Click on the Send to Back button after you have selected an object to push the object behind any overlapping objects.
	Group	After you select multiple objects with the Drawing Selection tool, click on the Group button to combine all the objects into a single group. When you group a collection of objects, you create a complex object made up of many other objects. You can move, resize, and reformat the complex object as a single entity. Grouping objects makes editing complex drawings easier; as you get an area of the object finished, group the objects together to keep from disturbing the object relationships.
	Ungroup	Click on the Ungroup tool after selecting a complex object to break the complex object up into its component objects.
	Reshape	For freehand or polygon drawings, select the drawing and click on the Reshape button to create editing handles at each curve or angle (called *vertexes*). Drag on the handles to reshape the drawing in more complex ways than are available using the normal handles. Figure 13.8 shows a freehand squiggle with the numerous Reshape handles displayed.

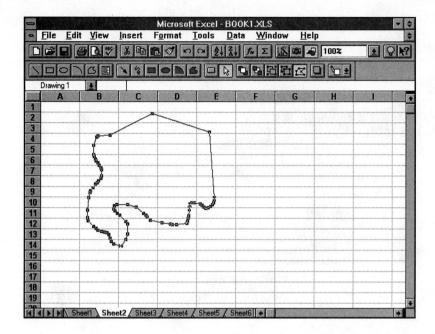

Figure 13.8
Freehand object
with reshape
handles.

Importing Graphics Images

Excel can import and display many different types of graphics images, including images in these formats:

✔ AutoCAD 2D drawings (DXF)

✔ DrawPerfect and WordPerfect Graphics format (WPG)

✔ HP Graphics Language format (HGL)

✔ Micrographix Draw and Designer (DRW)

✔ Windows bitmaps (BMP)

✔ Windows metafile (WMF)

You can import graphics directly as long as they are stored in one of these formats. Pull down the Insert menu and choose Picture. You see the dialog box shown in figure 13.9.

Use the File Name, Directories, and Drives boxes to navigate to the file you want to open. If the directory contains many files, you can view a thumbnail of the file by selecting the Preview Picture checkbox. After you have found the file you want to open, click on the OK button to insert the picture into your worksheet or chart.

Charts

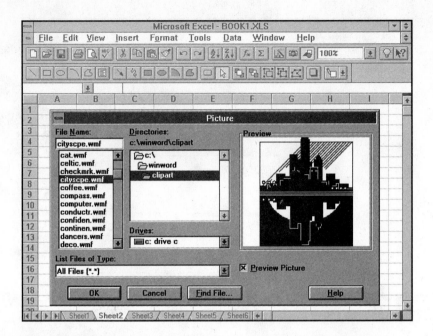

Figure 13.9

Picture dialog box.

AUTHOR'S NOTE

The Preview Picture feature can save you a great deal of time. Instead of wading through the list of files by opening them one at a time, you can just sneak a peek at the preview to see what each file contains.

Inserting Graphics Using the Paste Special Command

You can insert graphics objects from virtually any Windows-based drawing program by using the program's Cut or Copy option. After the object is in the Windows clipboard, use Paste Special in Excel to insert the object. When you do this, the Paste Special dialog box appears, as shown in figure 13.10.

You can choose between the two option buttons on the left of the dialog box: Paste and Paste Link. Paste simply pastes the image in the format you select, but Paste Link creates a DDE link back to the application that created the drawing (in this case, Windows Paintbrush). When you Paste Link a drawing, changing the drawing in the source application automatically updates the drawing in Excel. Also, you can double-click on a drawing that has been pasted using Paste Link to automatically load the source application with the drawing ready for editing.

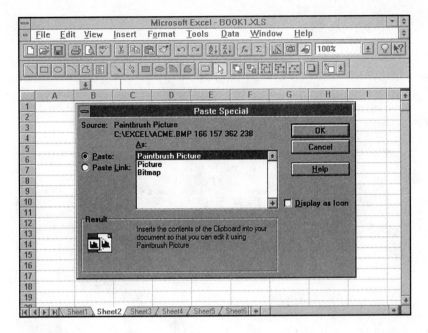

Figure 13.10
Paste Special
dialog box.

 NOTE *DDE* stands for Dynamic Data Exchange, one of the methods that Excel can use to communicate with other Windows programs. For a complete discussion of DDE, see *Inside Windows 3.1*, also from New Riders Publishing.

In the As list box, the various options for pasting the data are listed. Click on each choice to see the comments about that type of graphics discussed in the Result box at the bottom of the dialog box.

If you select the Display as Icon checkbox, the graphic does not appear on the worksheet. Instead, an icon appears that represents the image's source application (the familiar Windows Paintbrush palette icon, for example). Use this feature to conserve space and reduce memory requirements in complex documents. The image does not appear, but the worksheet user can click on this icon to easily open the image in its source application.

Changing Imported Images

You can resize and move imported pictures just like any other graphics objects in Excel. Because imported images likely are more complex than the other objects you work with, however, remember to hold down the Shift key as you resize the pictures to constrain the object to its original proportions. Failing to do so can ruin the quality of the image.

III

Charts

Using an Image for Chart Patterns

One of the more interesting features of Excel is that it enables you to use an imported image as charts patterns.

Consider the chart shown in figure 13.11. This chart could be improved and made more interesting to the audience by replacing the bars in the bar chart with an appropriate symbol. One possibility is shown in figure 13.12.

Figure 13.11
Recycling chart.

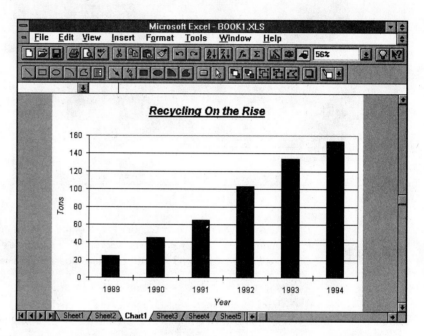

You can replace chart markers (for Line, Radar, and Scatter charts) or area fills (for Bar and Column charts) with graphics images using either of two methods. One option is to copy the image to the clipboard in the source application, switch to your chart, select the data series you want to change, and choose Paste from the Edit menu.

You also can import the images directly. To do this, follow these steps:

1. Select the series you want to modify.

2. Pull down the Insert menu and choose Picture. You see the Picture dialog box shown in figure 13.13.

3. Use this dialog box to find the picture file you want to use. After you have found it, click on the OK button to replace the chart symbol with the graphics image.

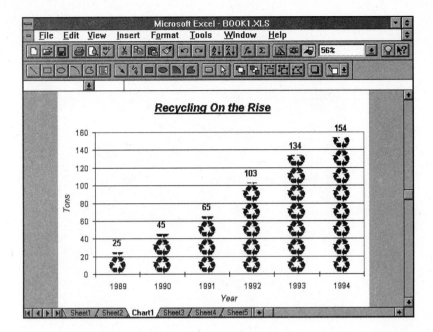

Figure 13.12
Recycling chart
with symbol.

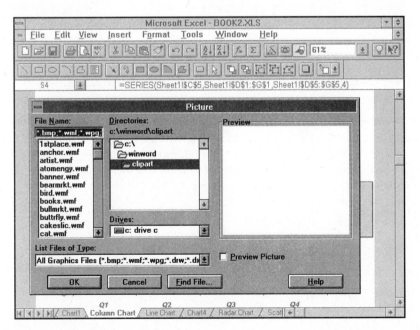

Figure 13.13
Picture dialog box.

A series that has had its symbol replaced with a graphics image has some additional settings available on the Patterns page of its formatting notebook (see fig. 13.14).

Figure 13.14
Patterns page for
chart symbols.

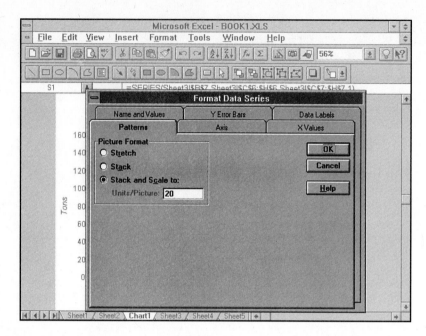

The Patterns page has these new settings available:

✔ **Stretch.** Stretches the image to cover the entire area in the bar or column rectangle. Figure 13.15 shows the graph with this choice selected.

✔ **Stack.** Keeps the image size the same but stacks as many images as are necessary to fill up the bar or column rectangle. The preceding figure 13.12 uses the Stack option.

✔ **Stack and Scale.** Enables you to control the number of units of the Value axis that are represented by each chart image. When you select this option button, you can type a number in the Units/Picture field to control the number of axis units represented per picture. By default, Excel chooses the number that shows the picture as large as possible. Figure 13.16 shows the Stack and Scale option with each picture set to represent 10 units on the chart.

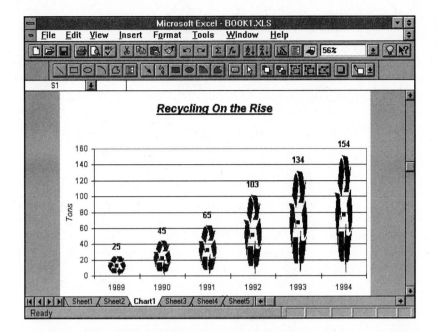

Figure 13.15
Stretch option.

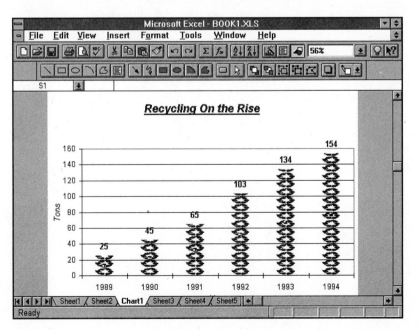

Figure 13.16
Stack option.

III

Charts

Chapter Snapshot

Excel has many advanced charting capabilities applicable to the more advanced business or technical user. In this chapter, you learn to accomplish the following:

✔ Editing the series formula for a chart

✔ Creating stock High-Low-Close stock charts

✔ Plotting trend lines

✔ Creating charts that use logarithmic scales

✔ Plotting missing data

✔ Creating multi-axis charts with dual X or Y axes

✔ Creating error bars for many Excel chart types

As you will see, Excel has the capability to generate just about any type of chart you could want. After you have mastered the basics of Excel charts, use the information in this chapter as a reference for these more advanced chart types and for the more advanced editing tasks.

Advanced Charts for Business and Science

A t times you probably need to generate charts that require something a little more complex than simply grabbing a chunk of your worksheet and hitting the ChartWizard button. Perhaps you want to control which parts of a series of numbers are plotted, or you want to use different category references for different data series. The next sections show you ways to accomplish these tasks.

Understanding Series Formulas

When you plot data from a worksheet to a chart, Excel uses a *series formula* in the chart to indicate each series. Although you usually don't have to work directly with this series formula, understanding how to read it and how to change it can be an important step in advancing your charting skills.

The series formula indicates the workbook name, the name of the sheet in the workbook, and the cells that contain the data being charted. To display a series formula for a particular chart series, click on the series. The formula is shown in the formula bar. Figure 14.1 shows a series formula for the bottom chart series. Figure 14.2 shows the data from which the example chart was plotted.

Figure 14.1
Series formula
example.

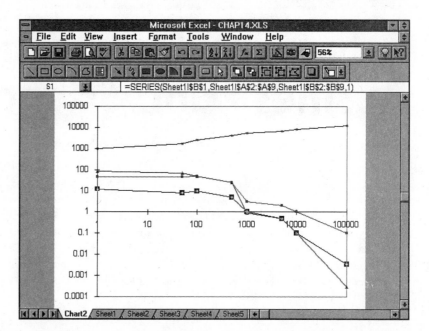

The series formula is divided into four major parameters, each separated by commas. The series formula parameters are arranged in this order:

1. **Series Name.** This parameter references the name of the series, which you also can see in the legend of your chart. In this case, the reference points to cell B1, giving the series the name "Red."

2. **Category Reference.** The second reference in the formula is to the range of cells that define the categories for the plotted data. For this series formula, the reference is to cells A2 through A9—the categories against which the data was plotted.

3. **Values Reference.** The Values Reference is the actual data that is plotted—in this case, cells B2 to B9.

4. **Order Number.** The Order Number in the series formula defines where in the order of the plotted data the series belongs. The sample series formula is for the first data series on the chart.

You can edit the series formula directly to change the data that the chart is plotting, but far easier methods are available.

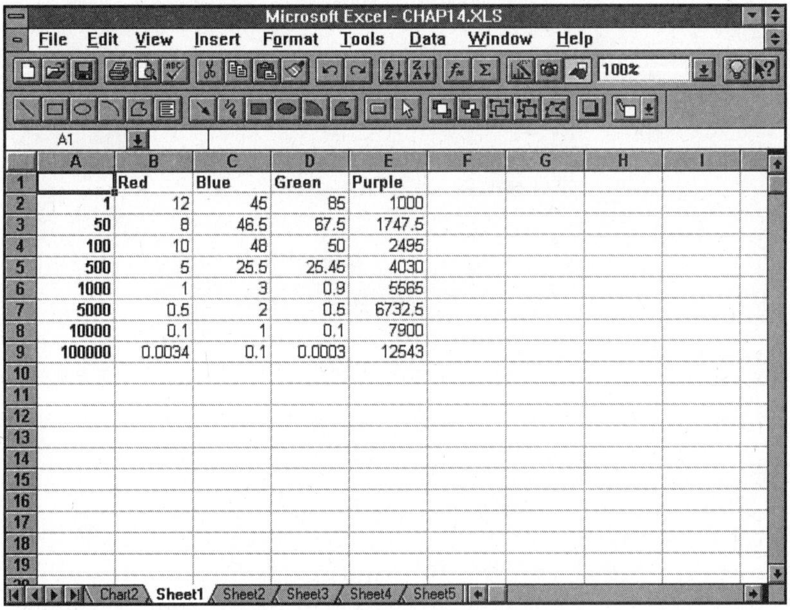

Figure 14.2
Data for example chart.

	A	B	C	D	E	F	G	H	I
1		Red	Blue	Green	Purple				
2	1	12	45	85	1000				
3	50	8	46.5	67.5	1747.5				
4	100	10	48	50	2495				
5	500	5	25.5	25.45	4030				
6	1000	1	3	0.9	5565				
7	5000	0.5	2	0.5	6732.5				
8	10000	0.1	1	0.1	7900				
9	100000	0.0034	0.1	0.0003	12543				

III

Charts

Changing the Series Using the Notebook

You can change the series formula easily by using the formatting notebook.

1. Select the series you want to control.

2. Pull up the formatting notebook for that series. Press Ctrl+1 to do this quickly.

3. Click on the X Values tab. You see the page shown in figure 14.3.

When you click on the X Values tab and then click in the series formula shown, you return to the source of the series data behind the notebook. To change the range used for X Values, move the formatting page so that you can see the source data, then use your mouse to reselect the range.

Figure 14.3
X Values page.

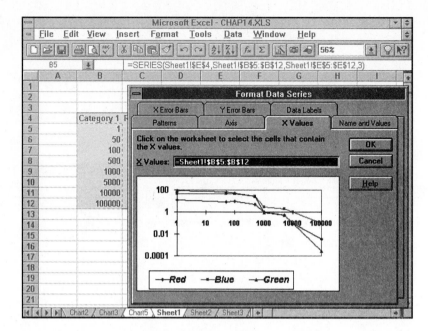

You also can change the cells used for the series name and for the Y Values by using the Name and Values page in the notebook, shown in figure 14.4.

Figure 14.4
Name and
Values page.

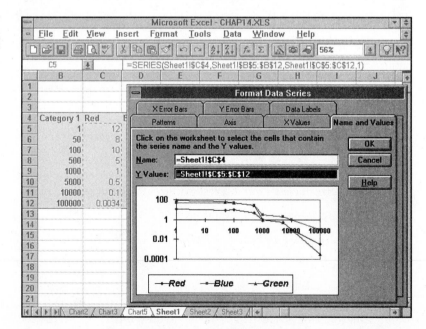

Plotting or Adding Noncontiguous Ranges

You do not necessarily need to arrange your data so that it is contiguous before you create a chart. Excel enables you to plot noncontiguous ranges of data (such as the selection shown in fig. 14.5) or add data to an existing chart using a range that is not next to the original data. To try this procedure, follow these steps:

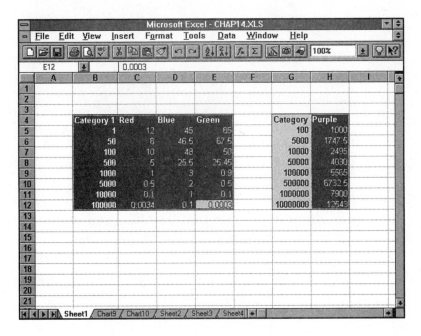

Figure 14.5
Noncontiguous ranges.

1. Select the first set of data to plot. If the data is not organized so that you can select the set, hold down the Ctrl key as you select each part of the set.

2. Plot the data from the first set.

3. Return to the worksheet and select the second set of data.

4. Use the Copy command on the Edit menu.

5. Switch to the chart and select the chart.

6. Use the Paste Special command in the Edit menu. You see the dialog box shown in figure 14.6.

Figure 14.6
Paste Special
dialog box.

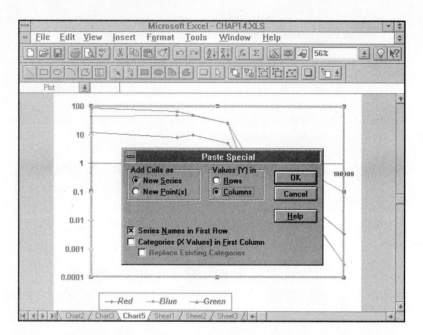

In the Paste Special dialog box, you can choose to add the new data as a New Series or as New Point(s) in existing series. You also can specify whether the values are organized in Rows or Columns. Finally, use the three checkboxes at the bottom of the dialog box to define what part of the pasted data contains the labels for the data.

When you click on OK in the Paste Special dialog box, your second set of data is added to the chart. At this point, you might want to designate that the second set of data use a different Value (Y) axis. See the section in this chapter titled "Creating a Dual Y-Axis Chart."

Changing a Chart Using the ChartWizard

With a chart selected, click on the ChartWizard button in the Standard Toolbar to redefine the chart choices. Clicking on the ChartWizard button starts a two-step process to redefine the chart. The first dialog box is shown in figure 14.7.

Use the first dialog box to reselect the range of cells to plot. When satisfied with your choice, click on the Next button to proceed to the second step, shown in figure 14.8.

On the second dialog box of the redefinition process using the ChartWizard, you can keep or change the choices you made when the chart was originally created. See Chapter 12, "Complete Guide to Charts," for more information about these choices.

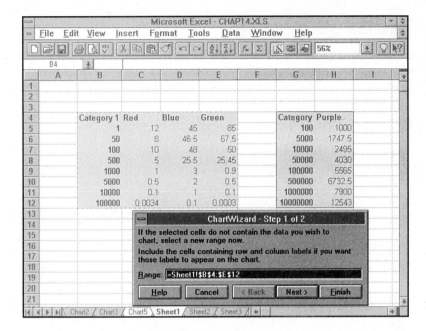

Figure 14.7
ChartWizard
redefinition:
step 1.

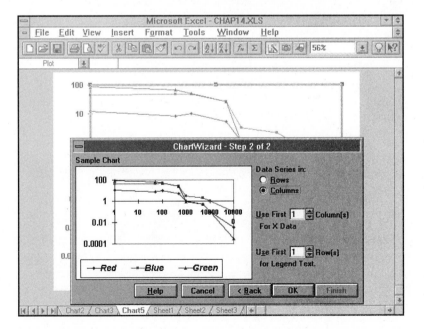

Figure 14.8
ChartWizard
redefinition:
step 2.

III

Charts

Using Advanced Charts

The remainder of this chapter shows you some of the more esoteric charts Excel can produce as well as some charting features that are not commonly used but that can be of great benefit when you need them.

Creating High-Low-Close Stock Charts

Excel includes a special type of line chart specifically for plotting stock market data over time in a High-Low-Close fashion. Start with your data in a format similar to the format shown in figure 14.9.

Figure 14.9
Stock market data.

	A	B	C	D	E	F	G	H	I
	A1		Date						
1	Date	Volume	High	Low	Close				
2	6/29/93	13240	91.75	88.50	89.00				
3	6/30/93	17630	90.25	87.25	88.00				
4	7/1/93	18100	88.50	86.50	87.13				
5	7/2/93	7940	87.50	86.50	87.25				
6	7/6/93	14910	87.75	85.25	86.00				
7	7/7/93	56000	84.25	81.25	83.38				
8	7/8/93	21910	85.50	84.00	84.88				
9	7/9/93	15630	85.00	83.50	84.63				
10	7/12/93	8290	84.75	83.50	83.75				
11	7/13/93	11400	84.00	82.50	82.75				
12	7/14/93	13590	85.50	82.50	84.25				
13	7/15/93	10760	84.25	82.75	83.50				
14	7/16/93	26950	83.25	80.75	81.13				
15	7/19/93	38260	80.25	78.00	78.75				
16	7/20/93	23380	80.50	78.00	80.50				
17	7/21/93	55930	79.00	76.75	79.00				
18	7/22/93	46100	81.75	76.75	77.63				
19	7/23/93	29000	78.25	76.75	77.63				
20	7/26/93	20560	79.25	77.75	78.25				
21	7/27/93	35070	78.75	75.50	75.50				

Microsoft Excel — File Edit View Insert Format Tools Data Window Help — 100%

Chart2 / Chart3 / Chart5 / Sheet1 \ Sheet2 / Sheet3

AUTHOR'S NOTE

This data was downloaded from the CompuServe MicroQuoteII system, which is capable of creating comma-separated files of stock history and downloading them to your computer.

Create the chart normally, but select the Line chart type and choose the High-Low-Close subformat shown in figure 14.10, which results in the chart shown in figure 14.11.

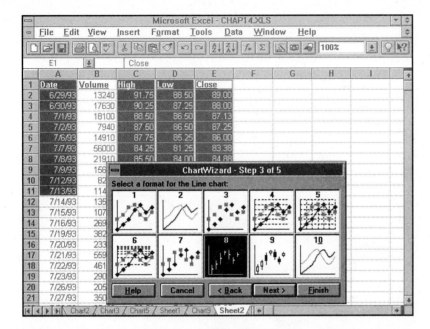

Figure 14.10
High-Low-Close
chart type.

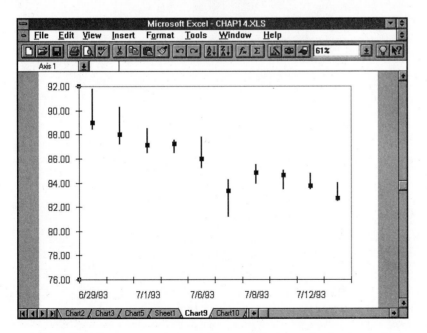

Figure 14.11
High-Low-Close
chart.

You also can create a combination chart showing the High-Low-Close chart superimposed on a column chart that shows the trading volume. To begin, make sure your data is organized in this order:

1. Date

2. Volume

3. High

4. Low

5. Close

Select the data and create the chart normally. Choose the Combination Chart type and the High-Low-Close-Volume subtype, shown in figure 14.12. The finished chart (with some minor formatting added) is shown in figure 14.13.

Figure 14.12
High-Low-Close-
Volume subtype.

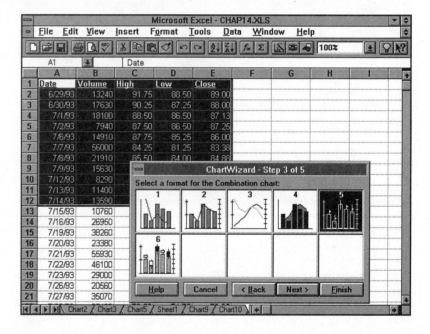

Creating a Dual Y-Axis Chart

When you need to compare two sets of data that are based on different scales, you do this with a dual Y-axis chart. Generally, these types of charts are used to look for correspondence between two sets of data. A dual Y-axis chart shows one set of data against values on the left axis of the chart, whereas the second set of data is shown against the right axis of the chart.

Examine the chart shown in figure 14.14. The top line of the chart contains numbers that are dramatically higher than the rest of the series (if the Value axis wasn't set to Logarithmic scale, you wouldn't even be able to see all the series). When this sort of spread happens, you lose the ability to discern some of the detail for both sets of data, because the chart must cover a much larger range.

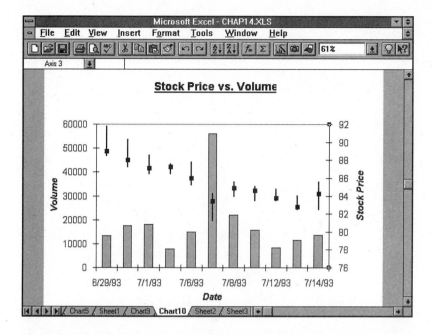

Figure 14.13
High-Low-Close-
Volume chart.

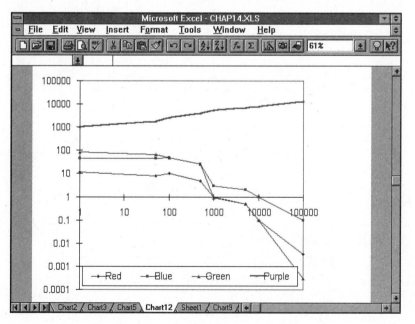

Figure 14.14
Line chart.

III

Charts

In cases like these, you might want to consider plotting the series that are different against another value category. To plot a second Y-axis, follow these steps:

1. Select the series that you want to plot against the second Y-axis.

2. Pull up the formatting notebook for that series. (Press Ctrl+1 or double-click on the series.)

3. Click on the Axis tab. The Axis page is shown in figure 14.15.

Figure 14.15
Axis page.

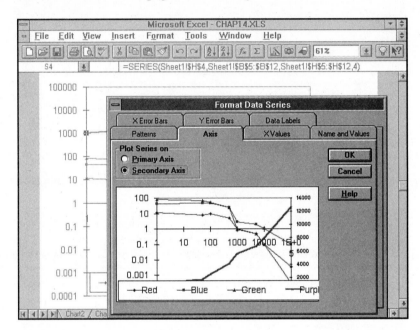

4. Click on the option marked Secondary Axis. The change is previewed on the Axis page.

5. Click on OK to save your changes and return to the chart. The results are shown in figure 14.16.

Working with Error Bars

One of the major frustrations with Excel 4 was that it did not have the capability to plot error bars easily. Fortunately, this has been resolved with a robust error bar feature in Excel 5.

Error bars are used to show visually the amount of uncertainty—or error—in plotted data. Excel enables you to calculate the amount of error in a number of ways:

✔ Fixed value that you enter

✔ Percentage that you enter

✔ Calculated Standard Deviation based on the mean of the plotted values

✔ Calculated Standard Error

✔ Calculated cell-by-cell error values from a worksheet

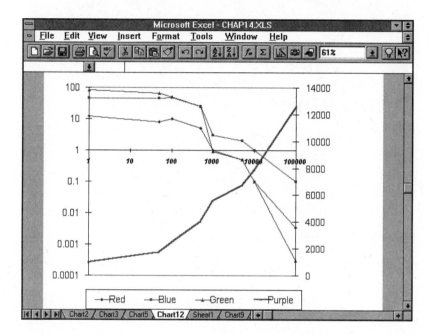

Figure 14.16
Dual Y-axis chart.

You can add error bars to area, bar, column, line, and scatter charts only. In addition, scatter charts can contain both Y-axis error bars and X-axis error bars.

If you change the chart type on a chart containing error bars from one of the allowed chart types to a different chart type, the error bars are deleted from the chart.

To add error bars to a chart, follow these steps:

1. Create the chart using one of the allowed chart types.

2. Select the series you want to show the error bars.

3. Pull down the Insert menu and choose Error Bars. You see the formatting page shown in figure 14.17.

4. Set the parameters for the desired error bars and click on OK to add the error bars.

Figure 14.17
Error Bars
formatting
page.

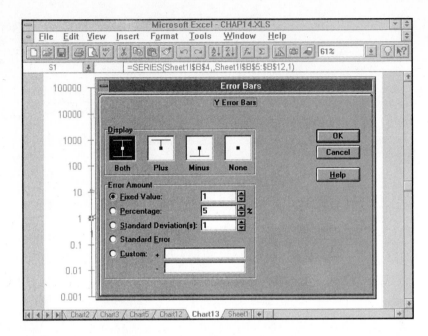

Table 14.1 details the options on the Error Bars formatting page.

Table 14.1
Error Bar Settings

Setting	Description
Display	In the Display section, you can choose whether you want error bars shown in both the positive and negative direction, either direction alone, or none at all.
Fixed Value	Enter an amount here to force all the error bars to be shown based on the entered number. Fixed error amounts are often given with various testing equipment, for example.
Percentage	Enter a number in the Percentage field to show what percentage of each value to use as the error amount.
Standard Deviation	This choice calculates the standard deviation based on the plotted series, which then is multiplied by the value you enter in the field next to the Standard Deviation option.
Standard Error	Select Standard Error to calculate the standard error for the plotted values using a least squares method.

Setting	Description
Custom	Use the Custom setting to define the error amount based on values stored in the worksheet. Click on either the + or – field, then select the range in the worksheet that contains the appropriate error values. You must select the same number of error values as the plot contains. You also can use an array formula in these fields, such as {12,15,3,4.5,12.1}.

Figure 14.18 shows a chart with error bars calculated to plus or minus 15 percent.

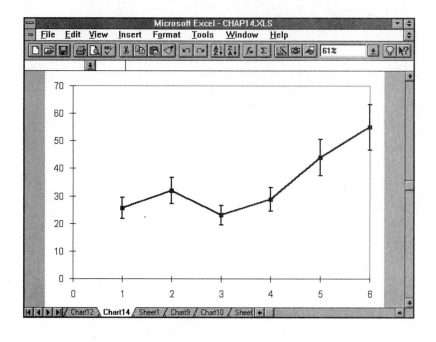

Figure 14.18
Percentage-based error bars.

Plotting with Missing Data

If you are using Excel as a technical graphing tool, you often have to work with charts that have some of the data missing. Excel provides three different methods for accounting for missing data:

✔ Don't plot them at all

✔ Assume that the missing data are zero

✔ Interpolate the missing data

You control the way Excel handles missing data through the Options notebook. Access the Options notebook by selecting the Options command in the Tools menu, then click on the Chart page of the notebook. The Chart page is shown in figure 14.19.

Figure 14.19
Chart page.

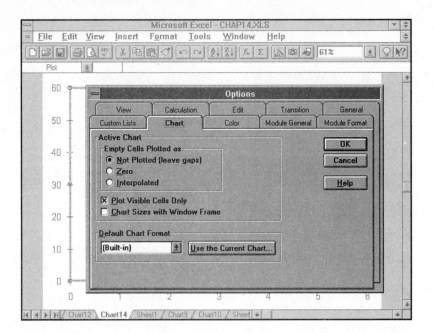

Table 14.2 discusses the three methods of plotting empty data points.

Table 14.2
Missing Data Settings

Setting	Description
Not Plotted	Often the most appropriate for bar charts or column charts, this choice simply leaves the data out of the chart. If this option is selected on line charts, two segments of the line are missing in the chart—the line before the missing data point and the line from the missing data point to the next data point. For that reason, avoid this setting on line charts.
Zero	This choice assumes the missing data are set to zero. This choice is rarely appropriate, but it might come in handy for some situations.

Setting	Description
Interpolated	For line charts or scatter charts that use lines to connect the data points, Interpolated is often the most appropriate choice. Excel continues the line through any missing data points. The point itself is not plotted for missing data.

Creating Trend Lines

New to Excel 5 is the capability to add trend lines to your plots. *Trend lines* can be used to smooth fluctuations in the plotted data or to predict values forward or backward. You can base the trend lines on a number of different statistical models.

5

Trend lines are calculated using *regression analysis*. Regression analysis uses the values provided to predict the relationship between the values. After the relationship is known, it can be used to display the data in a "smoothed" fashion or to predict values that aren't given.

Note that the Moving Average trend line is not a regression-based trend line; it is used only for data smoothing and cannot be used for prediction.

To create a trend line, select the series on which you want to base the trend line. Then pull down the Insert menu and choose Trend line. You see the Trend line notebook shown in figure 14.20.

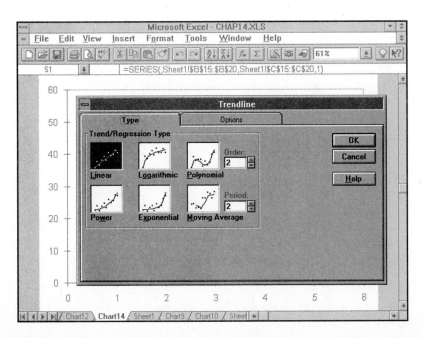

Figure 14.20
Trend line notebook.

III

Charts

In the Type notebook page, choose the regression method that best suits your data. You might need to try different methods depending on the data you are using. To find out how well the regression method fits your data, look at the R-Squared value, which is set on the Options page of the notebook.

The Options page also includes a variety of other settings for controlling the trend line. Figure 14.21 shows the Options page. Table 14.3 details these settings.

Figure 14.21
Options page for
Trend lines.

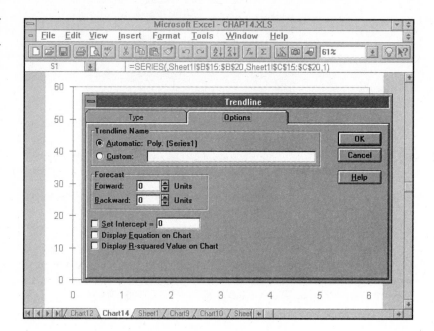

Table 14.3
Trend Line Options Settings

Setting	Description
Trend line Name	Use this area to define the name of the trend line, which is used for the legend on the chart.
Forecast	The Forecast section can contain the number of periods to forecast the data either Forward or Backward.
Set Intercept	Enter a value here to force the first location of the trend line against the Y axis.
Display Equation on Chart	Select this checkbox to place the formula used for the regression calculation on the chart, as shown in figure 14.22.

Setting	Description
Display <u>R</u>-Square Value on Chart	Select this checkbox to display the R-Squared value on the chart. An R-Squared value closer to 0 indicates that the regression is not matching the curve closely; an R-Squared value close to 1 indicates increasing accuracy in the trend line. The R-Squared value is displayed in the chart in figure 14.22.

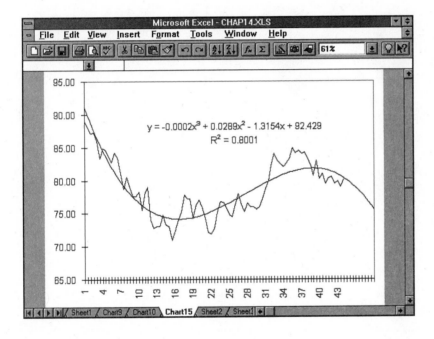

Figure 14.22
Chart with Trend line, Formula, and R-Squared Value.

III

Charts

Part IV

Macros

Chapter Snapshot

Macros can save you a great deal of time and effort. After you complete the examples in this chapter, you will be able to record and execute macros to automate repetitive tasks. In this chapter, you learn the following:

✔ Working with techniques for recording and writing macros that are new to Excel 5

✔ Recording a macro to repeat keystrokes, menu, and dialog box operations

✔ Assigning a macro to a shortcut key

✔ Creating macros for use with every workbook

✔ Saving macros

✔ Printing macros

✔ Editing existing macros

✔ Deleting macros

✔ Understanding Excel's macro languages

✔ Assigning macros to toolbar buttons

✔ Assigning macros to graphics objects

Macros make your work with Excel faster, more efficient, and even fun! In fact, the more you create and use macros, the more uses you find for them. One day you'll wonder how you ever got along without them.

15

CHAPTER

Understanding Macros

Despite Excel's impressive power and capabilities, you still might find yourself performing some operations over and over. You might begin several worksheets with the same column and row headings or apply the same series of formats to cells time and again. Macros automate these repetitive tasks for you. A *macro* contains a series of keystrokes, menu selections, or formulas. After you create a macro, you can repeat all the operations by pressing a shortcut key combination or by selecting the macro from a list. You can even customize a toolbar to run a macro by clicking on a toolbar button.

Macros also help you design consistently formatted worksheets. You probably want each part of a multipage worksheet to have the same overall appearance, for example. If you apply the formats manually, you might format one page of the worksheet differently from another. By recording the formats in a macro, you can apply the same formats to common elements on different pages or in different worksheets.

Macro recording and writing procedures have changed quite a bit in this version. Read this chapter even if you are an experienced macro programmer in Excel 4.

Table 15.1 describes the tools you learn about in this chapter.

Table 15.1
The Macro Tools

Tool	Name	Purpose
▶	Run	Displays the Macro dialog box to run a macro
■	Stop	Stops recording macro instructions
●	Record	Displays the Record New Macro dialog box for recording a macro

Recording a Simple Macro

The easiest way to create a macro is to record it. When you record a macro, Excel saves each of the keystrokes or mouse actions that you perform so that you can quickly repeat the steps another time. Macros are recorded live, meaning Excel performs the instructions you are recording. If you are recording a macro that prints a selected portion of a worksheet, for example, Excel actually prints that portion of the worksheet as you record the macro.

If you want to create a macro without performing the actions, you have to write the macro, as explained in Chapters 16, "Using the Excel 4 Macro Language," and 20, "Creating Custom Menus and Dialog Boxes."

Before you record a macro, make sure that Excel, Windows, and your worksheet are set up exactly as you want them. Otherwise, you might have to stop recording the macro, change your settings, then record the macro again. If you want to print a worksheet, for example, make sure your printer is set up properly in the Windows environment before you start recording the macro.

To record a macro, select Record Macro from the Tools menu, then choose Record New Macro. The dialog box shown in figure 15.1 appears.

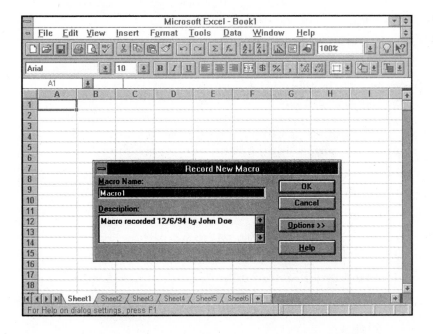

Figure 15.1
The Record New Macro dialog box.

Macro Names

In the Macro Name text box, you enter the macro's name. Excel suggests the name Macro1 for the first macro you record, Macro2 for the second, and so on. You can accept the suggested name or create one of your own. Enter a name that clearly illustrates the macro's function. Several months from now, you might forget the function that Macro1 performs, but you will know exactly what task is performed by the macro named Print_Worksheet.

Excel reserves some special macro names for automatic executing macros. A macro named Auto_Open, for example, will run as soon as you open the Workbook. If you usually start Excel and change to full-screen display, name the macro Auto_Open, then record the selection View Full Screen. Other reserved macro names are Auto_Close, Auto_Activate, and Auto_Deactivate.

Macro names must start with a letter and cannot contain any spaces or punctuation marks other than the underline character. Use uppercase letters or the underline character to designate separate words, such as Print_Worksheet or OpenBudget.

Excel displays a warning message if you try to use a macro name that already exists. You can select Yes to replace the existing macro with a new macro or select No to enter another macro name.

Macro Description

In the Description box, type a brief description of the macro. By default, the description includes the date you recorded the macro and the user name inserted when Excel was installed. If you don't care about that information, you can press the Del or Backspace keys to delete the default entry. Otherwise, place the cursor at the end of the default description and add your own comments there. If you can't remember the name of the macro after you create it, you can use the description to help you determine which macro you want to run.

After you have completed all the selections in the dialog box, click on OK to begin recording the macro. Follow these steps to record a macro that prints a worksheet:

1. Turn on your printer.

2. Select Tools, Record Macro, Record New Macro to display the Record New Macro dialog box. The Macro Name text box is automatically selected.

3. Type **QuickPrint** as the macro name, replacing Excel's suggested name, Macro1.

4. Select the Description text box and type **Prints an entire worksheet**.

5. Select OK.

6. Select File, Print, then select OK.

7. Because your worksheet is empty, a warning box reports that there is nothing to print. Select OK to close the warning box without affecting the macro.

8. To stop recording, click on the Stop button or select Tools, Record Macro, Stop Recording.

You cannot stop recording a macro while you are entering text in the formula bar—the options in the Macro submenu are dimmed. Click on the Enter box to accept your entry or press Esc to cancel it, then select Stop Recording.

TIP

If you press an arrow key or press the Enter key to move to another cell, then stop recording, the selection of that cell is recorded in the macro. When you later run the macro, Excel will make the same selection. If you want to stop recording without moving to another cell, click on the formula bar Enter box to accept the text you just entered, then stop recording.

Do not forget to click on the Stop button or select Tools, Record Macro, Stop Recording to stop recording your actions. If you forget, Excel continues to record all your operations.

Playing a Macro

To play a macro, select Tools, Macro to display the dialog box shown in figure 15.2. Double-click on the name of the macro in the list, or choose the macro and click on Run.

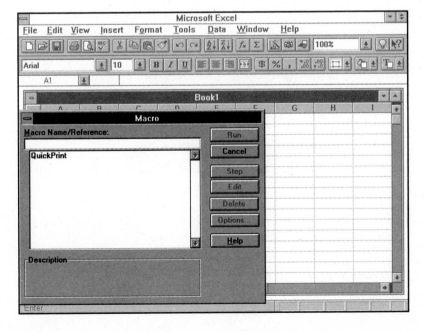

Figure 15.2
The Macro dialog box.

IV

Macros

When you select a macro in the list, its description appears in the Description box. Make sure you select the proper macro before you run it.

Excel beeps and displays a message box if it encounters an error in the macro. This beep should not occur if you recorded the macro properly. (Do not confuse an error beep with the normal system beep that sometimes occurs when computing is complete.)

Most of your macros run so quickly that they will appear to perform their task almost instantaneously. To stop a longer macro while it is running, however, press Esc. A dialog box appears with options to end the macro, continue running it, debug the macro to locate errors, or to go to the cell where the macro stopped. Select End to stop the macro, or select Continue to continue from where it stopped. Debugging macros is discussed in later chapters.

NOTE   Like figure 15.2, the option buttons in the Macro dialog box remain dimmed until you select a macro in the list box. These options are discussed later in this chapter.

When you run a macro, Excel repeats the keystrokes, menu, and dialog box actions you recorded. The pull-down menus and dialog boxes you used to record the macro do not appear, however—only the results of selecting them are repeated. Suppose, for example, that you use the Font dialog box to record a macro that formats a number of cells. When you run the macro, the fonts are applied to the cells, but the Font dialog box does not appear on-screen.

Using the Visual Basic Toolbar

You can streamline your work with macros by displaying the Visual Basic toolbar, shown in figure 15.3. Select View, Toolbars, click on Visual Basic, and select OK.

Figure 15.3
Visual Basic
toolbar.

For fundamental work, you only need the Run, Stop, and Record buttons. The other buttons are used for more advanced programming tasks.

NOTE   The toolbar is called Visual Basic because macro instructions are recorded in the Visual Basic for Applications (VBA) language. You learn more about VBA later in this chapter and again in Chapter 19, "Using Excel Visual Basic."

Macro Record Options

You can make your macros more efficient by selecting macro options. In the Record New Macro dialog box, click on Options to expand the box as shown in figure 15.4.

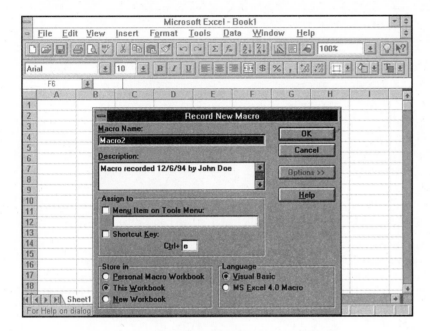

Figure 15.4
Macro record options.

Assigning Macros for Easy Play

In the Assign To section of the dialog box, you can choose to attach the macro to the Tools menu, to a shortcut key combination, or both.

Assigning to the Tools menu

To add the macro to the Tools menu, click on the checkbox next to the Menu Item in Tools Menu option. Click on the text box under the prompt, then type the text you want to appear on the menu.

Use a brief name, but one that clearly explains the task the macro performs. For example, if you were creating the QuickPrint macro and wanted to add it to the menu, use the name QuickPrint or the words "Print Worksheet."

The entry you make appears at the bottom of the Tools menu. To run the macro, select Tools, then click on the item, or select it and press Enter.

IV

Macros

NOTE   The macro appears in the Tools menu only when the workbook is open.

Assigning Shortcut Keys

The quickest way to run a macro is to assign it to a *shortcut key*: a key you can press along with the Ctrl key to execute the macro.

To assign a shortcut key, select the Shortcut <u>K</u>ey checkbox. Excel suggests a default letter starting with the lowercase e. For each macro that you assign a shortcut key, it increments the letter, skipping over those already assigned to the built-in shortcut keys, such as "a" for Select All (Ctrl+a) and "b" for Boldface (Ctrl+b). Excel displays the letters in this order:

     e j k l m q t w y

These letters are followed by all 26 uppercase letters from A to Z. If you want to assign a key different from the suggested letter, click in the box next to C<u>t</u>rl+ and enter the letter you want to use.

Shortcut keys are case-sensitive. An uppercase shortcut letter actually assigns the combination Ctrl+Shift plus the letter to the macro. If you press Shift+E to enter the uppercase "e" as the shortcut key, you have to press Ctrl+Shift+E to run the macro. If you enter the lowercase "e" as the shortcut key, you only have to press Ctrl and the "e" key to run the macro.

AUTHOR'S NOTE

In the Excel help system, shortcut keys are shown with uppercase letters. For example, if you look up help on how to use the keyboard with Excel, you'll see that Ctrl+A is the shortcut key for the "select all" function and that Ctrl+B is the shortcut key for boldface. (To agree with the Excel convention, the built-in shortcut keys shown in this book also include uppercase letters.) These letters refer to the letter printed on the face of the keyboard key.

In actuality, Microsoft has assigned its built-in shortcut keys to lowercase letters. To bold, you press Ctrl and the B key by itself, not Ctrl+Shift+B. If you press Ctrl+Shift+B, Excel sounds a little warning beep reporting that the key combination is not assigned—unless, of course, you assigned it one of your own macros.

Keep this in mind when you are creating your own macros. You can assign the key combination Ctrl+Shift+B to one of your own macros, even though Ctrl+B is already used by Excel.

When you select OK in the Record New Macro dialog box, Excel displays a warning box asking if you used a shortcut key letter already assigned to another macro. The warning box asks if you want to assign the key anyway. Select No to return to the Record New Macro dialog box so that you can enter a different letter; select Yes if you want to assign the same letter to another macro. You can record several macros assigned to the same shortcut key. When you press the shortcut key combination, however, Excel runs the macro whose name is first alphabetically. To execute another macro assigned to the same shortcut key, you must select its name from a list.

You can attach a macro to any letter key, even if the letter is assigned to a built-in Excel function. The new macro overrides the built-in function; the original assignment does not run. If you create a macro assigned to Ctrl+P, for instance, your macro runs—you can no longer use the default Ctrl+P combination to display the Print dialog box. To return the shortcut key to its original purpose, you must delete the macro, as explained later in this chapter.

TIP Don't worry if you have already recorded a macro without assigning it to the menu or to a shortcut key. Later in this chapter, you learn to set the options for a previously recorded macro.

Macro Locations

You can store a macro in any of three locations. By default, your macros are stored with the current workbook. You can use the macros whenever you open the workbook.

In Excel 5, global macros are no longer stored in the global macro sheet. If you have macros from version 4, however, you can still use them. See Chapter 16, "Programming Macros," for additional information.

If you want to use the macro with every workbook, store the macro in the Personal Macro Workbook, a file called PERSONAL.XLS in the EXCEL\XLSTART directory. Each time you start Excel, the workbook is automatically opened and its macros are made available for use.

NOTE If you just installed Excel, don't bother looking for the PERSONAL.XLS file. The file does not exist until you create a macro and save it in the personal workbook.

You also can record the macro in a new workbook. If you select this option, Excel opens another workbook just to record the macro. If you store your macro in a workbook other than the Personal Macro Workbook, you must open the workbook to access the macro; Excel does not open it automatically.

You might want to create individual workbooks for categories of macros. If you have several macros you use just to create budget worksheets, for example, you can store them together in one workbook. When you need to create a budget, open the workbook to access the macros.

AUTHOR'S NOTE

It might seem more convenient to store all of your macros in the Personal Macro Workbook so that you can use them without opening a workbook first. However, the use of other workbooks to divide your macros into logical groups makes sense for several reasons. A workbook crammed with rarely used macros takes up needed system memory and other resources. In addition, you quickly run out of unique key assignments and have to spend time scrolling through a list of macro names to locate the one you want to run.

Use the Personal Macro Workbook for macros you use on a regular basis. Use other workbooks for macros you use only periodically.

Running Macros from Workbooks

You can run a macro in any worksheet of the workbook. You might, for example, use the Title macro created later in this chapter to add headings to any worksheet in the same workbook. Keep in mind, however, that any text, numbers, or formulas entered by the macro replace contents already in the cells.

To use a macro in another workbook, you must open the workbook first. Macros in any open workbook are available for use. You can run macros in the Personal Macro Workbook in any workbook.

Before you run a macro, make sure the correct worksheet is active. Do not run a macro that sets up standard headings, for example, when the active worksheet already has headings.

If the macro you want to run is not listed in the dialog box or does not run when you press the shortcut key, the workbook in which it is located is not open. Use the File, Open option to open the workbook.

Macro Language

Excel gives you two options for the language used to record your macros. By default, macros are saved in the Visual Basic language (known as VBA). Microsoft uses this powerful programming language in many of its application programs and as a stand-alone development tool. The option to select a recorded macro language is new in Excel 5.

You also can select to record your macros in the Excel 4 Macro Language. This programming language is used exclusively with Excel 4. If you are an experienced macro programmer in Excel 4, you might want to select this option.

NOTE For more information on using the Excel 4 Macro Language, see Chapter 16, "Programming Macros."

AUTHOR'S NOTE

Even if you are an experienced Excel 4 macro programmer, take the time to learn VBA. At some time in the future, VBA will become the common macro language for all Microsoft applications. By learning VBA now, you can transfer your new skills to other programs and build complete custom applications.

To compare the two approaches quickly, record the same macro using both languages. Then use the Arrange menu option to display both on the screen at the same time.

Changing Macro Properties

Excel makes it easy to change the name, shortcut key, or menu assignment of an existing macro:

1. Select Tools, Macro.

2. Click on the name of the macro you want to modify, then select Options to display the dialog box shown in figure 15.5.

3. Set or change the desired options in the dialog box, then select OK.

NOTE The options in the Help Information section are used for creating custom applications. Refer to Chapters 19,"Using Excel Visual Basic," and 20,"Creating Custom Menus and Dialog Boxes," for more information.

IV

Macros

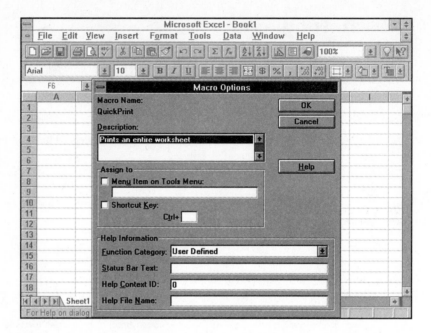

Figure 15.5
Macro Options
dialog box.

Relative and Absolute Selection

When you record a macro that includes cell selection, you can record the operation in two ways. By default, Excel records cell selections on an *absolute* basis. If you select a cell when recording the macro, the same cell is selected when you later execute the macro. Suppose you begin recording a macro when you are in cell A1, for example. You click on cell B2 to select it, then continue recording your macro instructions. When you later run the macro, cell B2 is selected no matter where in the worksheet you are when you run the macro. If you are in cell C5, cell B2 is still selected when you run the macro.

Alternatively, you can choose to select cells using a relative reference. When you select a cell *relatively*, the macro selects a cell in relation to the currently active cell. If you start in cell A1 and select cell B2 using a relative reference, Excel selects the cell one column over and one row down from whichever cell is currently active when you later run the macro. If you run the macro when cell C5 is active, for example, cell D6 is selected. You select the method in the Record Macro submenu.

You select cells by relative reference by choosing Tools, Record Macro and selecting the option Use Relative Reference. The option is turned on when a checkmark appears next to it. To change to absolute selection, deselect the option so that no checkmark appears there.

Use Relative Reference is a *toggle*—a setting you turn off or on. It does not affect the way you select the cells when you record the macro, just the way they are selected when you run it.

As another example, suppose you duplicate a series of column and row headings in several locations within an individual worksheet or on a number of separate worksheets. Rather than type the headings yourself, you record a macro to do it for you. If you used the default absolute reference, however, the headings would always appear in the same rows and columns. You would not be able to use the macro to place the headings in other locations.

In the following steps, you record a macro that enters standard row and column headings using a relative reference. You should be in Excel with a blank worksheet. Record the macro in the Personal Macro Workbook.

When you first start an Excel session, the Use Relative References option is dimmed in the macro submenu. The option becomes active after you record, or begin to record, a macro.

1. Select cell A1.

2. Select Tools, Record Macro, Record New Macro to display the Record New Macro dialog box.

3. Type **Standard_Headings** as the macro name.

4. Select Options.

5. Click on the Menu Item on Tools Menu check box.

6. Select the text box under the prompt and type **Headings**.

7. Select the Ctrl+ text box and type **h**.

8. Click on Personal Macro Workbook.

9. Click on OK.

10. Select Tools, Record Macro, then select Use Relative Reference if it is not already selected.

11. Select cell B1.

12. Type **1st Qtr**.

13. Drag the fill handle in the lower right corner of cell B2 to cell E1.

14. Select cell A2 and type **Sales**.

15. Select cell A3 and type **Rentals**.

16. Select cell A4, type **Total**, and press Enter.

17. Click on the Stop button, or select Tools, Record Macro, Stop Recording to stop recording your actions.

IV

Macros

The cell selections were recorded using a relative reference. When you later run this macro, Excel inserts the text 1st Qtr in the cell to the right of the active cell and uses AutoFill to complete the series in the next three cells. The row headings appear in the three rows below the starting cell position.

To change back to absolute cell selection, deselect the Use Relative Reference option.

Adding to a Macro

While you are recording a macro, you can stop the recorder to perform actions you don't want to record. For example, suppose that while recording a macro you want to open another worksheet to check a reference. If you open the worksheet while recording, the open instructions are recorded as part of the macro. When you later run the macro, the worksheet is opened, even though you only needed to open it as a reference that one time. To pause the recording, click on the Stop button or select Tools, Record Macro, Stop Recording to stop recording your actions. When you want to continue adding instructions to the same macro, select Tools, Record Macro, Record at Mark.

You can use this feature if you realize that you stopped recording a macro before you performed all the operations you wanted to record. When you select Record at Mark, Excel begins recording your actions again, adding them to the end of the last macro you created.

To add instructions to a previously recorded macro, see "Setting the Recording Location" later in this chapter.

Follow these steps to insert additional instructions into the macro named Standard_Headings that you recorded in the last exercise.

1. Select cell A4.

2. Select Tools, Record Macro, then select Use Relative Reference, if it is not already selected.

3. Select Tools, Record Macro, Record at Mark.

4. Select cell A6 and type **Salaries**.

5. Select cell A7 and type **Supplies**.

6. Select cell A8 and type **Total**.

7. Select cell A10, type **Profit**, and click on the Enter box.

8. Click on the Stop button, or select <u>T</u>ools, <u>R</u>ecord Macro, <u>S</u>top Recording to stop recording your actions.

Exploring the Recorded Macro

When Excel records a macro, it inserts special instructions into the workbook. If you recorded your macro correctly and you are not interested in learning more about the advanced macro features discussed in Chapter 16,"Using the Excel 4 Macro Language," and Chapter 19, "Using Excel Visual Basic," you don't need to view these commands.

If you want to confirm that the macro was recorded properly, or if you want to edit or delete a macro, you must display the text of the macro.

When you use the VBA language (the default setting), macros are recorded in a module. A *module* is a special type of object attached to the workbook. To display a module, click on the Last Tab button (see fig. 15.6) to see a tab called Module1. Then click on the Module1 tab to display the module. The Visual Basic toolbar automatically appears when you display the module.

Figure 15.6
Macro module.

Last tab button

Macros

TIP

You can also select <u>T</u>ools, <u>M</u>acro, select the macro you want to see, then click on <u>E</u>dit to see the workbook's module.

Your macros are listed in the order that you created them. The commands are written in VBA.

By tiling the macro sheet and your worksheet, you can get a feel for the way Excel records macros. Follow these steps to display the module and the worksheet to record an additional macro:

1. Make the worksheet the active window, then select <u>W</u>indow, <u>N</u>ew Window.

2. Click on the Last Tab button, then click on the Module1 tab to display the text of your macro.

3. Select <u>W</u>indow, <u>A</u>rrange, <u>T</u>iled and click on OK.

4. Click in the worksheet window, or press Ctrl+F6.

5. Select cell A25.

Now record a macro and watch the instructions appear in the Module window.

6. Select <u>T</u>ools, <u>R</u>ecord Macro, <u>R</u>ecord New Macro to display the Record New Macro dialog box.

7. Type **Title** as the macro name.

8. Select <u>O</u>ptions.

9. Click on the This <u>W</u>orkbook button.

10. Select OK. The macro name is added to the end of the list of existing macros. Excel scrolls the list automatically to display the macro name in the window.

11. Type **Wilson Automotive, Inc.** and press the down arrow. The recorded instruction appears in the macro sheet.

12. Type **Annual Budget**, then click on the Enter box.

13. Select cells A25 and A26.

14. Select Forma<u>t</u>, <u>C</u>ells, <u>A</u>lignment, <u>C</u>enter, then click on OK.

15. Click on the Stop button.

16. Click anywhere on the worksheet to deselect the cells. Your screen should look something like figure 15.7.

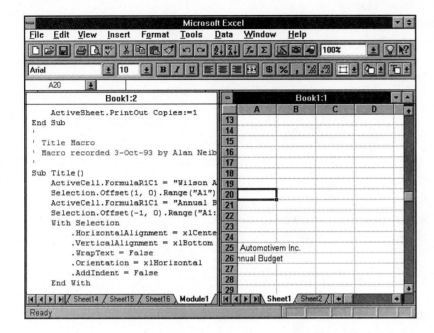

Figure 15.7
Module and worksheet tiled.

Displaying the Personal Macro Workbook

Unlike workbooks, modules, and other windows, Excel does not normally display the Personal Macro Workbook on the screen—it is hidden. To open the Personal Macro Workbook, select Window, Unhide to display a dialog box listing the names of hidden windows. Click on PERSONAL.XLS, then select OK. Excel displays the personal workbook that contains your macros.

You can use the Arrange command to display the personal workbook and your other workbook on the screen at the same time.

Printing Macros

Although the macro instructions might not mean much to you, they can serve as an excellent source of reference, particularly when you record a large number of operations.

As your macros become longer and more sophisticated, you should print a hard copy of the macro list as a reference. You can study the hard copy, writing notes where you'd like to make changes.

To print a copy of your macros, display the macro sheet, or make it active if its windows are tiled, then select File, Print and click on OK.

IV

Macros

TIP Make sure the Selected Sheets option is chosen in the Print dialog box when you want to print macros.

Setting the Recording Location

You can add instructions to a macro you have already recorded by setting the recording location. When you set the recording location, you can place the newly recorded instructions at any point within a macro.

Display the Module or the Personal Macro Workbook that contains the macro to which you want to add instructions. Move the cursor to the point at which you want to insert the instructions, then select Tools, Record Macro, Mark Position for Recording.

TIP To add instructions to the end of the macro, place the insertion point before the End Sub command (see fig. 15.8).

Figure 15.8
Placement of insertion point to add to the macro.

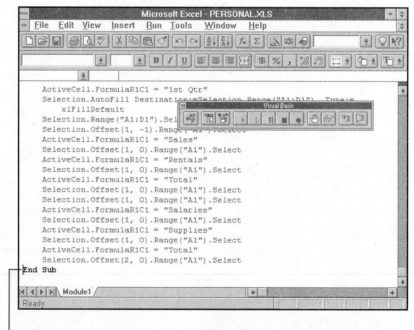

Click here to add to the macro

Display the sheet where you want to record the macro, then select Tools, Record Macro, Record at Mark and begin recording your macro. The new instructions are recorded at the position you set.

Make sure you set the position correctly. If you record instructions in the wrong location, your macro will not operate correctly. Suppose, for example, your macro selects a cell and enters some information into the cell. If you record new commands between these instructions, the contents will not appear where you originally intended.

Follow these steps to add instructions at the end of the Standard_Headings macro in the Personal Macro Workbook:

1. Maximize one of the workbook windows.

2. Select Window, Unhide, OK to unhide the Personal Macro Workbook.

3. Scroll until you see the End Sub command of the Standard_Headings macro.

4. Place the cursor before End Sub, as you saw in figure 15.8.

5. Select Tools, Record Macro, Mark Position for Recording.

6. Press Ctrl+F6 to return to the worksheet window.

7. Select cell A10.

   Because you are recording the macro using relative reference, you must position the insertion point in the correct cell. When you run this part of the macro, you want it to select the proper cell in relation to the previously recorded section.

8. Select Tools, Record Macro, then select Use Relative Reference, if it is not already selected.

9. Select Tools, Record Macro, Record at Mark.

10. Select cell A15.

11. Type **All budget figures are subject to audit** and click on the Enter box.

12. Click on the Stop button.

The new instructions appear at the end of the macro, as in figure 15.9.

IV

Macros

Figure 15.9
Added
instructions.

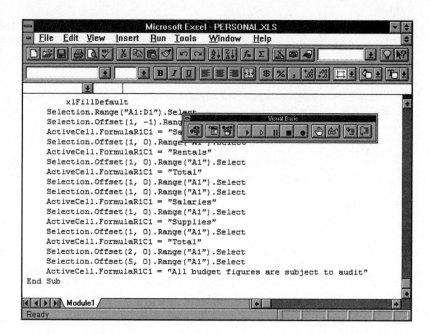

```
        xlFillDefault
    Selection.Range("A1:D1").Select
    Selection.Offset(1, -1).Rang
    ActiveCell.FormulaR1C1 = "Sa
    Selection.Offset(1, 0).Range
    ActiveCell.FormulaR1C1 = "Rentals"
    Selection.Offset(1, 0).Range("A1").Select
    ActiveCell.FormulaR1C1 = "Total"
    Selection.Offset(1, 0).Range("A1").Select
    Selection.Offset(1, 0).Range("A1").Select
    ActiveCell.FormulaR1C1 = "Salaries"
    Selection.Offset(1, 0).Range("A1").Select
    ActiveCell.FormulaR1C1 = "Supplies"
    Selection.Offset(1, 0).Range("A1").Select
    ActiveCell.FormulaR1C1 = "Total"
    Selection.Offset(2, 0).Range("A1").Select
    Selection.Offset(5, 0).Range("A1").Select
    ActiveCell.FormulaR1C1 = "All budget figures are subject to audit"
End Sub
```

Saving Macros

A macro module is part of the workbook. When you save the workbook, the module is saved along with it. If you want to save the macros without saving the sheets, you have several alternatives. You can delete the contents of the sheets, then save the workbook. You also can copy the module to a new workbook. To copy the module, click on the module tab, then select Edit, Move or Copy Sheet. Pull down the To Book list and select (new book). Excel creates a new book that contains the module.

TIP

You also can display two workbooks on the screen, then drag the Module tab to the other workbook.

Hiding and Saving the Personal Macro Workbook

The Personal Macro Workbook is not saved when you save other workbooks. You must save the Personal Macro Workbook before you exit Excel. Display the workbook, then select File, Save.

If you close the Personal Macro Worksheet when it is unhidden, its macro is not available, and you must open it again. Rather than closing it, hide it again. This removes the workbook from the display but makes its macros accessible. To hide the worksheet, make it active and select Window, Hide. If you don't hide the Personal Macro Worksheet, it appears on-screen the next time you start Excel.

Remember to display and select the Personal Macro Workbook before you select Window, Hide. If you don't, the active worksheet window is hidden.

Deleting a Macro

You can delete a macro if you change your mind after recording it, or if you just want to clean out unused macros from a workbook.

To delete a macro, select Tools, Macro, click on the macro name in the list box, then select Delete. You also can display the module or Personal Macro Workbook, then delete the macro code by selecting it and pressing Del. Remember, you must unhide the Personal Macro Workbook if it is not listed in the Window menu.

If you delete a macro that has been added to the Tools menu, the list still appears in the menu. Before you delete the macro, select Tools, Macro, then select the macro in the list box. Finally, select Options. Deselect the Menu Item on Tools Menu box, then select OK. This action removes the item from the menu. You can now delete the macro itself. If you delete the item before removing it from the menu, you must use the Tools, Menu Editor option to edit the menu.

To delete all your personal macros, delete the file PERSONAL.XLS from the disk. Excel creates a new one the next time you save a macro using that option.

Classifications of Macros

Excel's macro language is a powerful tool for automating worksheets. Recorded macros, however, only touch on their power and versatility. When you record a macro, you are creating a command macro, which is one of two types of macros you can create. The other type of macro is a function macro.

IV

Macros

Command Macros

A *command macro* performs some action on the worksheet. It repeats keystrokes or selections from menus or dialog boxes. Command macros save you from repeating the same series of operations.

Macros that you record are always command macros. You can also write a command macro if you want to create it without actually performing the instructions. By writing macros, you can repeat a series of steps, make decisions based on the contents of cells, and even create interactive macros that accept input from the keyboard. You learn to write, edit, and delete command macros Chapter 16, "Programming Macros."

Function Macros

A *function macro* creates a user-defined function. The macro operates the same way as Excel's built-in functions to perform a calculation and return a value. It does not perform any action on the worksheet except to insert a value into a cell.

Some complex calculations that you perform might require formulas in several cells. Each formula is actually another step in the overall calculation. If you add the formulas directly in the worksheet, they could occupy a considerable amount of space. By adding all of the formulas into a function macro, you can perform the calculation using a single worksheet cell.

You cannot record an entire user-defined function macro. You have to write the macro, or perform extensive editing on a record macro. You learn more about this in Chapters 16, "Programming Macros," and 19, "Using Excel Visual Basic."

Understanding Macro Code

Unless you decide to record macros in the Excel 4 format, your macros are constructed using the Visual Basic for Applications (VBA) language.

A *keyword* is a word that represents a macro language command or instruction. Every macro begins with the keyword Sub followed by the macro name and ends with the keyword End Sub. The macro instructions are called *statements*. Each statement tells Excel to perform a specific action. VBA instructions are combinations of objects, methods, properties, and variables.

Technically, the Sub and End Sub commands indicate a subroutine. You learn more about VBA in Chapter 19, "Using Excel Visual Basic," but some of its basic concepts are discussed here.

The VBA statement to select cell D9, for example, appears like this:

```
Range("D9").Select
```

Range is a VBA object that represents a cell or a range of cells. The range object, however, requires an argument that further identifies the object being referred to, giving the specific cell or range of cells. In this case, the object is cell D9.

The VBA statement also must specify the *method* of dealing with or using the object. The keyword select is the method. It tells Excel what action to perform on the object—in this case, to select the cell. In the statement Range("D9:G9").Select, the object to be selected is the range of cells D9 through G9.

The statement for entering contents into a cell appears like this:

```
ActiveCell.FormulaR1C1 = "Profit"
```

The object is the currently active cell. In this case, however, you are not performing a method on the cell but defining its properties. A *property* explains the conditions or state of the object. In this statement, the property is FormulaR1C1, and it indicates that the following text will be contained in the object.

In some cases, the object has a number of properties. For example, the command to format a cell in a font is as follows:

```
Selection.Font.Name = "Arial"
```

Selection is an object that refers to the currently selected object in the worksheet. Font also is an object to be applied to the selections. But the Font object needs a property (Name) to explain the way in which it is applied. In this case, the selected cells are assigned the font named Arial.

NOTE Macros are not simply a record of keystrokes. The command to change a font has no reference to the Format Cell selection which is needed to display the Font dialog box. Macro instructions are the results of your recorded actions.

A definite pattern exists for performing Excel tasks. Usually, a cell (or range of cells) is selected, then one or more properties are assigned to the selection. Suppose, for example, you record the instructions that use AutoFill to complete a series of entries. Here is a typical process:

```
Range("D9").Select
ActiveCell.FormulaR1C1 = "1st Qtr"
Selection.AutoFillDestination:=Range("D9:G9"),Type:=xlFillDefault
```

These VBA statements select a cell, enter the starting value (1st Qtr), then assign properties to the cell that complete the series.

When you select items from a dialog box, any number of properties can be included in the VBA statement. For instance, when you use the Font dialog box, you can select a font name, size, and various other character attributes. Rather than repeating the object names for every property, Excel places them in a with structure:

```
With Selection.Font
    .Name = "Arial"
    .FontStyle = "Regular"
    .Size = 10
    .Strikethrough = False
    .Superscript = False
    .Subscript = False
    .OutlineFont = False
    .Shadow = False
    .Underline = xlNone
    .ColorIndex = xlAutomatic
End With
```

The statement With Selection.Font indicates that all of the following properties refer to the same object. Name, FontStyle, Size, and so on are properties of the Selection.Font object.

You can use a similar technique to format the position of text within a cell. In this example, the five properties are applied to the Selection object:

```
With Selection
    .HorizontalAlignment = xlCenter
    .VerticalAlignment = xlBottom
    .WrapText = False
    .Orientation = xlHorizontal
    .AddIndent = False
End With
```

Streamlining Macro Selection

If you use a macro often, you can add it to a toolbar or to a graphics object. This procedure makes the macro visible on-screen so that you don't have to remember its shortcut key or select it from a list.

Adding a Macro to a Toolbar

Pressing the shortcut key combination is a quick way to run a macro. Still, it is easy to forget what key you assigned to every macro you created. As you build a library of macros, you also might run out of keys to assign.

Rather than try to remember the shortcut keys or scroll through the Run Macro dialog box to locate the macro, you can assign the macro to a toolbar. You can then run the macro by clicking on the toolbar button.

AUTHOR'S NOTE

Assigning a macro to a toolbar has one great advantage. When you click on the tool assigned to the macro, Excel opens the workbook in which the macro is located if it is not already open. You don't have to remember to open the workbook yourself.

You assign a macro to the toolbar using the dialog box shown in figure 15.10. Select the desired tool, then drag it onto the toolbar. You then can select the macro you want to assign to the toolbar or record a macro to assign to it. The macro sheet that contains the macro you want to assign must be open.

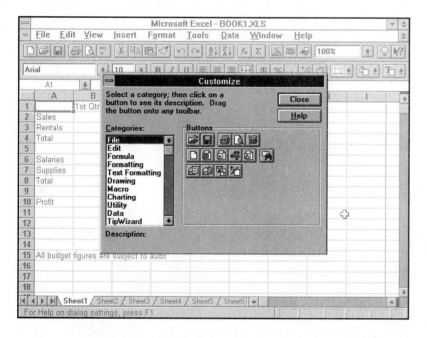

Figure 15.10
The Customize dialog box.

Follow these steps to add the Standard_Headings macro to the toolbar:

1. Point to the toolbar and click the right mouse button to display the toolbar shortcut menu. Alternatively, use the keyboard to select View, Toolbars.

2. Select Customize to display the Customize dialog box.

3. Click on Custom in the Categories list. (You have to scroll the list to display the option.) The tools shown in the dialog box are unassigned. They are not connected with any Excel function.

4. Drag one of the tools to the toolbar. When you release the mouse button, the Assign Macro dialog box appears.

5. Select PERSONAL.XLS!Standard_Headings or any other macro you want to assign to the tool, then click on OK. Click on Record to record and assign the macro to the tool at the same time.

6. Select Close to close the Customize dialog box.

If you select Cancel or Close in the Assign Macro dialog box, the tool is not associated with a macro. When you first click on the macro, however, the Assign Macro dialog box appears so that you can make the assignment or record a macro.

TIP Alternatively, you can use the keyboard to assign a macro using the View, Toolbars, Tools, Assign Macro.

Reassigning Tools

You also can assign a macro to a tool already displayed on the toolbar. Like preset key combinations, making the assignment cancels the built-in function—when you click on the tool, your macro runs instead. To assign a macro to an existing tool, follow these steps:

1. Display the toolbar that contains the button.

2. Point to the toolbar and click the right mouse button to display the toolbar shortcut menu.

3. Select Customize.

4. Point to the button you want to change, then click the right mouse button to display the shortcut menu shown in figure 15.11.

5. Select Assign Macro.

6. Select the macro you want to assign to the tool, then click on OK.

7. Close the Customize dialog box.

Only the tool on that toolbar is affected. If the same tool appears on another toolbar, it retains its original value. To reassign the tool to its original function, follow these steps:

1. Display the toolbar that contains the button.

2. Point to the toolbar and click the right mouse button to display the toolbar shortcut menu.

3. Select Customize.

4. Drag the tool off the toolbar to delete it.

5. In the Categories box, select the category of the function originally performed by the tool. The tools in that category appear in the Tools panel.

6. Drag the tool to its original position on the toolbar.

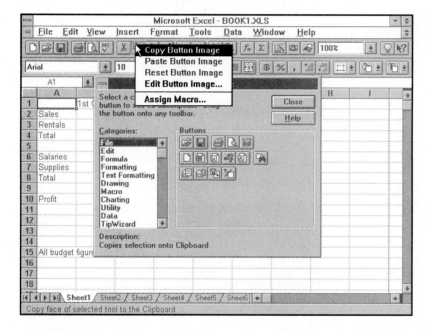

Figure 15.11
Customize toolbar shortcut menu.

Macros

Adding a Macro to a Graphics Object

In Chapter 13, "Drawing and Adding Graphics to Worksheets," you learned to create graphics objects. You can assign a macro to a graphics object and then run the macro by selecting the object. To assign a macro to a graphics object, follow these steps:

1. Select the graphics object.

2. Select Tools, Assign Macro.

3. Select the macro from the list, or select Record and then record the macro.

Chapter Snapshot

When you need to create macros, Excel gives you a choice. You can create macros in Visual Basic for Applications (VBA) or the Microsoft Excel 4 macro language. Even if you want to program in VBA, you should know how to use the alternative. In this chapter, you learn the following tasks and concepts:

✔ Recording a macro using the Excel 4 macro language

✔ Using existing Excel 4 macros and macro sheets

✔ Adding instructions to existing macros

✔ Deleting macros

✔ Understanding macro arguments

✔ Writing command macros

✔ Writing user-defined functions

✔ Understanding macro flow control

✔ Writing macros that make decisions

✔ Writing macros that repeat instructions

✔ Writing macros that input values

If you are new to the world of macros and programming, you should find this chapter to be a perfect introduction to programming logic and techniques. The programming skills you learn here can be applied to VBA or any other programming language.

16 CHAPTER

Using the Excel 4 Macro Language

A lthough Visual Basic for Applications (VBA) is a powerful automation and development tool, you should be familiar with another Microsoft language: the Excel 4 Macro Language. If you already are an experienced Excel macro programmer, you'll discover the convenience of developing important macros in the familiar environment while you learn VBA. You then can switch to VBA when your programming skills increase.

But even if you are not a programmer, you might have Excel macros that were written by others, copied from magazines, or downloaded from a bulletin board. You can use these macros in Excel 5 and record and write macros in the Excel 4 macro language. (From this point on, this chapter refers to the Excel 4 Macro Language as *the macro language.*)

> ### AUTHOR'S NOTE
>
> If you skipped Chapter 15 because you are an experienced macro language programmer, or because you did not want to learn VBA, go back! Excel 5 incorporates some new features that can streamline recording and writing macros.

Recording a Macro

As you learned in Chapter 15, you record a macro in the macro language the same way you do in VBA. When the Record New Macro dialog box appears, however, select Options, then click on the MS Excel 4.0 Macro button in the Language section.

Give the macro a name, enter a description, and assign a shortcut key just as you do for any other macro. From the recording standpoint, the process is the same as the one you learned earlier.

Table 16.1 describes the toolbar icons you use in this chapter.

Table 16.1
Macro Toolbar Icons

Tool	Name	Purpose
▷	Step	Steps through macro instructions one at a time
‖	Resume	Resumes a paused macro
☞	Step Into	Steps through a macro, including subroutines
☞	Step Over	Steps through a macro, skipping over subroutines

NOTE   Remember, macro names must start with a letter and cannot contain any spaces or punctuation marks other than the underline character.

Macro Locations

You can select to store a macro in one of three locations. By default, macros are stored in the current workbook. These macros are available whenever the workbook is open. You can open the workbook to access its macros from other workbooks.

If you want to be able to use the macro with every worksheet, select the Personal Macro Workbook option. The macro is recorded in the file PERSONAL.XLS, along with any VBA macros that you have written or recorded. The Personal Macro Workbook operates according to the description in Chapter 15:

✔ It is opened automatically when you start Excel

✔ It is hidden until you select Windows Unhide

✔ It must be saved when you exit Excel

If you select New Workbook, Excel opens a new workbook and records your macro there. You must save the workbook before you exit Excel, and you must open the workbook to access the macros.

NOTE Each time you select New Workbook, Excel opens another workbook. After you open a workbook, record other macros in it by setting the macro location.

Running Macros

You can run a macro written in the macro language just as you learned to in Chapter 15.

✔ If the macro is assigned to a shortcut key, press the key combination.

✔ If the macro is assigned to the menu, pull down the menu and select the item.

✔ If the item is assigned to a toolbar button or graphic object, point and click. If necessary, Excel opens the workbook in which the macro is located.

✔ Select <u>T</u>ools <u>M</u>acro, then double-click on the macro in the list box, or select the macro and choose Run.

NOTE All the cautions and warnings that apply to running VBA macros apply equally to macro language macros. Refer to Chapter 15 for additional information.

IV

Macros

Follow these steps to record a macro that enters your name on a worksheet.

1. Select cell A1.

2. Select Tools, Record Macro, Record New Macro to display the Record Macro dialog box.

3. Type **Title** as the macro name.

4. Select Options.

5. Select the Menu Item on Tools Menu option.

6. Select the text box under the prompt, then type **Title**.

7. Click on the Shortcut Key checkbox.

8. Click on MS Excel 4.0 Macro.

9. Click on OK.

10. Select cell A1.

11. Select Insert, Rows.

12. Type your name, then press Enter.

13. Click on the Stop button, or select Tools, Record Macro, Stop Recording to stop recording your actions.

Do not forget to stop recording when you have completed the operations that you want to record. If you forget, Excel continues to record all your operations.

You can record Excel 4 macros using either relative or absolute cell references, as explained in Chapter 15.

Using Existing Macros

You can use macros written in Excel 4 without any conversion or editing. Open the macro sheet just as you did in Excel 4 and run the macro using the explanation in Chapter 15.

If you have an Excel 4 global macro sheet (the file GLOBAL.XLM in the EXCEL\XLSTART subdirectory), it opens automatically when you start Excel, and its macros are available. By default, however, the global macro sheet is hidden.

NOTE

GLOBAL.XLM is a worksheet created by Excel 4 that stores macros in the Excel 4 macro language. Both the GLOBAL.XLM worksheet and the PERSONAL.XLS workbook open automatically, which might cause Excel to start slowly.

Transferring Macros

If you have macros in the global macro sheet, you can transfer them to PERSONAL.XLS. This step avoids the necessity of having both open in order to access all your global macros. To transfer the macros, open and unhide both GLOBAL.XLM and PERSONAL.XLS. Display the sheet that contains your macros in GLOBAL.XLM, then select Edit, Move or Copy Sheet to display the dialog box shown in figure 16.1. Pull down the To Book list and select PERSONAL.XLS, then OK.

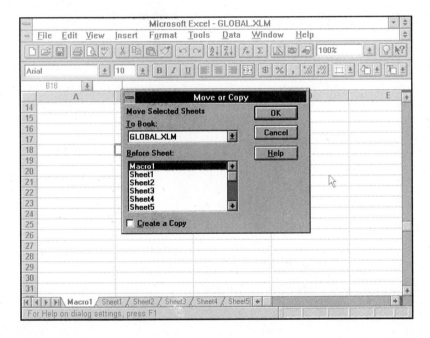

Figure 16.1

The Move or Copy Sheet dialog box.

TIP

If you want to copy the macros so that they remain in the global macro sheet, click on the Create a Copy check box.

AUTHOR'S NOTE

The Personal Macro Workbook in Excel 5 replaces the global macro sheet function-
ally in Excel 4. You can use both if desired, and both can store VBA and Excel 4
macros. The only reason to retain the global macro sheet, however, is for compatibility with earlier Excel versions.

If you have Excel 5 on your office computer and you have Excel 4 on your home
computer, for instance, recording macros in the global macro sheet enables you to
use them with both versions.

Excel 5 has features and functions not available in earlier versions, however. Macros
that contain commands for these functions do not run in Excel 4.

Exploring the Recorded Macro

As you read in Chapter 15, VBA macros are stored in modules. A module is attached to a
workbook, but it does not contain the rows and columns of a worksheet.

Macro language macros are saved in macro sheets that look the same as regular worksheets.
The sheets are added at the end of the workbook, following any VBA modules. Sheet tabs for
worksheets that contain Excel 4 macros are labeled Macro rather than Module. Module
sheets are reserved for VBA macros. To display the sheet, click on the Last Tab button on the
far left of the horizontal scroll bar to find a tab called Macro1. Then click on the Macro1 tab.
Your Title macro appears as in figure 16.2.

NOTE   Macro sheets do not exist until you record an Excel 4 macro.

Each macro is listed in a column of the worksheet. The first macro you recorded is in column
A, the second in column B, and so on. Row A contains the macro names and shortcut key
assignments. Cell A1 in figure 16.2, for example, indicates that the column contains the
macro called Title and that is it assigned to the key combination Ctrl+E.

TIP   The columns settings might prevent you from seeing the full text of each macro
instruction. Widen the columns if necessary.

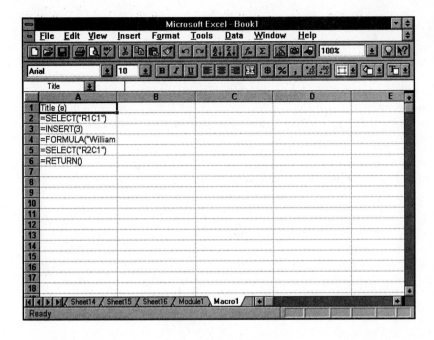

Figure 16.2
The Excel 4 macro in macro sheet.

The remaining rows contain instructions in Excel's macro language. The instruction =RETURN() must end every macro. It tells Excel where to stop looking for instructions to repeat when you run the macro.

By tiling the macro sheet and your worksheet, you can get a feel for the way Excel records macros.

Printing Macros

To print a copy of all the macros in the macro sheet, display the sheet and select File, Print, OK. To print a copy of a specific macro, select the instructions that make up the macro and select File, Print, Selection, then OK.

Widen the columns and/or change fonts to see the full text of the instructions on the printout.

Macros

Setting the Recording Location

You can use the Mark Position for Recording option to add commands to any macro in the macro sheet.

To add commands to the *end* of a macro, click on any cell in the macro that already contains a command, then select Tools, Record Macro, Mark Position for Recording. Return to the worksheet, then select Tools, Record Macro, Record at Mark. The instructions you record will be added to the end of the macro.

To add commands within a macro, first insert enough blank rows to hold the macro commands you are adding. Select the first blank row, and then select Tools, Record Macro, Mark Position for Recording.

If you set a recording position to start in a blank cell, make sure there are enough empty cells below that position to store the entire macro. If Excel encounters a cell that already contains any contents, it will stop recording your macro and display a warning box with the message Recorder Range is Full. To continue, click on OK to remove the warning box, then insert additional blank cells in the macro.

You waste space if you record a large number of short macros and start each in a new column. This method is particularly troublesome if you want to print your macro sheet. If you record 20 short macros, for example, you must print all 20 columns for a hard copy of the macros. Instead, you can use unused rows that follow a macro's RETURN() command to record other macros.

When you set the recording position, you can start a macro in a row other than the first one. To set the position, display the macro sheet, click on the empty cell where you want to begin recording instructions, then select Tools, Record Macro, Mark Position for Recording. Change to a worksheet window, then select Tools, Record Macro, Record at Mark. The instructions are recorded beginning in the selected cell.

Before using the macro, you must give it a name. Change to the macro window and select the cell in which you began the macro. Select Insert, Name, Define to display the dialog box shown in figure 16.3. Type a name for the macro, then click the Command option button in the macro section. You can assign the macro a shortcut key by entering the keystroke in the Key:Ctrl+ box. Click on OK.

The set recorder feature works only for one macro at a time. The next macro that you record is saved in the next available column.

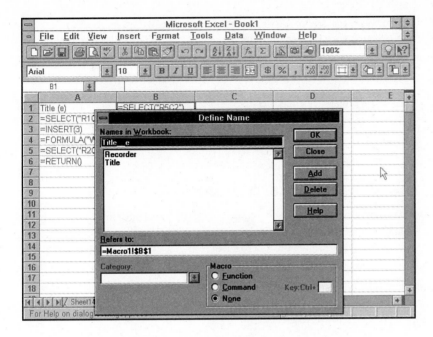

Figure 16.3
The Name dialog box.

NOTE

If you select a range of cells in the macro sheet (rather than clicking on just one cell), then select **T**ools, **R**ecord Macro, **M**ark Position for Recording, Excel limits the macro to that number of instructions. If you select 10 cells, for example, you can only record a macro with eight steps. Remember, one cell is needed for the macro name and another cell for the RETURN() command. If you try to record more instructions than will fit in the cells, the `Recorder Range is Full` message appears, and the recorder stops.

To add macros to a previously recorded macro sheet, you must open it. Select **F**ile, **O**pen, then double-click on the name of the workbook that contains the macros.

Recording to the Global Macro Sheet

Even with the global macro sheet open and unhidden, the macro is stored in PERSONAL.XLS when you select Personal Macro Sheet as the recording location.

To store a macro in the Excel 4 global macro sheet, you must open and unhide it, then choose a cell in the sheet as the starting, recording position. Record and name the macro according to the previous explanation.

Excel 4 created the global macro sheet when you selected the option from the Record Macro dialog box. Excel 5 does not create a global macro sheet for you automatically. If you want to

create a global macro sheet, select <u>N</u>ew Workbook as the location. Before exiting Excel, save the workbook that contains your macros with the name GLOBAL.XLM and store it in the XLSTART subdirectory.

NOTE

Remember, references in this chapter to the global macro sheet relate to the file GLOBAL.XLM, not to the personal macro workbook of Excel 5.

Hiding the Global Macro Sheet

If the global macro sheet is not hidden when you exit Excel, it appears automatically when you start Excel again. Before exiting Excel, display the sheet and select <u>W</u>indow, <u>H</u>ide. When you exit, Excel asks if you want to save the macro sheet changes, even if you saved the sheet before hiding it.

The hidden attribute is actually stored with the sheet itself. Hiding the sheet after you saved it changes the attribute. Select <u>Y</u>es to exit Excel. If you select <u>N</u>o, the sheet appears when you next start Excel, even though it was hidden.

STOP

If you fail to display and select the global macro sheet before you select <u>W</u>indow, <u>H</u>ide, the active worksheet window will be hidden.

When you exit Excel, Excel asks if you want to save the changes to the Global Macro sheet. Select <u>Y</u>es to keep the sheet hidden when you start Excel again.

Deleting an Excel Macro

You can delete a macro if you change your mind after recording it, or if you just want to clean out macros from a macro sheet.

TIP

You cannot use the <u>D</u>elete option in the Macro dialog box to delete an Excel 4 macro. The delete dialog box option only deletes Visual Basic macros.

To delete an Excel 4 macro, make the macro sheet in which the macro is stored the active window. (Remember, you must unhide GLOBAL.XLM if it is not listed in the Window menu.) Delete the contents of the cells in which the macro is stored, or delete the entire column.

Next, with the macro sheet still active, select <u>I</u>nsert, <u>N</u>ame, <u>D</u>efine, click on the macro name, then choose <u>D</u>elete.

If you simply delete the macro from the sheet, its name still appears when you list macros that can be run. If you delete just the name, the macro instructions still occupy space in the macro sheet.

TIP To delete all the macros, delete the macro sheet file from the disk. If you delete the global macro sheet file, Excel creates a new one the next time you save a macro using that option.

Understanding Excel's Macro Language

Excel's macro language is a powerful tool for automating worksheets. Like VBA, you can use it to create command macros and function macros.

Macro Command Arguments

The macro instructions recorded in the macro sheet are functions. Each macro function represents the results of a series of actions. If, for example, you select <u>F</u>ile, <u>O</u>pen to record the actions that open a worksheet called Budget, the macro instruction might be `=OPEN("C:\EXCEL\BUDGET.XLS")`.

The instruction contains no reference to the <u>F</u>ile menu, just the results of the operation. The function OPEN represents the selection <u>F</u>ile, <u>O</u>pen, or clicking on the open tool.

You should be familiar with the concept of functions. In Chapter 7, you learned to use Excel's built-in functions to perform mathematical and other operations. When you used a built-in function, you entered the equal sign, the name of the function, and an argument or arguments that explained the details of the operation. If you use the SUM function to total the values in cells A1 through A13, for instance, you enter the function like this:

`=SUM(A1:A13)`

The name of the function is SUM, and the argument is A1:A13, which tells Excel the way to apply the function.

Macro functions are very similar. Each macro command contains two parts, the macro function name and one or more arguments. The name indicates the type of action to be performed, such as Open to open a worksheet, Print to print a worksheet, or Select to select a cell. A macro function name is assigned to every action that you can perform using Excel.

The arguments give specific details of the action. The macro command Open, for example, needs an argument that specifies which worksheet should be opened. The arguments are

IV

Macros

contained in parentheses following the macro function name. Without the argument, Excel wouldn't know what to do with the function, just as entering **=SUM()** would be meaningless.

AUTHOR'S NOTE

If you plan only to record macros, don't worry about understanding macro arguments. Excel inserts the correct arguments for you when it records your menu and dialog box actions.

Some macro functions require only one argument; others might require quite a few. Arguments are separated by commas. Every macro function has a specific number of arguments that it can accept. The number of arguments used in the instruction depends on the task you are performing.

The macro function to select cells, for example, is named Select, and it is followed by an argument that indicates which cell should be selected. The argument lists the row, then the column of the cell. In recorded macros, columns are designated by numbers, not letters. The instruction =SELECT("R1C2"), for example, selects cell B1 using absolute reference. Think of the argument as meaning "row 1, second column." The second column is column B.

NOTE Recorded Excel macros use R1C1 references even if you are working in A1 mode. The cell references must be enclosed in quotation marks.

Instructions for selecting cells by relative references appear like this:

    =SELECT("R[1]C[1]")

The numbers in brackets indicate the distance away from the cell currently active. In this case, the notation specifies the selection of a cell one row and one column away from the current cell. The instruction =SELECT("RC[1]") means to select a cell in the same row, but one column to the right. Use positive numbers to indicate positions to the right of or below the current cell. Use negative numbers to indicate cell positions to the left of or above the cell. The instruction =SELECT("R[-1]C"), for example, indicates the cell one row above the active cell in the same column.

Both of these examples contain only one argument. If you select a range of cells, however, the command includes two arguments. The first argument is the range of cells selected, the second is the active cell in the selected group, as in =SELECT("R1C1:R5C2","R2C1").

Arguments must be in a prescribed order. You do not need to use all the arguments, but the ones that are used must appear in their proper position. Excel knows what each argument means by its position in the parentheses.

When Excel encounters an Open macro function, for example, it knows that the first argument lists the name of the file to open. The Open command can take up to 10 arguments, but only the first is absolutely necessary. In fact, when you record a macro that opens a workbook using the default values in the open dialog box, only one argument is listed.

NOTE The other arguments in the Open command specify the way in which links are updated, the text file format, and the source of the file.

When you record a macro that opens a worksheet in read-only mode, however, it appears like this:

```
=OPEN("C:\EXCEL\BUDGET.XLS",,TRUE)
```

The argument TRUE indicates read-only. The extra comma between the arguments is a placeholder, indicating that TRUE is the third possible argument. The second parameter, which specifies the way links are updated, was not recorded, but a place must be left for it. This precaution ensures that Excel knows that the word TRUE refers to the third argument. When you use a placeholder, Excel applies the default arguments that would appear in that position in the command.

When the macro represents a dialog box action, the arguments specify your selections from the dialog box. But even if you select OK to accept all the default dialog box values, several arguments might be recorded. If you record the command to print a worksheet using all the default settings, for instance, it appears as follows:

```
=PRINT(1,,,1,FALSE,FALSE,1,,,300)
```

Many arguments have been omitted, but their positions are marked by placeholders. In this case, the arguments listed are the minimum that Windows needs to print the worksheet. The omitted arguments are optional.

The first argument tells Windows the range of pages you want to print. If you select the default values, the argument indicates that you want to print the entire worksheet. Because you are printing the entire worksheet, the second and third arguments, which specify a range of pages, are unnecessary. Their places are left blank.

The fourth argument in the Print command is required because it indicates the number of copies to be printed. Excel expects the value to be in the fourth argument position. The extra commas indicate the empty positions of the second and third arguments, ensuring that the fourth argument is interpreted correctly.

If you select to print specific pages in the dialog box, the value of the second argument is 2 and the next two arguments are required.

```
=PRINT(2,1,3,1,FALSE,FALSE,1,,,300)
```

IV

Macros

NOTE Some macro functions, such as Return(), can contain no arguments, although the opening and closing parentheses are still included.

Entering Data into Cells

In the macro language, the command for entering data into cells is FORMULA. The information to insert is the command's argument, enclosed in quotation marks. To insert a text string in a cell, add the text as the argument as follows:

```
=FORMULA("1st Qtr")
```

To insert a cell reference or formula, precede it with an equal sign, but also enclose it in quotation marks:

```
=FORMULA("=R1C1+R2C1")
```

The command inserts the formula to add cells A1 and A2 into the cell currently selected.

You also can designate a specific cell, other than the active cell, to enter the data. The syntax is =FORMULA("*text*", *cell*).

The command =FORMULA("1st Qtr", "R10C3"), for example, inserts the text in cell C10.

Writing Macros

In addition to recording a macro, you can write one directly in the macro sheet. Writing a macro enables you to take advantage of functions and commands that are not recordable.

Both VBA and the macro language contain a large number of programming commands that extend the capabilities of your macros. These commands control the flow of your macro, make decisions based on cell contents, and can repeat a series of commands.

AUTHOR'S NOTE

In order to write macros, you must be familiar with the macro language. Excel 5's Function Wizard helps you select and enter macro commands, but you still need a basic understanding of the language.

Writing a macro requires a series of steps:

1. Planning and outlining the steps or functions you want the macro to perform

2. Displaying or opening the macro sheet

3. Writing the macro instructions

4. Naming the macro

5. Testing the macro

In the following sections, you learn the details behind each of these basic steps.

Designing A Macro

Before you write a macro, you should plan exactly what tasks the macro should perform. Most macros automate routine tasks that you perform often, such as inserting labels, formatting cells, or printing worksheets, reports, and database operations. You can also use macros to repeat a complex series of tasks that require many actions. By performing the tasks using a macro, you can ensure that the correct operations are performed each time the macro is run. You also can use macros to create complete, automated applications that include custom dialog boxes, menus, and buttons.

> ### AUTHOR'S NOTE
>
> You can create an application using the macro language, but VBA is better suited for sophisticated systems.

Write the steps of your macro in sentence form, each sentence explaining another step in the macro. Suppose, for instance, you have a series of workbooks that contain budget reports, and you need a macro that opens the workbooks and prints the first worksheet of each. You can outline the macro like this:

1. Open worksheet Budget1.

2. Select File, Print, Selected Sheets, OK.

3. Open worksheet Budget2.

4. Select File, Print, Selected Sheets, OK.

5. Open worksheet Budget 3.

6. Select File, Print, Selected Sheets, OK.

IV

Macros

As your macros become more complex, you might need to design them in a flow chart form. A *flow chart* shows graphically the steps of the macro and the relationship between them. Flowcharting is an art in itself and requires knowledge of program flow and design.

Opening a Macro Sheet

The next step is to open the macro sheet that will contain your macro. You can use a macro sheet already attached to the workbook, or you can open a new one. To begin a new macro sheet in the current workbook, select Insert, Macro, MS Excel 4.0 Macro. The sheet appears before the worksheet already displayed. If Sheet1 is active, for example, the macro sheet appears at the start of the workbook, before Sheet1.

Excel numbers macro sheets consecutively. If you have recorded a macro already, the new sheet is labeled Macro2, the next is Macro3, and so forth.

You can write the macro by opening a macro sheet in PERSONAL.XLS, GLOBAL.XLM, or any other workbook. If you want to use the macro with every workbook, however, use the Personal Macro Workbook or the global macro sheet.

While creating and testing a macro, use a separate workbook to ensure that your work-in-progress does not interfere with macros that you use every day. After you complete the macro and thoroughly test it, you can copy it to any other workbook or sheet.

Writing the Macro

To write the macro, move to an empty cell. Make sure that enough empty cells are available below it to store the entire macro. Type the name you want to assign the macro in the first cell, then continue writing the macro commands, beginning each with the = sign.

The macro name is optional. You assign the macro name when you use Insert, Name, Define to name the macro.

The last line of the macro usually is =RETURN(). The line might, however, be =HALT() or even a Goto command, depending on the flow of your program logic.

TIP   Remember to start commands with the = symbol.

When you move to a cell after you complete a macro instruction, Excel checks the command to make sure it conforms to the proper syntax. It changes lowercase characters in command names to uppercase and ensures that the instruction contains the proper arguments. It displays a message box if it detects an error. Click on OK to remove the box, then correct the mistake. The checking process is not foolproof, however. It checks for syntax of commands, not for proper logic. Excel does not know if you are entering the wrong command as long as the command is properly structured.

If you are uncertain of a command's syntax, you can paste the command in the macro rather than writing it. To paste a command, select Insert, Function, scroll the Function Category list and select the category that contains the command you want to insert. Programming and flow control commands are in the Macro Control category. In the Function Name list, double-click on the command you want to insert, or select the command, then choose next.

Excel displays one or more dialog boxes from which you can select the syntax desired or enter arguments.

Naming the Macro

Before using the macro, you must define its name. Select the cell that contains the macro name, then select Insert, Name, Define. Click on the Command button in the macro section, assign a shortcut key, if desired, then select OK.

This procedure assigns the name that you use to run the macro from the Macro dialog box.

Follow these steps to write a command macro:

1. Select Sheet1.

2. Select Insert, Macro, MS Excel 4.0 Macro to display a new macro sheet, Macro2.

3. Select cell A1, type **DateSheet**, then press Enter to select cell A2.

4. Type **=Select("R1C1")** and press Enter. Excel uppercases the command.

5. Type **=Insert(3)** and press Enter. This command inserts a row in the worksheet. The arguments correspond to the options in the Insert dialog box: 1 to shift cells to the right; 2 to shift cells down; 3 to insert a row; and 4 to insert a column.

6. Type **=FORMULA("=TODAY()")** and press Enter. The TODAY() function returns the current date. By using it as the argument of the FORMULA command, the date appears in the active cell.

Macros

7. Type **=RETURN()** and press Enter.

8. Select cell A1, the cell that contains the macro name.

9. Select Insert, Name, Define. The label in cell A1 appears as the suggested macro name. You can enter another name if you want, but using the same label as the name makes it easier to identify your macros if you need to edit.

10. Click on the Command button in the macro section.

11. Click on OK.

12. Select File, Save, type **MYMAC**, and select OK twice.

TIP

Do not forget to select the Command button. If you fail to select it, the macro name does not appear in the Macros dialog box.

To run the macro, select Tools, Macro, then double-click on the macro name.

1. Click on the Sheet2 tab.

2. Select cell A1.

3. Type **BUDGET** and press Enter.

4. Select Tools, Macro, then double-click on the name DateSheet.

Excel runs the macro, which inserts a row and the current date.

Function Macros

A command macro performs some action on the worksheet. You also can create a function macro. A function macro operates in much the same way as Excel's built-in functions. When you want to perform some task that is not available in a built-in function, write your own.

Like a built-in function, a custom function might have arguments. An argument contains information you are "sending" to the function to process. Suppose you want to create a function that subtracts a six-percent discount. The argument needed by the function is the amount of the order. The function can then multiply the amount by 0.94 to arrive at the discounted price. The complete function is shown in figure 16.4. Refer to it as you read the following discussion.

You specify the argument by following the name of the macro with the ARGUMENT command. The argument of ARGUMENT is the name of the variable that contains the sales amount:

```
=ARGUMENT("amount").
```

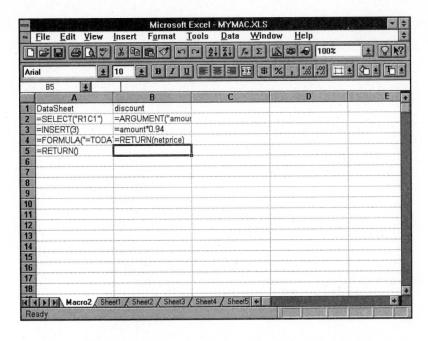

Figure 16.4
The Function macro.

Notice that the argument is in quotation marks. The next instruction performs the computation:

```
=amount * 0.94
```

Finally, the RETURN command sends the computed value to the worksheet. The argument of the RETURN command is the variable that contains the value, the result of the calculation:

```
=RETURN(netprice)
```

To use this function macro, you need to define two names: the macro name (discount) and the returned variable name (netprice). If you want to list the macro in the Function dialog box, you must define the macro as a function in the Define Name dialog box.

NOTE

You do not need to define the name of the receiving argument, such as *amount*; the argument statement defines the name.

To create the macro, follow these steps:

1. Click on the Macro2 tab to display the macro sheet.

2. Select cell B1.

3. Type **discount** and press Enter.

4. Type **=ARGUMENT("amount")** and press Enter.

5. Type **=amount*0.94** and press Enter.

6. Type **=RETURN(netprice)** and press Enter.

Next, name the macro and the return variable.

7. Select cell B1.

8. Select Insert, Name, Define.

9. Click on the Function button in the macro section.

10. Click on OK.

11. Select cell B3, the cell that contains the formula.

12. Select Insert, Name, Define.

13. Type **netprice**, then select OK. The name must be the same as the returned variable in the RETURN command.

14. Click on the Sheet1 tab to return to the worksheet.

TIP   When defining the name of the RETURN variable, leave the macro section set at None.

Using a Function Macro

To use custom function, you must call it from the worksheet. If the function is defined in the same workbook, you simply use its name and the proper argument.

1. Select cell C3.

2. Type **100** and press Enter.

3. Type **=discount(C3)** and press Enter.

Excel executes the function, displaying the results in the cell. Here's what Excel does:

✔ Transfers processing to the discount function

✔ Assigns the value in cell C3, the argument, to the variable amount

✔ Computes the value of amount*.94 and assigns the result to the variable netprice

✔ Returns to the worksheet, and inserts the value of netprice into the active cell

NOTE Like built-in functions, you can use your custom functions anywhere in the workbook, as often as you need them.

If you defined the macro as a function in the Define Name dialog box, you can paste the function using the Function Wizard. Select Insert, Function, scroll the Function category list and select User-defined. Your custom functions are listed in the Function Name list. Double-click on the function to insert it into the worksheet.

TIP If your function does not appear in the Function Wizard, confirm that you clicked on the Function option in the Name dialog box. Return to the macro sheet, select the function label, then select Insert, Name, Define. If the option is not selected, click on it, then select OK.

Using Global Functions

If you created the function in the Personal Macro Workbook, the global macro sheet, or another open workbook, you must specify the sheet name in the function call. If you added the discount function to the Personal Macro workbook, for example, call it using this syntax:

```
=PERSONAL.XLS!discount(B3)
```

If the function is in any other workbook, the workbook must be opened before it can be accessed.

Multiple Arguments

Custom functions are not limited to a single argument. If you need to send more than one cell or value to the function, you can create multiple arguments. Each argument must be included in its own ARGUMENT command, and arguments must appear in the order in which you want to call them. Suppose you want to compute the discount on the amount of the sale less any special reduction, such as a manufacturer's coupon or special promotion. You need to pass two values to the function. If the amount is in cell A3 and the reduction is in cell A4, you call the function as follows:

```
=discount(A3,A4)
```

The first argument sent to the function contains the amount of the sale; the second argument contains the reduction. The function, then, needs two arguments:

```
discount
=ARGUMENT("amount")
=ARGUMENT("reduction")
```

IV

Macros

```
=(amount-reduction)*0.94
=RETURN(netprice)
```

If you reverse the order of the receiving or calling arguments, the function does not return the correct results. If you call the macro using the syntax =discount(A4,A3), the function assumes cell A4 contains the amount of the sale and that cell A3 contains the reduction.

The amount of the sale then is subtracted from the reduction amount. A sale of $100, for example, and a $15 reduction is calculated as 15–100, rather than 100–15. You would be charging the customer a negative amount!

Make the change to the function macro and test it.

1. Click on the Macro2 tab to display the macro sheet.

2. Select cell B3.

3. Click the right mouse button to display the shortcut menu and select Insert.

4. Select OK to shift the cells down.

5. Type **=ARGUMENT("reduction")** and press Enter.

6. Type **=(amount-reduction)*0.94**, then press Enter.

7. Click on the Sheet1 tab.

8. Select cell C4.

9. Type **15** and press Enter.

10. Type **=discount(C3,C4)** and press Enter. Excel calculates and displays the correct results.

11. Select File, Save to save the workbook.

Your macros can be as simple or as complex as they need to be.

Handling Macro Errors

When you record a macro, Excel always inserts the proper commands using the appropriate syntax. Unfortunately, mistakes can occur in our own command or function macros. Three types of errors are common:

✔ **Language.** Occurs because you used the incorrect syntax or arguments. In many cases, Excel detects the language error when you enter the command, so you can correct it before you run the macro. You can avoid these errors by inserting commands with the Function Wizard. Select the Commands option in the Function Category list to display programming commands.

✔ **Run-time.** Occurs when the macro attempts to perform a function that cannot be completed. These errors might occur, for example, when you attempt to reference a cell that contains text in a mathematical formula. When you wrote the macro, Excel had no way of knowing what the actual contents of the cell would be at run-time.

✔ **Logic.** Occurs when your commands follow the proper syntax but do not perform the intended task. These errors include calling multiple arguments in the incorrect order, using the wrong arithmetic operators in a formula, or constructing the formula incorrectly.

When Excel encounters a language or run-time error, it stops executing the macro and displays a dialog box such as the one shown in figure 16.5. The message contains the location of the macro and the cell in which the error occurs.

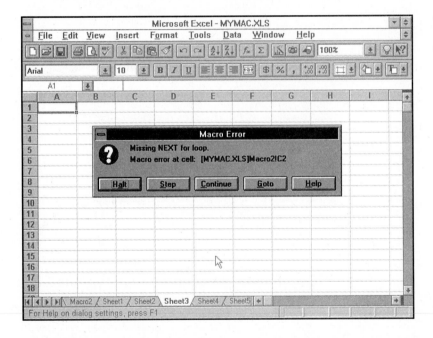

Figure 16.5
A Macro Error dialog box.

Macros

TIP

In most cases, Excel does not detect a logic error unless it results in a run-time error. If you enter a formula with the wrong operators (such as adding rather than subtracting numbers), for example, Excel performs the operation and displays the results without stopping. Logic errors are the most difficult to detect and correct. The best way to find logic errors is to check the results of your macros very carefully. Make certain mathematical results are correct and that the macro performs the tasks for which it was designed.

✔ **Ha lt.** Stops the macro. Before you select this option, note the location of the error, so you can return to the macro sheet to correct the problem.

✔ **S tep.** Continues executing the macro one command at a time. It begins with the command after the one that caused the error condition.

✔ **C ontinue.** Continues running the macro, ignoring the error. In most cases, however, a macro does not continue to run without additional errors after one error has occurred and has been ignored.

✔ **G oto.** Stops the macro and returns to the macro sheet where the command error has occurred. This method is the best way to correct errors.

✔ **H elp.** Displays help information.

Stepping Through Macros

When you select the **S**tep option, Excel displays the Single Step dialog box, shown in figure 16.6, after each command is executed. Use the options in this box to help find additional errors in the macro or to further investigate the current error.

 The Debug window is available only when viewing VBA modules.

Figure 16.6
The Step dialog box.

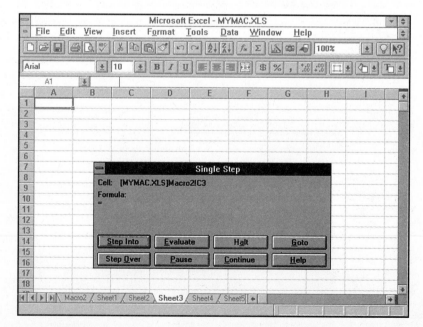

The box displays four additional command buttons:

✔ **Step Into**. Performs the next command shown. If the next command calls a subroutine, the subroutine is performed step by step. You learn about subroutines later in this chapter.

✔ **Step Over**. Performs the next command that is not a subroutine call.

✔ **Evaluate**. Calculates and displays the results of each expression of a formula. Use this option if the error is in a formula.

✔ **Pause**. Removes the Single Step dialog box from the screen. To continue the macro, display the Visual Basic toolbar and click on the Resume button.

You also can find errors using the VBA toolbar, even with macro language macros. To display the toolbar, select **V**iew, Toolbars, Visual Basic, OK. Display the macro sheet, then click on the Step button to single-step through the macro. The toolbar also contains Resume, Step Into, and Step Over buttons.

Understanding Flow Control

The macros you have designed so far have been linear. They perform each step of the macro in the order it appears in the macro sheet.

Recorded macros are always linear; thus, recorded macros are limited. By writing a macro, however, you can control the flow of the *program logic*, the order in which instructions are performed. You also can perform some steps based on the contents of a cell or the status of Excel at a certain point.

Designing non-linear macros requires some understanding of programming logic. If you are familiar with any computer programming language, such as BASIC, C, or PASCAL, then you should feel comfortable with the Excel 4 Macro Language or with VBA. The programming concepts are the same in every language; only the syntax of the commands varies.

If you are unfamiliar with programming logic, Excel's macro language serves as a good introduction. The language is easy to learn, and you can observe program results immediately by running the macro. If you understand the macro concepts already discussed in this chapter, you learn quickly the way to program in the macro language. In fact, you can transfer the skills and concepts you learn here to VBA or any other programming language.

Function Subroutines

One way to streamline your macros is to use subroutines. A subroutine is a section of macro instructions stored outside of the macro in which they are used. A subroutine, however, is just another macro. Any macro can be used as a subroutine, even if it is not entered or designed in any special way.

You can even use VBA macros as subroutines in macro language macros, and macro language macros as subroutines in VBA macros. If you already have macro language macros, you can use them in VBA macros without converting or retyping them.

Suppose, for example, you want to perform the functions of the DateSheet macro within another macro. Rather than retype the instructions or copy them from macro to macro, call the macro as a subroutine. This not only saves typing, but makes your macros smaller and easier to read and understand.

To call the DateSheet macro in a macro, for example, use the command `=Datesheet()`. When Excel encounters the line in a macro, it performs the command DateSheet, then returns to the calling macro. It then continues with the commands following the call to DateSheet.

If the macro is not in the current workbook, precede the name with the workbook name, as in `=GLOBAL.XLM!Datesheet()`.

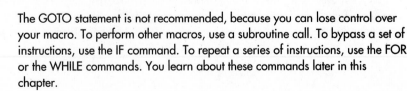

AUTHOR'S NOTE

By building a library of subroutines, you can write complex macros quickly and easily. In fact, some macros might contain little more than function calls to other macros.

Jumping to Other Instructions

One other way to perform another macro or set of instructions is to use the GOTO command. You can use GOTO to leave one macro and perform another or to begin following the commands at a named reference in the same macro. The syntax is `=GOTO(reference)`. When Excel encounters a GOTO command, it moves to the referenced location and begins to follow the macro instructions found there. After completing the instructions at that location, however, the macro does not return to the instructions after the GOTO command. This behavior is the opposite of a subroutine call, which performs the instructions in the subroutine, then returns to the instruction after the call.

The GOTO statement is not recommended, because you can lose control over your macro. To perform other macros, use a subroutine call. To bypass a set of instructions, use the IF command. To repeat a series of instructions, use the FOR or the WHILE commands. You learn about these commands later in this chapter.

Making Decisions

You might not always want to perform every instruction in a macro. Some commands might be *conditional*, meaning you might want to perform them in some situations, but not in others.

The discount function macro illustrated previously subtracted a six-percent discount on a sales amount. Each time you called the function, the reduction was taken regardless of the sale amount. A purchase of $1000 would be reduced by the same percentage as a purchase of just one dollar.

In reality, the discount might be applied only to purchases over a certain amount, or a different discount rate might be applied to various levels of purchases.

You can write separate functions for each discount amount, but you need to know which function to call when you create the worksheet. You cannot, for instance, use the same function call for every purchase.

The solution is to write a function macro that contains conditional instructions. The percentage of the discount, or whether one is subtracted or not, varies with the amount of the order. The same function can be called no matter what the purchase amount. The function decides the proper discount rate. The command that performs this decision is the IF command. The IF command has several forms, but they all are based on a condition:

```
if(condition)
```

The condition is a logical test that can be TRUE or FALSE. Usually, the test compares two values, as in `if(amount > 100)` or `if(B4 < B5)`.

In the first example, the condition is TRUE if the value of the amount is greater than 100. In the second example, the condition is TRUE if the contents in cell B4 are less than the contents of cell B5. The condition can use the following operators:

=	equal
>	greater than
<	less than
>=	greater than or equal
<=	less than or equal
<>	not equal

Making Fundamental Choices

The most basic use of the IF command decides between two alternatives. The syntax is as follows:

```
If(condition, TRUE-command, FALSE-command)
```

If the condition is TRUE, the TRUE-command is performed. If the condition is FALSE, the FALSE-command is performed:

```
if(amount>100, amount * 0.94, amount)
```

In this command, if the value of amount is greater than 100, then amount is multiplied by 0.94 to apply the discount. If amount is 100 or less, then no discount is applied. The command could be used in a function macro like this:

```
discount
=ARGUMENT("amount")
=if(amount>100, amount * 0.94, amount)
=RETURN(netprice)
```

You also can use the command to perform alternate subroutines. One subroutine would be performed if the condition were TRUE, another if the condition were FALSE, as in the following example:

```
=if(amount>1000, specialrate(), standardrate())
```

When the condition is TRUE, because the amount is over $1000, the specialrate macro is called and performed. Otherwise, the standardrate macro is called.

Any macro or macro command can be performed as part of the conditional.

Change the discount macro to provide a decision based on the purchase amount. The macro uses two arguments, but you need to consider only the value of amount in the condition.

1. Click on the Macro2 tab to display the macro sheet.

2. Select cell B4, the cell that contains the formula in the discount macro.

3. Edit the formula so that it reads: **=if(amount>100, (amount-reduction)*0.94, amount-reduction)**, then press Enter.

4. Press Enter.

5. Click on the Sheet1 tab.

6. Select cell C3.

7. Type **101** then click on the Enter box.

8. Select cell C4, type **0**, then click on the Enter box. Notice the results of the function call reflect the discount, 94.94.

9. Select cell C3 again, type **100**, then click on the Enter box. Now no additional discount is applied.

10. Select <u>F</u>ile, <u>S</u>ave to save the workbook.

Performing Multiple Commands

The basic syntax of the IF command allows it to perform only one command or subroutine call on a TRUE or FALSE condition. Often, the logic of your macro requires that a number of commands be executed. You can use another syntax of the IF command, called IF END.IF():

```
IF(condition)
    instructions
END.IF()
```

You can have as many instructions between the IF and END.IF commands as you need. When the condition is TRUE, all the instructions are performed, then the macro continues with the command following END.IF. When the condition is FALSE, none of the instructions between the IF and END.IF commands are performed, and the macro goes directly to the command following END.IF.

You must understand that the instructions following the END.IF command are *always* executed. They are not dependent upon the condition being TRUE or FALSE. You might, however, want to perform an alternate series of commands only when the condition is FALSE. For this, use the IF ELSE END.IF structure:

```
IF(condition)
    instructions to perform when the condition is true
ELSE()
    instructions to perform when the condition is false
END.IF()
```

This structure provides alternate sets of commands. If the condition is TRUE, the commands between the IF and the ELSE() instructions are performed. Those commands between the ELSE() and the END.IF are ignored.

When the condition is FALSE, the commands between the ELSE() and the END.IF() are performed, and those commands between the IF and ELSE() are ignored.

You can use the command in all types of macros, even command macros such as the following:

```
=IF(amount>100)
=    (amount-reduction)*0.94
=    send.mail(client,"Special discount",FALSE)
=ELSE()
=    (amount)
=    printinvoice()
```

IV

Macros

```
=END.IF()
=SAVE()
=CLOSE()
```

If the condition is TRUE, the special discount is applied and the worksheet is transmitted via Microsoft Mail. If the condition is FALSE, no discount is applied and a custom function, called printinvoice, is called.

In either case, the worksheet is saved, then closed using Excel's built-in functions.

> **TIP** The instructions following the END.IF are performed regardless of the condition.

Yet another possible use of the command is to combine IF with the ELSE.IF structure:

```
IF(condition)
    instructions
ELSE.IF(condition)
  instructions
END.IF()
```

Using this syntax, one set of instructions is performed when the condition is TRUE. If the condition is FALSE, however, a second IF condition is tested.

> **TIP** For the second set of instructions to be performed, the first condition must be FALSE and the second condition must be TRUE. If both are FALSE, no instructions between the IF and END.IF() commands are executed.

Repeating Commands with Loops

In addition to making decisions, a macro can repeat a series of instructions. Programming commands that cause repetition are called *loops*. Why would you want to repeat commands? Perhaps you might want to insert text or values in a series of cells, or perform a step repeatedly until some condition is TRUE or a certain event occurs. Excel provides several ways to repeat instructions.

Fixed Repetitions

When you know or can determine the exact number of times you want to repeat the instructions, use the FOR-NEXT loop. The syntax is for this loop is as follows:

```
FOR(counter_text, starting_value, ending_value, step_value)
```

The functions of the arguments follow:

- ✔ Counter_text is a name, similar to a variable, which counts the number of repetitions. Its value changes with each repetition of the loop so that Excel will know when the maximum value has been reached.

- ✔ Starting_value sets the first value that the counter_text will contain.

- ✔ Ending_value determines the last value of the counter text. The repetition stops when the counter_text is above this value.

- ✔ Step_value determines the way in which the counter_text value is incremented with each repetition. The value is optional. If you omit it, the counter increments by one with each loop.

When the step value is not included or is set at 1, the loop repeats from the starting to the ending value. The command FOR("counter",1,10) would repeat a series of instructions 10 times. During the first repetition, the value of counter is set at 1. During the second repetition, the value is 2. After the tenth repetition, the value of counter is 11, and the process stops.

Every FOR command must be matched with a NEXT() command. During the loop, Excel repeats all the instructions between the FOR and NEXT() commands. Consider this macro:

```
=SELECT("R1C1")
=FORMULA("1")
=FOR("counter",1,19)
=SELECT("RC[1]")
=FORMULA("=RC[-1]+1")
=NEXT()
=RETURN()
```

The macro numbers the top row of the worksheet from 1 to 20. Enter it now.

1. Click on the Macro2 tab to display the macro sheet.

2. Select cell C1.

3. Type **loop** and press Enter.

4. Type **=SELECT("R1C1")** and press Enter.

5. Type **=FORMULA("1")** and press Enter. Now use the Function Wizard to enter the FOR loop.

6. Select Insert Function.

7. Scroll the Function Category list and select Macro Control.

Macros

8. Scroll the Function Name list and select For.

9. Select Next to display the dialog box shown in figure 16.7.

10. Type **count** in the counter_text box, then press Tab.

11. Type 1 in the start_num box and press Tab.

12. Type 19 in the end_num box, then select Finish. The completed command is inserted in the cell.

13. Press Enter.

14. Type **=SELECT("RC[1]")** and press Enter.

15. Type **=FORMULA("=RC[-1]+1")** and press Enter.

16. Type **=NEXT()** and press Enter.

17. Type **=RETURN()** and press Enter.

18. Now name the macro. Select cell C1.

19. Select Insert, Name, Define.

20. Click on the Command button in the macro section.

21. Click on OK.

22. Click on the Sheet4 tab to return to the worksheet.

23. Select Tools, Macro, and double-click on the loop macro. The macro numbers the first 20 columns.

Here is the way that the macro works.

1. The SELECT command selects cell A1.

2. The FORMULA command inserts the number 1 in cell A1.

3. The FOR command sets up a loop that repeats 19 times, incrementing the value of counter from 1 to 19. When counter becomes 20, the loop stops.

4. The SELECT command selects the cell in the next column. This relative reference means "one cell over in the same row."

5. The FORMULA command inserts into the cell the value of the previous cell plus 1.

6. The NEXT command repeats the loop.

7. The RETURN command ends the macro.

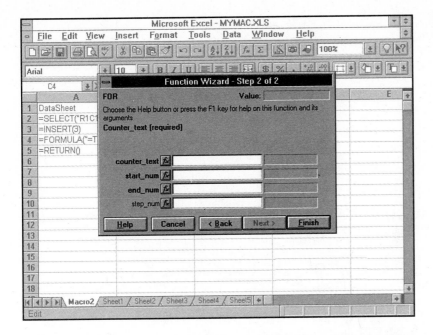

Figure 16.7
The Function Wizard box for the FOR command.

You can perform any number of instructions between the FOR and NEXT() commands, even call other macros as subroutines.

While you are learning to write loops, practice with a small number of repetitions. When your are certain your macro operates correctly, increase the number of repetitions to the final setting.

A variation of the FOR-NEXT loop is FOR.CELL-NEXT. This loop repeats once for each cell in a designated range of cells using the following syntax:

```
FOR.CELL(reference, area, skip_blanks)
  instructions
NEXT()
```

With each repetition, Excel uses the next cell in the range. The loop stops after it reaches the last cell. The reference is the name Excel gives to the currently selected cell. The actual cell being referenced changes with each repetition.

Skip_blanks is either set at TRUE or FALSE. When set at TRUE, Excel skips blank cells that it encounters in the range. When set at FALSE, Excel operates on blank cells. The default setting is FALSE.

As an example, suppose you have a worksheet that contains price information in the first 20 columns of row 5. To increase all prices by 10 percent, create a macro with these commands:

```
=FOR.CELL("prices","R5C1:R5C20",TRUE)
=FORMULA(prices*1.1,prices)
=NEXT()
=RETURN()
```

The FOR.CELL loop repeats for each of the cells in the range. It does not perform any operation on blank cells—only on those that already contain values.

Using the WHILE Loop

Sometimes you do not know the exact number of times you want to repeat a series of instructions. In these instances, use the WHILE-NEXT loop. The loop using this syntax:

```
WHILE(condition)
    instructions
NEXT()
```

The instructions within the loop are repeated as long as the condition is TRUE.

 You must ensure that the condition eventually becomes FALSE, otherwise the loop continues until you press Esc to stop it.

The condition can reference a cell value or a named variable. Before using the loop, however, you must know the initial state of the condition. If you want to perform the loop at least one time, you must ensure that the condition is initially TRUE. This task usually is accomplished using the SET.VALUE command. The command assigns an initial value to a named cell on the macro sheet.

Suppose you want to create a macro that enables the user to select the number of columns to number. Rather than include the ending number in the FOR loop, you want to input a number and use it as a variable. The command to input a number is as follows:

```
=INPUT("Enter a number",1,"Input Macro",,,,)
```

The syntax for this command is the following:

```
=INPUT(text, type, title, default, x-position, y-position,
help-reference)
```

 The INPUT command inputs a value into a cell in the macro sheet, not into the worksheet. You must name the INPUT command cell, then you can use the name as a variable in another macro command.

The *type* represents the type of value expected:

✔ 0 Formula

✔ 1 Number

✔ 2 Text

✔ 3 Logical

✔ 4 Reference

✔ 8 Error

✔ 64 Array

TIP

Most of the parameters of the INPUT command are used for special purposes. Include the first three parameters, then omit or use placeholders for the rest, as shown in the example.

You must enter a number greater than zero, however, to actually number the columns. You want to design a macro that repeats the INPUT command until a number greater than zero has been entered. Follow these steps:

1. Click on the Macro2 tab to display the macro sheet.

2. Select cell C2.

3. Select Insert, Cells, OK.

4. Type **=SET.VALUE(count,0)** and press Enter. This command ensures that the input is performed.

5. Select cell C5, then select Insert, Cells, OK.

6. Type **=WHILE(count<1)** and press Enter.

7. Select Insert, Cells, OK.

8. Type **=INPUT("Enter a number:,1,"Input Macro",,,,)**, then press Enter.

9. Select Insert, Cells, OK.

10. Type **=NEXT()** and press Enter.

11. Select cell C8, the cell that contains the FOR loop.

12. Edit the contents to **=FOR("COUNTER",1,COUNT-1)**, then click on the Enter box.

The completed macro is shown in figure 16.8. The FOR loop now contains a variable for the ending number. The value is the amount entered in response to the INPUT command less 1.

IV

Macros

Now name the INPUT command as the count variable.

13. Select cell C6.

14. Select Insert, Name, Define.

15. Type **count**, then select OK.

16. Click on the Sheet5 tab to return to the worksheet.

17. Select Tools, Macro, and double-click on the loop macro. A dialog box appears as in figure 16.9.

18. Type 10, to number 10 columns, then press Enter.

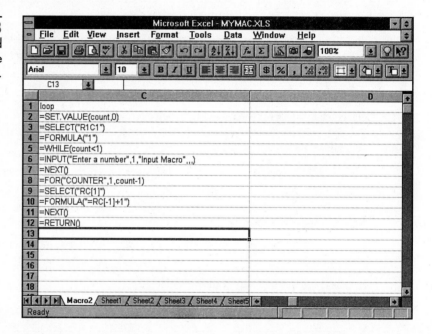

Figure 16.8
The completed macro using the WHILE command.

Programming in the macro language can be a rewarding experience. Take your time and try to record as many of the instructions as possible. Then, display the macro sheet, insert cells, and enter additional commands that you need to perform the desired task.

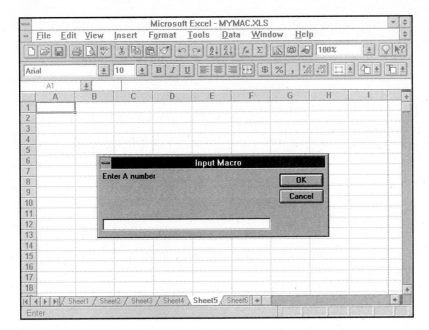

Figure 16.9
The Input Macro dialog box.

Chapter Snapshot

You can use this chapter as a quick guide to finding descriptions of Excel's macro functions. Specifically, this chapter contains the following:

- ✔ A list of the available macro functions in excel

- ✔ Variable names associated with each function

- ✔ One-line descriptions of each function

For information on Visual Basic for Application commands and topics, see the *Visual Basic for Applications Command Reference* at the back of this book.

Complete Macro Language Function Reference

This chapter provides a list of Excel 5's macro functions and a brief description of each function's purpose. This chapter is not intended to serve as a complete startup guide to using macros, but as a ready reference for you to use after you become familiar with the functions.

Each function's variable names (shown in italic next to the function name) are verbose enough to be reasonably self-explanatory. You don't need to use these exact variable names in your macros—you can use any name, or simply a value. For those variables that take a TRUE or FALSE value, a 0 indicates FALSE, and a 1 or nonzero number indicates TRUE. Further information about macro functions can be found in the *Excel 5 User's Guide* or Excel 5's Help system.

The parameter list of certain functions only references the manual because those functions have multiple permissible syntaxes. See your Excel 5 user manual or on-line Help for greater detail.

A1.R1C1(A1OrR1C1)

Sets display of row and column headings to A1 or R1C1 format.

ABSREF(Offset, Reference)

Returns the absolute reference of the cells that are offset from the reference cells by a given amount.

ACTIVATE(WindowToSwitchTo, PaneNumber)
or
ACTIVATE?(WindowToSwitchTo, PaneNumber)

Switches to a different window or pane.

ACTIVATE NEXT(WorkbookName)

Switches to the next window or the next worksheet in the workbook.

ACTIVATE PREV(WorkbookName)

Switches to the previous window or the previous worksheet in the workbook.

ACTIVE CELL()

Returns the full reference of the active cell.

ADD.ARROW()

Adds an arrow to the active chart.

ADD.BAR(MenuBarNumber)

Creates a new menu bar and returns the menu bar ID number.

ADD.CHART.AUTOFORMAT(FormatName, FormatDescription)

Adds the format of the active chart to the AutoFormat list of custom formats.

ADD.COMMAND*(MenuBarNumber, MenuID, CommandDefReference, CommandPlacement, CommandPlacementSubmenu)*

Adds a command to a menu.

ADD.MENU*(MenuBarNumber, MenuDefReference, MenuPlacement, SubmenuPlacement)*

Adds a menu to a menu bar.

ADD.OVERLAY()

Adds an overlay to a 2D chart.

ADD.TOOLBAR*(ToolbarName, ToolbarDefReference)*

Creates a new toolbar with specified buttons.

ADD.TOOL*(ToolbarID, ButtonPosition, ToolDefReference)*

Adds buttons to a toolbar.

ALERT*(MessageText, DialogBoxType, HelpTopicReference)*

Displays a dialog box and waits for user button press.

ALIGNMENT*(HorizAlignmentType, WrapTextInCells, VertAlignmentType, TextOrientation)*

Aligns the text of the selected cells.

ANOVA1*(InputRange, OutputTopLeftCell, RowOrColumn, FirstRowLabels, Alpha)*
or
ANOVA1?*(InputRange, OutputTopLeftCell, RowOrColumn, FirstRowLabels, Alpha)*

Performs single-factor analysis of variance.

ANOVA2*(InputRangeWithLabels, OutputTopLeftCell, NumRowsPerSample, Alpha)*
or
ANOVA2?*(InputRangeWithLabels, OutputTopLeftCell, NumRowsPerSample, Alpha)*

Performs two-factor analysis of variance with replication.

Macros

ANOVA3(InputRange, OutputTopLeftCell, FirstRowLabels, Alpha)
or
ANOVA3?(InputRange, OutputTopLeftCell, FirstRowLabels, Alpha)

Performs two-factor analysis of variance without replication.

APP.ACTIVATE.MICROSOFT(ApplicationID)

Activates a different Microsoft application.

APP.ACTIVATE(ApplicationTitle, ImmediateOrWaitToSwitch)

Switches to another application.

APP.MAXIMIZE()

Maximizes the Excel window.

APP.MINIMIZE()

Minimizes the Excel window.

APP.MOVE(NewXPosition, NewYPosition)

Moves the Excel window.

APP.RESTORE()

Restores the Excel window to its previous size and location.

APP.SIZE(NewWidth, NewHeight)

Changes the size of the Excel window.

APP.TITLE(NewTitle)

Changes the title of the Excel 5 workspace.

APPLY.NAMES(NameArray, IgnoreRelativeAbsolute, UseRowColumnNames, OmitColumnName, OmitRowName, OrderNumber, AppendLast)

Replaces definitions with their respective names.

APPLY.STYLE(NameOfStyle)

Applies a style to the current selection.

ARGUMENT(*ArgumentOrCellName, DataType, [DestinationCellReference]*)

Describes the arguments used in a custom function.

ARRANGE.ALL(*HowToArrangeWindows, ActiveDocument, SyncHoriz, SyncVert*)

Rearranges or resizes open windows and icons.

ASSIGN.TO.OBJECT(*MacroID*)

Assigns a macro to the currently selected object.

ASSIGN.TO.TOOL(*ToolbarID, ButtonPosition, MacroAssignedToTool*)

Assigns a macro to a tool.

ATTACH.TEXT(*ItemToAttach, NumberOfSeries, NumberOfPoint*)

Attaches text to parts of the selected chart.

AXES(*XPrimary, YPrimary, XSecondary/ZPrimary, [YSecondary]*)

Sets chart axes to visible or hidden.

BEEP(*TypeOfBeep*)

Sounds a tone.

BORDER(*OutlineLine, LeftLine, RightLine, TopLine, BottomLine, Shading, OutlineColor, LeftLineColor, RightLineColor, TopLineColor, BottomLineColor*)

Adds a border and background color to selected cells.

BREAK()

Interrupts a program loop.

BRING.TO.FRONT()

Places the selected object on top of all other objects.

CALCULATE.DOCUMENT()

Calculates the active worksheet.

IV

Macros

CALCULATE.NOW()

Calculates all open workbooks.

CALCULATION(TypeOfCalc, Iterate, MaxIterations, MaxChangeIterate, UpdateRemote, PrecisionAsDisplayed, Date1904, RecalcBeforeSave, SaveExtLinkValues, ExcelOrLotusCalc, ExcelOrLotusFormulas)

Controls calculation.

CALLER()

Returns information about the item that called the macro currently running.

CANCEL.COPY(Render)

Cancels the marquee after copy or cut.

CANCEL.KEY(EnableEscape, MacroToRunOnCancel)

Specifies action taken when user interrupts a macro.

CELL.PROTECTION(Locked, Hidden)

Controls cell protection and display.

CHANGE.LINK(OldLink, NewLink, TypeOfLinkToChange)
or
CHANGE.LINK?(OldLink, NewLink, TypeOfLinkToChange)

Changes a link from one workbook to another.

CHART.TREND(Type, OrderPeriods, Forecast, Backcast, Intercept, DisplayEquation, DisplayRSquared, LineName)

Adds a trendline to the active chart.

CHART.WIZARD(LongRoutine, SourceDataReference, TypeOfChart, FormatNumber, DataInRowsOrColumns, FirstRowLabels, FirstRowSeriesTitles, LegendYesOrNo, TitleText, XAxisTitle, YAxisTitle, ZAxisTitle, NumberCategoryLabels, NumberTitles)
or
CHART.WIZARD?(LongRoutine, SourceDataReference, TypeOfChart, FormatNumber, DataInRowsOrColumns, FirstRowLabels, FirstRowSeriesTitles, LegendYesOrNo, TitleText, XAxisTitle, YAxisTitle, ZAxisTitle, NumberCategoryLabels, NumberTitles)

Assists in formatting a chart.

CHECK.COMMAND(MenuBarNumber, MenuID, CommandToCheck, CheckOnOrOff, SubmenuCommandToCheck)

Adds or removes a check mark from a command in a menu.

CLEAR(TypeToClear)

Clears series or formats from selection.

CLEAR.ROUTING.SLIP(ResetWithoutClear)

Clears the routing slip.

CLOSE(SaveBeforeClose, RouteAfterClose)

Closes the active window.

CLOSE.ALL()

Closes all windows.

COLOR.PALETTE(FileNameToCopyFrom)

Copies a color palette from another workbook.

COLUMN.WIDTH(*Width, [ColumnReference], SetStandardWidth, ColumnTypeNumber, StandardWidth*)
or
COLUMN.WIDTH?(*Width, [ColumnReference], SetStandardWidth, ColumnTypeNumber, StandardWidth*)

Changes column widths.

COMBINATION(*CombinationChartNumber*)
or
COMBINATION?(*CombinationChartNumber*)

Changes the format of the active chart.

CONSOLIDATE(*SourceReferences, FunctionUsed, TopRow, LeftColumn, CreateLinks*)

Consolidates data on multiple worksheets to a single worksheet.

CONSTRAIN.NUMERIC(*NumericConstraint*)

Constrains handwriting recognition to numbers and punctuation only.

COPY(*FromReference, ToReference*)

Copies data or objects into the Clipboard.

COPY.CHART(*HowToCopy*)

Copies a chart.

COPY.PICTURE(*AppearanceCopy, SizeCopy, DataFormat*)
or
COPY.PICTURE?(*AppearanceCopy, SizeCopy, DataFormat*)

Copies chart or cells to Clipboard as graphic.

COPY.TOOL(*ToolbarID, ButtonPosition*)

Copies a button face to the Clipboard.

CREATE.NAMES(*TopRow, LeftColumn, BottomRow, RightColumn*)
or
CREATE.NAMES?(*TopRow, LeftColumn, BottomRow, RightColumn*)

Creates names from text labels.

CREATE.OBJECT

Draws an object on a worksheet. (See manual for parameters.)

CREATE.PUBLISHER(*NewFile, Appearance, Size, Format*)
or
CREATE.PUBLISHER?(*NewFile, Appearance, Size, Format*)

Publishes selection to an edition file (Macintosh).

CUSTOM.REPEAT(*[MacroToRepeat, RepeatCommandText,] [FormulaToRecord]*)

Allows custom commands to be repeated using the Repeat command.

CUSTOM.UNDO(*MacroDefReference, UndoMenuText*)

Enables you to customize the Undo and/or Redo commands.

CUT(*FromReference, ToReference*)

Cuts data or objects into the Clipboard.

DATA.DELETE()
or
DATA.DELETE?()

Deletes data that matches the current criteria in the current database.

DATA.FIND(*EnterOrExitFindMode*)

Selects records in the database range that match criteria in the criteria range.

DATA.FIND.NEXT()
or
DATA.FIND.NEXT?()

Finds the next matching record in the database.

DATA.FIND.PREV()
or
DATA.FIND.PREV?()

Finds the previous matching record in the database.

DATA.FORM()

Displays the data form.

DATA.SERIES(RowsOrColumns, TypeOfSeries, DateUnit, Step, Stop, TrendCheck)
or
DATA.SERIES?(RowsOrColumns, TypeOfSeries, DateUnit, Step, Stop, TrendCheck)

Enables you to enter an incremental series on a worksheet.

DEFINE.NAME(Name, RefersTo, MacroType, ShortcutKey, HiddenName, FunctionCategory, LocalOrGlobalDef)
or
DEFINE.NAME?(Name, RefersTo, MacroType, ShortcutKey, HiddenName, FunctionCategory, LocalOrGlobalDef)

Defines a name on the active worksheet.

DEFINE.STYLE

Creates and changes styles. (See manual for parameters.)

DELETE.ARROW()

Deletes the selected arrow.

DELETE.BAR(MenuBarNumber)

Deletes a custom menu bar.

DELETE.CHART.AUTOFORMAT(TemplateName)

Deletes a custom format from AutoFormat.

DELETE.COMMAND(MenuBarNumber, MenuID, CommandOrSubmenu, [Subcommand])

Removes a command from a menu.

DELETE.FORMAT(FormatName)

Deletes a given custom number format.

DELETE.MENU(MenuBarNumber, MenuID, [Submenu])

Deletes a menu or submenu.

DELETE.NAME(Name)

Deletes a name.

DELETE.OVERLAY()

Deletes all overlays from a chart.

DELETE.STYLE*(StyleName)*

Deletes a style from the active workbook.

DELETE.TOOL*(ToolbarID, ButtonPosition)*

Deletes a button from a toolbar.

DELETE.TOOLBAR*(ToolbarName)*

Deletes a custom toolbar.

DEMOTE*(GroupRowsOrColumns)*
or
DEMOTE?*(GroupRowsOrColumns)*

Demotes (groups) the selected rows or columns in an outline.

DEREF*(CellReference)*

Returns the value of the cells in a reference.

DESCR*(InputRange, OutputTopLeftCell, RowOrColumn, FirstRowLabels, SummaryStatistics, ReportLargestData, ReportSmallestData, ConfidenceLevel)*
or
DESCR?*(InputRange, OutputTopLeftCell, RowOrColumn, FirstRowLabels, SummaryStatistics, ReportLargestData, ReportSmallestData, ConfidenceLevel)*

Generates descriptive statistics.

DIALOG.BOX*(DialogBoxDefReference)*

Displays a predefined dialog box.

DIRECTORY*(PathToChangeTo)*

Sets a directory path or returns the current path.

DISABLE.INPUT*(EnableOrDisable)*

Disables all mouse and keyboard input.

IV

Macros

DISPLAY

Controls screen displays. (See manual for parameters.)

DOCUMENTS*(IncludeAddInWorkbooks, [NameSelectionCriteria])*

Returns the names of the open workbooks, sorted alphabetically.

DUPLICATE()

Duplicates the selected object.

ECHO*(UpdatingOnOrOff)*

Specifies whether screen updating is on or off while a macro is running.

EDIT.COLOR*(PaletteBoxNumber, RedValue, GreenValue, BlueValue)*
or
EDIT.COLOR?*(PaletteBoxNumber, RedValue, GreenValue, BlueValue)*

Defines a color.

EDIT.DELETE*(ShiftDirection)*
or
EDIT.DELETE?*(ShiftDirection)*

Removes cells from the worksheet.

EDIT.OBJECT*(VerbNumberForApplication, MacroPauseWhileEditing)*

Starts the application to edit the selected object.

EDIT.REPEAT()

Repeats prior action.

EDIT.SERIES*(SeriesNumber, SeriesName, XRef, YRef, ZRef, PlotOrder)*
or
EDIT.SERIES?*(SeriesNumber, SeriesName, XRef, YRef, ZRef, PlotOrder)*

Adds a new series formula to chart.

EDITION.OPTION*(PublisherOrSubscriber, EditionName, CellReference, EditionOption, PublishScreenOrPrint, ChartSize, FileFormatNumber)*

Sets options or actions to a specified publisher or subscriber.

ELSE.IF*(TestLogical)*

Begins a group of formulas to be executed if the preceding IF function returns a FALSE value and if TestLogical is TRUE.

ELSE()

Begins a group of formulas to be executed if the preceding IF function returns a FALSE value.

EMBED*(ObjectCreatorClass, AreaToCopy)*

Displayed in the formula bar when an embedded object is selected.

ENABLE.COMMAND*(MenuBarNumber, MenuID, CommandToEnableOrDisable, EnableOrDisable, SubmenuCommandToEnableOrDisable)*

Enables or disables a custom menu command or custom menu.

ENABLE.TOOL*(ToolbarNumber, ButtonPosition, ButtonEnableOrDisable)*

Enables or disables a button on a toolbar.

END.IF()

Ends a group of formulas associated with the preceding IF function.

ENTER.DATA*(DataEntryModeOnOrOff)*

Enables data entry into unlocked cells in the current selection.

ERROR*(ErrorTrapOnOrOff, MacroToRunIfError)*

Specifies action to be taken when an error is encountered during execution of a macro.

EVALUATE*(ExpressionToEvaluate)*

Evaluates a formula or expression and returns the result.

EXECUTE*(DDEChannel, CommandText)*

Executes commands over an existing DDE link.

IV

Macros

EXEC(*ProgramName, WindowMaxOrMin, [RunInBackground]*)

Starts another program.

EXPON(*InputRange, OutputTopLeftCell, DampingFactor, StandardErrors, GenerateChart*)

Performs exponential smoothing; predicts a value based on the forecast for the prior period.

EXTEND.POLYGON(*ArrayOrCellReference*)

Adds vertices to a polygon.

EXTRACT(*UniqueRecordsOnly*)
or
EXTRACT?(*UniqueRecordsOnly*)

Finds database records that match the criteria defined in the criteria range and copies all found records into a separate extract range.

FCLOSE(*FileNumber*)

Closes the specified file.

FILE.CLOSE(*SaveBeforeClose, RouteAfterClose*)

Closes the active workbook.

FILE.DELETE(*FileName*)
or
FILE.DELETE?(*FileName*)

Deletes a file from disk.

FILES(*SourceDirectory*)

Returns the names of all files in the specified directory.

FILL.AUTO(*DestinationReference, CopyOrAutoFill*)

Copies a cell into a range of cells.

FILL.DOWN()

Copies the top cell row into the rest of the selection.

FILL.GROUP*(TypeNumber)*
or
FILL.GROUP?*(TypeNumber)*

Copies the contents of the current selection to the same area on all other worksheets in the group.

FILL.LEFT()

Copies the right cell column into the rest of the selection.

FILL.RIGHT()

Copies the left cell column into the rest of the selection.

FILL.UP()

Copies the bottom cell row into the rest of the selection.

FILTER*(FieldNumber, Criteria1, Operation2With1, Criteria2)*
or
FILTER?*(FieldNumber, Criteria1, Operation2With1, Criteria2)*

Filters lists of data by column.

FILTER.ADVANCED*(CopyList, SourceRef, CriteriaRange, CopyRange, UniqueOnly)*
or
FILTER.ADVANCED?*(CopyList, SourceRef, CriteriaRange, CopyRange, UniqueOnly)*

Sets options for filtering a list.

FILTER.SHOW.ALL()

Displays all items in a filtered list.

FIND.FILE?()

Enables searching for files.

FONT*(Name, Size)*

Sets the font for the Normal style.

FOPEN*(FileName, ReadWriteAccess)*

Opens a file and returns a file ID number.

FOR*(LoopCounterName, StartNumber, EndNumber, StepNumber)*

Defines a program loop.

FOR.CELL*(NameOfReferenceCell, RangeOfCells, SkipBlankCells)*

Defines a program loop.

FORMAT.AUTO*(FormatNumber, Number, Font, Alignment, Border, Pattern, Width)*
or
FORMAT.AUTO?*(FormatNumber, Number, Font, Alignment, Border, Pattern, Width)*

Formats the selection from a format gallery.

FORMAT.CHART*(ChartNumber, View, Overlap, GapWidth, VaryByCategories, DropLines, HiLoLines, FirstSliceAngle, GapDepth, ChartDepth, UpDownBars, SeriesLines, RadarAxisLabels, DoughnutSize)*
or
FORMAT.CHART?*(ChartNumber, View, Overlap, GapWidth, VaryByCategories, DropLines, HiLoLines, FirstSliceAngle, GapDepth, ChartDepth, UpDownBars, SeriesLines, RadarAxisLabels, DoughnutSize)*

Formats a chart.

FORMAT.FONT

Sets font formatting. (See manual for parameters.)

FORMAT.LEGEND*(Position)*
or
FORMAT.LEGEND?*(Position)*

Formats a legend on a chart.

FORMAT.MAIN(*ChartNumber, View, Overlap, GapWidth, VaryByCategories, DropLines, HiLoLines, FirstSliceAngle, GapDepth, ChartDepth, UpDownBars, SeriesLines, RadarAxisLabels, DoughnutSize*)
or
FORMAT.MAIN?(*ChartNumber, View, Overlap, GapWidth, VaryByCategories, DropLines, HiLoLines, FirstSliceAngle, GapDepth, ChartDepth, UpDownBars, SeriesLines, RadarAxisLabels, DoughnutSize*)

Formats a chart.

FORMAT.MOVE

Moves the selected object. (See manual for parameters.)

FORMAT.NUMBER(*FormatString*)
or
FORMAT.NUMBER?(*FormatString*)

Formats numbers in selected cells.

FORMAT.OFFSET(*XPosition, YPosition*)

Moves the selected object.

FORMAT.OVERLAY()

Formats an overlay chart.

FORMAT.SHAPE(*VertexNumber, InsertVertex, VertexReference, XOffset, YOffset*)

Reshapes a polygon.

FORMAT.SIZE

Changes the size of a selected object. (See manual for parameters.)

FORMAT.TEXT(*HorizAlign, VertAlign, OrientNumber, AutoText, AutoSize, ShowKey, ShowValue*)
or
FORMAT.TEXT?(*HorizAlign, VertAlign, OrientNumber, AutoText, AutoSize, ShowKey, ShowValue*)

Formats the selection.

IV

Macros

FORMULA

Enters a formula into the active cell or reference. (See manual for parameters.)

FORMULA.ARRAY(*Text, CellReference*)

Enters an array formula into the active cell or range.

FORMULA.CONVERT(*FormulaText, A1ToR1C1, R1C1ToA1, FormulaReferenceType, BaseForRelativeReferences*)

Converts cell references between styles or types.

FORMULA.FILL(*FormulaString, CellDestination*)

Enters a formula in a range of cells.

FORMULA.FIND(*Text, WhereSearch, ExactText, RowOrColumnSearch, DirectionNum, MatchCase*)
or
FORMULA.FIND?(*Text, WhereSearch, ExactText, RowOrColumnSearch, DirectionNum, MatchCase*)

Selects the text to find.

FORMULA.FIND.NEXT()

Finds the next cell meeting the FORMULA.FIND criteria.

FORMULA.FIND.PREV()

Finds the previous cell meeting the FORMULA.FIND criteria.

FORMULA.GOTO(*Reference, Corner*)
or
FORMULA.GOTO?(*Reference, Corner*)

Sets the cursor to a named area or reference.

FORMULA.REPLACE(*FindText, ReplaceText, ExactText, RowOrColumnSearch, ActiveCell, MatchCase*)
or
FORMULA.REPLACE?(*FindText, ReplaceText, ExactText, RowOrColumnSearch, ActiveCell, MatchCase*)

Finds and replaces characters.

FOURIER*(InputRange, OutputTopLeftCell, Inverse, FirstRowLabels)*
or
FOURIER?*(InputRange, OutputTopLeftCell, Inverse, FirstRowLabels)*

Performs a Fourier transform.

FPOS*(FileNumber, SetPosition)*

Sets the current position within an open file.

FREADLN*(FileNumber)*

Reads characters from the open file, beginning at the current position within the file and continuing to the end of the line.

FREAD*(FileNumber, NumberOfBytesToRead)*

Reads a specified number of characters from the open file, beginning at the current position within the file.

FREEZE.PANES*(Freeze, ColumnSplit, RowSplit)*

Freezes or unfreezes existing panes.

FSIZE*(FileNumber)*

Returns the number of bytes in the open file.

FTESTV*(DataSetOneInputRange, DataSetTwoInputRange, OutputTopLeftCell, FirstRowLabels)*
or
FTESTV?*(DataSetOneInputRange, DataSetTwoInputRange, OutputTopLeftCell, FirstRowLabels)*

Performs a two-sample F-test.

FULL*(Full)*

Sets Full size.

FULL.SCREEN*(Full)*

Sets Full screen.

IV

Macros

FWRITELN*(FileNumber, TextToWrite)*

Writes text to the open file, beginning at the current position in the file. Text is followed by a carriage return and linefeed.

FWRITE*(FileNumber, TextToWrite)*

Writes text to the open file, beginning at the current position in the file.

GALLERY.3D.AREA*(FormatNumber)*
or
GALLERY.3D.AREA?*(FormatNumber)*

Changes the active chart to a 3D area chart.

GALLERY.3D.BAR*(FormatNumber)*
or
GALLERY.3D.BAR?*(FormatNumber)*

Changes the active chart to a 3D bar chart.

GALLERY.3D.COLUMN*(FormatNumber)*
or
GALLERY.3D.COLUMN?*(FormatNumber)*

Changes the active chart to a 3D column chart.

GALLERY.3D.LINE*(FormatNumber)*
or
GALLERY.3D.LINE?*(FormatNumber)*

Changes the active chart to a 3D line chart.

GALLERY.3D.PIE*(FormatNumber)*
or
GALLERY.3D.PIE?*(FormatNumber)*

Changes the active chart to a 3D pie chart.

GALLERY.3D.SURFACE*(FormatNumber)*
or
GALLERY.3D.SURFACE?*(FormatNumber)*

Changes the active chart to a 3D surface chart.

GALLERY.AREA*(FormatNumber, DeleteOverlay)*
or
GALLERY.AREA?*(FormatNumber, DeleteOverlay)*

Changes the active chart to an area chart.

GALLERY.BAR*(FormatNumber, DeleteOverlay)*
or
GALLERY.BAR?*(FormatNumber, DeleteOverlay)*

Changes the active chart to a bar chart.

GALLERY.COLUMN*(FormatNumber, DeleteOverlay)*
or
GALLERY.COLUMN?*(FormatNumber, DeleteOverlay)*

Changes the active chart to a column chart.

GALLERY.CUSTOM*(TemplateName)*

Changes the active chart to a custom format.

GALLERY.DOUGHNUT*(FormatNumber)*
or
GALLERY.DOUGHNUT?*(FormatNumber)*

Changes the active chart to a doughnut chart.

GALLERY.LINE*(FormatNumber, DeleteOverlay)*
or
GALLERY.LINE?*(FormatNumber, DeleteOverlay)*

Changes the active chart to a line chart.

GALLERY.PIE*(FormatNumber, DeleteOverlay)*
or
GALLERY.PIE?*(FormatNumber, DeleteOverlay)*

Changes the active chart to a pie chart.

GALLERY.RADAR*(FormatNumber, DeleteOverlay)*
or
GALLERY.RADAR?*(FormatNumber, DeleteOverlay)*

Changes the active chart to a radar chart.

IV

Macros

GALLERY.SCATTER*(FormatNumber, DeleteOverlay)* or GALLERY.SCATTER?*(FormatNumber, DeleteOverlay)*

Changes the active chart to an XY (scatter) chart.

GET.BAR()

Returns the number of the active menu bar.

GET.CELL*(InformationType, CellsToGetInfo)*

Returns information about a cell.

GET.CHART.ITEM*(CoordinatesToReturn, PointIndexOnChart, ItemText)*

Returns the position of a point on a chart item.

GET.DEF*(DefinedName, SheetContainingName, TypesOfNames)*

Returns the name of an area, value, or formula in a workbook.

GET.DOCUMENT*(TypeOfInformation, [DocumentName])*

Returns information about a worksheet in a workbook.

GET.FORMULA*(CellReference)*

Returns the full contents of a cell.

GET.LINK.INFO*(LinkPath, TypeOfInformation, TypeOfLink, CellReference)*

Returns information about the specified link.

GET.NAME*(DefinedName, [TypeOfInformation])*

Returns the definition of a name.

GET.NOTE*(CellReferenceAttached, StartingCharNumber, NumberOfCharactersToReturn)*

Returns a note.

GET.OBJECT*(TypeOfInformation, ObjectID, StartingCharNumber, NumberOfCharactersToReturn)*

Returns information about the specified object.

GET.PIVOT.FIELD*(TypeNumber, PivotFieldName, PivotTableName)*

Returns information about a field in a pivot table.

GET.PIVOT.ITEM*(TypeNumber, PivotItemName, PivotFieldName, PivotTableName)*

Returns information about an item in a pivot table.

GET.PIVOT.TABLE*(TypeNumber, PivotTableName)*

Returns information about a pivot table.

GET.TOOLBAR*(TypeOfInformation, ToolbarID)*

Returns information about a toolbar(s).

GET.TOOL*(TypeOfInformation, ToolbarID, ButtonPosition)*

Returns information about a toolbar button(s).

GET.WINDOW*(TypeOfInformation, [WindowTitle])*

Returns information about a window.

GET.WORKBOOK*(TypeOfInformation, [WorkbookName])*

Returns information about a workbook.

GET.WORKSPACE*(TypeOfInformation)*

Returns information about the workspace.

GOAL.SEEK*(FormulaCellRef, TargetValue, CellToChange)*

Calculates values necessary to achieve a specific goal.

GOTO*(CellReference)*

Redirects the execution of a macro to a specified label.

GRIDLINES*(XMajor, XMinor, YMajor, YMinor, ZMajor, ZMinor)*

Enables you to turn chart gridlines on or off.

GROUP()

Creates one object from selected objects.

IV

Macros

HALT*(CloseAutoYesOrNo)*

Stops all macros.

HELP*(HelpTopicReference)*

Starts or switches to Help and displays the custom Help topic specified.

HIDE()

Hides the active window.

HIDE.OBJECT*(ObjectID, HideOnOrOff)*

Hides or displays the given object.

HISTOGRAM*(InputRange, OutputTopLeftCell, BinRangeReference, IncludePareto, CumulativePercents, GenerateChart, FirstRowLabels)*
or
HISTOGRAM?*(InputRange, OutputTopLeftCell, BinRangeReference, IncludePareto, CumulativePercents, GenerateChart, FirstRowLabels)*

Performs a histogram calculation.

HLINE*(NumberOfColumns)*

Scrolls through the active window by a given number of columns.

HPAGE*(NumberOfWindows)*

Scrolls horizontally through the active window by a given number of windows.

HSCROLL*(DestinationPosition, ScrollMode)*

Scrolls horizontally through the active window by percentage or by column number.

IF*(TestLogical)*

Begins a group of formulas to be executed if TestLogical is TRUE.

INITIATE*(ApplicationName, TopicText)*

Opens a DDE channel and returns the channel number.

INPUT*(MessageText, DataType, TitleBarText, DefaultInput, HorizPosition, VertPosition, HelpTopicReference)*

Displays a dialog box and waits for user input.

INSERT*(ShiftCellsBy)*

Inserts blank cells in the active worksheet.

INSERT.OBJECT*(ObjectClass, SourceFileName, LinkToFile, DisplayAsIcon , FileContainingIcon, IconNumber, LabelBelowIcon, AttachedTemplateName)*
or
INSERT.OBJECT?*(ObjectClass, SourceFileName, LinkToFile, DisplayAsIcon , FileContainingIcon, IconNumber, LabelBelowIcon, AttachedTemplateName)*

Creates an embedded object whose data is supplied by another application.

INSERT.PICTURE*(FileName, FilterNumber)*

Inserts a picture into the active worksheet.

LAST.ERROR()

Returns the cell reference in which the last macro worksheet error occurred.

LEGEND*(AddOrRemove)*

Adds or removes a legend from a chart.

LINKS*(SourceWorkbookName, TypeOfLink)*

Returns an array of the names of all workbooks referenced in the specified workbook.

LIST.NAMES()

Lists all names defined on the active worksheet.

MAIN.CHART*(TypeNumber, Stack, 100, Vary, Overlay, Drop, HiLo, Overlap%, Cluster, Angle)*
or
MAIN.CHART?*(TypeNumber, Stack, 100, Vary, Overlay, Drop, HiLo, Overlap%, Cluster, Angle)*

Same as FORMAT.MAIN.

IV

Macros

MCORREL(InputRange, OutputTopLeftCell, RowOrColumn, FirstRowLabels)
or
MCORREL?(InputRange, OutputTopLeftCell, RowOrColumn, FirstRowLabels)

Performs a correlation calculation.

MCOVAR(InputRange, OutputTopLeftCell, RowOrColumn, FirstRowLabels)
or
MCOVAR?(InputRange, OutputTopLeftCell, RowOrColumn, FirstRowLabels)

Performs a covariance calculation.

MERGE.STYLES(SourceDocumentName)

Merges all styles from another workbook into the active workbook.

MESSAGE(DisplayOrRemove, MessageText)

Displays messages in the status bar.

MOVE(NewXPosition, NewYPosition, WindowName)

Same as WINDOW.MOVE.

MOVE.TOOL(SourceToolbarID, SourceButtonPosition, DestToolbarID, DestButtonPosition, MoveOrCopy, WidthOfDropDownList)

Moves or copies a toolbar button to another toolbar.

MOVEAVG(InputRange, OutputTopLeftCell, Interval, StdErrors, GenerateChart, FirstRowLabels)
or
MOVEAVG?(InputRange, OutputTopLeftCell, Interval, StdErrors, GenerateChart, FirstRowLabels)

Performs a moving averages calculation.

NAMES(WorkbookName, IncludeHiddenNames, [NameSelectionCriteria])

Returns the specified names defined in the specified workbook.

NEW*(TypeOfWorkbook, ChartXYSeries, AddToOpenWorkbook)*
or
NEW?*(TypeOfWorkbook, ChartXYSeries, AddToOpenWorkbook)*

Creates a new workbook or opens a template.

NEW.WINDOW()

Creates a new window for the active workbook.

NEXT()

Ends a program loop.

NOTE*(TextToAdd, CellReference, StartCharacter, NumberOfCharacters)*
or
NOTE?*(TextToAdd, CellReference, StartCharacter, NumberOfCharacters)*

Creates or edits a note.

OBJECT.CONVERT*(ConvertToClass)*

Converts an OLE object to another class type.

OBJECT.PROPERTIES*(PlacementType, PrintObject)*

Determines the way in which the selected object(s) is attached to cells beneath.

OBJECT.PROTECTION*(Locked, TextLocked)*

Changes the protection of the selected object(s).

ON.DATA*(RemoteSheetName, MacroCellReference)*

Runs a macro when data is received via a DDE link.

ON.DOUBLE.CLICK*(SheetName, MacroCellReference)*

Runs a macro when you double-click or any cell, object, or item.

ON.ENTRY*(SheetName, MacroCellReference)*

Runs a macro when data is entered into any cell.

IV

Macros

ON.KEY(KeyCombination, MacroCellReference)

Assigns a macro to a key combination.

ON.RECALC(SheetName, MacroCellReference)

Runs a macro when a given worksheet is recalculated.

ON.TIME(DateAndTimeSerialNumber, MacroCellReference, TimeTolerance, SetTimer)

Runs a macro at a given time.

ON.WINDOW(WindowName, MacroCellReference)

Runs a macro when a given window has the focus.

OPEN(FileName, UpdateLinks, ReadOnly, Format, AccessPassword, WritePassword, IgnoreReadOnlyRecommend, FileOrigin, CustomDelimiter, AddToOpenWorkbook) or OPEN?(FileName, UpdateLinks, ReadOnly, Format, AccessPassword, WritePassword, IgnoreReadOnlyRecommend, FileOrigin, CustomDelimiter, AddToOpenWorkbook)

Opens a workbook.

OPEN.LINKS(FileName1, ... FileName12, ReadOnly, LinkType) or OPEN.LINKS?(FileName1, ... FileName12, ReadOnly, LinkType)

Opens workbooks linked to a particular worksheet.

OPEN.MAIL(Subject, Comments)

Opens the mail utility.

OPEN.TEXT(FileName, FileOrigin, StartRow, FileType, TextQualifier, ConsecDelims, TabDelim, SemicolonDelim, CommaDelim, SpaceDelim, OtherDelim, OtherChar, [FieldInfo1...])

Uses the TextWizard to open a text file in Excel 5.

OPTIONS.CALCULATION*(TypeOfCalc, Iterate, MaxIterations, MaxChangeIterate, UpdateRemote, PrecisionAsDisplayed, Date1904, RecalcBeforeSave, SaveExtLinkValues)*
or
OPTIONS.CALCULATION?*(TypeOfCalc, Iterate, MaxIterations, MaxChangeIterate, UpdateRemote, PrecisionAsDisplayed, Date1904, RecalcBeforeSave, SaveExtLinkValues)*

Sets worksheet calculation settings.

OPTIONS.CHART*(DisplayBlanks, PlotVisible, ResizeWithWindow, DefaultChartFormat)*
or
OPTIONS.CHART?*(DisplayBlanks, PlotVisible, ResizeWithWindow, DefaultChartFormat)*

Sets chart settings.

OPTIONS.EDIT*(InCellEditing, DragAndDrop, AlertBeforeOverwrite, MoveAfterEnter, FixedDecimals, DecimalPlaces, CopyObjects, UpdateLinks)*
or
OPTIONS.EDIT?*(InCellEditing, DragAndDrop, AlertBeforeOverwrite, MoveAfterEnter, FixedDecimals, DecimalPlaces, CopyObjects, UpdateLinks)*

Sets worksheet editing options.

OPTIONS.GENERAL*(A1OrR1C1, DDEOn, SummaryInfo, ShowTips, RecentlyUsedFiles, UseOldMenus, UserInfo, StandardFontName, FontSize, DefaultFileLocation, AlternateFileLocation, SheetsInNewWorkbook, [EnableMenuUnderline])*
or
OPTIONS.GENERAL?*(A1OrR1C1, DDEOn, SummaryInfo, ShowTips, RecentlyUsedFiles, UseOldMenus, UserInfo, StandardFontName, FontSize, DefaultFileLocation, AlternateFileLocation, SheetsInNewWorkbook, [EnableMenuUnderline])*

Sets general Excel 5 settings.

IV

Macros

OPTIONS.LISTS.ADD*(StringArray/ImportReference, [ListByRowOrColumn])*
or
OPTIONS.LISTS.ADD?*(ImportReference, [ListNumberToActivate])*

Adds a new custom list.

OPTIONS.LISTS.DELETE*(ListNumber)*

Deletes a custom list.

OPTIONS.TRANSITION*(MenuKey, AltMenuOption, TransitionNavigation, TransitionFormulaEvaluation, TransitionFormulaEntry)*
or
OPTIONS.TRANSITION?*(MenuKey, AltMenuOption, TransitionNavigation, TransitionFormulaEvaluation, TransitionFormulaEntry)*

Sets compatibility with other spreadsheets.

OPTIONS.VIEW*(FormulaBar, StatusBar, Notes, ShowInfo, ObjectOption, AutoPageBreaks, ShowFormulas, Gridlines, ColorNumber, Headers, OutlineSymbols, ZeroValues, HorizScrollBar, VertScrollBar, SheetTabs)*
or
OPTIONS.VIEW?*(FormulaBar, StatusBar, Notes, ShowInfo, ObjectOption, AutoPageBreaks, ShowFormulas, Gridlines, ColorNumber, Headers, OutlineSymbols, ZeroValues, HorizScrollBar, VertScrollBar, SheetTabs)*

Sets various view settings.

OUTLINE*(AutoStyles, SumRowsDirection, SumColsDirection, CreateOrApply)*
or
OUTLINE?*(AutoStyles, SumRowsDirection, SumColsDirection, CreateOrApply)*

Creates an outline and defines settings.

PAGE.SETUP(Header, Footer, LeftMgn, RightMgn, TopMgn, BottomMgn, RowColHeading, CellGrid, CenterHoriz, CenterVert, Orient, PaperSize, Scale, FirstPageNumber, PageOrder, Black&WhiteCells, Quality, HeaderMargin, FooterMargin, PrintNotes, Draft)
or
PAGE.SETUP?(Header, Footer, LeftMgn, RightMgn, TopMgn, BottomMgn, RowColHeading, CellGrid, CenterHoriz, CenterVert, Orient, PaperSize, Scale, FirstPageNumber, PageOrder, Black&WhiteCells, Quality, HeaderMargin, FooterMargin, PrintNotes, Draft)

Controls the appearance of the worksheet on the page.

PARSE(Text, DestinationReference)

Distributes the contents of the current selection to fill multiple columns.

PASTE(DestinationReference)

Pastes data or objects from the Clipboard into the active cell(s).

PASTE.LINK()

Pastes data or objects from the Clipboard into the active cell(s) and establishes a link to the source of the data or objects.

PASTE.PICTURE()

Pastes a picture from the Clipboard into the active cell(s).

PASTE.PICTURE.LINK()

Pastes a picture from the Clipboard into the active cell(s) and establishes a link to the source of the data or objects.

PASTE.SPECIAL

Pastes the given components from the copy area into the current selection. (See manual for parameters.)

PASTE.TOOL(ToolbarID, ButtonPosition)

Pastes a button face from the Clipboard to a toolbar position.

PATTERNS

Changes the appearance of the selection. (See manual for parameters.)

PAUSE*(PromptForResumeMacro)*

Pauses a macro.

PIVOT.ADD.DATA*(TableName, PivotFieldName, NewName, FieldPosition, FieldFunction, CalculationToField, BaseField, BaseFieldItem)*

Adds data to a PivotTable.

PIVOT.ADD.FIELDS*(TableName, RowArray, ColumnArray, PageArray, AddToTable)*

Adds fields to a PivotTable.

PIVOT.FIELD*(TableName, PivotFieldName, Orientation, DestinationPosition)*

Pivots a field within a PivotTable.

PIVOT.FIELD.GROUP*(StartDate, EndDate, SizeOfGroups, Periods)*
or
PIVOT.FIELD.GROUP?*(StartDate, EndDate, SizeOfGroups, Periods)*

Creates groups within a PivotTable.

PIVOT.FIELD.PROPERTIES*(TableName, PivotFieldName, NewName, Orientation, CalculationToApply, Formats)*

Changes the properties of a field inside a PivotTable.

PIVOT.FIELD.UNGROUP()

Ungroups all selected groups within a PivotTable.

PIVOT.ITEM*(TableName, PivotFieldName, PivotItemName, Position)*

Moves an item within a PivotTable.

PIVOT.ITEM.PROPERTIES*(TableName, PivotFieldName, PivotItemName, NewName, Position, Show, ActivePage)*

Changes the properties of an item within a PivotTable.

PIVOT.REFRESH*(TableName)*

Refreshes a PivotTable.

PIVOT.SHOW.PAGES*(TableName, PageField)*

Creates new worksheets in the workbook that contains the active cell.

PIVOT.TABLE.WIZARD*(TypeOfData, Source, Destination, TableName, RowGrandTotal, ColGrandTotal, SaveData, ApplyAutoFormat, AutoPage)*
or
PIVOT.TABLE.WIZARD?*(TypeOfData, Source, Destination, TableName, RowGrandTotal, ColGrandTotal, SaveData, ApplyAutoFormat, AutoPage)*

Creates an empty PivotTable.

PLACEMENT*(Type)*
or
PLACEMENT?*(Type)*

Same as OBJECT.PROPERTIES.

POKE*(DDEChannel, DestinationItem, DataSourceReference)*

Sends data to another application via DDE.

PRECISION*(UseAsDisplayed)*

Sets precision to be precision displayed.

PREFERRED()

Changes the format of the active chart to the default.

PRESS.TOOL*(ToolbarID, ButtonPosition, ButtonNormalOrPressed)*

Formats a button to appear normal or pressed.

PRINT*(Range, FromPage, ToPage, Copies, Draft, Preview, PrintWhat, Color, Feed, Quality, YResolution, Selection)*
or
PRINT?*(Range, FromPage, ToPage, Copies, Draft, Preview, PrintWhat, Color, Feed, Quality, YResolution, Selection)*

Prints the active workbook.

PRINT.PREVIEW()

Previews pages of the active workbook on the screen prior to printing.

PRINTER.SETUP*(PrinterName)*

Changes the default printer.

PROMOTE*(PromoteRowsOrColumns)*
or
PROMOTE?*(PromoteRowsOrColumns)*

Promotes (ungroups) the selected rows or columns in an outline.

PROTECT.DOCUMENT*(ProtectContents, Windows, Password, Objects)*

Adds or removes document, worksheet, or object protection.

PTTESTM*(DataSetOneInputRange, DataSetTwoInputRange, OutputTopLeftCell, FirstRowLabels, Alpha, MeanDifference)*
or
PTTESTM?*(DataSetOneInputRange, DataSetTwoInputRange, OutputTopLeftCell, FirstRowLabels, Alpha, MeanDifference)*

Performs a paired two-sample t-Test for means.

PTTESTV*(DataSetOneInputRange, DataSetTwoInputRange, OutputTopLeftCell, FirstRowLabels, Alpha)*
or
PTTESTV?*(DataSetOneInputRange, DataSetTwoInputRange, OutputTopLeftCell, FirstRowLabels, Alpha)*

Performs a two-sample t-Test assuming unequal variances.

QUERY.GET.DATA*(ConnectionString, QueryText, KeepQueryDefn, KeepFieldNames, KeepRowNumbers, Destination)*
or
QUERY.GET.DATA?*(ConnectionString, QueryText, KeepQueryDefn, KeepFieldNames, KeepRowNumbers, Destination)*

Builds a new SQL query using supplied information.

QUERY.REFRESH*(CellReference)*

Refreshes data in a data range written by a query.

QUIT()

Exits Excel.

RANDOM*(OutputRange, NumberOfVariables, NumberOfDataPoints, DistributionType, Seed, From/Mean/ Probability/Lambda/InputRange, To/StdDev/NumberOfTrials, [Step, NumberOfRepeats, NumberOfSeqsRepeat])*
or
RANDOM?*(OutputRange, NumberOfVariables, NumberOfDataPoints, DistributionType, Seed, From/Mean/ Probability/Lambda/InputRange, To/StdDev/NumberOfTrials, [Step, NumberOfRepeats, NumberOfSeqsRepeat])*

Generates a given number of pseudorandom numbers.

RANKPERC*(InputRange, OutputTopLeftCell, RowOrColumn, FirstRowLabels)*
or
RANKPERC?*(InputRange, OutputTopLeftCell, RowOrColumn, FirstRowLabels)*

Performs a rank and percentile calculation on a set of data.

REFTEXT*(ReferenceToConvert, A1OrR1C1)*

Converts a cell reference to an absolute reference.

IV

Macros

REGISTER(DLLName, DLLFunctionName, DataTypes, FunctionNameToWizard, ArgumentNames, FunctionOrCommand, FunctionCategory, ShortcutKey, ReferenceToHelp, FunctionDescription, Argument1, ..., Argument21)

Registers the given DLL and returns the ID.

REGRESS(InputYRange, InputXRange, YInterceptZero, FirstRowLabels, ConfidenceLevel, SummaryOutputTopLeftCell, IncludeResiduals, IncludeStdzdResiduals, ResidualsPlots, RegressionLinePlots, ResidualsOutputTopLeftCell, NormalProbPlots, ProbOutputTopLeftCell)
or
REGRESS?(InputYRange, InputXRange, YInterceptZero, FirstRowLabels, ConfidenceLevel, SummaryOutputTopLeftCell, IncludeResiduals, IncludeStdzdResiduals, ResidualsPlots, RegressionLinePlots, ResidualsOutputTopLeftCell, NormalProbPlots, ProbOutputTopLeftCell)

Performs linear regression analysis.

RELREF(Offset, Reference)

Returns the reference of a cell relative to a given cell.

REMOVE.PAGE.BREAK()

Removes manual page breaks.

RENAME.COMMAND(MenuBarNumber, MenuID, CommandID, NewCommandName, [SubmenuCommandID])

Changes the name of a menu or menu command.

RENAME.OBJECT(NewName)

Renames the selected object or group.

REPORT.DEFINE(ReportName, SectionsArray, ContinuousPageNumbers)

Creates or replaces a report definition.

REPORT.DELETE*(ReportName)*

Removes a report definition from the active workbook.

REPORT.GET*(TypeOfInformation, ReportName)*

Returns information about reports defined for the active workbook.

REPORT.PRINT*(ReportName, NumberCopies, ShowPrintDialog)* or
REPORT.PRINT?*(ReportName, ShowPrintDialog)*

Prints a report.

REQUEST*(DDEChannel, TypeOfInformationRequested)*

Requests an array from a DDE link.

RESET.TOOL*(ToolbarID, ButtonPosition)*

Resets a tool button to its default button face.

RESET.TOOLBAR*(ToolbarID)*

Resets toolbars to the defaults.

RESTART*(NumberOfReturnsToIgnore)*

Removes a given number of Return statements from the return stack.

RESULT*(DataType)*

Sets the type of data a macro or custom function returns.

RESUME*(HowToResume)*

Resumes a paused macro.

RETURN*(ValueToReturn)*

Returns a macro to its calling routine.

ROUTE.DOCUMENT()

Routes the document using its routing slip.

IV

Macros

ROUTING.SLIP(Recipients, Subject, Message, RoutingMethod, ReturnToSender, TrackStatus)
or
ROUTING.SLIP?(Recipients, Subject, Message, RoutingMethod, ReturnToSender, TrackStatus)

Adds or edits the routing slip attached to the current workbook.

ROW.HEIGHT(Height, RowReference, StandardHeight, HideOrFit)
or
ROW.HEIGHT?(Height, RowReference, StandardHeight, HideOrFit)

Changes the row height in a reference.

RUN(MacroCellReference, SingleStep)

Runs a macro.

SAMPLE(InputRange, OutputTopLeftCell, SamplingMethod, SamplingRateOrNumber, FirstRowLabels)
or
SAMPLE?(InputRange, OutputTopLeftCell, SamplingMethod, SamplingRateOrNumber, FirstRowLabels)

Performs sampling of a set of data.

SAVE()

Saves the active workbook.

SAVE.AS(NewName, FileFormat, AccessPassword, MakeBackup, WritePassword, ReadOnlyRecommend)

Saves a file under new name or attributes.

SAVE.TOOLBAR(ToolbarID, DestinationFileName)

Saves toolbar definitions to a given file.

SAVE.WORKBOOK(NewName, FileFormat, AccessPassword, MakeBackup, WritePassword, ReadOnlyRecommend)

Same as SAVE.AS.

SAVE.WORKSPACE*(NameOfWorkspace)*

Saves the current workbook(s) as a workspace.

SCALE

Scales a chart. (See manual for parameters.)

SCENARIO.ADD*(ScenarioName, ValueArray, ChangingCellsReference, ScenarioComment, Locked, Hidden)*

Defines a scenario.

SCENARIO.CELLS*(CellReference)*
or
SCENARIO.CELLS?*(CellReference)*

Defines the changing cells for a scenario model.

SCENARIO.DELETE*(ScenarioName)*

Deletes a scenario.

SCENARIO.EDIT*(ScenarioName, NewName, ScenarioComment, ChangingCellsReference, ValueArray, Locked, Hidden)*
or
SCENARIO.EDIT?*(ScenarioName, NewName, ScenarioComment, ChangingCellsReference, ValueArray, Locked, Hidden)*

Edits a scenario.

SCENARIO.GET*(TypeOfInformation, ScenarioName)*

Returns information about defined scenarios.

SCENARIO.SHOW*(ScenarioName)*

Recalculates using a scenario and displays the result.

SCENARIO.SHOW.NEXT()

Recalculates using the next scenario and displays the result.

SCENARIO.SUMMARY*(ResultReference, ReportType)*
or
SCENARIO.SUMMARY?*(ResultReference, ReportType)*

Generates a table summarizing the results of all scenarios.

IV

Macros

SELECT

Selects a cell(s) or changes the active cell. (See manual for parameters.)

SELECT.CHART()

Selects a chart.

SELECT.END*(Direction)*

Selects the cell at the edge of the range in a given direction.

SELECT.LAST.CELL()

Selects the last cell that has data.

SELECT.PLOT.AREA()

Selects the plot area of the active chart.

SELECT.SPECIAL*(SelectType, TypeOfConstantsOrFormulas, LevelsToSelect)*
or
SELECT.SPECIAL?*(SelectType, TypeOfConstantsOrFormulas, LevelsToSelect)*

Selects groups of cells that have similar characteristics.

SELECTION()

Returns the full reference of the current selection.

SEND.KEYS*(KeyCombination, WaitForActions)*

Sends a series of keystrokes to the active application.

SEND.MAIL*(Recipients, Subject, ReturnReceipt)*

Sends the active workbook to recipients.

SEND.TO.BACK()

Sends selected object(s) to behind all other objects.

SERIES*(NameReference, CategoriesReference, ValuesReference, PlotOrder)*

Represents a data series in the active chart.

SET.CRITERIA()

Defines the name Criteria for the selected range.

SET.DATABASE()

Defines the name Database for the selected range.

SET.EXTRACT()

Defines the name Extract for the selected range.

SET.NAME*(Name, Value)*

Defines a name to refer to a value.

SET.PAGE.BREAK()

Sets manual page breaks.

SET.PREFERRED*(FormatName)*

Changes the default format used to create a new chart.

SET.PRINT.AREA*(Range)*

Defines the print area for the workbook.

SET.PRINT.TITLES*(ColTitlesReference, RowTitlesReference)*

Defines the print titles for the active worksheet.

SET.UPDATE.STATUS*(LinkedFilePath, UpdateMethod, TypeOfLink)*

Sets automatic or manual updating of a link.

SET.VALUE*(CellReferences, Values)*

Changes the value of cells on the macro worksheet without changing any formulas within those cells.

SHORT.MENUS*(OnOff)*

Sets short menus.

SHOW.ACTIVE.CELL()

Scrolls the window until the active cell is visible.

SHOW.BAR(*MenuBarNumber*)

Displays a menu bar.

SHOW.CLIPBOARD()

Displays the Clipboard contents in a new window.

SHOW.DETAIL(*RowsOrColumns, RowColNumber, ExpandOrCollapse, AddField*)

Expands or collapses detail.

SHOW.INFO(*Mode*)

Controls the display of the Info window.

SHOW.LEVELS(*RowLevelNumber, ColumnLevelNumber*)

Displays row and column levels of an outline.

SHOW.TOOLBAR(*ToolbarID, VisibleOrHidden, DockPosition, HorizPosition, VertPosition, ToolbarWidth*)

Hides or displays a toolbar.

SIZE(*Width, Height, WindowName*)

Same as WINDOW.SIZE.

SLIDE.COPY.ROW()

Copies the selected slides to the Clipboard.

SLIDE.CUT.ROW()

Cuts the selected slides to the Clipboard.

SLIDE.DEFAULTS(*EffectNumber, Speed, AdvanceRate, SoundFileName*)
or
SLIDE.DEFAULTS?(*EffectNumber, Speed, AdvanceRate, SoundFileName*)

Specifies the default values for transitions in a slide show.

SLIDE.DELETE.ROW()

Deletes the selected slides.

SLIDE.EDIT*(EffectNumber, Speed, AdvanceRate, SoundFileName)*
or
SLIDE.EDIT?*(EffectNumber, Speed, AdvanceRate, SoundFileName)*

Modifies attributes of the selected slide.

SLIDE.GET*(TypeOfInformation, SlideShowDocName, [SlideNumber])*

Returns information about a slide or the entire slide show.

SLIDE.PASTE*(EffectNumber, Speed, AdvanceRate, SoundFileName)*
or
SLIDE.PASTE?*(EffectNumber, Speed, AdvanceRate, SoundFileName*

Pastes the Clipboard as the next available slide.

SLIDE.PASTE.ROW()

Pastes multiple slides from the Clipboard into the current selection.

SLIDE.SHOW*(InitialSlideNumber, Repeat, DialogTitle, AllowNavigationKeys, AllowDialogBoxControl)*

Starts a slide show.

SOLVER.ADD*(ConstraintCellReference, Relation, Formula)*

Adds a constraint to the current problem.

SOLVER.CHANGE*(ConstraintCellReference, Relation, Formula)*

Changes the right side of an existing constraint.

SOLVER.DELETE*(ConstraintCellReference, Relation, Formula)*

Deletes a constraint from the current problem.

SOLVER.FINISH*(KeepFinalSolution, ReportArgumentsArray)*

Displays a dialog box with the arguments and results when solver is finished.

SOLVER.GET*(TypeOfInformation, ScenarioSheetName)*

Returns information about the current settings for Solver.

IV

Macros

SOLVER.LOAD(*LoadSourceReference*)

Loads previously saved Solver problem specifications.

SOLVER.OK(*SetTargetCell, MaxMinValue, ValueOf, ByChanging*)

Specifies basic Solver options.

SOLVER.OPTIONS(*MaxTime, Iterations, Precision, AssumeLinear, StepThrough, Estimates, Derivatives, Search, IntTolerance, Scaling*)

Specifies the available Solver options.

SOLVER.RESET()

Removes all cell selections and constraints from the Solver parameters and restores all Solver option settings.

SOLVER.SAVE(*DestinationReference*)

Saves the Solver problem specification on the worksheet.

SOLVER.SOLVE(*UserFinish, ShowMacroReference*)

Begins Solver.

SORT(*ByRowsOrColumns, SortKey1, Order1, SortKey2, Order2, SortKey3, Order3, Header, CustomSorting, MatchCase*)

Sorts rows or columns within the selection.

SOUND.NOTE(*CellReference, Erase*)

Records or erases sound in a cell note.

SOUND.PLAY(*CellReference, FileName, [Resource]*)

Plays the sound from a cell note or a file.

SPELLING(*CustomDictName, IgnoreUppercaseWords, AlwaysSuggest*)

Checks the spelling of words in the current selection.

SPELLING.CHECK*(WordOrReference, CustomDictName, IgnoreUppercaseWords)*

Checks the spelling of a word.

SPLIT*(ColumnSplit, RowSplit)*

Splits the active window into panes.

SQL.BIND*(ConnectionNumber, ResultColumn, CellReference)*

Specifies the location at which results from an SQL query are placed.

SQL.CLOSE*(ConnectionNumber)*

Closes a connection to an external data source.

SQL.ERROR()

Returns error information from an SQL operation.

SQL.EXEC.QUERY*(ConnectionNumber, QueryText)*

Queries an external data source.

SQL.GET.SCHEMA*(ConnectionNumber, InfoType, QualifierText)*

Returns information about the structure of a data source in a given connection.

SQL.OPEN*(ConnectionString, OutputReference, DriverPrompt)*

Establishes a connection with an external data source.

SQL.RETRIEVE.TO.FILE*(ConnectionNumber, DestinationFile, FirstRowColumnNames, ColumnDelim)*

Retrieves results from data source and places them in a file.

SQL.RETRIEVE*(ConnectionNumber, DestinationCellReference, MaxColumns, MaxRows, FirstRowColumnNames, FirstColumnRowNumbers, NamedRange, FetchFirst)*

Retrieves results from data source.

IV

Macros

STEP()

Single-steps a macro — useful for debugging.

STYLE*(Bold, Italic)*
or
STYLE?*(Bold, Italic)*

Same as FORMAT.FONT.

SUBSCRIBE.TO*(SourceFileName, SourceFileFormat)*

Inserts contents of a given edition at the current selection point.

SUBTOTAL.CREATE*(AtEachChangeIn, UseFunctionNumber, AddSubtotalTo, Replace, PageBreakBetweenGroups, SummaryBelowData)*
or
SUBTOTAL.CREATE?*(AtEachChangeIn, UseFunctionNumber, AddSubtotalTo, Replace, PageBreakBetweenGroups, SummaryBelowData)*

Generates a subtotal in a list or a database.

SUBTOTAL.REMOVE()

Removes all subtotals.

SUMMARY.INFO*(Title, Subject, Author, Keywords, Comments)*

Generates summary info for the active workbook.

TABLE*(RowCellReference, ColumnCellReference)*
or
TABLE?*(RowCellReference, ColumnCellReference)*

Creates a table based upon input values and formulas.

TERMINATE*(DDEChannel)*

Closes a DDE channel.

TEXT.BOX*(TextToAdd, ObjectID, StartingCharacterNumber, NumberOfCharacters)*

Replaces characters in a text box or button.

TEXT.TO.COLUMNS*(DestinationReference, DataType, TextDelimiter, ConsecutiveDelimsAsOne, TabDelims, SemicolonDelims, CommaDelims, SpaceDelims, CustomDelims, OtherCharDelims, FieldInfo)*

Parses text into columns of data.

TEXTREF*(ReferenceAsText, A1OrR1C1)*

Converts text to absolute cell references.

TRACER.CLEAR()

Clears all tracer arrows on the worksheet.

TRACER.DISPLAY*(Direction, NextArrowLevel)*

Activates formula tracers showing relationships among cells.

TRACER.ERROR()

Activates formula tracers showing error values in cells.

TRACER.NAVIGATE*(Direction, FormulaReferenceNumber, [LinkToFollow])*

Moves the selection from one end of the tracer arrow to the other.

TTESTM*(DataSetOneInputRange, DataSetTwoInputRange, OutputTopLeftCell, FirstRowLabels, Alpha, MeansDifference)* or TTESTM?*(DataSetOneInputRange, DataSetTwoInputRange, OutputTopLeftCell, FirstRowLabels, Alpha, MeansDifference)*

Performs a two-sample t-Test for means, assuming equal variances.

UNDO()

Reverses (in most cases) the last action.

UNGROUP()

Separates a grouped object into individual objects.

UNHIDE*(WindowName)*

Displays a hidden window.

UNLOCKED.NEXT()

Moves the next unlocked cell in a protected worksheet.

UNLOCKED.PREV()

Moves the previous unlocked cell in a protected worksheet.

UNREGISTER*(RegisterID)*

Unregisters the given DLL.

UPDATE.LINK*(LinkPath, TypeOfLink)*

Updates a link.

VIEW.3D*(Elevation, Perspective, Rotation, Axes, Height%, AutoScale)*
or
VIEW.3D*(Elevation, Perspective, Rotation, Axes, Height%, AutoScale)*

Adjusts the view of the active 3D chart.

VIEW.DEFINE*(ViewName, PrintSettingsInView, RowColumnSettingsInView)*

Defines or redefines a view.

VIEW.DELETE*(ViewName)*

Deletes a view from the active workbook.

VIEW.GET*(TypeOfInformation, NameOfView)*

Returns an array of views from the active workbook.

VIEW.SHOW*(ViewName)*
or
VIEW.SHOW?*(ViewName)*

Shows a view.

VLINE*(NumberOfRows)*

Scrolls through the active window by a given number of rows.

VOLATILE*(VolatileOrNonvolatile)*

Defines whether a custom function is recalculated whenever a calculation occurs on the worksheet.

VPAGE*(NumberOfWindows)*

Scrolls vertically through the active window by a given number of windows.

VSCROLL*(DestinationPosition, ScrollMode)*

Scrolls vertically through the active window by percentage or by row number.

WAIT*(DateAndTimeSerialNumber)*

Pauses a macro until a given time.

WHILE*(TestLogical)*

Defines a program loop.

WINDOW.MAXIMIZE*(WindowName)*

Changes the active window to full size.

WINDOW.MINIMIZE*(WindowName)*

Changes the active window to an icon.

WINDOW.MOVE*(NewXPosition, NewYPosition, WindowName)*

Moves the active window.

WINDOW.RESTORE*(WindowName)*

Changes the active window from maximized or minimized to its previous size.

WINDOW.SIZE*(Width, Height, WindowName)*

Changes the size of the active window.

WINDOW.TITLE*(NewTitle)*

Changes the title of the active window.

WINDOWS*(TypesOfWorkbooks, [NameSelectionCriteria])*

Returns the names of the given Excel windows.

WORKBOOK.ACTIVATE*(SheetName)*

Activates a worksheet.

IV

Macros

WORKBOOK.ADD(NameArrayToMove, DestinationWorkbookName, NewPosition)
or
WORKBOOK.ADD?(NameArrayToMove, DestinationWorkbookName, NewPosition)

Moves a worksheet between workbooks.

WORKBOOK.COPY(NameArrayToCopy, DestinationWorkbookName, NewPosition)
or
WORKBOOK.COPY?(NameArrayToCopy, DestinationWorkbookName, NewPosition)

Copies a worksheet between workbooks.

WORKBOOK.DELETE(SheetName)

Deletes a worksheet or group of worksheets from the current workbook.

WORKBOOK.HIDE(SheetName, VeryHidden)

Hides worksheets in the active workbook.

WORKBOOK.INSERT(SheetTypeNumber)

Inserts a worksheet or worksheets into the current workbook.

WORKBOOK.MOVE(NameArrayToMove, DestinationWorkbookName, NewPosition)

Moves a worksheet or worksheets between workbooks or within a workbook.

WORKBOOK.NAME(OldName, NewName)

Renames a worksheet in a workbook.

WORKBOOK.NEW()
or
WORKBOOK.NEW?()

Adds a worksheet to a workbook.

WORKBOOK.NEXT()

Activates the next worksheet in the active workbook.

WORKBOOK.OPTIONS*(OldName, Bound, NewName)*

Renames a worksheet in a workbook.

WORKBOOK.PREV()

Activates the previous worksheet in the active workbook.

WORKBOOK.PROTECT*(ProtectStructure, ProtectWindows, AccessPassword)*

Controls the protection of workbooks.

WORKBOOK.SCROLL*(NumberOfSheets, [ToFirstOrLast])*

Scrolls through the worksheets in a workbook.

WORKBOOK.SELECT*(NameArray, ActiveSheetName, Replace)*

Selects a worksheet or worksheets in the active workbook.

WORKBOOK.TAB.SPLIT*(TabRatio)*

Sets the ratio of the tabs to the horizontal scrollbar.

WORKBOOK.UNHIDE*(SheetName)*
or
WORKBOOK.UNHIDE?*(SheetName)*

Unhides a worksheet or worksheets in the active workbook.

WORKGROUP*(NameArray)*
or
WORKGROUP?*(NameArray)*

Creates a group.

IV

Macros

WORKSPACE(FixedDecimal, DecimalPlaces, A1OrR1C1, ScrollBars, StatusBar, FormulaBar, AltMenuKey, IgnoreRemote, MoveAfterEnter, [CommandUnderlines], StandardToolbar, NoteIndicator, NavKeys, MenuKeyAction, Drag&Drop, ShowInfo, InCellEditing)
or
WORKSPACE?(FixedDecimal, DecimalPlaces, A1OrR1C1, ScrollBars, StatusBar, FormulaBar, AltMenuKey, IgnoreRemote, MoveAfterEnter, [CommandUnderlines], StandardToolbar, NoteIndicator, NavKeys, MenuKeyAction, Drag&Drop, ShowInfo, InCellEditing)

Changes the workspace settings for a workbook.

ZOOM(Magnification)

Zooms the display in the active window.

ZTESTM(DataSetOneInputRange, DataSetTwoInputRange, OutputTopLeftCell, FirstRowLabels, Alpha, MeansDifference, DataSetOneVariance, DataSetTwoVariance)
or
ZTESTM?(DataSetOneInputRange, DataSetTwoInputRange, OutputTopLeftCell, FirstRowLabels, Alpha, MeansDifference, DataSetOneVariance, DataSetTwoVariance)

Performs a two-sample z-Test for means, assuming known variances.

Part V

Building Applications

Chapter Snapshot

Working in the Windows environment has several advantages over working in the DOS environment. In addition to its more obvious features like the graphical user interface and the ability to run more than one application at the same time, Windows provides you with yet another very powerful tool. Unlike DOS, Windows allows applications of completely different natures to communicate easily with each other. In this chapter, you see several ways in which Excel works with other applications:

✔ Importing files into Excel

✔ Exporting files to other applications

✔ Creating DDE links

✔ Creating OLE 2 links

✔ Using links with macros

✔ Diagnosing and correcting some common linking problems

Although this chapter is not comprehensive, you should at least gain a basic understanding of the different types of data transfer and why they are used. With some practice using Excel 5, Visual Basic, and other Windows applications, you soon can create stunning work that might amaze even yourself.

Linking Excel with Other Applications

With the extreme diversity in today's computer industry, no standardized versions of software exist. A multitude of word processors, spreadsheet packages, database managers, and other software are available. To be competitive, software developers must give their applications the capability to use, understand, and work with the many different file formats available.

Importing Files into Excel

The process of converting a file created using another application into a format you can use in your current application is referred to as *importing*. When you load data from another application into Excel, Excel employs an *import filter* to read the incoming data. The foreign file is filtered and converted into a format that Excel can use, much like a book might be translated from German to English before it can be read by the average American.

Several import filters are available in Excel 5. These filters enable you to load files of the following types:

- ✔ Excel files (earlier versions)
- ✔ dBase
- ✔ Quattro Pro for DOS
- ✔ Lotus 1-2-3
- ✔ SYLK files (Symbolic Link)
- ✔ Microsoft Works
- ✔ Data Interchange Format

To import a file of a different format into Excel 5, first choose File, Open from Excel's main menu. The Open dialog box appears, as shown in figure 18.1. If you know the name and path of the file you want to import, simply enter that information. Excel detects the file type and converts it as needed.

Consider, for example, that in the past you have used both dBase and Lotus 1-2-3, but you now want to work with the Lotus files only. You can tell Excel's Open dialog box to display files of only the Lotus type.

To display only Lotus files, open the pop-up list called List Files of Type, located in the lower left corner of the dialog box, by clicking once on the down arrow to its right and then choosing Lotus.

The list of Lotus files in the current directory will appear. To open one of these files, simply double-click on it, or mark the file by clicking it once, and press the Open button.

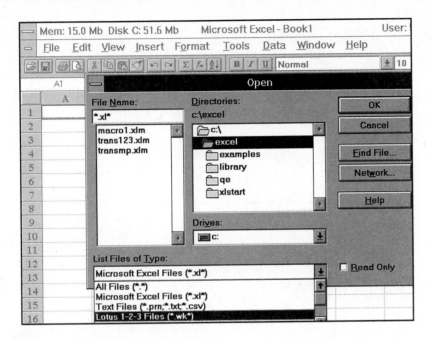

Figure 18.1
The Open
dialog box.

Building Applications

Exporting Files

Exporting files is the same as importing files, but in reverse. When you import a file, you convert it from another format into an Excel format. When you *export* a file, you convert it from an Excel format to a format used by another application. Exporting, like importing, uses filters to convert files.

Excel 5 enables you to export files to several different configurations. The following is a list of available export filters:

- ✓ Excel 4.0, 3.0, 2.1
- ✓ Data Interchange Format
- ✓ dBase II, III, IV
- ✓ Quattro Pro for DOS
- ✓ Lotus 1-2-3
- ✓ SYLK (Symbolic Link)

Notice that although you can import files from Microsoft Works, you cannot save Excel files in either of these formats. You can, however, save these files as text and then open them in Microsoft Works. Unfortunately though, this method has a tendency to change the structure or format of the document.

Exporting files is just as easy as importing files. To export a file to a specific format from Excel's main menu, choose File, Save As. The Save As dialog box appears (see fig. 18.2). Notice that in the lower left corner of this dialog box is another pop-up list labeled Save File as Type.

Figure 18.2
The Save As
dialog box.

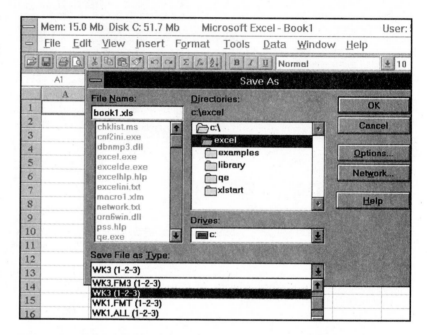

To save a file in the Lotus format, open the pop-up list by clicking once on the down arrow to the right of the box. A list of available formats appears. Simply click on the option you want, specify a file name, and click on OK.

If you open a file of a format other than Excel, and eventually want to save it again, Excel automatically saves the file in a form that matches its form when it was opened. That is, if you open a Lotus file, and then choose to save it, Excel saves it as a Lotus file again, and not as an Excel file. If you want to save the file in the Excel format, you must use the Save As option instead of the Save option.

Using DDE and OLE 2

Importing and exporting files are not the only ways to transport material between Excel and other Windows applications. DDE and OLE 2 also enable you to manipulate a variety of information from almost any Windows source.

Because DDE and OLE 2 were designed as bridges between Windows applications, please note that some of this chapter deals with DDE and OLE 2 as applied to Windows in general. A general understanding of the process gives you the flexibility to work with all your applications and to use DDE and OLE 2 as they were intended to be used.

DDE

Dynamic Data Exchange (DDE) is one way to transfer data of varied types into and out of Excel. *Dynamic Data Exchange* means just what its name implies: a data transfer in which data are in a *dynamic*, or changing, state. DDE places a pointer in the current (*destination*) document that points to the original source file. The data from the source file are not actually in the destination document, but the destination document maintains a record of where the source data are permanently located, saving time and memory.

OLE 2

Object Linking and Embedding (OLE 2) is another way to move data between Windows applications. Unlike DDE, *embedding* an object places an actual copy of the source data in the current application. OLE then assigns a pointer to the application that created the source data. If you use Microsoft Word to create a document and then embed it in an Excel document as an object, for example, Excel copies the whole file and then remembers that it was created by Word. OLE does not keep a record of the original object's location, only the application to which it is associated. If you want to edit the embedded object, you just double-click on the object, and the original application is started automatically.

Excel 5 is one of the first Windows applications to employ OLE 2. For differences between OLE and OLE 2, please see the "Added Features of OLE 2" section later in this chapter.

OLE 2 or DDE? Use DDE when the data source file is particularly large, when the source is not likely to change often, or when the source might be placed in several documents.

Building Applications

OLE 2 is best used when the source file is of a moderate size, when the source must be changed often, or when you are not sure that the source file is always certain to be present at the current location.

In the following sections, you learn to create DDE and OLE 2 links, create links into and out of Excel, and see several examples of links at work. Links are not hard to perform, but they can be difficult to understand. If you follow along on-screen as you read, links should become clearer to you.

DDE Links

DDE communicates between applications by using a link. *Links* are channels for communication, much like telephone lines. Just as a phone line enables two people to talk to each other, links allows Windows applications to converse. To set up a DDE environment, you must establish the link.

Establishing a DDE Link

DDE links are not difficult to establish. You simply follow these steps:

1. Open the source document.

2. Select the object in the source file that you want to link.

3. From the <u>E</u>dit menu of the object source application, choose <u>C</u>opy. Copying the object places an exact duplicate of the selected object on the Clipboard.

4. Return to the container or *destination* document. (Please do not let terminology confuse you. The destination document is nothing more than the document to which you are copying the object.)

5. From the <u>E</u>dit menu, choose Paste <u>S</u>pecial. The Paste Special dialog box appears, as shown in figure 18.3.

6. The following options are available in the Paste Special dialog box:

   ✔ **Paste <u>L</u>ink.** This option is absolutely essential for establishing a DDE link. (Merely pasting an object creates no link to the original. If you wish to establish a DDE link, you must use the Paste <u>L</u>ink option.) Activate the Paste <u>L</u>ink option by clicking on it once with the mouse or pressing Alt+L.

✔ **A**s. In this section, specify the type of object you are linking; in other words, the application with which you want the object to be associated.

✔ **D**isplay as Icon. Check this box if you want the linked object to appear as an icon. Displaying an object as an icon is particularly useful if the object is large and might clutter the destination document's window.

You are not required to use Paste **S**pecial to import objects into an Excel document. As with most Windows applications, you can use the normal **C**ut and **P**aste routine. Anything that you can place on the Clipboard can be cut and pasted. Note, however, that plain cut-and-paste object manipulation does not give you the luxury of automatic object updates or the ability to double-click on the object to run its parent application.

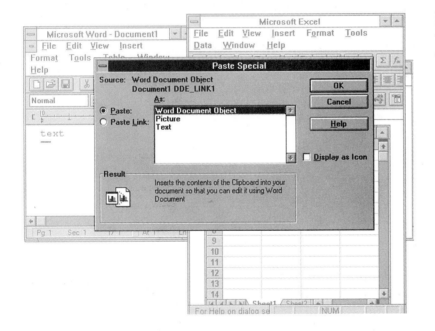

Figure 18.3
The Paste Special dialog box.

DDE Links and Inactive Applications

Imagine that an Excel document has links, and that the document is saved and then re-opened at a later time. What happens?

When the Excel document is re-opened, Excel tells you that links exist in the document. Excel then asks you if you want to re-establish the links. If you want to re-establish these DDE links, simply choose **Y**es, as shown in figure 18.4.

Figure 18.4
The Re-establish
links dialog box.

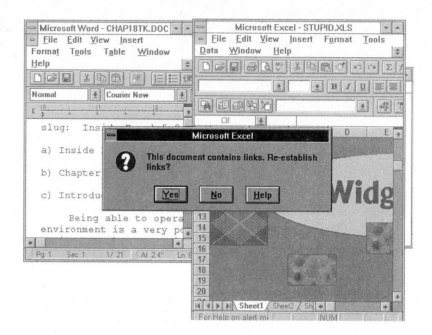

If you open a document that contains DDE links and you know that the source file is different from the image portrayed in your document (the source has changed), you need to *update* the link.

Updating a Link

To update a link manually, choose Edit, Links from the Excel main menu. The Links dialog box appears, as shown in figure 18.5. In the center area of this dialog box, you see a list of active links.

Link updates are done automatically if you have Update set to Automatic and the source application is active.

Highlight the link that you want to update by clicking on it once with the mouse. To update the highlighted link, press the Update Now button. Very quickly, the source application is activated, the container document is updated, and the source application is closed again.

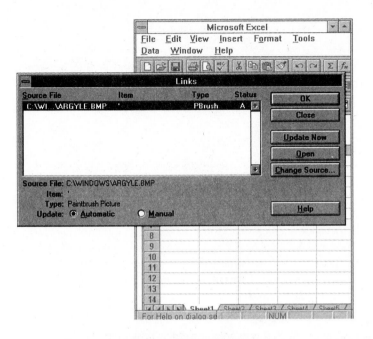

Figure 18.5
The Links
dialog box.

AUTHOR'S NOTE

Although automatic updating of DDE links is a wonderful tool, having Update set to **A**utomatic while both source and container applications are open can significantly slow down your CPU.

The first few times you try DDE linking, leave updating on **A**utomatic so that you can see the way changes in the source document affect the container document. After the first few times you use DDE links, however, you might want to switch update to **M**anual while both applications are active.

Particularly with graphics, any change in the source can take a large amount of processor time to update the container's object. This read-write time is time you must spend waiting for the mouse cursor to return from its hourglass shape.

For best results set update to **M**anual, make all your changes to the source object, and then choose **U**pdate Now.

Shortcuts and Tips

If you have many links in one Excel document, and you want to update several of them, you might want to know about some shorcuts that can save you time. When you are highlighting specific links, you can use the same shortcuts that can be used in the Windows File Manager.

✔ Click on one link to highlight it, and then Shift-click on the last link to mark all links between the first and last links.

✔ Hold down the Ctrl key as you click on individual links to mark links that are not consecutive.

✔ You also can use the combination of the Ctrl and Shift keys with the mouse to mark non-consecutive ranges.

✔ The Links dialog box offers an option to change the source file for a DDE linked object. You easily can change the source file from this dialog box. A shortcut is available, however.

Notice that when you select an object in an Excel document, and you have Formulas from the View Menu turned on, you see information about the object's source file. By editing this formula line, you can change the source file. Simply change the path to the one you want and press Enter at the end of the line.

Although this method is a valid shortcut, it is a very dangerous one. Do not try this method unless you are comfortable with it. In any case, you need to be sure that the path for the source file you are specifying is correct. If it is not, you might get unexpected results.

You should save your work before you attempt this method. Note also that this method works only if the link is to an object that is composed of an entire file. It works fine for a single graphic image in a file, but does not work for an object located in a file with more than one object.

A Practical DDE Example

Laura Woodward is a manager with Widgets Inc., and each year she is responsible for producing a report on regional sales. Laura usually represents this data in the form of a chart in a Word for Windows document.

Laura has become tired of constantly reproducing the same work. Because she uses this Excel chart in several documents, she decides to use a DDE link between her Word document and the Excel chart.

Using Excel, Laura imports the data for the various sales regions from exisiting Lotus 1-2-3 spreadsheet files. She formats the data to her liking, and creates what she hopes is an informative chart. Now that Laura has created the chart, she needs to connect it to her Word document, which contains the rest of the report.

First, she selects the chart image in Excel by clicking once on it. After the chart is selected, she can copy it to the Clipboard. To put a copy of the chart on the Clipboard, she chooses Edit, Copy from the main menu.

Now, Laura is finished with Excel for a while. She switches to her Word document and places the cursor where she wants the chart to be displayed. She chooses Edit, Paste Special from the main menu. The Paste Special dialog box appears, and she chooses Paste Link and Picture from the As box.

NOTE   Please notice that Excel and Word have very similar menus and dialog boxes. This property makes it much easier for you to switch between the two documents and perform similar tasks without having to learn any new system syntax.

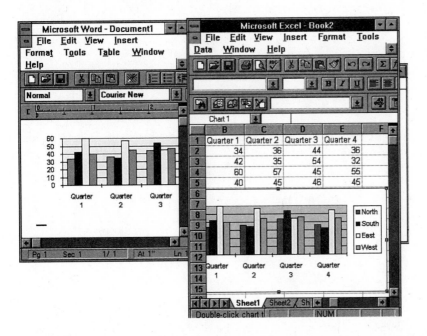

Figure 18.6
Sample chart linked between applications.

Now, Laura has chosen all the attributes for the link. The last thing she must do is formally establish the link. She clicks once on the OK button in the upper right corner of the Paste Special dialog box. An image of the chart is projected into her Word document.

As a final step, Laura wants to make sure that the image in her Word document will be updated whenever she changes the source chart in Excel. Under Edit, Links from the main menu, she sees that the link is set to Automatic. Now her document is ready to present to the vice president. Even if the north region's sales representative faxes in some last-minute corrections to his figures, Laura can update her report with only a few clicks of the mouse.

TIP

Every object in Excel has properties associated with it. To edit an object's properties quickly, you might want to use the object's *shortcut* menu. Place the cursor over the embedded or linked object and press the right mouse button. Notice the menu that appears. See figure 18.7 for an example of this shortcut menu.

Figure 18.7
The shortcut menu.

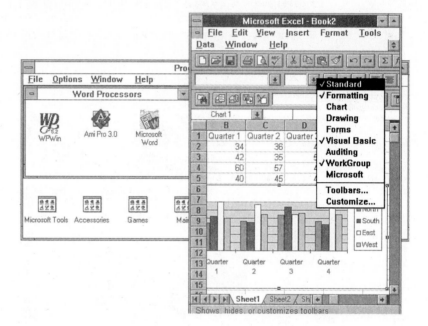

OLE 2 Links

OLE 2, like DDE, communicates between applications using links. OLE 2 links differ in some properties from DDE links, but the general idea is the same: links are just lines for communication.

Establishing an OLE 2 Link

Establishing an OLE 2 link is almost the same as establishing a DDE link, except that you choose Paste from the Paste Special dialog box rather than Paste Link.

To establish the OLE 2 link, follow these steps:

1. Open the source document.

2. Select the object in the source file that you want to link.

3. From the Edit menu, choose Copy to place a copy of the object on the Clipboard.

4. Return to the container document.

5. From the Edit menu, choose Paste Special. The Paste Special dialog box appears like the one you saw in figure 18.3.

6. The Paste Special dialog box offers several options:

   ✔ To establish an OLE link, choose Paste.

   ✔ In the As portion of the dialog box, specify the type of object you are linking.

   ✔ Check Display as Icon if you want the linked object to appear as an icon.

Although OLE 2 embedded objects are considered to be linked into the container document, OLE links differ from DDE links. DDE links point to the source file; OLE 2 links point to the source file's parent application. OLE 2 links do not appear when you edit the links in the Link Editor dialog box.

Another Method for Establishing OLE Links

Another way to establish OLE 2 links enables you to import objects without opening their associated application. This method also enables you to open an application without a source document, then create a new object as the source. The source in the latter case exists only within the destination document.

To import objects into Excel directly from a file, use the following steps:

1. From the Excel main menu, choose Insert, Object.

2. An **Object** dialog box appears with a list of available applications. The Object notebook contains two pages:

   ✔ The first page, called Create New, provides you with very few options (see fig. 18.8). If you want to create a new object using one of the applications shown, highlight the application by clicking on it, and then click on OK. The only other choice you have on this page is a toggle switch in the lower right corner that enables you to show the object as an icon. After you choose OK on this page, the application opens and you can create your new object.

   ✔ The second page, named Create from File, gives you more options than the Create New page (see fig. 18.9). Using the Create from File page, you can create new objects directly from the source file without opening the source file's parent application. The Create from File page offers an additional option not available on the Create New page: the option to create the object and use DDE to link it to the source file, instead of embedding it in your document.

Figure 18.8
The Create New
page of the
Object notebook.

Figure 18.9
The Create from
File page of the
Object notebook.

A Practical OLE Example

Suppose that Laura, after finishing her report, still is not satisfied with the chart that she linked into her Word for Windows document. She believes that she needs to add a little something to jazz up the document's appearance. She decides to embed a bit-mapped image of the company logo into her spreadsheet.

Because the bit map already exists, Laura decides to embed it directly from the file instead of opening the application first. From the Excel main menu, she chooses Insert, Object.

Because she is importing an image from an existing file, she brings the Create from File page to the foreground in the Object notebook by clicking on its page tab.

She specifies the file name of her bit map in the File Name box, then chooses the appropriate directory. Because Laura is embedding this object, she leaves the Link to File toggle switch blank.

Everything seems to be right, so she presses the OK button. After the CPU thinks about things for a few seconds, an image of the bitmap appears on her spreadsheet. Now she can manipulate the image for her needs by moving it around the worksheet, changing its size, or even editing it by double-clicking on the object itself.

Added Features of OLE 2

In the past, OLE worked in the following manner: after you established the link, if you double-clicked on the object in the destination document, the application used to create the object was activated. The original source file was not changed by this method—only the copy in the destination document was modified. OLE 2 performs the same function. OLE 2 offers some new features, however.

Dragging and Dropping Objects

One of the most interesting and potentially useful new tools in OLE 2 is the *Drag and Drop* feature. Drag and Drop enables you to click on an object in the source document and drag it to the destination document, eliminating the need to bother with Copy and Paste Special. Until more applications are developed that use OLE 2, though, this feature will not be very useful.

Drag and Drop is supported only when both the destination application and the source application support OLE 2. Most Windows applications do not support OLE 2 currently. But as new versions of applications are developed, the Drag and Drop tool should become very effective.

In-Place Application Activation

Another new feature of OLE 2 is *in-place activation* of applications. In the past, when you opened an OLE object, the source application opened in a separate window.

When you double-click on an OLE 2 object, the source application opens. Instead of opening in a separate window, however, the source application's menu options appear on the Excel main menu. And instead of choosing Exit and Return to go back to Excel when you finish editing the object, you just click anywhere outside of the object.

Like Drag and Drop, this feature of OLE 2 is supported only when both source and container applications support OLE 2 embedding.

Using Links with Macros

Excel enables you to automate linking and embedding through the use of macros, or more specifically, Visual Basic for Applications (VBA), which is Excel 5's macro programming language. This automation tool is particularly useful if you frequently transfer data between applications. Visual Basic gives you the power to automate these tasks and makes it simple enough for a non-programmer to understand. In the following sections, you will learn how to:

✔ Combine links with macros

✔ Create a sample link/macro

Combining Links with Macros

The following simple example demonstrates the way macros can make an impact on DDE and OLE 2 links. In this particular case, you place a bit-mapped image created by Windows PaintBrush in an Excel document, then assign a macro to a button to update the link. In other words, you automate the update of your image.

Note that Excel 5 is the first application to support VBA. Therefore, macros written in Excel 5 will not work with external applications that do not support VBA. As more applications are developed, though, this tool will be very useful. Although a specific example is given in the following section, it does not work as described. Macros in Excel 5 only work with external applications if that application also supports VBA. The current version of PaintBrush does not support VBA. The example is theoretically correct, except that the macro does not actually run with this external application after you have designed it. If, in the following example, you tried to access an application that supports Visual Basic, the example would work. The logic is sound, and the explanation is valid.

Although this list of steps might seem rather long, the linking process is very simple. Just follow these steps:

1. Enter PaintBrush and create a simple bit-mapped image.

2. Save the image and close PaintBrush.

3. Open Excel and place the cursor in the cell at the point at which you want to insert the new image.

4. From the main menu, choose Insert, Object. The Object notebook appears on the screen.

5. Click on the Create from File tab. This page appears, as shown in figure 18.9.

6. Insert the path and file name of the bit-mapped image you created in the appropriate area of the notebook.

7. Be sure Link to File is checked. (The Link to File option tells Excel to create a DDE link rather than embed the object.) Now click on the OK button. The image appears on your worksheet.

8. The next step is to record a macro that updates the image from the source file. From the main menu, choose Record Macro, Record New Macro.

9. When the Macro dialog box appears, give the macro any name that you desire and click on the OK button. You now are recording a macro. The Stop Recording button appears somewhere on your screen.

10. Now, you need to record the updating of your link. From the main menu, choose Edit, and then Links. The Links dialog box appears on the screen.

11. Highlight the link to your image by clicking once on the appropriate link name. The link probably is already highlighted.

12. After the link you want to update is highlighted, click on the Update Now button. After a few seconds, the image updates itself.

13. Choose the OK button to close the Links dialog box.

14. Click on the Stop Recording button. Your macro has been recorded.

15. After the macro is recorded, you need to associate it with a button on the Worksheet. To create a Button, you must use the Drawing toolbar, so activate it by placing the mouse pointer anywhere in the toolbar area and clicking the right mouse button. A list of toolbars appears. Choose Drawing. The Drawing toolbar appears.

16. Click once on the Create tool in the lower left corner of the toolbar. The cursor changes to a crosshair.

Building Applications

TIP

If you put the mouse cursor over any individual tool on the Drawing toolbar, a display under the cursor shows you the function of the button.

17. Drag the pointer across the area in the worksheet in which you want your button to appear (see fig 18.10). When you release the mouse button, the Assign Macro dialog box appears.

18. Enter the name of the macro you just defined into the Assign Macro dialog box.

19. Click on OK. The macro now is assigned to the button; each time you press the button, it updates your image.

NOTE

You can modify the physical appearance of the button easily, but that point is not relevant to this chapter. For more information on using macros, buttons, and their properties, please refer to Parts IV and V of this book.

Figure 18.10

A button assigned to a macro.

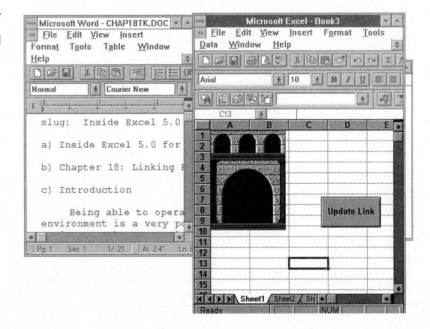

Diagnosing and Correcting Linking Problems

A few problems might occur when you are using DDE and OLE 2 with Excel. The majority of these problems come from the working environment, but Excel itself has a few problems. Software design is not always perfect, and might never be. The capability to work around a problem, however, is another trademark of good software.

Until the computer industry standardizes a particular data-exchange format, problems are sure to exist in interpreting data between applications. Humans, after all, have been speaking for thousands of years, and still miscommunicate, even when speaking the same language. Excel 5 has done an impressive job of implementing its DDE and OLE 2 utilities. There seem to be very few bugs in the application itself; most problems you have will probably occur as Excel works with external applications and the disk storage environment. Some of these problems are listed in the following sections.

Movement of DDE Linked Files

One of the main requirements for DDE is a static disk storage environment. Because the container document points to the source file specifically if that source file is moved or deleted, the container document cannot maintain the link. This problem is easy to fix, but if you store your DDE source files on a network, your files might be moved without your knowledge. Keep this potential problem in mind when you create your links.

The solution for this problem is simply to move the source file to the correct location specified by the link, or change the link address to the correct address for the source file.

You can choose any operating environment to move the file. If you want to change the link address, consult the section in this chapter titled "Updating a Link."

DDE Linked Data does not Update

Another problem that occasionally occurs with DDE is when the source file is changed and the container document does not automatically update. Again, the solution is not difficult.

The highest probability here is that the link was somehow changed to a Manual update. An error is not occurring, but Excel does not know that it is supposed to update the container image automatically.

To correct this problem, update the link properties as discussed in the "Updating a Link" section of this chapter.

No Response from Embedded Object

One area OLE 2 sometimes has problems in is the inactivity of embedded objects. When you double-click on the embedded object to edit it, sometimes nothing happens.

Infrequently, and without much reason, OLE 2 seems to forget to which application an embedded object is linked. In other words, OLE 2 might forget that a Word document should be associated with Microsoft Word.

Two explanations come to mind. One is that the linked object was not established correctly in the first place. The second is that OLE 2 cannot find the application at all. Check your system to make sure that the desired application is still there. Again, this might be a problem on networks when they are down for maintenance or are being remapped.

Inserting Graphics

One of the significant problems that Excel 5 seems to have is creating a DDE link with graphic images. When you try to use the Copy and then Paste Special method for creating a link, Excel tells you that it cannot paste the link. The Paste Picture Links option under Edit give you the same result.

Excel can link to a graphic, but for some reason, it does not like to do so using the Paste Special Option. If you experience a problem importing graphics, try the following method:

1. Choose Insert, Object from the Excel main menu.

2. When the Links dialog box appears, switch to Create from File.

3. Highlight the file that you want to link to your current document.

4. Before you click on OK, make sure that you select Link to File. Now, press OK. The selected object is now linked into your Excel document.

5. The source application probably activates itself at this point. It might not work correctly when Excel opens it. If the application is not working correctly, close the application and run it again. It should load correctly the second time. Open the source file in the application and the link should be established and correct.

This problem of importing graphics might be something specific with a non-OLE 2 application. As more applications become OLE 2-compliant, these importing problems are likely to cease.

Chapter Snapshot

This chapter introduces you to Microsoft's Visual Basic for Applications (VBA), Excel version. With VBA, you now can write applications in Excel and use them in other applications that will support VBA, such as Microsoft Powerpoint, Access, and future versions of Word for Windows. You'll learn the following in this chapter:

✔ Why Excel has Visual Basic for Applications

✔ Writing Visual Basic applications

✔ Debugging Visual Basic applications

✔ Using a sample VBA application provided on the *Inside Excel 5 for Windows* bonus disk

VBA represents an exciting new depature for Microsoft. *Inside Excel 5 for Windows* is one of the very first books to provide comprehensive coverage of this new inter-application programming technology.

Using Excel Visual Basic

Included with Excel 5 is the Microsoft Visual Basic Programming System, Applications Edition. This development system, more commonly referred to as *VB for Apps (or VBA)*, represents a radical departure from Excel's XLM Macro language (which you can still use in this version of Excel). VBA provides compatibility and functional equivalence with the XLM language, but it uses an object-oriented approach and a complete structured programming language, including explicitly declared variables.

VBA is considered a core technology by Microsoft and will be available in all of their major applications, such as Excel, Word for Windows, Powerpoint, and Project. It will be improved and enhanced in future releases of these products, while the current macro languages, like XLM, will remain static. It is recommended that you write new applications in VBA.

As you read this chapter and begin experimenting with this new programming system, you need to decide whether to switch to VBA. The benefits of making this change, however, might not be entirely obvious, because they are not as quantifiable as a simple improvement in speed or functionality.

A historical perspective is helpful in understanding the need for VBA, the problems it solves, and why it will be important for the types of applications you will be developing now and in the future.

The Rationale behind VBA

When the personal computer was first introduced, software and development tools were very much constrained by the limitations of the hardware. Processors were slow, memory was expensive, and disk storage was small. The early products that became successful provided a macro capability that enabled individuals to customize the products to deliver specific solutions.

These macro capabilities seem arcane by today's standards, but at the time, they were superior in their capabilities compared to mainframes or minicomputers.

In the Beginning: Macros

Typically, these solutions were singularly focused and provided a specific function for a specific problem. Macros were written in one application only; any integration between applications, such as a spreadsheet and a word processor, was done through files or simple cut and paste. Developers would often focus on learning one application and its macro language well, and then use that application as a tool to perform all types of solutions.

As the personal computer industry evolved and became more sophisticated, hardware and operating system limitations became less critical. The newer graphical interfaces made applications much easier to use. Multiple applications could be running at the same time. Each of these applications focused on a particular type of functionality, such as that of a spreadsheet, word processor, graphics, or database.

The focus in the industry was to produce the "best of breed" applications. In accordance with this, virtually every successful product developed its own macro language to allow customization, automation of repetitive tasks, and development of custom applications. Individuals used these macro languages to provide solutions to business problems, often combining several applications to provide the overall solution.

This resulted in an application-centric computing model in which functions were performed within an application. A business problem, for example, may require number crunching and graphing. On the application-centric model, this would be accomplished by using a spreadsheet application's macro language. The problem may also require text processing or letter generation, which would be handled with a macro language in a word processor.

Even though these different applications can be integrated closely using facilities such as DDE (Dynamic Data Exchange), the user is still aware when functionality switches from the spreadsheet to the word processor. Menus, display windows, and the presentation of data all change as the application changes.

The developer is even more aware of the change when processing switches between applications. Each application has a specific macro language unique to that application. Developing the overall solution often requires knowing and using several macro languages.

Application Compatibility Becomes Possible

The personal computer industry has evolved and created more sophisticated operating systems. Hardware limitations are no more than temporary. New standards, such as OLE Automation, allow the integration of several applications in a seamless manner. Products like Microsoft Office provide this capability right out of the box. The computing model is in the process of shifting from its current application-centric focus to a document-centric focus.

This new focus enables the user to view information in a context that brings together all the information about a specific subject. If part of the information is text-based, it will be handled by the word processor. If part of the information, by its nature, is presented in a chart or graph, the spreadsheet software will be responsible. To the user, these are just pieces of what appears to be one document.

This document-centric model will become more prevalent and commonplace. This level of integration might seem 'nice to have' today; soon it will be expected by the user community.

For the developer or sophisticated user, providing solutions in this model presents formidable challenges. A solution that would span three or four applications requires the provider to be fluent in the macro languages for each of these packages. The macro languages, developed with a 'best of breed' focus, may all be very different from each other. The solution provider does not only have to be able to develop in each of these languages, but has to maintain skill in each of them to provide ongoing support.

A simple, quick solution is often difficult to provide for users of several application customization languages. Much learning and testing has to be done first to make sure all these different applications and different macro languages can work together. Often, the solution is limited to the capabilities provided by the weakest of the macro languages.

This situation creates a barrier to moving forward and developing the solutions that people want. It also raises the level of skill required for someone to develop successfully in this environment. Removing barriers and making products easier to use are two things that Microsoft does extremely well. Hence, the development of VBA.

Taking Advantage of Visual Basic for Applications

The Visual Basic Programming System provides a common development environment across all major Microsoft applications. In many ways, the use of VBA is analogous to the graphical user interface. The first time you use a graphical user interface, it is not always obvious how to do things. The advantage of a GUI and the reason why it always is referred to as intuitive is that the second application is easy to learn because it works similarly to the first.

The same is true with VBA. There will be a traditionally lengthy learning curve for the first application (such as Excel), but the second application will be much easier. By investing the time to learn the Visual Basic Programming System, you will be developing a valuable skill, not only now, but in the years to come. With VBA, you will be able to develop sophisticated, supportable solutions without always being on the learning curve.

The purpose of this chapter is to make the learning curve as short and flat as possible. The areas of difficulty that you will experience depend greatly on your background.

Visual Basic for Experienced Macro Users

If you are an experienced Excel user who has programmed using the XLM macro language, you will probably have the most difficulty with the syntax and object-oriented nature of Visual Basic. You already know what Excel can do, but your challenge will be to figure out how to do it in this new language. Pay special attention to the concepts and programming models presented in this chapter. They differ from those used by the XLM language, and if you think in terms of XLM, you will probably have difficulties.

TIP

If you are familiar with the XLM macro language, you may find it helpful to use the macro recorder. This will generate Visual Basic macro code as tasks are performed. A review of this code can be a great learning aid.

If you are an experienced Visual Basic programmer, the concepts and programming language will already be familiar to you. Your challenge will be to become familiar with all the objects, properties, and methods available to you in Excel. In Visual Basic, you start with a blank form and begin adding controls. A finite number of objects, each with its own set of properties and methods, can easily be determined. In Excel Visual Basic, you may be overwhelmed by the number of objects. Even starting with a blank workbook, thousands of objects are available.

The best method for gaining object experience is to use the Object Browser. The Object Browser is available from the <u>V</u>iew menu or by pressing F2 while working in a Visual Basic module sheet. If you select the Excel library from the combo box on the top (see fig. 19.1), you will be shown a list box of all objects and another box of the properties and methods associated with the currently selected object in that list.

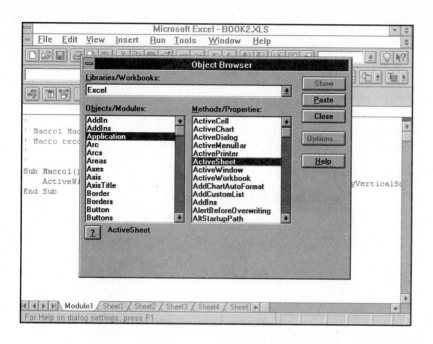

Figure 19.1
The Object
Browser.

V

Building Applications

Visual Basic for the Inexperienced Macro User

For an Excel user new to programming, the Basic language is an excellent choice as the first programming language to learn. It has a straightforward syntax that can be mastered quickly. The previous chapter contains a section on designing a macro that is referenced in this chapter. The concepts presented here also apply to Visual Basic programs.

Before you begin a project, define what you are going to do and sketch a quick flowchart of how you will accomplish it. Study the concepts and the sample program presented later in this chapter. Then select a task for your first Excel Visual Basic program.

The Structure of a VB Program

This section presents the concepts on which Microsoft Visual Basic for Applications are based. An understanding of these concepts makes it much easier to learn and recognize the approach used in Visual Basic applications.

The Microsoft Visual Basic Programming System is object-oriented and procedure based. It provides a standard, straightforward programming syntax to control program flow, assign values to the properties of objects, execute the methods of the objects (properties and methods are described later), and detect and handle errors.

A VB program is organized into small procedures. Each procedure should be limited in size and focused on performing a specific task. Procedures may call other procedures. This allows complex tasks to be broken down into small steps that are executed in order. Breaking programs into small pieces like this makes them easier to develop and debug, and much easier to support in the future.

> When you mentally picture a procedure, you should think of it as a black box. You pass it a limited amount of information (called *arguments*), it performs some processing on that information or executes instructions on available objects, then returns (at most) one piece of information.

The Use and Structure of Procedures in Visual Basic

Two basic types of procedures are in Visual Basic: Sub procedures and Function procedures. These two types of procedures are very similar and use the same programming syntax. Each serves a slightly different purpose. The differences between the two are highlighted in the following table.

Sub Procedures	Function Procedures
May be called directly from the macro menu or assigned to a tool-bar, button, or a graphic image.	Cannot be called directly. Must be called from another procedure.
Does not return a value.	Returns a value.
Generally used for main control procedures.	Generally used for small specific procedures that enable the calling procedure to check the returned result.

Recognizing Sub Procedures

The syntax for a Sub procedure is as follows:

```
w begin with the Sub command naming the procedure and its arguments,
w    explicit declarations of variables local to the procedure,
w    program code necessary to perform the task
w end the procedure with the End Sub command.
```

As an example, here is a simple Sub procedure to toggle the display of row and column headings:

```
Sub ToggleRowColHeadings()
    ' Comments begin with a single quote. It is a good idea to
    ' place comments in your program to explain what you are doing
    ' and why you are doing it. This will make it easier to
    ' support later on.
```

```
        ActiveWindow.DisplayHeadings = Not ActiveWindow.DisplayHeadings
    End Sub
```

The first line of this Sub procedure is the *Sub statement*. All Sub procedures begin with the word Sub. This command uniquely names the procedure so that it can be called by other procedures or assigned to buttons, menus, or toolbars. The name of this Sub procedure is ToggleRowColHeadings. The parentheses following the procedure name are to enclose any arguments passed to the Sub procedure. For this procedure, there are no arguments.

The next four lines of the preceding procedure are comments. *Comments* begin with a single quote, and they have no effect on the actual execution of the procedure. Comments are helpful for documenting the procedure, although placing four lines of comments for one line of code is overkill. Nevertheless, it is good practice to include comments in your programs because it makes it much easier to support and debug later.

The next line in the simple procedure is the only line of executable code: an *assignment statement*. This line assigns the DisplayHeadings property (object properties are discussed later in this section) to the opposite value of the current setting. If the heading is currently True (which means display row and column headings), it will be set to False.

The last line is the *End Sub statement*. This is required for all Sub procedures—it denotes the end of the procedure.

Recognizing Function Procedures

The syntax for a Function procedure is similar to that of a Sub procedure. A function procedure begins with the Function command and names the procedure and its arguments. A *function procedure* contains explicit declarations of variables local to the procedure. It also contains program code necessary to perform the task. A function procedure assigns the return value to the name of the function. The procedure ends with the End Function command. The following sample code helps illustrate a function procedure:

```
w begin with the Function command, naming the procedure and its
  ➥arguments,
w    contain explicit declarations of variables local to the procedure,
w    program code necessary to perform the task
w    assign the return value to the name of the function
w end the procedure with the End Function command.
```

As an example, here is a simple Function procedure to accept a date and convert it to the date of the Monday of the same week.

```
Function Monday(CheckDate As Date)
    ' Set Error Checking to Continue and return the error value
    On Error Resume Next
    ' Subtracting or adding an integer to a Date will move the date
    ' by that number of days. The WeekDay function returns the day
```

```
' of the week as an integer from 1 to 7, with 1 being Sunday.
' Assigning this value to Monday, which is the name of this
' function, will cause this value to be returned to the calling
' procedure.
Monday = CheckDate - (WeekDay(CheckDate) - 2)
End Function
```

The first line of this Function procedure is the *Function statement*. All Function procedures begin with this command. This command uniquely names the procedure so that it can be called by other procedures. In this case, the name of the Function procedure is Monday. Following the function name is one argument, called CheckDate, passed to the procedure. Specifying 'As Date' forces the argument to be a Date type when it is accessed in the procedure code.

The comments that follow the Function command have no effect on the execution of the code. The next line (**On Error Resume Next**), however, sets the error checking to continue if an error is encountered. In this case, as error would be caused by an invalid date being passed to the procedure. If a bad date is passed, this procedure will simply return a #VALUE error. The checking of this error, if required, is the responsibility of the calling program.

The next line of code contains an expression that calculates the date of the Monday of the week of the date passed. In the calculation, the standard mathematical precedence of operators is used—in other words, whatever is in parentheseis is calculated first, and then multiplication before addition. The calculation and assignment can reside and be processed on the same line, which is a common practice in the Visual Basic language.

To illustrate how the sample function procedure operates, suppose it is November 12, 1993 (a Friday). Here is how the line would be resolved:

Monday = "11/12/93" - (**WeekDay("11/12/93")** - 2)	First, resolve the WeekDay function which will be 6 since it is a Friday
Monday = "11/12/93" - (**6 - 2**)	Resolve the 6-2 because it is in parentheses.
Monday = **"11/12/93" - 4**	Subtract 4 days from the date passed as an argument
Monday = **"11/08/93"**	Assign the calculated date to Monday

By assigning the calculated date to a variable with the same name as the Function procedure name, this will cause Visual Basic to return the value of the calculated date to the calling Procedure. If this procedure were called from another procedure in this manner, as in the following, the variable sdate would be set to November 8, 1993 after the Monday procedure ends:

```
sdate = Monday("11/12/93")
```

The last line is the End Function statement. This is required for all Function procedures, denoting the end of the procedure.

Special Function Procedures

A special type of Function procedure can be used to create a function that can be called directly from a formula in a cell of an Excel worksheet. In the worksheet, it would appear no different from any of the standard Excel functions like SUM, MAX, or MIN.

A user-defined function has the same general syntax as a normal Function procedure. It is limited, though, in the types of things that can be done in the procedure. The purpose of a user-defined function is to accept information on arguments, perform calculations or manipulations on those arguments, and return a single value.

Hence, a user-defined function may not alter the state of Excel or the worksheet. If you attempt to perform those types of actions in a user-defined function, an error will be returned.

An example of a user-defined function is shown here. This function calculates a salary based on the hourly rate, the number of regular hours, the number of overtime hours, and the overtime pay factor.

```
Function Salary(PayRate As Double, RegHours As Double,
             OTHours As Double, OTFactor as Double)
    ' Assigning the value calculated to Salary, which is the name
    ' of this procedure will cause that value to be returned to the
    ' cell from which this function was called
    Salary = (RegHours * PayRate) + (OTHours * PayRate * OTFactor)
End Function
```

User-defined functions are not difficult to create and provide value to the Excel user. Instead of having long, cryptic formulas in the cells of the spreadsheet, a user-defined function can be used to make the sheet much more intuitive for the user and simpler to develop.

Working with Objects

As mentioned, VBA is an object-oriented programming system. The term object-oriented may evoke different images. Many attempts to provide an object-oriented programming system have been academic in nature, religiously adhering to the principals of object-oriented programming. The result was often a system that was not successful because it was extremely difficult to use and debug.

To program successfully in Visual Basic, you must think in terms of objects. An *object* is a general term that refers to anything you are able to control through a Visual Basic program. In Excel, a worksheet, a range, and a button are all examples of objects.

VBA is a practical implementation of the object-oriented model. Once you understand the concepts on which it is based, you should find it powerful, flexible, and easy to maintain.

Using Object Properties

In Excel, each object will have a set of characteristics that can be interrogated or assigned. These characteristics are called *properties*. Properties determine the appearance and function of an object.

For instance, a Range object has a Formula, Font, Row, Column, and Value property. By changing any of these properties, you would change the range on the worksheet; referring to any of these properties returns the current value of the property.

Referring back to the ToggleRowColHeadings example procedure gives an example of the use of object properties.

```
ActiveWindow.DisplayHeadings = Not ActiveWindow.DisplayHeadings
```

A window object—in the preceding example, the ActiveWindow—has a property called DisplayHeadings. On the right hand side of the expression is ActiveWindow.DisplayHeadings, which returns the current setting of that property. Naming the same property on the left hand side of the expression tells Visual Basic to assign a new value to that property.

Because the evaluation of the right hand side of the expression is the opposite of the current setting, the value of the DisplayHeadings property will be toggled. A change to this property causes the screen display to change; it either shows or does not show the row and column headings. The appearance of the object—in this case a window object—is changed as the property of the object is changed.

Using Object Methods

In Excel, objects also have methods. *Methods* are actions that objects can perform. For example, a worksheet object has a PrintOut method and a Calculate method. A range object has a CheckSpelling and a Sort method.

To have the object perform its action, you simply need to mention the name of the method (kind of like "There's no place like home" but you only have to say it once).

For example, the following line causes the active worksheet to recalculate its formulas:

```
ActiveSheet.Calculate
```

Some methods simply perform an action. Others perform an action and return an object that resulted from that action. For example, the following line first searches the range of cells from A1 through A15 to find the first occurrence of the string 'Office'.

```
Range("A1:A15").Find(What:="Office")
```

If this method successfully finds a match, it will return a Range object describing the cell in which it found the match.

Using Object Containers

In an object-oriented programming environment, one of the main tasks of the developer is to name the object correctly. In the preceding section, you read that if you can correctly name an object and its property, you can get or set the value of the property. If you can correctly name an object and its method, you can force that method to take its specific action.

NOTE This is the power of the object-oriented approach. If the developer can simply name an object, any of its properties or methods can be accessed. This is not always as simple as it seems, though, because of the large number of objects. As an abstract example, the process of finding the Phone Number property of a person object may seem like a simple task—you look in the phone book. If the person object is John Smith and 100 John Smiths are in the phone book, however, you quickly realize that more information is needed to find the John Smith you are looking for.

Fortunately, Visual Basic uses the container model to make unique naming of objects simpler. An Application object contains Workbook objects which contain Worksheet objects which contain Range objects.

The syntax for naming objects lists the containers left to right in order from the outermost container inward, with each container name separated by a period. Here is an example:

```
Application.Workbook("Timesht").Worksheet("Assignments").Range("A1")
```

This example identifies a Range object on the Assignment worksheet in the Timesht workbook in the Excel application.

It is not necessary to provide the full name for every container object all the way back to the Application. It is only necessary to supply the container names if they are required to identify specifically the object.

For instance, if the Assignments worksheet is the currently active worksheet, then either of the following two lines refer to the same Range object:

```
Application.Workbook("Timesht").Worksheet("Assignments").Range("A1")
```

```
Range("A1")
```

Declaring Variables and Constants

Whenever you work in Visual Basic, it is always a good practice to declare all the program variables you use. Program variables in Visual Basic are program elements that have a name, a data type and a value. To declare a variable one of three simple statements must be used: Dim (short for Dimension), Static, or Public. The syntax of these statements is as follows:

```
Dim variablename As variabledatatype
Static variablename As variabledatatype
Public variablename As variabledatatype
```

For example, to declare a variable called LastName that will hold a text string containing the last name of someone, use the following statement:

```
Dim LastName As String
```

In this statement, LastName is the variable name that will be referenced by the Visual Basic code. The data type is set to String, telling Visual Basic that this variable will contain text.

It is not as necessary to declare a variable in Visual Basic as it is in many other languages. If a variable name is referenced but was not explicitly declared, Visual Basic automatically creates a variable with that name and a datatype of Variant. A *Variant* is a wild card variable that can represent any of the Visual Basic standard data types.

Table 19.1 shows the data types available in Visual Basic for Excel.

Table 19.1
Data Types for Declaring Variables

Purpose	Visual Basic Data Type
Text Types	
Variable Strings	String
Fixed Length Strings	String * n (where n is length)
Number Types	
Small Whole numbers (between -32K and +32K)	Integer
Large Whole numbers	Long
Small Number with Fractional Parts	Single
Large Numbers with Fractional Parts	Double
Values of Money	Currency

Purpose	Visual Basic Data Type
Other Types	
Date and Time Values	Date
True/False or Yes/No Values	Boolean
Visual Basic Object	Object

If it is not required that variables be declared, and a program will run just fine if they are not, why declare them? By declaring variables, VBA can know more about your program and, therefore, provide a higher level of error checking. It is always better to have the computer catch errors.

To illustrate the benefits of declaring variables, examine a typical error. Suppose that you are calling a function that requires two arguments: a string and an integer. Inadvertently, you switch the order of the arguments so that the integer is placed where the string is supposed to go. If you had declared the variables so as to define explicitly the variable as an integer, Excel Visual Basic would be able to check the arguments and recognize that a string is expected where an integer is being passed. Excel would then return a Type Mismatch error and highlight the argument in error before it even calls the function. Declaring variables provides a much simpler means to correct the error than to take time stepping through the debugger, checking values, and trying to determine the cause of the problem.

Examining Different Scopes of Variables

How and where you declare a variable specifies the scope of the variable. The scope of the variable defines the areas of your program where the variable will have meaning.

A variable declared within a procedure is considered a local variable that is available only to that procedure. A variable declared outside a procedure (typically at the beginning of a module) is considered a module variable and is available to any procedure in that module. A variable declared outside a procedure that is declared with the Public statement instead of the Dim statement is available to all the procedures in all the modules in Excel.

The use of the Static statement instead of the Dim statement for a local variable enables that variable to retain its value between calls to that procedure.

Constants are very similar to variables. They can have the same local, module, and public scope as variables. The difference is that the value assigned to a constant may not be changed through the course of running the program. By convention, the name of the constant should be in all capital letters. This will help you identify constants in your programs.

In the following excerpt from a module, the variables newSheetName, sdate, and WeekCount are local variables that have a meaning only within the CopyTemplateForNewWeek procedure. Because WeekCount is declared Static, it will not be reinitialized each time the procedure is called. OTFACTOR is a constant declared with a value of 1.5 that is available to all procedures in the module. EmployeeID is a public string variable available to all procedures in all modules in Excel.

```
' Declare Public Variable
Public EmployeeID as String * 3      ' The ID of the Employee


' Declare Constants for this Module
Const OTFACTOR = 1.5 ' The Overtime factor is Time and a Half


Sub CopyTemplateForNewWeek()
     ' Declare Variables local to this procedure
     Dim newSheetName As String
     Dim sdate As Date
     Static WeekCount As Integer
     ' Procedure Code ...
End Sub
```

Controlling Program Execution

Visual Basic for Excel also provides a full programming language with constructs for conditionally executing parts of your procedure and looping.

The main statements for conditionally executing parts of a procedure are If and Select Case. The If statement should be used if only one or two actions are to be taken based on the evaluation of the test condition. The Select Case statement should be used if more than two actions will be taken based on the value of the test condition.

Here is an example of an appropriate use of If:

```
If CurrentHour > 12 Then
     greeting = "Good Afternoon"
Else
     greeting = "Good Morning"
End If
```

This construct will set a different value for greeting depending on whether it is before or after noon.

The select case statement enables the program to check for more conditions and respond accordingly. Here is an example of an appropriate use of Select:

```
Select Case CurrentHour
     Case Is < 4    ' earlier than 4 in the morning
     greeting = "What are you doing here now?"
     Case 5 To 11 ' the morning hours
     greeting = "Good Morning"
     Case 12 ' Noon time
     greeting = "Shouldn't you be at lunch?"
     Case 13, 14, 15, 16 ' afternoon hours
     greeting = "Good Afternoon"
     Case Else
     greeting = "Good Evening"
End Select
```

Looping is primarily accomplished through a Do-Loop structure or a For-Next structure. Do-Loop is used when the looping continues until a condition changes; For-Next is used when the exact number of loops is known before the loop begins.

This example illustrates the differences between these two structures:

```
' Loop until a blank cell is found
cRow = 1
Do Until ActiveSheet.Cells(cRow,1).Value = ""
     cRow = cRow + 1
Loop

' Beep three times
For BeepCount = 1 to 3
     Beep
Next BeepCount
```

Error Checking

Three types of errors can be encountered by your Visual Basic for Excel program:

✔ **Syntax errors.** Fundamental errors in the usage of the language of Visual Basic.

✔ **Run time errors.** Errors that occur during the running of the Visual Basic program that produce an error condition.

✔ **Logic errors.** Errors that are not be detected by Excel, but cause the wrong results.

Finding Syntax Errors

Syntax errors are the simplest to find. Excel sends notification when the error is detected so that it can be corrected. These errors will be detected either immediately after you enter the line and move to the next line, or immediately before the procedure is executed. These are the simplest to find and correct, and if you are going to have errors, these are the type to have. Explicitly declaring variables and arguments enables Excel to perform more in-depth checking of your code.

Finding Run Time Errors

Run time errors are not detected until the program is executed. The syntax of the code is correct, but something in the evaluation of the code is incorrect. These types of errors are commonly caused by passing invalid values of arguments to procedures, or by incorrectly naming an object. When an error of this type occurs, Excel immediately displays a message showing a description of the error detected (see fig. 19.2) and the line number of the code causing the error.

Figure 19.2
An error box.

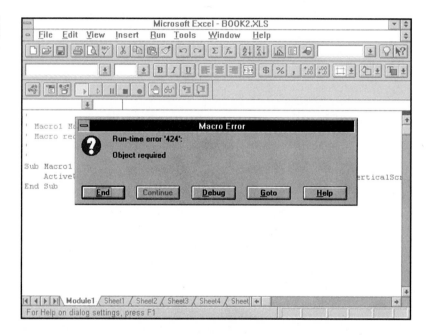

When the error is displayed, you are given the option to go to (use Goto) the line of your program causing the error. This is a great aid to the developer of a program in trying to detect and correct the error. If these types of errors are the result of mistakes in the program, they should be corrected so that this error does not occur again.

Sometimes, though, errors are encountered during the execution of a program that are normal. For instance, you need to check to see if a file exists before you write over it. If the file has not been previously created, the execution of the **Dir** command will result in a File Does Not Exist Error. In this case, it is not a good thing to present a novice user with a cryptic error message and the option to go from their spreadsheet directly into the Visual Basic module.

Excel for Visual Basic has a facility for detecting and handling run-time error conditions. The **On Error** command enables the developer to take control of an error situation and gracefully recover. The **On Error** command tells Excel what to do if it encounters a run-time error by providing two choices:

✔ **On Error Resume Next.** Just ignore the error and continue with the next line of code.

✔ **On Error Goto** *ErrorHandlingProcedure*. When the error occurs, automatically call the procedure named.

In an error handling procedure, a code denoting the error that occurred is stored in a Public variable named Err. Conditional execution (such as the **Select Case** statement) can be used to take different actions based on different errors. Three choices are available for proceeding from the Error handler:

✔ **Resume.** Return to the line causing the error and try again.

✔ **Resume Next.** Return to the line immediately following the one causing the error and continue execution.

✔ **End.** Halt execution of the program.

Here is a simple example of trapping and handling a run time error.

```
Sub DeleteFile(fname As String)
     'Set the Error trapping
     On Error GoTo ErrorRoutine

     'Delete the file
     Kill fname

     'Exit this procedure
     Exit Sub
ErrorRoutine:
     MsgBox "Unable to Delete " + fname + " - " + Error(Err)
     Resume Next
End Sub
```

Detecting Logic Errors

Logic errors (usually caused by the lack thereof) are generally the toughest to detect and fix. If the code is syntactically correct and the results, though valid, are incorrect, you probably have a logic problem.

If you write, for example, a function to calculate Monday's date of the current week and it returns September 23, 1955 after executing without error, you probably have a logic problem.

Often you can find logic problems by meticulously going over your program. It may be that you simply added when you should have subtracted. Occasionally, however, the problem is tougher to find and requires the use of better tools.

> Excel 5 contains an excellent debugging tool for Visual Basic. The debugger enables you to step line by line through your program examining variables and object property values as it is executed. This provides a powerful way to determine the cause of the logic error. This debugger is demonstrated in the next section.

Creating a Visual Basic Procedure

Now that you have been exposed to the concepts of programming in VBA, it is time to give it a test drive. This section will acquaint you with the programming environment used in Excel Visual Basic.

In Excel 5, the tab of a workbook that will store a Visual Basic program is called a *module*. A primary difference in the appearance of a module when compared to a worksheet is the Visual Basic program is not oriented to rows and columns of data, but rather to lines of code.

To begin a Visual Basic program, you first must follow a few steps to create a module.

1. Create a new workbook by selecting File, New from the Excel menu.

2. Insert a Visual Basic module into the workbook by selecting the Insert, Macro menu option, then select the Module option of the tearaway menu.

At this point, you should be looking at a blank Visual Basic Module sheet. If so, you are ready to begin writing aVisual Basic procedure. The best way to begin is by recording the procedure, then modifying it to perform a specific task.

Recording a Procedure

To record a procedure, follow these steps:

1. Begin by selecting the Tools, Record Macro, Mark Position for Recording menu option. This sets the current position in the Visual Basic module you just created as the spot where the recorded code will be placed.

2. Select the Tools, Record Macro, Record New Macro... option to display the Record New Macro dialog box shown in figure 19.3. In this dialog box, you can name your macro.

3. Click on OK to select the default macro name. You are ready to begin recording your macro. Notice that on the left side of the Excel status bar, the word **Recording** displays to show that you are in record mode. A button also appears that enables you to stop recording at any time.

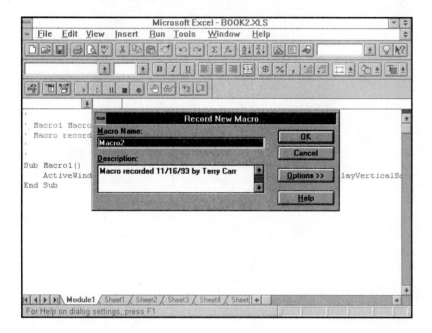

Figure 19.3
Give your macro a name and a brief description.

4. Again, access the Tools menu and select the Options button. When the dialog box displays, select the View tab. On this tab (see fig. 19.4), an area named Window Options contains a toggle switch to determine whether the vertical scroll bar is displayed. Click on the Vertical Scroll Bar switch to toggle its value.

5. Click on OK to accept the change in the View options you just made. Notice that the code you recorded now appears in the Visual Basic module.

6. Click on the Stop button to end the recording of the macro. The Stop button is the button that appeared in its own toolbar when you first selected the Tools, Record Macro menu. Your Visual Basic module should now look something like this:

```
'
' Macro1 Macro
' Macro recorded 11/16/93 by Terry Carr
'
'
Sub Macro1()
      ActiveWindow.DisplayVerticalScrollBar = False
End Sub
```

Figure 19.4
The Options
dialog box has a
number of tabbed
sections.

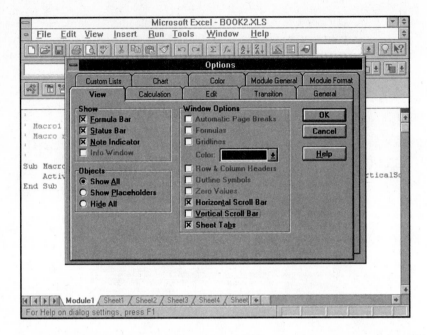

You now have a working procedure in a Visual Basic module. Notice in the programming interface that comments are displayed in green and keywords to the Visual Basic language are displayed in blue. In this case, the words Sub, False, and End Sub should all be displayed in blue. The remainder of the code is displayed in black.

TIP

The use of color in the display makes the code much easier to read, support, and debug. Visual Basic automatically changes the code to these colors when you complete a line and move to another line. This helps you catch errors quickly. For example, if you accidently type False as Flase, Visual Basic would interpret it as a variable name and automatically create a variable for it. As a variable, it would display in black. This may visually cue you to an error if you expected it to be blue.

The editing of a VB procedure conforms to the Windows standards for editing text. Recording a macro to create a starting point for a procedure, then modifying it to perform the specific task you desire is a good process for learning and writing Visual Basic programs.

Suppose that you want to have the macro toggle the display of the vertical scroll bar back and forth each time it is run. To do this, modify the assignment statement so that it does not simply set the DisplayVerticalScrollBar property to False, but rather sets it to the opposite of the current setting.

```
ActiveWindow.DisplayVerticalScrollBar =
              Not ActiveWindow.DisplayVerticalScrollBar
```

Running a Visual Basic Procedure

Now that the procedure is written, you will want to execute the procedure. There are many ways to run a macro in Visual Basic.

To begin, make sure the caret is placed in the macro you just recorded and modified. From the menu, select Run, Start (a short cut for this is to press the F5 function key). This executes the procedure you currently are editing. You should notice that the vertical scroll bar appears and disappears each time you press the F5 key. If the display of the vertical scroll bar does not toggle on and off, you may want to pay special attention to the debugging overview later in this section.

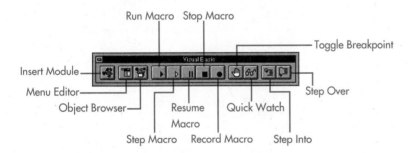

Figure 19.5
The Visual Basic toolbar.

The Run menu is only available from the VB Module sheet. A more general method for running macros is to use the Tools, Macro menu option. This displays a dialog box containing a list of all available macros that can be selected and run. This menu is available on worksheets and macro sheets in an Excel workbook.

Another method to execute macros is to use the Visual Basic Toolbar. This toolbar, shown in figure 19.5 provides a shortcut method for calling the functions used to run and debug macros.

The run macro button performs the Run, Start function if you are in a module sheet, or the Tools, Macro function if you are not.

You may also assign a macro to custom toolbar, hotkey, button, graphic object, text object, or menus. This will make them easier to execute and will give the application you develop a much more polished look. Assigning macros to some of these objects is discussed in more detail in the final section of this chapter.

Debugging a Visual Basic Procedure

This is the good news-bad news section of this chapter. The bad news is that if you write Visual Basic procedures of even moderate complexity, you will probably need the information in this section. Few large macros do everything correctly the first time.

Fortunately, the good news is that Excel Visual Basic provides a professional, easy to use debugging facility that greatly simplifies this task.

You can aid yourself in the process of writing Excel applications by keeping procedures small and focused, explicitly declaring variables and arguments, and using comments that describe the logic. However, you still will be confronted when the program does not produce the desired results for all cases.

The debugging process of writing a Visual Basic program often refers to a special terminology. Table 19.2 lists some terms you need to be familiar with.

Table 19.2
Debugging Terminology

Debugging Term	Definition
Step	"Stepping through a macro" means to execute the macro one line at a time. Each line is highlighted as it is about to be executed while it waits for you to tell it to execute that line.
Step Into	"Stepping into a procedure" means to execute that procedure line by line.
Step Over	"Stepping over a procedure" means to execute the procedure without showing the internals of that procedure.
Breakpoint	A breakpoint is set for a line of your code in that the macro will pause and bring up the debugging environment when encountered in the execution of the macro.
Watch	A watch expression is a Visual Basic expression that is moni tored by Excel as the macro executes. The value of the watch

Debugging Term	Definition
Watch (cont'd)	expression can be displayed in the debug window, or debug mode can be automatically entered when the watch expression reaches a specified value.
Quick Watch	A one time display of the value of a variable or object in the Visual Basic program.

Stepping through a macro is very similar to running a macro, except that you choose to execute one line at a time. To begin, start with the sample macro shown earlier to toggle the display of the vertical scroll bar. Make sure you are still in the Visual Basic module containing the macro, and that the caret is somewhere within that macro.

Now select <u>R</u>un, Step <u>I</u>nto (F8 is the shortcut for this function) from the menu bar. The Debug Window shown in figure 19.6 displays.

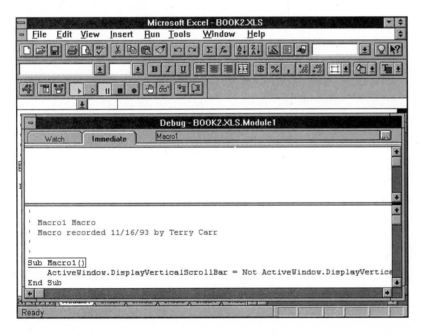

Figure 19.6
The debug window for stepping through your procedure.

The bottom half of the Debug window is the Code pane. It displays the current procedure and highlights the line of code about to be executed by drawing a box around that line. In this case, the Sub Macro1() line is about to be executed.

To step through the execution of this procedure, press the F8 key to step into it. Notice that the next line of code (the statement to assign the new value to the DisplayVerticalScrollBar property) is now highlighted.

Press F8 again to execute this line of code. Notice that the display of the scroll bar changes. This is a very powerful method for debugging your program because you can see the results as each line executes.

The End Sub line should now be highlighted. Press F8 one more time to execute this line. The debug window should disappear now that the procedure is complete.

Examining Values

In addition to being able to step through your program, the VBA debug facility enables you to inspect the value of any program variable or property as the program executes.

To do this, begin by Stepping through the sample macro used the preceding section. The debug window once again displays. From this point, click and drag in the Code pane to select the text ActiveWindow.DisplayVerticalScrollBar.

With this selected, press Shift+F9 (or from the menu, choose Tools, Instant Watch) to display the current value of this property.

The Instant Watch facility provides a quick way to view the value of any Excel Visual Basic expression. While viewing the Instant Watch window, you may press the Add button to add this expression to the normal watch window.

With the Watch tab of the top half of the Debug window, you can view watch expressions. Their values will change to reflect the current value of the expression as the program is executed.

In this sample, if you click on the Add button to make ActiveWindow. DisplayVertical ScrollBar a watch expression, you will be able to see its value change as you step through the program.

These debugging functions are also available through the Visual Basic toolbar. The toolbar makes it simple to run and interrogate your Visual Basic Procedures by using the following tools (see fig. 19.5):

- ✔ Step Macro
- ✔ Quick Watch
- ✔ Step Into
- ✔ Step Over
- ✔ Toggle Breakpoint

Applying Excel Visual Basic

The best way to get familiar with a new development tool is to take a sample application and experiment with it until you understand how it works. A sample Time Sheet application using Excel VBA is supplied on the *Inside Excel 5 for Windows* bonus disk in the back of the book. The file name is called TIMESHT.XLS.

The purpose of this sample application is to provide you with an environment for harmless experimentation and learning. As such, it has been designed to:

✔ Illustrate, in a simple form, many of the different types of procedures that can be written using VBA

✔ Enable you to concentrate on learning Visual Basic, not on the understanding of the problem addressed by the application

✔ Give you a feel for the power and flexibility of this language by providing a fairly robust and full-functioned application that requires minimal programming

With this in mind, don't be afraid to experiment with the sample program. Make changes to it, break it, and then fix it. This is a no risk opportunity. It is best to make as many mistakes here as you can, so that you don't repeat them later when you are developing a real application.

The Sample Application

The sample application is a Time Sheet application. It provides a simple way to log and keep track of time spent working on assigned tasks. Time is recorded by week; at the end of the week, the time is logged. *Logging* means adding the time for that week to the total for each assignment. The time sheet is then frozen so as not to allow future changes to the time sheet for that week.

Some of the functions required for the sheet include:

✔ Automatic totaling by assignment, day, and week

✔ Differentiation between regular and overtime hours

✔ Capability to add and close assignments

✔ Create a blank time sheet for a new week

✔ Print a time sheet

✔ Display hours or billable amounts on the time sheet

✔ Review previous week's time sheets

✔ Make it easy for a novice user

A Quick Tour of Inside Excel 5's Sample Application

The first thing to do to see the sample application is load it into Excel. Copy the file TIMESHT.XLS from the enclosed Excel 5 disk to your hard disk, then open the XLS file in Excel.

As the workbook is opened, you should notice that several things happen automatically. Excel goes to Full Screen view mode, a toolbar titled "Time Sheet" with four buttons displays, and the first time sheet in the workbook displays. The display should look something like figure 19.7.

Figure 19.7
The sample Visual Basic program's opening screen.

| File | Edit | View | Insert | Format | Tools | Data | Window | Help |

Time Sheet
Hours

Terry Carr   **11/29/93**

	Mon	Tues	Weds	Thurs	Fri	Sat	Sun	Reg.	OT	Total
Weekly Total:										
Administrative Tasks										
Sales/Bidding										
Vacation and Holidays										
Excel 5 VB Chapter										
SQL Server DB Setup										
Evaluate VBX Tools										

11-29-93 / Assignments / VB Module /

As you look at the time sheet, you will notice a list of assignments down the left side, plus an area for each day of the week and totals. The areas are shaded with a different color, with the light yellow area being the cells where time is entered. The active cell should be positioned to the Monday column of the first assignment, Administrative Tasks.

Enter the number 6 into the cell. Notice that the 6 totals for Monday, and into the Regular Hour totals for the assignment and the week, and that the Total Hours for the week is also updated.

Select the cell immediately to the right of the cell with the number 6. This is still within the Monday column. Enter a 2 into this cell. Notice that the 2 displays in red and the Overtime Totals are updated. The Total Hours for the week are also updated. Each day of the week has a column for regular hours and overtime hours.

Now select the Monday regular hours cell for the assignment "Excel 5 VB Chapter." Enter a 2 into this cell. The Time Sheet should now show that you have worked ten hours on Monday—eight regular and two overtime. The total for the week is also ten hours. Continue filling in the Time Sheet until it looks like figure 19.8.

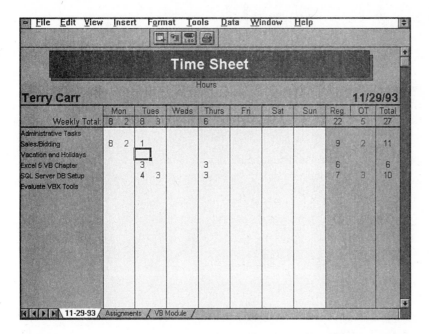

Figure 19.8
The time sheet lists the total hours worked on each project.

Now use the mouse to click on the label at the top of the workbook that says, "Time Sheet." Instead of saying "Hours" below the label, it now says "Billing." The totals column also changes: instead of showing a sum of the hours, it shows the billable amount for each assignment. Click on the "Time Sheet" label again, and the display will return to "Hours."

You are finished entering time for the week, so click on the Log button on the Time Sheet toolbar. This button takes the totals for the week for each assignment and adds them to current totals, then protects the worksheet so that it may not be changed again. A message denoting that the Time Sheet has been logged is placed on the worksheet.

Click on the toolbar button to create a new time sheet. This will cause a new worksheet to be created for the week immediately following the last Time Sheet. All the unclosed assignments are placed on the new Time Sheet. Finally, the new week's Time Sheet is displayed, ready for entry.

At any time, the previous week's time can be reviewed simply by clicking on the Excel worksheet tab related to that week. A hard copy of any week's Time Sheet can be printed by clicking on the toolbar Print button as the Time Sheet is displayed.

Click on the Excel worksheet tab named "Assignments". Assignments can also be added or closed out simply by modifying this worksheet. Notice that with each assignment, a billing rate, estimated hours, and totals to date are stored.

Examining the Sample Application

This sample, while simple, has a lot of functionality that was accomplished with a small amount of programming. It is best to start at the beginning when examining this application.

When the Timesht workbook was first opened, Excel automatically changed to display the Time Sheet in a mode that makes it easy for a novice user to log their time. This type of display gives the time sheet the feel of an application, not a spreadsheet. Accomplishing this is very simple.

When a workbook is opened, Excel will automatically look for a subroutine named Auto_Open in the workbook. If one is found, the subroutine is automatically executed.

The Auto_Open subroutine used in the sample looks like this:

```
Sub Auto_Open()
    ' Turn off Screen Updating to speed up macro
    Application.ScreenUpdating = False

    ' Set up display
    Application.DisplayFullScreen = True
    Toolbars("Full Screen").Visible = False
    Toolbars("Time Sheet").Visible = True
    Sheets(1).Select
    Range("A8").Select
    Range("C8").Select

    ' Turn Screen Updating back on
    Application.ScreenUpdating = True
End Sub
```

The first line of the Auto_Open sub procedure sets the Screen Updating property of the Application to False. This causes Excel not to redisplay until the property is set back to True. This is a technique used to speed up the execution of macros. It enables Excel to perform many functions and changes without slowing down to update the screen.

Next, several commands are issued to tailor the display of the workbook. Notice the simple object-oriented command syntax of setting properties and executing methods.

First, Excel is set to Full Screen mode by setting the DisplayFullScreen property to True. Next, the default Full Screen toolbar is forced not to display (if it already was set to display, this will have no effect), and the toolbar specific to this workbook is set to display. Notice

that you did not explicitly have to create the Time Sheet toolbar. It was created and attached to the workbook and goes with the workbook when it is copied to another machine. You will learn about creating toolbars later in the book. This is a powerful capability of Excel to make your applications professional and easy to use.

The syntax for setting this property is first to use the Toolbars method (such as Toolbars("Time Sheet")) to return the appropriate Toolbar object. The visible property of the Toolbar object is then set to True.

```
Toolbars("Time Sheet").Visible = True
```

The next three lines use the Select method to position the display to the first worksheet (the method Sheets(1) returns the worksheet object of the first sheet) and to ensure that the correct area of the worksheet is displayed with the correct cell active:

```
Sheets(1).Select
Range("A8").Select
Range("C8").Select
```

Finally, the screen updating is returned to True to display Excel in the desired state and the Sub procedure ends.

Hopefully, you are beginning to see the power of the Visual Basic approach to programming in Excel. This simple, understandable macro enables you to tailor Excel so that it automatically provides an easy to use interface when the workbook is opened.

In the same way that a Sub procedure named Auto_Open is executed when the workbook is opened, a Sub procedure named Auto_Close is executed when the workbook is closed. This procedure provides a convenient place to perform clean up functions that may be required by your application. The Auto_Close procedure used in the sample application sets Excel back to the way it was before the workbook was opened.

```
Sub Auto_Close()
    Application.DisplayFullScreen = False
    Toolbars("Time Sheet").Visible = False
End Sub
```

Special Procedures in the Sample Application

When the Time Sheet label of the workbook is clicked, the display is toggled between hours and billable amounts. This is accomplished by two procedures.

Sub Procedures

The first is a Sub procedure that is assigned to the "Time Sheet" text label. Macro procedures can be assigned to many types of objects in Excel, such as toolbar buttons, menus, and graphic or text objects. The procedure assigned to this label is as follows:

```
Sub ToggleTotalsDisplay()
    ' Turn off Screen Updating so it doesn't flash when changed
    Application.ScreenUpdating = False
    ' Turn protection off so we can update the DispType Field
    ActiveSheet.Unprotect
    ' Toggle the value in the DispType Cell of the current
    ' Timesheet. This will cause either Hours or Billable Amount
    ' To be displayed in the total column.
    If ActiveSheet.Range("DispType").Value = "Hours" Then
        ActiveSheet.Range("DispType").Value = "Billing"
    Else
        ActiveSheet.Range("DispType").Value = "Hours"
    End If
    ' Set protection back on
    ActiveSheet.Protect DrawingObjects:=True, Contents:=True, _
            Scenarios:=True
    ' Recalculate the totals using the Calculate Method
    Application.Calculate
    ' Turn Screen Updating back on
    Application.ScreenUpdating = True
End Sub
```

This subroutine toggles the value of the cell under the Time Sheet label that is defined by the range "DispType" to either Hours or Billing. After the cell value is changed, the Excel application is forced to recalculate so that all the total values will display the correct value.

Much of the syntax of this macro is similar to syntax discussed in earlier examples. The line to reset protection in the worksheet presents a new syntax for passing arguments to a method call named arguments.

```
ActiveSheet.Protect DrawingObjects:=True, Contents:=True, _
        Scenarios:=True
```

Naming the arguments often makes the procedure easier to read and use. In this case, DrawingObject, Contents, and Scenarios are all named arguments. In addition, this line uses the underscore character as a continuation character. This tells Visual Basic for Apps to treat the next line (Scenarios:=True) as though it were part of the current line.

User-Defined Functions

The second procedure in the sample application is a special type of Function procedure called a User-Defined function. This is a Function procedure that does not modify or change the appearance of Excel. The function then can be used as any other Excel function as part of a formula in a cell of a worksheet.

In this case, each cell in the Totals column of the Time Sheet has a formula similar to:

```
=TotalsFmt(T8,Q8,R8,DispType)
```

This calls the TotalsFmt function, which is a user-defined function. It will be called automatically when Excel recalculates that cell. The function looks like this:

```
Function TotalsFmt(BillRate As Double, RegHours As Double,
                        OTHours As Double, DisplayType As String)
      ' Declare a local variable to store the total reg and OT hours
      Dim TotHours As Double

      ' First add the Reg and OverTime Hours to get the total hours
      TotHours = RegHours + OTHours

      ' Next check to see if hours will be displayed or
      ' if the total hours is zero, in which case don't bother
      ' trying to calculate billing since it will also be zero.
      If DisplayType = "Hours" Or TotHours = 0 Then
              ' Assigning the value calculated to TotalsFmt, which is
the
          ' name of this procedure will cause that value to be
          ' returned to the calling procedure.
              TotalsFmt = TotHours
      Else
              ' Assigning the value calculated to TotalsFmt, which is
the
          ' name of this procedure will cause that value to be
          ' returned to the calling procedure.
              TotalsFmt = (RegHours*BillRate)+(OTHours*BillRate*OTFACTOR)
      End If
End Function
```

The first argument is the billing rate. This comes from the cell immediately to the right of the Totals column on the Time Sheet. It was loaded with the hourly billing rate for that assignment from the Assignment table when the Time Sheet was created. The next two arguments are the Regular and Overtime hour weekly totals for the assignment. These are precalculated on the Time Sheet. The final argument is the value of DispType.

This procedure checks the type of display, which was set by the ToggleTotalsDisplay procedure shown in the preceding example. This procedure conditionally returns a different result based on the value of DispType. If it is Hours (or no time has been logged for that assignment), the total number of hours logged is returned. Otherwise, the total amount billable for this assignment is calculated with this expression:

```
TotalsFmt = (RegHours*BillRate) + (OTHours*BillRate*OTFACTOR)
```

All the components of this expression were passed as arguments to the procedure, with the exception of OTFACTOR. This is a global constant that is declared in the beginning of the module with the following line:

```
Const OTFACTOR = 1.5 ' The Overtime factor is Time and a Half
```

The value returned by the TotalsFmt function is displayed in the cell from which it was called.

The next function enables the program to create a new time sheet. This demonstrates some of the versatility of Excel. This process could start with a blank worksheet and use the power of Visual Basic for Applications to format and set up the Time Sheet, but there is an easier way.

The Time Sheet Workbook

In the Timesht workbook, there is a hidden worksheet that is preformatted with the formulas, formats, and named ranges required by the Time Sheet. To create a new Time Sheet, the hidden worksheet is used as a template and copied to a new worksheet. The next date is calculated, stored in the worksheet, and the new Time Sheet is saved with the correct name.

NOTE If you are already familiar with Visual Basic, you will find this technique similar to setting the properties of a form and its objects at design time.

By using the standard capabilities of Excel to create a template, the procedure to create a new Time Sheet becomes much simpler. This also enables future flexibility and adaptability. Many changes can simply be made to the template.

The procedure to create a new Time Sheet is as follows:

```
Sub CopyTemplateForNewWeek()
    Dim newSheetName As String
    Dim sd As String
    Dim sdate As Date

    ' Turn off Screen Updating while copy occurs
    Application.ScreenUpdating = False

    ' Disable automatic calculation of cells while setting
    ' up the time sheet.
    Application.Calculation = xlManual

    ' Copy the Template Sheet to a new Time Sheet
    Sheets("Timesheet Template").Visible = True
```

```
Sheets("Timesheet Template").Copy Sheets(1)
Sheets("Timesheet Template").Visible = False

' Set up the name of the sheet so that it is one week after the
' last time sheet.
On Error Resume Next
sd = Sheets(2).Range("WeekBegin").Value
If sd = "" Then
        sdate = Monday(Date)
Else
        sdate = CDate(sd) + 7
End If
newSheetName = Format$(sdate, "mm-dd-yy")
On Error Goto 0

' Make sure the new sheet is active
Sheets(1).Select
' Do not let the user change the date after sheet creation
ActiveSheet.Unprotect
ActiveSheet.Range("WeekBegin").Select
ActiveCell.Value = " " + Format$(sdate, "mm/dd/yy")
Selection.Locked = True

' The beauty of the procedural nature of Visual Basic is that
' this procedure will be called to load the new assignments to
' the time sheets. How the RetrieveOpenAssignments procedure
' actually works or where it gets its information doesn't
' really matter to this procedure.
RetrieveOpenAssignments

Range("A8").Select
Range("C8").Select
' Protect the sheet
ActiveSheet.Protect DrawingObjects:=True, Contents:=True, _
        Scenarios:=True

' Set the Name to the new Time Sheet to the date
Sheets(1).Name = newSheetName

' Return the calculation mode to automatic
Application.Calculation = xlAutomatic
' Redisplay the screen
Application.ScreenUpdating = True
End Sub
```

In this procedure, three local variables are declared. Explicitly declaring them is a good technique because it simplifies debugging if it is required.

Next, two application properties are set to speed up this process. The ScreenUpdating property that will stop intermediate screen display was previously discussed. Setting the Calculation property to xlManual disables Excel's capability to calculate the value of cells automatically when it thinks it is required. It will greatly speed up this procedure to have Excel wait until the copy and setup of the template is complete before recalculating.

The following three lines are really the guts of the CopyTemplateForNewWeek procedure.

```
Sheets("Timesheet Template").Visible = True
Sheets("Timesheet Template").Copy Sheets(1)
Sheets("Timesheet Template").Visible = False
```

The first line makes the template visible. Because ScreenUpdating is set to False, you will not see it as you run the procedure. The next line copies the Timesheet Template and places it before Sheet 1 in the workbook. The final line hides the template again so that the user doesn't have to deal with it.

The week that this Time Sheet applies to must then be calculated. This is accomplished by first looking to see if another Time Sheet already exists in the workbook. If so, the program gets the date from the last sheet and adds seven to it. If this is the first Time Sheet, take the Monday of the current week. The following Visual Basic code performs this task.

```
On Error Resume Next
sd = Sheets(2).Range("WeekBegin").Value
If sd = "" Then
        sdate = Monday(Date)
Else
        sdate = CDate(sd) + 7
End If
newSheetName = Format$(sdate, "mm-dd-yy")
On Error Goto 0
```

First, error checking is turned off. If there are no other Time Sheets, retrieving the WeekBegin value from the second sheet will return an error. Because this condition is handled by the procedure, it is not desirable to have an error message appear. Next, a text string containing the date of the beginning of the week of the previous Time Sheet is assigned to the local variable sd.

If sd is blank (meaning this is the first Time Sheet in the workbook), get the date of the start of the current week using the Monday function (this function was discussed earlier in this chapter).

If the date from the previous Time Sheet has been returned, it needs to be converted from a text string stored to a Visual Basic date so that seven (the number of days in a week) can be

added to it. This is done by using the CDate function. Visual Basic has many built-in functions like the CDate function.

After sdate is assigned the correct date value, it can be used to create the name for the Time Sheet. The Format$ command will convert the Visual Basic date variable back into a string in the format specified. This value is then assigned to the string variable newSheetName. Finally, error checking is returned to the standard Excel error checking.

Now that the Time Sheet is created and the correct date has been determined, the information for the sheet must be loaded onto it. First, the date displayed on the sheet must be set. To do this, the protection must be removed from the sheet and the date formatted to a text string.

Next, assignments must be loaded to the time sheet. One of the beauties of the procedural nature of Visual Basic is that the RetrieveOpenAssignments (shown as follows) can be called in one line from this procedure. How this procedure actually accomplishes its task is not important to the current procedure. This allows for flexibility and adaptability. If the format for assignments, or where they are stored (such as in a database) changes later, the RetrieveOpenAssignments procedure must change, not the rest of the procedures.

```
Sub RetrieveOpenAssignments()
Dim AssignRow As Integer
Dim TimesheetRow As Integer

        'The first assignment on the Assignment sheet is in row 2
        AssignRow = 2
        ' The first assignment on a Time Sheet is in row 8
        TimesheetRow = 8


        'Loop through all the assignments and select any
        'that are not closed
        While (Sheets("Assignments").Cells(AssignRow, 1).Value <> "")
        If (Sheets("Assignments").Cells(AssignRow,
➥ASSGNSTATUS).Value <> "Closed") Then
                        ActiveSheet.Cells(TimesheetRow, 1).Value =
Sheets("Assignments").Cells(AssignRow, 1).Value
                        ActiveSheet.Cells(TimesheetRow, 20).Value =
Sheets("Assignments").Cells(AssignRow, BILLINGRATE).Value
                        TimesheetRow = TimesheetRow + 1
                End If
                AssignRow = AssignRow + 1
        Wend


    End Sub
```

Building Applications

After the assignments are loaded to the Time Sheet, the first cell is selected, the Time Sheet is protected and the name changed to reflect the week it is recording. Lastly, calculation and screen display are returned to their normal settings.

Saving the Time Sheet Hours Worked

Only one function remains to be performed by this demonstration application: take the time entered and log it back to the Assignment Table. This is accomplished through two procedures. The first, LogTimeRecords, controls the logging of the time values. LogTimeRecords locks the Time Sheet so that it cannot be changed again. Next, it loops through all the assignments.

When an assignment with time logged against it is encountered, the other procedure, UpdateTotals, is called. Finally, the sheet is flagged to show it has already been logged, and it is protected again so that it will not be accidentally changed.

```
Sub LogTimeRecords()
Dim TimesheetRow As Integer
Dim RegTotal As Double
Dim OTimeTotal As Double
    'First Lock down Recorded Time Values
    ActiveSheet.Unprotect
    Application.Goto Reference:=Range("MonReg:SunOT")
    Selection.Locked = True

    'Now, update the database
    TimesheetRow = 8
    While (ActiveSheet.Cells(TimesheetRow, 1).Value <> "")
    RegTotal = ActiveSheet.Cells(TimesheetRow,
TIMEREGTOTAL).Value
    OTimeTotal = ActiveSheet.Cells(TimesheetRow,
TIMEOTTOTAL).Value
            If RegTotal + OTimeTotal > 0 Then
            UpdateTotals
Assignment:=ActiveSheet.Cells(TimesheetRow, 1).Value, _
                            RegHours:=RegTotal, OTHours:=OTimeTotal
            End If
            TimesheetRow = TimesheetRow + 1
    Wend
    'Set the flag to show time has already been logged
    Range("LogStatus").Select
    ActiveCell.Value = "Effort for this week has been logged"
    Selection.Locked = True
    ActiveSheet.Protect DrawingObjects:=True, Contents:=True,
```

```
            Scenarios:=True
      End Sub
```

The UpdateTotals function takes the assignment name, the regular hour total, and the overtime hour total as arguments. It uses the name to look up the correct assignment in the assignment table, then increments the totals for that assignment with the new ones for this week.

```
      Function UpdateTotals(Assignment As String, RegHours As Double, OTHours
   ➡As Double)
      Dim LookupRow As Integer

            On Error Resume Next
            'Find the assignment in the table and return the appropriate
            ➡value.
            LookupRow =
   ➡Sheets("Assignments").Columns("A").Find(What:=Assignment, _
                          LookIn:=xlValues, LookAt:=xlWhole,
                          ➡MatchCase:=True).Row

            If LookupRow = 0 Then
                  ' There was no match for this assignment
                  MsgBox ("There was no matching assignment information.")
                  UpdateTotals = False
            Else
                  Sheets("Assignments").Cells(LookupRow, REGHOURTOT).Value = _
                        Sheets("Assignments").Cells(LookupRow,
   ➡REGHOURTOT).Value + RegHours
                  Sheets("Assignments").Cells(LookupRow, OTHOURTOT).Value = _
                  Sheets("Assignments").Cells(LookupRow, OTHOURTOT).Value +
   ➡OTHours
                  UpdateTotals = True
            End If
      End Function
```

There are many more capabilities and functions available through the Visual Basic for Applications Programming System. Hopefully, this introduction gives you an idea of the power and flexibility of this facility.

V

Building Applications

Chapter Snapshot

You already have learned the mechanics of creating macros, and you've read about some features that add something extra to Excel. One of the most intriguing features of Excel 5 is that it provides you with the ability to create custom menus and dialog boxes that you can use to make your macros and applications more user-friendly. In this chapter, you learn the following:

✔ Adding new commands to a new or existing menu

✔ Creating a dialog box

✔ Using Excel's new dialog editor

✔ Building and editing a custom dialog box

✔ Setting the defaults for the dialog box

✔ Linking the dialog box to a worksheet

✔ Setting hot keys, default buttons, and tab orders for the dialog box

✔ Adding functions to a dialog box

Although a dialog box has a much better appearance than a command line, this chapter is not about making your macro look pretty; it is about making your macros easy to use and making Excel look the way you want it to look—rather than just the way someone else designed it.

20 CHAPTER

Creating Custom Menus and Dialog Boxes

S uppose that you have come up with an idea for a macro you can write that would make your life easier. You have figured out what the spreadsheet should look like and some of the things you want the macro to do. A big hole is left, however; namely, how does the macro talk to you, and how can you talk to it?

These communication issues are related to the *user interface*, the way in which a program works and interacts with the person using it. A well-designed user interface can make the difference between clumsy, cumbersome macros and ones that are slick and easy to use. Not only can you create your macros entirely within Excel, you also can assign them to new or existing menus to make them easy to find and use. You also can create custom-designed dialog boxes that work within your macros.

Adding New Commands to Existing Menus

Suppose that you have created a macro that sets a certain formatting for a selected cell, and you use this macro so often that you wish someone had designed it into Excel so that you could simply pick it out of a menu. After you complete this chapter, you will be able to add your macro anywhere (to the Format menu, perhaps?) and make it look as if Excel came that way right out of the box.

The first step is to bring up the Visual Basic toolbar (if it's not already visible). Excel offers two methods to display this toolbar. One method is to select the View menu, and choose the Toolbars option. In the Toolbars dialog box that appears (see fig. 20.1), check Visual Basic, and click on OK. The other method is to right-click with the pointer anywhere on any toolbar, then select the Visual Basic entry.

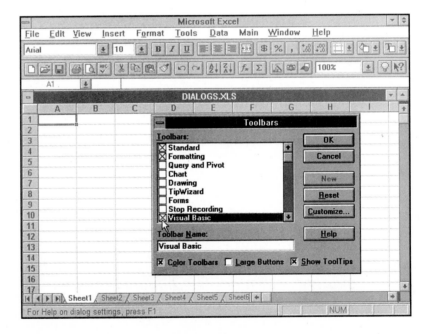

Figure 20.1
The Toolbars dialog box.

After the Visual Basic toolbar is active, select the Menu Editor tool (the tool has a picture of a menu on it) shown in figure 20.2. The Menu Editor dialog box appears. This dialog box enables you to make changes to any menu or submenu that activates when you open the workbook to which it is attached.

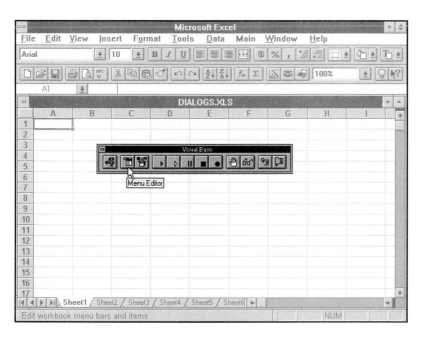

Figure 20.2
The Visual Basic toolbar with the Menu Editor selected.

After you decide to which menu you want to attach your macro, select the menu title from the Menus list (see fig. 20.3). Notice that the Menu Items list contains all the menu entries under the selected menu.

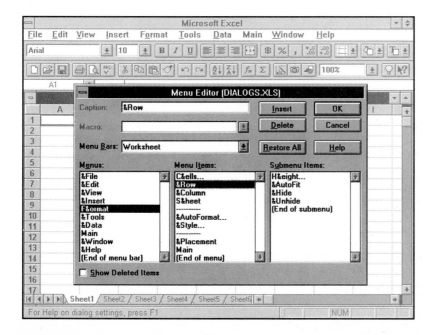

Figure 20.3
The Menu Editor dialog box.

To add an item to a menu, follow these steps:

1. Select the menu to modify.

2. Select the menu item you want to immediately follow your new item, then click on Insert. A blank line is inserted in the Menu Items list at the point where your new menu item will be placed.

3. In the Caption field, enter the words you want to appear in the actual menu. The caption can include an ampersand (&) to indicate that the character following the ampersand can be recognized from the keyboard and should be underlined on the menu (like the F in the File menu).

4. In the Macro text box, enter the name of the macro you want to attach to that menu item (if any). To display a list of all macros that are a part of the current workbook, click on the down arrow to the right of the Macro text box. You can select any macro, or you can enter an external macro reference in the Macro text box.

5. If you do not want to attach a macro but want the new menu item to have a submenu, then leave the Macro text box blank. Excel adds the submenu arrow to the menu when submenu items have been entered, indicating that a submenu is available.

6. When you have finished entering text in the text boxes, click on a menu item (the same one or another one), and the new item is added to the menu.

If you add more items to a menu than fit on a screen, Excel cheerfully adds them to your desired menu, even though you cannot to see them. Don't make your customized menus too long, especially if you have an SVGA or other high-resolution screen. Others who use your program might have a lower-resolution screen—in which case, part of their menu might run off the screen, never to be used.

If you want to delete a menu item, simply select the item from the Menu Items list and click on the Delete button. (Careful: no Undo is available!)

To rename an item, edit the item's text in the Caption field, then click on a menu item (the same one or another one). Note that you can only rename items that you have added, not Excel's built-in ones.

Adding New Menus

If all your menus are full, or your macro does not really fall under any of the existing categories, you might want to create a new menu altogether. Essentially, adding a new menu is simple: you insert a new menu into the Menus list just as you inserted a new menu item into the Menu Items list. In the Menus list, however, only a caption is allowed because you cannot run a macro directly from the menu bar.

To add a new menu, repeat the steps to open the Menu Editor dialog box, then continue on as follows:

1. Select the menu caption you want to immediately follow (to the right of) your new menu, then select the Insert button.

2. Enter the title of the menu in the Caption field.

3. Select the (End of menu) entry in the Menu Items list. This step enters the new menu into Excel's list of menus.

4. As before, you can attach the macro you want to reference or add as many items and submenus as you like (within reason).

Creating Dialog Boxes

After you have mastered the art of creating dialog boxes, you will never want to go back to writing command-line programs again (such as MS-DOS). Admittedly, creating dialog boxes takes more work than simply asking the user a series of questions, but the results far outweigh the effort. One immediate and perceptible difference—dialog boxes look good. To anyone using the macro, a good set of dialog boxes makes the macro look like a polished product.

Dialog boxes also serve the additional function of mini-Help screens for those macros you use infrequently (for example, once a year around the night of April 15) and do not remember exactly what you need to enter when a command-line prompt says Filename?. In a dialog box, the command-line prompt Filename? might become a combination list box-edit box with all available file names in the current subdirectory, a neighboring list box with the names of all subdirectories, a drop-down list of file formats, text stating the file name last used, and a group surrounding the whole thing entitled Output File. Well-designed dialog boxes should be almost self-explanatory, with judicious use of entry boxes, text, buttons, and groups. All these elements are possible—and easy to accomplish—using Excel.

Dialog boxes are best created by first figuring out what kind of input is required of the user (in other words, good programming practice) and then putting that scheme into action. After the user requirements are known, the dialog box needs to be mapped out. You now can lay out the dialog box from within Excel 5—the layout becomes just another sheet in your workbook.

After you have the dialog box laid out to your satisfaction, you can create a function, if desired, for each item in the dialog box. These functions become part of the macro; their results are the user input used by the rest of the macro. Dialog boxes can operate without functions, however, by using only dynamic links between dialog box items and worksheet cells.

Excel 5's dialog boxes are *dynamic*, which means that the settings you change take effect immediately—while the dialog box is still on the screen. Dynamic dialog boxes are in contrast to *static* dialog boxes, which must disappear for a while to change objects. Dynamic dialog boxes give an added dimension to your macros because parts of the dialog box can be changed, depending upon certain user input (or even something external like the time of day). You might, for example, design the OK button to be gray until the user has entered all the right data, or you could display a file name list box only if the user has selected an option button with the caption "Save As File."

Using the Dialog Editor

In Excel 5, the Dialog Editor has been built-in for ease of use. Earlier versions of Excel had an external Dialog Editor program that used the Clipboard to transfer a dialog table between Excel and the Dialog Editor. In the new version of the software, you can design your dialog boxes visually within Excel, using one screen per dialog worksheet. You do not have to contend with the cryptic numbers and syntax of dialog tables (although you still can if you want to). You even can have a separate workbook that contains only your macros and dialog boxes, and reference this workbook from another one.

To begin defining a dialog box, select <u>M</u>acro from the <u>I</u>nsert menu, and then select Dialog from the Macro submenu. Excel inserts a new Dialog worksheet, a blank dialog box opens, and the Forms toolbar appears beside the dialog box (see fig. 20.4).

Figure 20.4
The Dialog editing screen.

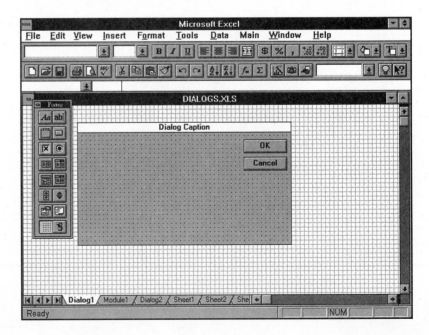

Using the Dialog Editor, you can add, position, edit, or delete objects in the new dialog box. You can manipulate any portion of the dialog box until you get it just the way you want it.

Building the Dialog Box

Using the Dialog Editor is similar to using a Windows drawing package such as Paintbrush. Add an object to the dialog box by clicking on the tool you want (for example, the Create Button tool). The cursor changes to a cross. Next, move to the dialog box and select a starting corner for your object. Hold the left mouse button down, and drag it to the opposite corner of the button. An outline of the new button's shape appears (see fig. 20.5). Release the mouse button. Dont panic if you don't get it right the first time because you can always move and resize items at any time.

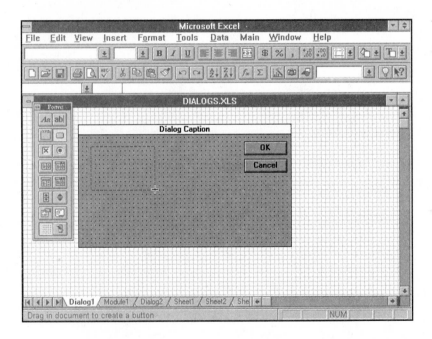

Figure 20.5
Adding a new button.

The tools on the Forms toolbar are used to add each object to your dialog box. These tools are described in table 20.1.

Table 20.1
Forms Toolbar Icons

Icon	Name	Description
	Label	Creates a text label for user information
	Edit Box	Creates an edit box for user input
	Group Box	Creates a group box to group associated objects
	Pushbutton	Creates a pushbutton for immediate actions
	Check Box	Creates a check box for user selection
	Option Button	Creates an option button for user choices
	List box	Creates a list box containing user choices available
	Drop down	Creates a drop-down list box
	Combination List Box	Creates a list box with a connected edit box
	Combination Drop-Down Edit Box	Creates a drop-down list box with a connected edit box
	Scroll Bar	Creates an independent scroll bar
	Spin	Creates an independent spin button
	Control Properties	Allows changing the properties of the selected object

Icon	Name	Description
	Edit Code	Allows editing or creating code for the selected object
	Toggle Grid	Displays or hides the grid in the dialog definition worksheet
	Run Dialog	Runs the dialog box (useful for testing)

To move or resize an object, select the object by clicking on it. A border with sizing handles appears around the object. Drag any of the handles to resize the object, as shown in figure 20.6. You also can drag any side of the border (not a handle) to move the entire object.

To delete an item, select the item and either press the Del key or select Clear All from the Edit menu.

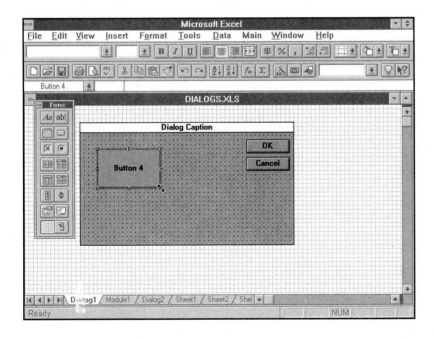

Figure 20.6
Sizing the button.

You can select multiple objects by clicking on the first object, then holding down the Shift key and clicking on the other objects. The selected objects can be sized and moved as if they were one object. Note, however, that only the sizing handles appear—the sizing border is not visible as it is when only one object is selected. When you need to move more than one object on the dialog box, this technique is a convenient way to maintain the same relative position of the objects.

Setting Default Properties

After you have defined all the objects in your dialog box, you need to define their properties. Select an object, then select the Control Properties tool (see fig. 20.7). You also can double-click on the border of any object to edit its control properties, or you can double-click anywhere within list box, pull-down menu, or scroll item.

Figure 20.7
Setting Control Properties for an object.

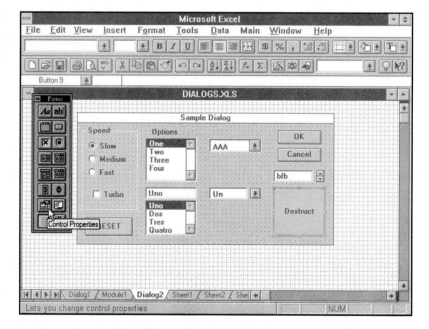

The Control page of the Format Object notebook appears as shown in figure 20.8 for a pushbutton. This dialog box enables you to set various properties for the object. The properties vary according to the object selected. Select the properties you want to set for the object, and then click on OK.

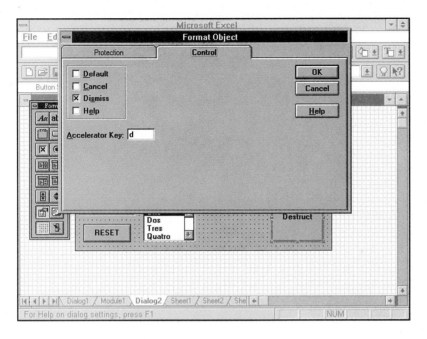

Figure 20.8
The Pushbutton
Control Pages.

Figure 20.9 shows the Control page for a drop-down list. In the Input Range field, you can reference cells on a worksheet that contain the list items. The range of cells in the Input Range field must be a column, not a row, because Excel might not recognize a row reference.

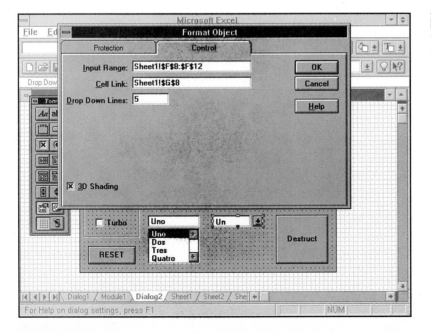

Figure 20.9
The Drop-down list
Control page.

Linking Worksheet Cells to the Object

The Cell Link field designates the single-cell reference where the number of the selected choice is stored (the first entry in the drop-down box is output to $G$8 as number 1, the second entry in number 2, and so on). This cell link is a two-way link: not only does the dialog box write to the cell, but the cell's value when the dialog box starts determines the default choice.

An edit box cannot be linked; it must have a function behind it to operate fully.

Like dialog boxes, all cell links are *dynamic*. Any change to a worksheet value is immediately reflected in the dialog box, and a change in the dialog box results in a change to the worksheet value. Excel automatically recalculates the worksheet after any value changes in the dialog box. The linked worksheet(s) must be open while the dialog box is active. Figure 20.10 shows the worksheet that is linked to the example dialog box.

You can use a single dialog box with linked items to create "what if" calculations on a worksheet. Use the input ranges as the results of calculations and the cell links as results or variables in calculations.

Figure 20.10
The worksheet linked to the example dialog box.

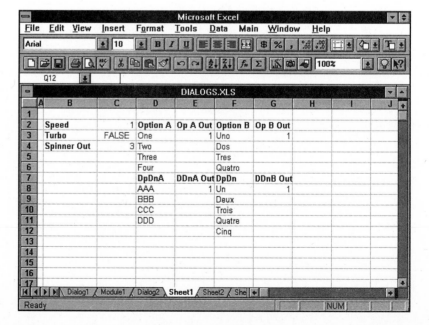

Cancel does not restore linked cells to their original value. The linked cells retain the last change that was made to them from within the dialog box or from the worksheet calculations. If you want to have Cancel restore all original settings, you need to use two separate worksheet cells for each of the same data: one that is linked and dedicated only to the dialog box, and one that received a copy of all the dialog box dates when OK is selected.

The type of input to be accepted by input boxes must be defined (Edit Validation) under the Tools menu. Edit Validation enables you to set the allowed type of user input that the selected box will accept. For instance, you can set a box to only accept numerical input. If the user input is different from its setting, Excel notifies the user that the setting is in error and highlights the offending box. The dialog box cannot be dismissed until the input type is satisfied.

Adding an Accelerator Key

An *accelerator key* is an Alt+*key* combination that sets the focus to that item. Accelerator keys also are known as *shortcut keys* or "hot keys" because they give you quick access to commands and buttons without using the mouse. Nearly all Excel menus and commands have accelerator keys. A few examples include the File menu, the Save command, and the Help menu. You designate this key in the Accelerator Key field of the button or option's Control page.

Designating the Default Button

Next, you need to decide which button should be the default (the one activated when the Enter key is pressed). You also need to decide which button or buttons (if any) can dismiss (accept) the dialog box during runtime and which buttons can cancel it. (Remember that you always have the Close option on the Control menu in the upper left corner of any dialog box.) Normally, the OK button is the default and can dismiss the dialog box, and the Cancel button can (oddly enough) cancel the dialog box. You can set the desired attributes of the proper buttons in the Control Page of the Format Object notebook.

Setting the Tab Order

Another property you probably want to set in your dialog boxes is a tab order. *Tab order* defines which dialog box item is selected next when the user presses the Tab key. Tabs are a way for the user to enter data quickly in a dialog box without having to switch constantly between the mouse and the keyboard to select the next item. You define a tab order by selecting the Tab Order selection under the Tools menu. The Tab Order dialog box appears, as shown in figure 20.11.

Building Applications

Figure 20.11
The Tab Order
dialog box.

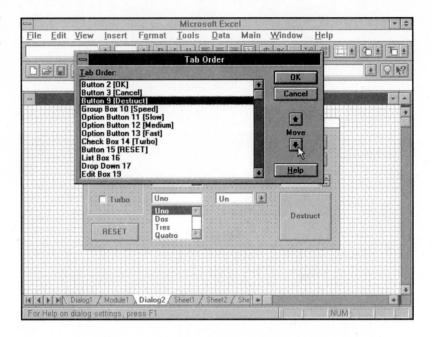

Tabs are ordered from top to bottom, with the top item selected (highlighted) when the dialog box opens. You can move any item up or down in the list by selecting the item and using the Move arrow buttons in the Tab Order dialog box. Moving an item in the list does not change its physical location on the dialog box, but simply determines the item's order in the tab sequence.

Do not confuse the top tab item with the default object. A dialog box always contains one of each. You can make the default object be the top tab item, or the top tab item be the default object in the Control page of the Format Object notebook if you want to, but it is not necessary to do so.

Finishing the Dialog Box

Now that you have built a dialog box, you need to make it work. Excel dialog boxes enable you to add software behind them to make them come alive. You don't have to add macro functions behind any dialog box item, but the dialog box can do only a limited amount without such functions. Without some instructions behind it, a dialog box button cannot do anything except dismiss or cancel the dialog box (if that is set).

An edit box, for example, does nothing (besides accept and validate data) without a function. Changing the data within the edit box activates the function, which can then distribute or recall data as needed.

In a finished dialog box, each item has its own function that operates when the item is activated. You must create each function, but the programming is not as frightening as it sounds. (You would have to do all the same operations in the main program.) You don't have to add functions behind every item—only those items you decide need a function. A list box, for instance, can be used solely to pass data between a worksheet and the user; no extra functions are needed to make this happen.

To create a function for the Destruct button in our example, select the Destruct button, then click on the Edit Code tool in the Forms toolbar (see fig. 20.12). Excel then creates a function in the dialog's Module sheet. When the user activates the object (selects the option, clicks on the button, and so on), this function runs.

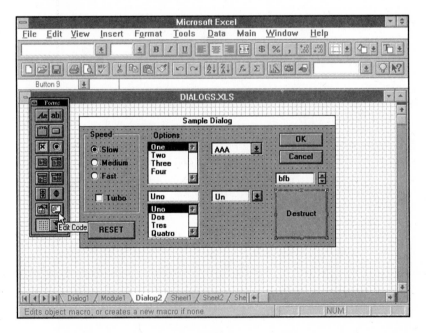

Figure 20.12
The Forms toolbar with the Edit Code tool selected.

Excel creates one Module sheet for each dialog box. Enter your Visual Basic routine or Excel macro code in the blank function created as shown in figure 20.13, and then return to the Dialog sheet to select the next item. For more specifics on writing the routines or entering and editing them, refer to Chapter 7 or Chapter 19.

Figure 20.13
Visual Basic
functions for
dialog box
objects.

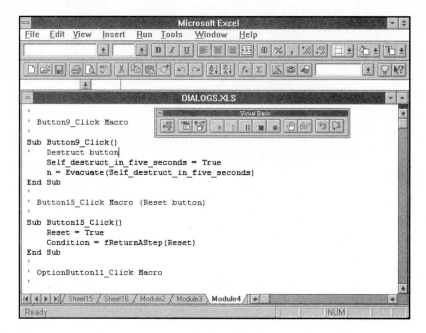

After you have created functions for all the items in the dialog box, you are ready to incorporate the dialog box into the macro.

1. Click on the module sheet that contains the code for your macro and locate the point in the code at which you want the dialog box to open.

2. Enter the DialogSheets command code with the .Show method, as follows:

```
DialogSheets("Dialog2").Show
```

The name in the Daily Sheets command (`"Dialog2"`) is the name of the worksheet containing the dialog box you want to activate. Figure 20.12 shows the Dialog2 worksheet.

Any function in the dialog box's Module sheet can call any other functions or simply set a variable and return. If the user selects the OK button from the dialog box, the .Show method returns TRUE; otherwise, FALSE is returned. You can use these TRUE and FALSE values in your macro to quickly determine the way your dialog box was closed.

TIP

You can define a macro that starts when the dialog box is initiated but before it appears. You might want to do this to set up certain defaults, or to check for the existence of certain files, before the user sees it.

To define such a macro, click on the border of the dialog definition to assign, and then select Assign Macro from the **T**ools menu. Pick the name of the macro you want to begin running when the dialog box is initiated.

You can display a standard (built-in) Excel dialog box by using the following command:

```
Application.DialogSheets(xlBuiltInDialog).Show(Path$)
```

In this command, *xlBuiltInDialog* is the name of the dialog box; and *Path$* is the full path name, including drive, of the directory in which the built-in dialog boxes are stored. If the *Path$* statement is omitted (no parentheses, either), the standard Excel dialog box is assumed.

You can reference a given dialog box item, either for storing or for reading, by substituting its control (item) for the .Show method. Any of the contents of the dialog box controls (items) can be changed from any function initiated by any other control (item).

A complete listing of all the controls is available under the Visual Basic (Objects) reference in Excel Help. You also can find this information in the Excel Visual Basic Command Reference at the end of this book.

Any object's control properties can be changed or read from any function. The following statement, for example, disables all checkboxes in the dialog box:

```
DialogSheets("Dialog2").CheckBoxes.Enabled = False
```

Dialog boxes, as well as controls of dialog boxes, can have properties; and as such, the property name is placed immediately after the dialog box reference. The statement `DialogSheets(x).Hide`, for example, dismisses the dialog box.

Part VI

Excel Tools

Chapter Snapshot

Microsoft includes additional Excel tools that are not part of the basic Excel software. The tools covered in this chapter are broken out into "add-ins," which you can choose to enable and use if you want. These tools provide a variety of added functions, including the following:

- ✔ Examining Excel's additional financial, statistical and engineering functions

- ✔ Saving workbooks automatically

- ✔ Managing reporting on multiple views and scenarios

- ✔ Performing an electronic slide show with Excel charts and worksheets

- ✔ Exploring a tool called the Solver, which performs more advanced What-If functions than Goal Seek performs (Goal Seek is built into Excel, whereas Solver is an add-in)

- ✔ Examining View Manager, which saves multiple versions of the same workbook

Getting the most out of these tools is an important aspect of mastering Excel. The Solver, for example, is a powerful tool that can be used to solve difficult problems. Likewise, the View Manager is an invaluable tool for performing various analysis functions in Excel. And enabling the AutoSave add-in frees you from worrying about saving your workbooks every so often.

Using Excel Add-ins

Excel 5 for Windows contains many additional features that are not part of the core Excel program. You can add these additional capabilities to Excel selectively, so that you use only the features you want. This chapter shows you the way to add, remove, and use the various add-ins that Excel provides.

Installing Excel Add-ins

You can install the optional add-in tools at the same time you install Excel. If you did not choose to install them at that time, however, you can make them a part of Excel by using the Microsoft Excel Setup program in your Excel folder. See Appendix A for instructions on installing parts of Excel that you didn't choose during your initial installation.

Using the Add-in Manager

After the add-ins are installed on your computer, you can incorporate them into Excel so that they appear on the Excel menus just like any other command. You control the status of the add-ins by using the Add-in Manager. Access the Add-in Manager by pulling down the Tools menu and choosing the Add-Ins command. The Add-ins dialog box is shown in figure 21.1.

Figure 21.1
The Add-ins
dialog box.

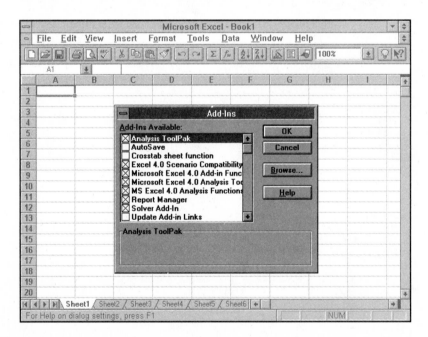

In the dialog box, select or deselect the checkboxes to control which add-ins appear on the Excel menus. You also can click on the Help button to find out more about the add-ins available for Excel.

NOTE

Depending on the speed of your computer, accessing the Add-ins menu might take a while. Also, selecting new add-ins might take several minutes when Excel installs them after you click on the OK button from the Add-ins dialog box.

Analysis

Access the analysis tools by pulling down the Tools menu and choosing Data Analysis from the menu. This operation causes the Analysis dialog box to appear, as shown in figure 21.2.

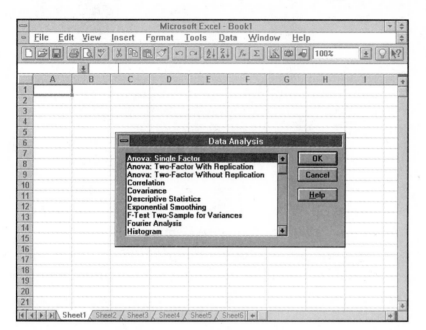

Figure 21.2
The Analysis dialog box.

To use any of the analysis tools, select a tool in the list and then click on the OK button. This procedure causes the dialog box for that tool to appear on your screen. For example, selecting Random Number Generator shows the dialog box in figure 21.3.

The data analysis tools are very extensive. They are covered in detail in Chapter 9, "Mastering Excel Analytical Tools."

AutoSave

Nothing is more frustrating than spending lots of time on a workbook, only to have your computer crash for some reason with your work unsaved. Although you can help prevent this problem by learning to do frequent saves of your work, you also can use the AutoSave add-in to save automatically.

Access the AutoSave function by pulling down the Tools menu and choosing AutoSave. You can see the dialog box shown in figure 21.4.

Figure 21.3
The Random
Number
Generator dialog
box.

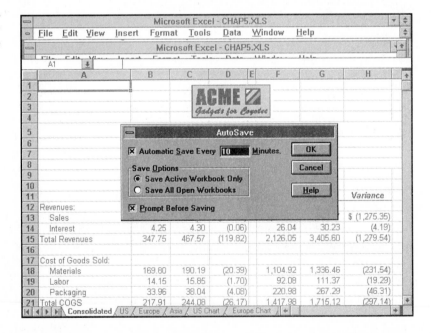

Figure 21.4
The AutoSave
dialog box.

In this dialog box, you can control several functions:

✔ Whether to perform the automatic save. Select or deselect the checkbox marked
   Automatic Save.

✔ The number of minutes between automatic saves. Change the value in the <u>M</u>inutes field.

✔ Whether to save the active workbook or all open workbooks. Use the two option buttons in the Save <u>O</u>ptions box to choose. If you have many workbooks open, but are not modifying more than one of them at a time, you can speed up the AutoSave process by choosing to save only the active workbook. If, however, you are using a single workbook that modifies the other workbooks (by means of a macro, for instance), choose to save all open workbooks to ensure that all of your work is saved.

✔ Whether you are prompted before every automatic save. Select or deselect the checkbox marked <u>P</u>rompt before saving in order to control this option.

Report Manager

Excel enables you to define separate reports in your workbooks. You can use these defined reports to generate multiple reports from your workbooks in one operation.

To set up the reports, access the Report Manager by pulling down the <u>F</u>ile menu and choosing Print R<u>e</u>port. You can see the Print Report dialog box, shown in figure 21.5.

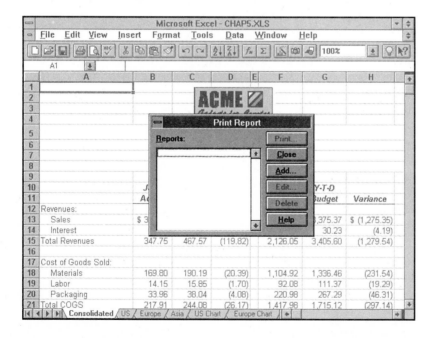

Figure 21.5
The Print Report dialog box.

To print predefined reports, select the reports from the dialog box and click on the Print button. To add new reports to the dialog box, click on the <u>A</u>dd button, which brings up the dialog box shown in figure 21.6.

Figure 21.6
Add Report
dialog box.

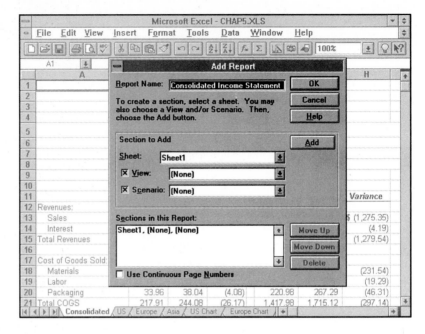

You define each report by specifying its name, the sheet in the workbook, on which scenario the report is located, and which view you want to show. After you have defined the first report, click on the Add button to create it. When you have several reports defined, use the Move Up and Move Down buttons to reorganize the order of the reports.

See the last section in this chapter for more information about the View Manager.

Slideshow

You can use the Excel Slideshow add-in to prepare and present slide shows by preparing slide images and then pasting them on a special slide show sheet.

To open a new slide show worksheet, pull down the File menu and choose New. From the dialog box that appears, select Slides and click on the OK button. You see the Slideshow workbook shown in figure 21.7.

You prepare each slide for the slide show by copying the data from the source workbook into the clipboard using the Copy command in the Edit menu. Then, switch to the Slideshow workbook and click on the Paste Slide button. You can copy and paste both charts and ranges of worksheets.

When you click on the Paste Slide button, a dialog box appears that asks you to define the way in which the slide should be displayed. This dialog box is shown in figure 21.8.

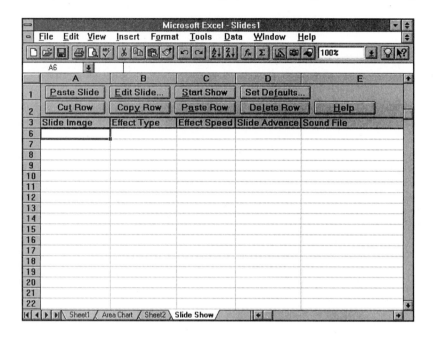

Figure 21.7
The Slideshow workbook.

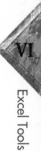

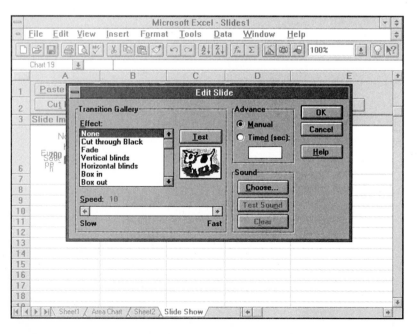

Figure 21.8
The Edit Slide dialog box.

Table 21.1 shows the options on the Edit Slide dialog box.

Table 21.1
Edit Slide Dialog Box Settings

Setting	Description
Effect	This list box lists a variety of special effects that you can use to set a transition from one slide to the next. To see the way each effect works, select it in the list box and click on the Test button.
Speed	You can choose a transition speed from 1 to 10.
Advance	The Advance section enables you to choose the way in which Excel can know to switch from one slide to the next. You can choose Manual, which requires you to click the mouse or press the spacebar to advance to the next slide, or you can choose the Timed option, which enables you to define the number of seconds during which the slide should be displayed.
Sound	You also can choose a sound effect that plays when the slide is transitioned. Click on the Choose button to select the WAV file that contains the sound and the Test Sound button to play the sound.

When you have defined a slide show, the worksheet displays thumbnail sketches of each slide, along with their settings, as shown in figure 21.9.

Table 21.2 shows the buttons that control this worksheet.

Table 21.2
Slideshow Worksheet Buttons

Button	Description
Paste Slide	Pastes the contents of the clipboard into the next available slide position.
Cut Row	Removes the selected slide. You must select the row that contains the slide you want to cut before you choose this button.
Edit Slide	Click on this button to open the Edit Slide dialog box, in which you can change the settings for the selected slide.
Copy Row	Copies the selected row to the clipboard.

Button	Description
Start Show	Begins the slide show. If the slides are set to manual transitions, click on the mouse button or press the spacebar to advance from slide to slide.
Paste Row	Pastes the copied slide into the current row.
Set Defaults	Brings up the equivalent of the Edit Slide dialog box. The Set Defaults dialog box enables you to choose the default slide settings for the Edit Slide dialog box.
Delete Row	Choose this button to delete the slide from the slide worksheet.

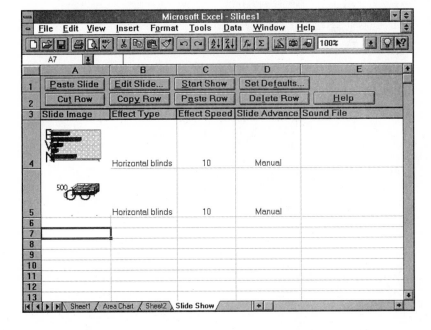

Figure 21.9
The Slideshow worksheet.

Excel Tools

Solver

The Goal Seek function in Excel is fairly limited when you need to solve problems that have many factors influencing the outcome or when you need to apply constraints to the solution. Excel 5 contains an Add-in called the Solver, however, which can deal with finding optimal solutions to such problems. Examples of problems to which the Solver might be applied include:

✔ Finding optimal scheduling for employees

✔ Maximizing return on investment while keeping within a defined risk in a complex portfolio

✔ Modeling engine performance, given certain physical constraints and engineering data

✔ Maximizing profit by choosing product mix

These examples suggest only a few of the uses for the Excel Solver. It is an incredibly powerful tool that you can use to help solve extraordinarily difficult problems. Figure 21.10 shows an example problem for which the Solver is suited.

Figure 21.10
The example Solver problem.

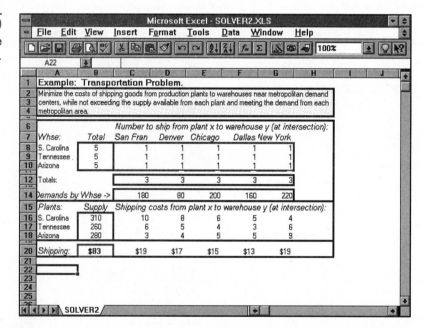

In order to understand the way Solver works, you must understand the structure of the example problem.

Row 7 shows the five warehouses: San Francisco, Denver, Chicago, Dallas, and New York. Cells A8:A10 show the three plants. The numbers at the intersection of the plants and warehouses contain the number of packages to ship to each warehouse from each plant. These numbers are *seeded* with 1s to give the Solver something from which to start. To the left and bottom of the table are the totals shipped from each plant and the totals received from each warehouse. To begin, each warehouse ships five packages, one to each plant.

Below the ship table, cells C14:G14 contain the numbers of packages demanded by each warehouse. One constraint for a successful solution is to find a method that makes certain that each warehouse gets the number of packages it requires.

The bottom table, cells C16:G18, contains the shipping costs from each warehouse to each plant. Cells B16:B18 contain the amount available to ship from each plant.

The bottom line in the worksheet contains the total shipping cost for each warehouse, with the total of all shipping costs shown in cell B20.

At first glance, the worksheet looks somewhat complex, but when you study it, you probably realize that it really is quite simple. It contains no complex math and should be understood easily.

The problem for the Solver can be stated as follows:

✔ Minimize total shipping costs

✔ Meet the demands of each warehouse

✔ Do not exceed the supply available from each plant

This worksheet is perfect for this discussion. In real life, however, you are likely to need to add timing constraints, along with production rate at the plants, and so forth. Models such as this one can always be made more complicated, however! The real trick in modeling a complex problem is in finding the least complicated way for you to meet your goals.

After the worksheet is set up, you can access the Solver by pulling down the Tools menu and choosing Solver. This operation displays the main dialog box of the Solver, as shown in figure 21.11.

Table 21.3 discusses the settings in the Solver dialog box.

Table 21.3
Solver Dialog Box Settings

Setting	Description
Set Target Cell	The key goal to be met by the Solver, it indicates a single cell on the worksheet.
Equal to	The Equal to box enables you to tell the Solver what you want it to do with the target cell. You can choose to find the maximum value possible by choosing the Max button, the minimum value possible by choosing the Min button, or a set goal amount defined in the Value field. In this example, you want to minimize shipping costs, so the Min button is selected.

continues

VI

Excel Tools

Table 21.3, Continued
Solver Dialog Box Settings

Setting	Description
By Changing Cells	Indicate in this field which cells on the worksheet should be changed in an attempt to find the optimal solution, or click on the **G**uess button.
Guess	Click on the **G**uess button to cause the Solver to determine which non-formula cells go into the cell indicated in S**e**t Target Cell. These cells are entered automatically into the **B**y Changing Cells field. When you choose **G**uess, Excel examines the target cell, and then moves back through all calculated cells until it finds the cells that do not contain formulas, but are part of the target cell's solution.
S**u**bject to the Constraints	This list box lists all of the constraints in the problem. As you can see, three are set already. The first constraint, B8:B10 <= B16:B18, indicates that the cells in B8:B10 (the total shipped from each plant) must be less than or equal to the values in cells B16:B18 (the amount each plant has available). The second constraint, C12:G12 >= C14:G14, indicates that the total amount shipped to each warehouse must be greater than or equal to the amount required by the warehouse. The final constraint, C8:G10 >= 0, tells the Solver that the amount shipped to each warehouse must be greater than or equal to zero for each plant. This constraint (obvious in real life) keeps the Solver from suggesting solutions that include some negative shipments to certain plants but still meet the other constraints.

To define a constraint, click on the **A**dd button. The Add Constraint dialog box appears, as shown in figure 21.12.

Indicate the cell reference for the constraint in the field provided. Then select a constraint type by clicking on the down arrow in the middle of the dialog box. Possible constraints are >=, =, <=, and Int. Int requires that the values in the cell reference cells be full integers. (If you are trying to find optimal schedules, for example, you can't very well schedule part of a truck, or part of a person.) After you have chosen the constraint, you can enter in the value of the constraint in the **C**onstraint field. Click OK to return to the Solver dialog box, or click on **A**dd to store the constraint but keep the Add Constraint dialog box on screen to define additional constraints.

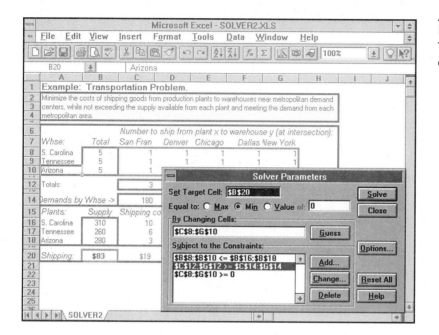

Figure 21.11
The Solver
dialog box.

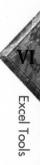

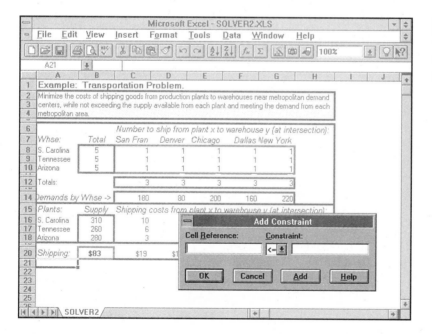

Figure 21.12
The Add
Constraint
dialog box.

You can control the behavior of the Solver with the Options dialog box, accessed through the Options button. Figure 21.13 shows the Options dialog box and Table 21.4 shows its settings.

Figure 21.13
The Options
dialog box.

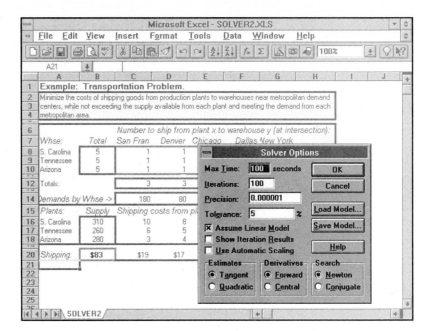

Table 21.4
Solver Options Dialog Box Settings

Setting	Description
Max Time	Sets the maximum amount of time that the Solver can use to solve the problem. You can enter a value as high as 32,767 seconds in this field.
Iterations	Limits the maximum number of iterations that the Solver can take. You can enter up to 32,767 in this field.
Precision	This field controls the precision that the Solver uses to find solutions. You can enter a value here between 0 and 1. A smaller number (fewer decimal places) indicates greater precision. This value controls the tolerance used for constraints.
Tolerance	The Tolerance settings are used when you solve problems that have integer constraints. When you add integer constraints, you require the Solver to solve many subproblems in finding the answer to the larger problem. The value you enter in this field controls the percentage error allowed in the optimal solution. Use this field to speed up the Solver for problems with integer constraints.

Setting	Description
Assume Linear Model	If all of the relationships in a particular problem are linear, selecting this checkbox can make the Solver run faster.
Show Iteration Results	If this checkbox is selected, the Solver stops on each iteration to show you the results in progress. This option can be useful in learning why the Solver is arriving at solutions, which do not seem to be correct, and can suggest additional constraints that keep the Solver on the right track for a correct solution.
Use Automatic Scaling	When you solve a problem where the inputs and outputs have an order of magnitude differences (such as percentage yield on very large dollar investments), you can get more accurate results by enabling this checkbox.
Estimates	The two choices in the Estimates box tell the Solver how to come up with the initial estimates used for the solving process. Choose Tangent for the Solver to use linear extrapolation from a tangent vector. Choose Quadratic for the Solver to use Quadratic Extrapolation.
Derivatives	You can choose between Forward differencing and Central differencing for estimating partial derivatives for the target and constraints. Use Central differencing when the Solver gives you a message saying that it cannot improve on the results already obtained.
Search	When the Solver comes up with an estimate during an iteration, it must decide in which direction to search to proceed to the optimal solution. Newton searching is the default method, but it can consume large amounts of memory for complex problems. In such cases, use Conjugate searching, which is slower, but requires less memory.
Save Model	Click on this button to save the Solver parameters for the problem to a cell range. This operation saves the information on the main Solver dialog box, such as the target cell and constraints, but not the options set in the options dialog box. To work on a Solver

VI

Excel Tools

continues

Table 21.4, Continued
Solver Options Dialog Box Settings

Setting	Description
	problem over multiple sessions with Excel, use this option to save your parameters, and then use the Load Model option to reload the parameters when you return to your workbook.
Load Model	Click on this button to load a model from a cell range.

After changing the Solver options, click on the OK button to return to the main Solver dialog box. To solve for the optimal solution, click on the Solve button. When the Solver has finished calculating it shows you the results, as shown in figure 21.14.

Figure 21.14

The Solver completion dialog box.

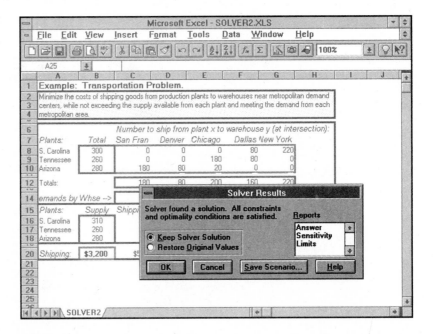

In the completion dialog box, you can choose to view reports of the actions taken by the Solver. Click on each type of report you want to see in the Reports box before clicking on OK to complete the Solving process. The results of the example worksheet are shown in figure 21.15.

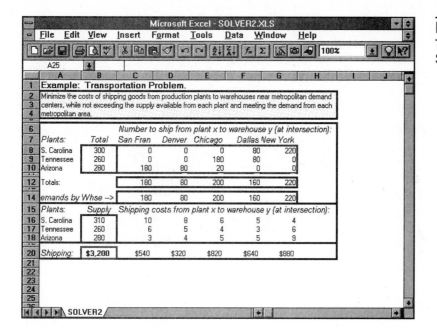

Figure 21.15
The completed
Solver example.

View Manager

You can use the View Manager to store different *views* of your worksheet without being required to maintain different sheets in your workbook. You might, for example, create different views that show various levels of detail and use the View Manager to switch quickly between the different views. The View Manager stores aspects of your current view, such as zoom level, pane and window positions, gridline appearance, and so on.

First, you should create a view of the completed worksheet so that you can quickly switch back to it at any time. To create this first view, follow these steps:

1. Pull down the View menu and choose View Manager. You see the View Manager dialog box shown in figure 21.16.

2. Click on the Add button to bring up a new dialog box (shown in fig. 21.17), which enables you to control which aspects of the current view to save.

3. In the Add View dialog box, enter the name to be used for the current view in the Name field.

4. If you want current print settings stored in the view, select the Print Settings checkbox. If you want hidden row and column status to be saved, select the Hidden Rows and Columns checkbox. Click on the OK button to save the view and exit the View Manager.

Figure 21.16
The View
Manager
dialog box.

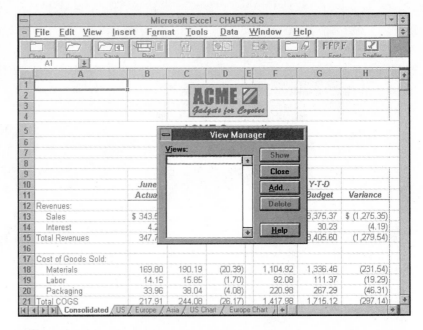

Figure 21.17
The Add View
dialog box.

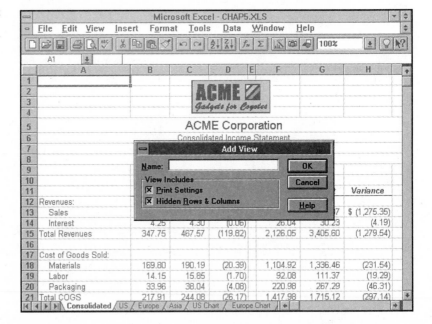

Now, you can create another view that you would like to store. When you have completed changing the worksheet viewing components to suit your taste, activate the View Manager again and add the new view.

After you have added the views you want to store, switch between them by activating the View Manager, choosing the view you want in the dialog box, and then click on the $\underline{S}$how button to display the worksheet instantly in the stored fashion.

Excel Tools

Part VII

Appendixes

APPENDIX

Installing Excel and Included Disk

F or most users, installing Excel is an easy and relatively straightforward task. Because of Excel's versatility, however, you can approach the installation from many different angles. You can install Excel from a network, for example, or add and subtract program components from your installed copy of Excel. This appendix covers the basic Excel for Windows installation process along with the other capabilities of the Excel installation program. The second half of the appendix tells you how to install the bonus disk included with this book.

System Requirements

Before installing Excel 5 for Windows, you must have the following system capabilities:

- ✔ An Intel-based computer (also called *IBM-compatible*) that uses at least an 80286 processor.

- ✔ 4M of installed memory.

- ✔ A 3 ½ -inch or 5 ¼ inch floppy disk drive (or both).

- ✔ A hard disk with at least 10M of free space. (To install *all* Excel features, you need 23M of free disk space.)

- ✔ DOS version 3.1 or later and Windows 3.1 or later. Note that Excel 5 for Windows does not function properly with Windows 3.0.

Installing Excel

To begin installing Excel, follow these steps:

1. Start Windows.

2. Insert Disk 1 of Excel into the appropriate floppy drive.

3. In the Program Manager, pull down the File menu and choose Run. In the dialog box that appears, type *x*:**SETUP**, where *x* is the drive letter in which the Excel disk is inserted. If you are using drive A, for example, type **A:SETUP** and press Enter.

After a moment, the initial installation screen appears, as shown in figure A.1.

After you click on the OK button to continue, Excel prompts you for your name and company name. Type the information in the fields provided and click on the OK button to proceed.

After you enter your name and company name, that information is permanently stored on the disks and will be used for all future installations of Excel from that set of disks. Make sure you are entering the correct information before proceeding.

Next, a screen appears that shows you the serial number for your copy of Excel. You should write down that information someplace safe, because you will need it if you ever need to call Microsoft for assistance. In general, it is a good idea to write the serial number on disk 1 and inside the cover of the Excel manual.

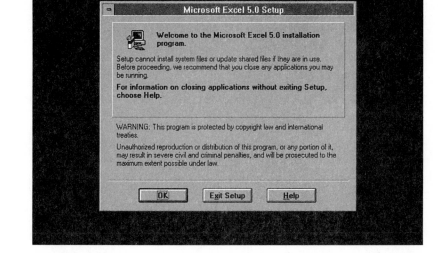

Figure A.1
Opening installation screen.

If you don't write down the serial number, you still can access it from within Excel. Pull down the Help menu and choose About. The serial number appears in the dialog box.

Upgrading Excel

At this point in the installation, if you are installing an upgrade version of Excel, you need to provide some additional information in order to proceed. If you are installing a full copy of Excel, you can skip to the next section.

Normally, when you are installing an upgrade version of Excel, it scans your hard disk to locate the previous version. If, however, you have removed the previous version of Excel from your computer, you need to have access to the disks from the previous version to continue with the installation.

If the installation program cannot find a previous version of Excel on your hard disk, you see the screen shown in figure A.2.

VII

Appendixes

Figure A.2
Upgrade
message.

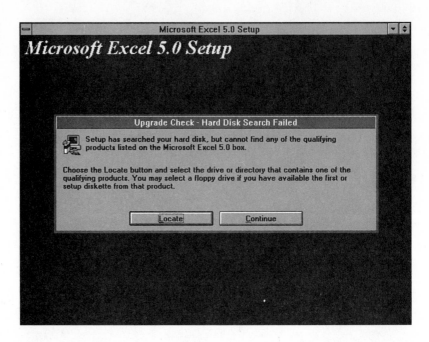

To proceed from the dialog box shown in figure A.2, click on the Locate button. You then see the dialog box shown in figure A.3.

Figure A.3
Locate dialog box.

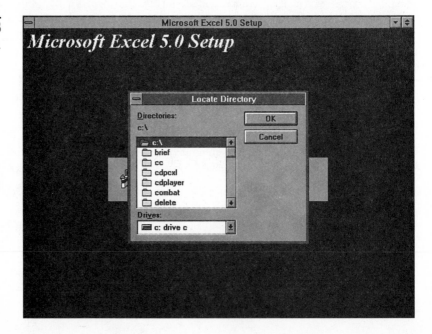

Use this dialog box to indicate to the installation program where the previous version of Excel is installed. Alternately, insert Disk 1 from the previous version, click on the Drives list box, then choose the appropriate disk drive where you have inserted the disk. Next, click on the OK button to proceed with the installation. If the installation program cannot find the files it needs, it asks you to insert another disk.

Continuing the Installation

The Excel installation program now asks you in which directory you want to install Excel. See figure A.4, which shows this screen.

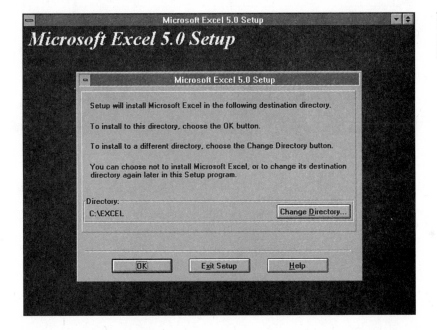

Figure A.4
Directory dialog box.

If the directory shown in the Directory box is not where you want to install Excel, click on the Change Directory button, then indicate where you want Excel to be installed. Otherwise, click on the OK button to go on.

Selecting Options

You now come to the main screen, which enables you to select which options you want to install, as shown in figure A.5.

Figure A.5
Selection screen.

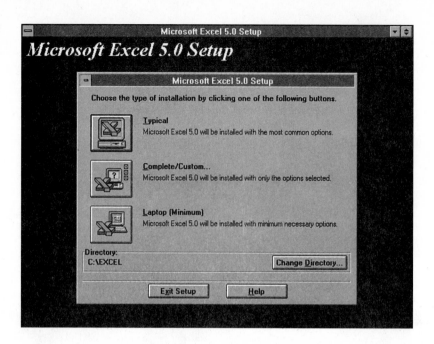

You have three types of installation available to you:

- ✔ **Typical.** Choose this option to install the most common Excel options.

- ✔ **Complete/Custom.** Choose this option to control exactly which options of Excel to install or to install all Excel options.

- ✔ **Laptop (Minimum).** If you are installing on a system with limited disk space, choose this installation option.

If you choose a Typical or Laptop installation, the installation process continues. If, however, you select the Complete/Custom option, you see the dialog box shown in figure A.6.

The Options window shows you each major component of Excel, along with the amount of space that component will take up on your hard disk. Click on a particular component to see a description of that component in the Description area of the dialog box. Click on the check boxes to select or deselect a particular component. Or, if you only want parts of a particular component, click once on the component, then click on the Change Option button to view the details of that particular component. In this way, you can select exactly which features you want to install. At the bottom of the dialog box, you see the amount of disk space your selected configuration will take as well as how much free disk space is available. After you have selected all the components you want, click on the Continue button to continue with the installation.

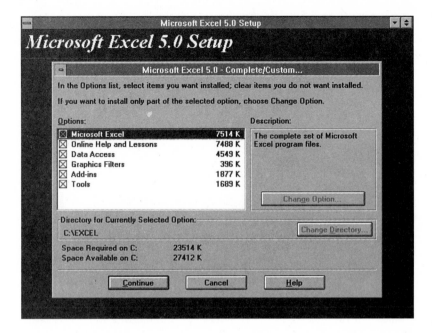

Figure A.6
Complete/Custom
dialog box.

After you have selected one of the three installation options, Excel prompts you for the name of the Program Manager group in which you want to install the Excel 5 icons. By default, it selects a group called Microsoft Office. If you want to install the icons in a different program group, select it from the list (or type it into the field provided), then click on the OK button.

The installation now begins. At certain points in the installation, Setup asks you to insert each of the Excel disks in turn. When the installation is complete, the new icons are created in the program group you selected. Also, if you don't already have SHARE.EXE loaded in your AUTOEXEC.BAT file, the Excel installation program adds it for you. SHARE.EXE is required for Excel 5 for Windows.

After Excel is installed, an icon labelled Microsoft Excel Read Me appears in your Excel program group. You should double-click on the Read Me icon to read last-minute notes about Excel that did not make it into the program documentation.

Changing Installed Components

You can add or delete Excel components with the MS Excel Setup icon in the Excel program group. When you start the Setup program, you see the screen shown in figure A.7.

5   VII

Appendixes

Figure A.7
Installation
maintenance
program.

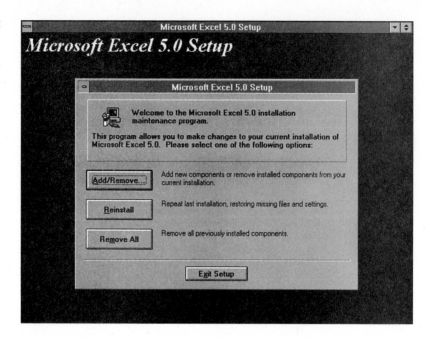

The installation maintenance program includes the following options:

✔ **A**dd/Remove. Choose this button to add or remove Excel components.

✔ **R**einstall. If you think you might have accidentally erased part of Excel, or if Excel does not seem to be functioning correctly, and you think one of the program files might have become damaged, select this option to reinstall Excel.

✔ **Re**move All. Choose this button to completely remove Excel from your computer.

Installing the *Inside Excel 5 for Windows* Bonus Disk

This part of the appendix shows you how to install the *Inside Excel 5 for Windows* bonus disk that accompanies this book. For further information on ordering the upgrade to the Baarns Utilities that are on this disk, see the back of the book. Also, a Word for Windows 2.0 formatted documented (\BAARNS\BAARNDOC.ZIP) is provided on the disk for you to read as a reference on getting the most out of these utilities.

What's on the Bonus Disk?

The *Inside Excel 5 for Windows* bonus disk contains several files that can help you get the most out of your Excel 5 investment. As you go through this book, some chapters reference specific exercise files that are on the bonus disk. These files are stored on the disk under specific chapter subdirectories, such as \CHAP03 or \CHAP19.

Also contained on the bonus disk is New Riders Publishing exclusive Excel 5 On-Screen Advisor, a Windows Help file designed to aid you in getting up and running on Excel 5. The On-Screen Advisor is a separate .HLP file that you can add to your Excel 5 toolbar or run it from Program Manager.

As an exclusive offer to Prentice Hall Computer Publishing and New Riders Publishing, the *Inside Excel 5 for Windows* bonus disk contains a special Version 1 of The Baarns Utilities. The Baarns Utilities are Excel productivity enhancements aimed at making you more productive while working in Excel 5. You can upgrade to Version 5 for only $19.95 by following the directions provided in the back of the book.

The Baarns Utilities provided on the bonus disk contain the following items:

- ✔ **Baarns AutoSave.** Automatically saves your current documents to minimize the chances of losing your work.

- ✔ **Baarns Clock.** This is a simple utility that places either the time or the time and date in a separate window on your screen.

- ✔ **Baarns Express Math.** Designed to enable you to change a group of numbers by a constant amount.

- ✔ **Baarns New.** Similar to the File, New command in Excel 5, this utility opens a new document or template. Additionally, this utility enables you to save custom templates with long, 31 character, descriptive names and store them in any directory you choose.

- ✔ **Baarns Print Cleanser.** This utility removes all the left over printing setups that are "stored" with a document. Really handy for all those manual page breaks inserted in documents.

- ✔ **Baarns Print Special.** Enables you to print parts of your documents that are not currently defined as a print area.

- ✔ **Baarns Reminders.** Enables you to keep track of events in the future.

- ✔ **Baarns Save As Icon.** Saves your current document and creates an icon for it in the Windows Program Manager. You then can double-click on the icon in Program Manager to start Excel and load that document.

✔ **Baarns Set Standard Font.** Provides a shortcut for setting the standard font in a document and optionally setting the standard font on all future documents.

✔ **Baarns Sticky Notes.** Creates an on-screen note similar to Post-It Notes.

✔ **Baarns Template Wizard.** Assists you in building templates.

✔ **Baarns Timer.** Enables you to set a timer as you work on your documents. Handy if you are working on a billable project.

✔ **Baarns Utilities Options.** Enables you to control the display of its menus and toolbar, and to change the startup settings for specific utilities.

✔ **Baarns Zoom.** Enables you to change the magnification of your document.

Using Specific Exercise Files

Included on the *Inside Excel 5 for Windows* bonus disk are the sample applications and spreadsheets that accompany specific exercises or chapters in the book. These files are stored on the bonus disk in separate subdirectories that correspond to their chapter names. The sample application for Chapter 19, for instance, is stored in the subdirectory named CHAP19. Simply copy the file(s) from the specific subdirectory onto your hard drive as you work through the exercises.

Installing the Baarns Utilities

You can install the Baarns Utilities from the bonus disk itself or copy the contents onto your hard drive and install them from there. If you want to install the Baarns Utilities from your hard drive, use the following instructions (see Step 3 if you are installing from the bonus disk):

1. Find the following directory on the *Inside Excel 5 for Windows* bonus disk:

   \BAARNS\DISK1

2. You then need to copy the \DISK1 subdirectory and its contents onto your hard drive. Make sure that you copy or make a subdirectory called DISK1 on your hard drive. Without it, the utilities will not be able to install.

3. After you have the contents copied onto your hard disk, select File, Run from the Windows Program Manager or File Manager. In the Command Line text box in

the Run dialog box, enter the complete path where you have placed the Baarns Utilities and include \SETUP.EXE at the end of the path. This will run the installation program that installs the Baarns Utilities on your hard drive.

You might, for instance, have the Baarns Utilities stored in a BAARNS directory. If this is the case, you would type the following:

```
C:\BAARNS\DISK1\SETUP.EXE
```

If you are installing straight from the bonus disk, enter the drive letter in which the floppy disk resides (usually A: or B:) and type the command **\BAARNS\DISK1\SETUP.EXE**.

4. Click on OK. This starts the installation and displays the Baarns Utilities Setup dialog box.

5. Click on <u>C</u>ontinue. This opens the Baarns Utilities Installation Option dialog box, in which you have the following two choices:

   ✔ **<u>E</u>xpress Installation (Recommended).** This installs all the utilities on your hard drive in the default directory, which usually is the \LIBRARY subdirectory in your EXCEL directory.

If you still have Excel 4 on your hard drive, the default directory for the utilities might be in the Excel 4 directory rather than Excel 5. If you want them in your Excel 5 directory, use the following installation option.

   ✔ **<u>C</u>ustom Installation (or Uninstall).** This option enables you to select several options, such as installing the Help file, installing the Baarns Utilities, or uninstalling the utilities. You also can set the location where you want to place the utilities on your hard drive.

6. Depending on the choice you made in the preceding step, the setup routine starts copying all or some of the files onto your hard drive. If you selected to have the utilities start when Excel starts, you now can activate Excel and start using the utilities.

See the DOC file provided on the bonus disk for more information on using specific utilities. You should also consult the Help file provided with the Baarns Utilities if you have any problems.

Installing the Excel 5 On-Screen Advisor

Included on the *Inside Excel 5 for Windows* bonus disk is the NRP On-Screen Advisor. To install the Excel 5 On-Screen Advisor on your hard disk, use the following steps.

1. Change to the \OSA directory on the bonus disk and copy the OSA-XL.HLP file into the directory on your hard drive in which you want to place the On-Screen Advisor, such as C:\EXCEL5.

2. Create an icon in Program Manager by choosing File, New in Program Manager and clicking on the New Item option. Click OK.

3. In the Program Item Properties dialog box, type **Excel 5 On-Screen Advisor** in the Description box.

4. In the Command Line field, type in the full path of the IWP60OSA.HLP file, such as **C:\EXCEL5\OSA-XL.HLP**.

5. Click on OK. You now can double-click on the Help icon to run the On-Screen Advisor.

APPENDIX

Getting Excel Help

When you are learning and using Excel 5 for Windows, questions inevitably arise, and your work comes to a screeching halt until you find answers. As a general rule, you should become at least a little familiar with where and how to find information before you really need it. This appendix uncovers all those places you can go for help, including the following:

- ✔ The Excel program

- ✔ Reference materials

- ✔ On-line help

- ✔ Microsoft support

If you know where to look, you can get fast, fast relief and proceed with work as planned.

Experts estimate that as many as 98 percent of the people who call for software support already had the answer to their questions available in the manuals that came with their programs. You should not be surprised, then, to learn that Microsoft charges for telephone support—after all, it costs money to hire all those employees to read the manual to people who call.

Why do so many people call for software support, anyway? With a large, complex program like Excel 5, it sometimes is hard to know where to begin to look for answers.

Running the Tutorial

One of the first things to know is the correct terminology. Clearly, you might find it difficult to look up an answer when you are having a problem with a "whatchamacalit" only to find out that the Excel program refers to it as a "thingy." Utilizing the tutorial that comes with Excel is a good way to start learning the correct terminology.

The first time you start Excel after installing it on your computer, Excel automatically presents you with its built-in tutorial. If you are new to Excel, spend the time to run this tutorial. It is a good way to get your feet wet with Excel.

To start the tutorial, use the following steps:

1. Pull down the Help menu.

2. Choose Quick Preview.

The Quick Preview function is divided into four lessons; each one takes about seven minutes to complete. These lessons cover getting started, new features in Excel 5, getting help while you work, and a special preview for people moving to Excel from Lotus 1-2-3. After you have mastered the information in the Quick Preview, choose Examples and Demos from the Help menu to get more comprehensive information about a wide variety of Excel topics. Many of these topics include demonstrations on ways to accomplish different tasks, along with explanatory text and pictures.

Using Excel Help

After you have progressed through the tutorial, take some time to browse through the Help feature that comes with the Excel 5 program. If you did not install Help (yes, it does take up some extra disk space), you should install it now. To begin the Excel 5 Help, simply click on the word Help in the upper right corner of the Excel Window.

You also can access help for specific parts of the screen, toolbar buttons, and so on, by clicking on the Help button on the Standard toolbar. Your cursor changes to a pointer with a question mark. Point to the part of Excel with which you want additional help, then click the left mouse button. You also can use this method to choose menu commands to get help.

Using Excel Wizards

In version 5 of Excel, Microsoft has included Wizards for various functions. A Wizard (ChartWizard, Function Wizard, TextWizard, and so on) automatically starts up when you begin using the tool it accompanies. Each Excel Wizard is discussed in its appropriate place in this book. They help make Excel more "user-friendly" by walking you through different procedures step by step.

Viewing Demonstrations of Excel Features

You do not need to go to the nearest computer store for a quick demonstration of ways to use various functions. Click on Help, then select Examples & Demos for a helpful sneak preview.

Reading the Manual

The manuals that come with Excel actually are quite good and are fairly complete, unlike many computer software manuals. Their only real shortcoming is that various topics are not explained terribly well; they are, however, well laid out. The manuals are a good place to look when you have a question about Excel (if you can't find it in *this* book, of course!).

Reading this Book

Inside Excel 5 for Windows is a good resource for you, also. The book is written and organized for maximum reference value. See the introduction for organization information, type conventions, and special icons. Whether you are a beginner or an advanced Excel user, this book can provide a wide range of helpful information and valuable advice.

Getting Excel Help on CompuServe

If none of the help resources already mentioned answer your questions, do not pick up the phone to call (and pay for) Microsoft's Excel help line just yet. Instead, pick up the phone and call CompuServe Information Service (CIS) to get a CompuServe account.

Nearly all large (or even moderately-sized) software or hardware companies today provide help on CIS, and Microsoft is no exception. This support is a win-win situation: companies that have their own CIS forums find that it takes far fewer people to support *a lot* more users; and, it costs you considerably *less* money to get support on CIS than it does to call the help line.

Understanding CompuServe

If you are not familiar with CIS, take a few minutes to read this section.

You can think of CompuServe as the world's largest computer bulletin board system (BBS). A real bulletin board contains messages to specific people and general information for everyone. CIS has everything a real bulletin board has and a whole lot more. In addition to the business-related forums, it has many hobby- and interest-related categories as well as tremendous databases of information.

The cost to access CompuServe varies with the pricing plan you select as well as the country in which you reside. For United States residents, it costs approximately $10–18 per hour.

You can greatly reduce your costs by using an autonavigational program. An *autonav* program can go on- and off-line very quickly, picking up most of the information you need at full speed—because you told it what to get before it went on-line. Most autonav programs are available for downloading from CompuServe, although they are published independently. Good programs to evaluate include OzCIS and TapCIS, although there are other good programs as well. If you decide to keep and use these shareware programs, you need to register and pay for the programs with the respective software companies.

The best part about CompuServe is that the nearest node is usually only a local telephone call away. Every major city, and lots and lots of smaller ones, have a CompuServe node. (A node is a bank of modems ready for your telephone call to access CompuServe.)

In addition to accessing CompuServe and all it has to offer, you can do the following:

- ✔ Send and receive Internet, MCI, and MHS mail
- ✔ Send postal letters (which later are printed at certain CompuServe locations and mailed as regular U.S. Postal mail)
- ✔ Send faxes

CompuServe provides a lot of different services. Some of these services cost a little extra.

For a complete guide to CompuServe and its many uses, see New Riders Publishing's *Inside CompuServe*, by Richard Wagner. In addition to hundreds of pages of valuable information, this book includes a coupon for a free introductory CompuServe membership.

Getting Started on CompuServe

You can open a CompuServe account in a number of ways:

- ✔ Contact a friend who already has a CompuServe account—your friend receives some usage credit for referring you, and you receive a usage credit for signing up.
- ✔ Call CompuServe Information service at 1-800-848-8990 or 1-614-529-6887.
- ✔ Browse your local computer software store for a box that says "CompuServe" on the side. It contains all the information and software you need to go on-line and get started immediately.

As soon as you get a CompuServe account, go to the Practice area (**GO PRACTICE**) to practice posting and reading messages. This forum is free of connect time charges so that you do not have to pay to learn. You can find some useful information in the libraries there, also. (Libraries are discussed later in this appendix.)

Setting up Your Computer

All you need to use CompuServe is a modem attached to your computer. If you do not have a CompuServe access program, you also need some communications software, which you can find in any computer retail store or catalog. That's it!

Talking to Microsoft on CompuServe

If you have other Microsoft programs, you should be happy to know that Microsoft supports all of them on CIS without a surcharge other than the normal CIS fees. To get to the top level menu of all the Microsoft services on CompuServe, type **GO MICROSOFT** from any ! prompt.

You navigate through CompuServe using "GO" commands. CompuServe is not pretty, and it might seem a little cryptic. CompuServe uses an exclamation mark for its prompt. At any ! prompt, you can type **HELP** to get the help you need. The prompt also is where you type **GO** words.

Three main areas in the Microsoft forums provide the support you need for getting help with Excel. These areas are discussed in the next three sections.

Accessing the Excel Forum

Each forum on CompuServe is divided into several sections to better categorize questions and answers and the conversations that occur. The Excel forum sections (at the time this book was written) are set up as shown in Figure B.1.

You can see that your questions should be posted in Section 3, "Excel for the PC." In case you are wondering, the numbers beside the menu selection (in parentheses) indicate the number of *message threads* (or conversations) on the message board, followed by the total number of messages in that section.

Appendixes

Figure B.1
CompuServe's
main Excel forum
menu.

```
The Microsoft Excel Forum+ Messages Menu

Message age selection = [All]

  1 SELECT (Read by section and subject)
  2 READ or search messages

  3 CHANGE age selection

  4 COMPOSE a message
  5 UPLOAD a message

Enter choice !1

The Microsoft Excel Forum+ Sections Menu

Section names (#subjs/# msgs)
  1 General Information  (42/77)
  2 Excel for the Mac  (29/55)
  3 Excel for the PC  (143/322)
 14 nonTech Cust Ser  (5/11)
 16 MS Office Setup (2/3)

Enter choice(s) or ALL !_
  Alt-Z FOR HELP| ANSI        | FDX | 19200 E71 | LOG CLOSED | PRINT OFF | ON-LINE
```

If you need to post a question on the message board, keep the following guidelines in mind:

✔ **Be Polite.** Even if you are frustrated, keep your temper in check. That old adage "You can catch more flies with honey than with vinegar" applies just as much on CompuServe as it does anywhere else. People are more willing to be helpful if you are courteous.

✔ **Once is enough.** Do not post the same message more than once on a forum. If your message is in the wrong place, the *SysOp* (System Operator, or overseer of the forum), moves it to the correct message section or lets you know where you might post the message for a better response. Remember that people do not like to pay to download or read the same message more than once.

✔ **Be concise.** Provide all the pertinent information, but do not wander from the point too much. For instance, including such items as "I stayed up for 82 hours straight trying to solve this problem" does not help in providing people with the information they need to answer your question. You should include the following information in your message:

    ✔ The version of Excel you are using.

    ✔ Your operating system (DOS, OS/2, and so on) and version number.

    ✔ Your hardware manufacturer and model.

    ✔ The keystrokes that you used just prior to having a problem (if applicable). Try to reproduce the problem before you report it.

    ✔ If you receive an error message, write down the exact wording so that you can include it in your message.

Most forums try to provide answers within 24 hours. Some questions are answered in a matter of an hour or two, and most are answered within the targeted 24-hour period. Do not despair, however, if your question is not answered immediately.

In addition to the SysOps, a lot of knowledgeable people tend to "hang out" on the forums (including many of the people involved in writing and producing this book). If your question is answered by someone other than a Microsoft employee, chances are fairly high that the person is well-informed. Very rarely do you receive incorrect answers or bad advice anywhere on CompuServe. Because the messages are visible to read by anyone with a CompuServe account, people correct information they know is wrong.

> One of the things that makes a support forum on CompuServe so viable is that advice to one person can be read by all people who choose to read the messages. If you pay attention to what other people are asking, you might not need to post your own question, because it might have already been asked and answered. You might also be able to avoid some pitfalls or mistakes by reading what others are doing.

Using the Microsoft Knowledge Base

You might not even need to post a question on Microsoft's Excel forum if you utilize Microsoft's Knowledge Base. The Knowledge Base is a special database that formerly was available only to Microsoft Technical Support personnel—the people you talk to when you call Microsoft Support. Now, you can use it in your own home or office at no cost over and above the regular CompuServe charges.

To get to the Microsoft Knowledge Base, simply type **GO MSKB**, or select it from the Microsoft main menu (**GO MICROSOFT**). However you get there, you should end up at a menu that looks like figure B.2.

VII

Appendixes

```
Exiting at 31-Oct-93 18:25:08
Thank you for visiting The Microsoft Excel Forum


One moment please...

Knowledge Base+

Welcome to The Microsoft Knowledge Base
Copyright (c) 1993 Microsoft Corporation

 1 What's New in the Knowledge Base
 2 Description of Database
 3 Online User's Guide

 4 Search the Knowledge Base
 5 Search using Expert Mode
 6 Quick Search - By Document Id Number

 7 Microsoft Software Library

!
Alt-Z FOR HELP| ANSI       | FDX | 19200 E71 | LOG CLOSED | PRINT OFF | ON-LINE
```

Figure B.2
The Knowledge Base main menu.

You should read item 2—Description of Database—and item 3—Online User's Guide—before you try to use the database. This area cannot be automated with an autonavigational program, and the clock is ticking while you are on-line. Learning the way in which the Knowledge Base works before spending lots of time with it pays off in reduced connect-time charges.

Accessing the Microsoft Software Library

Another valuable area is the Microsoft Software Library. As you can see from the menu shown in figure B.2, you can choose selection number 7, or you can go there directly by typing **GO MSL**. This library contains all sorts of files including device drivers, samples, information files, sample spreadsheets, and even macro code samples. These sample files not only serve as good examples, but might also be a good starting point for a project.

You can utilize this area much better by finding out what information you want to download beforehand in the Knowledge Base. (You cannot automate access to this area, either.) This area is particularly cryptic, as shown in figure B.3.

Figure B.3
The Microsoft
Software Library
main menu.

```
One moment please...

CompuServe+    MSL-1


MICROSOFT SOFTWARE LIBRARY

1 BROWSE thru files
2 SCAN
3 KEYWORD list

4 DOWNLOAD a file
5 READ a file




Enter choice !_
Alt-Z FOR HELP| ANSI      | FDX | 19200 E71 | LOG CLOSED | PRINT OFF | ON-LINE
```

Finding Other Files

CompuServe is rich with all types of resources, including many shareware programs, add-ons, and files. (*Shareware* is try-it-before-you-buy-it software—Excel is *not* shareware, although many of the tools available for download from CIS are.)

CompuServe File Finder is the central place to go to find out where all the Excel shareware files might be found. Type **GO FILEFINDER** to get there, and start with a keyword search of **EXCEL**. You need to have additional selection criteria in mind because so many files containing keywords of Excel exist. As of the date of this book, a keyword search for EXCEL in Filefinder found 407 files that had the word "Excel" in their descriptions.

Again, this area of CompuServe cannot be autonavigated. Have some idea of what you are looking for before you go there.

Talking to Prentice Hall Computer Publishing

Prentice Hall Computer Publishing also maintains a forum on CompuServe where many of the authors, editors, and other readers hang out (**GO PHCP**). New Riders Publishing is a division of Prentice Hall Computer Publishing, and you can post a message there if you have a question or comment about the book. This area is not intended for technical support for Excel, but rather for comments about Prentice Hall Computer Publishing books.

If you do not want everyone with a CompuServe account (more than one million people) to see your comments about this book, you can send messages directly to persons involved with this book. New Riders can be reached at CompuServe ID {70031,2231}. Author Bruce Hallberg's private CompuServe ID is {76376,515}. The technical editor, Bob Greenblatt, is on-line at {71540,3362} (**GO MAIL**).

Calling Microsoft

If you still have not found the answer to your question in the Microsoft Excel help system, demos, tutorial, wizard, manual, or this book, and you cannot find what you are looking for on CompuServe (which is very unlikely), you should call Microsoft for support.

> **NOTE** Before you call Microsoft, take a look at the Common Questions in the Help files as well as the README file that was installed with Excel. You might be able to save yourself some time and money by finding the answers you need there.

Like your CompuServe messages, make sure you have the following information handy before you call:

✔ The version of Excel you are using, along with the serial number, which you can find in the Excel box or by accessing <u>A</u>bout from the <u>H</u>elp menu.

✔ Your operating system and version number.

✔ Your hardware manufacturer and model.

✔ The keystrokes you used just prior to having a problem (if applicable). Try to reproduce the problem before you report it.

✔ If you receive an error message, write down the exact wording so that you can include it in your message.

Microsoft has two calling plans; each one costs a lot more money and takes more time than any of the options listed previously.

Accessing Free Support

Between the hours of 6:00 a.m. and 6:00 p.m. Pacific time, Microsoft has a free support line available (although you do have to pay for the long-distance phone charges). This number is 206-635-7070. Because this number is for free support, you should expect a fair amount of time on hold. You hear status messsages regarding the average time spent waiting, so you can judge whether to stay on the line or try again later.

Accessing Paid Support

Microsoft offers "priority access" support 24 hours a day, seven days a week, excluding holidays. The numbers vary depending on the payment plan you choose. Here are the numbers:

- ✔ 1-900-555-2100. The cost is $2 per minute ($25 maximum), and the charges appear on your telephone bill.

- ✔ 1-800-936-5700. The charge is $25 per "incident" and can be billed to your VISA, MasterCard, or American Express.

An "incident" means that if the question or problem cannot be taken care of with one telephone call, no additional fee is charged for calls until the problem is resolved.

If you want to tell Microsoft what you would like to see in the next version of Excel, then you need to call 1-206-936-WISH.

Using Other Telephone Support

Microsoft offers telephone support to people with special needs. If you have hearing difficulties, you can call Microsoft's text telephone (TT/TDD) at 1-206-635-4948 between 6:00 a.m. and 6:00 p.m. Pacific time, Monday through Friday (excluding holidays).

For faxes, and to receive recorded answers to questions commonly asked, you can dial Microsoft's FastTips telephone number at 1-800-936-4100, 24 hours a day, seven days a week. You also can receive articles concerning technical subjects (solving installation problems, resolving compatability problems, and so on) via the FastTips line.

Finding Excel Training

If you are really stumped about all this Excel business, you might want to consider some formal training courses. In addition to local PC stores that offer many training courses, Microsoft has officially sanctioned training courses and centers around the United States. Call 1-800-227-4679 between 6:30 a.m. and 5:30 p.m. Pacific time to find out the location nearest you.

Closing Advice

As you can see by browsing this appendix, lots of help options are open to you when working with Excel. To overcome likely problems, keep the following advice in mind when you are working with any software program:

- ✔ **Be patient.** Expect to take some time to look through this book, the help files in the Excel program, and the manuals. Excel is a large, complex program, and it might take some time and experimentation to find the right answers.

- ✔ **Take frequent breaks.** It does not matter if you walk your kids or pet your dog, but do take frequent breaks. You are better off in the long run.

- ✔ **Take small steps.** Try one thing at a time—do not make lots of changes all at the same time. Lots of changes can cause confusion and can make a mess even worse. It also makes it harder to retrace your steps if you have a crash or get an error message.

- ✔ **Look out for bugs.** Programmers are human, and humans do make mistakes. Although Excel is exceptionally clean compared to many software programs, you might run into an occasional problem that is rooted in the program itself. Again, patience is the key here. If you think you have found a software bug, it is very important that you write down all the information concerning the bug and report it to Microsoft. Often, they have fixes for bugs already reported and can send those fixes to you for a nominal fee.

- ✔ **Have fun!** Remember, the future of Western civilization is not at stake here. Maintain your perspective.

VII

Appendixes

Keyboard Shortcuts

This appendix contains a number of useful keyboard shortcuts. Learning the following keys can make you more productive with Excel. Use the following tables as a handy reference guide.

Microsoft Excel 5 for Windows includes a number of key changes from version 4. Some of these key changes accommodate new features, while others make the Excel keys more compatible with other Microsoft products.

Table C.1
Excel 5 Key Combination Changes

Key or Key Combination	Action
F4	Repeat last action
F7	Check spelling
Ctrl+F	Find
Ctrl+H	Replace
Shift+F4	Find
Ctrl+Shift+F4	Find previous
Ctrl+N	Open new workbook
Ctrl+O	Open
Ctrl+S	Save
Ctrl+P	Print
Ctrl+Tab	Next window
Ctrl+Shift+Tab	Previous window
Ctrl+PgDn	Moves to the next worksheet
Ctrl+PgUp	Moves to the previous worksheet
Ctrl+A	Select all

Tables C.2–C.4 lists the keys you use to enter and edit data. Use these keys to navigate your documents, access the clipboard functions, and control calculations in your documents. You'll use these shortcuts more often than others.

Table C.2
Entering Data

Key or Key Combination	Action
F2	Edits the current cell
Enter	Completes an action
Esc	Cancels an act
F4	Repeats the last act (Redo)

Key or Key Combination	Action
Ctrl+Z	Undoes the last act (Undo)
Ctrl+Shift++ (plus sign)	Inserts new blank cells
Ctrl+– (hyphen)	Deletes the selected object or cells
Del	Clears the selected area of formulas and data; when editing a cell, deletes the character to the right of the current cursor position
Ctrl+X	Cuts the selection
Ctrl+C	Copies the selection
Ctrl+V	Pastes to the selection
Backspace	Edits the formula after clearing the cell entry, or backspaces over a character; when editing a cell, erases the previous character
Shift+F2	Edits a cell note
F3	Pastes a name into a formula
Shift+F3	Activates the function wizard
Ctrl+F3	Defines a name
Ctrl+Shift+F3	Creates names from cell text
F9 or Ctrl+= (equals sign)	Calculates all documents in all open workbooks; if you highlight a section, calculates only that section
Shift+F9	Calculates the active document
Alt+=	Inserts the AutoSum formula
Ctrl+; (semicolon)	Enters the date
Ctrl+Shift+: (colon)	Enters the time
Ctrl+D	Fills down
Ctrl+R	Fills right
Enter	Moves down through a selection
Shift+Enter	Moves up through a selection

VII

Appendixes

continues

Table C.2, Continued
Entering Data

Key or Key Combination	Action
Tab	Moves right through a selection
Shift+Tab	Moves left through a selection
Ctrl+Shift+A	Completes the punctuation for you when you first type in a valid function name in a formula

Table C.3
Editing Data

Key or Key Combination	Action
Ctrl+X	Cuts the selection to the clipboard
Ctrl+C	Copies the selection to the clipboard
Ctrl+V	Pastes the selection from the clipboard
Del	Clears the selection of formulas and data
Ctrl+Shift++	Inserts blank cells
Ctrl+−	Deletes the selected calls
Ctrl+Z	Undoes the last act

Table C.4
Working in Cell Entries

Key or Key Combination	Action
=	Starts a formula
Alt+Enter	Inserts a carriage return
Arrow keys	Moves one character up, down, left, or right
Backspace	Deletes the character to the left of the insertion point, or deletes the selection

Key or Key Combination	Action
Ctrl+' (apostrophe)	Copies the formula from the cell above the active cell into the current cell
Ctrl+' (single quote, usually found above the Tab key)	Alternates between displaying results or formulas in cells
Ctrl+Alt+=	Displays the Function Wizard if typed after entering in a function name in a cell
Ctrl+Alt+Tab	Inserts a tab
Ctrl+Delete	Cuts text to the end of the line
Ctrl+Enter	Fills a selection of cells with the current entry. Select the cells, type the information, then press Ctrl+Enter.
Ctrl+Shift+"	Copies the value from the cell above the active cell into the current cell
Ctrl+Shift+:	Inserts the time
Ctrl+Shift+Enter	Enters the formula as an array formula
Del	Deletes the character to the right of the cursor, or deletes the entire selection
Enter	Completes a cell entry
Esc	Cancels an entry
F2	Edits cell entry
F4	Toggles current reference between absolute and relative references
Home	Moves to the start of a line
Shift+Tab	Stores the cell entry and moves to the previous cell in the row or range
Tab	Stores the cell entry and moves to the next cell in the row or range

The new workbook metaphor in Excel 5 created the need for new key shortcuts for moving between your workbook documents. Table C.5 shows the keys that accomplish these moves as well as the keys for navigating among and within open Excel windows.

Table C.5
Moving In and Between Documents

Key or Key Combination	Action
Alt+PgDn	Moves right one screen
Alt+PgUp	Moves left one screen
Arrow key	Moves one cell in the direction of the arrow key pressed
Ctrl+6	Toggles between hiding objects, displaying objects, and displaying placeholders for graphic objects
Ctrl+7	Toggles the Standard toolbar
Ctrl+A	Selects the entire worksheet
Ctrl+Down arrow	Moves down to the edge of any filled cells or to end of document
Ctrl+End	Moves to the lower right corner of the worksheet
Ctrl+Home	Moves to cell A1
Ctrl+Left arrow	Moves left to the edge of any filled cells
Ctrl+PgDn	Moves to the next sheet in the workbook
Ctrl+PgUp	Moves to the previous sheet in the workbook
Ctrl+Right arrow	Moves right to the edge of any filled cells or by one screen width
Ctrl+Shift+* (asterisk)	Selects the current region (contiguous filled cells)
Ctrl+Shift+Arrow key	Extends the selection to the edge of any contiguous filled cells in the direction of the arrow key pressed
Ctrl+Shift+End	Extends the selection to the lower right corner of the worksheet
Ctrl+Shift+Home	Extends the selection to the beginning of the worksheet
Ctrl+Shift+Spacebar	With an object selected, selects all objects on a sheet
Ctrl+Spacebar	Selects the entire column or all columns for the current selection

Key or Key Combination	Action
Ctrl+Up arrow	Moves up to the edge of the current data region
Home	Moves to the beginning of the row (Column A)
PgDn	Moves down one screen
PgUp	Moves up one screen
Scroll Lock	Turns scroll lock on or off
Shift+Arrow key	Extends the selection by one cell in the direction of the arrow key pressed
Shift+Backspace	Collapses the selection to the active cell
Shift+Home	Extends the selection to the beginning of the row
Shift+PgDn	Extends the selection down one screen
Shift+PgUp	Extends the selection up one screen
Shift+Spacebar	Selects the entire row
Tab	Moves among the unlocked cells in a protected worksheet

Excel contains a special shortcut key mode called End mode, which you enter by pressing the End key. When End mode is active, the END indicator appears on the right side of the Status bar. Use the keys listed in table C.6 to jump around your document in ways that you cannot accomplish with other shortcut keys.

Table C.6
End Mode Keys

Key or Key Combination	Action
End	Turns End mode on or off
End,Arrow key	Moves by one block of data within a row or column
End,Enter	Moves to the last filled cell in the current row
End,Home	Moves to the lower right corner of the worksheet
End,Shift+Arrow key	Extends the selection to the end of the data block in the direction of the arrow

continues

VII

Appendixes

Table C.6, Continued
End Mode Keys

Key or Key Combination	Action
End,Shift+Enter	Extends the selection to the last cell in the current row
End,Shift+Home	Extends the selection to the lower right corner of the worksheet

Similar to End mode, Excel also allows a different keyboard mode when you activate the Scroll Lock key. To use any of the keys in table C.7, make sure Scroll Lock is on.

Table C.7
Scroll Lock Keys

Key or Key Combination	Action
End	Moves to the lower right cell in the window
Home	Moves to the upper left cell in the window
Left or right arrow	Scrolls the screen left or right one column
Shift+End	Extends the selection to the lower right cell in the window
Shift+Home	Extends the selection to the upper left cell in the window
Up or down arrow	Scrolls the screen up or down one row

Primarily used for data entry, the keys listed in table C.8 show you how to move around a data-entry area—any series of cells you have selected before entering data.

Table C.8
Moving Within Selected Cells

Key or Key Combination	Action
Enter	Moves from top to bottom within the selection
Shift+Enter	Moves from bottom to top within the selection

Key or Key Combination	Action
Tab	Moves from left to right within the selection; if at far right in selection, wraps to left side of next row
Shift+Tab	Moves from right to left within the selection or to far right of previous row
Ctrl+. (period)	Moves clockwise to the next corner of the selection

The shortcut keys listed in table C.9 do not really fall into any single category, but are miscellaneous Excel key shortcuts that you will rarely use. When you do need them, however, they can really come in handy. Of particular interest are the shortcuts that use the left and right brackets ([or]). These keys select cells that contribute to the active cell or that rely on the data in the active cell.

Table C.9
Special Cells

Key or Key Combination	Action
Ctrl+Shift+? (question mark)	Selects all cells that contain notes
Ctrl+Shift+*	Selects a range of filled cells around the active cell
Ctrl+/ (forward slash)	Selects the entire array, if any, to which the active cell belongs
Ctrl+[(left bracket)	Selects all cells which are referred to by the formula in the selected cell
Ctrl+Shift+{ (left brace)	Selects all cells directly or indirectly referred to by cells in the selection
Ctrl+] (right bracket)	Selects all cells who's formulas refer to the active cell
Ctrl+Shift+} (right brace)	Selects all cells that directly or indirectly refer to the active cell
Alt+;	Selects all visible cells in the current selection

The shortcuts listed in table C.10 are not Excel shortcut keys, but are Windows shortcuts that you might find helpful.

Table C.10
Switching Windows

Key or Key Combination	Action
Alt+Esc	Moves to next application
Alt+Shift+Esc	Moves to previous application
Alt+Tab	Shows the next Windows application
Alt+Shift+Tab	Shows the previous Windows application
Ctrl+Esc	Activates the Windows Task List
Ctrl+F4	Closes document
Ctrl+F5	Restores window size
Ctrl+F6	Moves to next window
Ctrl+Shift+F6	Moves to previous window
Ctrl+F7	Move window command
Ctrl+F8	Size window command
Ctrl+F9	Minimize window
Ctrl+F10	Maximize window

Excel power users quickly learn that using the mouse actually slows them down. Having to move your hands away from the keyboard is an impediment to the fastest possible use of Excel. If you are trying to use your mouse as little as possible, use the keys in table C.11 to navigate Excel (or Windows) dialog boxes.

Table C.11
Dialog Boxes

Key or Key Combination	Action
Tab	Moves to the next section in the dialog box
Shift+Tab	Moves to the previous section in the dialog box
Arrow key	Moves within the section of the dialog box (radio buttons, list boxes)
Spacebar	Selects the active button

Key or Key Combination	Action
Any letter key	Moves to the item beginning with that letter in an active list box
Alt+any letter key	Selects the item with that underlined letter (hot keys)
Enter	Chooses the default command button (it is surrounded with a thick black line)
Esc	Cancels the dialog box

Most people spend quite a bit of time formatting their worksheets. The keys in table C.12 are useful for performing a variety of quick formatting tasks.

Table C.12
Formatting Data

Key or Key Combination	Action
Alt+' (apostrophe)	Activates the style dialog box
Ctrl+Shift+~ (tilde)	Applies the General number format
Ctrl+Shift+$ (dollar sign)	Applies the currency format with two decimal places
Ctrl+Shift+% (percent sign)	Applies the percentage format
Ctrl+Shift+^ (carat)	Applies the exponential number format
Ctrl+Shift+# (pound sign)	Applies the standard date format
Ctrl+Shift+@ (at sign)	Applies the standard time format
Ctrl+Shift+&	Applies the outline border
Ctrl+Shift+_ (underscore)	Removes all borders
Ctrl+B	Toggles bold
Ctrl+I	Toggles italic
Ctrl+U	Toggles underline
Ctrl+5	Toggles strikethrough

continues

VII

Appendixes

Table C.12, Continued
Formatting Data

Key or Key Combination	Action
Ctrl+9	Hides rows
Ctrl+Shift+((open parenthesis)	Unhides rows
Ctrl+0 (zero)	Hides columns
Ctrl+Shift+) (close parenthesis)	Unhides columns

If you are using the Excel outlining features, use the shortcuts in table C.13 to quickly promote and unhide selected outline groups.

Table C.13
Outlining

Key or Key Combination	Action
Alt+Shift+Left Arrow	Ungroups a row or a column
Alt+Shift+Right Arrow	Groups a row or a column
Ctrl+8	Displays or hides the outline symbols
Ctrl+9	Hides selected rows
Ctrl+Shift+(	Unhides selected rows
Ctrl+0 (zero)	Hides selected columns
Ctrl+Shift+)	Unhides selected columns

Table C.14 lists keys you can use to control printing your selection and navigate the Print Preview function.

Table C.14
Printing and Print Previewing

Key or Key Combination	Action
Ctrl+P	Activates the Print dialog box
Arrow keys	Moves around page when zoomed in

Key or Key Combination	Action
Up or down arrow	Moves by one page when zoomed out
PgUp, PgDn	Moves by one page when zoomed out

Sometimes you might have trouble selecting certain chart items. The item you want might be very small or too close to another chart item. When this problem arises, switch to the keys in table C.15 for assistance.

Table C.15
Selecting Chart Items

Key or Key Combination	Action
Down arrow	Selects the previous group of items
Up arrow	Selects the next group of items
Right arrow	Selects the next item within the group
Left arrow	Selects the previous item within the group

Most Windows users should already be familiar with the keystrokes used to speed up working with menus. Take a quick look at table C.16, however, to make sure that you are making full use of the shortcut keys available for navigating menus.

Table C.16
Keys for Working in Menus

Key or Key Combination	Action
Alt or F10	Activates the menu bar
Shift+F10	Activates the shortcut menu
Alt+Backspace or Ctrl+Z	Undoes the last command
F4	Repeats the last command
Esc or Ctrl+. (period)	Cancels the menu
Spacebar	Displays Control menu
Letter key	Selects the menu or option that contains the under-lined letter

VII

Appendixes

continues

Table C.16, Continued
Keys for Working in Menus

Key or Key Combination	Action
Left or right arrow	Selects the menu to the left or right
Down or up arrow	Selects the next or previous command on the menu
Enter	Chooses the selected command
Down or up arrow	Selects the next or previous command on the menu
Left or right arrow	Toggles selection between main menu and submenu

Use the shortcut keys in table C.17 to access the most frequently used items in the Excel File menu.

Table C.17
File Commands

Key or Key Combination	Action
Ctrl+N	New workbook
Ctrl+O	Open
Ctrl+S	Save
F12	Save As
Ctrl+P	Print
Alt+F4	Closes Excel

Use the shortcut keys in table C.18 to access the most frequently used items in the Excel Edit menu.

Table C.18
Edit Menu Command Keys

Key or Key Combination	Action
Ctrl+Z	Undo
F4	Repeat
Ctrl+X	Cut

Key or Key Combination	Action
Ctrl+C	Copy
Ctrl+V	Paste
Ctrl+D	Fill Down
Ctrl+R	Fill Right
Delete	Clear Contents
Ctrl+−	Deletes the selected cells
Ctrl+F	Displays the Find dialog box
Ctrl+H	Displays the Replace dialog box
Ctrl+Shift+F	Find Next
Ctrl+Shift+E	Find Previous
F5	Go To

Table C.19
Insert Commands

Key or Key Combination	Action
Ctrl+Shift++	Activates Insert dialog box
Shift+F11	Inserts new worksheet
F11	Inserts new chart sheet
Ctrl+F11	Inserts new Excel 4.0 macro sheet
Ctrl+F3	Activates the Define Name dialog box
F3	Activates the Paste Name dialog box
Shift+Ctrl+F3	Activates the Create Names dialog box

New to Excel 5 is the Insert menu, which helps you organize the most common object-based tasks. Use the keys in table C.19 to access these functions.

VII

Appendixes

5

Use the shortcuts in table C.20 to access the most common items in the Excel Format menu.

Table C.20
Format Menu Commands

Key or Key Combination	Action
Ctrl+1	Format Cells tabbed dialog box
Ctrl+9	Hide rows
Ctrl+Shift+(	Unhide rows
Ctrl+0 (zero)	Hide columns
Ctrl+Shift+)	Unhide columns
Alt+' (apostrophe)	Activates the Style dialog box

Although many of the keys listed in table C.21 are listed in other sections of this appendix, this table contains all the function key shortcuts for easy reference.

Table C.21
Function Keys

Key or Key Combination	Action
F1	Help
Shift+F1	Help for current function
F2	Activates the formula bar
Shift+F2	Edit Note
Ctrl+F2	Info window
F3	Paste Name dialog box
Shift+F3	Function Wizard
Ctrl+F3	Define Name command
Ctrl+Shift+F3	Create command
F4	Toggles between relative and absolute references
Ctrl+F4	Closes the window
Alt+F4	Closes Excel

Key or Key Combination	Action
F5	Go To command
Ctrl+F5	Restore window size
F6	Next pane
Shift+F6	Previous pane
Ctrl+F6	Next window
Ctrl+Shift+F6	Previous window
F7	Check spelling
Ctrl+F7	Move command
F8	Toggle Extend Mode
Shift+F8	Toggle Add mode
Ctrl+F8	Size command
F9	Calculate all
Shift+F9	Calculates active sheet
Ctrl+F9	Minimize the workbook
F10 *	Activate the menu bar
Shift+F10	Activate the shortcut menu
Ctrl+F10	Maximize the workbook
F11	Insert new chart sheet
Shift+F11	Insert new worksheet
Ctrl+F11	Inserts new Excel 4.0 macro sheet
F12	Save As command
Shift+F12	Save command
Ctrl+F12	Open command
Ctrl+Shift+F12	Print command

COMMAND REFERENCE

Visual Basic for Applications Command Reference

Abs   Function

Explanation: Returns the absolute value of a number.

Syntax: Abs (*number*)

The *number* argument can be any valid numeric expression. When *number* does not contain valid data, Null is returned. When *number* is an uninitialized variable, Empty is returned.

Note: The absolute value of a number is its unsigned magnitude. The expressions ABS(–1) and ABS(1), for instance, both return 1.

Related Topics: Math Function, Sgn Function

Accelerator   Property

Applies To: Button, Buttons, CheckBox, CheckBoxes, DrawingObjects, GroupBox, GroupBoxes, Label, Labels, OptionButton, OptionButtons

Explanation: Returns or sets the keyboard hot key character for the control. Read-write.

Syntax: `object.Accelerator`

The `object` parameter is the object to which this Property applies.

Notes: You can assign one hot key character to a control so a user can can press ALT and the hot key character to activate a control while a dialog is running.

The first text character of the control that matches the first hot key text character is underlined. The comparison for underlining is case-sensitive, but case is not considered when the user presses the hot key combination.

If the hot key key doesn't match any text in the control, the hot key is non-functional.

Activate   Method

Applies To: Chart, ChartObject, DialogSheet, MenuBar, Module, OLEObject, Pane, Range, Window, Workbook, Worksheet

Explanation: Activates the object, as shown in the following table.

Object	Explanation
Chart, ChartObject	Makes the chart the active chart.
DialogSheet, Module, Worksheet	Makes the sheet the active sheet, which is the same as clicking the tab.
MenuBar	Activates the menu bar. See the Notes section for limitations.
OLEObject	Activates the object.
Pane	Activates the pane. When the pane is not in the active window, the window that the pane belongs to also is activated.
Range	Activates a single cell (the cell must be inside the current selection). Use the Select Method when you want to select a range of cells.

Object	Explanation
Window	Orders the window to the front of the z-order. You cannot run Auto_Activate or Auto_Deactivate macros that are attached to the workbook with this object. To run those macros, use the RunAutoMacros Method.
Workbook	Activates the first window associated with the workbook. You cannot run Auto_Activate or Auto_Deactivate macros that are attached to the workbook. You should use the RunAutoMacros Method to run those macros.

Syntax: `object.Activate`

In the preceding syntax, *object* is the object to activate.

Notes: You can display only a menu bar that is appropriate for the object when you use the Activate Method. You might, for instance, try to return a chart menu bar for a worksheet. This results in an error and will stop the current macro.

When you activate a custom menu bar, the automatic menu bar switching is diabled when different types of documents are selected. If, for example, you have a custom menu bar displayed and you switch to a chart, the two chart menus are not displayed, as is the case if you are using built-in menu bars instead of the custom menu bars. The automatic menu bar switching reenables when you display a built-in menu bar.

Related Topics: RunAutoMacros Method, Select Method

ActivateMicrosoftApp   Method

Applies To: Application

Explanation: Starts a Microsoft application, unless it is already running (then it starts the application that is already running).

Syntax: `object.ActivateMicrosoftApp(index)`

In the preceding syntax, *object* is the Application object. The *index* parameter specifies the Microsoft application to activate, such as xlMicrosoftAccess, xlMicrosoftWord, xlMicrosoftFoxPro, xlMicrosoftPowerPoint, xlMicrosoftMail, xlMicrosoftProject, or xlMicrosoftSchedulePlus.

Related Topics: AppActivate Statement, Shell Function

ActivateNext   Method

Applies To: Window

Explanation: Use this Method to bring the next window to the front of the z-order and diplaying the next window. This in turn sends the specified window to the back of the z-order.

Syntax: `object.ActivateNext`

The *object* is the Window object.

Related Topics: ActivatePrevious Method, Next Property

ActivatePrevious   Method

Applies To: Window

Explanation: Use this Method to bring the previous window to the front of the z-order and to display the previous window. This in turn sends the specified window to the back of the z-order.

Syntax: `object.ActivatePrevious`

The *object* is the Window object.

Related Topics: ActivateNext Method, Previous Property

ActiveCell   Property

Applies To: Application, Window

Explanation: Displays the active cell of the active windows. The *active cell* is a Range object. ActiveCell is a read-only Property.

Syntax: `object.ActiveCell`

The *object* is the object to which this Property applies and is optional for Application, but required for Window.

Notes: The *active cell* is a single cell inside the current selection. The *selection* can contain more than one cell, of which only one is the active cell.

These expressions return the active cell and are all equivalent: ActiveCell, Application.ActiveCell, ActiveWindow.ActiveCell, and Application.ActiveWindow.ActiveCell

ActiveChart   Property

Applies To: Application, Window, Workbook

Explanation: Returns the currently active Chart. The active Chart can be an embedded chart or a chart sheet. Embedded charts are active when they are selected or activated. If a chart is not active, Nothing is returned. This Property is read-only.

Syntax: *object*.`ActiveChart`

The **object** parameter is the object to which this Property applies. It is optional for Application, but is required for Window and Workbook.

ActiveDialog   Property

Applies To: Application

Explanation: Use this Property to return the topmost currently running DialogSheet. This Property returns Nothing if a dialog is not running and is a read-only Property.

Syntax: *object*.`ActiveDialog`

The *object* parameter is the Application object.

Note: The active dialog is not necessarily the active sheet.

ActiveMenuBar   Property

Applies To: Application

Explanation: The ActiveMenuBar displays or sets the active MenuBar. It is a read-write Property.

Syntax: *object*.`ActiveMenuBar`

object is the Application object.

ActivePane   Property

Applies To: Window

Explanation: This Property is the active Pane of the window and is a read-only Property.

Syntax: *object*.`ActivePane`

The **object** parameter is the Window object.

Notes: You can use ActivePane only with worksheets and macro sheets.

ActivePane returns a Pane object. If you to obtain the index of the active pane, you must use the Index Property.

ActivePrinter   Property

Applies To: Application

Explanation: You use this Property to return or set the name of the current printer. The name is a string. ActivePrinter is a read-write Property.

Syntax: *object*.`ActivePrinter`

object is the Application object.

Note: This Property cannot be set on the Apple Macintosh.

ActiveSheet   Property

Applies To: Application, Window, Workbook

Explanation: You can return the active sheet of the active workbook by using the ActiveSheet Property. It returns Nothing if no sheet is active. This Property is read-only.

The object type returned by the ActiveSheet Property depends on the active sheet, as shown in the following table:

Active sheet	Object type returned
Worksheet	Worksheet
Visual Basic module	Module
Chart	Chart
Dialog sheet	DialogSheet

Syntax: *object*.`ActiveSheet`

In the preceding syntax, **object** is the object to which this Property applies and is optional for Application, but is required for Window and Worksheet.

Note: The ActiveSheet Property may be different in different windows when a workbook appears in more than one window.

Related Topics: Activate Method, Select Method

ActiveWindow   Property

Applies To: Application

Explanation: Returns the active Window, which is the top window and is a read-only Property. ActiveWindow returns Nothing if no windows are open.

Syntax: `object.ActiveWindow`

object is the Application object.

Related Topics: Activate Method, Select Method

ActiveWorkbook   Property

Applies To: Application

Explanation: Use this Property to return the Workbook in the active window.
ActiveWorkbook is a read-only workbook. This Property returns Nothing if you do not have
any windows open or if the active window is the info window or the clipboard window.

Syntax: `object.ActiveWorkbook`

object is the Application object.

Add   Method

Explanation: As shown in the following table, the Add Method adds a member to a
collection. To get a description of the Add Method for a particular object, select that object.

Object	Description
AddIns	Adds a new add-in file to the current list of add-ins.
Arcs, Buttons, ChartObjects, Drawings, Lines, Ovals, Pictures, Rectangles, TextBoxes	Creates a new drawing object Lines. Add, for example, creates a new line. The type of the object depends on the collection on which you call Add.
CheckBoxes, DropDowns, EditBoxes, GroupBoxes, Labels, ListBoxes, OptionButtons, ScrollBars, Spinners	Creates a new control. The type of the object depends on the collection on which you call Add.
Charts	Creates a new chart.
DialogSheets	Creates a new dialog sheet.
MenuBars	Creates a new menu bar.

continues

Object	Description
MenuItems	Adds a new menu item to the menu. You can use this Method also to restore a built-in menu item that has been deleted.
Menus	Adds a new menu. (You cannot build a new shortcut menu, but you can alter a built-in shortcut menu.). You can use this Method also to restore a built-in menu item that has been deleted.
Modules	Lets you create a new module.
Names	Enables you to create a new defined name.
OLEObjects	Adds a new OLE object to the current sheet.
Scenarios	Applies to the current worksheet and enables you to create a new scenario and add it to the list of scenarios available.
SeriesCollection	Lets you add one or more new series to the the SeriesCollection.
Sheets	Enables you to create a new sheet, including a worksheet, chart, module, dialog sheet, or macro sheet.
Styles	Enables you to build a new style and add it to the list of styles available for the current workbook.
ToolbarButtons	Lets you place a new button on the existing toolbar.
Toolbars	Enables you to create a new toolbar.
Trendlines	Creates a trendline with specified parameters.
Workbooks	Creates a new workbook, which becomes the active workbook.
Worksheets	Creates a new worksheet, which becomes the active worksheet.

AddChartAutoFormat　　　　　　　　**Method**

Applies To: Application

Explanation: This Method enables you to add a custom chart autoformat to the list of available chart autoformats.

Syntax: `object.AddChartAutoFormat(chart, name, description)`

The AddChartAutoFormat Method has the following arguments:

- ✔ `object`. The Application object.

- ✔ `chart`. A chart object that contains the format that will be applied when the new chart autoformat is applied.

- ✔ `name`. A string that represents the name of the autoformat.

- ✔ `description`. A string that describes the custom autoformat.

Related Topics: DeleteAutoFormat Method, SetDefaultChart Method

AddCustomList　　　　　　　　　　**Method**

Applies To: Application

Explanation: Use this Method to add a custom list for custom autofill and/or custom sort.

Syntax: `object.AddCustomList(listArray, byRow)`

The AddCustomList Method has the following arguments:

- ✔ `object`. The Application object.

- ✔ `listArray`. Denotes an array of strings, or a Range.

- ✔ `byRow`. You use this argument if `listArray` is a Range. If True, Excel creates a custom list from each row in the range. If False, Excel creates a custom list from each column in the range. If this argument is omitted and more rows than columns (or an equal number of rows and columns) are in the range, then Excel creates a custom list from each column in the range. If this argument is omitted and more columns than rows are in the range, then Excel creates a custom list from each row in the range.

Note: The AddCustomList Method does not do anything when the list you are trying to add already exists.

Related Topics: CustomListCount Property, DeleteCustomList Method, GetCustomListNum Method, GetCustomListContents Method

AddFields   Method

Applies To: PivotTable

Explanation: Use this Method to add row, column, and page fields to the pivot table.

Syntax: *object*.AddFields(*rowFields*, *columnFields*, *pageFields*, *addToTable*)

The AddFields Method has the following arguments:

- ✔ *object*. The PivotTable object.

- ✔ *rowFields*. Denotes a PivotField or an array of PivotFields to be added as rows.

- ✔ *columnFields*. Denotes a PivotField or an array of PivotFields to be added as columns.

- ✔ *pageFields*. Denotes a PivotField or an array of PivotFields to be added as pages.

- ✔ *addToTable*. If True, the fields are added to the pivot table (none of the existing fields are replaced). If False, the new fields replace existing fields. The default is False if this argument is not specified.

Note: You must specify one of the field arguments.

Related Topics: ColumnFields Method, DataFields Method, HiddenFields Method, PageFields Method, RowFields Method, VisibleFields Method

AddIn   Object

Explanation: An add-in, either installed or not installed.

To create an add-in when you are in a Visual Basic module, choose Tools, Make Add-In. The AddIn object provides a programming interface to the Add-In Manager. The AddIn object, however, does not create an object.

AddIndent   Property

Applies To: Button, Buttons, DrawingObjects, GroupObject, GroupObjects, Range, Style, TextBox, TextBoxes

Explanation: This Property is true if text with the distributed text alignment style has extra space added at the beginning and end of each line. AddIndent is a read-write Property.

Syntax: *object*.AddIndent

object is the object to which this Property applies.

Note: This Property is available only in Far East versions of Excel, and only works for text with the xlDistributed alignment style in the direction of the text (indent is added if the text Orientation is xlVertical and the VerticalAlignment is xlDistributed, or if the text Orientation is xlHorizontal and the HorizontalAlignment is xlDistributed).

Related Topics: HorizontalAlignment Property, Orientation Property, VerticalAlignment Property

AddIns   Method

Applies To: Application

Explanation: This Method returns a single add-in (an AddIn object, Syntax 1) or the collection of add-ins (an AddIns object, Syntax 2) that appears in the Add-Ins dialog box. It is read-only.

Syntax 1: `object.AddIns(index)`

Syntax 2: `object.AddIns`

object is the Application object.

index is the number of the add-in, or the title of the add-in, as a string.

AddIns   Object

Explanation: A collection of Addin Objects.

AddItem   Method

Applies To: DrawingObjects, DropDown, DropDowns, ListBox, ListBoxes

Explanation: Adds an item to a list box or dropdown list box.

Syntax: `object.AddItem(text, index)`

object is the object to which this Method applies. The *text* parameter denotes the text string to add. The *index* parameter specifies the position at which to add the new entry. If the list has fewer entries than the specified index, blank items are added from the end of the list to the specified position. If this argument is omitted, the item is appended to the existing list.

Note: By using this Method, you clear any ListFillRange.

Related Topics: List Property, RemoveItem Method

AddMenu   Method

Applies To: MenuItems

Explanation: Use this Method to add a new submenu to the menu. Set the restore argument to True to restore a built-in submenu that was previously deleted.

Syntax: *object*.AddMenu(*caption, before,* **restore**)

In the preceding syntax, *object* is the MenuItems object. *caption* is the caption to use for the new submenu. To create an access key, put an ampersand (&) before the access-key letter. When you use *before*, it specifies the menu item before which this submenu should be inserted. May be a string containing the caption of the menu item (without the ampersand), a number indicating the position of the menu item, or a reference to the menu item. If the restore argument is True, Excel restores the previously deleted built-in submenu named by the caption argument. If False or omitted, Excel adds a new submenu.

Address   Method

Applies To: Range

Explanation: Returns the range reference as a string in the language of the macro.

Syntax: *object*.Address(*rowAbsolute, columnAbsolute, referenceStyle, external, relativeTo*)

In the preceding syntax, *object* returns a reference to this range. If *rowAbsolute* is True or omitted, the row part of the reference is returned as an absolute reference. If *columnAbsolute* is True or omitted, the column part of the reference is returned as an absolute reference. If *referenceStyle* is set to xlA1 or is omitted, the Method returns an A1-style reference. If set to xlR1C1, the Method returns an R1C1-style reference. If *external* is True, the Method returns an external reference. If False, the Method returns a local reference. The default is False. For the relativeTo argument, if rowAbsolute and columnAbsolute are False, and *referenceStyle* is xlR1C1, you must include a starting point for the relative reference. This argument is a Range object type that defines the starting point.

Note: If the reference contains more than one cell, rowAbsolute and columnAbsolute apply to all rows and columns.

Related Topics: AddressLocal Method, Offset Method

AddressLocal   Method

Applies To: Range

Explanation: Use this Method to return the range reference, as a string in the language of the user.

Syntax: *object*.AddressLocal(*rowAbsolute, columnAbsolute, referenceStyle, external, relativeTo*)

In the preceding syntax, *object* returns a reference to this range. If *rowAbsolute* is True or omitted, the row part of the reference is returned as an absolute reference. If *columnAbsolute* is True or omitted, the column part of the reference is returned as an absolute reference. If *referenceStyle* is set to xlA1 or omitted, the Method returns an A1-style reference. If set to xlR1C1, the Method returns an R1C1-style reference. If *external* is True, the Method returns an external reference. If False, the Method returns a local reference. For *relativeTo,* if rowAbsolute and columnAbsolute are False, and referenceStyle is xlR1C1, then you must include a starting point for the relative reference. This argument is a Range object type that defines the starting point.

Note: If the reference contains more than one cell, rowAbsolute and columnAbsolute apply to all rows and columns.

Related Topics: Address Method, Offset Method

AddVertex   Method

Applies To: Drawing

Explanation: Adds a vertex to the end of the drawing.

Syntax: `object.AddVertex(left, top)`

In the preceding syntax, **object** is the Drawing object. The **left** parameter is left position of the new vertex in points (1/72 inch), relative to the upper left corner of the sheet. **top** is the top position of the new vertex in points, relative to the upper left corner of the sheet.

Related Topics: Add Method (Drawings Collection), Reshape Method

AdvancedFilter   Method

Applies To: Range

Explanation: Use the AdvancedFilter Method to filter or copy from a list based on a criteria range. If the initial selection is a single cell, its current region is used.

Syntax: `object.AdvancedFilter(action, criteriaRange, copyToRange, unique)`

In the preceding syntax, **object** the Range object. The **action** argument specifies the operation (either xlFilterInPlace or xlFilterCopy). *criteriaRange* sets the criteria range. If omitted, there are no criteria. The **copyToRange** is required if action is xlFilterCopy, ignored otherwise. The destination range for the copied rows. In reference to the *unique* parameter, True means unique records only; False means all records that meet the criteria. If omitted, assumed False.

Related Topics: AutoFilter Method, FilterMode Property, ShowAllData Method

AlertBeforeOverwriting   **Property**

Applies To: Application

Explanation: This Property is set to True if Excel displays a message before overwriting non-blank cells during a drag and drop editing operation. AlertBeforeOverwriting is a read-write Property.

Syntax: *object*`.AlertBeforeOverwriting`

object is the Application object.

AltStartupPath   **Property**

Applies To: Application

Explanation: Returns or sets the name of the alternate startup directory or folder. This is a read-write Property. The name is a string.

Syntax: *object*`.AltStartupPath`

object is the Application object.

AppActivate   **Statement**

Explanation: Activates an application window.

Syntax: `AppActivate(`*title*`,`*wait*`)`

The AppActivate statement syntax has these named-argument parts:

Part	Description
title	In Windows, the title argument is the string in the title bar of the application window you want to activate. On the Macintosh (System 7.0 or later), the title argument is the application name. You can use the MacID function to specify an application's signature instead of the application name, such as AppActivate MacID("MSWD").
	You also can use the task ID returned by the Shell function to activate an application, in place of title.
wait	This argument is a Boolean value specifying whether the calling application has the focus before activating another. If set to False (default), the specified application is immediately activated, even if the calling application does not have the focus. If True, the calling application waits until it has the focus, then activates the specified application.

Notes: The AppActivate statement changes the focus to the named application or window but does not affect whether it is maximized or minimized. Focus moves from the activated application window when the user takes some action to change the focus or close the window. Use the Shell function to start an application and set the window style. In trying to find the application to activate, a comparison is made to try to find an application whose title string is an exact match with title. If unsuccessful, any application's title string that begins with title is activated. In Windows, if more than one instance of the application is named by title, one is arbitrarily activated.

If you use the MacID function with AppActivate in Windows, you will experience an error.

Related Topics: MacID Function, Shell Function, SendKeys Statement

Application   Object

Explanation: The Application object contains the following:

- ✔ Application-wide settings and options, such as options in the Tools Options dialog box

- ✔ Built-in worksheet functions, such as SUM, AVERAGE, and COUNTA

- ✔ Methods that return top-level objects, such as ActiveCell, ActiveSheet, and so on

Many of the properties and Methods that return the most common user-interface objects, such as the active cell (ActiveCell Property) can be used without the Application object qualifier. For example, instead of writing Application.ActiveCell.Font.Bold = True, you can write ActiveCell.Font.Bold = True. These properties and Methods appear in the Object Browser under both the Application object and the Global object.

Application   Property

Applies To: All objects

Explanation: Returns the Application that created this object. This is a read-only Property.

Syntax: `object.Application`

In the preceding syntax, `object` is the object to which this Property applies.

Note: The value of this Property is "Microsoft Excel" if the object was created by Excel.

Related Topic: Creator Property

ApplyDataLabels   Method

Applies To: Chart, Point, Series

Explanation: Use this Method to apply data labels to the point, the series, or to all series on the chart.

Syntax: `object.ApplyDataLabels(type, legendKey)`

In the preceding syntax, **object** is the Chart, Point, or Series object. **type** is the type of data label, as shown in the following list.

Value	Meaning
xlNone	No data labels.
xlShowValue	Value for the point (assumed if this argument is not specified).
xlShowPercent	Percentage of the total. Only available for pie and doughnut charts.
xlShowLabel	Category for the point.
xlShowLabelAndPercent	Percentage of the total and category for the point. Only available for pie and doughnut charts.

If the legendKey parameter is set to True, Excel shows the legend key next to the point.

Related Topics: DataLabel Property, HasDataLabel Property, HasDataLabels Property

ApplyNames   Method

Applies To: Range

Explanation: Use this Method when you want to apply names to the cells in the range.

Syntax: `object.ApplyNames(names, ignoreRelativeAbsolute, useRowColumnNames, omitColumn, omitRow, order, appendLast)`

In the preceding syntax, *object* is the range where names will be applied. The *names* parameter contains an array of the names to apply. If omitted, all names on the sheet are applied to the range. If *ignoreRelativeAbsolute* is True or omitted, Excel replaces references with names regardless of the reference types of either the names or references. If False, Excel replaces absolute references only with absolute names, relative references only with relative names, and mixed references only with mixed names.

If *useRowColumnNames* is set to True or omitted, Excel uses the names of row and column ranges containing the specified range if names for the range cannot be found. If False, the *omitColumn* and *omitRow* arguments are ignored. If *omitColumn* is True or omitted, Excel replaces the reference with the row-oriented name without including a column-oriented name if the referenced cell is in the same column as the formula and within a row-oriented named range. If *omitRow* is True or omitted, Excel replaces the reference with the column-oriented name without including a row-oriented name if the referenced cell is in the same row as the formula within a column-oriented named range.

The *order* argument determines which range name is listed first when a cell reference is replaced by a row-oriented and column-oriented range name (either xlRowThenColumn or xlColumnThenRow). If *appendLast* is True, Excel replaces the definitions of the names in names and also replaces the definitions of the last names defined. If *appendLast* is False or omitted, Excel replaces the definitions of the *names* in names only.

Notes: You can use the Array function to create the list of names for the *names* argument.

If you want to apply names to the entire sheet, use `Cells.ApplyNames`.

Use the Delete Method if you want to un-apply names.

Related Topics: Add Method, Array Function, Delete Method

ApplyOutlineStyles   Method

Applies To: Range

Explanation: Applies outlining styles to the range.

Syntax: `object.ApplyOutlineStyles`

In the preceding syntax, **object** is the range where outlining styles is to be applied.

Arc   Object

Explanation: The Arc object is an arc graphic object drawn on a chart or worksheet.

Arcs   Method

Applies To: Chart, DialogSheet, Worksheet

Explanation: Returns a single arc (an Arc object, Syntax 1) or a collection of arcs (an Arcs object, Syntax 2) on the chart or sheet. This is a read-only Method.

Syntax 1: `object.Arcs(index)`

Syntax 2: object.Arcs

In the preceding syntax lines, **object** is the object to which this Method applies and **index** (in Syntax 1) is the name or number of the arc.

Arcs   Object

Explanation: A collection of Arc objects.

Area3DGroup   Property

Applies To: Chart

Explanation: Returns the area ChartGroup on a 3D chart.

Syntax: `object.Area3DGroup`

In the preceding syntax, **`object`** is the Chart object.

Related Topic: AreaGroups Method

AreaGroups   Method

Applies To: Chart

Explanation: On a 2D chart, this Method returns a single area chart group (a ChartGroup object, see the following Syntax 1), or a collection of the area chart groups (a ChartGroups collection, see the following Syntax 2).

Syntax 1: `object.AreaGroups(index)`

Syntax 2: `object.AreaGroups`

In the preceding syntax lines, **`object`** is the Chart object. The **`index`** parameter in Syntax 1 specifies the chart group.

Related Topic: Area3DGroup Property

Areas   Method

Applies To: Range

Explanation: Returns a single range (a Range object, Syntax 1), or a collection of all ranges (an Areas object, Syntax 2) in a multiple selection.

Syntax 1: `object.Areas(index)`

Syntax 2: `object.Areas`

In the preceding syntax lines, **`object`** is the multiple-selection range. **`index`** is the number of the range within the multiple selection.

Note: For a single selection, the Areas Method returns a collection of one object, the original Range object itself. For a multiple selection, the Areas Method returns a collection that contains one object for each selection.

Related Topic: Union Method

Areas   Object

Explanation: This object is a collection of the areas in a Range (each area is a Range). Areas objects are returned by the Areas Method. Each area corresponds to the sections of a multiple selection.

Arrange   Method

Applies To: Windows

Explanation: Use this Method to arrange the windows on your screen.

Syntax: *object*.`Arrange`(*arrangeStyle, activeWorkbook, syncHorizontal, syncVertical*)

In the preceding syntax, *object* denotes the Windows object. The *arrangeStyle* argument enables you to arrange windows in this style, and has one of the following values:

Value	Meaning
xlTiled	Tells Excel to tile windows. This is the default value if you do not specifiy an arrangeStyle.
xlCascade	Cascades the windows.
xlHorizontal	Windows are arranged horizontally.
xlVertical	Arranges the windows vertically.
xlIcons	Arranges the icons (not available on the Apple Macintosh).

When set to True, the *activeWorkbook* argument arranges only the visible windows of the active workbook, instead of all the windows in Excel. It arranges all of the windows if set to False or is omitted. The *syncHorizontal* argument is ignored if *activeWorkbook* is False or omitted and the windows are not synchronized. If True, the windows of the active workbook are synchronized when scrolling horizontally. The *syncVertical* argument is ignored if *activeWorkbook* is False or omitted and the windows are not synchronized. If True, the windows of the active workbook are synchronized when scrolling vertically.

Array   Function

Explanation: Returns a Variant containing an array.

Syntax: `Array`(*arglist*)

The *arglist* consists of a comma-delimited list of an arbitrary number of values that are assigned to the elements of the array contained within the Variant. An array of zero-length is created when no arguments are specified.

Notes: Although a Variant containing an array is conceptually different from an array whose elements are of type Variant, the way the array elements are accessed is the same.

Related Topics: Dim Statements, Let Statement, Option Base Statement

ArrowHeadLength   Property

Applies To: DrawingObjects, GroupObject, GroupObjects, Line, Lines

Explanation: Use this Property to return or set the length of arrow heads, including xlShort, xlMedium, or xlLong. This is a read-write Property.

Syntax: *object*`.ArrowHeadLength`

In the preceding syntax, *object* is the object to which this Property applies.

Related Topics: ArrowHeadStyle Property, ArrowHeadWidth Property

ArrowHeadStyle   Property

Applies To: DrawingObjects, GroupObject, GroupObjects, Line, Lines

Explanation: Use this Property to return or set arrow head types, such as xlNone, xlOpen, xlClosed, xlDoubleOpen, or xlDoubleClosed. This is a read-write Property.

Syntax: *object*`.ArrowHeadStyle`

In the preceding syntax, *object* is the object to which this Property applies.

Related Topics: ArrowHeadLength Property, ArrowHeadWidth Property

ArrowHeadWidth   Property

Applies To: DrawingObjects, GroupObject, GroupObjects, Line, Lines

Explanation: Use this Property to return or set arrow head widths, such as xlNarrow, xlMedium, or xlWide. This is a read-write Property.

Syntax: *object*`.ArrowHeadWidth`

In the preceding syntax, *object* is the object to which this Property applies.

Related Topics: ArrowHeadLength Property, ArrowHeadStyle Property

Asc   Function

Explanation: Use the Asc function to return the character code of the first letter in a string.

Syntax: `Asc(string)`

In the preceding syntax, ***string*** is any valid string expression. A run-time error happens when the string contains no characters.

Related Topic: Chr Function

Atn   Function

Explanation: Use this function to return the arctangent of a number.

Syntax: `Atn(number)`

In the preceding syntax, ***number*** can be any valid numeric expression.

Notes: The Atn function takes the ratio of two sides of a right triangle (number) and returns the corresponding angle in radians. The ratio is the length of the side opposite the angle divided by the length of the side adjacent to the angle. The range of the result is –pi/2 to pi/2 radians.

You have to multiply degrees by pi/180 to convert degrees to radians. Multiply radians by 180/pi to convert radians to degrees.

Related Topics: Cos Function, Sgn Function, Tan Function

Author   Property

Applies To: AddIn, Workbook

Explanation: This Property is used when you want to return or set the author of an object, as a string. This Property is read-only for AddIn and read-write for Workbook.

Syntax: *object*`.Author`

In the preceding syntax, ***object*** is the AddIn or Workbook object.

Related Topics: Comments Property, Keywords Property, Subject Property, Title Property

AutoFill   Method

Applies To: Range

Explanation: Performs an autofill on the cells in the range.

Syntax: *object*`.AutoFill(destination, type)`

In the preceding syntax, *object* denotes the source range. The destination argument is a Range object that represents the cells to fill. The object must include the source range. The *type* argument can be one of many, including xlFillDefault, xlFillSeries, xlFillCopy, xlFillFormats, xlFillValues, xlFillDays, xlFillWeekdays, xlFillMonths, xlFillYears, xlLinearTrend, xlGrowthTrend. If *type* is set to xlFillDefault or is omitted, the Method selects the most appropriate type based on the source range.

AutoFilter   Method

Applies To: Range

Explanation: In the following syntax line, **Syntax 1:** displays or hides the AutoFilter drop-down arrows. **Syntax 2:** filters a list using the AutoFilter.

Syntax 1: `object.AutoFilter`

Syntax 2: `object.AutoFilter(field, criteria1, operator, criteria2)`

In the preceding syntax lines, *object* is the Range object. The *field* argument is the integer offset of the field on which to base the filter. From the left of the list, the leftmost field is field one. The *criteria1* argument is the criteria (a string). Use "=" to find blank fields and "<>" to find non-blank fields. If this argument is omitted, the criteria is All. The *operator* argument is used with *criteria1* and *criteria2* to construct compound criteria. You can set this to xlAnd or xlOr. When you don't set it, xlAnd is used. The *criteria2* argument is the second criteria (a string) and is used with *criteria1* and *operator* to construct compound criteria.

Related Topics: AdvancedFilter Method, AutoFilterMode Property, FilterMode Property, ShowAllData Method

AutoFilterMode   Property

Applies To: Worksheet

Explanation: The AutoFilterMode is set to true if the drop-down arrows for AutoFilter are displayed on the sheet. This Property is independent of the FilterMode Property and is a read-write Property.

Syntax: `object.AutoFilterMode`

In the preceding syntax, *object* is the the Worksheet object.

Notes: You can set this Property to False to remove the arrows, but you cannot set it to True. Use the AutoFilter Method to filter a list and display the drop-down arrows.

Related Topics: AutoFilter Method, FilterMode Property

AutoFit   Method

Applies To: Range

Explanation: Use this Method if you want the rows and columns to be set for the best fit. AutoFit lets you change the width of the columns in the range or the height of the rows in the range.

Syntax: `object.AutoFit`

In the preceding syntax, *object* is the range (such as a row or a range of rows, or a column or a range of columns). If you specify any other range, Excel displays an error. One unit of column width is equal to the width of one character of the Normal style.

Related Topics: ColumnWidth Property, RowHeight Property

AutoFormat   Method (Chart object)

Applies To: Chart

Explanation: Use this Method when you want to apply a built-in or custom autoformat to a chart.

Syntax: `object.AutoFormat(gallery, format)`

In the preceding syntax, *object* denotes the Chart object. The *gallery* argument denotes the built-in gallery and can be xl3DArea, xl3DBar, xl3DColumn, xl3DLine, xl3DPie, xl3DSurface, xlArea, xlBar, xlColumn, xlCombination, xlCustom, xlDefaultAutoFormat, xlDoughnut, xlLine, xlPie, xlRadar, or xlXYScatter. The *format* argument specifies the option number for the built-in autoformats or a string containing the name of the custom autoformat if *gallery* is xlCustom.

Related Topics: AutoFormat Method (Range Object)

AutoFormat   Method (Chart object)

Applies To: Chart

Explanation: You can use this Method to apply a built-in or custom autoformat to a chart.

Syntax: `object.AutoFormat(gallery, format)`

In the preceding syntax, *object* is the Chart object. The *gallery* argument denotes the Excel gallery, which is xl3DArea, xl3DBar, xl3DColumn, xl3DLine, xl3DPie, xl3DSurface, xlArea, xlBar, xlColumn, xlCombination, xlCustom, xlDefaultAutoFormat, xlDoughnut, xlLine, xlPie, xlRadar, or xlXYScatter. The *format* argument specifies the option number for the Excel autoformats or a string containing the name of the custom autoformat if gallery is xlCustom.

Related Topic: AutoFormat Method (Chart Object)

AutomaticStyles   Property

Applies To: Outline

Explanation: This Property is set to True if the outline uses automatic styles. This is a read-write Property.

Syntax: *object*.`AutomaticStyles`

In the preceding syntax, object is the Outline object.

AutoOutline   Method

Applies To: Range

Explanation: Use this Method when you want to automatically set up an outline for a range (the new outline will replace the existing outline). You can create an outline for the whole sheet by specifying a range of a single cell.

Syntax: *object*.`AutoOutline`

In the preceding syntax, *object* is the Range object.

Related Topics: ApplyOutlineStyles Method, ClearOutline Method

AutoScaling   Property

Applies To: Chart

Explanation: Use this Property when you want to scale your 3D chart to make it closer in size to the 2D chart it's based on. The RightAngleAxes Property must be True. This is a read-write Property.

Syntax: *object*.`AutoScaling`

In the preceding syntax, *object* is the Chart object.

AutoSize   Property

Applies To: Button, Buttons, DrawingObjects, GroupObject, GroupObjects, TextBox, TextBoxes

Explanation: This Property is set to True if the object is automatically resized to fit any text that is contained within it. It is a read-write Property.

Syntax: *object*.`AutoSize`

In the preceding syntax, *object* the object to which this Property applies.

Note: When you resize the object manually (or it is resized by the Height or Width properties), this Property is set to False ().

AutoText   Property

Applies To: DataLabel, DataLabels

Explanation: The AutoText Property is set to True if the object automatically generates appropriate text based on context. This is a read-write Property.

Syntax: `object.AutoText`

In the preceding syntax, **object** is the DataLabel or DataLabels object.

AutoUpdate   Property

Applies To: OLEObject

Explanation: This Property is True if the OLE object updates automatically when the source changes and is valid only if the object is linked (its OLEType Property must be xlOLELink). It is a read-only Property.

Syntax: `object.AutoUpdate`

In the preceding syntax, **object** the OLEObject.

Axes   Method

Applies To: Chart

Explanation: This Method returns a single axis if you use an Axis object as shown in Syntax 1, or as collection of the axes on the chart if you use an Axes object as shown in Syntax 2. This is a read-only Method.

Syntax 1: `object.Axes(index, axisGroup)`

Syntax 2: `object.Axes`

In the preceding syntax, **object** is the Chart object. The **index** argument specifies the axis to return and can set as xlValue, xlCategory, or xlSeries. The xlSeries is valid for 3D charts. The **axisGroup** argument specifies the axis group (either xlPrimary or xlSecondary). If this argument is omitted, the primary group is used. 3D charts have only one axis group.

Axes   Object

Explanation: This object is a collection of axis objects.

Axis   Object

Explanation: This object is an axis on a chart.

AxisBetweenCategories   Property

Applies To: Axis

Explanation: This Property is set to True if the value axis crosses the category (x) axis between categories.

Syntax: `object.AxisBetweenCategories`

In the preceding syntax, **object** denotes the Axis object.

Note: AxisBetweenCategories applies to category axes, but not to 3D charts.

AxisGroup   Property

Applies To: Axis, ChartGroup, Series

Explanation: Returns the group (either xlPrimary or xlSecondary) for the specified axis, chart group, or series. This is a read-write Property for Series and read-only for Axis and ChartGroup.

Syntax: `object.AxisGroup`

In the preceding syntax, **object** is the Axis, ChartGroup, or Series object.

Note: only xlPrimary is valid for 3D charts.

AxisTitle   Object

Explanation: This object is an axis title, which is a graphic object, on a chart.

AxisTitle   Property

Applies To: Axis

Explanation: This Property returns the AxisTitle for the specified axis and is read-only.

Syntax: `object.AxisTitle`

In the preceding syntax, object is the Axis object.

Note: When you set AxisTitle.Caption to any string, such as a blank string, the HasTitle Property for that axis sets to True.

Related Topics: ChartTitle Property, HasTitle Property, Title Property

Background Property

Applies To: Font

Explanation: Used only for text on charts, this Property returns or sets the text background type (can be one of xlAutomatic, xlOpaque, or xlTransparent). This is a read-write Property.

Syntax: *object*.`Background`

In the preceding syntax, *object* is the Font object.

Backward Property

Applies To: Trendline

Explanation: This Property returns or sets the number of periods (or units on a scatter chart) that the trendline extends backward. It is a read-write Property.

Syntax: *object*.`Backward`

In the preceding syntax, *object* is the Trendline object.

Related Topics: Add Method, Forward Property

Bar3DGroup Property

Applies To: Chart

Explanation: This Property returns the bar ChartGroup on a 3D chart.

Syntax: *object*.`Bar3DGroup`

In the preceding syntax, object is the Chart object.

Related Topic: BarGroups Method

BarGroups Method

Applies To: Chart

Explanation: In Syntax 1, this Method returns a single bar chart group on a 2D chart. In Syntax 2, this Method returns a collection of the bar chart groups (a ChartGroups collection).

Syntax 1: *object*.`BarGroups(`*index*`)`

Syntax 2: *object*.`BarGroups`

In the preceding syntax, *object* is the Chart object. The *index* argument specifies the chart group.

Related Topic: Bar3DGroup Property

BaseField   Property

Applies To: PivotField

Explanation: The BaseField Property is used only for data fields and returns or sets the base field for the custom calculation. It is a read-write Property.

Syntax: `object.BaseField`

In the preceding syntax, *object* denotes the PivotField object.

BaseItem   Property

Applies To: PivotField

Explanation: Returns or sets the item in the base field for the custom calculation. Valid only for data fields. It is a read-write Property.

Syntax: `object.BaseItem`

In the preceding syntax, *object* is the PivotField object.

BCCRecipients   Property

Applies To: Mailer

Explanation: Returns or sets the blind carbon copy recipients of the mailer. It is a read-write Property.

Syntax: `object.BCCRecipients`

In the preceding syntax, *object* is the Mailer object.

Related Topics: CCReciptients Property, Enclosures Property, Mailer Property, Received Property, SendDateTime Property, Sender Property, SendMailer Method, Subject Property, ToRecipients Property

Beep   Statement

Explanation: Use this statement when you want to sound a tone through the computer's speaker.

Syntax: `Beep`

Note: The beep duration and frequency depend on the type of hardware that you have.

BlackAndWhite   **Property**

Applies To: PageSetup

Explanation: This Property is True if elements of the document will be printed in black -and-white. It is a read-write Property.

Syntax: `object.BlackAndWhite`

In the preceding syntax, object is the PageSetup object.

Notes: This Property applies only to worksheet pages.

Bold   **Property**

Applies To: Font

Explanation: This Property is True if the font is bold. It is a read-write Property.

Syntax: `object.Bold`

In the preceding syntax, *object* is the font object.

Border   **Object**

Explanation: The Border object is the border of a cell or graphic.

Border   **Property**

Applies To: Arc, Arcs, Axis, AxisTitle, ChartArea, ChartObject, ChartObjects, ChartTitle, CheckBox, CheckBoxes, DataLabel, DataLabels, DownBars, Drawing, DrawingObjects, Drawings, DropLines, ErrorBars, Floor, Gridlines, GroupObject, GroupObjects, HiLoLines, Legend, LegendKey, Line, Lines, OLEObject, OLEObjects, OptionButton, OptionButtons, Oval, Ovals, Picture, Pictures, PlotArea, Point, Rectangle, Rectangles, Series, SeriesLines, TextBox, TextBoxes, Trendline, UpBars, Walls

Explanation: Use this Property when you want to set the Border of the object. It is a read-write Property.

Syntax: `object.Border`

In the preceding syntax, *object* is the object to which this Property applies.

BorderAround   Method

Applies To: Range

Explanation: When you want to add a border to a Range and set the Color, LineStyle, and Weight properties for a new border, use this Method.

Syntax: `object.BorderAround(lineStyle, weight, colorIndex, color)`

In the preceding syntax, `object` is the Range object. The `lineStyle` argument denotes the border line style (such as xlContinuous, xlDash, xlDot, or xlDouble). The `weight` argument denotes the border weight (such as xlHairline, xlThin, xlMedium, or xlThick). xlThin is the default setting (even if you omit it from the syntax). The `colorIndex` argument specifies the border color as a color index into the current color palette. You can use a number from 1 to 56. You also can use the constant xlAutomatic to use the window text color. The `color` argument denotes the border color as an RGB value.

Notes: You cannot use both `colorIndex` and `color` in your syntax. Excel uses the xlAutomatic `color` index when you do not specify either.

Also, you cannot use both `lineStyle` and `weight` in your syntax. Excel creates a default border when you do not specify either.

Borders   Method

Applies To: Range, Style

Explanation: Use this Method to returns a single border (a Border object, see Syntax 1) or a collection of borders (a Borders object, see Syntax 2). It is a read-write Property.

Syntax 1: `object.Borders(index)`

Syntax 2: `object.Borders`

In the preceding syntax, object is the Range or Style object. In Syntax 1, index denotes the border, such as xlTop, xlBottom, xlLeft, or xlRight.

BottomMargin   Property

Applies To: PageSetup

Explanation: Use this Property when you want to return or set the size of the bottom margin in points, which are 1/72 of an inch. It is a read-write Property.

Syntax: `object.BottomMargin`

In the preceding syntax, `object` are the PageSetup object, such as ActiveSheet.PageSetup.

Notes: Margins are set or returned in points. You might want to see the Application.InchesToPoints or Application.CentimetersToPoints function to convert inches and centimeters to points.

Related Topics: LeftMargin Property, RightMargin Property, TopMargin Property

BottomRightCell   Property

Applies To: Arc, Button, ChartObject, CheckBox, Drawing, DropDown, EditBox, GroupBox, GroupObject, Label, Line, ListBox, OLEObject, OptionButton, Oval, Picture, Rectangle, ScrollBar, Spinner, TextBox

Explanation: This propery returns the cell that lies under the bottom right corner of the object. When you are referring to drawing objects, this Property applies only when the drawing object is on a worksheet. Read-only.

Syntax: *object*`.BottomRightCell`

In the preceding syntax, *object* is the object to which this Property applies.

Related Topic: TopLeftCell Property

BringToFront   Method

Applies To: Arc, Arcs, Button, Buttons, ChartObject, ChartObjects, CheckBox, CheckBoxes, Drawing, DrawingObjects, Drawings, DropDown, DropDowns, EditBox, EditBoxes, GroupBox, GroupBoxes, GroupObject, GroupObjects, Label, Labels, Line, Lines, ListBox, ListBoxes, OLEObject, OLEObjects, OptionButton, OptionButtons, Oval, Ovals, Picture, Pictures, Rectangle, Rectangles, ScrollBar, ScrollBars, Spinner, Spinners, TextBox, TextBoxes

Explanation: Use this Method to bring an object to the front of the z-order.

Syntax: *object*`.BringToFront`

In the preceding syntax, *object* is the object to which this Method applies.

Related Topics: SendToBack Method, Zorder Property

BuiltIn   Property

Applies To: MenuBar, Toolbar, ToolbarButton

Explanation: This Property is set to True if the object is part of Excel and not a custom object. This is a read-only Property.

Syntax: *object*`.BuiltIn`

In the preceding syntax, *object* is the MenuBar, Toolbar, or ToolbarButton object.

Related Topics: BuiltInFace Property

BuiltInFace   Property

Applies To: ToolbarButton

Explanation: This Property is set to True if the button is using its built-in face, but set to False if the button has a custom face. It is a read-write Property.

Syntax: `object.BuiltInFace`

In the preceding syntax, *object* is the ToolbarButton object.

Notes: Although this Property can be set to False, you cannot set it to False. You can only set it to True. Use the CopyFace and PasteFace Methods to use a custom face, which sets this Property to False.

Related Topic: BuiltIn Property

Button   Object

Explanation: This object is a custom button graphic object on a chart or worksheet.

Buttons   Method

Applies To: Chart, DialogSheet, Worksheet

Explanation: This Method returns a single button (as shown in Syntax 1) or a collection of buttons (as shown in Syntax 2) on the chart or sheet. This is a read-only Method.

Syntax 1: `object.Buttons(index)`

Syntax 2: `object.Buttons`

In the preceding syntax, *object* is the object to which this Method applies. The *index* argument is the name or number of the button.

Calculate   Method

Applies To: Application, Range, Worksheet

Explanation: Calculates all open workbooks, a specific worksheet in a workbook, or a specified range of cells in a sheet, as the following table shows:

To calculate	Example
All open workbooks	Enter *Application.*`Calculate` or just `Calculate`
A specific worksheet	Enter *Worksheets(1).*`Calculate`
A specified range	*Worksheets(1).Rows(2).Calculate*

Syntax: *Object.*`Calculate`

The *Object* is optional for Application, required for Worksheet and Range and specifies where the calculation occurs.

CalculateBeforeSave   Property

Applies To: Application

Explanation: If workbooks are calculated before they are saved to disk (if the Calculation Property is set to xlManual), returns True. This Property is preserved even if you change the Calculation Property. Read-write.

Syntax: *Object.*`CalculateBeforeSave`

The *Object* is the Application Object and is required.

Call   Statement

Explanation: Transfers control to a Sub, Function, dynamic-link library (DLL), or a Macintosh code resource procedure.

Syntax: `Call name` (*argumentlist*)

Call is an optional keyword. If specified, you must enclose *argumentlist* in parentheses. An example is `Call MyProc(0)`

name is the name of the procedure to call.

(*argumentlist*) is the comma-delimited list of variables, arrays, or expressions to pass to the procedure. Components of *argumentlist* can include the keywords ByVal or ByRef to describe the way the arguments are to be treated by the called procedure. ByVal and ByRef, however, can be used with Call only when making a call to a DLL procedure or a Macintosh code resource.

Notes: You are never required to use the Call keyword when calling a procedure. If you use the Call keyword to call a procedure that requires arguments, however, *argumentlist* must be enclosed in parentheses. If you omit the Call keyword, you also must omit the parentheses around *argumentlist*. If you use either Call syntax to call any intrinsic or user-defined function, the function's return value is discarded.

To pass a whole array to a procedure, enter the array name followed by empty parentheses.

Related Topics: Declare Statement

Caller   Property

Applies To: Application

Explanation: Returns information about the way in which Visual Basic was called. Read-only.

Syntax: `Object.Caller`

The Object is required and is the Application Object.

Notes: This Property returns information about the way in which Visual Basic was called, as shown in the following list.

- ✔ A custom function entered in a single cell returns a Range specifying that cell.

- ✔ A custom function, part of an array formula in a range of cells, returns a Range specifying that range of cells.

- ✔ An Auto_Open, Auto_Close, Auto_Activate, or Auto_Deactivate macro returns the name of the document as text.

- ✔ A command on a menu returns an array of three elements specifying the command's position number, the menu number, and the menu bar number.

- ✔ The user clicked on a drawing Object returns the specifier of that Object as a string.

- ✔ A tool on a toolbar returns an array of two elements, specifying the tool position number and the toolbar name as text.

- ✔ A macro set by the OnDoubleClick or OnEntry properties returns the name of the chart Object identifier or cell reference, if applicable, to which the macro applies.

- ✔ Run manually from the Tools Macro dialog box, or for any reason not described above, returns the #REF! error value.

This Property returns information about the way in which Visual Basic was called, not about how the current procedure was called. If the user presses button 4, for example, which calls Macro1, and Macro1 calls Macro2, and Macro2 uses the Caller Property, the Property returns Button 4.

If you need to write a macro that behaves differently, based on whether it is called from a button or a menu item, you should specify an argument for the macro in the Assign Macro To Object dialog box.

CancelButton   Property

Applies To: Button, Buttons, DrawingObjects

Explanation: Applies only to buttons in a user-defined dialog. If the button is automatically selected when Esc is pressed, or when the system menu close box or menu item is selected, returns true. If the user presses Esc, the Cancel button is selected, and Excel runs the macro identified by the button's OnAction Property.

Syntax: `Object.CancelButton`

The `Object` is required and is the Object to which this Property applies.

Notes: Set this Property for a button if you want some code to always run when the dialog is canceled, even if it is cancelled by the Esc key or the system menu.

Only one button in the dialog can have the Cancel Property set to True at any given time. Setting one will reset this Property for all other buttons on the sheet.

Related Topic: DismissButton Property

CanPlaySounds   Property

Applies To: Application

Explanation: Returns true if the computer can play sound notes. Read-only.

Syntax: `Object.CanPlaySounds`

The `Object` is required and is the Application Object.

Related Topic: CanRecordSounds Property

CanRecordSounds   Property

Applies To: Application

Explanation: Returns true if the computer can record sound notes. Read-only.

Syntax: `Object.CanRecordSounds`

The `Object` is required and is the Application Object.

Related Topic: CanPlaySounds Property

Caption   Property

Applies To: Application, AxisTitle, Button, Buttons, Characters, ChartTitle, CheckBox, CheckBoxes, DataLabel, DataLabels, DialogFrame, DrawingObjects, DropDown, DropDowns, EditBox, EditBoxes, GroupBox, GroupBoxes, Label, Labels, Menu, MenuBar, MenuItem, OptionButton, OptionButtons, TextBox, TextBoxes, Window

Explanation: The Caption Property has different meanings, depending on the Object type to which it is applied. The Caption Property is read-write, except as noted in the following table.

Object type	Meaning
Application	The name that appears in the title bar of the main Excel window. If you don't specify a name, or if you set the name to Empty, then this Property returns `Microsoft Excel`. This Property is read-only on the Apple Macintosh.
AxisTitle	The axis title text.
Button	The button text.
Characters	The text contained in this range of characters.
ChartTitle	The chart title text.
Controls	The control text (check box, dialog frame, drop down, edit box, group box, label, and option button).
DataLabel	The data label text.
Menu	The name of the menu. Use an ampersand (&) before the letter that you want to be the command underline (for example, `&File`).
MenuBar	The menu bar text.
MenuItem	The name of the menu item (command). Use an ampersand (&) before the letter that you want to be the command underline (for example, `E&xit`).
TextBox	The text in the text box.
Window	The name that appears in the title bar of the document window. When you set the name, you can use that name as the index to the Windows Property. You can restore the default document name by setting the Caption Property to Empty.

Syntax: `Object.Caption`

The `Object` is required and is the Object to which this Property applies.

Related Topic: Text Property

Category   Property

Applies To: Name

Explanation: If the name refers to a custom function or command, this Property returns or sets the category for this name as a string translated to the language of the macro. Read-write.

Syntax: `Object.Category`

The `Object` is required and is the Name Object.

Related Topic: MacroType Property

CategoryLocal   Property

Applies To: Name

Explanation: If the name refers to a custom function or command, this Property returns or sets the category for this name as a string in the language of the user. Read-write.

Syntax: `Object.CategoryLocal`

The `Object` is required and is the Name Object.

Related Topics: Category Property, MacroType Property

CategoryNames   Property

Applies To: Axis

Explanation: Returns or sets all the category names for the specified axis as a text array. You can set this Property to an array or a Range containing the category names. Read-write.

Syntax: `Object.CategoryNames`

The `Object` is required and is the Axis Object.

Notes: Category names are a Property of the special series in an axis grouping. If you delete or modify that special series, you will cause the category names for all series using the axis to chang.

Related Topics: Formula Property, Values Property, Xvalues Property

CBool   Function

Explanation: Converts an expression to a Boolean operation.

Syntax: `CBool (expression)`

The *expression* argument is any valid numeric expression.

Note: If *expression* is zero, False is returned; otherwise, True is returned. If **expression** can't be interpreted as a numeric value, a run-time error occurs.

CCRecipients   Property

Applies To: Mailer

Explanation: Returns or sets the carbon copy (indirect) recipients of the mailer. Read-write.

Syntax: `Object.CCRecipients`

The `Object` is required and is the Mailer Object.

Notes: This Property is an array of strings that specify the address, in one of the following formats:

✔   A record in the Preferred Personal Catalog. These names are one level deep. Examples include the record of Fred or June.

✔   A full path that specifies a record in a personal catalog, such as HD:Excel Folder:My Catalog:Barney or a plain record, such as HD:Folder:Martin.

✔   A relative path from the current working directory that specifies a personal catalog record, such as My Catalog:Barney or a plain record, such as Martin.

✔   A path in a PowerShare catalog tree of the form CATALOG_NAME:<node>:RECORD_NAME where <node> is a path to a PowerShare catalog. An example of a complete path is AppleTalk:North Building Zone:George's Mac.

Related Topics: BCCRecipients Property, Enclosure Property, Mailer Property, Received Property, SendDateTime Property, Sender Property, SendMailer Method, Subject Property, ToRecipients Property

CCur   Function

Explanation: Converts an expression to a Currency.

Syntax: `CCur(expression)`

The expression argument is any valid numeric or string expression.

Notes: Generally, you can document your code by using the data type conversion functions to show that the result of some operation should be expressed as a particular data type rather than the default data type. You can, for example, use CCur to force currency arithmetic in cases where single-precision, double-precision, or integer arithmetic normally would occur.

You should use the CCur function rather than Val to provide internationally-aware conversions from any other data type to a Currency. Different decimal separators are properly recognized, depending on the country setting of your computer, as are different thousand separators and various currency options.

Note that if an expression lies outside the acceptable range for the Currency data type, an error occurs.

CDate   Function

Explanation: Converts an expression to a Date.

Syntax: `CDate(date)`

The date argument is any valid date expression.

Notes: Use the IsDate function to determine if date can be converted to a date or time. CDate recognizes date and time literals as well as some numbers that fall within the range of acceptable dates. If you are converting a number to a date, the whole number portion is converted to a date. Any fractional part of the number is converted to a time of day, starting at midnight.

CDate recognizes date formats according to the international settings of your system. The correct order of day, month, and year may not be determined if it is provided in a format other than one of the recognized date settings. In addition, a long date format is not recognized if it also contains the day-of-the-week string.

A CVDate function also is provided for compatibility with previous versions of Visual Basic. Because there is now an intrinsic Date type, however, there is no further need for CVDate. Although the CVDate function syntax is identical to the CDate function syntax, CVDate returns a Variant whose subtype is Date rather than an actual Date type. The same effect can be achieved by converting an expression to a Date and then assigning it to a Variant. This technique is consistent with the conversion of all other intrinsic types to their equivalent Variant subtypes.

Related Topic: IsDate Function

CDbl   Function

Explanation: Converts an expression to a Double.

Syntax: `CDbl(expression)`

The expression argument is any valid numeric or string expression.

Notes: Generally, you can document your code by using the data type conversion functions to show that the result of some operation should be expressed as a particular data type rather than the default data type. Use CDbl or CSng, for example, to force double- or single-precision arithmetic in cases in which currency or integer arithmetic normally would occur.

You should use the CDbl function rather than Val to provide internationally aware conversions from any other data type to a Double. Different decimal separators and thousands separators, for example, are properly recognized depending on the locale setting of your system.

CellDragAndDrop   Property

Applies To: Application

Explanation: Returns true if Cell Drag and Drop editing is on. Read-write.

Syntax: `Object.CellDragAndDrop`

The Object parameter is required and is the Application Object.

Cells   Method

Applies To: Application, Range, Worksheet

Explanation: Returns a single cell (Syntax 1 and 2) or a collection of cells (Syntax 3) as a Range. The action of the Cells Method depends on the Object to which it is applied, as shown in the following table:

Object type	Action
Application	If the active document is a worksheet, Application.Cells is equal to ActiveSheet.Cells, which returns a collection of cells on the active worksheet. Otherwise, the Cells Method returns an error.
Range	Returns a collection of cells from the range. Worksheet Returns a collection of cells from the worksheet.

Syntax 1: `Object.Cells(rowIndex, columnIndex)`

Syntax 2: `Object.Cells(rowindex)`

Syntax 3: `Object.Cells`

The Cells Method has the following Object qualifier and named arguments:

✔ The ***Object*** is optional for Application, required for Worksheet and Range. The Object that contains the cells. If you omit the Object qualifier, the Cells Method applies to the active worksheet of the active workbook.

✔ The ***rowIndex*** is required for Syntax 1 and is the row number of the cell you want to access, starting with 1 for row 1 (for Application and Worksheet) or the first row in the Range.

The ***rowIndex*** is required for Syntax 2 and is a long integer that specifies the index number of the cell you want to access, in row-major order. A1 is Cells(1), A2 is Cells(257) for Application and Worksheet; Range.Cells(1) is the top left cell in the Range.

✔ The ***columnIndex*** is required for Syntax 1 and is a number or string that indicates the column number of the cell you want to access, starting with 1 or "A" for column A (for Application or Worksheet) or the first column in the Range.

Notes: Syntax 1 uses a row number and a column number or letter as index arguments. For more information about this syntax, see the Range Object.

Syntax 2 uses a single number as an index argument. The index is 1 for cell A1, 2 for cell B1, 3 for cell C1, 257 for cell A2, and so on.

The rowIndex and columnIndex arguments are relative offsets when you apply the Cells Method to a Range Object. In other words, specifying a rowIndex of 1 returns cells in the first row of the range, not the first row of the worksheet. For example, if the selection is cell C3, then Selection.Cells(2, 2) returns cell D4 (you can use the Method to index outside the original range).

If you apply Syntax 3 to a Range, it returns the same Range Object (in other words, it does nothing).

If you apply Syntax 3 to a Worksheet, it returns a collection of all the cells in the worksheet (all the cells, not just the cells that are currently in use).

Related Topic: Range Method

CenterFooter   Property

Applies To: PageSetup

Explanation: Returns or sets the center part of the footer. Read-write.

Syntax: *Object*.CenterFooter

The ***Object*** qualifier is required and is the PageSetup Object (ActiveSheet.PageSetup, for example).

Notes: Special format codes can be used in the footer text.

Related Topics: CenterHeader, LeftFooter, LeftHeader, RightHeader, RightFooter

CenterHeader   Property

Applies To: PageSetup

Explanation: Returns or sets the center part of the header. Read-write.

Syntax: `Object.CenterHeader`

The `Object` is rquired and is the Page Setup Object. An example is `ActiveSheet.PageSetup`.

Note: You can us special format codes in the header text.

Related Topics: CenterFooter Property, LeftFooter Property, RightHeader Propereety, RightFooter Property

CenterHorizontally   Property

Applies To: PageSetup

Explanation: True if the sheet is centered horizontally on the page. Read-write.

Syntax: `Object.CenterHorizontally`

The `Object` is required and is the PageSetup Object. An example is `ActiveSheet.PageSetup`.

Related Topic: CenterVertically Property

CenterVertically   Property

Applies To: PageSetup

Explanation: True if the sheet is centered vertically on the page. Read-write.

Syntax: `Object.CenterVertically`

The `Object` is required and is the PageSetup Object. An example is `ActiveSheet.PageSetup`.

Related Topic: InchesToPoints Method

CentimetersToPoints   Method

Applies To: Application

Explanation: Converts a measurement that is in centimeters to points (0.035 centimeters).

Syntax: `Object.CentimetersToPoints(centimeters)`

The `Object` is required and is the Application Object.

The `centimeters` argument is required. It specifies the centimeter value to convert to points.

Related Topic: InchesToPoints Method

ChangeFileAccess   Method

Applies To: Workbook

Explanation: Changes the access permissions for the workbook. This may require loading an updated version from the disk.

Syntax: *Object*.`ChangeFileAccess`(*mode*, `writePassword`, `notify`)

The ChangeFileAccess Method has the following Object qualifier and named arguments:

The *Object* is required and is the Workbook Object.

The *mode* argument is required. It specifies the new access mode (one of xlReadWrite or xlReadOnly).

The `writePassword` argument is optional. If the file is write-reserved and mode is xlReadWrite, this argument specifies the write-reserved password. Ignored if there is no password for the file or mode is xlReadOnly.

The `notify` argument is optional. It returns a True if you want to be notified when the file cannot be immediately accessed. Assumed to be True if omitted.

Note: If you have a file open in read-only mode, you do not have exclusive access to the file. If you change a file from read-only to read-write, Excel must load a new copy of the file to ensure that no changes were made while you had the file open as read-only.

ChangeLink   Method

Applies To: Workbook

Explanation: Changes a link from one document to another.

Syntax: *Object*.`ChangeLink`(*name*, `newName`, `type`)

The ChangeLink Method has the following Object qualifier and named arguments:

The *Object* is required and is the Workbook Object.

The *name* argument is required. It specifies the name of the Excel or DDE/OLE link to change, as returned from the LinkSources Method.

The `newName` argument is required. The new name of the link.

The `type` argument is optional. It specifies the link type (either xlExcelLinks or xlOLELinks). If omitted, the default is xlExcelLinks. Use xlOLELinks for both DDE and OLE links.

ChangeScenario   Method

Applies To: Scenario

Explanation: Changes the scenario to have a new set of changing cells and (optionally) scenario values.

Syntax: *Object*.ChangeScenario(*changingCells*, *values*)

The ChangeScenario Method has the following Object qualifier and named arguments:

The *Object* is required and is the Scenario Object.

The *changingCells* argument is required and is a range that specifies the new set of changing cells for the scenario. The changing cells must be on the same sheet as the scenario.

The *values* argument is optional and is an array that contains the new scenario values for the changing cells. If omitted, the scenario values are assumed to be the current values in the changing cells.

Note: If you specify values, the array must contain an element for each cell in the changingCells range, or Excel generates an error.

Related Topics: ChangingCells Property, Comment Property

ChangingCells   Property

Applies To: Scenario

Explanation: Returns a Range that contains the changing cells for a scenario. Read only.

Syntax: *Object*.ChangingCells

The *Object* is required and is the Scenario Object.

Related Topics: ChangeScenario Method, Comment Property

Characters   Method

Applies To: AxisTitle, Button, Buttons, ChartTitle, CheckBox, CheckBoxes, DataLabel, DialogFrame, DrawingObjects, DropDown, DropDowns, EditBox, EditBoxes, GroupBox, GroupBoxes, Label, Labels, OptionButton, OptionButtons, Range, TextBox, TextBoxes

Explanation: Returns a range of Characters within the Object text and enables you to format characters within a text string.

Syntax: *Object*.Characters(*start*, *length*)

The Characters method has the following Object qualifier and named arguments:

The *Object* is required and is the Object to which this Method applies.

The *start* argument is optional and is the first character to return. If this argument is one or omitted, this Method returns a range of characters starting with the first character.

The *length* argument is optional and is the number of characters to return. If this argument is omitted, this Method returns the remainder of the string after the start character.

Notes: For a Range Object, this Method will fail if it is used with arguments and the cell does not contain a text value. You can use this Method without arguments to obtain a set of characters for the entire range, but you cannot use the Method with arguments.

Characters   Object

Explanation: A collection of characters (in other words, the text or a subset of the text) in a cell, text box, or custom button graphic Object.

Chart   Object

Explanation: A chart in a workbook.

Chart   Property

Applies To: ChartObject

Explanation: Returns the Chart contained in the Object. Read-only.

Syntax: `Object.Chart`

The *Object* is required and is the Object to which this Property applies.

ChartArea   Object

Explanation: The chart area of a chart.

ChartArea   Property

Applies To: Chart

Explanation: Returns the complete ChartArea for the chart. Read-only.

Syntax: `Object.ChartArea`

The *Object* is required and is the Chart Object.

ChartGroup   Object

Explanation: A chart group on a chart.

ChartGroups   Method

Applies To: Chart

Explanation: Returns a single chart group (a ChartGroup Object, Syntax 1) or a collection of all the chart groups in the chart (a ChartGroups Object, Syntax 2). Every type of group is included in the returned collection.

Syntax 1: `Object.ChartGroups(index)`

Syntax 2: `Object.ChartGroups`

The ChartGroups Method has the following Object qualifier and named arguments:

The *Object* is required and is the Chart Object.

The *index* argument is required for Syntax 1. The number of the chart group.

ChartGroups   Object

Explanation: A collection of ChartGroups objects.

ChartObject   Object

Explanation: An embedded chart on a sheet. The ChartObject acts as a container for a chart. The ChartObject provides the size.

ChartObjects   Method

Applies To: Chart, DialogSheet, Worksheet

Explanation: Returns a single chart (a ChartObject Object, Syntax 1) or a collection of all the embedded charts (a ChartObjects Object, Syntax 2) on the chart or sheet.

Syntax 1: `Object.ChartObjects(index)`

Syntax 2: `Object.ChartObjects`

The ChartObjects Method has the following Object qualifier and named arguments:

The *Object* is required and is the Object to which this Method applies. If you specify a Chart Object, it must be a chart sheet (it cannot be an embedded chart).

The *index* argument is required for Syntax 1. The name or number of the chart (can be an array to specify more than one).

Notes: This Method is not equivalent to the Charts Method. This Method returns embedded charts; the Charts Method returns chart sheets. Use the Chart Property to return the chart sheet for an embedded chart Object.

Related Topic: Charts Method

ChartObjects   Object

Explanation: A collection of ChartObjects objects.

ChartSize   Property

Applies To: PageSetup

Explanation: Returns or sets the Method used when scaling a chart to fit on a page, as shown in the following table. Read-write.

Value	Meaning
xlScreenSize	Print the chart the same size as it appears on the screen.
xlFitToPage	Print the chart as large as possible, while retaining the chart's height-to-width ratio as shown on the screen.
xlFullPage	Print the chart to fit the page, adjusting the height-to-width ratio as necessary.

Syntax: `Object.ChartSize`

The Object is required and is the PageSetup Object. An example is `ActiveSheet.PageSetup`.

Notes: This Property applies only to chart sheets (it cannot be used with embedded charts).

Charts   Method

Applies To: Application, Workbook

Explanation: Returns a single chart (a Chart Object, Syntax 1) or a collection of the charts (a Charts Object, Syntax 2) in the workbook.

Syntax 1: `Object.Charts(index)`

Syntax 2: `Object.Charts`

The Charts Method has the following Object qualifier and named arguments:

The `Object` is optional for Application, required for Workbook. It is the Object to which this Method applies.

The *index* argument is required for Syntax 1. It is the name or number of the chart (can be an array to specify more than one).

Notes: If you use this Method with no Object qualifier, it is equivalent to ActiveWorkbook.Charts.

Related Topic: ChartObjects Object

Charts   Object

Explanation: A collection of charts in a workbook.

ChartTitle   Object

Explanation: The title of the chart.

ChartTitle   Property

Applies To: Chart

Explanation: Returns the ChartTitle for the specified chart. Read-only.

Syntax: `Object.ChartTitle`

The `Object` is required and is the Chart Object.

Related Topics: AxisTitle, HasTitle, Title

ChartWizard   Method

Applies To: Chart

Explanation: Modifies the properties of the given chart. Allows a chart to be quickly formatted without setting all the individual properties. This Method is noninteractive, and changes only the specified properties.

Syntax: `Object.ChartWizard`(*source, gallery, format, plotBy, categoryLabels, seriesLabels, hasLegend, title, categoryTitle, valueTitle, extraTitle*)

The ChartWizard Method has the following Object qualifier and named arguments:

The `Object` is required and is the Chart Object.

The *source* argument is optional. It specifies a range that contains the source data for the chart. If this argument is omitted, Excel uses the current selection.

The *gallery* argument is optional. It specifies the chart type (one of xlArea, xlBar, xlColumn, xlLine, xlPie, xlRadar, xlXYScatter, xlCombination, xl3DArea, xl3DBar, xl3DColumn, xl3DLine, xl3DPie, xl3DSurface, or xlDoughnut).

The *format* argument is optional. It specifies the option number for the built-in autoformats and can be a number from 1 to 10, depending on the gallery type. If this argument is omitted, Excel chooses a default value based on the gallery type and data source.

The *plotBy* argument is optional. It specifies whether the data for each series is in rows or columns (either xlRows or xlColumns).

The *categoryLabels* argument is optional. It is an integer specifying the number of rows or columns within the source range containing category labels. Legal values are from zero to one less than the maximum number of the corresponding categories or series.

The *seriesLabels* argument is optional. It is an integer specifying the number of rows or columns within the source range containing series labels. Legal values are from zero to one less than the maximum number of the corresponding categories or series.

The *hasLegend* argument is optional. True to include a legend.

The *title* argument is optional and is the Chart title text.

The *categoryTitle* argument is optional and is the Category (x) axis title text.

The *valueTitle* argument is optional and is the Value axis title text.

The *extraTitle* argument is optional. It is the Series axis title for 3D charts, second value axis title for 2D charts.

ChDir   Statement

Explanation: Changes the current directory or folder.

Syntax: `ChDir (path)`

The **path** named argument is a string expression that identifies which directory or folder becomes the new default directory or folder. It may include drive. If no drive is specified, **ChDir** changes the default directory or folder on the current drive.

Notes: In Windows, the ChDir Statement changes the default directory but not the default drive. For example, if the default drive is C, the following Statement changes the default directory on drive D, but C remains the default drive:

```
ChDir D:\TMP
```

On the Macintosh, the default drive always changes to whatever drive is specified in path.

Related Topics: ChDrive Statement, CurDir Method, Dir, MkDir, RmDir

ChDrive   Statement

Explanation: Changes the current drive.

Syntax: `ChDrive (drive)`

The *drive* named argument is a string expression that specifies an existing drive. If you supply a zero-length argument (""), the current drive doesn't change. In Windows, if the argument drive is a multiple-character string, ChDrive uses only the first letter. On the Macintosh, ChDrive changes the current folder to the root folder of the specifed drive.

Related Topics: ChDir, CurDir, MkDir, RmDir

CheckBox   Object

Explanation: A check box control on a worksheet or dialog sheet.

Notes: Check boxes have position and dimension but no formatting properties. The background and font of the check box is fixed.

CheckBoxes   Method

Applies To: Chart, DialogSheet, Worksheet

Explanation: Returns a single check box (a CheckBox Object, Syntax 1) or a collection of check boxes on the chart or sheet (a CheckBoxes Object, Syntax 2).

Syntax 1: `Object.CheckBoxes(index)`

Syntax 2: `Object.CheckBoxes`

The CheckBoxes Method has the following Object qualifier and named arguments:

The *Object* is required and is the Chart, DialogSheet, or Worksheet Object.

The *index* argument is required for Syntax 1. It specifies the name or number of the check box (can be an array to specify more than one).

CheckBoxes   Object

Explanation: A collection of CheckBox objects.

Checked   Property

Applies To: MenuItem

Explanation: True if the menu item is checked. Read-write.

Syntax: `Object.Checked`

The *Object* is required and is the MenuItem Object.

CheckSpelling   Method

Applies To: Application, Button, Buttons, Chart, CheckBox, CheckBoxes, DialogFrame, DialogSheet, DrawingObjects, GroupBox, GroupBoxes, GroupObject, GroupObjects, Label, Labels, OptionButton, OptionButtons, Range, TextBox, TextBoxes, Worksheet

Explanation: Syntax 1 checks the spelling of an Object. This form has no return value; Excel displays the Spelling dialog box.

Syntax 2 checks the spelling of a single word. Returns True if the word is found in one of the dictionaries, False if it is not.

Syntax 1: *Object*.**CheckSpelling**(*customDictionary*, *ignoreUppercase*, *alwaysSuggest*)

Syntax 2: *Object*.**CheckSpellingword**, (*customDictionary*, *ignoreUppercase*)

The CheckSpelling Method has the following Object qualifier and named arguments:

The *Object* is required and is the Object to which this Method applies. Use the Application Object to check a single word (Syntax 2).

The *customDictionary* argument is optional. It is a string indicating the file name of the custom dictionary to examine if the word is not found in the main dictionary. If omitted, the currently specified dictionary is used.

The *ignoreUppercase* argument is optional. If True, Excel will ignore words that are in all uppercase. If False, Excel will check words that are in all uppercase. If omitted, the current setting will be used.

The *alwaysSuggest* argument is optional. If True, Excel will display a list of suggested alternate spellings when an incorrect spelling is found. If False, Excel will wait for you to input the correct spelling. If omitted, the current setting will be used.

The *word* argument is required (used with Application Object only) and is the word you want to check.

Notes: To check headers, footers, and objects, use Worksheet.CheckSpelling.

To check only cells and notes, use Worksheet.Cells.CheckSpelling.

ChildField   Property

Applies To: PivotField

Explanation: Returns the child pivot field for the specified field (if the field is grouped and has a child field). Read-only.

Syntax: *Object*.**ChildField**

The *Object* is required and is the PivotField Object.

Notes: If the specified field has no child field, this Property causes an error.

ChildItems   Method

Applies To: PivotField, PivotItem

Explanation: Returns one pivot item (a PivotItem Object, Syntax 1) or a collection of all the pivot items (a PivotItems Object, Syntax 2) that are group children in the specified field, or children of the specified item. Read-only.

Syntax 1: `Object.ChildItems(index)`

Syntax 2: `Object.ChildItems`

The ChildItems Method has the following Object qualifier and named arguments:

The **`Object`** is required and is the PivotField or PivotItem Object.

The **`index`** argument is required for Syntax 1 and is the number or name of the pivot item to return (can be an array to specify more than one).

Chr   Function

Explanation: Returns the character associated with the specified character code.

Syntax: `Chr(charcode)`

The **`charcode`** named argument is a number in the range 0 to 255, inclusive, that identifies a character.

Notes: Numbers from 0 to 31 are the same as standard, nonprintable ASCII codes. For example, `Chr10` returns a linefeed character.

Related Topics: Asc, Str

CInt   Function

Explanation: Converts an expression to an Integer.

Syntax: `CInt(expression)`

The `expression` argument is any valid numeric or string expression.

Notes: In general, you can document your code by using the data type conversion functions to show that the result of some operation should be expressed as a particular data type, rather than the default data type. Use CInt or CLng, for example, to force integer arithmetic in cases where currency, single-precision, or double-precision arithmetic normally would occur.

You should use the CInt function rather than Val to provide internationally aware conversions from any other data type to an Integer. For example, different decimal separators are properly recognized depending on the locale setting of your system, as are different thousand separators.

If expression lies outside the acceptable range for the Integer data type, an error occurs.

CInt differs from the Fix and Int functions that truncate, rather than round, the fractional part of a number. When the fractional part is exactly 0.5, the CInt function always rounds it to the nearest even number. For example, 0.5 rounds to 0, and 1.5 rounds to 2.

Related Topics: Fix, Int

CircularReference   Property

Applies To: Worksheet

Explanation: Returns the Range containing the first circular reference on the sheet, or Nothing if there is no circular reference present. The circular reference must be removed before calculation can proceed. Read-only.

Syntax: `Object.CircularReference`

The `Object` is required and is the Worksheet Object.

Clear   Method

Applies To: ChartArea, Range

Explanation: Clears the entire range or chart area.

Syntax: `Object.Clear`

The `Object` is required and is the ChartArea or Range Object.

Related Topics: ClearFormats, ClearContents

ClearArrows   Method

Applies To: Worksheet

Explanation: Clears the tracer arrows on the worksheet. Tracer arrows are added by the auditing feature.

Syntax: `Object.ClearArrows`

The `Object` is required and is the Worksheet Object.

Related Topics: ShowDependents, ShowErrors, ShowPrecedents

ClearContents   Method

Applies To: ChartArea, Range

Explanation: Clears the formulas from the range. Clears the data from a chart but leaves the formatting.

Syntax: `Object.ClearContents`

The `Object` is required and is the Chart or Range Object.

ClearFormats   Method

Applies To: ChartArea, Floor, LegendKey, PlotArea, Point, Range, Series, Trendline, Walls

Explanation: Clears the formatting of the Object.

Syntax: `Object.ClearFormats`

The `Object` is required and is the Object to which this Method applies.

Related Topics: Clear, ClearContents

ClearNotes   Method

Applies To: Range

Explanation: Clears the note and the sound notes from all the cells in the range.

Syntax: `Object.ClearNotes`

The `Object` is required and is the clear notes and sound notes from this range.

Related Topics: NoteText Method, SoundNote Property

ClearOutline   Method

Applies To: Range

Explanation: Clears the outline for the specified range.

Syntax: `Object.ClearOutline`

The `Object` is required and is the Range Object.

Related Topics: AutoOutline Method

ClipboardFormats   Property

Applies To: Application

Explanation: Returns the formats currently on the Clipboard as an array of numeric values. Read-only.

Syntax: `Object.ClipboardFormats`

The `Object` is required and is the Application Object.

Notes: This Property is available in Windows and on the Macintosh. Some formats may be available only on the Macintosh, or only in Windows.

CLng .... Function

Explanation: Converts an expression to a Long.

Syntax: `CLng(expression)`

The *expression* argument is any valid numeric or string expression.

Notes: In general, you can document your code by using the data type conversion functions to show that the result of some operation should be expressed as a particular data type rather than the default data type. For example, use CInt or CLng to force integer arithmetic in cases where currency, single-precision, or double-precision arithmetic normally would occur.

You should use the CLng function instead of Val to provide internationally aware conversions from any other data type to a Long. For example, different decimal separators are properly recognized depending on the locale setting of your system, as are different thousand separators.

If expression lies outside the acceptable range for the Long data type, an error occurs.

CLng differs from the Fix and Int functions that truncate, rather than round, the fractional part of a number. When the fractional part is exactly 0.5, the CLng function always rounds it to the nearest even number. For example, 0.5 rounds to 0, and 1.5 rounds to 2.

Related Topics: Fix Function, Int Function

Close .... Method

Applies To: Window, Workbook, Workbooks

Explanation: Closes the Object. The Workbooks collection uses Syntax 1. Window and Workbook objects use Syntax 2.

Syntax 1: `Object.Close`

Syntax 2: `Object.Close(saveChanges, fileName, routeWorkbook)`

The Close Method has the following Object qualifier and named arguments:

The **Object** is required and is the Object to close.

The *saveChanges* argument is optional. If there are no changes to the workbook in the window, this argument is ignored. If there are changes to the workbook, and there are other windows open on the workbook, this argument is ignored. If there are changes to the workbook, and there are no other windows open on the workbook, this argument takes the following action:

Value	Action
True	Saves the changes to the workbook. If there is not yet a file name associated with the workbook, then fileName is used. If fileName is omitted, the user is asked to supply a file name.
False.	Does not save the changes to this file.
Omitted	Displays a dialog box asking the user whether to save changes.

The `fileName` argument is optional. Save changes under this file name.

The `routeWorkbook` argument is optional. If the workbook does not need to be routed to the next recipient (has no routing slip, or is already routed), this argument is ignored. Otherwise, Excel routes the workbook as shown in the following table:

Value	Meaning
True	Sends the workbook to the next recipient.
False	Does not send the workbook.
Omitted	Displays a dialog box asking the user if the workbook should be sent.

Notes: Closing a workbook from Visual Basic does not run any Auto_Close macros in the workbook. Use the RunAutoMacros Method to run the auto close macros.

Close   Statement

Explanation: Concludes input/output (I/O) to a file opened using the Open Statement.

Syntax: `Close (filenumberlist)`

The `filenumberlist` argument can be one or more file numbers using the following syntax, where filenumber is any valid file number.

Notes: If you omit `filenumberlist`, all active files opened by the Open Statement are closed.

When you close files that were opened for Output or Append, the final buffer of output is written to the operating system buffer for that file. All buffer space associated with the closed file is released.

When the Close Statement executes, the association of a file with its file number ends.

Related Topics: End Statement, Open Statement, Reset Statement, Stop Statement

Color   **Property**

Applies To: Border, Borders, Font, Interior

Explanation: Returns or sets the primary color of the Object, as shown in the following table. The color is a long integer, created with the RGB function. Read-write.

Object	Color
Border	The color of the border.
Borders	The color of all four borders of a range. If they are not the same, returns Null.
Font	The color of the font.
Interior	The cell shading color or drawing Object fill color.

Syntax: `Object.Color`

The `Object` is required and is the Object to which this Property applies.

Note: If the color is Automatic, the Color Property returns the automatic color as an RGB value (a long integer). Use the ColorIndex Property to determine whether the color is Automatic.

ColorButtons   **Property**

Applies To: Application

Explanation: True if toolbars are displayed using colored faces. Read-write.

Syntax: `Object.ColorButtons`

The `Object` is required and is the Application Object.

Related Topic: LargeButtons Property

ColorIndex   **Property**

Applies To: Border, Borders, Font, Interior

Explanation: Returns or sets the color of the border, font, or interior, as shown in the following table. The color is specified as an index value into the current color palette, or the special constant xlAutomatic to use the automatic fill style. Read-write.

Object	ColorIndex
Border	Color of the border.
Borders	Color of all four borders. Returns Null if all four colors are not the same.
Font	Color of the font. Specify xlAutomatic to use the automatic color.
Interior	Color of the interior fill. Set this Property to xlNone to specify no fill. Set this Property to xlAutomatic to specify the automatic fill (for drawing objects).

Syntax: `Object.ColorIndex`

The `Object` is required and is the Object to which this Property applies.

Notes: This Property specifies a color as an index into the workbook color palette. You can use the Colors Property to return the current color palette.

Related Topics: Color Property, Colors Property, PatternColor Property

Colors   Property

Applies To: Workbook

Explanation: Returns or sets an array of colors (from one to 56) in the palette for the workbook. Read-write.

Syntax: `Object.Colors`

The `Object` is required and is the Workbook Object.

Related Topic: ColorIndex Property

Column   Property

Applies To: Range

Explanation: Returns the first column of the first area in the range, as a number. Read-only.

Syntax: `Object.Column`

The `Object` is required and is the range containing the column to return.

Notes: Column A returns 1, column B returns 2, and so on. To return the number of the last column in the range, use myRange.Columns(myRange.Columns.Count).Column

Related Topics: Columns Method, Column Property, Rows Method

Column3DGroup   Property

Applies To: Chart

Explanation: Returns the column ChartGroup on a 3D chart.

Syntax: `Object.Column3DGroup`

The `Object` is required and is the Chart Object.

Related Topic: ColumnGroups Method

ColumnDifferences   Method

Applies To: Range

Explanation: Returns a Range that contains all the cells whose contents are different than the comparison cell in each column. The comparison cell is the one in the same row as comparison.

Syntax: `Object.ColumnDifferences(comparison)`

The ColumnDifferences Method has the following Object qualifier and named arguments:

The `Object` is required and is the range that contains the cells to compare.

The `comparison` argument is required and is a cell in the comparison row.

Related Topic: RowDifferences Method

ColumnFields   Method

Applies To: PivotTable

Explanation: Returns a single pivot field (a PivotField Object, Syntax 1) or a collection of the pivot fields (a PivotFields Object, Syntax 2) that are currently showing as column fields. Read-only.

Syntax 1: `Object.ColumnFields(index)`

Syntax 2: `Object.ColumnFields`

The ColumnFields Method has the following Object qualifier and named arguments:

The `Object` is required and is the PivotTable Object.

The `index` argument is required for Syntax 1. The name or number of the pivot field to return (can be an array to specify more than one).

Related Topics: DataFields Method, HiddenFields Method, PageFields Method, PivotFields Method, RowFields Method, VisibleFields Method

ColumnGrand   Property

Applies To: PivotTable

Explanation: True if the pivot table shows column grand totals. Read-write.

Syntax: `Object.ColumnGrand`

The `Object` is required and is the PivotTable Object.

Related Topic: RowGrand Property

ColumnGroups   Method

Applies To: Chart

Explanation: On a 2D chart, returns a single column chart group (a ChartGroup Object, Syntax 1), or a collection of the column chart groups (a ChartGroups collection, Syntax 2).

Syntax 1: `Object.ColumnGroups(index)`

Syntax 2: `Object.ColumnGroups`

The ColumnGroups Method has the following Object qualifier and named arguments.

The `Object` is required and is the Chart Object.

The `index` argument is required for Syntax 1. Specifies the chart group.

Related Topic: Column3DProperty

ColumnRange   Property

Applies To: PivotTable

Explanation: Returns the Range that contains the pivot table column area. Read-only.

Syntax: `Object.ColumnRange`

The `Object` is required and is the PivotTable Object.

Related Topics: DataBodyRange Property, DataLabelRange Property, PageRange Property, RowRange Property

Columns   Method

Applies To: Application, Range, Worksheet

Explanation: Returns a single column (Syntax 1) or a collection of columns (Syntax 2). A column is a Range Object.

Syntax 1: `Object.Columns(index)`

Syntax 2: `Object.Columns`

The Columns Method has the following Object qualifier and named arguments:

The `Object` is optional for Application; the `Object` is required for Range and Worksheet and is the Object that contains the columns.

The `index` argument is required for Syntax 1 and is the name or number of the column.

Notes: When applied to a Range Object that is a multiple selection, this Method returns columns from the first area of the range only. If the Range Object is a multiple selection with two areas, for example, A1:B2 and C3:D4, Selection.Columns.Count, returns 2, not 4.

To use this Method on a range that may contain a multiple selection, test Areas.Count to determine if the range is a multiple selection, and if it is, then loop over each area in the range.

Related Topics: Range Method, Rows Method

ColumnWidth   Property

Applies To: Range

Explanation: Returns or sets the width of all columns in the range. Read-write.

Syntax: `Object.ColumnWidth`

The `Object` is required. Return or set column widths for this range.

Notes: One unit of column width is equal to the width of a character of the Normal style. For proportional fonts, the width of the character 0 (zero) is used.

Use the Width Property to return the width of a column in points.

If all columns in the range have the same width, the ColumnWidth Property returns the width. If columns in the range have different widths, the Property returns Null.

Related Topic: RowHeight Property

CommandUnderlines   Property

Applies To: Application

Explanation: Returns or sets the state of the command underlines, as shown in the following list.

Value	Meaning
xlOn	Command underlines are on.
xlOff	Command underlines are off.
xlAutomatic	Command underlines appear when you activate the menus.

Syntax: `Object.CommandUnderlines`

The `Object` is required and is the Application Object.

Note: In Excel, reading this Property always returns xlOn, and setting this Property to anything but xlOn is an error.

Comment   Property

Applies To: Scenario

Explanation: Returns or sets the comment associated with the scenario. The comment text cannot exceed 255 characters. Read-write.

Syntax: `Object.Comment`

The `Object` is required and is the Scenario Object.

Related Topics: ChangeScenario Method, ChangingCells Property

Comments   Property

Applies To: AddIn, Workbook

Explanation: Returns or sets the comments for an Object as a string. Read-only for AddIn, read-write for Workbook.

Syntax: `Object.Comments`

The `Object` is required and is the AddIn or Workbook Object.

Related Topics: Author Property, Keyword Property, Subject Property, Title Property

Consolidate   **Method**

Applies To: Range

Explanation: Consolidates data from multiple ranges on multiple worksheets into a single range on a single worksheet.

Syntax: *Object*.Consolidate(*sources, function, topRow, leftColumn, createLinks*)

The *Object* is required and is the destination range.

The *sources* argument is optional. It specifies the sources of the consolidation as an array of text reference strings in R1C1-style notation. The references must include the full path of sheets to consolidate.

The *function* argument is optional. The consolidation function (one of xlAverage, xlCount, xlCountNums, xlMax, xlMin, xlProduct, xlStDev, xlStDevP, xlSum, xlVar, or xlVarP).

The *topRow* argument is optional. If True, data is consolidated based on column header titles in the top row of the consolidation ranges. If False or omitted, data is consolidated by position.

The *leftColumn* argument is optional. If True, data is consolidated based on row titles in the left column of the consolidation ranges. If False or omitted, data is consolidated by position.

The *createLinks* argument is optional. If True, the consolidation uses worksheet links. If False, the consolidation copies the data.

Related Topics: ConsolidationFunction Property, ConsolidationOptions Property, ConsolidationSources Property, Style Property

ConsolidationFunction   **Property**

Applies To: Worksheet

Explanation: Returns the function code used for the current consolidation (one of xlAverage, xlCount, xlCountNums, xlMax, xlMin, xlProduct, xlStDev, xlStDevP, xlSum, xlVar, or xlVarP). Read-only.

Syntax: *Object*.ConsolidationFunction

The *Object* is required and is the Worksheet Object.

Related Topics: Consolidate Method, ConsolidationOptions Property, ConsolidationSources Property

ConsolidationOptions   Property

Applies To: Worksheet

Explanation: Returns a three-element array of consolidation options, as shown in the following table. If the element is True, that option is set. Read-only.

Element	Meaning
1	Labels in top row.
2	Labels in left column.
3	Create links for data.

Syntax: `Object.ConsolidationOptions`

The `Object` is required and is the Worksheet Object.

Related Topics: Consolidate Method, ConsolidationFunction Property, ConsolidationSources Property

ConsolidationSources   Property

Applies To: Worksheet

Explanation: Returns an array of string values that name the source sheets for the worksheet's current consolidation. Returns Empty if there is no consolidation on the sheet. Read-only.

Syntax: `Object.ConsolidationSources`

The `Object` is required and is the Worksheet Object.

Related Topics: Consolidate Method, ConsolidationFunction Property, ConsolidationOptions Property

Const   Statement

Explanation: Declares constants for use in place of literal values.

Syntax: `Public` or `Private Const (constname As type = expression)`

The Const Statement syntax has these parts:

Part	Description
Public	Used at module level to declare constants that are available to all procedures in all modules. Not allowed in procedures.
Private	Used at module level to declare constants that are available only within the module where the declaration is made. Not allowed in procedures.
constname	Name of the constant; follows standard variable-naming conventions.
type	Data type of the constant; may be Boolean, Integer, Long, Currency, Single, Double, Date, String, or Variant. Use a separate As type clause for each constant being declared.
expression	Literal, other constant, or any combination including arithmetic or logical operators except Is.

Notes: If not explicitly specified using either Public or Private, constants are Private by default.

Several constant declarations can be combined on the same line by separating each constant assignment with a comma. If constant declarations are combined in this way, the Public or Private keywords, if used, apply to all of them.

You can't use string concatenation, variables, user-defined or intrinsic functions (such as Chr) in expressions assigned to constants.

The special characters left bracket ([), question mark (?), number sign (#), and asterisk (*) can be used to match themselves directly only by enclosing them in brackets. The right bracket (]) can't be used within a group to match itself, but it can be used outside a group as an individual character. Constants can make your programs self-documenting and easier to modify. Unlike variables, constants can't be inadvertently changed while your program is running.

If you don't explicitly declare the constant type (using As type), the constant is given a data type that is most appropriate for the expression provided. Constants declared in Sub, Function, or Property procedures are local to that procedure. A constant declared outside a procedure is defined throughout the module in which it is declared. You can use constants anywhere you would use an expression.

Related Topics: Def Type Statements, Let Statement

ConstrainNumeric   Property

Applies To: Application

Explanation: True if handwriting recognition is limited to numbers and punctuation only. Read-write. This Property is available only if you are using Windows for Pen Computing. If you try to return or set this Property under any other operating system, an error occurs.

Syntax: `Object.ConstrainNumeric`

The **Object** is required and is the Application Object.

ConvertFormula   Method

Applies To: Application

Explanation: Converts cell references in a formula between the A1 and R1C1 reference styles, between relative and absolute references, or both.

Syntax: `Object.ConvertFormula(formula fromReferenceStyle toReferenceStyle toAbsolute relativeTo)`

The ConvertFormula Method has the following Object qualifier and named arguments:

The **Object** is required and is the Application Object.

The **formula** argument is required and is a string that contains the formula that you want to convert. This must be a valid formula and it must begin with an equal sign.

The **fromReferenceStyle** argument is required and is the reference style of the formula. May be either xlA1 or xlR1C1.

The **toReferenceStyle** argument is optional. The reference style you want returned. It may be either xlA1 or xlR1C1. If omitted, the reference style is not changed (the formula stays in the style specified by fromReferenceStyle).

The **toAbsolute** argument is optional. It specifies the converted reference type (one of xlAbsolute, xlAbsRowRelColumn, xlRelRowAbsColumn, or xlRelative). If this argument is omitted, the reference type is not changed.

The **relativeTo** argument is optional and is a Range Object that contains one cell. This Object determines the cell to which relative references relate.

Copy   Method

Applies To: Arc, Arcs, Button, Buttons, Chart, ChartArea, ChartObject, ChartObjects, Charts, CheckBox, CheckBoxes, DialogSheet, DialogSheets, Drawing, DrawingObjects, Drawings, DropDown, DropDowns, EditBox, EditBoxes, GroupBox, GroupBoxes, GroupObject, GroupObjects, Label, Labels, Line, Lines, ListBox, ListBoxes, Module,

Modules, OLEObject, OLEObjects, OptionButton, OptionButtons, Oval, Ovals, Picture, Pictures, Point, Range, Rectangle, Rectangles, ScrollBar, ScrollBars, Series, Sheets, Spinner, Spinners, TextBox, TextBoxes, ToolbarButton, Worksheet, Worksheets

Explanation: Syntax 1 copies the control or drawing Object to the Clipboard. Copies a picture of the point or series to the Clipboard.

Syntax 2 copies the Range to the specified range, or to the Clipboard.

Syntax 3 copies the sheet to another location in the workbook.

Syntax 4 copies a toolbar button to another position, either on the same toolbar or to another toolbar.

Syntax 1: *Object*.Copy

Syntax 2: *Object*.Copy(*destination*)

Syntax 3: *Object*.Copy(*before, after*)

Syntax 4: *Object*.Copy*toolbar*, (*before*)

The Copy Method has the following Object qualifier and named arguments:

The *Object* is required and is the Object to which this Method applies. Copying a Chart Object uses Syntax 3, and copies the entire chart sheet. To copy only the chart area, use Syntax 1 with the ChartArea Object.

The *destination* argument is optional. It specifies the new range where the specified range will be copied. If this argument is omitted, Excel copies the range to the Clipboard.

The *before* argument in syntax 3 is optional. It represents the sheet before which this sheet will be copied. You cannot specify *before* if you specify *after*.

In syntax 4, the *before* argument is required. Specifies the new button position as a number from one to the number of exisiting buttons + one. Gaps count as one position. Buttons to the right of this position are moved right (or down) to make room for the copied button.

The *after* argument is optional. It represents the sheet after which this sheet will be copied. You cannot specify *after* if you specify *before*.

The *toolbar* argument is required for Syntax 4. Specifies the toolbar Object to copy the button to.

Notes: If you do not specify either before or after, Excel creates a new workbook containing the copied sheet.

To copy a button and insert a gap before the copied button, first insert a gap on the destination toolbar by using the ToolbarButtons Add Method, then copy the button to the position after the new gap.

Related Topics: Move Method, Paste Method

CopyFace   Method

Applies To: ToolbarButton

Explanation: Copies the specified button face to the Clipboard. This Method copies only the bitmap button face, not the button itself.

Syntax: *Object*.CopyFace

The *Object* is required and is the ToolbarButton Object.

Related Topics: Builtin Property, BuiltInFace Property, PasteFace Method

CopyObjectsWithCells   Property

Applies To: Application

Explanation: True if drawing objects are cut, copied, extracted, and sorted with cells. Read-write.

Syntax: *Object*.CopyObjectsWithCells

The *Object* is required and is the Application Object.

CopyPicture   Method

Applies To: Arc, Arcs, Button, Buttons, Chart, ChartObject, ChartObjects, CheckBox, CheckBoxes, DialogFrame, Drawing, DrawingObjects, Drawings, DropDown, DropDowns, EditBox, EditBoxes, GroupBox, GroupBoxes, GroupObject, GroupObjects, Label, Labels, Line, Lines, ListBox, ListBoxes, OLEObject, OLEObjects, OptionButton, OptionButtons, Oval, Ovals, Picture, Pictures, Range, Rectangle, Rectangles, ScrollBar, ScrollBars, Spinner, Spinners, TextBox, TextBoxes

Explanation: Copies the Object to the Clipboard as a Picture. Syntax 2 is used for the Chart Object. Syntax 1 is used for all other objects.

Syntax 1: *Object*.CopyPicture*appearance*, *format*

Syntax 2: *Object*.CopyPicture*appearance*, *format*, *size*

The CopyPicture Method has the following Object qualifier and named arguments:

The *Object* is required and is the Object to copy.

The *appearance* argument is optional and specifies how the picture should be copied. If xlScreen or omitted, the picture is copied as closely as possible to the picture displayed on the screen. If xlPrinter, the picture is copied as it would be printed.

The *format* argument is optional and specifies the format of the picture (one of xlPicture or xlBitmap). If omitted, picture format is used.

The *size* argument is optional and specifies the size of the copied picture when the Object is a chart that is on a chart sheet (not embedded on a worksheet). If xlPrinter or omitted, the picture is copied as closely as possible to the printed size. If xlScreen, the picture is copied as closely as possible to the size as displayed on the screen.

Notes: This Method creates a Picture Object on the Clipboard, regardless of the copied Object.

If you copy a range, it must be made up of adjacent cells.

Related Topics: Copy Method, Paste Method

Corners   Property

Applies To: Chart

Explanation: Returns the Corners of a 3D chart. The corners cannot be formatted; this Property can be used only to select the corners of the chart. Read-only.

Syntax: *Object*.Corners

The *Object* is required and is the Chart Object.

Cos   Function

Explanation: Returns the cosine of an angle.

Syntax: Cos(*number*)

The *number* named argument can be any valid numeric expression that expresses an angle in radians.

Notes: The Cos function takes an angle and returns the ratio of two sides of a right triangle. The ratio is the length of the side adjacent to the angle divided by the length of the hypotenuse.

The result lies in the range –1 to 1.

To convert degrees to radians, multiply degrees by pi/180. To convert radians to degrees, multiply radians by 180/pi.

Related Topics: Atn Function, Sin Function, Tan Function

Count   Property

Applies To: All collections

Explanation: Returns the number of items in the collection. Read-only.

For help about using the Count worksheet function in Visual Basic, see Using Worksheet Functions in Visual Basic.

Syntax: `Object.Count`

The *Object* is required and is the Object to which this Property applies.

CreateBackup   Property

Applies To: Workbook

Explanation: True if a backup will be created when this file is saved. Read-only.

Syntax: `Object.CreateBackup`

The *Object* is required and is the Workbook Object.

CreateNames   Method

Applies To: Range

Explanation: Creates names in the given range based on text labels in the sheet.

Syntax: `Object.CreateName(top, left, bottom, right)`

The CreateNames Method has the following Object qualifier and named arguments:

The *Object* is required to create names in this range.

The *top* argument is optional and corresponds to the Top Row checkbox in the Create dialog box. Can be True or False.

The *left* argument is optional and corresponds to the Left Column checkbox in the Create dialog box. Can be True or False.

The *bottom* argument is optional and corresponds to the Bottom Row checkbox in the Create dialog box. Can be True or False.

The *right* argument is optional and corresponds to the Right Column checkbox in the Create dialog box. Can be True or False.

Related Topics: Add Method, Delete Method

CreateObject   Function

Explanation: Creates an OLE Automation Object.

Syntax: `CreateObject(class)`

The class named argument uses the syntax *appname.objecttype* and has these parts:

Part	Description
appname	The name of the application providing the Object.
objecttype	The type or class of Object to create.

Notes: If an application that supports OLE Automation exposes an Object library, it is preferable to use the functions defined within the library for Object creation rather than use CreateObject.

Each application that supports OLE Automation provides at least one type of Object. For example, a word processing application may provide an application Object, a document Object, and a toolbar Object.

Use this function to create an OLE Automation Object and assign the Object to an Object variable. To do this, use the Set Statement to assign the Object returned by CreateObject to the Object variable. For example:

```
Set WordBasicObject = CreateObjectWord.Basic
```

When this code is executed, the application creating the Object is started, if it is not already running (Word in this example), and an Object of the specified type is created. Once an Object is created, you reference it in code using the Object variable you defined. In the above example, you access properties and methods of the new Object using the Object variable, WordBasicObject. For example:

```
WordBasicObject.Insert "Hello, world."
```

```
WordBasicObject.FilePrint
```

```
WordBasicObject.FileSaveAs "C:\DOCS\TEST.DOC"
```

Related Topics: GetObject Function, Set Statement

CreatePublisher   Method

Applies To: Chart, Range

Explanation: Creates a publisher based on a Chart or a Range. Available only on the Macintosh with System 7 or later.

Syntax: *Object*.**CreatePublisher**(*edition*, *appearance*, *size*, *containsPICT*, *containsBIFF*, *containsRTF*, *containsVALU*)

The CreatePublisher Method has the following Object qualifier and named arguments:

The *Object* is required and is the Chart or Range Object.

The *edition* argument is optional and is the file name of the edition to be created. If omitted, a default of *Document Name Edition #n* is used.

The *appearance* argument is optional and is one of xlPrinter or xlScreen.

The *size* argument is optional (used only with Chart objects). One of xlPrinter or xlScreen.

The *containsPICT* argument is optional. True if the publisher should include PICT format. Assumed True if not specified.

The *containsBIFF* argument is optional. True if the publisher should include BIFF format. Assumed True if not specified for a Range, False for a Chart.

The *containsRTF* argument is optional. True if the publisher should include RTF format. Assumed True if not specified for a Range, False for a Chart.

The *containsVALU* argument is optional. True if the publisher should include VALU format. Assumed True if not specified for a Range, False for a Chart.

CreateSummary   Method

Applies To: Scenarios

Explanation: Creates a new worksheet containing a summary report for the scenarios on the specified worksheet.

Syntax: *Object*.CreateSummary(*reportType, resultCells*)

The CreateSummary Method has the following Object qualifier and named arguments:

The *Object* is required and is the Scenarios collection Object.

The *reportType* argument is optional. It specifies the report type (either xlStandardSummary or xlPivotTable). If this argument is omitted, a standard report is created.

The *resultCells* argument is optional and is a range containing the result cells on the specified worksheet. Normally, this range refers to one or more cells that contain the formulas that depend on the changing cell values for your model (the cells that show the results of a particular scenario). If this argument is omitted, no result cells are included in the report.

Creator   Property

Applies To: All objects

Explanation: Returns the application that created this Object, as a 32-bit integer. If the Object was created by Excel, this Property returns the string XCEL, which is the hexadecimal number 5843454C. Read-only.

Syntax: *Object*.Creator

The *Object* is required and is the Object to which this Property applies.

Note: The Creator Property is designed to be used in Excel for the Macintosh, where each application has a four-character creator code. For example, Excel has the creator code XCEL.

Related Topics: Application Property

Crosses   Property

Applies To: Axis

Explanation: Returns or sets the point on the specified axis where the other axis crosses, as shown in the following list. Read-write.

Value	Meaning
xlAutomatic	Excel sets the axis crossing.
xlMinimum	The axis crosses at the minimum value.
xlMaximum	The axis crosses at the maximum value.
xlCustom	The CrossesAt Property specifies the crossing point.

Syntax: `Object.Crosses`

The `Object` is required and is the Axis Object.

Notes: This Property is not available for 3D charts or radar charts.

This Property can be used for both category and value axes. On the category axis, xlMinimum sets the value axis to cross at the first category, and xlMaximum sets the value axis to cross at the last category.

xlMinimum and xlMaximum can have different meanings, depending on the axis.

Related Topic: CrossesAt Property

CrossesAt   Property

Applies To: Axis

Explanation: Returns or sets the point on the value axis where the category (x) axis crosses. Applies only to the value axis. Read-write.

Syntax: `Object.CrossesAt`

The `Object` is required and is the Axis Object.

Notes: Setting this Property causes the Crosses Property to change to xlCustom.

This Property is not available for 3D charts or radar charts.

Related Topic: Crosses Property

CSng   Function

Explanation: Converts an expression to a Single.

Syntax: CSng(*expression*)

The *expression* argument is any valid numeric or string expression.

Notes: In general, you can document your code by using the data type conversion functions to show that the result of some operation should be expressed as a particular data type rather than the default data type. For example, use CDbl or CSng to force double- or single-precision arithmetic in cases where currency or integer arithmetic normally would occur.

You should use the CSng function instead of Val to provide internationally aware conversions from any other data type to a Single. For example, different decimal separators are properly recognized depending on the locale setting of your system, as are different thousand separators.

If an expression lies outside the acceptable range for the Single data type, an error occurs.

CStr   Function

Explanation: Converts an expression to a String.

Syntax: CStr(*expression*)

The *expression* argument is any valid numeric or string expression.

Notes: In general, you can document your code by using the data type conversion functions to show that the result of some operation should be expressed as a particular data type rather than the default data type. For example, use CStr to force the result to be expressed as a String.

You should use the CStr function instead of Str to provide internationally aware conversions from any other data type to a String. For example, different decimal separators are properly recognized depending on the locale setting of your system.

The data in expression determines what is returned according to the following table:

If expression is	CStr returns
Boolean	String containing True or False (translated as appropriate for locale).
Date	String containing a date in the short-date format of your system.
Null	A run-time error.

If expression is	CStr returns
Empty	A zero-length String ("").
Error	A String containing the word Error (translated as appropriate for locale) followed by the error number.
Other Numeric	A String containing the number.

CurDir   Function

Explanation: Returns the current path.

Syntax: CurDir(*drive*)

The drive argument is a string expression that specifies an existing drive. In Windows, if no drive is specified or if drive is zero-length (""), CurDir returns the path for the current drive. On the Macintosh, CurDir ignores any drive specified and simply returns the path for the current drive.

CurrentArray   Property

Applies To: Range

Explanation: If this cell is part of an array, returns a Range that is the entire array. Read-only.

Syntax: *Object*.CurrentArray

The *Object* is required and is a single cell to test.

Related Topics: CurrentRegion Property, HasArray Property

CurrentPage   Property

Applies To: PivotField

Explanation: Returns or sets the current page showing for the page field (only valid for page fields). Read-write.

Syntax: *Object*.CurrentPage

The *Object* is required and is the PivotField Object.

Notes: To set this Property, set it to the name of the page. Set it to "All" to set all pages showing.

CurrentRegion   Property

Applies To: Range

Explanation: Returns a Range that is the current region. The current region is a range bounded by any combination of blank rows and blank columns. Read-only.

Syntax: `Object.CurrentRegion`

The `Object` is required and is the range inside the region.

Notes: This Property is useful for many operations that automatically expand the selection to include the entire current region, such as the AutoFormat Method.

Related Topic: CurrentArray Property

CustomListCount   Property

Applies To: Application

Explanation: Returns the number of defined custom lists (including built-in lists). Read-only.

Syntax: `Object.CustomListCount`

The `Object` is required and is the Application Object.

Related Topic: CurrentArray Property

Cut   Method

Applies To: Arc, Arcs, Button, Buttons, ChartObject, ChartObjects, CheckBox, CheckBoxes, Drawing, DrawingObjects, Drawings, DropDown, DropDowns, EditBox, EditBoxes, GroupBox, GroupBoxes, GroupObject, GroupObjects, Label, Labels, Line, Lines, ListBox, ListBoxes, OLEObject, OLEObjects, OptionButton, OptionButtons, Oval, Ovals, Picture, Pictures, Range, Rectangle, Rectangles, ScrollBar, ScrollBars, Spinner, Spinners, TextBox, TextBoxes

Explanation: Cuts the Object to the Clipboard or to a specified destination.

Syntax: `Object.Cut(destination)`

The Cut Method has the following Object qualifier and named arguments:

The `Object` is required and is the Object to cut.

The `destination` argument is optional (used only with Range objects). It specifies the range where the Object should be pasted. If omitted, the Object is cut to the Clipboard. The destination range must be a single cell or an enlarged multiple of the range to be cut.

Notes: The cut range must be made up of adjacent cells.

Only embedded charts can be cut.

Related Topics: Copy Method, Paste Method

CutCopyMode   Property

Applies To: Application

Explanation: Returns or sets the Cut or Copy mode status, as shown in the following list. Read-write.

Return value	Description
False	Not in Cut or Copy mode.
xlCopy	In Copy mode.
xlCut	In Cut mode.
Set value	Description.
True	Cancels Cut or Copy mode and removes the moving border. In Excel or the Macintosh, this also places the contents of the selection in the Macintosh clipboard.

Syntax: `Object.CutCopyMode`

The `Object` is required and is the Application Object.

CVar   Function

Explanation: Converts an expression to a Variant.

Syntax: `CVar(expression)`

The `expression` argument is any valid numeric or string expression.

Notes: In general, you can document your code by using the data type conversion functions to show that the result of some operation should be expressed as a particular data type rather than the default data type. For example, use CVar to force the result to be expressed as a Variant.

CVErr   Function

Explanation: Returns a Variant of subtype Error containing an error number specified by the user.

Syntax: `CVErr(errornumber)`

The *errornumber* argument is any valid error number.

Notes: Use the CVErr function to create user-defined errors in user-created procedures. For example, if you create a function that accepts several arguments and normally returns a string, you can have your function evaluate the input arguments to ensure they are within acceptable range. If they are not, it is likely that your function will not return what you expect. In this event, CVErr allows you to return an error number that tells you what action to take.

Note that implicit conversion of an Error is not allowed. For example, you can't directly assign the return value of CVErr to a non-Variant variable. However, you can perform an explicit conversion (using CInt, CDbl, and so on) of the value returned by CVErr and assign that to a variable of the appropriate data type.

DataBodyRange   Property

Applies To: PivotTable

Explanation: Returns the Range that contains the pivot table data area. Read-only.

Syntax: `Object.DataBodyRange`

The `Object` is required and is the PivotTable Object.

Related Topics: ColumnRange Property, DataLabelRange Property, PageRange Property, RowRange Property

DataEntryMode   Property

Applies To: Application

Explanation: Returns or sets Data Entry mode, as shown in the following list. When in Data Entry mode, you can enter data only in the unlocked cells of the currently selected range. Read-write.

Value	Meaning
xlOn	Data Entry mode on.
xlOff	Data Entry mode off.
xlStrict	Data Entry mode on, and ESC will not exit the Data Entry mode.

Syntax: `Object.DataEntryMode`

The *Object* is required and is the Application Object.

DataFields   Method

Applies To: PivotTable

Explanation: Returns a single pivot field (a PivotField Object, Syntax 1) or a collection of the pivot fields (a PivotFields Object, Syntax 2), which are currently showing as data fields. Read-only.

Syntax 1: `Object.DataFields(index)`

Syntax 2: `Object.DataFields`

The DataFields Method has the following Object qualifier and named arguments:

The *Object* is required and is the PivotTable Object.

The *index* argument is required for Syntax 1. The name or number of the pivot field to return (can be an array to specify more than one).

Related Topics: ColumnFields Method, HiddenFields Method, PageFields Method, PivotFields Method, RowFields Method, VisibleFields Method

DataLabel   Object

Explanation: A data label on a chart series, or a data label on a single point of a chart series.

DataLabel   Property

Applies To: Point, Trendline

Explanation: Returns the DataLabel associated with the point or trendline. Read-only.

Syntax: `Object.DataLabel`

The *Object* is required and is the Point or Trendline Object.

DataLabelRange   Property

Applies To: PivotTable

Explanation: Returns the Range that contains the pivot table data field labels. Read-only.

Syntax: `Object.DataLabelRange`

The *Object* is required and is the PivotTable Object.

Related Topics: ColumnRange Property, DataBodyRange Property, PageRange Property, RowRange Property

DataLabels   Method

Applies To: Series Description Returns a single data label (a DataLabel Object, Syntax 1) or a collection of all data labels for the series (a DataLabels collection, Syntax 2).

Syntax 1: *Object*.DataLabels*index*

Syntax 2: *Object*.DataLabels

The DataLabels Method has the following Object qualifier and named arguments:

The *Object* is required and is the Series Object.

The *index* argument is required for Syntax 1 and is the number of the data label.

Notes: If the series has the Show Value option on for the data labels, the returned collection can contain up to one label for each point. Data labels can be turned on or off for individual points in the series.

If the series is on an area chart and has the Show Label option on for the data labels, the returned collection contains only a single label, which is the label for the area series.

Related Topic: DataLabel Property

DataLabels   Object

Explanation: A collection of all the DataLabel objects for the points on a series.

DataRange   Property

Applies To: PivotField, PivotItem

Explanation: Returns a Range as shown in the following table. Read-only.

Object	DataRange
Data field	Data contained in the field.
Row, Column, or Page field	Items in the field.
Item	Data qualified by the item.

Syntax: *Object*.DataRange

The *Object* is required and is the PivotField or PivotItem Object.

DataSeries   Method

Applies To: Range

Explanation: Creates a data series in the range.

Syntax: *Object*.**DataSeries**(*rowcol, type, date, step, stop, trend*)

The DataSeries Method has the following Object qualifier and named arguments:

The *Object* is required and is the location where the data series will be created.

The *rowcol* argument is optional. It can be xlRows or xlColumns to enter the data series in rows or columns, respectively. If omitted, the size and shape of the range is used.

The *type* argument is optional. It can be xlLinear, xlGrowth, xlChronological, or xlAutoFill. If omitted, it is xlLinear.

The *date* argument is optional. If the type argument is xlChronological, this indicates the date unit by which to step, either xlDay, xlWeekday, xlMonth, or xlYear. If omitted, it is xlDay.

The *step* argument is optional and is the step value for the series. If omitted, it is assumed to be 1.

The *stop* argument is optional. The stop value for the series. If omitted, the Method fills to the end of the range.

The *trend* argument is optional. If True, the Method creates a linear or growth type of trend. If False or omitted, the Method creates a standard data series.

DataType   Property

Applies To: PivotField

Explanation: Returns a constant describing the type of data in the pivot field. Can be xlText, xlNumber, or xlDate. Read-only.

Syntax: *Object*.**DataType**

The *Object* qualifier is required and is the PivotField Object.

Date   Function

Explanation: Returns the current system date.

Syntax: **Date**

Notes: To set the system date, use the Date Statement.

Related Topics: Cdate Function, Date Property, Format Function, Now Function, Time Function, Time Statement

Date

Statement

Explanation: Sets the current system date.

Syntax: `Date = date`

For MS-DOS computers, the date argument must be a date from January 1, 1980 through December 31, 2099, or an error occurs. For the Macintosh, date must be a date from January 1, 1904 through December 31, 2040. For all other systems, date is limited to dates from January 1, 100 through December 31, 9999.

Notes: If you use the Date Statement to set the date on computers using versions of MS-DOS earlier than version 3.3, the change remains in effect only until you change it again or turn off your computer. Many computers have a battery-powered CMOS RAM that retains date and time information when the computer is turned off. However, to permanently change the date on computers running earlier versions of MS-DOS, you may have to use your Setup disk or perform some equivalent action. Refer to the documentation for your particular system.

Related Topics: Date Function, Time Function, Time Statement

Date1904

Property

Applies To: Workbook

Explanation: True if this workbook uses the 1904 date system. Read-write.

Syntax: `Object.Date1904`

The `Object` qualifier is required and is the Workbook Object.

DateSerial

Function

Explanation: Returns a date for a specified year, month, and day.

Syntax: `DateSerial(year,month,day)`

The DateSerial function syntax has these named-argument parts:

Part	Description
year	Number between 100 and 9999, inclusive, or a numeric expression.
month	Number between 1 and 12, inclusive, or a numeric expression.
day	Number between 1 and 31, inclusive, or a numeric expression.

Notes: To specify a date, such as December 31, 1991, the range of numbers for each DateSerial argument should be in the normally accepted range for the unit; that is; 1–31 for days and 1–12 for months. You can also specify relative dates for each argument by using any numeric expression that represents some number of days, months, or years before or after a certain date.

The following example uses numeric expressions instead of absolute date numbers. Here the DateSerial function returns a date that is the day before the first day (1 – 1) of two months before August (8 – 2) of 10 years before 1990 (1990 – 10); in other words, May, 31, 1980.

```
DateSerial(1990 - 10, 8 - 2, 1 - 1)
```

For the year argument, values between 0 and 99, inclusive, are interpreted as the years 1900–1999. For all other year arguments, use a complete four-digit year (for example, 1800).

If the date specified by the three arguments, either directly or by expression, falls outside the acceptable range of dates, an error occurs.

Related Topics: Date Function, Date Statement, DateValue Function, Day Function, Month Function, Now Function, TimeSerial Function, TimeValue Function, Weekday Function, Year Function

DateValue   Function

Explanation: Returns a date.

Syntax: `DateValue(date)`

The *date* named argument normally is a string expression that represents a date from January 1, 100 through December 31, 9999. A date also can be any expression that can represent a date, a time, or both a date and time, in that range.

Notes: If the date argument includes time information, DateValue doesn't return it. However, if date includes invalid time information (such as "89:98"), an error occurs.

If *date* is a string that includes only numbers separated by valid date separators, DateValue recognizes the order for month, day, and year according to the Short Date format you specified for your system. DateValue also recognizes unambiguous dates that contain month names, either in long or abbreviated form. For example, in addition to recognizing 12/30/1991 and 12/30/91, DateValue also recognizes December 30, 1991 and Dec 30, 1991.

If the year part of date is omitted, DateValue uses the current year from your computer's system date.

Related Topics: Cdate Function, Date Function, Date Statement, DateSerial Function, Day Function, Month Function, Now Function, TimeSerial Function, TimeValue Function, Weekday Function, Year Function

Day   Function

Explanation: Returns a whole number between 1 and 31, inclusive, representing the day of the month.

Syntax: `Day(date)`

The *date* named argument is limited to a date or numbers and strings, in any combination, that can represent a date. If date contains no valid data, Null is returned.

Related Topics: Date Function, Date Statement, Hour Function, Minute Function, Month Function, Now Function, Second Function, Weekday Function, Year Function

DDEAppReturnCode   Property

Applies To: Application

Explanation: Returns the application-specific DDE return code that was contained in the last DDE acknowledge message received by Excel. Read-only.

Syntax: `Object.DDEAppReturnCode`

The *Object* qualifier is optional and is the Application Object.

DDEExecute   Method

Applies To: Application

Explanation: Runs a command or takes other actions in another application via the specified DDE channel.

Syntax: `Object.DDEExecute(channel, string)`

The DDEExecute Method has the following Object qualifier and named arguments:

The *Object* qualifier is optional and is the Application Object.

The *channel* argument is required and is the channel number returned by the DDEInitiate Method.

The *string* argument is required and is the message defined in the receiving application.

Notes: An error occurs if the Method call is not successful.

The DDEExecute Method is designed to send commands to another application. You can also use it to send keystrokes to an application, although the SendKeys Method is the preferred way to send keystrokes. The string argument can specify any single key, or any key combined with ALT, CTRL, or SHIFT, or any combination of those keys (in Excel for Windows) or COMMAND, CTRL, OPTION, or SHIFT or any combination of those keys (in Excel for the Macintosh). Each key is represented by one or more characters, such as "a" for the character a, or "{ENTER}" for the ENTER key.

To specify characters that aren't displayed when you press the key, such as Enter or Tab, use the codes shown in the following table. Each code in the table represents one key on the keyboard.

Key	Code
Backspace	"{BACKSPACE}" or "{BS}" BREAK "{BREAK}"
Caps Lock	"{CAPSLOCK}"
Clear	"{CLEAR}"
Delete or Del	"{DELETE}" or "{DEL}"
Down Arrow	"{DOWN}"
End	"{END}"
Enter (numeric keypad)	"{ENTER}"
Enter	"~" (tilde)
Esc	"{ESCAPE}" or "{ESC}"
Help	"{HELP}"
Home	"{HOME}"
Ins	"{INSERT}"
Left Arrow	"{LEFT}"
Num Lock	"{NUMLOCK}"
Page Down	"{PGDN}"
Page Up	"{PGUP}"
Return	"{RETURN}"
Right Arrow	"{RIGHT}"
Scroll Lock	"{SCROLLLOCK}"
Tab	"{TAB}"
Up Arrow	"{UP}"
F1 through F15	"{F1}" through "{F15}"

In Excel for Windows, you can also specify keys combined with Shift and/or Ctrl and/or Alt. In Excel for the Macintosh, you can also specify keys combined with SHIFT and/or Ctrl and/or Option and/or Command. To specify a key combined with another key or keys, use the following table.

To combine with	Precede the key code by
Shift	"+" (plus sign)
Ctrl	"^" (caret)
Alt or Option	"%" (percent sign)
Command	"*" (asterisk)

DDEInitiate   Method

Applies To: Application

Explanation: Opens a DDE channel to an application.

Syntax: *Object*.**DDEInitiate**(*app, topic*)

The DDEInitiate Method has the following Object qualifier and named arguments:

The *Object* qualifier is optional and is the Application Object.

The *app* argument is required and is a string containing the application name.

The *topic* argument is required and is a string that describes something in the application to which you are opening a channel, usually a document of that application.

Notes: If successful, the DDEInitiate Method returns the number of the open channel. All subsequent DDE functions use this number to specify the channel.

DDEPoke   Method

Applies To: Application

Explanation: Sends data to an application.

Syntax: *Object*.**DDEPoke**(*channel, item, data*)

The DDEPoke Method has the following Object qualifier and named arguments.

The *Object* qualifier is optional and is the Application Object.

The *channel* argument is required and is the channel number returned by the DDEInitiate Method.

The *item* argument is required and is the item to which the data is to be sent.

The *data* argument is required and is the data to send to the application.

Notes: An error occurs if the Method call is not successful.

DDERequest   Method

Applies To: Application

Explanation: Requests information from the specified application. This Method always returns an array.

Syntax: *Object*.**DDERequest**(*channel, item*)

The DDERequest Method has the following Object qualifier and named arguments.

The *Object* qualifier is optional and is the Application Object.

The *channel* argument is required and is the channel number returned by the DDEInitiate Method.

The *item* argument is required and is the item to request.

DDETerminate   Method

Applies To: Application

Explanation: Closes a channel to another application.

Syntax: *Object*.**DDETerminate**(*channel*)

The DDETerminate Method has the following Object qualifier and named arguments.

The *Object* qualifier is optional and is the Application Object.

The *channel* argument is required and is the channel number returned by the DDEInitiate Method.

Debug   Object

Explanation: The Debug Object is accessed with the keyword Debug, and is used to send output to the Debug window at run time.

Declare   Statement

Explanation: Used at module level to declare references to external procedures in a dynamic link library (DLL) or Macintosh code resource.

Syntax 1:

```
Public or Private Declare Sub name CDecl Lib "libname" [Alias
"aliasname" ][([arglist])]
```

Syntax 2:

```
[Public ¦ Private ] Declare Function name [CDecl] Lib "libname" [Alias
"aliasname" ] [([arglist])][As type]
```

The Declare Statement syntax has these parts:

Part	Description
Public	Used to declare procedures that are available to all other procedures in all modules.
Private	Used to declare procedures that are available only within the module where the declaration is made.
Sub	Indicates that the procedure doesn't return a value.
Function	Indicates that the procedure returns a value that can be used in an expression.
name	Any valid procedure name.
CDecl	For the Macintosh only. Indicates that the procedure uses C language argument order, naming conventions, and calling conventions.
Lib	Indicates that a DLL or code resource contains the procedure being declared. The Lib clause is required for all declarations.
libname	Name of the DLL or code resource that contains the declared procedure.
Alias	Indicates that the procedure being called has another name in the DLL or is in a Macintosh code resource. This is useful when the external procedure name is the same as a keyword. You can also use Alias when a DLL procedure has the same name as a Public variable or constant or any other procedure in the same scope. Alias is also useful if any characters in the DLL procedure name aren't allowed in names.
aliasname	Name of the procedure in the DLL or code resource. In Windows, if the first character is not a #, aliasname is the name of the procedure's entry point in the DLL. If # is the first character, all characters that follow must indicate the ordinal number of the procedure's entry point. On the Macintosh, the syntax to specify the code resource type

Part	Description
	is as follows: "[*resourcetype*]$[*resourcename*]" The resourcetype is any valid 4-character constant. If omitted, the default resourcetype is CODE. The resourcename is the procedure name in the code resource. If resourcename is omitted, it is assumed to be the same as name.
arglist	List of variables representing arguments that are passed to the procedure when it is called.
type	Data type of the value returned by a Function procedure; may be Boolean, Integer, Long, Currency, Single, Double, Date, String (variable length only), Object, Variant, a user-defined type, or an Object type.

The arglist argument has the following syntax and parts:

*Optional*By Val `|` or Ref*ParamArray* **varname**( )As **type**

Part	Description
Optional	Indicates that an argument is not required. If used, all subsequent arguments in arglist must also be optional and declared using the Optional keyword. All Optional arguments must be Variant. Optional can't be used for any argument if ParamArray is used.
ByVal	Indicates that the argument is passed by value.
ByRef	Indicates that the argument is passed by reference.
ParamArray	Used only as the last argument in arglist to indicate that the final argument is an Optional array of Variant elements. The ParamArray keyword allows you to provide an arbitrary number of arguments. May not be used with ByVal, ByRef, or Optional.
varname	Name of the variable representing the argument being passed to the procedure; follows standard variable naming conventions.
type	Data type of the argument passed to the procedure; may be Boolean, Integer, Long, Currency, Single, Double, Date, String (variable length only), Object, Variant, a user-defined type, or an Object type.

Notes: For Function procedures, the data type of the procedure determines the data type it returns. You can use an As clause following the arglist to specify the return type of the function. Within arglist you can use an As clause to specify the data type of any of the arguments passed to the procedure. In addition to specifying any of the standard data types, you can specify As Any in the arglist to inhibit type checking and allow any data type to be passed to the procedure.

Empty parentheses indicate that the Sub or Function procedure has no arguments and that arguments should be checked to ensure that none are passed. In the following example, First takes no arguments. If you use arguments in a call to First, an error occurs:

```
Declare Sub First Lib "MyLib" ()
```

If you include an argument list, the number and type of arguments are checked each time the procedure is called. In the following example, First takes one Long argument:

```
Declare Sub First Lib "MyLib" (X As Long)
```

Notes: You can't have fixed-length strings in the argument list of a Declare Statement because only variable-length strings can be passed to procedures. Fixed-length strings can appear as procedure arguments, but they are converted to variable-length strings before being passed.

Related Topic: Call Statement

DefaultButton   Property

Applies To: Button, Buttons, DialogSheet, DrawingObjects

Explanation: Applies only to buttons in a user-defined dialog.

For Button objects, this Property is True if the button is the default button for a user-defined dialog. The default button is indicated by a thick border. When the user presses the Enter key, the default button is selected, and Excel runs the macro identified by the button's OnAction Property. Read-write.

For DialogSheet objects, this Property is the name of the button that is the default while a dialog is running. Read-write.

Syntax: `Object.DefaultButton`

The `Object` qualifier is required and is the Object to which this Property applies.

Notes: When the dialog is not displayed, this Property can be used with the Button Object to return or set the initial default button (the default button when the dialog is first displayed). Only one button on the dialog can be the default button. Setting this Property resets the Property for all other buttons on the dialog sheet.

When the dialog is displayed, use this Property in an event procedure to return or set the current default button. In this case, the Property is the button ID as a string, and the Property is applied to the DialogSheet Object. You cannot apply this Property to a Button Object when the dialog is displayed.

Related Topic: CancelButton Property

DefaultFilePath   **Property**

Applies To: Application

Explanation: Returns or sets the default path Excel uses when it opens files. Read-write.

Syntax: *Object*`.DefaultFilePath`

The *Object* qualifier is required and is the Application Object.

Deftype   **Statements**

Explanation: Used at module level to set the default data type for variables and Function procedures whose names start with the specified characters.

Syntax:

        `DefBool` *letterrange1,letterrange2* . . .

        `DefInt` *letterrange1,letterrange2.* . .

        `DefLng` *letterrange1,letterrange2* . . .

        `DefCur` *letterrange1,letterrange2* . . .

        `DefSng` *letterrange1,letterrange2* . . .

        `DefDbl` *letterrange1,letterrange2* . . .

        `DefDate` *letterrange1,letterrange2* .` . .

        `DefStr` *letterrange1,letterrange2* . . .

        `DefObj` *letterrange1,letterrange2* . . .

        `DefVar` *letterrange1,letterrange2* . . .

The argument letterrange has the following syntax:

The arguments *letterrange1* and *letterrange2* specify the name range for which you can set a default data type. Each argument represents the first letter of the variable or Function procedure name and can be any letter of the alphabet. The case of letters in letterrange isn't significant.

Notes: The Statement name determines the data type:

Statement	Data type
`DefBool`	Boolean
`DefInt`	Integer
`DefLng`	Long

continues

Statement	Data type
DefCur	Currency
DefSng	Single
DefDbl	Double
DefDate	Date
DefStr	String
DefObj	Object
DefVar	Variant

A Deftype Statement affects only the module where it is used. For example, a DefInt Statement in one module affects only the default data type of variables and Function procedures declared in that module; the default data type of variables in other modules is unaffected. If not explicitly declared with a Deftype Statement, the default data type for all variables and all Function procedures is Variant.

When you specify a letter range, it usually defines the data type for variables that begin with letters in the lower 128 characters of the character set. However, when you specify the letter range A–Z, you set the default to the specified data type for all variables, including any that begin with international characters from the extended part of the character set (128 –255).

Once the range A–Z has been specified, you can't further redefine any subranges of variables using Deftype statements. In fact, once a range has been specified, if you include a previously defined letter in another Deftype Statement, an error occurs. However, you can explicitly specify the data type of any variable, defined or not, using a Dim Statement with an As type clause. For example, you can use the following code at module level to define a variable as a Double even though the default data type is Integer:

```
DefInt A-Z
```

```
Dim TaxRate As Double
```

Deftype statements don't affect elements of user-defined types since they must be explicitly declared.

Related Topic: Let Statement

Delete   Method

Applies To: Arc, Arcs, Axis, AxisTitle, Button, Buttons, Characters, Chart, ChartObject, ChartObjects, Charts, ChartTitle, CheckBox, CheckBoxes, DataLabel, DataLabels, DialogSheet, DialogSheets, DownBars, Drawing, DrawingObjects, Drawings, DropDown, DropDowns, DropLines, EditBox, EditBoxes, ErrorBars, Gridlines, GroupBox, GroupBoxes,

GroupObject, GroupObjects, HiLoLines, Label, Labels, Legend, LegendEntry, LegendKey, Line, Lines, ListBox, ListBoxes, Menu, MenuBar, MenuItem, Module, Modules, Name, OLEObject, OLEObjects, OptionButton, OptionButtons, Oval, Ovals, Picture, Pictures, Point, Range, Rectangle, Rectangles, Scenario, ScrollBar, ScrollBars, Series, SeriesLines, Sheets, SoundNote, Spinner, Spinners, Style, TextBox, TextBoxes, TickLabels, Toolbar, ToolbarButton, Trendline, UpBars, Worksheet, Worksheets

Explanation: Deletes the Object. Syntax 2 applies only to Range objects.

Syntax 1: `Object.Delete`

Syntax 2: `Object.Delete(shift)`

The `Object` qualifer is required. The Object to which this Method applies. Syntax 2 applies only to Range objects.

The `shift` argument is optional. It specifies how to shift cells to replace the deleted cells (either xlToLeft, or xlUp). If this argument is omitted, Excel selects a default based on the shape of the range.

Notes: Attempts to delete a built-in Toolbar or MenuBar Object will fail, but will not cause an error. This allows you to use a For Each loop to delete all custom tool bars or menu bars.

Deleting a Point or LegendKey deletes the entire series.

DeleteChartAutoFormat   Method

Applies To: Application

Explanation: Removes a custom chart autoformat from the list of available chart autoformats.

Syntax: `Object.DeleteChartAutoFormat(name)`

The DeleteChartAutoFormat Method has the following Object qualifier and named arguments:

The `Object` qualifier is required and is the Application Object.

The `name` argument is required and specifies the name of the custom autoformat to remove.

Related Topics: AddChartAutoFormat Method, SetDefaultChart Method

DeleteCustomList   Method

Applies To: Application

Explanation: Deletes a custom list.

Syntax: `Object.DeleteCustomList(listNum)`

The DeleteCustomList Method has the following Object qualifier and named arguments:

The *Object* qualifier is required and is the Application Object.

The *listNum* argument is required and is the custom list number. This number must be greater than or equal to five (Excel has four built-in custom lists that cannot be deleted).

Notes: This Method generates an error if the list number is less than five or a matching custom list does not exist.

Related Topics: AddCustomList Method, CustomListCount Property, GetCustomListNum Method, GetCustomListContents Method

DeleteNumberFormat   Method

Applies To: Workbook

Explanation: Deletes a custom number format from the workbook.

Syntax: *Object*.DeleteNumberFormat(*numberFormat*)

The DeleteNumberFormat Method has the following Object qualifier and named arguments:

The *Object* qualifier is required and is the Workbook Object.

The *numberFormat* argument is required and is a string that names the number format to delete.

Delivery   Property

Applies To: RoutingSlip

Explanation: Returns or sets the delivery Method used when routing (one of xlOneAfterAnother or xlAllAtOnce). Read-write before routing starts, read-only once routing is in progress.

Syntax: *Object*.Delivery

The *Object* qualifier is required and is the RoutingSlip Object.

Dependents   Property

Applies To: Range

Explanation: Returns a Range that contains all of the dependents of a cell. This may be a multiple selection (a union of Range objects) if there is more than one dependent. Read-only.

Syntax: *Object*.Dependents

The *Object* qualifier is required and returns dependents for this cell.

Related Topics: DirectDependents Property, DirectPrecedents Property, Precedents Property, ShowDependents Method

DepthPercent   Property

Applies To: Chart

Explanation: Returns or sets the depth of a 3D chart as a percentage of the chart width (between 20 and 2000 percent). Read-write.

Syntax: `Object.DepthPercent`

The `Object` qualifier is required and is the Chart Object.

Related Topic: HeightPercent Property

Deselect   Method

Applies To: Chart

Explanation: Cancels the selection for the specified chart.

Syntax: `Object.Deselect`

The `Object` qualifier is required and is the Chart Object.

Related Topics: Select Method, Selection Property

DialogBox   Method

Applies To: Range

Explanation: Displays a dialog box defined by a dialog-box definition table on a Excel version 4.0 macro sheet. Returns the number of the chosen control, or False if the user chooses the Cancel button.

Syntax: `Object.DialogBox`

The `Object` qualifier is required and is a dialog-box definition table.

Note: This Method is included for backward compatibility with the Excel version 4.0 macro language.

DialogFrame   Object

Explanation: The dialog frame provides the backdrop for user-defined dialogs. It has no formatting properties, only a position, a size, and a caption. Only one dialog frame exists per dialog sheet, and it cannot be deleted or moved in front of any other graphic Object. Dialog frames do not exist on the worksheet.

DialogFrame   Property

Applies To: DialogSheet

Explanation: Returns the DialogFrame associated with this dialog sheet. Read only.

Syntax: `Object.DialogFrame`

The `Object` qualifier is required and is the DialogSheet Object.

Dialogs   Method

Applies To: Application

Explanation: Returns a single built-in dialog (a Dialog Object, Syntax 1) or a collection of all built-in dialogs (a Dialogs Object, Syntax 2). Read-only.

Syntax 1: `Object.Dialogs(index)`

Syntax 2: `Object.Dialogs`

The Dialogs Method has the following Object qualifier and named arguments:

The `Object` qualifier is required and is the Application Object.

The `index` argument is required for Syntax 1 and is a built-in constant. See the following Notes section for more information.

Notes: Using the Dialogs and Show methods, you can display approximately 200 built-in dialog boxes. Each dialog box has a constant assigned to it; these constants all begin with xlDialog. You can use the Object Browser to browse the list of dialog box constants. From the View menu, choose Object Browser, select the Excel library, and then select the Constants Object. Scroll the list in the Methods/Properties box until you find the constants that begin with xlDialog. The constants correspond to dialog box names; for example, the constant for the Find File dialog box is xlDialogFindFile.

The Dialogs Method may fail if you try to show a dialog box in an incorrect context. For example, to display the Format Data Labels dialog box (using the Visual Basic expression Application.Dialogs(xlDialogDataLabel).Show), the active sheet must be a chart, otherwise the Method fails.

Related Topic: Show Method

Dialogs   Object

Explanation: A collection of Dialog objects.

DialogSheet   Object

Explanation: A dialog sheet in a workbook.

DialogSheets   Method

Applies To: Application, Workbook

Explanation: Returns a single dialog sheet (a DialogSheet Object, Syntax 1) or a collection of all dialog sheets (a DialogSheets Object, Syntax 2) in the workbook. Read-only.

Syntax 1: *Object*.DialogSheets(*index*)

Syntax 2: *Object*.DialogSheets

The DialogSheets Method has the following Object qualifier and named arguments:

The *Object* qualifier is optional for Application, required for Workbook. The Object that contains dialog sheets.

The *index* argument is required for Syntax 1. The name or number of the dialog sheet to return.

Notes: Using this Method with no Object qualifier is a shortcut for ActiveWorkbook.DialogSheets.

Dim   Statement

Explanation: Declares variables and allocates storage space.

Syntax: Dim *varname*(*subscripts*)As *type*,*varname*(*subscripts*)As *type* . . .

The Dim Statement syntax has these parts:

Part	Description
varname	Name of the variable; follows standard variable naming conventions.
subscripts	Dimensions of an array variable; up to 60 multiple dimensions may be declared. The subscripts argument uses the following syntax:
	[lower To] upper [,[lower To] upper] . . .
type	Data type of the variable; may be Boolean, Integer, Long, Currency, Single, Double, Date, String (for variable-length strings), String * length (for fixed-length strings), Object, Variant, a user-defined type, or an Object type. Use a separate As type clause for each variable you declare.

Notes: Variables declared with Dim at the module level are available to all procedures within the module. At the procedure level, variables are available only within the procedure.

Use the Dim Statement at module or procedure level to declare the data type or Object type of a variable. For example, the following Statement declares a variable as an Integer:

```
Dim NumberOfEmployees As Integer
```

If you do not specify a data type or Object type, and there is no Deftype Statement in the module, the variable is Variant by default.

When variables are initialized, a numeric variable is initialized to 0, a variable-length string is initialized to a zero-length string, and a fixed-length string is filled with zeros. Variant variables are initialized to Empty. Each element of a user-defined type variable is initialized as if it was a separate variable. A variable that refers to an Object must be assigned an existing Object using the Set Statement before it can be used. Until it is assigned an Object, the declared Object variable has the special value Nothing, which indicates that it does not refer to any particular instance of an Object.

You can also use the Dim Statement with empty parentheses to declare dynamic arrays. After declaring a dynamic array, use the ReDim Statement within a procedure to define the number of dimensions and elements in the array. If you try to redeclare a dimension for an array variable whose size was explicitly specified in a Private, Public, or Dim Statement, an error occurs.

When you use the Dim Statement in a procedure, it is a generally accepted programming practice to put the Dim Statement at the beginning of the procedure.

Related Topics: Array Function, Option Base Statement, Private Statement, Public Statement, ReDim Statement, Set Statement, Static Statement, Type Statement

Dir   Function

Explanation: Returns the name of a file, directory, or folder that matches a specified pattern or file attribute, or the volume label of a drive.

Syntax: Dir(*pathname*,*attributes*)

The Dir function syntax has these parts:

Part	Description
pathname	String expression that specifies a file name and may include directory or folder, and drive. Null is returned if pathname is not found.
attributes	Constant or numeric expression, the sum of which specifies file attributes. If omitted, all normal files are returned that match pathname.

The attributes argument has these constants and values:

Constant	Value	File Attribute
vbNormal	0	Normal.
vbHidden	2	Hidden.
vbSystem	4	System not available on the Macintosh.
vbVolume	8	Volume label; if specified, all attributes are ignored; not available on the Macintosh.
vbDirectory	16	Directory or folder.

These constants are specified by Visual Basic. As a result, the names can be used anywhere in your code in place of the actual values.

Notes: Dir supports the use of '*' (multiple character) and '?' (single character) wild cards to specify multiple files. However, on the Macintosh, these characters are treated as valid file name characters and can't be used as wild cards to specify multiple files.

Since the Macintosh does not support wild cards, use the file type to identify groups of files. You can use the MacID function to specify file type instead of using the file names. For example, the following Statement returns the name of the first "TEXT" file in the current folder.

If you use the MacID function with Dir in Windows, an error occurs.

Any attribute value greater than 256 is considered a MacID value. You must specify pathname the first time you call the Dir function, or an error occurs. If you also specify file attributes, pathname must be included.

Dir returns the first file name that matches pathname. To get any additional file names that match pathname, call Dir again with no arguments. When no more file names match, Dir returns a zero-length string. Once a zero-length string is returned, you must specify pathname in subsequent calls or an error occurs. You can change to a new pathname without retrieving all of the file names that match the current pathname. However, you can't recursively call the Dir function.

Because file names are retrieved in no particular order, you may want to store returned file names in an array and then sort the array.

Related Topics: ChDir Statement, CurDir Function, MaCID Function

DirectDependents   Property

Applies To: Range

Explanation: Returns a Range that contains all of the direct dependents of a cell. This may be a multiple selection (a union of Range objects) if there is more than one dependent. Read-only.

Syntax: `Object.DirectDependents`

The `Object` qualifier is required and returns direct dependents for this cell.

Related Topics: Dependents Property, DirectDependents Property, Precedents Property, ShowDependents Method

DirectPrecedents   Property

Applies To: Range

Explanation: Returns a Range that contains all of the direct precedents of a cell. This may be a multiple selection (a union of Range objects) if there is more than one precedent. Read-only.

Syntax: `Object.DirectPrecedents`

The `Object` qualifier is required and returns direct precedents for this cell.

Related Topics: Dependents Property, DirectDependents Property, Precedents Property, ShowPrecedents Method

DismissButton   Property

Applies To: Button, Buttons, DrawingObjects

Explanation: True if the button will automatically close a user-defined dialog when the button is clicked. Any number of buttons on the dialog can have the DismissButton Property set to True. Read-write.

Syntax: `Object.DismissButton`

The `Object` qualifier is required and is the Object to which this Property applies.

When you click a button that has the DismissButton Property set to True, three steps are taken:

✔   The button's OnAction procedure runs. If you want to do any custom data validation, then do it in this procedure. If validation fails, you can set the DismissButton Property to False, in which case the dialog remains visible. Remember to reset the DismissButton Property to True when validation passes.

✔   When the OnAction procedure ends and the DismissButton Property is True, edit fields on the dialog are automatically validated to ensure that they contain data of the type specified by their InputType properties. If automatic validation fails, Excel displays an alert, the offending edit box gets the focus, and the dialog remains visible.

✔ If automatic validation passes, the dialog box closes and the Show Method that called the dialog returns True. If no button in the dialog has the DismissButton Property set to True, then you must explicitly call the Hide Method or cancel the dialog to close it.

Related Topics: Cancel Property, Hide Method, InputType Property, OnAction Property, Show Method

Display3DShading   Property

Applies To: CheckBox, CheckBoxes, DrawingObjects, DropDown, DropDowns, GroupBox, GroupBoxes, ListBox, ListBoxes, OptionButton, OptionButtons, ScrollBar, ScrollBars, Spinner, Spinners

Explanation: True if the control uses 3D visual effects. This Property applies only to controls on worksheets and charts. Read-write.

Syntax: `Object.Display3DShading`

The `Object` qualifier is required and is the Object to which this Property applies.

DisplayAlerts   Property

Applies To: Application

Explanation: True if Excel displays certain alerts and messages while a macro is running. Read-write.

Syntax: `Object.DisplayAlerts`

The `Object` qualifier is required and is the Application Object.

Notes: Defaults to True. Set this to False if you do not want to be disturbed by prompts and alert messages while a macro is running, and want Excel to choose the default response.

If you set this Property to False, Excel sets it back to True when your macro stops running.

DisplayAutomaticPageBreaks   Property

Applies To: DialogSheet, Worksheet

Explanation: True if automatic page breaks should be displayed for this sheet. Read-write.

Syntax: `Object.DisplayAutomaticPageBreaks`

The `Object` qualifier is required and is the Object to which this Property applies.

DisplayBlanksAs   Property

Applies To: Chart

Explanation: Returns or sets how blank cells are plotted on a chart (one of xlNotPlotted, xlInterpolated, or xlZero). Read-write.

Syntax: `Object.DisplayBlanksAs`

The `Object` qualifier is required and is the Chart Object.

DisplayClipboardWindow   Property

Applies To: Application

Explanation: Macintosh only. True if the Cipboard window is displayed. Set this Property to True to display the Clipboard window. Read-write.

Syntax: `Object.DisplayClipboardWindow`

The `Object` qualifier is required and is the Application Object.

Notes: In Windows, this Property retains its value, but does nothing.

DisplayDrawingObjects   Property

Applies To: Workbook

Explanation: Returns or sets how drawing objects are displayed, as shown in the following table. Read-write.

Value	Meaning
xlAll	Show all drawing objects.
xlPlaceholders	Show only placeholders.
xlHide	Hide all drawing objects.

Syntax: `Object.DisplayDrawingObjects`

The `Object` qualifier is required and is the Workbook Object.

DisplayEquation   Property

Applies To: Trendline

Explanation: True if the equation for the trendline is displayed on the chart (in the same data label as the R-squared value). Setting this Property to True automatically turns on data labels. Read-write.

Syntax: `Object.DisplayEquation`

The **Object** is required and is the Trendline Object.

Related Topics: Add Method, DisplayRSquared Property

DisplayExcel4Menus   Property

Applies To: Application

Explanation: True if Excel displays Excel 4 menu bars; False if Excel displays the Excel 5 menu bars. Read-write.

Syntax: `Object.DisplayExcel4Menus`

The **Object** qualifier is required and is the Application Object.

DisplayFormulaBar   Property

Applies To: Application

Explanation: True if the formula bar is displayed. Read-write.

Syntax: `Object.DisplayFormulaBar`

The **Object** is required and is the Application Object.

DisplayFormulas   Property

Applies To: Window

Explanation: True if the window is displaying formulas, or False if the window is displaying values. Read-write.

Syntax: `Object.DisplayFormulas`

The **Object** qualifier is required and is the Window Object.

Notes: This Property applies only to worksheets and macro sheets.

DisplayFullScreen   Property

Applies To: Application

Explanation: True if Excel is in full-screen mode. Read-write.

Syntax: `Object.DisplayFullScreen`

The **Object** qualifier is required and is the Application Object.

Notes: Full-screen mode maximizes the application window to cover the entire screen and hides the application title bar (in Windows). Toolbars, the status bar, and the formula bar maintain separate display settings for full-screen and normal modes.

DisplayGridlines   Property

Applies To: Window

Explanation: True if gridlines are displayed. Read-write.

Syntax: `Object.DisplayGridlines`

The `Object` qualifier is required. The Window Object.

Notes: This Property applies only to worksheets and macro sheets.

This Property affects only displayed gridlines. Use the PrintGridlines Property to control gridline printing.

DisplayHeadings   Property

Applies To: Window

Explanation: True if both row and column headings are displayed, False if no headings are displayed. Read-write.

Syntax: `Object.DisplayHeadings`

The `Object` qualifier is required and is the Window Object.

Notes: This Property applies only to worksheets and macro sheets.

This Property affects only displayed headings. Use the PrintHeadings Property to control heading printing.

DisplayHorizontalScrollBar   Property

Applies To: Window

Explanation: True if the horizontal scrollbar is displayed. Read-write.

Syntax: `Object.DisplayHorizontalScrollBar`

The `Object` qualifier is required and is the Window Object.

Related Topics: DisplayVerticalScrollBar Property, DisplayScrollBars Property, TabRatio Property

DisplayInfoWindow   Property

Applies To: Application

Explanation: True if the Info window is displayed. Set this Property to True to display the Info window. Read-write.

Syntax: *Object*.`DisplayInfoWindow`

The *Object* qualifier is required and is the Application Object.

DisplayNoteIndicator   Property

Applies To: Application

Explanation: True if cells containing notes contain note indicators (small dots in their upper right corners). Read-write.

Syntax: *Object*.`DisplayNoteIndicator`

The *Object* qualifier is required and is the Application Object.

DisplayOutline   Property

Applies To: Window

Explanation: True if outline symbols are displayed. Read-write.

Syntax: *Object*.`DisplayOutline`

The *Object* qualifier is required and is the Window Object.

Notes: This Property applies only to worksheets and macro sheets.

DisplayRecentFiles   Property

Applies To: Application

Explanation: True if the most recently used (MRU) file list is displayed in the File menu. Read-write.

Syntax: *Object*.`DisplayRecentFiles`

The *Object* qualifier is required and is the Application Object.

DisplayRightToLeft   Property

Applies To: Window

Explanation: True if the window displays right-to-left instead of left-to-right. Read-write.

Syntax: *Object*`.DisplayRightToLeft`

The *Object* qualifier is required and is the Window Object.

Notes: This Property is only available in Arabic and Hebrew Excel.

DisplayScrollBars   Property

Applies To: Application

Explanation: True if scroll bars are visible for all workbooks. Read-write.

Syntax: *Object*`.DisplayScrollBars`

The *Object* qualifier is required and is the Application Object.

Related Topics: DisplayHorizontalScrollBar Property, DisplayVerticalScrollBar Property

DisplayStatusBar   Property

Applies To: Application

Explanation: True if the status bar is displayed. Read-write.

Syntax: *Object*`.DisplayStatusBar`

The *Object* qualifier is required and is the Application Object.

Related Topics: DisplayHorizontalScrollBar Property, DisplayVerticalScrollBar Property

DisplayVerticalScrollBar   Property

Applies To: DrawingObjects, EditBox, EditBoxes, Window

Explanation: True if the vertical scrollbar is displayed. Read-write.

Syntax: *Object*`.DisplayVerticalScrollBar`

The *Object* qualifier is required and is the Object to which this Property applies.

DisplayWorkbookTabs   Property

Applies To: Window

Explanation: True if the workbook tabs are displayed. Read-write.

Syntax: *Object*`.DisplayZeros`

The *Object* qualifier is required and is the Window Object.

Notes: This Property applies only to worksheets and macro sheets.

DisplayZeros   Property

Applies To: Window

Explanation: True if zero values are displayed. Read-write.

Syntax: *Object*.`DisplayZeros`

The *Object* qualifier is required and is the Window Object.

Notes: This Property applies only to worksheets and macro sheets.

DoubleClick   Method

Applies To: Application

Explanation: Equivalent to double-clicking the active cell or currently selected Object.

Syntax: *Object*.`DoubleClick`

The *Object* qualifier is required and is the Application Object.

DoughnutGroups   Method

Applies To: Chart

Explanation: On a 2D chart, returns a single doughnut chart group (a ChartGroup Object, Syntax 1), or a collection of the doughnut chart groups (a ChartGroups collection, Syntax 2).

Syntax 1: *Object*.`DoughnutGroups(`*index*`)`

Syntax 2: *Object*.`DoughnutGroups`

The DoughnutGroups Method has the following Object qualifier and named arguments:

The *Object* qualifier is required and is the Chart Object.

The *index* argument is required for Syntax 1. Specifies the chart group.

DoughnutHoleSize   Property

Applies To: ChartGroup

Explanation: Returns or sets the size of the hole in a doughnut chart group. The hole size is expressed as a percentage of the chart size from 10 to 90 percent. Read-write.

Syntax: *Object*.`DoughnutHoleSize`

The *Object* qualifier is required and is the ChartGroup Object.

DownBars   Property

Applies To: ChartGroup

Explanation: Returns the DownBars on a line chart. Applies only to line charts. Read-only.

Syntax: `Object.DownBar`

The `Object` qualifier is required and is the ChartGroup Object.

Draft   Property

Applies To: PageSetup

Explanation: True if the sheet will be printed without graphics. Read-write.

Syntax: `Object.Draft`

The `Object` qualifier is required and is the PageSetup Object.

Notes: Setting this Property to True makes printing faster (at the expense of not printing graphics).

DrawingObjects   Method

Applies To: Chart, DialogSheet, Worksheet

Explanation: Returns a single drawing Object (Syntax 1) or a collection of all the drawing objects (Syntax 2) on the chart, worksheet, or dialog sheet. Returns all drawing objects, including graphic objects, pictures, embedded objects, and embedded charts.

Syntax 1: `Object.DrawingObjects(index)`

Syntax 2: `Object.DrawingObjects`

The DrawingObjects Method has the following Object qualifier and named arguments:

The `Object` qualifier is required and is the Chart, DialogSheet, or Worksheet Object.

The `index` argument is required for Syntax 1. The name or number of the drawing Object. Can be an array to return several drawing objects.

Drawings   Method

Applies To: Chart, DialogSheet, Worksheet

Explanation: Returns a single drawing (a Drawing Object, Syntax 1) or a collection of drawings (a Drawings Object, Syntax 2) on the chart, dialog sheet, or worksheet. Drawings are created by the Freeform, Freehand, and Filled Freeform buttons on the Drawing toolbar.

Syntax 1: `Object.Drawings(index)`

Syntax 2: *Object*.`Drawings`

The Drawings Method has the following Object qualifier and named arguments:

The *Object* qualifier is required and is the Chart, DialogSheet, or Worksheet Object.

The *index* argument is required for Syntax 1. The name or number of the drawing to return. More than one index can be specified.

DropDownLines   Property

Applies To: DrawingObjects, DropDown, DropDowns

Explanation: Returns or sets the number of list lines displayed in the drop-down portion of a drop-down list box. Read-write.

Syntax: *Object*.`DropDownLines`

The *Object* qualifier is required and is the Object to which this Property applies.

Notes: This Property is ignored on the Macintosh.

DropDowns   Method

Applies To: Chart, DialogSheet, Worksheet

Explanation: Returns a single drop-down list box control (a DropDown Object, Syntax 1) or a collection of drop-down list box controls on the chart or sheet (a DropDowns Object, Syntax 2).

Syntax 1: *Object*.`DropDowns`*index*

Syntax 2: *Object*.`DropDowns`

The DropDowns Method has the following Object qualifier and named arguments:

The *Object* is required and is the Chart, DialogSheet, or Worksheet Object.

The *index* argument is required for Syntax 1. It specifies the name or number of the drop-down list box control (can be an array to specify more than one).

DropLines   Property

Applies To: ChartGroup

Explanation: Returns or sets the DropLines for a series on a line or area chart. Applies only to line or area charts. Read-write.

Syntax: *Object*.`DropLines`

The *Object* is required and is the ChartGroup Object.

Duplicate   Method

Applies To: Arc, Arcs, Button, Buttons, ChartObject, ChartObjects, CheckBox, CheckBoxes, Drawing, DrawingObjects, Drawings, DropDown, DropDowns, EditBox, EditBoxes, GroupBox, GroupBoxes, GroupObject, GroupObjects, Label, Labels, Line, Lines, ListBox, ListBoxes, OLEObject, OLEObjects, OptionButton, OptionButtons, Oval, Ovals, Picture, Pictures, Rectangle, Rectangles, ScrollBar, ScrollBars, Spinner, Spinners, TextBox, TextBoxes

Explanation: Duplicates the Object and returns a reference to the new copy.

Syntax: `Object.Duplicate`

The `Object` is required and is the Object to which this Method applies.

Edit   Method

Applies To: ToolbarButton

Explanation: Starts the button editor for the specified toolbar button.

Syntax: `object.Edit`

In this syntax, `object` is the ToolbarButton object.

EditBoxes   Method

Applies To: DialogSheet

Explanation: EditBoxes returns a single edit box control (an EditBoxes object, as shown in the first sample syntax, which follows) or a collection of edit box controls on the sheet (as shown in Syntax 2).

Syntax 1: `object.EditBoxes(index)`

Syntax 2: `object.EditBoxes`

In either syntax, `object` is required, and is the DialogSheet object. In Syntax 1, `index` is required, and specifies the edit box's name or number. (You can use an array to specify more than one.)

EditDirectlyInCell   Property

Applies To: Application

Explanation: This property is true if Excel permits you to edit within a cell. EditDirectlyInCell is read-write.

Syntax: `object.EditDirectlyInCell`

In this syntax, `object` is the Application object.

EditionOptions   Method

Applies To: Workbook

Explanation: This method—which is available only on Macintosh computers running System 7—sets options for publishers and subscribers in the workbook.

Syntax: `object.EditionOptions(type, option, name, reference, appearance, chartSize, formats)`

In this syntax, `object` is the Workbook object.

The `type` argument is required. It specifies the edition type to change (either xlPublisher or xlSubscriber).

The `option` argument is required. It specifies the type of information to set for the edition. If `type` is xlPublisher, `option` can be xlCancel, xlSendPublisher, xlSelect, xlAutomaticUpdate, xlManualUpdate, or xlChangeAttributes. If `type` is xlSubscriber, `option` can be xlCancel, xlUpdateSubscriber, xlOpenSource, xlAutomaticUpdate, or xlManualUpdate.

The `name` argument is optional, and specifies the name of the edition as returned from the LinkSources method. If you leave out the `name` argument, you must specify a `reference`.

The `reference` argument is optional, but is required if you do not specify a name. The `reference` specifies the edition reference as text in R1C1-style form. This argument is required if more than one publisher or subscriber uses the same edition name in the workbook, or if the `name` argument is omitted.

The `appearance` argument is optional. If `option` is xlChangeAttributes, `appearance` determines whether the edition is published as shown on screen (xlScreen) or as shown when printed (xlPrinter).

The `chartSize` argument is optional. If `option` is xlChangeAttributes and the published object is a chart, the `chartSize` determines the size of the edition (either xlScreen or xlPrinter). You should omit the `chartSize` argument if the edition is not a chart.

The `formats` argument is optional. If `option` is xlChangeAttributes, the `formats` argument determines the published edition's format. The format can be any combination of xlPICT, xlBIFF, or xlRTF.

Elevation   Property

Applies To: Chart

Explanation: Returns or sets a 3D chart's elevation, in degrees. This property is read-write.

Syntax: `object.Elevation`

In this syntax, `object` is the Chart object.

Notes: A chart's elevation is the height, in degrees, from which you view the chart. For most kinds of charts, the default elevation is 15 degrees. You must set this property's value between –90 and 90. When using 3D bar charts, however, the setting should be between 0 and 44.

EnableCancelKey   Property

Applies To: Application

Explanation: Controls handling of the Ctrl+Break, Esc, or Command+period user interruptions when a procedure is running, as shown in the following table. This property is read-write.

Value	Meaning
xlDisabled	Disables cancel-key trapping.
xlInterrupt	Interrupts the current procedure so that the user can debug or end the procedure.
xlErrorHandler	Sends the interrupt to the running procedure as an error, which is trappable by an error handler set up with an On Error GoTo statement. The trappable error code is 18.

Syntax: `object.EnableCancelKey`

In this syntax, *object* is the Application object.

Notes: Use this property very carefully. If you use xlDisabled, you cannot interrupt a runaway loop or other code that does not terminate itself. If you use xlErrorHandler but your error handler always returns using the Resume statement, you cannot stop runaway code.

The EnableCancelKey property always resets to xlInterrupt when Excel returns to the idle state and no code is running. If you want to trap or disable cancellation in your procedure, you must change the EnableCancelKey property every time the procedure is called.

Enabled   Property

Applies To: CheckBox, CheckBoxes, Drawing, DrawingObjects, Drawings, DropDown, DropDowns, EditBox, EditBoxes, GroupBox, GroupBoxes, GroupObject, GroupObjects, Label, Labels, Line, Lines, ListBox, ListBoxes, Menu, MenuItem, OLEObject, OLEObjects, OptionButton, OptionButtons, Oval, Ovals, Picture, Pictures, Rectangle, Rectangles, ScrollBar, ScrollBars, Spinner, Spinners, TextBox, TextBoxes, ToolbarButton

Explanation: This property is True if the control, drawing object, or menu item is enabled. The Enabled property is read-write, except when it applies to Menu, in which case Enabled is write-only.

Syntax: *object*.`Enabled`

In this syntax, *object* is the object to which this property applies.

Note: Disabled menu items and disabled toolbars are gray. A disabled toolbar button beeps when it is pressed.

EnableTipWizard   Property

Applies To: Application

Explanation: This property is True if the TipWizard is enabled. EnableTipWizard is read-write.

Syntax: *object*.`EnableTipWizard`

In this syntax, *object* is the Application object.

Enclosures   Property

Applies To: Mailer

Explanation: Returns or sets the enclosed files attached to the workbook mailer, as an array of strings. Each string indicates the path name of a file to attach as an enclosure. Relative paths are allowed, and should be based on the current directory. This property is read-write.

Syntax: *object*.`Enclosures`

In this syntax, *object* is the Mailer object.

End   Method

Explanation: End returns a cell (a Range object) at the end of the region that contains the source range. End is equivalent to pressing End+Up arrow, End+Down arrow, End+Left arrow, or End+Right arrow.

Syntax: *object*.`End(`*direction*`)`

In this syntax, *object* is a cell in the range.

The *direction* argument is required. This argument specifies the direction in which to move. The *direction* argument can be set as xlToLeft, xlToRight, xlUp, or xlDown.

EndStyle   Property

Explanation: EndStyle returns or sets the end style for the error bars (either xlCap or xlNoCap). This property is read-write.

Syntax: `object.EndStyle`

In this syntax, **object** is the ErrorBars object.

EntireColumn   Property

Applies To: Range

Explanation: EntireColumn returns the entire column, or columns that contain the range. A column is a Range object. EntireColumn is read-only.

Syntax: `object.EntireColumn`

In this syntax, **object** is the range that contains the column or columns to return.

EntireRow   Property

Applies To: Range

Explanation: EntireRow returns the entire row or rows that contain the range. A row is a Range object. This property is read-only.

Syntax: `object.EntireRow`

In this syntax, **object** is the range that contains the row or rows to return.

ErrorBar   Method

Applies To: Series

Explanation: ErrorBar applies error bars to a series.

Syntax: `object.ErrorBar`(*direction, include, type, amount, minusValues*)

In this syntax, **object** is the Series object.

The *direction* argument is optional. It specifies the error bar's direction, which can be xlX or xlY. (X is available only for scatter charts.) If you omit *direction*, error bars are applied in the Y direction.

The *include* argument is optional. It specifies the error bar parts to be included (one of xlPlusValues, xlMinusValues, xlNone, or xlBoth). If you omit *include*, both error bars are included.

The *type* argument is optional. It specifies the type of error bar type to be included (either xlFixedValue, xlPercent, xlStDev, xlStError, or xlCustom).

The *amount* argument is optional, and determines the error amount. This argument is used only for the positive error amount when the *type* argument's value is xlCustom.

The *minusValues* argument is optional. This is the negative error amount when the *type* argument's value is xlCustom.

ErrorBars   Property

Applies To: Series

Explanation: ErrorBars returns the error bars for the series. This property is read-only.

Syntax: `object.ErrorBars`

In this syntax, **object** is the Series object.

Evaluate   Method

Applies To: Application, Chart, DialogSheet, Worksheet

Explanation: Evaluate converts an Excel name to an object or to a value.

Syntax: `object.Evaluate(name)`

In this syntax, **object** is optional for Application, but is required for Chart, DialogSheet, and Worksheet. It contains the named object.

The **name** argument is required, and is the name of the object, using Excel's naming convention.

Note: You can use the following names with the Evaluate method:

✔ **A1-style references.** This is any reference to a single cell using A1 notation. All references are considered absolute references.

✔ **Ranges.** You can use the range, intersect, and union operators (colon, space, and comma) with references.

✔ **Defined names** in the language of the macro.

✔ **External references using the ! operator.** These references can point to a cell or to a name that is defined in another workbook, such as Evaluate("[BOOK1.XLS]Sheet1!A1"). Graphic objects using their Microsoft Excel name (such as "Oval 3"). You cannot use the number alone.

Note: Square brackets (as in [A1:C5]) are identical to calling the Evaluate method with a string argument. For example, the following expression pairs are equivalent:

✔ `[a1].Value = 25`

✔ `Evaluate("A1").Value = 25`

```
✔ trigVariable = [SIN(45)]

✔ trigVariable = Evaluate("SIN(45)")

✔ Set firstCellInSheet = Workbooks("BOOK1.XLS").Sheets(4).[A1]

✔ Set firstCellInSheet = Workbooks("BOOK1.XLS").Sheets(4).Evaluate("A1")
```

Excel4IntlMacroSheets   Method

Applies To: Application, Workbook

Explanation: This method returns an Excel 4 international macro sheet (a Worksheet object, in Syntax 1) or a collection of all Excel 4 international macro sheets (a Worksheet object, as in Syntax 2) in the workbook. This method is read-only.

Syntax 1: `object.Excel4IntlMacroSheets(index)`

Syntax 2: `object.Excel4IntlMacroSheets`

The *object* is optional for Application, but is required for Workbook. This is the object that contains Excel 4 international macro sheets.

The *index* argument is required for Syntax 1. It is the name or number of the Excel 4 international macro sheet to return.

ExecuteExcel4Macro   Method

Applies To: Application

Explanation: This method runs an Excel 4 macro function and returns the function's results. The type returned depends on the function. This method is read-write.

Syntax: `object.ExecuteExcel4Macro(string)`

In this syntax, *object* is the Application object.

The *string* argument is required. It is an Excel 4 macro language function without the equal sign. All references must be given as R1C1 strings. If *string* contains embedded double quotation marks, then you must double them. For example, to run the macro function `=MID("text",1,4)`, *string* must be `"MID(""text"",1,4)"`.

Explosion   Property

Applies To: Point, Series

Explanation: Explostion returns or sets the percentage of explosion for pie chart or doughnut chart slices. If its value is zero, there is no explosion (the tip of the slice is in the center of the pie). This property is read-write.

Syntax: `object.Explosion`

In this syntax, **`object`** is the Point or Series object.

Extend   Method

Applies To: Series, Collection

Explanation: Extends data points to an existing collection in a series.

Syntax: `object.Extend(source, rowcol, categoryLabels)`

In this syntax, **`object`** is the SeriesCollection object.

The **`source`** argument is required. It specifies the data that is to be added to the SeriesCollection, either as a Range or as an array of data points.

The `rowcol` argument is optional. It specifies whether the new values are in the rows (xlRows) or columns (xlColumns) of the given range source. If you leave out `rowcol`, Excel determines where the values should go according to the size and orientation of the selected range or dimensions of the array. This argument is ignored if the source data is in an array.

The `categoryLabels` argument is optional. It is ignored if the `source` is an array. This argument is true if the first row or column contains the name of the category labels; it is false if the first row or column contains the first data point of the series. If you leave out `categoryLabels`, Excel determines where the category label should go according to the contents of the first row or column.

FileConverters   Property

Applies To: Application

Explanation: FileConverters displays a list of installed file converters, which appear formatted as a text array. In this array, each row provides information about one of the file converters, as shown in the following table. This property returns Null if no converters are installed. FileConverters is read-only.

Column	Contents
1	The long name of the converter, including the file-type search string in Windows—for example "Lotus 1-2-3 Files (*.wk*)".
2	The path name of the converter DLL or code resource.
3	The file-extension search string in Windows, or the four-character file type on the Macintosh.

Syntax: `object.FileConverters`

In this syntax, **`object`** is the Application object.

FileFormat   Property

Applies To: Workbook

Explanation: FileFormat displays the file format and type of the workbook, as shown in the following list.

```
xlAddInxlCSVxlCSVMacxlCSVMSDOSxlCSVWindowsxlDBF2xlDBF3xlDBF4xlDIFxlExcel2

xlExcel3xlExcel4xlExcel4WorkbookxlIntlAddInxlIntlMacroxlNormalxlSYLKxlTemplatexlTextxlTextMac

xlTextMSDOSxlTextWindowsxlTextPrinterxlWK1xlWK3xlWKSxlWQ1xlWK3FM3xlWK1FMTxlWK1A
```

The FileFormat property is read-only.

Syntax: `object.FileFormat`

In this syntax, **object** is the Workbook object.

FillAcrossSheets   Method

Applies To: Sheets, Worksheets

Explanation: This method copies a range to the same area on all the other worksheets in a collection of worksheets.

Syntax: `object.FillAcrossSheets(range, type)`

In this syntax, **object** is the Sheets or Worksheets object.

The **range** argument is required. It specifies the range that is to be filled across each of the worksheets in the collection. The specified range must be from one of the worksheets within the collection.

The *type* argument is optional. It specifies how to copy the range (either xlAll, xlContents, or xlFormulas). If you omit the *type* argument, Excel defaults to xlAll.

FillDown   Method

Applies To: Range

Explanation: FillDown fills a range from the top cell or cells down to the bottom. This method copies the contents and formats of the cells in the top row of the range into the rest of the rows in the range.

Syntax: `object.FillDown`

In this syntax, **object** is the range to be filled.

FillLeft   Method

Applies To: Range

Explanation: FillLeft fills a range from the rightmost cell or cells to the left. This method copies the contents and formats of the cells in the right column of the range into the rest of the columns in the range.

Syntax: *object*`.FillLeft`

In this syntax, *object* is the range to be filled.

FillRight   Method

Applies To: Range

Explanation: FillRight fills a range from the leftmost cell or cells to the right. This method copies the contents and formats of the cells in the left column of the range into the rest of the columns in the range.

Syntax: *object*`.FillRight`

In this syntax, *object* is the range to be filled.

FillUp   Method

Applies To: Range

Explanation: FillUp fills a range from the bottommost cell or cells to the top. This method copies the contents and formats of the cell or cells in the bottom row of the range into the rest of the rows in the range.

Syntax: *object*`.FillUp`

In this syntax, *object* is the range to be filled.

FilterMode   Property

Applies To: Worksheet

Explanation: The FilterMode property's value is True if the worksheet is in filter mode. FilterMode is read-only.

Syntax: *object*`.FilterMode`

In this syntax, *object* is the Worksheet object.

Notes: This property is True if the worksheet includes a filtered list that contains hidden rows.

Find   Method

Applies To: Range

Explanation: Find finds a cell that contains specific information in a range, and returns the first cell (a Range object) where it is found. This does not affect the selection or active cell.

Syntax: `object.Find(what, after, lookIn, lookAt, searchOrder, searchDirection, matchCase)`

In this syntax, `object` is the range to be searched.

The `what` argument is required. It is the contents you want to search for. The `what` argument can be a string or any Excel data type.

The `after` arugment is optional. It is the first cell after which you want to search. This corresponds to the position of the active cell when a search is done from the user interface. If you leave out the `after` argument, the search automatically starts at the top left cell of the range. The value of `after` must be one of the cells in the range.

The `lookIn` argument is optional, and can be either xlFormulas, xlValues, or xlNotes. If you leave out the `lookIn` argument, Excel uses xlFormulas as the default value.

The `lookAt` argument is optional, and can be xlWhole or xlPart. If you leave out the `lookAt` argument, Excel uses xlPart as the default value.

The `searchOrder` argument is optional. It can be either xlByRows (to search row-major) or xlByColumns (to search column-major). If you leave out the `searchOrder` argument, Excel uses xlByRows as the default value.

The `searchDirection` argument is optional. It can be either xlNext or xlPrevious. If you leave out the `searchDirection` argument, Excel uses xlNext as the default value.

The `matchCase` argument is optional. If it is True, Excel performs a case-sensitive search. If it is False or omitted, the search is case-insensitive.

Notes: You can use either the FindNext or FindPrevious methods to repeat a search.

FindFile   Method

Applies To: Application

Explanation: FindFile displays the Find File command's dialog box. This dialog box, however, is only displayed interactively; that is, you cannot preset it.

Syntax: `object.FindFile`

In this syntax, `object` is the Application object.

FindNext   Method

Applies To: Range

Explanation: FindNext continues a search that was started with the Find method. This method finds the next cell that matches the same conditions used by the Find method, and then returns that cell as a Range object. FindNext does not affect the selection or the active cell.

Syntax: *object*`.FindNext(`*after*`)`

In this syntax, *object* is the range to be searched.

The *after* argument is optional. It is the first cell after which you want to search. This corresponds to the position of the active cell when a search is done from the user interface. If you leave out the *after* argument, the search automatically starts at the top left cell of the range.

FindPrevious   Method

Applies To: Range

Explanation: FindPrevious continues a search that was started with the Find method. FindPrevious finds the previous cell that matches the same conditions that were used in the Find method, and then returns that cell as a Range object. FindPrevious does not affect the selection or the active cell.

Syntax: *object*`.FindPrevious(`*after*`)`

In this syntax, *object* is the range to be searched.

The *after* argument is optional. It is the first cell before which you want to search. This corresponds to the position of the active cell when a search is done from the user interface. If you leave out the after argument, the search automatically starts at the top left cell of the range.

FirstPageNumber   Property

Applies To: PageSetup

Explanation: This property returns or sets the first page number that will be used for printing this sheet. The default value is xlAutomatic. FirstPageNumber is read-write.

Syntax: *object*`.FirstPageNumber`

In this syntax, *object* is the PageSetup object.

FirstSliceAngle   Property

Applies To: ChartGroup

Explanation: This property returns or sets the angle of the first pie or doughnut slice for a pie, 3D pie, or doughnut chart. The angle is set in degrees, moving clockwise from vertical. This property applies only to pie, 3D pie, and doughnut charts. FirstSliceAngle is read-write.

Syntax: *object*.`FirstSliceAngle`

In this syntax, *object* is the ChartGroup object.

FitToPagesTall   Property

Applies To: PageSetup

Explanation: This property returns or sets how many pages tall the worksheet will be scaled to when it is printed. Excel ignores this property unless the Zoom property is False. If FitToPagesTall is False, Excel scales the worksheet according to the FitToPagesWide property. This property applies only to worksheets. FitToPagesTall is read-write.

Syntax: *object*.`FitToPagesTall`

In this syntax, *object* is the PageSetup object.

FitToPagesWide   Property

Applies To: PageSetup

Explanation: This property returns or sets how many pages wide the worksheet will be scaled when it is printed. Excel ignores this property unless the Zoom is False. If this property is False, Excel scales the worksheet according to the FitToPagesTall property. This property applies only to worksheets. FitToPagesWide is read-write.

Syntax: *object*.`FitToPagesWide`

In this example, *object* is the PageSetup object.

FixedDecimal   Property

Applies To: Application

Explanation: When FixedDecimal is True, all data entered is formatted with the number of fixed decimal places set by the FixedDecimalPlaces property.

Syntax: *object*.`FixedDecimal`

In this syntax, *object* is the Application object.

FixedDecimalPlaces   Property

Applies To: Application

Explanation: When the FixedDecimal property is True, FixedDecimalPlaces returns or sets the number of fixed decimal places to be used. This property is read-write.

Syntax: *object*`.FixedDecimalPlaces`

In this syntax, *object* is the Application object.

Floor   Property

Applies To: Chart

Explanation: Floor returns the floor of a 3D chart. This property is read-only.

Syntax: *object*`.Floor`

In this syntax, *object* is the Chart object.

Focus   Property

Applies To: DialogSheet

Explanation: Focus returns or sets the current dialog box's dynamic focus as a string containing the ID for the control with the focus. The control with the focus is where user keyboard input is directed. The focus is visually indicated by a dashed rectangle around the control or around selections within the control. The Focus property is read-write.

Syntax: *object*`.Focus`

In this syntax, *object* is the DialogSheet object.

Notes: An error will result if you read or set this property while the dialog is not running. While the dialog is running, setting this property will attempt to change the focus to the specified control. Not all controls will accept the focus, and the dialog manager may refuse to move the focus under certain conditions. Reading this property always returns the ID of the control with the focus.

Font   Property

Applies To: AxisTitle, Button, Buttons, Characters, ChartArea, ChartTitle, DataLabel, DataLabels, DrawingObjects, GroupObject, GroupObjects, Legend, LegendEntry, PlotArea, Range, Style, TextBox, TextBoxes, TickLabels

Explanation: The Font property returns or sets an object's font. This property is read-write.

Syntax: *object*`.Font`

In this syntax, *object* is the object to which this property applies.

FontStyle   Property

Applies To: Font

Explanation: FontStyle returns or sets the font style as a string. This property is read-write.

Syntax: *object*.`FontStyle`

In this syntax, *object* is the Font object.

Note: Other Font properties (such as Bold and Italic) may be changed when you modify FontStyle. This property is always in the language of the system because the system determines which fonts are available.

FooterMargin   Property

Applies To: PageSetup

Explanation: FooterMargin returns or sets the amount of space between the bottom of the page and the footer. The distance is set in points (1/72 inch). This property is read-write.

Syntax: *object*.`FooterMargin`

In this syntax, *object* is the PageSetup object.

Formula   Property

Applies To: Button, Buttons, Picture, Pictures, Range, Series, TextBox, TextBoxes

Explanation: This property returns or sets the object's formula, in A1-style notation and the language of the macro. Formula is read-write.

Syntax: *object*.`Formula`

In this syntax, *object* is the object to which this property applies.

FormulaArray   Property

Applies To: Range

Explanation: FormulaArray returns or sets the formula of a range, entered as an array. Returns (or can be set to) a single formula or a Visual Basic array. If the specified range is not array entered, this property returns Null. FormulaArray is read-write.

Syntax: *object*.`FormulaArray`

In this syntax, *object* is the range for which an array formula is returned.

FormulaLocal   Property

Applies To: Range, Series

Explanation: FormulaLocal returns or sets the formula for the object, using A1-style references in the user's language. This property is read-write.

Syntax: *object*.FormulaLocal

In this syntax, *object* is the Range or Series object.

FormulaR1C1   Property

Applies To: Range, Series

Explanation: FormulaR1C1 returns or sets the formula for an object, using R1C1-style notation in the language of the macro.

Syntax: *object*.FormulaR1C1

In this syntax, *object* is the Range or Series object.

FormulaR1C1Local   Property

Applies To: Range, Series

Explanation: FormulaR1C1Local returns or sets the formula for an object, using R1C1-style notation in the user's language.

Syntax: *object*.FormulaR1C1Local

In this syntax, *object* is the Range or Series object.

Forward   Property

Applies To: Trendline

Explanation: Forward returns or sets the number of periods (or units on a scatter chart) from which the trendline extends. This property is read-write.

Syntax: *object*.Forward

In this syntax, *object* is the Trendline object.

ForwardMailer   Method

Applies To: Workbook

Explanation: ForwardMailer sets up the workbook mailer for forwarding. It creates a new mailer that is preset with the subject and enclosures of the existing mailer. This method is valid only when the workbook has a received mailer attached—that is, you can only forward a workbook you have received. ForwardMailer is available only in Excel for the Macintosh with the PowerTalk mail system extension.

Syntax: `object.ForwardMailer`

In this syntax, *object* is the Workbook object.

FreezePanes   Property

Applies To: Window

Explanation: FreezePanes' value is True if split panes are frozen. This property is read-write.

Syntax: `object.FreezePanes`

In this syntax, *object* is the Window object.

Notes: FreezePanes can be True while Split is False, and vice versa. This property applies only to worksheets and macro sheets.

FullName   Property

Applies To: AddIn, Workbook

Explanation: FullName returns the object's name, including its path on disk, as a string. This property is read-only.

Syntax: `object.FullName`

In this syntax, *object* is the AddIn or Workbook object.

Note: This property is equivalent to the Path property, followed by the current file system separator, followed by the Name property.

Function   Property

Applies To: PivotField

Explanation: Function returns or sets the function that is used to summarize the PivotField. You can use only data fields. Function can use one of these values: xlAverage, xlCount, xlCountNums, xlMax, xlMin, xlProduct, xlStDev, xlStDevP, xlSum, xlVar, or xlVarP. This property is read-write.

Syntax: `object.Function`

In this syntax, *object* is the PivotField object.

GapDepth   Property

Applies To: Chart

Explanation: GapDepth returns or sets the distance between the data series in a 3D chart. The distance is a percentage of the marker width (between 0 and 500). GapDepth is read-write.

Syntax: `object.GapDepth`

In this syntax, `object` is the Chart object.

GapWidth   Property

Applies To: ChartGroup

Explanation: Returns or sets the space between bar or column clusters as a percentage of the width of a bar or column. This property must be between 0 and 500. Read-write.

Syntax: `object.GapWidth`

The `object` is the ChartGroup object and is required.

GetCustomListContents   Method

Applies To: Application

Explanation: Returns a custom list (an array of strings) for a specified list number.

Syntax: `object.GetCustomListContents(listNum)`

The GetCustomListContents method has the following object qualifier and named arguments:

The `object` is the Application object and is required.

The `listNum` is the list number and is required.

Notes: This method generates an error if a corresponding list does not exist.

GetCustomListNum   Method

Applies To: Application

Explanation: Returns the custom list number for an array of strings. Both built-in and custom defined lists can be matched using this method.

Syntax: `object.GetCustomListNum(listArray)`

The GetCustomListNum method has the following object qualifier and named arguments:

The *object* is the Application object and is required.

The *listArray* is an array of strings and is required.

Notes: This method generates an error if a corresponding list does not exist.

GetOpenFilename   Method

Applies To: Application

Explanation: Displays the standard Open dialog box and gets a file name from the user without actually opening any files.

Syntax: *object*.**GetOpenFilename**(*fileFilter, filterIndex, title, buttonText*)

The GetOpenFilename method has the following object qualifier and named arguments:

The *object* is the Application object and is required.

The *fileFilter* argument is an optional string specifying file filtering criteria. In Windows, this string consists of pairs of file filter strings followed by the MS-DOS wild card file filter specification, with each part and each pair separated by commas. Each separate pair is listed in the File Type drop-down list box. For example, the following string specifies two file filters—text and addin:

```
"Text Files (*.txt),*.txt,Add-In Files (*.xla),*.xla"
```

To use multiple MS-DOS wild card expressions for a single file filter type, separate the wild card expressions with semicolons. For example:

```
"Visual Basic Files (*.bas; *.txt),*.bas;*.txt".
```

If omitted on Windows, this argument defaults to "All Files (*.*),*.*".

On the Macintosh, this string is a list of comma-separated file type codes, ("TEXT,XLA,XLS4"). Spaces are significant and should not be inserted before or after the comma separators unless they are part of the file type code. If omitted, this argument defaults to all file types.

The *filterIndex* argument is an optional string, Windows only (ignored on the Macintosh), and specifies the index number of the default file filtering criteria from one to the number of filters specified in fileFilter. If this argument is omitted or greater than the number of filters present, the first file filter is used.

The *title* argument is optional, Windows only (ignored on the Macintosh), and specifies the dialog title. If this argument is omitted, the dialog title is "Open".

The *buttonText* argument is optional, Macintosh only (ignored in Windows), and specifies the text used for the Open button in the dialog box. If this argument is omitted, the button text is "Open."

Note: This method returns the selected file name or the name entered by the user. The returned name may include a path specification. Returns False if the user cancels the dialog box.

This method may change the current drive or directory.

GetSaveAsFilename   **Method**

Applies To: Application

Explanation: Displays the standard Save As dialog box and gets a file name from the user without actually saving any files.

Syntax: `object.GetSaveAsFilename`(*initialFilename,fileFilter, filterIndex, title, buttonText*)

The GetSaveAsFilename method has the following object qualifier and named arguments:

The *object* is the Application object and is required.

The *initialFilename* argument specifies the suggested file name and is optional. If this argument is omitted, Excel uses the active workbook's name.

The *fileFilter* argument is a string specifying file filtering criteria and is optional. In Windows, this string consists of pairs of file filter strings followed by the MS-DOS wild card file filter specification, with each part and each pair separated by commas. Each separate pair is listed in the File Type drop-down list box. For example, the following string specifies two file filters—text and addin:

```
"Text Files (*.txt), *.txt, Add-In Files (*.xla), *.xla"
```

To use multiple MS-DOS wild card expressions for a single file filter type, separate the wildcard expressions with semicolons. For example:

```
"Visual Basic Files (*.bas; *.txt),*.bas;*.txt"
```

If omitted on Windows, this argument defaults to "All Files (*.*),*.*".

On the Macintosh, this string is a list of comma-separated file type codes, ("TEXT,XLA,XLS4"). Spaces are significant and should not be inserted before or after the comma separators unless they are part of the file type code. If omitted, this argument defaults to all file types.

The *filterIndex* argument is optional and is Windows only (ignored on the Macintosh). It specifies the index number of the default file filtering criteria from one to the number of filters specified in fileFilter. If this argument is omitted or greater than the number of filters present, the first file filter is used.

The *title* argument is optional, Windows only (ignored on the Macintosh), and specifies the dialog title. If this argument is omitted, the dialog title is "Save As."

The `buttonText` argument is optional, Macintosh only (ignored in Windows), and Specifies the text used for the Save button in the dialog box. If this argument is omitted, the button text is "Save."

Notes: This method returns the selected file name or the name entered by the user. The returned name may include a path specification. Returns False if the user cancels the dialog box.

This method may change the current drive or directory.

GoalSeek   Method

Applies To: Range

Explanation: Calculates the values necessary to achieve a specific goal. If the goal is an amount returned by a formula, this calculates a value that, when supplied to your formula, causes the formula to return the number you want. Returns True if the goal seek is successful.

Syntax: `object.GoalSeek(goal, changingCell)`

The GoalSeek method has the following object qualifier and named arguments:

The `object` is required. The specified range must be a single cell.

The `goal` argument is the value you want returned in this cell, and is required.

The `changingCell` argument is a required range object indicating which cell should be changed to achieve the target value.

Goto   Method

Applies To: Application

Explanation: Selects any range or Visual Basic procedure in any workbook, and activates that workbook if it is not already active.

Syntax: `object.Goto(reference, scroll)`

The Goto method has the following object qualifier and named arguments:

The `object` is the Application object and is required.

The `reference` argument is required, and specifies the destination. This can be a range or a string containing a Visual Basic procedure name.

The `scroll` argument is optional. If this argument is True, Excel scrolls the window so that the top left corner of the range appears in the top left corner of the window. If False or omitted, Excel does not scroll the window.

Notes: This method differs from the Select method in the following ways:

✔ If you specify a range on a sheet that is not on top, Excel will switch to that sheet before selecting. (If you use Select with a range on a sheet that is not on top, the range will be selected but the sheet will not be activated.)

✔ This method has a scroll argument that lets you scroll the destination window.

✔ When you use the Goto method, the previous selection (before the Goto method runs) is added to the array of previous selections (for more information, see the PreviousSelections property). You can use this feature to quickly jump among up to four selections.

✔ The Select method has a replace argument; the Goto method does not.

GridlineColor   Property

Applies To: Window

Explanation: Returns or sets the gridline color as an RGB value. Read-write.

Syntax: *object*.`GridlineColor`

The *object* is the Window object and is required.

GridlineColorIndex   Property

Applies To: Window

Explanation: Returns or sets the gridline color as an index into the current color palette. Read-write.

Syntax: *object*.`GridlineColorIndex`

The *object* is the Window object and is required.

Notes: Set this property to xlAutomatic to specify the automatic color.

Group   Method

Applies To: Arcs, Buttons, ChartObjects, CheckBoxes, DrawingObjects, Drawings, DropDowns, EditBoxes, GroupBoxes, GroupObjects, Labels, Lines, ListBoxes, OLEObjects, OptionButtons, Ovals, Pictures, Range, Rectangles, ScrollBars, Spinners, TextBoxes

Explanation: Syntax 1: Demotes a range in an outline (in other words, increases its outline level). The range should be an entire row or column, or a range of rows or columns.

Groups a discontiguous range in a pivot table.

Groups multiple controls or drawing objects together; returns a new GroupObject.

Syntax 2: Performs numeric or date grouping in a pivot table field.

Syntax 1: `object.Group`

Syntax 2: `object.Group(start, end, by, periods)`

The Group method has the following object qualifier and named arguments:

The **object** is the object to which this method applies, and is required.

The *start* argument is optional, and is the first value to be grouped. If omitted or True, the first value in the field is used.

The *end* argument is optional, and is the last value to be grouped. If omitted or True, the last value in the field is used.

The *by* argument is optional; if the field is numeric, it specifies the size of each group.

If the field is a date, it specifies the number of days in each group if periods is set to days. Otherwise, *by* is ignored.

If this argument is omitted, a default group size is automatically chosen.

The *periods* argument is optional, and is an array of Boolean values specifying the period for the group, as shown in the following table.

- ✔ Seconds 1
- ✔ Minutes 2
- ✔ Hours 3
- ✔ Days 4
- ✔ Months 5
- ✔ Quarters 6
- ✔ Years 7

If an element of the array is True, a group is created for the corresponding time. If the element is False, no group is created. This argument is ignored if the field is not a date field.

GroupBoxes   Method

Applies To: Chart, DialogSheet, Worksheet

Explanation: Returns a single group box control (a GroupBox object, Syntax 1) or a collection of group box controls on the chart or sheet (a GroupBoxes object, Syntax 2).

Syntax 1: `object.GroupBoxes(index)`

Syntax 2: `object.GroupBoxes`

The GroupBoxes method has the following object qualifier and named arguments:

The *object* is the Chart, DialogSheet, or Worksheet object, and is required.

The *index* is required for Syntax 1, and specifies the name or number of the group box.

GroupLevel   Property

Applies To: PivotField

Explanation: Returns the placement of the specified field within a group of fields (if the field is a member of a grouped set of fields). Read-only.

Syntax: *object*.GroupLevel

The *object* is the PivotField object, and is required.

Notes: The highest-level parent field (leftmost parent field) is GroupLevel one, its child is GroupLevel two, and so on.

GroupObjects   Method

Applies To: Chart, DialogSheet, Worksheet

Explanation: Returns a single group (a GroupObject object, Syntax 1) or a collection of all the groups (a GroupObjects object, Syntax 2) on the chart, worksheet, or dialog sheet.

Syntax 1: *object*.GroupObjects(*index*)

Syntax 2: *object*.GroupObjects

The GroupObjects method has the following object qualifier and named arguments:

The *object* is the Chart, DialogSheet or Worksheet object, and is required.

The *index* is required for Syntax 1, and is the name or number of the group (can be an array to specify more than one).

HasArray   Property

Applies To: Range

Explanation: True if the specified cell is a part of an array. Read-only.

Syntax: *object*.HasArray

The *object* is the cell to test and is required.

HasAutoFormat   **Property**

Applies To: PivotTable

Explanation: True if the pivot table is automatically formatted when it is refreshed or when fields are moved. Read-write.

Syntax: *object*.AutoFormat

The *object* is the PivotTable object and is required.

HasAxis   **Property**

Applies To: Chart

Explanation: Indicates which axes exist on the current chart, as a two-dimensional array of Boolean values. Read-write.

The first array dimension indicates the axis (one of xlCategory, xlValue, or xlSeries). Series axes apply only to 3D charts.

The second array dimension indicates the axis group (xlPrimary or xlSecondary). Read-write. 3D charts have only one set of axes.

Syntax: *object*.HasAxis

The *object* is the Chart object and is required.

Notes: Excel may create or delete axes if you change the chart type or change the AxisGroup property.

HasDataLabel   **Property**

Applies To: Point

Explanation: True if the point has a data label. Read-write.

Syntax: *object*.HasDataLabel

The *object* is the Point object and is required.

HasDataLabels   **Property**

Applies To: Series

Explanation: True if the series has data labels. Read-write.

Syntax: *object*.HasDataLabels

The *object* is the Series object and is required.

HasDropLines Property

Applies To: ChartGroup

Explanation: True if the line or area chart has drop lines. Applies only to line and area charts. Read-write.

Syntax: *object*.HasDropLines

The *object* is the ChartGroup object and is required.

HasErrorBars Property

Applies To: Series

Explanation: True if the series has error bars. This property is not available on 3D charts. Read-write.

Syntax: *object*.HasErrorBars

The *object* is the Series object and is required.

HasFormula Property

Applies To: Range

Explanation: True if all cells in the range contain formulas; False if no cell in the range contains a formula; Null otherwise. Read-only.

Syntax: *object*.HasFormula

The *object* is the range to test and is required.

HasHiLoLines Property

Applies To: ChartGroup

Explanation: True if the line chart has high-low lines. Applies only to line charts. Read-write.

Syntax: *object*.HasHiLoLines

The *object* is the ChartGroup object and is required.

HasLegend Property

Applies To: Chart

Explanation: True if the chart has a legend. Read-write.

Syntax: *object*`.HasLegend`

The *object* is the Chart object and is required.

HasMailer   Property

Applies To: Workbook

Explanation: True if the workbook has a mailer. Available only in Excel for the Macintosh with the PowerTalk mail system extension installed. Read-write.

Syntax: *object*`.HasMailer`

The *object* is the Workbook object and is required.

HasMajorGridlines   Property

Applies To: Axis

Explanation: True if the axis has major gridlines. Only axes in the primary axis group can have gridlines. Read-write.

Syntax: *object*`.HasMajorGridlines`

The *object* is the Axis object and is required.

HasMinorGridlines   Property

Applies To: Axis

Explanation: True if the axis has minor gridlines. Only axes in the primary axis group can have gridlines. Read-write.

Syntax: *object*`.HasMinorGridlines`

The *object* is the Axis object and is required.

HasPassword   Property

Applies To: Workbook

Explanation: True if the workbook has a protection password. Read-only.

Syntax: *object*`.HasPassword`

The *object* is the Workbook object and is required.

Notes: You can assign a protection password to a workbook with the SaveAs method.

HasRadarAxisLabels
Property

Applies To: ChartGroup

Explanation: True if a radar chart has axis labels. Applies only to radar charts. Read-write.

Syntax: *object*.`HasRadarAxisLabels`

The *object* is the ChartGroup object and is required.

HasRoutingSlip
Property

Applies To: Workbook

Explanation: True if the workbook has a RoutingSlip. Read-write.

Syntax: *object*.`HasRoutingSlip`

The *object* is the Workbook object and is required.

Notes: Setting this property to True creates a routing slip with default values. Setting the property to False deletes the routing slip.

HasSeriesLines
Property

Applies To: ChartGroup

Explanation: True if a stacked column or bar chart has series lines. Applies only to stacked column and bar charts. Read-write.

Syntax: *object*.`HasSeriesLines`

The *object* is the ChartGroup object and is required.

HasTitle
Property

Applies To: Axis, Chart

Explanation: True if the axis or chart has a visible title. Read-write.

Syntax: *object*.`HasTitle`

The *object* is the Axis or Chart object and is required.

Notes: An axis title is an AxisTitle object. A chart title is a ChartTitle object.

HasUpDownBars   Property

Applies To: ChartGroup

Explanation: True if a line chart has up and down bars. Applies only to line charts. Read-write.

Syntax: *object*`.HasUpDownBars`

The *object* is the ChartGroup object and is required.

HeaderMargin   Property

Applies To: PageSetup

Explanation: Returns or sets the distance from the top of the page to the header, in points (1/72 inch). Read-write.

Syntax: *object*`.HeaderMargin`

The *object* is the PageSetup object and is required.

Height   Property

Applies To: Application, Arc, Arcs, Button, Buttons, ChartArea, ChartObject, ChartObjects, CheckBox, CheckBoxes, DialogFrame, Drawing, DrawingObjects, Drawings, DropDown, DropDowns, EditBox, EditBoxes, GroupBox, GroupBoxes, GroupObject, GroupObjects, Label, Labels, Legend, Line, Lines, ListBox, ListBoxes, OLEObject, OLEObjects, OptionButton, OptionButtons, Oval, Ovals, Picture, Pictures, PlotArea, Range, Rectangle, Rectangles, ScrollBar, ScrollBars, Spinner, Spinners, TextBox, TextBoxes, Toolbar, Window

Explanation: Returns or sets the height of an object, in points (1/72 inch).

Syntax: *object*`.Height`

The *object* is the object to which this property applies, and is required. Read-write for all objects, except as shown in the following table.

Note: The height set or returned depends on the specified object.

Object type	Height
Application	Height of the main Application window. On the Macintosh this is always equal to the total height of the screen, in points. Setting this value to something else on the Macintosh will have no effect. Under

Object type	Height
	Microsoft Windows, if the window is minimized, this property is read-only and refers to the height of the icon. If the window is maximized, this property cannot be set. Use the WindowState property to determine the window state.
Range	Height of the range. Read-only.
Toolbar	Height of the toolbar. Returns the exact height of the toolbar in points. Use the Width property to change the size of the toolbar. Read-only.
Window	Height of the window. Use the UsableHeight property to determine the maximum size for the window. You cannot set this property if the window is maximized or minimized. Use the WindowState property to determine the window state.
Arc, Button, ChartArea, ChartObject, CheckBox, DialogFrame, Drawing, DrawingObjects, DropDown, EditBox, GroupBox, GroupObject, Label, Legend, Line, ListBox, OLEObject, OptionButton, Oval, Picture, PlotArea, Rectangle, ScrollBar, Spinner, TextBox	Height of the object.

Height of the object. |

You can use negative numbers to set the Height and Width properties of the following drawing objects: Arc, Button, CheckBox, Drawing, DropDown, EditBox, GroupBox, GroupObject, Label, Line, ListBox, OLEObject, OptionButton, Oval, Picture, Rectangle, ScrollBar, Spinner, and TextBox. This causes the object to reflect or translate (the behavior depends on the object), after which the Top and Left properties change to describe the new position. The Height and Width properties always return positive numbers.

HeightPercent   Property

Applies To: Chart

Explanation: Returns or sets the height of a 3D chart as a percentage of the chart width (between 5 and 500 percent). Read-write.

Syntax: `object.HeightPercent`

The `object` is the Chart object and is required.

Help   Method

Applies To: Application

Explanation: Displays a Help topic.

Syntax: `object.Help(helpFile, helpContextID)`

The Help method has the following object qualifier and named arguments:

The `object` is the Application object and is required.

The `helpFile` argument is the name of the online Help file you wish to display, and is optional. If this argument is not specified, Excel's Help file is used.

The `helpContextID` argument is optional and specifies the context ID for the Help topic. If this argument is not specified, the contents topic is displayed.

HelpButton   Property

Applies To: Button, Buttons, DrawingObjects

Explanation: Applies only to buttons in a user-defined dialog box. If True, then pressing the Help key runs the macro identified by the button's OnAction property. If False, pressing the Help key does nothing. The Help key is F1 in Excel for Windows and COMMAND+? in Excel for the Macintosh. Read-write.

Syntax: `object.HelpButton`

The `object` is the object to which this property applies and is required.

Notes: Only one button in the dialog box can have the HelpButton property set to True at any given time; setting the property resets it for all other buttons in the dialog box.

If the user presses the Help key in a dialog box that has no Help button, nothing happens.

Hidden   Property

Applies To: Range, Scenario

Explanation: Range object: True if the rows or columns are hidden. The specified range must span an entire column or row. Read-write.

Scenario object: True if the scenario is hidden. The default value is False. Read-write.

Syntax: `object.Hidden`

The **object** is the object to which this property applies and is required.

Notes: Do not confuse this property with the FormulaHidden property.

HiddenFields   Method

Applies To: PivotTable

Explanation: Returns a single pivot field (a PivotField object, Syntax 1) or a collection of the pivot fields (a PivotFields object, Syntax 2) that are currently not showing as row, column, page, or data fields. Read-only.

Syntax 1: `object.HiddenFields(index)`

Syntax 2: `object.HiddenFields`

The HiddenFields method has the following object qualifier and named arguments:

The **object** is the PivotTable object and is required.

The **index** is the name or number of the pivot field to return (can be an array to specify more than one) and is required for Syntax 1.

HiddenItems   Method

Applies To: PivotField

Explanation: Returns one hidden pivot item (a PivotItem object, Syntax 1) or a collection of all the hidden pivot items (a PivotItems object, Syntax 2) in the specified field. Read-only.

Syntax 1: `object.HiddenItems(index)`

Syntax 2: `object.HiddenItems`

The HiddenItems method has the following object qualifier and named arguments:

The **object** is the PivotField object and is required.

The **index** is the number or name of the pivot item to return (can be an array to specify more than one) and is required for Syntax 1.

Hide   Method

Applies To: DialogSheet

Explanation: Hides a dialog. If the dialog is not currently displayed, an error occurs.

Syntax: *object*.Hide(*cancel*)

The Hide method has the following object qualifier and named arguments:

The *object* is the DialogSheet object and is required.

The *cancel* argument is optional. If True, the dialog is cancelled without validating edit-box contents. If False or omitted, edit box contents are validated before returning. No macros assigned to Cancel or OK buttons are run in either case.

Notes: If *cancel* is False and edit fields in the dialog could not be validated, then this method returns False, and the dialog does not exit. Otherwise, this method returns True.

HiLoLines   Property

Applies To: ChartGroup

Explanation: Returns or sets the HiLoLines for a series on a line chart. Applies only to line charts. Read-write.

Syntax: *object*.HiLoLines

The *object* is the ChartGroup object and is required.

HorizontalAlignment   Property

Applies To: AxisTitle, Button, Buttons, ChartTitle, DataLabel, DataLabels, DrawingObjects, GroupObject, GroupObjects, Range, Style, TextBox, TextBoxes

Explanation: Returns or sets the horizontal alignment for the object. Can be one of xlCenter, xlDistributed, xlJustify, xlLeft, or xlRight for all objects. In addition, the Range or Style object can be set to xlCenterAcrossSelection, xlFill, or xlGeneral. Read-write.

Syntax: *object*.HorizontalAlignment

The *object* is the object to which this property applies and is required.

Notes: The xlDistributed alignment style works only in Far East versions of Excel.

Hour   Function

Explanation: Returns a whole number between 0 and 23, inclusive, representing the hour of the day.

Syntax: Hour(*time*)

The *time* named argument is limited to a time or numbers and strings, in any combination, that can represent a time. If time contains no valid data, Null is returned.

Id   Property

Applies To: ToolbarButton

Explanation: The button identification number of the button (built-in buttons only). Read-only.

Syntax: `object.Id`

The **object** is required and is the ToolbarButton object.

IgnoreRemoteRequests   Property

Applies To: Application

Explanation: True if remote DDE requests are ignored. Read-write.

Syntax: `object.IgnoreRemoteRequests`

The **object** is required and is the Application object.

Import   Method

Applies To: SoundNote

Explanation: Imports a sound note from a file.

Syntax: `object.Import(file,resource)`

The Import method has the following object qualifier and named arguments:

The **object** is required and is the SoundNote object.

The **file** is required and is the name of the file containing sounds.

The **resource** is required for the Macintosh (not for Windows). It is the name or number of the sound resource in the file to import.

InchesToPoints   Method

Applies To: Application

Explanation: Converts a measurement in inches into points (1/72 inch).

Syntax: `object.InchesToPoints(inches)`

The InchesToPoints method has the following object qualifier and named arguments:

The *object* argument is required and is the Application object.

The *inches* argument is required and specifies the inch value to convert to points.

IncludeAlignment   Property

Applies To: Style

Explanation: True if the style includes the AddIndent, HorizontalAlignment, VerticalAlignment, WrapText, and Orientation properties. Read-write.

Syntax: *object*.`IncludeAlignment`

The *object* is required and is the Style object.

IncludeBorder   Property

Applies To: Style

Explanation: True if the style includes the Borders properties. Read-write.

Syntax: *object*.`IncludeBorder`

The *object* is required and is the Style object.

IncludeFont   Property

Applies To: Style

Explanation: True if the style includes the Font property. Read-write.

Syntax: *object*.`IncludeFont`

The *object* is required and is the Style object.

IncludeNumber   Property

Applies To: Style

Explanation: True if the style includes the NumberFormat property. Read-write.

Syntax: *object*.`IncludeNumber`

The *object* is required and is the Style object.

IncludePatterns   Property

Applies To: Style

Explanation: True if the style includes the Interior properties. Read-write.

Syntax: *object*.`IncludePatterns`

The *object* is required and is the Style object.

IncludeProtection   Property

Applies To: Style

Explanation: True if the style includes the FormulaHidden and Locked protection properties. Read-write.

Syntax: *object*.`IncludeProtection`

The *object* is required and is the Style object.

Index   Property

Applies To: Arc, Button, Chart, ChartObject, CheckBox, DialogSheet, Drawing, DropDown, EditBox, GroupBox, GroupObject, Label, LegendEntry, Line, ListBox, Menu, MenuBar, MenuItem, Module, Name, OLEObject, OptionButton, Oval, Pane, Picture, Rectangle, Scenario, ScrollBar, Spinner, TextBox, Trendline, Window, Worksheet

Explanation: Returns the index number of the object within the collection of similar objects. Read-only.

For help about using the Index worksheet function in Visual Basic, see "Using Worksheet Functions in Visual Basic."

Syntax: *object*.`Index`

The *object* is required and is the object to which this property applies.

InnerDetail   Property

Applies To: PivotTable

Explanation: Returns or sets the name of the field which will be shown as detail when the ShowDetail property is True for the innermost row or column field. Read-write.

Syntax: *object*.`InnerDetail`

The *object* is required and is the PivotTable object.

Input   Function

Explanation: Returns characters (bytes) from an open sequential file.

Syntax: `Input`(*number* `[#]`, *filenumber*)

The Input function syntax has these parts:

Part	Description
number	Any valid numeric expression specifying the number of characters to return.
filenumber	Any valid file number.

Use this function only with files opened in Input or Binary mode.

Unlike the Input # statement, the Input function returns all of the characters that it reads, including commas, carriage returns, linefeeds, quotation marks, and leading spaces.

Another function (InputB) is provided for use with the double-byte character sets (DBCS) that are used in some Asian locales. Instead of specifying the number of characters to return, number specifies the number of bytes. In areas where DBCS is not used, InputB behaves the same as Input.

InputBox   Method

Applies To: Application

Explanation: Displays a dialog box for user input. Returns the information entered in the dialog box.

Syntax: *object*.InputBox(*prompt, title, default, left, top, helpFile, helpContextID, type*)

The InputBox method has the following object qualifier and named arguments:

The *object* is required and is the Application object.

The *prompt* argument is required. The message to be displayed in the dialog box. This may be a string, a number, a date, or a Boolean value.

The *title* argument is optional and is the title for the input box. If this argument is omitted, the title bar is empty.

The *default* argument is optional. It specifies a value to be put in the edit box when the dialog box is initially displayed. If this argument is omitted, the edit box is left empty. This value may be a Range.

The *left* argument is optional. It specifies an x position for the dialog box, in points, from the top left of the screen. One point is 1/72 inch.

The *top* argument is optional. It specifies a y position for the dialog box, in points, from the top left of the screen.

The *helpFile* argument is optional. The name of the online Help file for this input box. If the helpFile and helpContextID arguments are present, a Help button will appear in the dialog.

The *helpContextID* argument is optional. The context ID of the Help topic in helpFile.

The *type* argument is optional and specifies the return data type. If this argument is omitted, the dialog box returns text. It might have one of the values in the following table:

Value	Meaning
0	A formula
1	A number
2	Text (a string)
4	A logical value (True or False)
8	A cell reference, as a Range object
16	An error value, such as #N/A
64	An array of values

You can use the sum of the allowable values for type. For example, for an input box that can accept text or numbers, set type equal to 1+2.

Use InputBox to display a simple dialog box so that you can enter information to be used in a macro. The dialog box has an OK and a Cancel button. If you choose OK, InputBox returns the value entered in the dialog box. If you choose Cancel, InputBox returns False.

If type=0, InputBox returns the formula in the form of text, for example: "=2*PI()/360". If there are any references in the formula, they are returned as A1-style references. (Use ConvertFormula to convert between reference styles.) If type=8, InputBox returns a Range. You must use the Set statement to assign the result to a Range, as shown in the following example.

Set myRange = InputBox(prompt := "Sample", type := 8)

If you do not use the Set statement, the variable is set to the value in the Range, rather than the Range itself.

If you use the InputBox method to ask the user for a formula, you must use the FormulaLocal property to assign the formula to a Range. The input formula will be in the user's language. The InputBox method differs from the InputBox function in that the InputBox method allows selective validation of the user's input, and can be used with Excel objects, error values, and formulas. Application.InputBox calls the InputBox method; InputBox with no object qualifier calls the InputBox function.

InputType   Property

Applies To: DrawingObjects, EditBox, EditBoxes

Explanation: Returns or sets what type of input validation is applied to the contents of an edit box (one of xlFormula, xlInteger, xlNumber, xlReference, or xlText). Read-write.

Syntax: `object.InputType`

The `object` is required and is the object to which this property applies.

Insert   Method

Applies To: Characters, Pictures, Range

Explanation: Syntax 1 (Range object): Inserts a cell or a range of cells into the worksheet or macro sheet and shifts other cells away to make space. Syntax 2 (Characters object): Inserts a string before the selected characters. Syntax 3 (Pictures object): Inserts the specified file as a picture.

Syntax 1: `object.Insert(shift)`

Syntax 2: `object.Insert(string)`

Syntax 3: `object.Insert(filename, converter)`

The Insert method has the following object qualifier and named arguments:

The `object` is required. Insert cells at this range (Syntax 1) or insert string before this character (Syntax 2).

The `shift` argument is optional and specifies the way to shift the cells: either xlToRight or xlDown. If `shift` is omitted, a default is used based on the shape of the range.

The `string` argument is required and is the string to insert.

The `filename` argument is required and it specifies the file to insert.

The `converter` argument is required and specifies the picture converter to use when loading the file. Can be one of xlBMP, xlWMF, xlPLT, xlCGM, xlHGL, xlPIC, xlEPS, xlDRW, xlTIF, xlWPG, xlDXF, xlPCX, or xlPCT.

InsertFile   Method

Applies To: Module

Explanation: Adds text from a file to the end of the module.

Syntax: `object.InsertFile(fileName, merge)`

The InsertFile method has the following object qualifier and named arguments:

The `object` is required and is the Module object.

The *fileName* argument is required and is the name of the file containing the text that you wish to insert.

The *Merge* argument is optional. If *merge* is True, the new file is merged so that all declarations are at the top of the module and all procedures are below the declarations. If it is False or omitted, the new file is inserted at the insertion point.

Notes: You cannot insert text into a running code module. This applies both to running procedures as well as modules containing code that is stacked waiting to run after the current procedure returns.

Installed   Property

Applies To: AddIn

Explanation: True if the add-in is installed. Read-write.

Syntax: *object*.Installed

The *object* is required and is the AddIn object.

Note: Setting this property to True installs the add-in and calls its Auto_Add functions. Setting this property to False removes the add-in and calls its Auto_Remove functions.

Interactive   Property

Applies To: Application

Explanation: This property is True if Excel is in interactive mode; this property is usually True. If you set it the property to False, Excel will block all input from the keyboard and mouse (except input to dialog boxes that are displayed by your code). Blocking user input prevents the user from interfering with the macro as it moves or activates Excel objects. Read-write.

Syntax: *object*.Interactive

The *object* is required and is the Application object.

Notes: This property is useful if you are using DDE, AppleEvents, or OLE Automation to communicate with Excel from another application.

If you set this property to False, don't forget to set it back to True.

Intercept   Property

Applies To: Trendline

Explanation: Returns or sets the point where the trendline crosses the value axis. Read-write.

For help about using the Intercept worksheet function in Visual Basic, see "Using Worksheet Functions in Visual Basic."

Syntax: *object*.Intercept

The *object* is required and is the Trendline object.

Notes: Setting this property causes the InterceptIsAuto property to be set to False.

InterceptIsAuto   Property

Applies To: Trendline

Explanation: True if the point where the trendline crosses the value axis is automatically determined by the regression. Read-write.

Syntax: *object*.InterceptIsAuto

The *object* is required and is the Trendline object.

Notes: Setting the Intercept property causes this property to be set to False.

Interior   Property

Applies To: Arc, Arcs, AxisTitle, ChartArea, ChartObject, ChartObjects, ChartTitle, CheckBox, CheckBoxes, DataLabel, DataLabels, DownBars, Drawing, DrawingObjects, Drawings, Floor, GroupObject, GroupObjects, Legend, LegendKey, OLEObject, OLEObjects, OptionButton, OptionButtons, Oval, Ovals, Picture, Pictures, PlotArea, Point, Range, Rectangle, Rectangles, Series, Style, TextBox, TextBoxes, UpBars, Walls

Explanation: Returns or sets the Interior of the object. Read-write.

Syntax: *object*.Interior

The *object* is required and is the object to which this property applies.

International   Property

Applies To: Application

Explanation: Returns a 45-element array containing information about the current country and international settings. Read-only.

Syntax: *object*.International(*index*)

The *object* is required and is the Application object.

The *index* argument is optional and specifies a single setting to return, as shown in the following table:

Index	Built-in constant	Type	Meaning
1	xlCountryCode	number	Country version of Excel.
2	xlCountrySetting	number	Current country setting in the Windows Control Panel, or the country number as determined by your Apple system software.
3	xlDecimalSeparator	text	Decimal separator.
4	xlThousandsSeparator	text	Zero or thousands separator.
5	xlListSeparator	text	List separator.
6	xlUpperCaseRowLetter	text	Uppercase Row letter (for R1C1 references).
7	xlUpperCaseColumnLetter	text	Uppercase Column letter.
8	xlLowerCaseRowLetter	text	Lowercase Row letter.
9	xlLowerCaseColumnLetter	text	Lowercase Column letter.
10	xlLeftBracket	text	Character used instead of the left bracket ([) in R1C1 relative references.
11	xlRightBracket	text	Character used instead of the right bracket (]).
12	xlLeftBrace	text	Character used instead of the left brace ({) in array literals.
13	xlRightBrace	text	Character used instead of the right brace (}).
14	xlColumnSeparator	text	Character used to separate columns in array literals.
15	xlRowSeparator	text	Character used to separate rows.

continues

Index	Built-in constant	Type	Meaning
16	xlAlternateArraySeparator	text	Alternate array item separator to use if the current array separator is the same as the decimal separator.
17	xlDateSeparator	text	Date separator (/ in US).
18	xlTimeSeparator	text	Time separator (: in US).
19	xlYearCode	text	Year symbol in number formats (y in US).
20	xlMonthCode	text	Month symbol (m).
21	xlDayCode	text	Day symbol (d).
22	xlHourCode	text	Hour symbol (h).
23	xlMinuteCode	text	Minute symbol (m).
24	xlSecondCode	text	Second symbol (s).
25	xlCurrencyCode	text	Currency symbol ($).
26	xlGeneralFormatName	text	Name of the General number format.
27	xlCurrencyDigits	number	Number of decimal digits to use in currency formats.
28	xlCurrencyNegative	number	Indicates the currency format for negative currencies: 0 = ($x) or (x$)1 = -$x or -x$2 = $-x or x-$3 = $x- or x$-**Note:** The position of the currency symbol is determined by 37.
29	xlNoncurrencyDigits	number	Number of decimal digits to use in non-currency formats.

Index	Built-in constant	Type	Meaning
30	xlMonthNameChars	number	Number of characters to use in month names.
31	xlWeekdayNameChars	number	Number of characters to use in weekday names.
32	xlDateOrder	number	Indicates the date order: 0 = month-day-year1 = day-month-year2 = year-month-day
33	xl24HourClock	Boolean	True if using 24-hour time; False if using 12-hour time.
34	xlNonEnglishFunctions	Boolean	True if not displaying functions in English.
35	xlMetric	Boolean	True if using the metric system; False if using the English measurement system.
36	xlCurrencySpaceBefore	Boolean	True if adding a space before the currency symbol.
37	xlCurrencyBefore	Boolean	True if the currency symbol precedes the currency values; False if it goes after.
38	xlCurrencyMinusSign	Boolean	True if using a minus sign for negative numbers; False if using parentheses.
39	xlCurrencyTrailingZeros	Boolean	True if trailing zeros are displayed for zero currency values.
40	xlCurrencyLeadingZeros	Boolean	True if leading zeros are displayed for zero currency values.

continues

Index	Built-in constant	Type	Meaning
41	xlMonthLeadingZero	Boolean	True if a leading zero is displayed in months when months are displayed as numbers.
42	xlDayLeadingZero	Boolean	True if a leading zero is displayed in days.
43	xl4DigitYears	Boolean	True if using 4-digit years; False if using 2-digit years.
44	xlMDY	Boolean	True if the date order is Month-Day-Year when dates are displayed in the long form; False if the date order is Day-Month-Year.
45	xlTimeLeadingZero	Boolean	True if the leading zero is shown in the time.

Intersect   Method

Applies To: Application

Explanation: Returns the rectangular intersection of two or more ranges.

Syntax: *object*.`Intersect(`*arg1, arg2,...*`)`

The Intersect method has the following object qualifier and named arguments:

The *object* is optional and is the Application object.

arg1, arg2,... are required and are the intersecting ranges. At least two Range objects must be specified.

IsGap   Property

Applies To: ToolbarButton

Explanation: True if the button is really a gap (an extended space between buttons). Read-only.

Syntax: *object*.`IsGap`

The *object* is required and is the ToolbarButton object.

Italic   Property

Applies To: Font

Explanation: True if the font is italic. Read-write.

Syntax: `object.Italic`

The `object` is required and is the Font object (ActiveCell.Font, for example).

Item   Method

Explanation: Returns part of a collection. The Item method works like the accessor method for a collection. As an example, see the following code:

```
ActiveWorkbook.Worksheets.Item(1)
```

The preceding code is equivalent to the following line of code:

```
ActiveWorkbook.Worksheets(1)
```

The Item method is not generally required; you can usually use the collection-accessor form. However, you might need to use the Item method to return part of a collection if you assign a variable to the collection and pass it to a function or subprocedure, as shown in the following example.

```
Sub UseItem(wk as Worksheets)
```

✔   wk.Item(1).PageSetup.BottomMargin = 120

✔   'must use Item here End S

Iteration   Property

Applies To: Application

Explanation: True if Excel will use iteration to resolve circular references. Read-write.

Syntax: `object.Iteration`

The `object` is required and is the Application object.

Justify   Method

Applies To: Range

Explanation: Rearranges the text in a range so that it fills the range evenly.

Syntax: `object.Justify`

The `object` is required and is the range to justify.

Notes: If the range is not large enough, Excel displays a message that text will extend below the range. If you choose OK , justified text replaces the contents in cells extending beyond the selected range. To prevent this message from appearing, set the DisplayAlerts property to False.

Keywords   Property

Applies To: AddIn, Workbook

Explanation: Returns or sets the keywords for an object, as a string. Read-only for AddIn, read-write for Workbook.

Syntax: `object.Keywords`

The **object** is required and is the AddIn or Workbook object.

LabelRange   Property

Applies To: PivotField, PivotItem

Explanation: PivotField returns the cell containing the field label. If there are multiple cells containing this label, they are all returned. Read-only.

PivotItem returns a Range containing all the cells in the pivot table that contain the item.

Syntax: `Object.LabelRange`

The **Object** is the PivotField or PivotItem Object and is required.

Labels   Method

Applies To: Chart, DialogSheet, Worksheet

Explanation: Returns a single label (a Label Object, Syntax 1) or a collection of labels on the sheet (a Labels Object, Syntax 2).

Syntax 1: `Object.Labels(index)`

Syntax 2: `Object.Labels`

The Labels Method has the following Object qualifier and named arguments:

The **Object** is the Chart, DialogSheet or Worksheet Object and is required.

The **index** argument specifies the name or number of the label (can be an array to specify more than one) and is required for Syntax 1.

LargeButtons   Property

Applies To: Application

Explanation: True if Excel is using large toolbar buttons. False if Excel is using standard toolbar buttons. Read-write.

Syntax: `Object.LargeButtons`

The `Object` is the Application Object and is required.

LargeChange   Property

Applies To: DrawingObjects, ScrollBar, ScrollBars

Explanation: Returns or sets the amount that the scroll box increments or decrements for a page scroll (when the user clicks in the scroll bar body region). Read-write.

Syntax: `Object.LargeChange`

The `Object` is the Object to which this Property applies and is required.

LargeScroll   Method

Applies To: Pane, Window

Explanation: Scrolls the window by pages.

Syntax: `Object.LargeScroll(down, up, toRight, toLeft)`

The LargeScroll Method has the following Object qualifier and named arguments:

The `Object` is the window to scroll and is required.

The `down` argument is the number of pages to scroll the window down and is optional.

The `up` argument is the number of pages to scroll the window up and is optional.

The `toRight` argument is the number of pages to scroll the window and is optional.

The `toLeft` argument is the number of pages to scroll the window left and is optional.

Notes: If down and up are both specified, the window is scrolled by the difference of the arguments. For example, if down is three and up is six, the window is scrolled up three pages.

If toLeft and toRight are both specified, the window is scrolled by the difference of the arguments. For example, if toLeft is three and toRight is six, the window is scrolled right three pages.

Any of the arguments can be a negative number.

Left   Function

Explanation: Returns a specified number of characters from the left side of a string.

Syntax: `Left(string,length)`

The Left function syntax has these named-argument parts:

Part	Description
string	String expression from which the leftmost characters are returned. If string contains no valid data, Null is returned.
length	Numeric expression indicating how many characters to return. If 0, a zero-length string is returned. If greater than or equal to the number of characters in string, the entire string is returned.

Notes: To determine the number of characters in string, use the Len function.

Another function (LeftB) is provided for use with the double-byte character sets (DBCS) used in some Asian locales. Instead of specifying the number of characters to return, length specifies the number of bytes. In areas where DBCS is not used, LeftB behaves the same as Left.

Left   Property

Applies To: Application, Arc, Arcs, AxisTitle, Button, Buttons, ChartArea, ChartObject, ChartObjects, ChartTitle, CheckBox, CheckBoxes, DataLabel, DataLabels, DialogFrame, Drawing, DrawingObjects, Drawings, DropDown, DropDowns, EditBox, EditBoxes, GroupBox, GroupBoxes, GroupObject, GroupObjects, Label, Labels, Legend, Line, Lines, ListBox, ListBoxes, OLEObject, OLEObjects, OptionButton, OptionButtons, Oval, Ovals, Picture, Pictures, PlotArea, Range, Rectangle, Rectangles, ScrollBar, ScrollBars, Spinner, Spinners, TextBox, TextBoxes, Toolbar, Window

Explanation: Returns or sets the position of the specified Object, in points (1/72 inch). Read-write, except for the Range Object.

Syntax: `Object.Left`

The `Object` is the Object to which this Property applies and is required.

Notes: The Left Property has several different meanings, depending on the Object it is applied to.

Object	Meaning
Application	The distance from the left edge of the physical screen to the left edge of the main Excel window, in points.
ClipboardWindow	Macintosh only. The left position of the window, in points, measured from the left edge of the usable area (below the menus, left-docked toolbars, and/or the formula bar).
Range	The distance from the left edge of column A to the left edge of the range, in points. If the range is discontinuous, the first area is used. If the range is more than one column wide, the leftmost column in the range is used. Read-only.
Toolbar	If the toolbar is docked (its Position Property is not xlFloating), the number of points from the left edge of the toolbar to the left edge of the toolbar's docking area. If the toolbar is floating, the number of points from the left edge of the toolbar to the left edge of the Excel workspace.
Window	The left position of the window, in points, measured from the left edge of the usable area.
Arc, AxisTitle, Button, ChartArea, ChartTitle, CheckBox, DataLabel, DialogFrame, Drawing, DrawingObjects, DropDown, EditBox, GroupObject, GroupBox, Label, Legend, Line, ListBox, OLEObject, OptionButton, Oval, Picture, PlotArea, Rectangle, ScrollBar, Spinner, TextBox	The left position of the Object, in points, measured from the left edge of column A (on a worksheet) or the upper left of the chart area (on a chart).

If the window is maximized, the Application.Left Property returns a negative number that varies based on the width of the window border. Setting Application.Left to zero will make the window a tiny bit smaller than it would if the application window were maximized. In other words, if Application.Left is zero, the left border of the main Excel window will just be visible on screen. On the Macintosh, Application.Left is always zero. Setting this value to something else on the Macintosh will have no effect.

With Windows, if the Excel window is minimized, Application.Left controls the position of the icon.

LeftFooter   Property

Applies To: PageSetup

Explanation: Returns or sets the left part of the footer. Read-write.

Syntax: `Object.LeftFooter`

The *Object* is the PageSetup Object (ActiveSheet.PageSetup, for example) and is required.

Notes: Special format codes can be used in the footer text.

LeftHeader   Property

Applies To: PageSetup

Explanation: Returns or sets the left part of the header. Read-write.

Syntax: `Object.LeftHeader`

The *Object* is the PageSetup Object (ActiveSheet.PageSetup, for example) and is required.

Notes: Special format codes can be used in the header text.

LeftMargin   Property

Applies To: PageSetup

Explanation: Returns or sets the size of the left margin, in points (1/72 inch). Read-write.

Syntax: `Object.LeftMargin`

The *Object* is the PageSetup Object (ActiveSheet.PageSetup, for example) and is required.

Notes: Margins are set or returned in points. Use the Application.InchesToPoints or Application.CentimetersToPoints function to convert.

Legend   Property

Applies To: Chart

Explanation: Returns the Legend for the chart. Read-only.

Syntax: *Object*.Legend

The *Object* is the Chart Object and is required.

LegendEntries   Method

Applies To: Legend

Explanation: Returns a single legend entry (a LegendEntry Object, Syntax 1) or a collection of legend entries for the legend (a LegendEntries Object, Syntax 2).

Syntax 1: *Object*.LegendEntries(*index*)

Syntax 2: *Object*.LegendEntries

The LegendEntries Method has the following Object qualifier and named arguments:

The *Object* is the Legend Object and is required.

The *index* argument is required for Syntax 1 and specifies the name or number of the legend entry.

LegendKey   Property

Applies To: LegendEntry

Explanation: Returns the LegendKey Object associated with the entry.

Syntax: *Object*.LegendKey

The *Object* is the LegendEntry Object and is required.

LibraryPath   Property

Applies To: Application

Explanation: Returns the path to the LIBRARY directory, not including the final separator. Read-only.

Syntax: *Object*.LibraryPath

The *Object* is the Application Object and is required.

Line3DGroup   Property

Applies To: Chart

Explanation: Returns the line ChartGroup on a 3D chart.

Syntax: *Object*.Line3DGroup

The *Object* is the Chart Object and is required.

LineGroups   Method

Applies To: Chart

Explanation: On a 2D chart, returns a single line chart group (a ChartGroup Object, Syntax 1), or a collection of the line chart groups (a ChartGroups collection, Syntax 2).

Syntax 1: `Object.LineGroups(index)`

Syntax 2: `Object.LineGroups`

The LineGroups Method has the following Object qualifier and named arguments:

The **Object** is the Chart Object and is required.

The **index** is required for Syntax 1, and specifies the chart group.

Lines   Method

Applies To: Chart, DialogSheet, Worksheet

Explanation: Returns a single line (a Line Object, Syntax 1) or a collection of lines (a Lines Object, Syntax 2) on the chart, dialog sheet, or worksheet. Read-only.

Syntax: 1: `Object.Lines(index)`

Syntax: 2: `Object.Lines`

The Lines Method has the following Object qualifier and named arguments:

The **Object** is the Object to which this Method applies and is required.

The **index** is required for Syntax 1, and is the name or number of the line.

Notes: This Property returns both lines and arrows. The only difference between a line and an arrow is the ArrowHeadStyle Property.

LineStyle   Property

Applies To: Border, Borders

Explanation: Returns or sets the line style of the border. Can be one of xlContinuous, xlDash, xlDot, xlDashDot, xlDashDotDot, xlGray50, xlGray75, xlGray25, xlDouble, xlNone, or xlAutomatic. Read-write.

Syntax: `Object.LineStyle`

The **Object** is the Border or Borders Object and is required.

LinkCombo   Method

Applies To: DrawingObjects

Explanation: Creates a combination list-edit box from a list box and an edit box. The edit box and list box to be linked must be the only two objects in the DrawingObjects collection.

Syntax: *Object*.LinkCombo(*link*)

The LinkCombo Method has the following Object qualifier and named arguments:

The *Object* is the DrawingObjects collection and is required.

The *link* argument is optional. If omitted or True, the objects are linked so that the edit box text is always updated to the current selection in the list box whenever the user selects a new list box item. If False, the link between the objects is broken.

Notes: This function is only useful on a dialog sheet, because edit boxes are not allowed on a worksheet or chart. To see how to use the LinkCombo Method, use the macro recorder to record creating a Combination List-Edit control on a dialog sheet.

LinkedCell   Property

Applies To: CheckBox, CheckBoxes, DrawingObjects, DropDown, DropDowns, ListBox, ListBoxes, OptionButton, OptionButtons, ScrollBar, ScrollBars, Spinner, Spinners

Explanation: Returns or sets the cell or cells (as a string reference) linked to the control's value. When a value is placed in the cell, the control takes this value. Likewise, if the value of the control changes, that value is also placed in the cell.

Syntax: *Object*.LinkedCell

The *Object* is the Object to which this Property applies and is required.

Notes: This Property cannot be used with multiselect list boxes.

LinkedObject   Property

Applies To: DropDown, EditBox, ListBox

Explanation: Returns the name of the Object linked to an edit box, list box, or drop-down control. For a DropDown Object, returns the name of the drop-down control if it can be edited, or False if it is not editable. Read-only.

Syntax: *Object*.LinkedObject

The *Object* is the Object to which this Property applies and is required.

LinkInfo   Method

Applies To: Workbook

Explanation: Returns information on link date and update state.

Syntax: *Object*`.LinkInfo(`*name*`,` *linkInfo*`,` *type*`,` *editionRef*`)`

The LinkInfo Method has the following Object qualifier and named arguments:

The ***Object*** is the Workbook Object and is required.

The ***name*** argument is required, and specifies the name of the link, as returned from the LinkSources Method.

The ***linkInfo*** argument is required, and specifies the type of information to be returned about the link (either xlUpdateState or xlEditionDate). xlEditionDate applies only to editions. For xlUpdateState, this Method returns 1 if the link updates automatically, or 2 if the link must be updated manually.

The *type* argument is optional, and specifies the type of link to return. Can be one of xlOLELinks (also handles DDE links), xlPublishers, or xlSubscribers.

The *editionRef* argument is optional. If the link is an edition, this argument specifies the edition reference as a string in R1C1-style form. This argument is required if there is more than one publisher or subscriber with the same name in the workbook.

LinkSources   Method

Applies To: Workbook

Explanation: Returns an array of links in the workbook. The names in the array are the names of the linked documents, editions, or DDE or OLE servers. Returns Empty if there are no links.

Syntax: *Object*`.LinkSources(`*type*`)`

The LinkSources Method has the following Object qualifier and named arguments:

The ***Object*** is the Workbook Object and is required.

The *type* argument is optional, and pecifies the type of link to return. Can be one of xlExcelLinks, xlOLELinks (also handles DDE links), xlPublishers, or xlSubscribers.

Notes: The format of the array is a single-dimensional array for all types but publisher and subscriber. The returned strings contain the name of the link source in the notation appropriate for the link type. For example, DDE links use the "Server | Document!Item" syntax.

For publisher and subscriber links, the returned array is two-dimensional. The first column of the array contains the names of the edition, and the second column contains the references of the editions as text.

List   **Property**

Applies To: DrawingObjects, DropDown, DropDowns, ListBox, ListBoxes

Explanation: Returns or sets the text entries in a list box or drop-down list box, as an array of strings (Syntax 1), or returns or sets a single text entry (Syntax 2). Returns an error if there are no entries in the list. Read-write.

Syntax 1: `Object.List`

Syntax 2: `Object.List(index)`

The `Object` is the Object to which this Property applies and is required.

The `index` argument is required for syntax 2, and is the text entry number.

Notes: Setting this Property clears any ListFillRange.

ListBoxes   **Method**

Applies To: Chart, DialogSheet, Worksheet

Explanation: Returns a single list-box control (a ListBox Object, Syntax 1) or a collection of list-box controls on the chart or sheet (a ListBoxes Object, Syntax 2).

Syntax 1: `Object.ListBoxes(index)`

Syntax 2: `Object.ListBoxes`

The ListBoxes Method has the following Object qualifier and named arguments:

The `Object` is the Chart, DialogSheet, or Worksheet Object and is required.

The `index` argument is required for Syntax 1. Specifies the name or number of the list box (can be an array to specify more than one).

ListCount   **Property**

Applies To: DropDown, ListBox

Explanation: Returns the number of entries in a list box or drop-down list box. Returns zero if there are no entries in the list. Read-only.

Syntax: `Object.ListCount`

The `Object` is the Object to which this Property applies and is required.

ListFillRange   **Property**

Applies To: DrawingObjects, DropDown, DropDowns, ListBox, ListBoxes

Explanation: Returns or sets the worksheet range used to fill the list box, as a string.

Setting this Property destroys any existing list in the list box. Read-write.

Syntax: `Object.ListFillRange`

The `Object` is the Object to which this Property applies and is required.

Notes: Excel reads the contents of every cell in the range and puts it into the list box. The list will track changes in the range cells.

If the list in the list box was created with the AddItem Method, this Property returns an empty string ("").

ListIndex   Property

Applies To: DrawingObjects, DropDown, DropDowns, ListBox, ListBoxes

Explanation: Returns or sets the index of the currently selected item in a list box or drop-down list box. Read-write.

Syntax: `Object.ListIndex`

The `Object` is the Object to which this Property applies and is required.

Notes: This Property cannot be used with multiselect list boxes. Use the Selected Property instead.

ListNames   Method

Applies To: Range

Explanation: Pastes a list of all nonhidden names on the worksheet, beginning at the first cell of the range.

Syntax: `Object.ListNames`

The `Object` is the the worksheet for which to list names, and the start of the range where the names will be listed. It is required.

Notes: Use the Names Method to return a collection of all the names on a worksheet.

LocationInTable   Property

Applies To: Range

Explanation: Returns a constant that describes the part of the PivotTable that contains the top left corner of the specified range. Can be one of xlRowHeader, xlColumnHeader, xlPageHeader, xlDataHeader, xlRowItem, xlColumnItem, xlPageItem, xlDataItem, or xlTableBody. Read-only.

Syntax: `Object.LocationInTable`

The `Object` is the Range Object and is required.

LockedText   Property

Applies To: Button, Buttons, CheckBox, CheckBoxes, DialogFrame, DrawingObjects, GroupBox, GroupBoxes, Label, Labels, OptionButton, OptionButtons, TextBox, TextBoxes

Explanation: True if the text in the Object will be locked to prevent changes when the document is protected. Read-write.

Syntax: `Object.LockedText`

The `Object` is the Object to which this Property applies and is required.

MacroType   Property

Applies To: Name

Explanation: Returns or sets what the name refers to, as shown in the following table. Read-write.

Value	Meaning
xlCommand	Name is a user-defined macro.
xlFunction	Name is a user-defined function.
xlNone	Name is not a function or macro.

Syntax: `Object.MacroType`

The `Object` is the Name Object and is required.

Mailer   Property

Applies To: Workbook

Explanation: Returns the PowerTalk Mailer attached to the workbook. Read-only.

Syntax: `Object.Mailer`

The `Object` is the Workbook Object and is required.

Notes: The Mailer Object contains the properties needed to mail workbooks with PowerTalk. To mail a workbook, turn on the mailer with the HasMailer Property, set the mailer properties, and then send the workbook and mailer with the SendMailer Method.

MailLogoff   Method

Applies To: Application

Explanation: Closes an established MAPI mail session.

Syntax: *Object*.MailLogoff

The *Object* is the Application Object and is required.

MailLogon   Method

Applies To: Application

Explanation: Logs into MAPI Mail and establishes a mail session. A mail session must be established before mail or document routing functions can be used.

Syntax: *Object*.MailLogon(*name, password, downloadNewMail*)

The MailLogon Method has the following Object qualifier and named arguments:

The *Object* is the Application Object and is required.

The *name* is optional, and is the mail account name. If omitted, the default mail account name is used.

The *password* is optional and is the mail account password.

The *downloadNewMail* is optional. If True, new mail is downloaded immediately.

Notes: Previously established mail sessions are logged off before an attempt is made to establish the new session.

Omit both the name and password parameters to piggyback on the system default mail session.

MailSession   Property

Applies To: Application

Explanation: Returns the MAPI mail session number as a hexadecimal string (if there is an active session), or Null if there is no session. Read-only.

Syntax: *Object*.MailSession

The *Object* is the Application Object and is required.

Notes: This Property is not used on PowerTalk mail systems.

MailSystem **Property**

Applies To: Application

Explanation: Returns the mail system installed on the host machine (one of xlNoMailSystem, xlMAPI, or xlPowerTalk). Read-only.

Syntax: *Object*.MailSystem

The *Object* is the Application Object and is required.

MajorGridlines **Property**

Applies To: Axis

Explanation: Returns the major Gridlines for the specified axis. Only axes in the primary axis group can have gridlines. Read-only.

Syntax: *Object*.MajorGridlines

The *Object* is the Axis Object and is required.

MajorTickMark **Property**

Applies To: Axis

Explanation: Returns or sets the type of major tick mark for the specified axis (one of xlNone, xlInside, xlOutside, or xlCross). Read-write.

Syntax: *Object*.MajorTickMark

The *Object* is the Axis Object and is required.

MajorUnit **Property**

Applies To: Axis

Explanation: Returns or sets the major units for the value axis. Applies only to the value axis. Read-write.

Syntax: *Object*.MajorUnit

The *Object* is the Axis Object and is required.

Notes: Setting this Property sets the MajorUnitIsAuto Property to False.

Use the TickMarkSpacing Property to set tick mark spacing on the category axis.

MajorUnitIsAuto   **Property**

Applies To: Axis

Explanation: True if Excel calculates major units for the value axis. Applies only to the value axis. Read-write.

Syntax: `Object.MajorUnitIsAuto`

The `Object` is the Axis Object and is required.

Notes: Setting the MajorUnit Property sets this Property to False.

MarkerBackgroundColor   **Property**

Applies To: LegendKey, Point, Series

Explanation: Returns or sets the marker background color as an RGB value. Line, scatter and radar charts only. Read-write.

Syntax: `Object.MarkerBackgroundColor`

The `Object` is the LegendKey, Point, or Series Object and is required.

MarkerBackgroundColorIndex   **Property**

Applies To: LegendKey, Point, Series

Explanation: Returns or sets the marker background color as an index into the current color palette (a value from one to 56, or xlNone if there is no background color). Line, scatter and radar charts only. Read-write.

Syntax: `Object.MarkerBackgroundColorIndex`

The `Object` is the LegendKey, Point, or Series Object and is required.

MarkerForegroundColor   **Property**

Applies To: LegendKey, Point, Series

Explanation: Returns or sets the foreground color of the marker, specified as an RGB value. Line, scatter, and radar charts only. Read-write.

Syntax: `Object.MarkerForegroundColor`

The `Object` is the LegendKey, Point, or Series Object and is required.

MarkerForegroundColorIndex   Property

Applies To: LegendKey, Point, Series

Explanation: Returns or sets the marker foreground color as an index into the current color palette (a value from one to 56, or xlNone if there is no foreground color). Line, scatter, and radar charts only. Read-write.

Syntax: *Object*.MarkerForegroundColorIndex

The *Object* is the LegendKey, Point, or Series Object and is required.

MarkerStyle   Property

Applies To: LegendKey, Point, Series

Explanation: Returns or sets the marker style for a point or series on a line chart, a scatter chart, or a radar chart. Read-write.

Syntax: *Object*.MarkerStyle

The *Object* is the LegendKey, Point or Series Object and is required.

Notes: This Property can have one of the following values:

Value	Meaning
xlNone	No markers.
xlAutomatic	Automatic markers.
xlSquare	Square markers.
xlDiamond	Diamond-shaped markers.
xlTriangle	Triangular markers.
xlX	Square markers with an X.
xlStar	Square markers with an asterisk.
xlDot	Short bar markers.
xlDash	Long bar markers.
xlCircle	Circular markers.
xlPlus	Square markers with a plus sign.
xlPicture	Picture markers.

MathCoprocessorAvailable   **Property**

Applies To: Application

Explanation: True if a math coprocessor is available. Read-only.

Syntax: *Object*.`MathCoprocessorAvailable`

The *Object* is the Application Object and is required.

Max   **Property**

Applies To: DrawingObjects, ScrollBar, ScrollBars, Spinner, Spinners

Explanation: Returns or sets the maximum value of a scroll bar or spinner range. The scroll bar or spinner will not take on values above this maximum value. Read-write.

For help about using the Max worksheet function in Visual Basic, see Using Worksheet Functions in Visual Basic.

Syntax: *Object*.`Max`

The *Object* is the Object to which this Property applies and is required.

Notes: The value of the Max Property must be greater than the value of the Min Property.

MaxChange   **Property**

Applies To: Application

Explanation: Returns or sets the maximum amount of change that is used in each iteration as Excel tries to resolve circular references. Read-write.

Syntax: *Object*.`MaxChange`

The *Object* is the Application Object and is required.

Notes: The MaxIterations Property sets the maximum number of iterations used when resolving circular references.

MaxIterations   **Property**

Applies To: Application

Explanation: Returns or sets the maximum number of iterations that will be allowed to resolve a circular reference. Read-write.

Syntax: *Object*.`MaxIterations`

The *Object* is the Application Object and is required.

Notes: The MaxChange Property sets the maximum amount of change used in each iteration when resolving circular references.

MaximumScale   Property

Applies To: Axis

Explanation: Returns or sets the maximum value on the value axis. Applies only to the value axis. Read-write.

Syntax: `Object.MaximumScale`

The `Object` is the Axis Object and is required.

Notes: Setting this Property sets the MaximumScaleIsAuto Property to False.

MaximumScaleIsAuto   Property

Applies To: Axis

Explanation: True if Excel calculates the maximum value for the value axis. Applies only to the value axis. Read-write.

Syntax: `Object.MaximumScaleIsAuto`

The `Object` is the Axis Object and is required.

Notes: Setting the MaximumScale Property sets this Property to False.

MemoryFree   Property

Applies To: Application

Explanation: Returns the amount of memory that is still available for Excel to use, in bytes. Read-only.

Syntax: `Object.MemoryFree`

The `Object` is the Application Object and is required.

MemoryTotal   Property

Applies To: Application

Explanation: Returns the total amount of memory that is available to Excel, including memory already in use, in bytes. Read-only.

Syntax: `Object.MemoryTotal`

The `Object` is the Application Object and is required.

Notes: MemoryTotal is equal to MemoryUsed + MemoryFree.

MemoryUsed   Property

Applies To: Application

Explanation: Returns the amount of memory that is currently in use by Excel, in bytes. Read-only.

Syntax: `Object.MemoryUsed`

The `Object` is the Application Object and is required.

MenuBars   Method

Applies To: Application

Explanation: Returns a single menu bar (a MenuBar Object, Syntax 1) or a collection of the top-level menu bars (the MenuBars Object, Syntax 2). Read-only.

Syntax 1: `Object.MenuBars(index)`

Syntax 2: `Object.MenuBars`

The MenuBars Method has the following Object qualifier and named arguments:

The `Object` is the Application Object and is required.

The `index` argument is required for Syntax 1, and is the name or number of the menu bar. Several predefined constants are available, as shown in the following list.

Constant	Description
xlWorksheet	Worksheet, macro sheet and dialog sheet.
xlChart	Chart.
xlModule	Visual Basic module.
xlNoDocuments	No documents open.
xlInfo	Info Window.
xlWorksheetShort	Short Worksheet menu (Excel version 3 compatibility).
xlChartShort	Short Chart menu (Excel version 3 compatibility).
xlWorksheet4	Old worksheet menu bar (Excel version 4 compatibility).
xlChart4	Old chart menu bar (Excel version 4 compatibility).

MenuItems Method

Applies To: Menu

Explanation: Returns a single menu item (a MenuItem Object, Syntax 1), or a collection of the menu items (a MenuItems Object, Syntax 2) on the menu. Read-only.

Syntax 1: `Object.MenuItems(index)`

Syntax 2: `Object.MenuItems`

The MenuItems Method has the following Object qualifier and named arguments:

The *Object* is the Menu Object and is required.

The *index* argument is required for Syntax 1, and is the name or number of the menu item.

Menus Method

Applies To: MenuBar

Explanation: Returns a single menu (a Menu Object, Syntax 1), or a collection of the menus (a Menus Object, Syntax 2) on the menu bar. Read-only.

Syntax 1: `Object.Menus(index)`

Syntax 2: `Object.Menus`

The Menus Method has the following Object qualifier and named arguments:

The *Object* is the MenuBar Object and is required.

The *index* argument is required for Syntax 1, and is the name or number of the menu. Can be one of the following constants:

Constant	Description
xlWorksheet	Worksheet, macro sheet, and dialog sheet.
xlChart	Chart.
xlModule	Visual Basic module.
xlNoDocuments	No documents open.
xlInfo	Info Window.
xlWorksheetShort	Short Worksheet menu (Excel 3 compatibility).
xlChartShort	Short Chart menu (Excel 3 compatibility).
xlWorksheet4	Old worksheet menu bar (Excel 4 compatibility).
xlChart4	Old chart menu bar (Excel 4 compatibility).

Merge   Method

Applies To: Scenarios, Styles

Explanation: Syntax 1: Merges the scenarios from another sheet into the collection of scenarios.

Syntax 2: Merges the styles from another workbook into the collection of styles.

Syntax 1: *Object*.Merge(*source*)

Syntax 2: *Object*.Merge(*workbook*)

The Merge Method has the following Object qualifier and named arguments:

The *Object* is the Scenarios or Styles Object and is required.

The *source* argument is required for Syntax 1, and is the Worksheet Object, or name of the sheet containing scenarios to merge.

The *workbook* argument is required for Syntax 2, and is the Workbook Object containing styles to merge.

Message   Property

Applies To: RoutingSlip

Explanation: Returns or sets the message text of the routing slip. This text is used as the body text of mail messages used to route the workbook. Read-write.

Syntax: *Object*.Message

The *Object* is the RoutingSlip Object and is required.

Mid   Function

Explanation: Returns a specified number of characters from a string.

Syntax: Mid(*string*,*start*,*length*)

The Mid function syntax has these parts:

Part	Description
string	String expression from which characters are returned. If string contains no valid data, Null is returned.
start	Character position in string at which the part to be taken begins. If start is greater than the number of characters in string, Mid returns a zero-length string.

Part	Description
length	Number of characters to return. If omitted or if there are fewer than length characters in the text (including the character at start), all characters from the start position to the end of the string are returned.

Notes: To determine the number of characters in string, use the Len function.

Another function (MidB) is provided for use with the double-byte character sets (DBCS) used in some Asian locales. Instead of specifying the number of characters to return, length specifies the number of bytes. In areas where DBCS is not used, MidB behaves the same as Mid.

Min   Property

Applies To: DrawingObjects, ScrollBar, ScrollBars, Spinner, Spinners

Explanation: Returns or sets the minimum value of a scroll bar or spinner range. The scroll bar or spinner will not take on values below this minimum value. Read-write.

For help about using the Min worksheet function in Visual Basic, see Using Worksheet Functions in Visual Basic.

Syntax: *Object*.Min

The *Object* is the Object to which this Property applies and is required.

Notes: The value of the Min Property must be less than the value of the Max Property.

MinimumScale   Property

Applies To: Axis

Explanation: Returns or sets the minimum value on the value axis. Applies only to the value axis. Read-write.

Syntax: *Object*.MinimumScale

The *Object* is the Axis Object and is required.

Notes: Setting this Property sets the MinimumScaleIsAuto Property to False.

MinimumScaleIsAuto   Property

Applies To: Axis

Explanation: True if Excel calculates the minimum value for the value axis. Applies only to the value axis. Read-write.

Syntax: *Object*.MinimumScaleIsAuto

The *Object* is the Axis Object and is required.

Notes: Setting the MinimumScale Property sets this Property to False.

MinorGridlines   Property

Applies To: Axis

Explanation: Returns the minor Gridlines for the specified axis. Only axes in the primary axis group can have gridlines. Read-only.

Syntax: *Object*.MinorGridlines

The *Object* is the Axis Object and is required.

MinorTickMark   Property

Applies To: Axis

Explanation: Returns or sets the type of minor tick mark for the specified axis (one of xlNone, xlInside, xlOutside, or xlCross). Read-write.

Syntax: *Object*.MinorTickMark

The *Object* is the Axis Object and is required.

MinorUnit   Property

Applies To: Axis

Explanation: Returns or sets the minor units on the value axis. Applies only to the value axis. Read-write.

Syntax: *Object*.MinorUnit

The *Object* is the Axis Object and is required.

Notes: Setting this Property sets the MinorUnitIsAuto Property to False.

Use the TickMarkSpacing Property to set tick mark spacing on the category axis.

MinorUnitIsAuto   Property

Applies To: Axis

Explanation: True if Excel calculates minor units for the value axis. Applies only to the value axis. Read-write.

Syntax: *Object*.MinorUnitIsAuto

The **Object** is the Axis Object and is required.

Notes: Setting the MinorUnit Property sets this Property to False.

Modules   Method

Applies To: Application, Workbook

Explanation: Returns a module (a Module Object, Syntax 1) or a collection of all modules (a Modules Object, Syntax 2) in the workbook. Read-only.

Syntax 1: `Object.Modules(index)`

Syntax 2: `Object.Modules`

The Modules Method has the following Object qualifier and named arguments:

The **Object** is the Workbook Object and is required.

The **index** argument is required for Syntax 1, and is the name or number of the module to return.

Month   Function

Explanation: Returns a whole number between 1 and 12, inclusive, representing the month of the year.

Syntax: `Month(date)`

The *date* named argument is limited to a date or numbers and strings, in any combination, that can represent a date. If date contains no valid data, Null is returned.

MouseAvailable   Property

Applies To: Application

Explanation: True if a mouse is available (always True on the Macintosh). Read-only.

Syntax: `Object.MouseAvailable`

The **Object** is the Application Object and is required.

Move   Method

Applies To: Chart, Charts, DialogSheet, DialogSheets, Module, Modules, Sheets, ToolbarButton, Worksheet, Worksheets

Explanation: Syntax 1: Moves the sheet to another location in the workbook.

Syntax 2: Moves a toolbar button to another position, either on the same toolbar or to another toolbar.

Syntax 1: `Object.Move(before, after)`

Syntax 2: `Object.Move(toolbar, before)`

The Move Method has the following Object qualifier and named arguments:

The **`Object`** is the Object to which this Method applies and is required.

The **`before`** argument is:

- ✔ Optional for Syntax 1. The sheet before which this sheet will be moved. You cannot specify before if you specify after.

- ✔ Required for Syntax 2. Specifies the new button position as a number from 1 to the number of existing buttons + 1. Gaps count as one position. Buttons to the right of this position are moved right (or down) to make room for the moved button.

The `after` argument is optional, and is the sheet after which this sheet will be moved. You cannot specify *after* if you specify *before*.

The **`toolbar`** argument is required for Syntax 2, and specifies the toolbar Object to move the button to.

Notes: If you do not specify either before or after, Excel creates a new workbook containing the moved sheet.

MoveAfterReturn   Property

Applies To: Application

Explanation: True if the selection will be moved as soon as the ENTER (RETURN) key is pressed. Read-write.

Syntax: `Object.MoveAfterReturn`

The **`Object`** is the Application Object and is required.

MultiLine   Property

Applies To: DrawingObjects, EditBox, EditBoxes

Explanation: True if the edit box is multiline enabled. Read-write.

Syntax: `Object.MultiLine`

The **`Object`** is the Object to which this Property applies and is required.

MultiSelect   Property

Applies To: DrawingObjects, ListBox, ListBoxes

Explanation: Returns or sets the selection mode of the list box (or collection of list boxes). Can be one of xlNone, xlSimple, or xlExtended. Read-write.

Syntax: *Object*.**MultiSelect**

The *Object* is the Object to which this Property applies and is required.

Notes: Single select (xlNone) allows only one item at a time to be selected. Any click or spacebar press deselects the currently selected item and selects the clicked-upon item.

Simple MultiSelect (xlSimple) toggles the selection on an item in the list when it is selected with the mouse or the spacebar is pressed when the focus is on the item. This mode is appropriate for pick lists where multiple items are often selected.

Extended MultiSelect (xlExtended) normally acts like a single-selection list box, so that mouse clicks on an item cancel all other selected items. When you hold down SHIFT while clicking the mouse or pressing an ARROW key, items are sequentially selected from the current item as the user navigates. When you hold down CTRL while clicking the mouse, single items are added to the list selection. This mode is appropriate when multiple items are allowed but not often used.

You can use the Value or ListIndex properties to get and set the selected item in a single-select list box. You must use the Selected Property to get and set the selected items in a multiselect list box.

Multiselect list boxes cannot be linked to cells with the LinkedCell Property.

Name   Property

Applies To: AddIn, Application, Arc, AxisTitle, Button, Chart, ChartArea, ChartObject, ChartTitle, CheckBox, Corners, DataLabel, DataLabels, DialogFrame, DialogSheet, DownBars, Drawing, DropDown, DropLines, EditBox, ErrorBars, Floor, Font, Gridlines, GroupBox, GroupObject, HiLoLines, Label, Legend, Line, ListBox, Module, Name, OLEObject, OptionButton, Oval, Picture, PivotField, PivotItem, PivotTable, PlotArea, Range, Rectangle, Scenario, ScrollBar, Series, SeriesLines, Spinner, Style, TextBox, TickLabels, Toolbar, ToolbarButton, Trendline, UpBars, Walls, Workbook, Worksheet

Explanation: Returns or sets the name of the object. See the Notes section for details.

Syntax: *object*.**Name**

The *object* is the object to which this property applies and is required.

Notes: The meaning of this property depends on the object, as shown in the following table. The name of a Range object is a Name object. For every other object, the name is a string.

Object	Name
AddIn	The file name of the add-in, not including its path on disk. Read-only.
Application	The name of the application. Read-only.
Chart	If the chart is a page in the workbook, this is the name of that page as shown on the tab. If the chart is an embedded object, it is the name of the object. Read-write.
Control or drawing object	The name of the control or drawing object, in the language of the macro. Read-write.
DialogSheet, Module, Worksheet	The name of the sheet, as shown on the tab. Read-write.
Font	The name of the font.
Name	The name itself. If it is one of the built-in names it will be translated to the language of the macro. Read-write.
OLEObject	The name of the object. Read-write.
PivotField	The name of the field in the pivot table. Read-write.
PivotItem	The name of the item in the pivot table field. Read-write.
PivotTable	The name of the pivot table. Read-write.
Range	The name of the range (this is a Name object). Assign to this property to define a name. If the range has multiple names, returns the first one. Read-write.
Scenario	The name of the scenario. Read-write.
Series	The name of the series. Read-write.
Style	The name of the style. If the style is a built-in style, this will return the name of the style in the language of the macro. Read only.
Toolbar	The name of the toolbar. If the toolbar is built-in, returns the name in the language of the macro. Read-write for custom toolbars, read-only for built-in toolbars.
ToolbarButton	The name of the button (as text), in the language of the macro writer. Only applies to built-in buttons. Read-only.

Object	Name
Trendline	The name of the trendline as it will appear in the legend. Read-write.
Workbook	The name of the workbook, not including its path on disk. Read-only.

NameIsAuto   Property

Applies To: Trendline

Explanation: True if Excel automatically determines the name of the trendline. Read-write.

Syntax: *object*.`NameIsAuto`

The *object* is the Trendline object and is required.

NameLocal   Property

Applies To: Name, Style

Explanation: Returns or sets the name of the object, in the language of the user. Read-write for Name, read-only for Style.

Syntax: *object*.`NameLocal`

The *object* is the Name or Style object and is required.

Notes: If the style is a built-in style, this property returns the name of the style in the language of the current locale.

Names   Method

Applies To: Application, Workbook

Explanation: Returns a single name (a Name object, Syntax 1) or a collection of names (the Names object, Syntax 2). Read-only.

Syntax 1: *object*.`Names`(*index, indexLocal, refersTo*)

Syntax 2: *object*.`Names`

The Names method has the following object qualifier and named arguments:

The *object* argument is optional for Application, required for Workbook. It specifies the object containing names to return.

The *index* argument is optional (Syntax 1 requires one of the three arguments), and is the name or number of the defined name to return.

The *indexLocal* argument is optional (Syntax 1 requires one of the three arguments), and is the name of the defined name, in the language of the user. No names will be translated if you use this argument.

The *refersTo* argument is optional (Syntax 1 requires one of the three arguments), and is what the name refers to. This allows you to get a name by what it refers to.

Notes: For Syntax 1, you must specify one (and only one) of the three arguments.

This method returns names in the active workbook for the Application object.

NavigateArrow   Method

Applies To: Range

Explanation: Navigates a tracer arrow for the specified range to the precedent, dependent, or error-causing cell or cells. Selects the precedent, dependent, or error cell and returns the new selection Range object. This method causes an error if applied to a cell without visible tracer arrows.

Syntax: `object.NavigateArrow(towardPrecedent, arrowNumber, linkNumber)`

The NavigateArrow method has the following object qualifier and named arguments:

The **object** is the Range object and is required.

The **towardPrecedent** argument is required, and specifies the direction to navigate (True to navigate toward precedents or False to navigate toward dependents).

The *arrowNumber* argument is optional, and specifies the arrow number to navigate, corresponding to the numbered reference in the cell's formula. If this argument is omitted, this first arrow is navigated.

The *linkNumber* argument is optional. If the arrow is an external reference arrow, this argument indicates which external reference to follow. If this argument is omitted, the first external reference is followed.

NewWindow   Method

Applies To: Window, Workbook

Explanation: Creates a new window for the workbook, or a copy of the specified window.

Syntax: `object.NewWindow`

The **object** is the Window or Workbook object and is required.

Next

Property

Applies To: Chart, DialogSheet, Module, Range, Worksheet

Explanation: Returns the next sheet or cell (a Range object). Read-only.

Syntax: `object.Next`

The **object** is the object to which this property applies and is required.

Notes: If the object is a range, this property emulates the TAB key, although the property returns the next cell without selecting it.

On a protected sheet, this property returns the next unlocked cell. On an unprotected sheet, this always returns the cell to the right of the specified cell.

NextLetter

Method

Applies To: Application

Explanation: Opens the oldest unread Excel letter from the In Tray. Available only in Excel for the Macintosh with the PowerTalk mail system extension installed.

Syntax: `object.NextLetter`

The **object** is the Application object and is required.

Notes: This method returns a Workbook object for the newly opened workbook, or Null if there are no more workbooks to open.

This method generates an error if it is used in Windows.

NoteText

Method

Applies To: Range

Explanation: Returns or sets the cell note associated with the upper left cell in this range. Read-write.

Syntax: `object.NoteText(text, start, length)`

The **object** is the range to which this property applies and is required.

The `text` argument is optional. If specified, it contains the text to add to the note (up to 255 characters). The text is inserted starting at position start, replacing length characters of the existing note. If this argument is omitted, this method returns the current text of the note starting at position start, for length characters.

The `start` argument is optional. It specifies the starting position for the set or returned text. If omitted, this method starts at the first character. This argument is omitted if there is no existing note. Specify a number larger than the number of characters in the existing note to append text to the note.

The *length* argument is optional. It specifies the number of characters to set or return. If this argument is omitted, Excel sets or returns characters from the start position to the end of the note (up to 255 characters). If there are more than 255 characters from start to the end of the note, this method returns only 255 characters.

Notes: To add a note containing more than 255 characters, use this method once to specify the first 255 characters, then append the remainder of the note 255 characters at a time.

NumberFormat   Property

Applies To: DataLabel, DataLabels, PivotField, Range, Style, TickLabels

Explanation: Returns or sets the format code for the object (as a string). Read-write.

Syntax: *object*.NumberFormat

The *object* is the object to which this property applies and is required.

Notes: For the PivotField object, the NumberFormat property can be set only for a data field.

The format code is the same string as the Format Codes option in the Format Cells dialog box. The Format function uses different format code strings than the NumberFormat and NumberFormatLocal properties.

NumberFormatLinked   Property

Applies To: DataLabel, DataLabels, TickLabels

Explanation: True if the number format is linked to the cells (so that the number format changes in the labels when it changes in the cells). Read-write.

Syntax: *object*.NumberFormatLinked

The *object* is the object to which this property applies and is required.

NumberFormatLocal   Property

Applies To: Range, Style

Explanation: Returns or sets the format code for the object as a string, in the language of the user (not the language of the macro writer). Read-write.

Syntax: *object*.NumberFormatLocal

The *object* is the Range or Style object and is required.

Notes: The Format function uses different format code strings than the NumberFormat and NumberFormatLocal properties.

Object   Property

Applies To: OLEObject

Explanation: Returns the OLE Automation object associated with this OLE object. Read-only.

Syntax: *object*.Object

The *object* is the Object object and is required.

Offset   Method

Applies To: Range

Explanation: Returns a range at an offset to the specified range.

Syntax: *object*.Offset(*rowOffset, columnOffset*)

The Offset method has the following object qualifier and named arguments:

The *object* is the a range offset to this one and is required.

The *rowOffset* argument is optional, and the number of rows (positive, negative, or zero) by which to offset the range. If omitted, zero is assumed.

The *columnOffset* argument is optional, and the number of columns (positive, negative, or zero) by which to offset the range. If omitted, zero is assumed.

OLEObjects   Method

Applies To: Chart, DialogSheet, Worksheet

Explanation: Returns a single OLE Object (an OLEObject, Syntax 1) or a collection of all OLE objects (an OLEObjects collection, Syntax 2) on the chart or sheet. Read-only.

Syntax 1: *object*.OLEObjects(*index*)

Syntax 2: *object*.OLEObjects

The OLEObjects method has the following object qualifier and named arguments:

The *object* is the Chart, DialogSheet, or Worksheet object and is required.

The *index* argument is required for Syntax 1, and is the name or number of the OLE object.

OLEType   Property

Applies To: OLEObject

Explanation: Returns xlOLELink if the object is linked (exists outside of the file), or xlOLEEmbed if the object is embedded (is entirely contained within the file). Read-only.

Syntax: `object.OLEType`

The *object* is the OLEObject and is required.

OnAction   Property

Applies To: Arc, Arcs, Button, Buttons, ChartObject, ChartObjects, CheckBox, CheckBoxes, DialogFrame, Drawing, DrawingObjects, Drawings, DropDown, DropDowns, EditBox, EditBoxes, GroupBox, GroupBoxes, GroupObject, GroupObjects, Label, Labels, Line, Lines, ListBox, ListBoxes, OLEObject, OLEObjects, OptionButton, OptionButtons, Oval, Ovals, Picture, Pictures, Rectangle, Rectangles, ScrollBar, ScrollBars, Spinner, Spinners, TextBox, TextBoxes, ToolbarButton

Explanation: Returns or sets the name of a macro that runs when the object is clicked. Read-write.

Syntax: `object.OnAction`

The *object* is the object to which this property applies and is required.

OnCalculate   Property

Applies To: Application, Worksheet

Explanation: Returns or sets the name of the macro that runs whenever you recalculate the worksheet. Read-write.

Syntax: `object.OnCalculate`

The *object* is the object to which this property applies and is required.

Notes: Setting this property for a worksheet overrides any macro that may be set for the application.

Set this property to empty text ("") to remove the macro.

A macro set to run by the OnCalculate property is not run by actions taken by other macros. For example, a macro set by OnCalculate will not run if a macro calls the Calculate method, but will be run if you change data in a sheet set to calculate automatically or choose the Calc Now button.

OnData   Property

Applies To: Application, Worksheet

Explanation: Returns or sets the name of the procedure that runs when DDE- or OLE-linked data arrives in Excel. The specified procedure runs only when data arrives from another application. Read-write.

Syntax: `object.OnData`

The *object* is the object to which this property applies and is required.

Notes: Set this property to empty text ("") to remove the procedure.

OnDoubleClick   Property

Applies To: Application, Chart, DialogSheet, Module, Worksheet

Explanation: Returns or sets the name of the macro that runs whenever you double-click anywhere on the chart or sheet. Read-write.

Syntax: *object*.`OnDoubleClick`

The *object* is the Application, Chart, DialogSheet, Module, and is required or Worksheet object.

Notes: Setting this property for a worksheet overrides any macro that may be set for the application.

This property overrides Excel's normal double-click behavior, such as editing data in a cell or displaying a formatting dialog box.

Set this property to empty text ("") to remove the macro.

OnEntry   Property

Applies To: Application, Worksheet

Explanation: Returns or sets the name of the procedure that runs whenever you enter data using the formula bar or when you edit data in a cell. Read-write.

Syntax: *object*.`OnEntry`

The *object* is the object to which this property applies and is required.

Notes: The procedure does not run when you use edit commands or macro functions.

Set this property to "" (empty text) to remove the procedure.

To determine which cell had data entered in it, use the Caller property.

OnKey   Method

Applies To: Application

Explanation: Runs a specified procedure when a particular key or key combination is pressed.

Syntax: *object*.`OnKey`(*key*, *procedure*)

The OnKey method has the following object qualifier and named arguments:

The *object* is the Application object and is required.

The *key* argument is the string indicating the keystroke and is required.

The *procedure* argument is optional, and is a string indicating the name of the procedure. If the procedure is "" (empty text), nothing happens when key is pressed. This form of OnKey disables the normal meaning of keystrokes in Excel. If the procedure is omitted, key reverts to its normal meaning in Excel, and any special key assignments made with previous OnKey methods are cleared.

Notes: The key argument can specify any single key, or any key combined with ALT, CTRL, or SHIFT, or any combination of those keys (in Excel for Windows) or COMMAND, CTRL, OPTION, or SHIFT or any combination of those keys (in Excel for the Macintosh). Each key is represented by one or more characters, such as "a" for the character a, or "{ENTER}" for the ENTER key.

To specify characters that aren't displayed when you press the key, such as ENTER or TAB, use the codes shown in the following table. Each code in the table represents one key on the keyboard.

Key	Code
BACKSPACE	"{BACKSPACE}" or "{BS}"
BREAK	"{BREAK}"
CAPS LOCK	"{CAPSLOCK}"
CLEAR	"{CLEAR}"
DELETE or DEL	"{DELETE}" or "{DEL}"
DOWN arrow	"{DOWN}"
END	"{END}"
ENTER (numeric keypad)	"{ENTER}"
ENTER	"~" (tilde)
ESC	"{ESCAPE} or {ESC}"
HELP	"{HELP}"
HOME	"{HOME}"
INS	"{INSERT}"
LEFT arrow	"{LEFT}"
NUM LOCK	"{NUMLOCK}"

Key	Code
PAGE DOWN	"{PGDN}"
PAGE UP	"{PGUP}"
RETURN	"{RETURN}"
RIGHT arrow	"{RIGHT}"
SCROLL LOCK	"{SCROLLLOCK}"
TAB	"{TAB}"
UP arrow	"{UP}"
F1 through F15	"{F1}" through "{F15}"

In Excel for Windows, you can also specify keys combined with SHIFT and/or CTRL and/or ALT. In Excel for the Macintosh, you can also specify keys combined with SHIFT and/or CTRL and/or OPTION and/or COMMAND. To specify a key combined with another key or keys, use the following table:

To combine with	Precede the key code by
SHIFT	"+" (plus sign)
CTRL	"^" (caret)
ALT or OPTION	"%" (percent sign)
COMMAND	"*" (asterisk)

To assign a procedure to one of the special characters (+, ^, %, and so on), enclose the character in braces. See the example for details.

OnRepeat   Method

Applies To: Application

Explanation: Sets the Repeat menu item and the name of the procedure that will run if you choose Repeat from the Edit menu after running the procedure that sets this property.

Syntax: `object.OnRepeat(text, procedure)`

The OnRepeat method has the following object qualifier and named arguments:

The *object* is the Application object and is required.

The *text* argument is the the text that appears with the Repeat command on the Edit menu and is required.

The *procedure* argument is required, and specifies the name of the procedure that will run when you choose Repeat from the Edit menu.

Notes: If a procedure does not use the OnRepeat method, the Repeat command repeats the most recently run procedure.

The procedure must use the OnRepeat and OnUndo methods last, to prevent the repeat or undo procedures from being overwritten by subsequent actions in the procedure.

OnSheetActivate   Property

Applies To: Application, Chart, DialogSheet, Module, Workbook, Worksheet

Explanation: Returns or sets the name of the macro that runs when the user activates the specified sheet (Chart, DialogSheet, Module, or Worksheet object), any sheet in the specified workbook (Workbook object), or any sheet in any open workbook (Application object). Read-write.

Syntax: *object*.`OnSheetActivate`

The *object* is the object to which this property applies and is required.

Notes: To disable an OnSheetActivate macro, set the property to an empty string.

OnSheetDeactivate   Property

Applies To: Application, Chart, DialogSheet, Module, Workbook, Worksheet

Explanation: Returns or sets the name of the macro that runs when the user deactivates the specified sheet (Chart, DialogSheet, Module, or Worksheet object), any sheet in the specified workbook (Workbook object), or any sheet in any open workbook (Application object). Read-write.

Syntax: *object*.`OnSheetDeactivate`

The *object* is the object to which this property applies and is required.

OnTime   Method

Applies To: Application

Explanation: Schedules a procedure to run at a specified time in the future (either at a specific time of day or after a specific period has passed).

Syntax: *object*.`OnTime`(*earliestTime*, *procedure*, *latestTime*, *schedule*)

The OnTime method has the following object qualifier and named arguments:

The **object** is the Application object and is required.

The **earliestTime** argument is the time when you want this procedure to run, and is required.

The **procedure** argument is the name of the procedure to run and is required.

The *latestTime* argument is optional, and is the latest time the procedure can be run. For example, if latestTime is set to earliestTime + 30 and Excel is not in Ready, Copy, Cut, or Find mode at earliestTime because another procedure is running, Excel will wait 30 seconds for the first procedure to complete. If Excel is not in Ready mode within 30 seconds, the procedure will not run. If this argument is omitted, Excel will wait until the procedure can be run.

The *schedule* argument is optional, and is False to clear a previously set OnTime procedure; True (or omitted) to schedule a new procedure.

Notes: Use Now + TimeValue(time) to schedule something at a time after the current time. Use TimeValue(time) to schedule something at a specific time.

OnUndo   Method

Applies To: Application

Explanation: Sets the Undo menu item and the name of the procedure that will run if you choose Undo from the Edit menu after running the procedure that sets this property.

Syntax: *object*.OnUndo(*text, procedure*)

The OnUndo method has the following object qualifier and named arguments:

The **object** argument is the Application object and is required.

The **text** argument is the text that appears with the Undo command on the Edit menu, and is required.

The *procedure* argument specifies the name of the procedure that runs when you choose Undo from the Edit menu, and is required.

Notes: If a procedure does not use the OnUndo method, the Undo command is disabled.

The procedure must use the OnRepeat and OnUndo methods last, to prevent the repeat or undo procedures from being overwritten by subsequent actions in the procedure.

OnWindow   Property

Applies To: Application, Window

Explanation: Returns or sets the name of the procedure that runs whenever you switch to a window. Read-write.

Syntax: `object.OnWindow`

The *object* is the object to which this property applies and is required.

Notes: The procedure specified by this property does not run when other procedures switch to the window or when a command to switch to a window is received through a DDE channel. Instead, the procedure responds to a user's actions, such as clicking a window with the mouse, choosing the Go To command from the Edit menu, and so on.

If a worksheet or macro sheet has an Auto_Activate or Auto_Deactivate macro defined for it, those macros will be run after the procedure specified by OnWindow.

Open   Method

Applies To: Workbooks

Explanation: Opens a workbook.

Syntax: `object.Open(fileName, updateLinks, readOnly, format, password, writeResPassword, ignoreReadOnlyRecommended, origin, delimiter, editable, notify, converter)`

The *object* is the Workbooks object and is required.

The *fileName* argument specifies the file name of the workbook to open.

The *updateLinks* argument is optional, and specifies how links in the file are updated. If this argument is omitted, the user is prompted to determine how to update links. Otherwise, this argument is one of the following:

✔ 0.

✔ No updates.

✔ 1.

✔ Updates external but not remote references.

✔ 2.

✔ Updates remote but not external references.

✔ 3.

✔ Updates both remote and external references. If Excel is opening a file in the WKS, WK1, or WK3 format and the updateLinks argument is 2, Excel generates charts from the graphs attached to the file. If the argument is 0, no charts are created.

The *readOnly* argument is optional. If True, the workbook is opened in read-only mode.

The *format* argument is optional. If Excel is opening a text file, this argument specifies the delimiter character, as shown in the following list. If this argument is omitted, the current delimiter is used.

Value	Delimiter
1	Tabs.
2	Commas.
3	Spaces.
4	Semicolons.
5	Nothing.
6	Custom character, see the delimiter argument.

The *password* argument is optional, and is a string containing the password required to open a protected workbook. If omitted and the workbook requires a password, the user is prompted for the password.

The *writeResPassword* argument is optional, and is a string containing the password required to write to a write-reserved workbook. If omitted and the workbook requires a password, the user will be prompted for the password.

The *ignoreReadOnlyRecommended* argument is optional. If True and the workbook was saved with the Read-Only Recommended option, Excel does not display the read-only recommended message.

The *origin* argument is optional. If the file is a text file, this indicates where it originated (so that code pages and CR/LF can be mapped correctly). It may be one of xlMacintosh, xlWindows, or xlMSDOS. If this argument is omitted, the current operating system is used.

The *delimiter* argument is optional. If the file is a text file and the format argument is 6, this is a string that specifies the character to use as the delimiter. For example, Chr(9) for tabs, "," for commas, ";" for semicolons, or a custom character. Only the first character of the string is used.

The *editable* argument is optional. If the file is an Excel 4.0 add-in, using True opens the addin so that it is a visible window. If False or omitted, the add-in is opened hidden and it cannot be unhidden. This option does not apply for Excel 5.0 Addins. If the file is not an addin, specifying True prevents the running of any Auto_Open macros.

The *notify* argument is optional. If the file cannot be opened in the mode requested by readOnly, specifying True adds the file to the file notification list. Excel will open the file read-only, poll the file notification list, and then notify the user when the file becomes available. If this argument is False or omitted, no notification is requested, and attempts to open an unavailable file will fail.

The *converter* argument is optional, and specifies the index of the first file converter to try when opening the file. The specified file converter is tried first, then all other converters are tried if the specified converter does not recognize the file. The converter index is the row number of the converters returned by the FileConverters property.

Notes: If the workbook being opened has any Auto_Open macros in it, they will not be run when you open the file from Visual Basic. If you want to run the Auto_Open macro, you must use the RunAutoMacros method.

OpenLinks   Method

Applies To: Workbook

Explanation: Opens the supporting documents for a link or links.

Syntax: `object.OpenLinks(name, readOnly, type)`

The OpenLinks method has the following object qualifier and named arguments:

The `object` is the Workbook object and is required.

The `name` argument is required, and specifies the name of the Excel or DDE/OLE link, as returned from the LinkSources method (can be an array of names to specify more than one link).

The `readOnly` argument is optional. True if the documents are opened read-only. False if omitted.

The `type` argument is optional, and specifies the link type. Can be one of xlExcelLinks, xlOLELinks (also handles DDE links), xlPublishers, or xlSubscribers.

OpenText   Method

Applies To: Workbooks

Explanation: Loads and parses a text file as a new workbook with a single sheet containing the parsed text-file data.

Syntax: `object.OpenText(filename, origin, startRow, dataType, textQualifier, consecutiveDelimiter, tab, semicolon, comma, space, other, otherChar, fieldInfo)`

The OpenText method has the following object qualifier and named arguments:

The `object` is the Workbooks object and is required.

The `filename` argument is the the file name of the text file to open and parse, and is required.

The `origin` argument is optional, and specifies the origin of the text file (one of xlMacintosh, xlWindows, or xlMSDOS). If this argument is omitted, the current system is assumed.

The `startRow` argument is optional, and is the row number at which to start parsing text. The first row is 1. If omitted, 1 is assumed.

The `dataType` argument is optional, and specifies the column format of the data within the file (either xlDelimited or xlFixedWidth). The default is xlDelimited.

The `textQualifier` argument is optional, and specifies the text qualifier. Can be one of xlDoubleQuote, xlSingleQuote, or xlNone. The default is xlDoubleQuote.

The *consecutiveDelimiter* argument is optional. True if consecutive delimiters should be considered as one delimiter. The default is False.

The *tab* argument is optional. True if dataType is xlDelimited and the tab character is a delimiter. The default is False.

The *semicolon* argument is optional. True if dataType is xlDelimited and the semicolon character is a delimiter. The default is False.

The *comma* argument is optional. True if dataType is xlDelimited and the comma character is a delimiter. The default is False.

The *space* argument is optional. True if dataType is xlDelimited and the space character is a delimiter. The default is False.

The *other* argument is optional. True if dataType is xlDelimited and the character specified by the otherChar argument is a delimiter. The default is False.

The *otherChar* argument is optional (required if other is True), and specifies the delimiter character when other is True. If more than one character is specified, only the first character of the string is used, remaining characters are ignored.

The *fieldInfo* argument is optional, and an array containing parse information for the individual columns of data. The interpretation depends on the value of dataType.

When the data is delimited, this argument is an array of two-element arrays, with each two-element array specifying the conversion options for a particular column. The first element is the column number (one based), and the second element is one of the following numbers specifying how the column in parsed:

- ✔ General 2
- ✔ Text 3
- ✔ MDY date 4
- ✔ DMY date 5
- ✔ YMD date 6
- ✔ MYD date 7
- ✔ DYM date 8
- ✔ YDM date 9
- ✔ Skip the column

The column specifiers may be in any order. If a column specifier is not present for a particular column in the input data, the column is parsed using the General setting. This example causes the third column to be skipped, the first column to be parsed as text, and the remaining columns in the source data to be parsed with the General setting:

```
Array(Array(3, 9), Array(1, 2))
```

If the source data has fixed-width columns, the first element of each two-element array specifies the starting character position in the column (as an integer; character zero is the first character). The second element of the two-element array specifies the parse option for the column as a number from one through nine, as listed previously.

The following example parses two columns from a fixed-width file, with the first column starting at the beginning of the line and extending for 10 characters. The second column starts at position 15 and goes to the end of the line. To avoid including the characters between position 10 and position 15, a skipped column entry is added.

```
Array(Array(0, 1), Array(10, 9), Array(15, 1))
```

OperatingSystem   Property

Applies To: Application

Explanation: Returns the name and version number of the current operating system. For example, "Windows 3.10" or "Macintosh 7.00". Read-only.

Syntax: *object*.OperatingSystem

The *object* is the Application Object and is required.

OptionButtons   Method

Applies To: Chart, DialogSheet, Worksheet

Explanation: Returns a single option button control (an OptionButton object, Syntax 1) or a collection of option button controls on the chart or sheet (an OptionButtons object, Syntax 2).

Syntax 1: *object*.OptionButtons(*index*)

Syntax 2: *object*.OptionButtons

The OptionButtons method has the following object qualifier and named arguments:

The *object* argument is the Chart, DialogSheet, or Worksheet object and is required.

The *index* argument is required for Syntax 1, and specifies the name or number of the option button (can be an array to specify more than one).

Order   Property

Applies To: PageSetup, Trendline

Explanation: PageSetup object: Returns or sets the order that Excel uses to number pages when printing a large worksheet (either xlDownThenOver or xlOverThenDown). Read-write.

Trendline object: Returns or sets the trendline order (an integer greater than one) when the trendline Type is xlPolynomial. Read-write.

Syntax: `object.Order`

The *object* is the PageSetup or Trendline object and is required.

Notes: For the PageSetup object, this property applies only to worksheets.

OrganizationName   Property

Applies To: Application

Explanation: Returns the registered organization name (as a string). Read-only.

Syntax: `object.OrganizationName`

The *object* is the Application object and is required.

Orientation   Property

Applies To: AxisTitle, Button, Buttons, ChartTitle, DataLabel, DataLabels, DrawingObjects, GroupObject, GroupObjects, PageSetup, PivotField, Range, Style, TextBox, TextBoxes, TickLabels

Explanation: Returns or sets the object's orientation, as shown in the following table.

Object	Orientation
PageSetup	Portrait or landscape printing mode. One of xlPortrait or xlLandscape.
PivotField	Location of the field in the pivot table. One of xlHidden, xlRowField, xlColumnField, xlPageField, or xlDataField.
AxisTitle, Button, ChartTitle, DataLabel, DrawingObjects, GroupObject, RadarAxisLabels, Range, Style, TextBox, TickLabels	The text orientation. One of xlHorizontal, xlVertical, xlUpward, or xlDownward. Can also be xlAutomatic for TickLabels only.

Syntax: `object.Orientation`

The *object* is the object to which this property applies and is required.

Outline   Property

Applies To: Worksheet

Explanation: Returns an Outline object for the specified worksheet.

Syntax: *object*.Outline

The *object* is the Worksheet object and is required.

OutlineFont   Property

Applies To: Font

Explanation: True if the font is an outline font. Read-write.

Syntax: *object*.OutlineFont

The *object* is the Font object (ActiveCell.Font, for example) and is required.

Notes: This property has no effect in Windows, but its value is retained (it can be set and returned).

OutlineLevel   Property

Applies To: Range

Explanation: Returns or sets the current row or column outline level of the specified row or column. Read-write.

Syntax: *object*.OutlineLevel

The *object* is the row or column for which to set outline level and is required. The range should be a row or a column, or a range of rows or columns.

Notes: Level one is the outermost summary level.

Ovals   Method

Applies To: Chart, DialogSheet, Worksheet

Explanation: Returns a single oval (an Oval object, Syntax 1) or a collection of ovals (an Ovals object, Syntax 2). Read-only.

Syntax 1: *object*.Ovals(*index*)

Syntax 2: *object*.Ovals

The Ovals method has the following object qualifier and named arguments:

The *object* is the object containing the ovals and is required.

The *index* argument is required in Syntax 1.

Overlap   **Property**

Applies To: ChartGroup

Explanation: Specifies how bars and columns are positioned. Can be a value from –100 to 100. Applies only to bar and column charts. Read-write.

Syntax: `object.Overlap`

The **object** is the ChartGroup object and is required.

Notes: If this property is set to –100, bars are positioned so that there is one bar width between them. With zero overlap, there is no space between bars (one bar starts immediately after the preceding bar). At 100 overlap, bars are positioned on top of each other.

PageBreak   **Property**

Applies To: Range

Explanation: Returns or sets the location of a page break (one of xlNone, xlManual, or xlAutomatic). Read-write.

Syntax: `object.PageBreak`

The **object** is required and controls page break location, as shown in the following table.

Specified range	Page break location
Entire column	Left of the column
Entire row	Above the row
Neither	Above and to the left of the range. In this case, you can set the page break, but not return it.

Notes: This property can return the location of either automatic or manual page breaks, but it can only set the location of manual breaks (it can only be set to xlManual or xlNone).

PageFields   **Method**

Applies To: PivotTable

Explanation: Returns a single pivot field (a PivotField object, Syntax 1) or a collection of the pivot fields (a PivotFields object, Syntax 2) that are currently showing as page fields. Read-only.

Syntax 1: `object.PageFields(index)`

Syntax 2: `object.PageFields`

The PageFields method has the following object qualifier and named arguments:

The *object* is required and is the PivotTable object.

The *index* argument is required for Syntax 1 and is the name or number of the pivot field to return (it can be an array to specify more than one).

PageRange   Property

Applies To: PivotTable

Explanation: Returns the Range that contains the pivot table page area. Read-only.

Syntax: *object*`.PageRange`

The *object* is required and is the PivotTable object.

PageSetup   Property

Applies To: Chart, DialogSheet, Module, Window, Worksheet

Explanation: Returns a PageSetup object that contains all of the page setup settings for this object. Read-only.

Syntax: *object*`.PageSetup`

The *object* is required and is the object to which this property applies.

Panes   Method

Applies To: Window

Explanation: Returns one pane (a Pane object, Syntax 1) or a collection of all the panes (a Panes object, Syntax 2) in a window. Read-only.

Syntax 1: *object*`.Panes(`*index*`)`

Syntax 2: *object*`.Panes`

The Panes method has the following object qualifier and named arguments:

The *object* is required and is the Window object.

The *index* argument is required for Syntax 1 and is the name or number of the pane.

Notes: This property is only available on windows that can be split (worksheets and Excel 4.0 macro sheets).

PaperSize   Property

Applies To: PageSetup

Explanation: Windows only. Returns or sets the size of the paper. Read-write.

Syntax: `object.PaperSize`

The **object** is required and is the PageSetup object (ActiveSheet.PageSetup, for example).

Notes: This property may have one of the following values:

Value	Meaning
xlPaperLetter	Letter (8 1/2 x 11 in.)
xlPaperLetterSmall	Letter Small (8 1/2 x 11 in.)
xlPaperTabloid	Tabloid (11 x 17 in.)
xlPaperLedger	Ledger (17 x 11 in.)
xlPaperLegal	Legal (8 1/2 x 14 in.)
xlPaperStatement	Statement (5 1/2 x 8 1/2 in.)
xlPaperExecutive	Executive (7 1/2 x 10 1/2 in.)
xlPaperA3	A3 (297 x 420 mm)
xlPaperA4	A4 (210 x 297 mm)
xlPaperA4Small	A4 Small (210 x 297 mm)
xlPaperA5	A5 (148 x 210 mm)
xlPaperB4	B4 (250 x 354 mm)
lPaperB5	B5 (182 x 257 mm)
xlPaperFolio	Folio (8 1/2 x 13 in.)
xlPaperQuarto	Quarto (215 x 275 mm)
xlPaper10x14	10 x 14 in.
xlPaper11x17	11 x 17 in.
xlPaperNote	Note (8 1/2 x 11 in.)
xlPaperEnvelope9	Envelope #9 (3 7/8 x 8 7/ in.)
xlPaperEnvelope10	Envelope #10 (4 1/8 x 9 1/2 in.)

continues

Value	Meaning
xlPaperEnvelope11	Envelope #11 (4 1/2 x 10 3/8 in.)
xlPaperEnvelope12	Envelope #12 (4 1/2 x 11 in.)
xlPaperEnvelope14	Envelope #14 (5 x 11 1/2 in.)
lPaperCsheet	C size sheet
xlPaperDsheet	D size sheet
xlPaperEsheet	E size sheet
xlPaperEnvelopeDL	Envelope DL (110 x 220 mm)
xlPaperEnvelopeC3	Envelope C3 (324 x 458 mm)
xlPaperEnvelopeC4	Envelope C4 (229 x 324 mm)
xlPaperEnvelopeC5	Envelope C5 (162 x 229 mm)
xlPaperEnvelopeC6	Envelope C6 (114 x 162 mm)
xlPaperEnvelopeC65	Envelope C65 (114 x 229 mm)
xlPaperEnvelopeB4	Envelope B4 (250 x 353 mm)
xlPaperEnvelopeB5	Envelope B5 (176 x 250 mm)
lPaperEnvelopeB6	Envelope B6 (176 x 125 mm)
xlPaperEnvelopeItaly	Envelope (110 x 230 mm)
xlPaperEnvelopeMonarch	Envelope Monarch (3 7/8 x 7 1/2 in.)
xlPaperEnvelopePersonal	Envelope (3 5/8 x 6 1/2 in.)
xlPaperFanfoldUS	U.S. Standard Fanfold (14 7/8 x 11 in.)
xlPaperFanfoldStdGerman	German Standard Fanfold (8 1/2 x 12 in.)
xlPaperFanfoldLegalGerman	German Legal Fanfold (8 1/2 x 13 in.)
xlPaperUser	User defined

Some printers may not support all paper sizes.

Parent   Property

Applies To: All objects

Explanation: Returns the parent object for the specified object. Read-only.

Syntax: *object*.`Parent`

The *object* is required and is the object to which this property applies.

ParentField   Property

Applies To: PivotField

Explanation: Returns the pivot field that is the group parent of the object. The field must be grouped and have a parent field. Read-only.

Syntax: *object*.`ParentField`

The *object* is required and is the PivotField object.

ParentItem   Property

Applies To: PivotItem

Explanation: Returns the parent pivot item in the parent PivotField (the field must be grouped so that it has a parent). Read-only.

Syntax: *object*.`ParentItem`

The *object* is required and is the PivotItem object.

ParentItems   Method

Applies To: PivotField

Explanation: Returns one pivot item (a PivotItem object, Syntax 1) or a collection of all the pivot items (a PivotItems object, Syntax 2) that are group parents in the specified field. The specified field must be a group parent of another field. Read-only.

Syntax 1: *object*.`ParentItems`(*index*)

Syntax 2: *object*.`ParentItems`

The ParentItems method has the following object qualifier and named arguments:

The *object* is required and is the PivotField object.

The *index* argument is required for Syntax 1. The number or name of the pivot item to return (can be an array to specify more than one).

ParentShowDetail   Property

Applies To: PivotItem

Explanation: True if the specified item is showing because one of its parents is showing detail; False if the specified item is not showing because one of its parents is hiding detail. This property is only available if the item is grouped. Read-only.

Syntax: *object*.`ParentShowDetail`

The *object* is required and is the PivotItem object.

Parse   Method

Applies To: Range

Explanation: Parses a range of data and breaks it into multiple cells. Distributes the contents of the range to fill several adjacent columns; the range can be no more than one column wide.

Syntax: *object*.`Parse`(*parseLine, destination*)

The Parse method has the following object qualifier and named arguments:

The *object* is required and is the range to parse.

The *parseLine* argument is optional and is the parse line, as a string. This is a string containing left and right brackets to indicate where the cells should be split. For example, "[xxx][xxx]" would put the first three characters into the first column, and the next three characters into the second column of the destination range. If omitted, Excel guesses where to split the columns, based on the spacing of the top left cell in the range. If you want to use a different range to guess the parse line, use a Range as the parseLine argument. That range must be one of the cells that is being parsed. The parseLine argument cannot be longer than 255 characters, including the brackets and spaces.

The *destination* argument is optional and is a range indicating the upper left corner of the destination for the parsed data. If the destination is omitted, Excel will parse in place.

Notes: Use a range as the parseLine argument to recognize data that you've read from files created by another application, such as a database (see the example for details).

PasteFace   Method

Applies To: ToolbarButton

Explanation: Pastes a bitmap button face from the Clipboard onto the specified button.

Syntax: `object.PasteFace`

The **object** is required and is the ToolbarButton object.

Path   Property

Applies To: AddIn, Application, Workbook

Explanation: Returns the complete path of the object (as a string), without including the final separator and name of the object. Read-only.

Syntax: `object.Path`

The **object** is optional for Application and is required for AddIn and Workbook. It is the object to which this property applies.

PathSeparator   Property

Applies To: Application

Explanation: Returns the character ":" in Excel for the Macintosh; "\" in Excel for Windows. Read-only.

Syntax: `object.PathSeparator`

The **object** is required and is the Application object.

Pattern   Property

Applies To: Interior

Explanation: Returns or sets the pattern of the interior. Read-write.

Syntax: `object.Pattern`

The **object** is required and is the Interior object.

PatternColor   Property

Applies To: Interior

Explanation: Returns or sets the interior pattern color as an RGB value. Read-write.

Syntax: *object*`.PatternColor`

The *object* is required and is the Interior object.

PatternColorIndex   Property

Applies To: Interior

Explanation: Returns or sets the interior pattern color as an index into the current color palette. Read-write.

Syntax: *object*`.PatternColorIndex`

The *object* is required and is the Interior object.

Notes: Set this property to xlAutomatic to specify the automatic pattern for cells or the automatic fill style for drawing objects. Set this property to xlNone to specify no pattern (this is the same as setting Interior.Pattern to xlNone).

Period   Property

Applies To: Trendline

Explanation: Returns or sets the period of the trendline (applies only if this is a moving average trendline; its Type property must be xlMovingAvg). Read-write.

Syntax: *object*`.Period`

The *object* is required and is the Trendline object.

PhoneticAccelerator   Property

Applies To: Button, Buttons, CheckBox, CheckBoxes, DrawingObjects, GroupBox, GroupBoxes, Label, Labels, OptionButton, OptionButtons

Explanation: Returns or sets the phonetic keyboard accelerator key character for the control (this property is available only in Far East Excel). The phonetic accelerator is used when the system accelerator mode is switched to phonetic characters (as opposed to roman characters, which use the Accelerator property). Read-write.

Syntax: *object*`.PhoneticAccelerator`

The *object* is required and is the object to which this property applies.

Pictures   Method

Applies To: Chart, DialogSheet, Worksheet

Explanation: Returns a single picture (a Picture object, Syntax 1) or a collection of pictures (a Pictures object, Syntax 2). Read-only.

Syntax 1: `object.Pictures(index)`

Syntax 2: `object.Pictures`

The Pictures method has the following object qualifier and named arguments:

The **object** is required and is the object containing the pictures.

The **index** argument is required in Syntax 1.

PictureType   Property

Applies To: Point, Series

Explanation: Returns or sets how pictures are displayed on a column or bar picture chart, as shown in the following table. Applies only to column and bar picture charts. Read-write.

Value	Meaning
xlStretch	Stretch the picture to reach the necessary value.
xlStack	Stack the pictures to reach the necessary value.
xlScale	Stack the pictures, but use the PictureUnit property to determine what unit each picture represents.

Syntax: `object.PictureType`

The **object** is required and is the Point or Series object.

PictureUnit   Property

Applies To: Point, Series

Explanation: Returns or sets the unit for each picture on a column or bar picture chart if the PictureType property is set to xlScale (if not, this property is ignored). Read-write.

Syntax: `object.PictureUnit`

The **object** is required and is the Point or Series object.

Pie3DGroup   Property

Applies To: Chart

Explanation: Returns the pie ChartGroup on a 3D chart. Read-write.

Syntax: `object.Pie3DGroup`

The `object` is required and is the Chart object.

PieGroups   Method

Applies To: Chart

Explanation: On a 2D chart, returns a single pie chart group (a ChartGroup object, Syntax 1), or a collection of the pie chart groups (a ChartGroups collection, Syntax 2).

Syntax 1: `object.PieGroups(index)`

Syntax 2: `object.PieGroups`

The PieGroups method has the following object qualifier and named arguments:

The `object` is required and is the Chart object.

The `index` argument is required for Syntax 1 and specifies the chart group.

PivotField   Property

Applies To: Range

Explanation: Returns the PivotField containing the top left corner of the range. Read-only.

Syntax: `object.Field`

The `object` is required and is the Range object.

PivotFields   Method

Applies To: PivotTable

Explanation: Returns a single pivot field (a PivotField object, Syntax 1) or a collection of the visible and hidden pivot fields (a PivotFields object, Syntax 2) in the pivot table. Read-only.

Syntax 1: object.PivotFields(index)

Syntax 2: `object.PivotFields`

The PivotFields method has the following object qualifier and named arguments:

The *object* is required and is the PivotTable object.

The *index* argument is required for Syntax 1 and is the name or number of the pivot field to return (can be an array to specify more than one).

PivotItem   Property

Applies To: Range

Explanation: Returns the PivotItem containing the top left corner of the range. Read-only.

Syntax: *object*.`PivotItem`

The *object* is required and is the Range object.

PivotItems   Method

Applies To: PivotField

Explanation: Returns a single pivot item (a PivotItem object, Syntax 1) or a collection of all the visible and hidden pivot items (a PivotItems object, Syntax 2) in the specified field. Read-only.

Syntax 1: *object*.`PivotItems`(*index*)

Syntax 2: *object*.`PivotItems`

The PivotItems method has the following object qualifier and named arguments:

The *object* is required and is the PivotField object.

The *index* argument is required for Syntax 1. The number or name of the pivot item to return (can be an array to specify more than one).

PivotTable   Property

Applies To: Range

Explanation: Returns the PivotTable containing the top left corner of the specified range. Read-only.

Syntax: *object*.`PivotTable`

The *object* is required and is the Range object.

PivotTables   Method

Applies To: Worksheet

Explanation: Returns a single pivot table (a PivotTable object, Syntax 1) or a collection of all the pivot tables (a PivotTables object, Syntax 2) in a worksheet. Read-only.

Syntax 1: `object.PivotTables(index)`

Syntax 2: `object.PivotTables`

The PivotTables method has the following object qualifier and named arguments:

The **object** is required and is the Worksheet object.

The **index** argument is required for Syntax 1. The name or number of the pivot table (can be an array to specify more than one).

PivotTableWizard   Method

Applies To: Worksheet

Explanation: Creates a PivotTable. This method does not display the Pivot Table Wizard.

Syntax: `object.PivotTableWizard(sourceType, sourceData, tableDestination, tableName, rowGrand, columnGrand, saveData, hasAutoFormat, autoPage)`

The PivotTableWizard method has the following object qualifier and named arguments:

The **object** is required and is the Worksheet object.

The *sourceType* argument is optional and describes the source of the pivot table data, as shown in the following list. If you specify this argument, you must also specify *sourceData*.

Value	Meaning
xlConsolidation	Multiple consolidation ranges.
xlDatabase	Microsoft Excel list or database.
xlExternal	Data from another application.
xlPivotTable	Same source as another pivot table.

If *sourceType* and *sourceData* are not specified, Excel assumes that the source type is xlDatabase, and the source data comes from the named range Database. If the named range does not exist, Excel uses the current region if the current selection is in a range of more than 10 cells containing data. If this is not true, this method will fail.

The *sourceData* argument is optional and is the data for the new pivot table. A Range, an array of ranges, or a text constant representing the name of another pivot table. For an external database, this is a two-element array. The first element is the connection string specifying the ODBC source for the data. The second element is the SQL query string used to get the data. If you specify this argument, you must specify sourceType. If the active cell is inside the sourceData range, you must specify tableDestination.

The `tableDestination` argument is optional. A Range specifying where the pivot table should be placed on the worksheet. If this argument is not specified, the pivot table is placed at the active cell.

The `tableName` argument is optional. The name of the pivot table to be created, given as a string.

The `rowGrand` argument is optional and if it is True, the new pivot table shows row grand totals. If it is False, row grand totals are omitted.

The `columnGrand` argument is optional. If True, the new pivot table shows column grand totals. If False, column grand totals are omitted.

The `saveData` argument is optional. If True, data is saved with the table. If False, only the table definition is saved.

The `hasAutoFormat` argument is optional. If True, Excel automatically formats the pivot table when it is refreshed or when fields are moved.

The `autoPage` argument is optional and is valid only if sourceType is xlConsolidation. If True, Excel creates a page field for the consolidation. If False, you must create the page field or fields.

Placement   Property

Applies To: Arc, Arcs, Button, Buttons, ChartObject, ChartObjects, CheckBox, CheckBoxes, Drawing, DrawingObjects, Drawings, DropDown, DropDowns, EditBox, EditBoxes, GroupBox, GroupBoxes, GroupObject, GroupObjects, Label, Labels, Line, Lines, ListBox, ListBoxes, OLEObject, OLEObjects, OptionButton, OptionButtons, Oval, Ovals, Picture, Pictures, Rectangle, Rectangles, ScrollBar, ScrollBars, Spinner, Spinners, TextBox, TextBoxes

Explanation: Returns or sets how the object is attached to the cells below it. Can be one of xlMoveAndSize, xlMove, or xlFreeFloating. Can be used only on objects in a worksheet. Read-write.

Syntax: `object.Placement`

The `object` is required and is the object to which this property applies.

Play   Method

Applies To: SoundNote

Explanation: Plays the sound note.

Syntax: `object.Play`

The `object` is required and is the SoundNote object.

Notes: To play sounds, you must have sound hardware installed in your computer.

PlotArea   Property

Applies To: Chart

Explanation: Returns the PlotArea of a chart. Read-only.

Syntax: *object*.`PlotArea`

The *object* is required and is the Chart object.

PlotOrder   Property

Applies To: Series

Explanation: Returns or sets the plot order for this series within the chart group. Read-write.

Syntax: *object*.`PlotOrder`

The *object* is required and is the Series object.

Notes: Plot order can only be set within a chart group (you cannot set the plot order for the entire chart if you have more than one chart type). A chart group is a collection of series with the same chart type and subtype.

Changing the plot order of one series will cause the plot orders of the other series on the chart group to adjust as necessary.

PlotVisibleOnly   Property

Applies To: Chart

Explanation: True if only visible cells are plotted (False if both visible and hidden cells are plotted). Read-write.

Syntax: *object*.`PlotVisibleOnly`

The *object* is required and is the Chart object.

Points   Method

Applies To: Series

Explanation: Returns a single point (a Point object, Syntax 1) or a collection of all of the points (a Points object, Syntax 2) in the series. Read-only.

Syntax 1: *object*.`Points(`*index*`)`

Syntax 2: *object*.`Points`

The *object* is required and is the Series object.

Position   Property

Applies To: Legend, PivotField, PivotItem, Toolbar

Explanation: Returns or sets the position of the specified object, as shown in the following table. Read-write.

Object	Position
Legend	Position of the legend on the chart. One of xlBottom, xlCorner, xlTop, xlRight, or xlLeft.
PivotField	Position of the field (first, second, third, and so on) among all the fields in its orientation (Rows, Columns, Pages, Data).
PivotItem	Position of the item in its field, if the item is currently showing.
Toolbar	Position of the toolbar. One of xlTop, xlLeft, xlRight, xlBottom, or xlFloating.

Syntax: *object*.`Position`

The *object* is required and is the object to which this property applies.

Precedents   Property

Applies To: Range

Explanation: Returns a Range that contains all of the precedents of a cell. This may be a multiple selection (a union of Range objects) if there is more than one precedent. Read-only.

Syntax: *object*.`Precedents`

The *object* is required and returns precedents for this cell.

PrecisionAsDisplayed   Property

Applies To: Workbook

Explanation: True if calculations in this workbook will be done using only the precision of the numbers as they are displayed. Read-write.

Syntax: *object*.`PrecisionAsDisplayed`

The *object* is required and is the Workbook object.

PrefixCharacter   Property

Applies To: Range

Explanation: Returns the prefix character for the cell. Read-only.

Syntax: *object*.`PrefixCharacter`

The *object* is required and returns the prefix character for this cell.

Notes: If the TransitionNavigKeys property is False, this character will be ' for a text label, or blank. If the TransitionNavigKeys property is True, this will be ' for a left-justified label, " for a right-justified label, ^ for a centered label, \ for a repeated label, or blank.

Previous   Property

Applies To: Chart, DialogSheet, Module, Range, Worksheet

Explanation: Returns the previous sheet or cell (a Range object). Read-only.

Syntax: *object*.`Previous`

The *object* is required and is the object to which this property applies.

Notes: If the object is a range, this property emulates SHIFT+TAB, although the property returns the previous cell without selecting it.

On a protected sheet, this property returns the previous unlocked cell. On an unprotected sheet, this always returns the cell to the left of the specified cell.

PreviousSelections   Property

Applies To: Application

Explanation: Returns an array of the four previous ranges or names selected. Read-only. Each time you go to a range or cell using the Name Box or GoTo command from the Edit Menu, (or each time a macro calls the Goto method), the range that was selected before is added to this array as element number one. The other items in the array are moved down.

Syntax: *object*.`PreviousSelections`

The *object* is required and is the Application object.

Print   Method

Applies To: Debug.

Explanation: Prints text in the Immediate pane of the Debug window.

Syntax: *object*.`Print(outputlist)`

The Print method syntax has these parts:

Part	Description
object	Object expression that evaluates to the Debug object.
outputlist	Expression or list of expressions to print. If omitted, a blank line is printed.

The outputlist argument has the following syntax and parts:

`[{Spc(n) ¦ Tab[(n)]}][expression][charpos]`

Part	Description
Spc(*n*)	Used to insert space characters in the output, where n is the number of space characters to insert.
Tab(*n*)	Used to position the insertion point at an absolute column number where n is the column number. Use Tab with no argument to position the insertion point at the beginning of the next print zone.
expression	Numeric or string expressions to print.
charpos	Specifies the insertion point for the next character. Use a semicolon to specify the insertion point to immediately follow the last character displayed. Use Tab(n) to position the insertion point at an absolute column number. Use Tab with no argument to position the insertion point at the beginning of the next print zone. If charpos is omitted, the next character is printed on the next line.

Notes: Multiple expressions can be separated with either a space or a semicolon. A space has the same effect as a semicolon. All data printed to the Immediate pane is internationally aware; that is, the data is properly formatted (using the appropriate decimal separator) and the keywords are output in the language appropriate for the international locale specified for your system.

For Boolean data, either True or False is printed. The True and False keywords are translated, as appropriate, according to the locale setting specified for your system.

Date data is written using the standard short date format recognized by your system. When either the date or the time component is missing or zero, only the data provided gets written.

Nothing is written if outputlist data is Empty. However, if outputlist data is Null, Null is output. Again, the Null keyword is translated, as appropriate, when output.

For error data, the output appears as Error errorcode. The Error keyword is translated, as appropriate, when output.

Notes: Because the Print method normally prints with proportionally spaced characters, it is important to remember that there is no correlation between the number of characters printed and the number of fixed-width columns those characters occupy. For example, a wide letter, such as a "W", occupies more than one fixed-width column, whereas a narrow letter, such as an "i", occupies less. To account for cases where wider than average characters are used, you must ensure that your tabular columns are positioned far enough apart. Alternatively, you can print using a fixed-pitch font (such as Courier) to ensure that each character uses only one column.

PrintArea   Property

Applies To: PageSetup

Explanation: Returns or sets the range to print, as a string using A1-style references in the language of the macro. Read-write.

Syntax: *object*.PrintArea

The *object* is required and is the PageSetup object.

Notes: Set this property to False or to the empty string ("") to set the print area to the entire sheet.

This property applies only to worksheet pages.

PrintGridlines   Property

Applies To: PageSetup

Explanation: True if cell gridlines are printed on the page. Read-write.

Syntax: *object*.PrintGridlines

The *object* is required and is the PageSetup object (ActiveSheet.PageSetup, for example).

Notes: This property applies only to worksheets.

PrintHeadings   Property

Applies To: PageSetup

Explanation: True if row and column headings are printed with this page. Read-write.

Syntax: *object*.PrintHeadings

The *object* is required and is the PageSetup object (ActiveSheet.PageSetup, for example).

Notes: This property applies only to worksheets.

The DisplayHeadings property controls on-screen heading display.

PrintNotes   Property

Applies To: PageSetup

Explanation: True if cell notes will be printed along with the sheet. Read-write.

Syntax: `object.PrintNotes`

The *object* is required and is the PageSetup object.

Notes: This property applies only to worksheet pages.

PrintObject   Property

Applies To: Arc, Arcs, Button, Buttons, ChartObject, ChartObjects, CheckBox, CheckBoxes, Drawing, DrawingObjects, Drawings, DropDown, DropDowns, EditBox, EditBoxes, GroupBox, GroupBoxes, GroupObject, GroupObjects, Label, Labels, Line, Lines, ListBox, ListBoxes, OLEObject, OLEObjects, OptionButton, OptionButtons, Oval, Ovals, Picture, Pictures, Rectangle, Rectangles, ScrollBar, ScrollBars, Spinner, Spinners, TextBox, TextBoxes

Explanation: True if the object will be printed when the document is printed. Read-write.

Syntax: `object.PrintObject`

The *object* is required and is the object to which this property applies.

PrintOut   Method

Applies To: Chart, Charts, DialogSheet, DialogSheets, Module, Modules, Range, Sheets, Window, Workbook, Worksheet, Worksheets

Explanation: Prints the object.

Syntax: `object.PrintOut`*(from, to, copies, preview)*

The PrintOut method has the following object qualifier and named arguments:

The *object* is required and is the object to print.

The *from* argument is optional and is the number of the page with which to start printing. If omitted, printing starts at the beginning.

The *to* argument is optional and is the number of the last page to print. If omitted, printing goes to the last page.

The *copies* argument is optional and is the number of copies to print. If *copies* is omitted, one copy is printed.

The *preview* argument is optional. If True, Excel invokes print preview before printing the object. If False (or omitted) the object is printed immediately.

Notes: "Pages" in the descriptions of from and to refers to printed pages, not overall pages in the sheet or workbook.

This method applies to the Window object only when it is the Info Window.

PrintPreview   Method

Applies To: Chart, Charts, DialogSheet, DialogSheets, Range, Sheets, Window, Workbook, Worksheet, Worksheets

Explanation: Shows a preview of the object as it would be printed.

Syntax: *object*.`PrintPreview`

The *object* is required and is the object to preview.

PrintQuality   Property

Applies To: PageSetup

Explanation: Returns or sets the print quality, as a two-element array containing both horizontal and vertical print quality. Some printers may not support vertical print quality. Read-write.

Syntax: *object*.`PrintQuality`

The *object* is required and is the PageSetup object.

Notes: This property always returns a two-element array, even if the printer does not support vertical print quality.

PrintTitleColumns   Property

Applies To: PageSetup

Explanation: Returns or sets the columns containing the cells to be repeated on the left of each page, as a string in A1-style notation in the language of the macro. Read-write.

Syntax: *object*.`PrintTitleColumns`

The *object* is required and is the PageSetup object.

Notes: If you specify only part of a column or columns, Excel expands the range to full columns.

Set this property to False or to the empty string ("") to turn off title columns.

This property applies only to worksheet pages.

PrintTitleRows   Property

Applies To: PageSetup

Explanation: Returns or sets the rows containing the cells to be repeated on the top of each page, as a string in A1-style notation in the language of the macro. Read-write.

Syntax: `object.PrintTitleRows`

The *object* is required and is the PageSetup object.

Notes: If you specify only part of a row or rows, Excel expands the range to full rows.

Set this property to False or to the empty string ("") to turn off title rows.

This property applies only to worksheet pages.

PromptForSummaryInfo   Property

Applies To: Application

Explanation: True if Excel asks for summary info when files are initially saved. Read-write.

Syntax: `object.PromptForSummaryInfo`

The *object* is required and is the Application object.

Protect   Method

Applies To: Chart, DialogSheet, Module, Workbook, Worksheet

Explanation: Protects a chart, dialog sheet, Visual Basic module or worksheet (Syntax 1), or a workbook (Syntax 2) so that it cannot be modified.

Syntax 1: `object.Protect`(*password*, `drawingObjects`, `contents`, `scenarios`)

Syntax 2: `object.Protect`(*password*, `structure`, `windows`)

The Protect method has the following object qualifier and named arguments:

The *object* is required and is the Chart, DialogSheet, Module, or Worksheet (Syntax 1) or Workbook object (Syntax 2).

The *password* argument is optional and is a string that specifies a case-sensitive password for the sheet or workbook. If omitted, you can unprotect the sheet or workbook without a password. If specified, you must specify the password to unprotect the sheet or workbook. If you forget the password, you cannot unprotect the sheet or workbook. It's a good idea to keep a list of your passwords and their corresponding document names in a safe place.

The *drawingObjects* argument is optional and are True to protect the drawing objects on the sheet. For a dialog sheet, this protects the layout of the controls. If this argument is omitted, the drawing objects are not protected. Ignored for Visual Basic modules.

The *contents* argument is optional. True (or omitted) to protect the contents of the object. For a Visual Basic Module, this protects the source code. For a chart, this protects the entire chart. For a dialog sheet, this protects the dialog layout and text of the dialog controls. For a worksheet, this protects the cells.

The *Scenarios* is optional and is True (or omitted) to protect scenarios. This argument is valid only for worksheets.

The *structure* argument is optional. True to protect the structure of the workbook (the relative position of the sheets). If this argument is omitted, the structure is not protected.

The *Windows* argument is optional and is True to protect the windows of the sheet or workbook. If omitted, the windows are not protected.

Notes: Using the Protect method causes an error if the workbook is already protected.

ProtectContents — Property

Applies To: Chart, DialogSheet, Module, Worksheet

Explanation: True if the contents of a sheet are protected. For a Visual Basic Module, this protects the source code. For a chart, this protects the entire chart. For a dialog sheet, this protects the dialog layout and text of the dialog controls. For a worksheet, this protects the cells. Read-only.

Syntax: *object*.ProtectContents

The *object* is required and is the Chart, DialogSheet, Module, or Worksheet object.

ProtectDrawingObjects — Property

Applies To: Chart, DialogSheet, Worksheet

Explanation: True if the drawing objects of a sheet are protected. On a dialog sheet, this protects the layout of the controls. Read-only.

Syntax: *object*.ProtectDrawingObjects

The *object* is required and is the Chart, DialogSheet, or Worksheet object.

ProtectScenarios — Property

Applies To: Worksheet

Explanation: True if the worksheet scenarios are protected. Read-only.

Syntax: *object*.`ProtectScenarios`

The *object* is required and is the Worksheet object.

ProtectStructure   Property

Applies To: Workbook

Explanation: True if the order of the sheets in the workbook is protected. Read-only.

Syntax: *object*.`ProtectStructure`

The *object* is required and is the Workbook object.

ProtectWindows   Property

Applies To: Workbook

Explanation: True if the windows of the workbook are protected. Read-only.

Syntax: *object*.`ProtectWindows`

The *object* is required and the Workbook object.

Pushed   Property

Applies To: ToolbarButton

Explanation: True if the button appears pressed down. Read-write.

Syntax: *object*.`Pushed`

The *object* is required and is the ToolbarButton object.

Notes: You cannot set this property for a built-in button. You can only set it for a custom button, and then only if the button has a procedure attached to it.

Quit   Method

Applies To: Application

Explanation: Quits Excel. Does not run any Auto_Close macros before quitting.

Syntax: *object*.`Quit`

The *object* is required and is the Application object.

Notes: If unsaved workbooks are open when you use this method, Excel displays a dialog box asking if you want to save the changes. You can prevent this by saving all workbooks before using the Quit method, or by setting the DisplayAlerts property to False. When the DisplayAlerts property is False, Excel does not display the dialog box when you quit with unsaved workbooks, and Excel quits without saving them.

If you set the Saved property for a workbook to True without saving it to the disk, Excel will quit without asking you to save the workbook.

RadarAxisLabels   Property

Applies To: ChartGroup

Explanation: Returns or sets the radar axis labels (a TickLabels collection) for this chart group. Read-write.

Syntax: *object*.`RadarAxisLabels`

The *object* is the ChartGroup object and is required.

RadarGroups   Method

Applies To: Chart

Explanation: On a 2D chart, returns a single radar chart group (a ChartGroup object, Syntax 1), or a collection of the radar chart groups (a ChartGroups collection, Syntax 2).

Syntax 1: *object*.`RadarGroups(`*index*`)`

Syntax 2: *object*.`RadarGroups`

The RadarGroups method has the following object qualifier and named arguments:

The *object* is the Chart object and is required.

The *index* argument is required for Syntax 1, and specifies the chart group.

ReadOnly   Property

Applies To: Workbook

Explanation: True if the workbook has been opened as read-only. Read-only.

Syntax: *object*.`ReadOnly`

The *object* is the Workbook object and is required.

ReadOnlyRecommended   Property

Applies To: Workbook

Explanation: True if the workbook was saved as read-only recommended. Read-only.

Syntax: *object*.ReadOnlyRecommended

The *object* is the Workbook object and is required.

Notes: When you open a document that was saved as read-only recommended, Excel displays a message recommending that you open the document as read-only. Use the SaveAs method to change this property.

Received   Property

Applies To: Mailer

Explanation: True if the workbook mailer has been received (it has been sent by another user to the current user) and the current user has not modified the mailer by using the Reply, ReplyAll, or ForwardMailer methods. PowerTalk requires that mailers be received before they can be forwarded or replied to. Read-only.

Syntax: *object*.Received

The *object* is the Mailer object and is required.

Recipients   Property

Applies To: RoutingSlip

Explanation: Returns or sets the recipients on the routing slip (as an array of strings). Read-write.

Syntax: *object*.Recipients

The *object* is the RoutingSlip object and is required.

Notes: The order of the recipient list defines the delivery order if the routing delivery option is xlOneAfterAnother. If a routing slip is in progress, only those recipients who have not already received and routed the document are returned or set.

Record   Method

Applies To: SoundNote

Explanation: Displays the Record dialog box so you can record a sound note.

Syntax: `object.Record`

The *object* is the SoundNote object and is required.

Notes: To record sounds, you must have sound hardware installed in your computer.

RecordMacro   Method

Applies To: Application

Explanation: Records code if the macro recorder is on.

Syntax: `object.RecordMacro(basicCode, xlmCode)`

The RecordMacro method has the following object qualifier and named arguments:

The *object* is the Application object and is required.

The *basicCode* argument is optional, and is a string that specifies the Visual Basic code that will be recorded if the macro recorder is recording into a Visual Basic module. The string will be recorded on one line. If the string contains a carriage return (ASCII character 10, or Chr$(10) in code), it will be recorded on more than one line.

The *xlmCode* argument is optional, and is a string that specifies the formula that will be recorded if the macro recorder is recording into a Excel version 4.0 macro sheet. The string will be recorded into one cell. If the string does not begin with an equal sign, a comment is recorded.

Notes: The RecordMacro method cannot record into the active module (the module in which the RecordMacro method exists).

If *basicCode* is omitted, and the application is recording into Visual Basic, Excel will record a suitable Application.Run statement.

If *xlmCode* is omitted, and the application is recording into Excel version 4.0, Excel will record a suitable RUN macro function.

RecordRelative   Property

Applies To: Application

Explanation: True if macros are recorded using relative references; False if recording is absolute. Read-only.

Syntax: `object.RecordRelative`

The *object* is the Application object and is required.

Rectangles   Method

Applies To: Chart, DialogSheet, Worksheet

Explanation: Returns a single rectangle (a Rectangle object, Syntax 1) or a collection of rectangles (a Rectangles object, Syntax 2). Read-only.

Syntax 1: *object*`.Rectangles(index)`

Syntax 2: *object*`.Rectangles`

The Rectangles method has the following object qualifier and named arguments:

The *object* is the object containing the rectangles and is required.

The *index* argument is required in Syntax 1.

ReferenceStyle   Property

Applies To: Application

Explanation: Returns or sets how Excel displays cell references and row and column headings in A1 or R1C1 reference style (either xlA1 or xlR1C1). Read-write.

Syntax: *object*`.ReferenceStyle`

The *object* is the Application object and is required.

RefersToLocal   Property

Applies To: Name

Explanation: Returns or sets a string containing the formula that the name is defined to refer to, in A1 notation, in the language of the user, beginning with an equal sign. Read-write.

Syntax: *object*`.RefersToLocal`

The *object* is the Application object and is required.

RefersToR1C1   Property

Applies To: Name

Explanation: Returns or sets a string containing the formula that the name is defined to refer to, in R1C1-style notation, in the language of the macro writer, beginning with an equal sign. Read-write.

Syntax: *object*`.RefersToR1C1`

The *object* is the Application object and is required.

RefersToR1C1Local   Property

Applies To: Name

Explanation: Returns or sets a string containing the formula that the name is defined to refer to, in R1C1-style notation, in the language of the user, beginning with an equal sign. Read-write.

Syntax: `object.RefersToR1C1Local`

The `object` is the Application object and is required.

RefreshDate   Property

Applies To: PivotTable

Explanation: Returns the date when the pivot table was last refreshed. Read-only.

Syntax: `object.RefreshDate`

The `object` is the PivotTable object and is required.

RefreshName   Property

Applies To: PivotTable

Explanation: Returns the name of the person who last refreshed the pivot table data. Read-only.

Syntax: `object.RefreshName`

The `object` is the PivotTable object and is required.

RefreshTable   Method

Applies To: PivotTable

Explanation: Refreshes the pivot table from the source data. Returns True if it is successful.

Syntax: `object.RefreshTable`

The `object` is the PivotTable object and is required.

RegisteredFunctions   Property

Applies To: Application

Explanation: Returns an array containing a list of functions in dynamic link libraries (DLLs) or code resources that were registered with the REGISTER or REGISTER.ID functions. Read-only. Each row in the array contains information about a single function, as shown in the following table.

Column	Contents
1	The name of the DLL or code resource.
2	The name of the procedure in the DLL or code resource.
3	Strings specifying the data types of the return values, and the number and data types of the arguments.

Syntax: `object.RegisteredFunctions`

The *object* is the Application object and is required.

Notes: If there are no registered functions, the property returns Null. Use the IsNull function to test the return value for Null.

RegisterXLL   Method

Applies To: Application

Explanation: Loads an XLL code resource and automatically registers the functions and commands that the resource contains.

Syntax: `object.RegisterXLL(filename)`

The RegisterXLL method has the following object qualifier and named arguments:

The *object* is the Application object and is required.

The *filename* argument is the the name of the XLL to load and is required.

Notes: This method returns True if the code resource is successfully loaded. Otherwise, the method returns False.

RemoveAllItems   Method

Applies To: DrawingObjects, DropDown, DropDowns, ListBox, ListBoxes

Explanation: Removes all entries from a list box or drop-down list box.

Syntax: `object.RemoveAllItems`

The *object* is the object to which this method applies and is required.

RemoveItem   Method

Applies To: DrawingObjects, DropDown, DropDowns, ListBox, ListBoxes

Explanation: Removes one or more items from a list box or drop-down list box.

Syntax: `object.RemoveItem(index, count)`

The RemoveItem method has the following object qualifier and named arguments:

The *object* is the object to which this method applies and is required.

The *index* argument specifies the number of the first item to remove, and is required. Valid values are from one to the number of items in the list (returned by the ListCount property).

The *count* argument is optional, and specifies the number of items to remove starting at item index. If this argument is omitted, one item is removed. If index + count exceeds the number of items in the list, all items from index through the end of the list are removed without an error.

Notes: This method fails if the object has a ListFillRange defined.

RemoveSubtotal   Method

Applies To: Range

Explanation: Removes subtotals from a list.

Syntax: `object.RemoveSubtotal`

The *object* is the Range object and is required.

Repeat   Method

Applies To: Application

Explanation: Repeats the last user-interface action.

Syntax: `object.Repeat`

The *object* is the Application object and is required.

Notes: This method can only be used to repeat the last action taken by the user before running the macro, and it must be the first line in the macro. It cannot be used to repeat Visual Basic commands.

Replace   Method

Applies To: Range

Explanation: Finds and replaces characters in cells within a range. Does not change the selection or active cell.

For help about using the Replace worksheet function in Visual Basic, see Using Worksheet Functions in Visual Basic.

Syntax: *object*`.Replace(`*what, replacement, lookAt, searchOrder, matchCase*`)`

The Replace method has the following object qualifier and named arguments:

The *object* is the characters or cells in this range and is required.

The *what* argument is the string indicating the contents for which you want to search, and is required.

The *replacement* argument is the string indicating the text with which you want to replace what, and is required.

The *lookAt* argument is optional. If xlWhole, what must match the entire contents of a cell. If xlPart or omitted, what must contain part of the contents of a cell.

The *searchOrder* argument is optional, and specifies whether to search by rows (xlByRows) or columns (xlByColumns). The default is xlByRows.

The *matchCase* argument is optional. If True, search is case-sensitive; if False or omitted, it is not.

Notes: If the contents of the what argument are found in at least one cell of the sheet, the method returns True.

Reply   Method

Applies To: Workbook

Explanation: Replies to the workbook by creating a copy of the workbook and pre-initializing the new workbook's mailer to send to the originator of the workbook. Valid only when the workbook has a received mailer attached (you can only reply to a workbook you have received). Available only in Excel for the Apple Macintosh with the PowerTalk mail system extension installed.

Syntax: *object*`.Reply`

The *object* is the Workbook object and is required.

Notes: To reply to a workbook, use this method to set up the mailer, use the Mailer property to adjust the mailer settings (if necessary), and then use the SendMailer method to send the reply.

This method generates an error if it is used in Windows.

ReplyAll   Method

Applies To: Workbook

Explanation: Replies to the workbook by creating a copy of the workbook and pre-initializing the new workbook's mailer to send to all recipients of the workbook. Valid only when the workbook has a received mailer attached (you can only reply to a workbook you have received). Available only in Excel for the Macintosh with the PowerTalk mail system extension installed.

Syntax: *object*.`ReplyAll`

The *object* is the Workbook object and is required.

Notes: To reply to all recipients of a workbook, use this method to set up the mailer, use the Mailer property to adjust the mailer settings (if necessary), and then use the SendMailer method to send the reply.

This method generates an error if it is used in Windows.

Reset   Method

Applies To: MenuBar, RoutingSlip, Toolbar, ToolbarButton

Explanation: Restores the built-in menu bar or toolbar to its original default configuration. Resets a toolbar button to its original face.

Resets the routing slip so that a new routing can be initiated with the same slip (using the same recipient list and delivery information). The routing must be completed before you use this method. Using this method at other times causes an error.

Syntax: *object*.`Reset`

The *object* is the object to which this property applies and is required.

Notes: Be careful when you reset a menu bar or toolbar—other macros may have added buttons or menu items, and resetting the bar will remove those as well. To avoid conflicting with other macros, remove the items or buttons your macro has added without resetting the menu bar or toolbar.

ResetTipWizard   Method

Applies To: Application

Explanation: Resets the TipWizard memory so that all tips will be shown. Normally tips that have been shown several times are disabled so that they do not become annoying.

Syntax: *object*.`ResetTipWizard`

The *object* is the Application object and is required.

Reshape   Method

Applies To: Drawing, DrawingObjects, Drawings

Explanation: Reshapes the drawing by inserting, moving, or deleting vertices.

Syntax: `object.Reshape(vertex, insert, left, top)`

The Reshape method has the following object qualifier and named arguments:

The **object** is the object to which this method applies and is required.

The **vertex** argument is required, and specifies the vertex you want to insert, move, or delete.

The **insert** argument is required. If True, Excel inserts a vertex between the vertices vertex and vertex –1. The number of the new vertex then becomes vertex. The number of the vertex previously identified by vertex becomes vertex +1, and so on. If insert is False, Excel deletes the vertex (if top and left are omitted) or moves the vertex to the position specified by the top and left arguments.

The `left` argument is optional, and is the left position for the new or moved vertex, in points (1/72 inch) relative to the upper left corner of cell A1 or the upper left corner of the chart.

The `top` argument is optional, and is the top position for the new or moved vertex, in points relative to the upper left corner of cell A1 or the upper-left corner of the chart.

Notes: You cannot delete a vertex if only two vertices remain.

Resize   Method

Applies To: Range

Explanation: Resizes the range.

Syntax: `object.Resize(rowSize, columnSize)`

The Resize method has the following object qualifier and named arguments:

The **object** is the Range object to resize and is required.

The `rowSize` argument is optional, and is the number of rows in the new range. If omitted, the range will keep the same number of rows.

The `columnSize` argument is optional, and is the number of columns in the new range. If omitted, the range will keep the same number of columns.

ReturnWhenDone   Property

Applies To: RoutingSlip

Explanation: True if the workbook is returned to the sender when the routing is finished. Read-write before routing begins; read-only when routing is in progress.

Syntax: `object.ReturnWhenDone`

The **object** is the RoutingSlip object and is required.

ReversePlotOrder   Property

Applies To: Axis

Explanation: True if Excel plots points from last to first. Read-write.

Syntax: *object*.`ReversePlotOrder`

The *object* is the Axis object and is required.

Notes: This property is not available for radar charts.

Right   Function

Explanation: Returns a specified number of characters from the right side of a string.

Syntax: `Right`(*string*,*length*)

The Right function syntax has these named-argument parts:

Part	Description
string	String expression from which the rightmost characters are returned. If string contains no valid data, Null is returned.
length	Numeric expression indicating how many characters to return. If 0, a zero-length string is returned. If greater than or equal to the number of characters in string, the entire string is returned.

Notes: To determine the number of characters in string, use the Len function.

Another function (RightB) is provided for use with the double-byte character sets (DBCS) used in some Asian locales. Instead of specifying the number of characters to return, length specifies the number of bytes. In areas where DBCS is not used, RightB behaves the same as Right.

RightAngleAxes   Property

Applies To: Chart

Explanation: True if the chart axes are at right angles, independent of chart rotation or elevation. Applies only to 3D line, column, and bar charts. Read-write.

Syntax: *object*.`RightAngleAxes`

The *object* is the Chart object and is required.

Notes: If this property is True, the Perspective property is ignored.

RightFooter   Property

Applies To: PageSetup

Explanation: Returns or sets the right part of the footer. Read-write.

Syntax: `object.RightFooter`

The *object* is the PageSetup object (ActiveSheet.PageSetup for example) and is required.

Notes: Special format codes can be used in the footer text.

RightHeader   Property

Applies To: PageSetup

Explanation: Returns or sets the right part of the header. Read-write.

Syntax: `object.RightHeader`

The *object* is the PageSetup object (ActiveSheet.PageSetup, for example) and is required.

Notes: Special format codes can be used in the header text.

RightMargin   Property

Applies To: PageSetup

Explanation: Returns or sets the size of the right margin, in points (1/72 inch). Read-write.

Syntax: `object.RightMargin`

The *object* is the PageSetup object (ActiveSheet.PageSetup, for example) and is required.

Notes: Margins are set or returned in points. Use the Application.InchesToPoints or Application.CentimetersToPoints function to convert.

Rotation   Property

Applies To: Chart

Explanation: Returns or sets the rotation of the 3D chart view (the rotation of the plot area around the z-axis, in degrees). The value of this property must be between 0 and 360, except for 3D Bar charts, where the value must be between 0 and 44. The default value is 20. Applies only to 3D charts. Read-write.

Syntax: `object.Rotation`

The *object* is the Chart object and is required.

RoundedCorners   Property

Applies To: ChartObject, ChartObjects, DrawingObjects, GroupObject, GroupObjects, Rectangle, Rectangles, TextBox, TextBoxes

Explanation: True if the drawing object has rounded corners. Read-write.

Syntax: *object*.RoundedCorners

The *object* is the object to which this property applies and is required.

Route   Method

Applies To: Workbook

Explanation: Routes the workbook using the workbook's current routing slip.

Syntax: *object*.Route

The *object* is the Workbook object and is required.

Notes: Routing a workbook forces the Routed property to True.

Routed   Property

Applies To: Workbook

Explanation: True if the workbook has been routed to the next recipient; False if the workbook needs to be routed. Read-only.

Syntax: *object*.Routed

The *object* is the Workbook object and is required.

RoutingSlip   Property

Applies To: Workbook

Explanation: Returns the RoutingSlip for the workbook. Reading this property if there is no routing slip causes an error. Read-only.

Syntax: *object*.RoutingSlip

The *object* is the Workbook object and is required.

Row   Property

Applies To: Range

Explanation: Returns the number of the first row of the first area of the range. Read-only.

Syntax: `object.Row`

The *object* is the Range object and is required.

RowDifferences   Method

Applies To: Range

Explanation: Returns a Range containing all the cells whose contents are different than the comparison cell in each of the rows. The comparison cell is a cell in the comparison column and is equal to the comparison argument.

Syntax: `object.RowDifferences(comparison)`

The RowDifferences method has the following object qualifier and named arguments:

The *object* is the object to which this method applies and is required.

The *comparison* argument is required, and is a cell in the comparison column. Use the ActiveCell property if you are finding the differences between the active cell's column and all rows in the range.

RowFields   Method

Applies To: PivotTable

Explanation: Returns a single pivot field (a PivotField object, Syntax 1) or a collection of the pivot fields (a PivotFields object, Syntax 2) that are currently showing as row fields. Read-only.

Syntax 1: `object.RowFields(index)`

Syntax 2: `object.RowFields`

The RowFields method has the following object qualifier and named arguments:

The *object* is the PivotTable object and is required.

The *index* argument is required for Syntax 1, and is the name or number of the pivot field to return (can be an array to specify more than one).

RowGrand   Property

Applies To: PivotTable

Explanation: True if the pivot table shows row grand totals. Read-write.

Syntax: `object.RowGrand`

The *object* is the PivotTable object and is required.

RowHeight   Property

Applies To: Range

Explanation: Returns the height of all of the rows in the range specified, measured in points (1/72 inch). Read-write.

Syntax: `object.RowHeight`

The `object` is the object to which this property applies and is required.

Notes: For a single row, the value of the Height property is equal to the value of RowHeight. However, you can also use the Height property to return the total height of a range of cells.

Other differences between RowHeight and Height are:

- ✔ Height is read-only.
- ✔ If you return the RowHeight of several rows, you will either get the row height of each of the rows (if they are the same), or Null if they are different. If you return the Height property of several rows, you will get the total height of all the rows.

RowRange   Property

Applies To: PivotTable

Explanation: Returns the Range that includes the pivot table row area. Read-only.

Syntax: `object.RowRange`

The `object` is the PivotTable object and is required.

Rows   Method

Applies To: Application, Range, Worksheet

Explanation: Returns a single row (Syntax 1) or a collection of rows (Syntax 2). A row is a Range object.

Syntax 1: `object.Rows(index)`

Syntax 2: `object.Rows`

The Rows method has the following object qualifier and named arguments:

The `object` is optional for Application, required for Range and Worksheet, and is the object to which this method applies.

The `index` argument is required for Syntax 1, and is the name or number of the row.

Notes: When applied to a Range object that is a multiple selection, this method returns rows from the first area of the range only. For example, if the Range object is a multiple selection with two areas, A1:B2 and C3:D4, Selection.Rows.Count, returns 2, not 4. To use this method on a range that may contain a multiple selection, test Areas.Count to determine if the range is a multiple selection, and if it is, then loop over each area in the range.

Run   Method

Applies To: Application, Range

Explanation: Syntax 1: Runs a macro or calls a function. This can be used to run a macro written in any language (Visual Basic, the Microsoft Excel 4.0 macro language, or a function in a DLL or XLL). Syntax 2: Runs the Excel 4.0 macro at this location. The range must be on a macro sheet.

Syntax 1: *object*.Run(*macro, arg1, arg2,...*)

Syntax 2: *object*.Run(*arg1, arg2,...*)

The Run method has the following object qualifier and named arguments:

The *object* is optional for Application, required for Range, and is the application that contains the macro, or a range on a macro sheet that contains an Excel 4.0 macro.

The *macro* argument is required for Syntax 1 (not used with Syntax 2), and is the macro to run. This can be a string with the macro name, or a Range indicating where the function is, or a register ID for a registered DLL (XLL) function. If a string is used, the string will be evaluated in the context of the active sheet.

The *arg1, arg2,...* arguments are optional, and are the arguments that should be passed to the function.

Notes: The Run method returns whatever the called macro returns.

RunAutoMacros   Method

Applies To: Workbook

Explanation: Runs the Auto_Open, Auto_Close, Auto_Activate, or Auto_Deactivate macros that are attached to the workbook.

These four auto macros do not run when workbooks are opened or closed (and when sheets are activated or deactivated) by a Visual Basic program. Use this method to run auto macros.

Syntax: *object*.RunAutoMacros(*which*)

The RunAutoMacros method has the following object qualifier and named arguments:

The *object* is the Workbook object and is required.

The *which* argument is required, and specifies which macros to run, as shown in the following table.

Value	Meaning
xlAutoOpen	Auto_Open macros.
xlAutoClose	Auto_Close macros.
xlAutoActivate	Auto_Activate macros.
xlAutoDeactivate	Auto_Deactivate macros.

Notes: The Auto_Activate and Auto_Deactivate macros are included for backward-compatibility with the Excel version 4.0 macro language. Use the OnSheetActivate and OnSheetDeactivate properties when you program in Visual Basic.

Save   Method

Applies To: Application, Workbook

Explanation: Workbook object (Syntax 1): Saves changes to the specified workbook. Application object (Syntax 2): Saves the current workspace.

Syntax 1: `object.Save`

Syntax 2: `object.Save(filename)`

The Save method has the following object qualifier and named arguments:

The **object** is the Workbook object (Syntax 1) or Application object (Syntax 2), and is required.

The `filename` argument is optional, and specifies the name of the saved workspace file. If this argument is omitted, a default name is used.

Notes: To open a workbook file, use the Open method.

To mark the workbook as saved without writing it to a disk, set its Saved property to True.

The first time you save a workbook, use the SaveAs method to specify a name for the file.

SaveAs   Method

Applies To: Chart, DialogSheet, Module, Workbook, Worksheet

Explanation: Saves changes to the sheet or workbook in a different file.

Syntax: `object.SaveAs(filename, fileFormat, password, writeResPassword, readOnlyRecommended, createBackup)`

The SaveAs method has the following object qualifier and named arguments:

The **object** is the object to which this method applies and is required.

The `filename` argument is optional, and is a string indicating the name of the file to save. You can include a full path; if you do not, Excel saves the file in the current directory or folder.

The `fileFormat` argument is optional, and is the file format to use when you save the file. See the FileFormat property for a list of valid choices.

The `password` argument is optional, and is a case-sensitive string indicating the protection password to be given to the file. Should be no more than 15 characters.

The `writeResPassword` argument is optional, and is a string indicating the write-reservation password for this file. If a file is saved with the password and the password is not supplied when the file is opened, the file is opened as read-only.

The `readOnlyRecommended` argument is optional. If True, when the file is opened, Excel displays a message recommending that you open the file as read-only.

The `createBackup` argument is optional. If True, Excel creates a backup file; if False, no backup file is created; if omitted, the status is unchanged.

Notes: To mark the workbook as saved without writing it to a disk, set the Saved property of the workbook to True.

This method can only be used to save worksheets in a non-3D format.

Basic modules can only be saved in Text format.

SaveCopyAs Method

Applies To: Workbook

Explanation: Saves a copy of the workbook to a file but does not modify the open workbook in memory.

Syntax: `object.SaveCopyAs(filename)`

The SaveCopyAs method has the following object qualifier and named arguments:

The `object` is the Workbook object and is required.

The `filename` argument is required, and specifies the file name for the copy.

Saved Property

Applies To: Workbook

Explanation: False if changes have been made to a workbook since it was last saved. Read-write.

Syntax: `object.Saved`

The `object` is the Workbook object and is required.

Notes: If a workbook has never been saved, its Path will return an empty string ("").

You can set this property to True if you want to close a modified workbook without saving it or being prompted to save it.

SaveData   Property

Applies To: PivotTable

Explanation: True if data for the pivot table is saved with the workbook; False if only the pivot table definition is saved. Read-write.

Syntax: `object.SaveData`

The `object` is the PivotTable object and is required.

SaveLinkValues   Property

Applies To: Workbook

Explanation: True if Excel will save external link values with this workbook. Read-write.

Syntax: `object.SaveLinkValues`

The `object` is the Workbook object and is required.

ScaleType   Property

Applies To: Axis

Explanation: Returns or sets the value axis scale type (xlLinear or xlLogarithmic). Applies only to the value axis. Read-write.

Syntax: `object.ScaleType`

The `object` is the Axis object and is required.

Notes: A logarithmic scale uses base-ten logarithms.

Scenarios   Method

Applies To: Worksheet

Explanation: Returns a single scenario (a Scenario object, Syntax 1) or a collection of scenarios (a Scenarios object, Syntax 2) on the worksheet.

Syntax 1: `object.Scenarios(index)`

Syntax 2: `object.Scenarios`

The Scenarios method has the following object qualifier and named arguments:

The *object* is the Worksheet object and is required.

The *index* argument is required for Syntax 1, and is the name or number of the scenario (can be an array to specify more than one).

ScreenUpdating   Property

Applies To: Application

Explanation: True if screen updating is on. Read-write.

Syntax: *object*.`ScreenUpdating`

The *object* is the Application object and is required.

Notes: Turn screen updating off to speed up your macro code. You will not be able to see what the macro is doing, but it will run faster.

ScrollBars   Method

Applies To: Chart, DialogSheet, Worksheet

Explanation: Returns a single scroll bar control (a ScrollBar object, Syntax 1) or a collection of scroll bar controls on the chart or sheet (a ScrollBars object, Syntax 2).

Syntax 1: *object*.`ScrollBars`(*index*)

Syntax 2: *object*.`ScrollBars`

The ScrollBars method has the following object qualifier and named arguments:

The *object* is the Chart, DialogSheet, or Worksheet object and is required.

The *index* argument is required for Syntax 1, and specifies the name or number of the scroll bar (can be an array to specify more than one).

ScrollColumn   Property

Applies To: Pane, Window

Explanation: Returns or sets the number of the column that appears at the left of the pane or window. Read-write.

Syntax: *object*.`ScrollColumn`

The *object* is the Pane or Window object and is required.

Notes: If the window is split, Window.ScrollColumn refers to the top left pane. If panes are frozen, Window.ScrollColumn excludes the frozen areas.

ScrollRow   Property

Applies To: Pane, Window

Explanation: Returns or sets the number of the row that appears at the top of the pane or window. Read-write.

Syntax: `object.ScrollRow`

The **object** is the Window object and is required.

Notes: If the window is split, Window.ScrollRow refers to the top left pane. If panes are frozen, Window.ScrollRow excludes the frozen areas.

ScrollWorkbookTabs   Method

Applies To: Window

Explanation: Scrolls the workbook tabs at the bottom of the window. Does not affect the active sheet in the workbook.

Syntax: `object.ScrollWorkbookTabs(sheets, position)`

The ScrollWorkbookTabs method has the following object qualifier and named arguments:

The **object** is the Window object and is required.

The `sheets` argument is optional, and is the number of sheets to scroll. Positive means scroll forward, negative means scroll backward, zero means don't scroll. You must specify sheets if you do not specify position.

The `position` argument is optional. xlFirst to scroll to the first sheet, or xlLast to scroll to the last sheet. You must specify position if you do not specify sheets.

Seek   Function

Explanation: Returns the current read/write position within a file opened using the Open statement.

Syntax: `Seek(filenumber)`

The **filenumber** named argument is any valid file number.

Notes: Seek returns a value between 1 and 2,147,483,647 (equivalent to $2^{31}-1$), inclusive. For files open in Random mode, Seek returns the number of the next record read or written. For files opened in Binary, Output, Append, or Input mode, Seek returns the byte position at which the next operation is to take place. The first byte in a file is at position 1, the second byte is at position 2, and so on.

Select
Method

Applies To: Arc, Arcs, Axis, AxisTitle, Button, Buttons, Chart, ChartArea, ChartObject, ChartObjects, Charts, ChartTitle, CheckBox, CheckBoxes, Corners, DataLabel, DataLabels, DialogFrame, DialogSheet, DialogSheets, DownBars, Drawing, DrawingObjects, Drawings, DropDown, DropDowns, DropLines, EditBox, EditBoxes, ErrorBars, Floor, Gridlines, GroupBox, GroupBoxes, GroupObject, GroupObjects, HiLoLines, Label, Labels, Legend, LegendEntry, LegendKey, Line, Lines, ListBox, ListBoxes, Module, Modules, OLEObject, OLEObjects, OptionButton, OptionButtons, Oval, Ovals, Picture, Pictures, PlotArea, Point, Range, Rectangle, Rectangles, ScrollBar, ScrollBars, Series, SeriesLines, Sheets, Spinner, Spinners, TextBox, TextBoxes, TickLabels, Trendline, UpBars, Walls, Worksheet, Worksheets

Explanation: Selects the object.

Syntax: `object.Select(replace)`

The `object` is the object to be selected and is required.

The `replace` argument is optional (used only with drawing objects and sheets). If True or omitted, the current selection is replaced with a new selection consisting of the specified object. If False, the current selection is extended to include any previously selected objects and the specified object.

Notes: To select a cell or range of cells, use the Select method. To make a single cell the active cell, use the Activate method.

Selected
Property

Applies To: DropDown, DropDowns, ListBox, ListBoxes

Explanation: Returns or sets an array of Boolean values indicating the selection state of items in the list box. Each entry in the array corresponds to an entry in the list box, and is True if the entry is selected or False if it is not selected. Use this property to obtain the selected items in a MultiSelect list box. Read-write.

Syntax: `object.Selected`

The `object` is the object to which this property applies and is required.

Notes: For single-selection list boxes, it is easier to use the Value or ListIndex properties to get and set the selection.

SelectedSheets
Method

Applies To: Window

Explanation: Returns a collection of all the selected sheets in the window (a Sheets collection).

Syntax: *object*`.SelectedSheets`

The *object* is the Window object and is required.

Selection   Property

Applies To: Application, Window

Explanation: Returns the object that is currently selected in the active window of the Application object, or the current selection in the given Window object. Read-only.

Syntax: *object*`.Selection`

The *object* is the object containing the selection and is required for Window.

Notes: The object type returned by the Selection property depends on the type of selection (for example, if a text box is selected, this property returns a TextBox object). The Selection property returns Nothing if nothing is selected.

SendDateTime   Property

Applies To: Mailer

Explanation: Returns the date and time that the mailer was sent. The mailer must be sent before this property is valid. Read-only.

Syntax: *object*`.SendDateTime`

The *object* is the Mailer object and is required.

Sender   Property

Applies To: Mailer

Explanation: Returns the name of the user (as text) who sent this workbook mailer. Read-only.

Syntax: *object*`.Sender`

The *object* is the Mailer object and is required.

SendKeys   Method

Applies To: Application

Explanation: Sends keystrokes to the active application.

Syntax: *object*`.SendKeys(`*keys*`, `*wait*`)`

The SendKeys method has the following object qualifier and named arguments:

The *object* is optional, and is the Application object.

The **keys** argument is required, and is the key or key combination you want to send to the application, as text.

The *wait* argument is optional. If True, Excel waits for the keys to be processed before returning control to the macro. If False or omitted, the macro continues to run without waiting for the keys to be processed.

Notes: This method places keystrokes into a key buffer. In some cases, you must call this method before you call the method that will use the keystrokes. For example, to send a password to a dialog box, you must call the SendKeys method before you display the dialog box.

The keys argument can specify any single key, or any key combined with Alt, CTRL, or Shift, or any combination of those keys (in Excel for Windows) or Command, CTRL, OPTION, or Shift or any combination of those keys (in Excel for the Macintosh). Each key is represented by one or more characters, such as "a" for the character a, or "{ENTER}" for the ENTER key.

To specify characters that aren't displayed when you press the key, such as ENTER or TAB, use the codes shown in the following table. Each code in the table represents one key on the keyboard.

Key	Code
BACKSPACE	"{BACKSPACE}" or "{BS}"
BREAK	"{BREAK}"
CAPS LOCK	"{CAPSLOCK}"
CLEAR	"{CLEAR}"
DELETE or DEL	"{DELETE}" or "{DEL}"
DOWN ARROW	"{DOWN}"
END	"{END}"
ENTER (numeric keypad)	"{ENTER}"
ENTER	"~" (tilde)
ESC	"{Esc} or {ESC}"
HELP	"{HELP}"
HOME	"{HOME}"
INS	"{INSERT}"

continues

Key	Code
LEFT ARROW	"{LEFT}"
NUM LOCK	"{NUMLOCK}"
PAGE DOWN	"{PGDN}"
PAGE UP	"{PGUP}"
RETURN	"{RETURN}"
RIGHT ARROW	"{RIGHT}"
SCROLL LOCK	"{SCROLLLOCK}"
TAB	"{TAB}"
UP ARROW	"{UP}"
F1 through F15	"{F1}" through "{F15}"

In Excel for Windows, you can also specify keys combined with Shift and/or CTRL and/or Alt. In Excel for the Macintosh, you can also specify keys combined with Shift and/or CTRL and/or OPTION and/or Command. To specify a key combined with another key or keys, use the following table.

To combine with	Precede the key code by
Shift	"+" (plus sign)
Ctrl	"^" (caret)
Alt or Option	"%" (percent sign)
Command	"*" (asterisk)

SendMail   Method

Applies To: Workbook

Explanation: Sends the workbook using the installed mail system.

Syntax: *object*.SendMail(*recipients*, *subject*, *returnReceipt*)

The SendMail method has the following object qualifier and named arguments:

The *object* is the Workbook object and is required.

The **recipients** argument is required, and specifies the name of the recipient as text, or an array of text strings if there are multiple recipients. At least one recipient must be specified, and all recipients are added as To recipients.

The *subject* argument is optional, and specifies the subject of the message. If omitted, the document name is used.

The *returnReceipt* argument is optional. If True, a return receipt is requested. If False or omitted, no return receipt is requested.

Notes: Use the SendMail method on Mail (MAPI or Mail for the Macintosh) electronic mail systems. Pass addressing information as parameters.

Use the SendMailer method on PowerTalk email systems on the Macintosh. The Mailer object contains the addressing information for PowerTalk.

SendMailer   Method

Applies To: Workbook

Explanation: Sends the workbook using the PowerTalk mailer. This method is available only on the Macintosh with the PowerTalk system extension installed and can only be used on a workbook with a mailer attached.

Syntax: *object*.**SendMailer**(*fileFormat, priority*)

The **object** is the Workbook object and is required.

The *fileFormat* argument is optional, and specifies the file format to use for the workbook that is sent. See the FileFormat property for a list of valid types.

The *priority* argument is optional, and specifies the delivery priority of the message (one of xlNormal, xlHigh, or xlLow). The default value is xlNormal.

Notes: Use the SendMail method on Mail (MAPI or Mail for the Macintosh) electronic mail systems. Pass addressing information as parameters.

SendToBack   Method

Applies To: Arc, Arcs, Button, Buttons, ChartObject, ChartObjects, CheckBox, CheckBoxes, Drawing, DrawingObjects, Drawings, DropDown, DropDowns, EditBox, EditBoxes, GroupBox, GroupBoxes, GroupObject, GroupObjects, Label, Labels, Line, Lines, ListBox, ListBoxes, OLEObject, OLEObjects, OptionButton, OptionButtons, Oval, Ovals, Picture, Pictures, Rectangle, Rectangles, ScrollBar, ScrollBars, Spinner, Spinners, TextBox, TextBoxes

Explanation: Sends the object to the back of the z-order.

Syntax: *object*.**SendToBack**

The **object** is the object to which this method applies and is required.

SeriesCollection   Method

Applies To: Chart, ChartGroup

Explanation: Returns a single series (a Series object, Syntax 1) or a collection of all the series (a SeriesCollection object, Syntax 2) in the chart or chart group. Read-only.

Syntax 1: `object.SeriesCollection(index)`

Syntax 2: `object.SeriesCollection`

The SeriesCollection method has the following object qualifier and named arguments:

The *object* is the Chart or ChartGroup object and is required.

The *index* argument is required for Syntax 1, and is the name or number of the series.

SeriesLines   Property

Applies To: ChartGroup

Explanation: Returns or sets the SeriesLines for a stacked bar or stacked column chart. Applies only to stacked bar and stacked column charts. Read-write.

Syntax: `object.SeriesLines`

The *object* is the ChartGroup object and is required.

SetDefaultChart   Method

Applies To: Application

Explanation: Specifies the name of the chart template that Excel will use when creating new charts.

Syntax: `object.SetDefaultChart(formatName)`

The SetDefaultChart method has the following object qualifier and named arguments:

The *object* is the Application object and is required.

The *formatName* argument is required, and specifies the name of a custom autoformat. This name can be a custom autoformat, as a string, or the special constant xlBuiltIn to specify the built-in chart template.

SetInfoDisplay   Method

Applies To: Window

Explanation: Sets the information displayed in the Info window (the specified window object must be the Info window).

Syntax: *object*.**SetInfoDisplay**(*cell, formula, value, format, protection, names, precedents, dependents, note*)

The SetInfoDisplay method has the following object qualifier and named arguments:

The *object* is the Window object and is required.

The *cell* argument is optional. True to display the cell reference text.

The *formula* argument is optional. True to display the cell formula.

The *value* argument is optional. True to display the cell value.

The *format* argument is optional. True to display cell formatting information.

The *protection* argument is optional. True to display cell protection information.

The *names* argument is optional. True to display cell name information.

The *precedents* argument is optional, and sets whether precedents are displayed (one of xlNone, xlDirect, or xlAll).

The *dependents* argument is optional, and sets whether dependents are displayed (one of xlNone, xlDirect, or xlAll).

The *note* argument is optional. True to display notes.

Notes: If this method is applied to any window other than Info window, an error occurs.

SetLinkOnData   **Method**

Applies To: Workbook

Explanation: Sets the name of a macro or procedure that runs whenever a link is updated.

Syntax: *object*.**SetLinkOnData**(*name, procedure*)

The SetLinkOnData method has the following object qualifier and named arguments:

The *object* is the Workbook object and is required.

The *name* argument is required, and specifies the name of the Excel or DDE/OLE link, as returned from the LinkSources method.

The *procedure* argument is optional, and specifies the name of the procedure to run when the link is updated. This can be either a Excel version 4 macro or a Visual Basic procedure. Set this argument to an empty string ("") to indicate that no procedure should run when the link is updated.

Notes: Use this method to set notification for a specific link. Use the OnData property if you wish to be notified when any link is updated.

Shadow   Property

Applies To: AxisTitle, ChartArea, ChartObject, ChartObjects, ChartTitle, DataLabel, DataLabels, Drawing, DrawingObjects, Drawings, Font, GroupObject, GroupObjects, Legend, OLEObject, OLEObjects, Oval, Ovals, Picture, Pictures, Rectangle, Rectangles, TextBox, TextBoxes

Explanation: True if the font is a shadow font or if the drawing object has a shadow. Read-write.

Syntax: `object.Shadow`

The `object` is the object to which this property applies and is required.

Notes: For the Font object, this property has no effect in Windows, but its value is retained (it can be set and returned).

Sheets   Method

Applies To: Application, Workbook

Explanation: Returns a single sheet (Syntax 1) or a collection of sheets (Syntax 2) in the workbook. Read-only. A sheet can be a Chart, DialogSheet, Module, or Worksheet.

Syntax 1: `object.Sheets(index)`

Syntax 2: `object.Sheets`

The Sheets method has the following object qualifier and named arguments:

The `object` is optional for Application, required for Workbook, and is the object to which this method applies.

The `index` argument is required for Syntax 1, and is the name or number of the sheet to return.

Notes: Using this method with no object qualifier is equivalent to ActiveWorkbook.Sheets.

SheetsInNewWorkbook   Property

Applies To: Application

Explanation: Returns or sets the number of sheets Excel automatically inserts in new workbooks. Read-write.

Syntax: `object.SheetsInNewWorkbook`

The `object` is the Application object and is required.

ShortcutKey   Property

Applies To: Name

Explanation: Returns or sets the shortcut key for a name defined as a custom Excel version 4.0 macro command. Read-write.

Syntax: *object*.ShortcutKey

The *object* is the Name object and is required.

ShortcutMenus   Method

Applies To: Application

Explanation: Returns a single shortcut menu. Read-only.

Syntax: *object*.ShortcutMenus(*index*)

The ShortcutMenus method has the following object qualifier and named arguments:

The *object* is optional, and is the Application object.

The *index* argument is required, and specifies the shortcut menu, as shown in the following list.

Constant	Description
xlAxis	Chart Axis
xlButton	Button
xlChartSeries	Chart Series
xlChartTitles	Chart Titles
xlColumnHeader	Column
xlDebugCodePane	Debug Code Pane
xlDesktop	Desktop
xlDialogSheet	Dialog Sheet
xlDrawingObject	Drawing Object
xlEntireChart	Entire Chart
xlFloor	Chart Floor
xlGridline	Chart Gridline

continues

Constant	Description
xlImmediatePane	Immediate Pane
xlLegend	Chart Legend
xlMacrosheetCell	Macro Sheet Cell
xlModule	Module
xlPlotArea	Chart Plot Area
xlRowHeader	Row
xlTextBox	Text Box
xlTitleBar	Title Bar
xlToolbar	Toolbar
xlToolbarButton	Toolbar Button
xlWatchPane	Watch Pane
xlWorkbookTab	Workbook Tab
xlWorksheetCell	Worksheet Cell

Show   Method

Applies To: Dialog, DialogSheet, Range, Scenario

Explanation: DialogSheet object (Syntax 1): Runs the dialog box. This method will not return to the calling procedure until the dialog box is closed or hidden, but event procedures assigned to the dialog box controls will run while the calling procedure is suspended.

Range object (Syntax 1): Scrolls the active window to move the range into view. The range must consist of a single cell which is a part of the currently active document

Scenario object (Syntax 1): Shows the scenario by inserting the scenario's values onto the worksheet. The affected cells are the changing cells of the scenario.

Dialog object (Syntax 2): Displays the dialog box and waits for the user to input data.

Syntax 1: *object*.Show

Syntax 2: *object*.Show(*arg1, arg2,..., arg30*)

The Show method has the following object qualifier and named arguments:

The *object* is required. For Syntax 1, the DialogSheet, Range, or Scenario object. For Syntax 2, the Dialog object.

The *arg1, arg2, . . . , arg30* argument is optional. For built-in dialog boxes only, provides the initial arguments for the command.

Notes: For built in dialog boxes, this method returns True if the user pressed OK, or False if the user pressed Cancel.

A single dialog box can change many properties at once. For example, the Format Cells dialog box can change all the properties of the Font object.

For some built-in dialog boxes (Open, for example), you can set initial values using arg1, arg2,..., arg30. To find the arguments to set, search Excel Macro Functions Help for the corresponding Excel 4.0 macro function. For example, search for the OPEN function to find the arguments for the Open dialog box. For more information about built-in dialog boxes, see Dialogs.

ShowAllData   Method

Applies To: Worksheet

Explanation: Makes all rows visible for the currently filtered list. If the AutoFilter is in use, this method changes the arrows to "All".

Syntax: *object*.`ShowAllData`

The *object* is the Worksheet object and is required.

ShowDataForm   Method

Applies To: Worksheet

Explanation: Displays the data form associated with the worksheet.

Syntax: *object*.`ShowDataForm`

The *object* is the Worksheet object and is required.

Notes: The macro pauses while you use the data form. When the user closes the data form, this macro will resume at the line following the ShowDataForm method.

This method will run the custom data form, if one exists.

ShowDependents   Method

Applies To: Range

Explanation: Draws tracer arrows to the direct dependents of the range.

Syntax: *object*.`ShowDependents`(*remove*)

The ShowDependents method has the following object qualifier and named arguments:

The *object* is the Range object. It must be a single cell, and is required.

The *remove* is optional. If True, removes one level of tracer arrows to direct dependents. If False or omitted, expands one level of tracer arrows.

ShowDetail   Property

Applies To: PivotItem, Range

Explanation: True if the outline is expanded for the specified range (the detail of the column or row is visible). The specified range must be a single summary column or row in an outline. Read-write.

For the PivotItem object (or the Range object if the range is in a pivot table), this property is True if the pivot item is showing detail.

Syntax: *object*.ShowDetail

The *object* is the PivotItem or Range object and is required.

Notes: If the specified range is not in a pivot table, the following comments apply:

The range must be in a single summary row or column.

This property returns False if any of the children of the row or column are hidden.

Setting this property to True is equivalent to unhiding all the children on the summary row or column.

Setting this property to False is equivalent to hiding all the children of the summary row or column.

If the specified range is in a pivot table, it is possible to set this property for more than one cell at once if the range is contiguous. To return this property, the range must be a single cell.

ShowErrors   Method

Applies To: Range

Explanation: Draws tracer arrows through the precedents tree to the cell that is the source of the error, and returns the range that contains the source of the error.

Syntax: *object*.ShowErrors

The *object* is the Range object and is required.

ShowLegendKey   Property

Applies To: DataLabel, DataLabels

Explanation: True if the data label legend key is visible. Read-write.

Syntax: `object.ShowLegendKey`

The *object* is the DataLabel or DataLabels object and is required.

ShowLevels   Method

Applies To: Outline

Explanation: Displays the specified number of row and/or column levels of an outline.

Syntax: `object.ShowLevels(rowlevels, columnlevels)`

The ShowLevels method has the following object qualifier and named arguments:

The *object* is the Outline object (ActiveSheet.Outline, for example) and is required.

The `rowLevels` argument is optional, and specifies the number of row levels of an outline to display. If the outline has fewer levels than specified, Excel shows all levels. If omitted or zero, no action is taken on rows.

The `columnLevels` argument is optional, and specifies the number of column levels of an outline to display. If the outline has fewer levels than specified, Excel shows all levels. If omitted or zero, no action is taken on columns.

Notes: You must specify at least one argument.

ShowPages   Method

Applies To: PivotTable

Explanation: Creates a new pivot table for each item in the page field. Each new pivot table is created on a new worksheet.

Syntax: `object.ShowPages(pageField)`

The ShowPages method has the following object qualifier and named arguments:

The *object* is the PivotTable object and is required.

The *pageField* argument is the string that names a single page field in the pivot table, and is required.

ShowPrecedents   Method

Applies To: Range

Explanation: Draws tracer arrows to the direct precedents of the range.

Syntax: *object*.ShowPrecedents(*remove*)

The ShowPrecedents method has the following object qualifier and named arguments:

The *object* is required, and is the Range object. It must be a single cell.

The *remove* argument is optional. If True, it removes one level of tracer arrows to direct precedents. If False or omitted, it expands one level of tracer arrows.

ShowToolTips   Property

Applies To: Application

Explanation: True if ToolTips are turned on. Read-write.

Syntax: *object*.ShowToolTips

The *object* is the Application object and is required.

Size   Property

Applies To: Font

Explanation: Returns or sets the size of the font. Read-write.

Syntax: *object*.Size

The *object* is the Font object and is required.

SizeWithWindow   Property

Applies To: Chart

Explanation: True if chart resizes to match the size of the chart sheet window. False if the chart size is not attached to the window size. Applies only to charts that are sheets in a workbook, not to embedded charts. Read-write.

Syntax: *object*.SizeWithWindow

The *object* is the Chart object and is required.

SmallChange   Property

Applies To: DrawingObjects, ScrollBar, ScrollBars, Spinner, Spinners

Explanation: Returns or sets the amount that the scroll bar or spinner increments or decrements for a line scroll (when the user clicks on an arrow). Read-write.

Syntax: *object*.`SmallChange`

The *object* is the object to which this property applies and is required.

SmallScroll   Method

Applies To: Pane, Window

Explanation: Scrolls the window by rows or columns.

Syntax: *object*.`SmallScroll`(*down, up, toRight, toLeft*)

The SmallScroll method has the following object qualifier and named arguments:

The *object* is the window to scroll and is required.

The *down* argument is optional, and is the number of rows to scroll the window down.

The *up* argument is optional, and is the number of rows to scroll the window up.

The *toRight* argument is optional, and is the number of columns to scroll the window right.

The *toLeft* argument is optional, and is the number of columns to scroll the window left.

Notes: If *down* and *up* are both specified, the window is scrolled by the difference of the arguments. For example, if *down* is three and *up* is six, the window is scrolled up three rows.

If *toLeft* and *toRight* are both specified, the window is scrolled by the difference of the arguments. For example, if *toLeft* is three and *toRight* is six, the window is scrolled right three columns.

Any of the arguments can be a negative number.

Smooth   Property

Applies To: LegendKey, Series

Explanation: True if the line or scatter chart has curve smoothing on. Applies only to line and scatter charts. Read-write.

Syntax: *object*.`Smooth`

The *object* is the LegendKey or Series object and is required.

Sort   Method

Applies To: Range

Explanation: Syntax 1 sorts the range, or the current region if the range contains only one cell.

Syntax 2 sorts a pivot table; see the argument list for more information.

Syntax 1: *object*.**Sort**(*key1*, *order1*, *key2*, *type*, *order2*, *key3*, *order3*, *header*, *orderCustom*, *matchCase*, *orientation*)

Syntax 2: *object*.**Sort**(*key1*, *order1*, *type*, *orderCustom*, *orientation*)

The Sort method has the following object qualifier and named arguments:

The *object* is the Range object and is required.

The *key1* argument is required (optional when sorting pivot tables), and is the first sort field, as text (a pivot field or range name) or a Range object ("Dept" or Cells(1, 1), for example).

The *order1* argument is optional. If xlAscending or omitted, *key1* is sorted in ascending order. If xlDescending, *key1* is sorted in descending order.

The *key2* argument is optional, and is the second sort field, as text (a pivot field or range name) or a Range object. If omitted, there is no second sort field. Not used when sorting pivot tables.

The *type* argument is optional, and is only used when sorting pivot tables. Specifies which elements are sorted, either xlSortValues or xlSortLabels.

The *order2* argument is optional, and is the sort order for *key2* (xlAscending or xlDescending); if omitted, xlAscending is assumed. Not used when sorting pivot tables.

The *key3* argument is optional, and is the third sort field, as text (a range name) or a Range object. If omitted, there is no third sort field. Not used when sorting pivot tables.

The *order3* argument is optional, and is the sort order for *key3* (xlAscending or xlDescending); if omitted, xlAscending is assumed. Not used when sorting pivot tables.

The *header* argument is optional. If xlYes, the first row contains headers (it is not sorted). If xlNo or omitted, no headers exist (the entire range is sorted). If xlGuess, Excel guesses if there is a header, and where it is if there is one. Not used when sorting pivot tables.

The *orderCustom* argument is optional, and is a one-based integer offset into the list of custom sort orders. If omitted, one (Normal) is used.

The *matchCase* argument is optional. If True, the sort is case sensitive. If False, the sort is not case sensitive. Not used when sorting pivot tables.

The *orientation* argument is optional. If xlTopToBottom or omitted, the sort is done from top to bottom (sort rows). If xlLeftToRight, the sort is done from left to right (sort columns).

SortSpecial   Method

Applies To: Range

Explanation: Syntax 1 uses Far-East sorting methods to sort the range, or the current region if the range contains only one cell. Syntax 2 uses Asian sorting methods to sort a pivot table; see the argument list for more information.

Syntax 1: *object*.SortSpecial(*key1*, *sortMethod*, *order1*, *key2*, *type*, *order2*, *key3*, *order3*, *header*, *orderCustom*, *matchCase*, *orientation*)

Syntax 2: *object*.SortSpecial(*key1*, *sortMethod*, *order1*, *type*, *orderCustom*, *orientation*)

The Sort method has the following object qualifier and named arguments:

The *object* is the Range object and is required.

The *key1* argument is required (optional when sorting pivot tables), and is the first sort field, as text (a pivot field or range name) or a Range object ("Dept" or Cells(1, 1), for example).

The *sortMethod* argument is optional, and specifies how to sort (xlSyllabary to sort phonetically or xlCodePage to sort by code page). The default value is xlSyllabary.

The *order1* argument is optional. If xlAscending or omitted, *key1* is sorted in ascending order. If xlDescending, key1 is sorted in descending order.

The *key2* argument is optional, and is the second sort field, as text (a pivot field or range name) or a Range object. If omitted, there is no second sort field. Not used when sorting pivot tables.

The *type* argument is optional, and is only used when sorting pivot tables. Specifies which elements are sorted, either xlSortValues or xlSortLabels.

The *order2* argument is optional, and is a sort order for *key2* (xlAscending or xlDescending); if omitted, xlAscending is assumed. Not used when sorting pivot tables.

The *key3* argument is optional, and is the third sort field, as text (a range name) or a Range object. If omitted, there is no third sort field. Not used when sorting pivot tables.

The *order3* argument is optional. Sort order for *key3* (xlAscending or xlDescending); if omitted, xlAscending is assumed. Not used when sorting pivot tables.

The *header* argument is optional. If xlYes, the first row contains headers (it is not sorted). If xlNo or omitted, no headers exist (the entire range is sorted). If xlGuess, Excel guesses if there is a header, and where it is if there is one. Not used when sorting pivot tables.

The *orderCustom* argument is optional, and is a one-based integer offset into the list of custom sort orders. If omitted, one (Normal) is used.

The *matchCase* argument is optional. If True, the sort is case sensitive. If False, the sort is not case sensitive. Not used when sorting pivot tables.

The *orientation* argument is optional. If xlTopToBottom or omitted, the sort is done from top to bottom (sort rows). If xlLeftToRight, the sort is done from left to right (sort columns).

SoundNote   Property

Applies To: Range

Explanation: Returns the SoundNote associated with the top left cell in the Range object. Read-only.

Syntax: `object.SoundNote`

The *object* is the Range object that contains the cell with and is required the sound note.

Notes: Your computer might require optional hardware to record and play sound notes.

SourceData   Property

Applies To: PivotTable

Explanation: Returns the data source for the PivotTable, as shown in the following table.

Data Source	Return Value
Microsoft Excel list or database	The cell reference as text.
External data source	An array. Each row consists of a SQL connection string with the remaining elements as the query string broken down into 200-character segments.
Multiple Consolidation ranges	A two-dimensional array. Each row consists of a reference and associated page field items.
Another pivot table	One of the preceding three kinds of information.

Syntax: `object.SourceData`

The *object* is the PivotTable object and is required.

SourceName   Property

Applies To: PivotField, PivotItem

Explanation: Returns the object name (a string) as it appears in the original source data for the pivot table. This might be different from the current item name if the user renamed the item after creating the pivot table. Read-only.

Syntax: `object.SourceName`

The *object* is the PivotField or PivotItem object and is required.

SpecialCells   Method

Applies To: Range

Explanation: Returns a range that refers to all the cells that match the specified type and value.

Syntax: *object*.**SpecialCells**(*type*, *value*)

The SpecialCells method has the following object qualifier and named arguments:

The *object* is the Range object and is required.

The *type* argument is required, and is the types of cells to include, as shown in the following table.

Value	Meaning
xlNotes	Cells containing notes.
xlConstants	Cells containing constants.
xlFormulas	Cells containing formulas.
xlBlanks	Empty cells.
xlLastCell	Last cell of the used range.
xlVisible	All visible cells.

The *value* argument is optional. If type is xlConstants or xlFormulas, the *value* argument is used to determine which types of cells to include in the result. These values can be added together to return more than one type. The default is to select all constants or formulas, no matter what the type.

Value	Meaning
xlNumbers	Numbers
xlTextValues	Text
xlLogical	Logical values
xlErrors	Error values

Spinners   Method

Applies To: Chart, DialogSheet, Worksheet

Explanation: Returns a single spinner control (a Spinner object, Syntax 1) or a collection of spinner controls on the chart or sheet (a Spinners object, Syntax 2).

Syntax 1: *object*.Spinners(*index*)

Syntax 2: *object*.Spinners

The Spinners method has the following object qualifier and named arguments:

The *object* is the Chart, DialogSheet, or Worksheet object and is required.

The *index* is required for Syntax 1, and specifies the name or number of the spinner (can be an array to specify more than one).

Split   Property

Applies To: Window

Explanation: True if the window is split. Read-write.

Syntax: *object*.Split

The *object* is the Window object and is required.

Notes: It is possible for FreezePanes to be True and Split to be False, or vice versa.

This property applies only to worksheets and macro sheets.

SplitColumn   Property

Applies To: Window

Explanation: Returns or sets the column number where the window is split into panes (the number of columns to the left of the split line). Read-write.

Syntax: *object*.SplitColumn

The *object* is the Window object and is required.

SplitHorizontal   Property

Applies To: Window

Explanation: Returns or sets the location of the horizontal window split, in points (1/72 inch). Read-write.

Syntax: *object*.SplitHorizontal

The *object* is the Window object and is required.

SplitRow   Property

Applies To: Window

Explanation: Returns or sets the row number where the window is split into panes (the number of rows above the split). Read-write.

Syntax: *object*.SplitRow

The *object* is the Window object and is required.

SplitVertical   Property

Applies To: Window

Explanation: Returns or sets the location of the vertical window split, in points (1/72 inch). Read-write.

Syntax: *object*.SplitVertical

The *object* is the Window object and is required.

SQLBind   Function

Explanation: Specifies where results are placed when they are retrieved using the SQLRetrieve function.

This function is designed to work exclusively with the SQLClose, SQLError, SQLExecQuery, SQLGetSchema, SQLOpen, and SQLRetrieve ODBC functions, to provide a way to create custom data access applications using Visual Basic.

This function is contained in the XLODBC add-in. Before you use the function, you must establish a reference to the XLODBC add-in using the References command from the Tools menu. For more information, see "Calling Procedures in Another Workbook" in the *Visual Basic User's Guide*.

Syntax: SQLBind(*connection*, *column*, *ref*)

The SQLBind function has the following named arguments:

The **connection** argument is required, and is the unique connection ID of the data source, returned by SQLOpen, for which you want to define storage.

The *column* argument is optional, and is the number of the result set that you want bound. Columns in the result set are numbered from left to right starting with 1. If you omit *column*, all bindings for connection are removed.

Column number 0 contains row numbers for the result set. If column number 0 is bound, SQLRetrieve returns row numbers in the bound location.

The *ref* argument is optional, and is the location of a single cell on a worksheet where you want the results bound, as a Range object. If *ref* is omitted, binding is removed for the column.

The Return Value function returns an array listing the bound columns for the current connection by column number.

If SQLBind is unable to bind the column to the cell in the specified reference, it returns the #N/A error value.

If **connection** is not valid or if you try to bind a cell that is not available, SQLBind returns the #VALUE! error value.

If *ref* refers to more than a single cell, SQLBind returns the #REF! error value.

If SQLRetrieve does not have a destination parameter, SQLBind places the result set in the location indicated by reference.

Notes: SQLBind tells the ODBC Control Panel Administrator where to place results when they are received using SQLRetrieve The results are placed in the reference cell and cells immediately below it.

Use SQLBind if you want the results from different columns to be placed in disjoint worksheet locations.

Use SQLBind for each column in the result set. A binding remains valid as long as the connection specified by connection is open.

SQLBind can be called any time there is a valid connection. Calls to SQLBind do not affect results that have already been retrieved.

SQLClose   Function

Explanation: Closes a connection to an external data source.

This function is designed to work exclusively with the SQLBind, SQLError, SQLExecQuery, SQLGetSchema, SQLOpen, SQLRetrieve, and SQLRetrieveToFile ODBC functions, to provide a way to create custom data access applications using Visual Basic.

This function is contained in the XLODBC add-in. Before you use the function, you must establish a reference to the XLODBC add-in using the References command from the Tools menu. For more information, see "Calling Procedures in Another Workbook" in the *Visual Basic User's Guide.*

Syntax: SQLClose(*connection*)

The SQLClose function has the following named argument:

The **connection** argument is the unique connection ID of the data source from which you want to disconnect, and is required.

If the connection argument is successfully closed, the Return Value function returns 0 (zero) and the connection ID is no longer valid.

If **connection** is not valid, this function returns the #VALUE! error value.

If SQLClose is unable to disconnect from the data source, it returns the #N/A error value.

SQLError   Function

Explanation: Returns detailed error information when called after one of the other ODBC functions fails. If SQLError itself fails, it cannot return error information.

Error information is defined and stored in memory whenever an ODBC function fails. To make the error information available, call the SQLError function.

SQLError provides detailed error information only about errors that occur when an ODBC function fails. It does not provide information about Excel errors.

This function is designed to work exclusively with the SQLBind, SQLClose, SQLExecQuery, SQLGetSchema, SQLOpen, SQLRetrieve, and SQLRetrieveToFile ODBC functions, to provide a way to create custom data access applications using Visual Basic.

This function is contained in the XLODBC add-in. Before you use the function, you must establish a reference to the XLODBC add-in using the References command from the Tools menu. For more information, see "Calling Procedures in Another Workbook" in the *Visual Basic User's Guide.*

Syntax: `SQLError()`

If there are errors, SQLError returns detailed error information in a two-dimensional array in which each row describes one error.

Each row has three fields for information obtained through the SQLError function call in ODBC. The fields are:

   ✔ A character string indicating the ODBC error class and subclass.

   ✔ A numeric value indicating the data source native error code.

   ✔ A text message describing the error.

If a function call generates multiple errors, SQLError creates a row for each error.

If there are no errors from a previous ODBC function call, this function returns only the #N/A error value.

SQLExecQuery   Function

Explanation: Executes a query on a data source with a connection that has been established using SQLOpen.

SQLExecQuery executes only the query. Use SQLRetrieve or SQLRetrieveToFile to get the results.

This function is designed to work exclusively with the SQLBind, SQLClose, SQLError, SQLGetSchema, SQLOpen, SQLRetrieve, and SQLRetrieveToFile macro functions, to provide a way to create custom data access applications using Visual Basic.

This function is contained in the XLODBC add-in. Before you use the function, you must establish a reference to the XLODBC add-in using the References command from the Tools menu. For more information, see "Calling Procedures in Another Workbook" in the *Visual Basic User's Guide.*

Syntax: SQLExecQuery(*connection, query*)

The SQLExecQuery function has the following named arguments:

The ***connection*** argument is required, and is the unique connection ID returned by SQLOpen that identifies the data source you want to query.

The ***query*** argument is required, and is the query to be executed on the data source. The query must follow the SQL syntax guidelines for the specific driver.

The value returned (return value) by SQLExecQuery depends on the type of SQL statement executed:

SQL statement executed	Return Value
SELECT	The number of columns in the result set.
UPDATE, INSERT or DELETE	The number of rows affected by the statement.
Any other valid SQL statement	0

If SQLExecQuery is unable to execute the query on the specified data source, it returns the #N/A error value.

If ***connection*** is not valid, SQLExecQuery returns the #VALUE! error.

Notes: Before calling SQLExecQuery you must establish a connection to a data source using SQLOpen The unique connection ID returned by SQLOpen is used by SQLExecQuery to send queries to the data source.

If you call SQLExecQuery using a previously used connection ID, any pending results on that connection are replaced by the new results.

SQLGetSchema   Function

Explanation: Returns information about the structure of the data source on a particular connection.

This function is designed to work exclusively with the SQLBind, SQLClose, SQLError, SQLExecQuery, SQLOpen, SQLRetrieve, and SQLRetrieveToFile ODBC functions, to provide a way to create custom data access applications using Visual Basic.

This function is contained in the XLODBC add-in. Before you use the function, you must establish a reference to the XLODBC add-in using the References command from the Tools menu. For more information, see "Calling Procedures in Another Workbook" in the *Visual Basic User's Guide.*

Syntax: `SQLGetSchema(`*`connection`*`, `*`action`*`, `*`qualifier`*`)`

The SQLGetSchema function has the following named arguments:

The *connection* argument is required, and is the unique connection ID of the data source you connected to using SQLOpen and for which you want information.

The *action* argument is required, and specifies the type of information you want returned, as shown in the following list.

Value	Meaning
1	A list of available data sources.
2	A list of databases on the current connection.
3	A list of owners in a database on the current connection.
4	A list of tables for a given owner and database on the current connection.
5	A list of columns in a particular table and their ODBC SQL data types in a two-dimensional array. The first field contains the name of the column and the second field is the ODBC SQL data type of the column.
6	The user ID of the current user.
7	The name of the current database.
8	The name of the data source defined during setup or by using the ODBC Control Panel Administrator.
9	The name of the DBMS the data source uses, for example, ORACLE, or SQL Server.
10	The server name for the data source.
11	The terminology used by the data source to refer to the owners, for example "owner," "Authorization ID," or "Schema."
12	The terminology used by the data source to refer a table, for example, "table" or "file."
13	The terminology used by the data source to refer to a qualifier, for example, "database" or "directory."
14	The terminology used by the data source to refer to a procedure, for example, "database procedure," "stored procedure," or "procedure."

The `qualifier` argument is optional, and is included only for action values of 3, 4 and 5. A string that qualifies the search, as shown in the following table:

Action	Qualifier
3	The name of the database in the current data source. SQLGetSchema returns the names of the table owners in that database.
4	Both a database name and an owner name. The syntax consists of the database name followed by the owner's name with a period separating the two; for example, "DatabaseName.OwnerName". This function returns an array of table names that are located in the given database and owned by the given owner.
5	The name of a table. SQLGetSchema returns information about the columns in the table.

The return value from a successful call to SQLGetSchema depends on the type of information requested.

If SQLGetSchema cannot find the requested information, it returns the #N/A error value.

If **connection** is not valid, this function returns the #VALUE! error value.

Notes: SQLGetSchema works with the ODBC functions SQLGetInfo and SQLTables to find the requested information.

SQLOpen   Function

Explanation: Establishes a connection to a data source.

This function is designed to work exclusively with the SQLBind, SQLClose, SQLError, SQLExecQuery, SQLGetSchema, SQLRetrieve, and SQLRetrieveToFile ODBC functions, to provide a way to create custom data access applications using Visual Basic.

This function is contained in the XLODBC add-in. Before you use the function, you must establish a reference to the XLODBC add-in using the References command from the Tools menu. For more information, see "Calling Procedures in Another Workbook" in the *Visual Basic User's Guide.*

Syntax: `SQLOpen(connectionString, output, prompt)`

The SQLOpen function has the following named arguments:

The **connectionString** argument is required, and supplies the information required by the driver being used to connect to a data source and must follow the driver's format.

You must define the data source name (DSN) used in **connectionString** before you try to connect to it.

The *output* argument is optional, and is a single cell, as a Range object, that contains the completed connection string.

Use *output* when you want SQLOpen to return the completed connection string to a worksheet.

The *prompt* argument is optional, and specifies when the driver dialog box is displayed and which options are available. Use one of the numbers described in the following table. If *prompt* is omitted, SQLOpen uses 2 as the default.

Value	Meaning
1	Driver dialog box is always displayed.
2	Driver dialog box is displayed only if information provided by the connection string and the data source specification are not sufficient to complete the connection. All dialog box options are available.
3	The same as 2 except that dialog box options that are not required are dimmed and unavailable.
4	Driver dialog box is not displayed. If the connection is not successful, SQLOpen returns an error.

If successful, SQLOpen returns a unique connection ID number (Return Value). Use the connection ID number with the other ODBC functions.

If SQLOpen is unable to connect using the information you provide, it returns the error value #N/A. Additional error information is placed in memory for use by SQLError.

SQLRequest   Function

Explanation: Connects to an external data source and runs a query from a worksheet, and then returns the result as an array.

This function is designed to work exclusively with the SQLBind, SQLClose, SQLError, SQLExecQuery, SQLGetSchema, SQLRetrieve, and SQLRetrieveToFile ODBC functions, to provide a way to create custom data access applications using Visual Basic.

This function is contained in the XLODBC add-in. Before you use the function, you must establish a reference to the XLODBC add-in using the References command from the Tools menu. For more information, see "Calling Procedures in Another Workbook" in the *Visual Basic User's Guide*.

Syntax: `SQLRequest(connectionString, query, output, prompt, columnNames)`

The SQLRequest function has the following named arguments:

The *connectionString* argument is required, and supplies information, such as the data source name, user ID, and passwords, required by the driver being used to connect to a data source and must follow the driver's format.

You must define the data source name (DSN) used in *connectionString* before you try to connect to it. If SQLRequest is unable to access the data source using *connectionString*, it returns the #N/A error value.

The *query* argument is required, and is the SQL statement that you want to execute on the data source.

If SQLRequest is unable to execute *query* on the specified data source, it returns the #N/A error value.

The *output* argument is optional, and is a single cell, as a range object, where you want the completed connection string placed.

Use *output* when you want SQLRequest to return the completed connection string to a worksheet.

The *prompt* argument is optional, and specifies when the driver dialog box is displayed and which options are available. Use one of the numbers described in the following table. If *prompt* is omitted, SQLRequest uses 2 as the default.

Value	Meaning
1	Driver dialog box is always displayed.
2	Driver dialog box is displayed only if information provided by the connection string and the data source specification is not sufficient to complete the connection. All dialog box options are available.
3	Driver dialog box is displayed only if information provided by the connection string and the data source specification is not sufficient to complete the connection. Dialog box options are dimmed and unavailable if they are not required.
4	Dialog box is not displayed. If the connection is not successful, it returns an error.

The *columnNames* argument is optional. True if you want the column names to be returned as the first row of results. It should contain False if you do not want the column names returned. The default value, if *columnNames* is omitted, is False.

If the Return Value function completes all of its actions, it returns an array of query results or the number of rows affected by the query.

If SQLRequest is unable to complete all of its actions, it returns an error value and places the error information in memory for SQLError.

If SQLRequest is unable to access the data source using connectionString, it returns the #N/A error value.

SQLRetrieve   Function

Explanation: Retrieves all or part of the results from a previously executed query. Before using SQLRetrieve, you must establish a connection with SQLOpen, execute a query with SQLExecQuery, and have the results pending.

This function is designed to work exclusively with the SQLBind, SQLClose, SQLError, SQLExecQuery, SQLGetSchema, and SQLOpen ODBC functions, to provide a way to create custom data access applications using Visual Basic.

This function is contained in the XLODBC add-in. Before you use the function, you must establish a reference to the XLODBC add-in using the References command from the Tools menu. For more information, see "Calling Procedures in Another Workbook" in the *Visual Basic User's Guide.*

Syntax: `SQLRetrieve(connection, destination, maxColumns, maxRows, columnNames, rowNumbers, namedRange, fetchFirst)`

The SQLRetrieve function has the following named arguments:

The **connection** argument is required, and is the unique connection ID returned by SQLOpen and for which you have pending query results generated by SQLExecQuery.

If **connection** is not valid, SQLExecQuery returns the #VALUE! error value.

The *destination* argument is optional, and is a Range object that specifies where the results should be placed. This function overwrites any values in the cells without confirmation.

If *destination* refers to a single cell, SQLRetrieve returns all of the pending results in that cell and in the cells to the right and below it.

If *destination* is omitted, the bindings established by previous calls to SQLBind are used to return results. If no bindings exist for the current connection, SQLRetrieve returns #REF! error value.

If a particular result column has not been bound and *destination* is omitted, the results are discarded.

The *maxColumns* argument is optional, and is the maximum number of columns returned to the worksheet starting at destination.

If *maxColumns* specifies more columns than are available in the result, SQLRetrieve places data in the columns for which data is available and clears the additional columns.

If *maxColumns* specifies fewer columns than are available in the result, SQLRetrieve discards the rightmost result columns until the results fit the specified size.

The order in which the data source returns the columns determines column position.

All of the results are returned if *maxColumns* is omitted.

The *maxRows* argument is optional. The maximum number of rows to be returned to the worksheet starting at destination.

If *maxRows* specifies more rows than are available in the results, SQLRetrieve places data in the rows for which data is available and clears the additional rows.

If *maxRows* specifies fewer rows than are available in the results, SQLRetrieve places data in the selected rows but does not discard the additional rows. Extra rows are retrieved by using SQLRetrieve again and by setting *fetchFirst* to False.

All of the rows in the results are returned if *maxRows* is omitted.

The *columnNames* argument is optional. True if you want the column names to be returned as the first row of results. False or omitted if you do not want the column names returned.

The *rowNumbers* argument is optional, and is used only when *destination* is included in the function call. If *rowNumbers* is True, the first column in the result set contains row numbers. If *destination* is False or omitted, the row numbers are not returned. You can also retrieve row numbers by binding column number 0 with SQLBind.

The *namedRange* argument is optional. True if you want each column of the results to be declared as a named range on the worksheet. The name of each range is the result column name. The named range includes only the rows that are returned with SQLRetrieve. The default is False.

The *fetchFirst* argument is optional, and allows you to request results from the beginning of the result set. If *fetchFirst* is False, SQLRetrieve can be called repeatedly to return the next set of rows until all the result rows are returned. When there are no more rows in the result set, SQLRequest returns 0. If you want to retrieve results from the beginning of the result set, set *fetchFirst* to True. To retrieve additional rows from the result set, set *fetchFirst* to False in subsequent calls. The default is False.

SQLRetrieve returns the number of rows (Return Value) in the result set.

If SQLRetrieve is unable to retrieve the results on the specified data source or if there are no results pending, it returns the #N/A error value. If no data is found, it returns 0.

Notes: Before calling SQLRetrieve, you must:

1. Establish a connection with a data source using SQLOpen.

2. Use the connection ID returned by SQLOpen to send a query with SQLExecQuery.

SQLRetrieveToFile   Function

Explanation: Retrieves all of the results from a previously executed query and places them in a file.

To use this function you must have established a connection with a data source using SQLOpen, executed a query using SQLExecQuery, and have the results of the query pending.

This function is designed to work exclusively with the SQLClose, SQLError, SQLExecQuery, SQLGetSchema, SQLOpen and SQLRetrieve ODBC functions, to provide a way to create custom data access applications using Visual Basic.

This function is contained in the XLODBC add-in. Before you use the function, you must establish a reference to the XLODBC add-in using the References command from the Tools menu. For more information, see "Calling Procedures in Another Workbook" in the *Visual Basic User's Guide.*

Syntax: `SQLRetrieveToFile(`*`connection`*`, `*`destination`*`, `*`columnNames`*`,`
`columnDelimiter`*`)`

The SQLRetrieveToFile function has the following named arguments:

The *connection* argument is required, and is the unique connection ID returned by SQLOpen and for which you have pending query results generated by SQLExecQuery.

If *connection* is not valid, SQLExecQuery returns the #VALUE! error value.

The *destination* argument is required, and is a string that specifies the name and path of the file where you want to place the results. If the file exists, its contents are replaced with the query results. If the file does not exist, SQLRetrieveToFile creates and opens the file and fills it with the results.

The format of the data in the file is compatible with the Excel.CSV (comma-separated value) file format.

Columns are separated by the character specified by *columnDelimiter*, and the individual rows are separated by a carriage return.

If the file specified by *destination* cannot be opened, SQLRetrieveToFile returns the #N/A error value.

The *columnNames* argument is optional. True if you want the column names to be returned as the first row of data. False or omitted if you do not want the column names returned.

The *columnDelimiter* argument is optional, and is a string that specifies the character used to separate the elements in each row. For example, use "," to specify a comma delimiter or ";" to specify a semicolon delimiter. If you omit *columnDelimiter*, a TAB is used.

If successful, SQLRetrieveToFile returns the query results (Return Value), writes them to a file, and then returns the number of rows that were written to the file.

If SQLRetrieveToFile is unable to retrieve the results, it returns the #N/A error value, and does not write the file.

If there are no pending results on the connection, SQLRetrieveToFile returns the #N/A error value.

Notes: Before calling SQLRetrieveToFile, you must:

1. Establish a connection with a data source using SQLOpen.

2. Use the connection ID returned by SQLOpen to send a query with SQLExecQuery.

StandardFont   Property

Applies To: Application

Explanation: Returns or sets the standard font name as a string. Read-write.

Syntax: *object*`.StandardFont`

The *object* is the Application object and is required.

Notes: If you change the standard font using this property, the change does not take effect until you restart Excel.

StandardFontSize   Property

Applies To: Application

Explanation: Returns or sets the standard font size in points (1/72 inch). Read-write.

Syntax: *object*`.StandardFontSize`

The *object* is the Application object and is required.

Notes: If you change the standard font size using this property, the change does not take effect until you restart Excel.

StandardHeight   Property

Applies To: Worksheet

Explanation: Returns the standard (default) height of all the rows in the worksheet, measured in points (1/72 inch). Read-only.

Syntax: *object*`.StandardHeight`

The *object* is the Worksheet object and is required.

StandardWidth   Property

Applies To: Worksheet

Explanation: Returns or sets the standard (default) width of all the columns in the worksheet, measured in characters of the normal font. Read-write.

Syntax: *object*`.StandardWidth`

The *object* is the Worksheet object and is required.

Notes: If the normal font is a proportional font, this property returns the column width measured in characters of the zero (0) character in the normal font.

StartupPath   Property

Applies To: Application

Explanation: Returns the complete path of the startup directory, not including the final separator. Read-only.

Syntax: `object.StartupPath`

The `object` is the Application object and is required.

Status   Property

Applies To: RoutingSlip

Explanation: Indicates the status of the routing slip (one of xlNotYetRouted, xlRoutingInProgress, or xlRoutingComplete). Read-only.

Syntax: `object.Status`

The `object` is the RoutingSlip object and is required.

StatusBar   Property

Applies To: Application

Explanation: Returns or sets the text in the status bar. Read-write.

Syntax: `object.StatusBar`

The `object` is the Application object and is required.

Notes: This property returns False if Excel has control of the status bar; set the property to False to restore the default status bar text. This works even if the status bar is hidden.

Strikethrough   Property

Applies To: Font

Explanation: True if the font is struck through. Read-write.

Syntax: `object.Strikethrough`

The `object` is the Font object (ActiveCell.Font, for example) and is required.

String   Function

Explanation: Returns a repeating character string of the length specified.

Syntax: `String(number,character)`

The String function syntax has these named-argument parts:

Part	Description
number	Length of the returned string. If number contains no valid data, Null is returned.
character	Character code specifying the character or string expression whose first character is used to build the return string. If character contains no valid data, Null is returned.

Notes: If you specify a number for character greater than 255, String converts the number to a valid character code using the formula: character Mod 256

Style   Property

Applies To: Range

Explanation: Returns or sets the Style of the range. Read-write.

Syntax: `object.Style`

The `object` is the Range object and is required.

Styles   Method

Applies To: Workbook

Explanation: Returns a single style (a Style object, Syntax 1) or a collection of all the styles (a Styles object, Syntax 2) in the workbook. Read-only.

Syntax 1: `object.Styles(index)`

Syntax 2: `object.Styles`

The Styles method has the following object qualifier and named arguments:

The `object` is the Workbook object and is required.

The `index` argument is required for Syntax 1, and is the name or number of the style to return.

Sub   Statement

Explanation: Declares the name, arguments, and code that form the body of a Sub procedure.

Syntax: `Private` or `Public.Static.Sub(name, arglist, statements)`

The Sub statement syntax has these parts:

Part	Description
Private	Indicates that the Sub procedure is accessible only to other procedures in the module where it is declared.
Public	Indicates that the Sub procedure is accessible to all other procedures in all modules. If used in a private module (one that contains an Option Private statement) the procedure is not available outside the project.
Static	Indicates that the Sub procedure's local variables are preserved between calls. The Static attribute doesn't affect variables that are declared outside the Sub, even if they are used in the procedure.
name	Name of the Sub; follows standard variable naming conventions.
arglist	List of variables representing arguments that are passed to the Sub procedure when it is called. Multiple variables are separated by commas.
statements	Any group of statements to be executed within the body of the Sub procedure.

The *arglist* argument has the following syntax and parts:

Optional ByVal or **ByRef ParamArray** (*varname*, As *type*)

Part	Description
Optional	Indicates that an argument is not required. If used, all subsequent arguments in arglist must also be optional and declared using the Optional keyword. All Optional arguments must be Variant. Optional can't be used for any argument if ParamArray is used.
ByVal	Indicates that the argument is passed by value.
ByRef	Indicates that the argument is passed by reference.
ParamArray	Used only as the last argument in arglist to indicate that the final argument is an Optional array of Variant elements. The ParamArray keyword allows you to provide an arbitrary number of arguments. May not be used with ByVal, ByRef, or Optional.
varname	Name of the variable representing the argument; follows standard variable naming conventions.

continues

Part	Description
type	Data type of the argument passed to the procedure; may be Boolean, Integer, Long, Currency, Single, Double, Date, String (variable length only), Object, Variant, a user-defined type, or an object type.

Notes: If not explicitly specified using either Public or Private, Sub procedures are Public by default. If Static is not used, the value of local variables is not preserved between calls.

All executable code must be in procedures. You can't define a Sub procedure inside another Sub, Function, or Property procedure.

The Exit Sub keyword causes an immediate exit from a Sub procedure. Program execution continues with the statement following the statement that called the Sub procedure. Any number of Exit Sub statements can appear anywhere in a Sub procedure.

Like a Function procedure, a Sub procedure is a separate procedure that can take arguments, perform a series of statements, and change the value of its arguments. However, unlike a Function procedure, which returns a value, a Sub procedure can't be used in an expression.

You call a Sub procedure using the procedure name followed by the argument list. See the Call statement for specific information on how to call Sub procedures.

Caution: Sub procedures can be recursive; that is, they can call themselves to perform a given task. However, recursion can lead to stack overflow. The Static keyword usually is not used with recursive Sub procedures.

Variables used in Sub procedures fall into two categories: those that are explicitly declared within the procedure and those that are not. Variables that are explicitly declared in a procedure (using Dim or the equivalent) are always local to the procedure. Other variables used but not explicitly declared in a procedure are also local unless they are explicitly declared at some higher level outside the procedure.

Caution: A procedure can use a variable that is not explicitly declared in the procedure, but a name conflict can occur if anything you have defined at the module level has the same name. If your procedure refers to an undeclared variable that has the same name as another procedure, constant or variable, it is assumed that your procedure is referring to that module-level name. Explicitly declare variables to avoid this kind of conflict. You can use an Option Explicit statement to force explicit declaration of variables.

Notes: You can't use GoSub, GoTo, or Return to enter or exit a Sub procedure.

Subject   Property

Applies To: AddIn, Mailer, RoutingSlip, Workbook

Explanation: Returns or sets the subject for an object, as a string. Read-only for AddIn, read-write for RoutingSlip and Workbook.

Syntax: `object.Subject`

The *object* is the object to which this property applies and is required.

Notes: The RoutingSlip subject is used as the subject of mail messages used to route the workbook.

PowerTalk requires that a subject be present before the mailer can be sent.

SubscribeTo   Method

Applies To: Range

Explanation: Macintosh (running System 7 or later) only. Subscribes to a published edition.

Syntax: `object.SubscribeTo(edition, format)`

The SubscribeTo method has the following object qualifier and named arguments:

The *object* is the Range object and is required.

The *edition* argument is required, and is the name of the edition, as a string, to which you want to subscribe.

The *format* argument is optional. xlPicture to subscribe to a picture, xlText to subscribe to text.

Subscript   Property

Applies To: Font

Explanation: True if the font is subscripted. Read-write.

Syntax: `object.Subscript`

The *object* is the Font object and is required.

Notes: This property is False by default.

SubType   Property

Applies To: Chart, ChartGroup

Explanation: Returns or sets the subtype for a single chart group or for all chart groups in the chart.

Syntax: `object.SubType`

The *object* is the Chart or ChartGroup object and is required.

Notes: Set the SubType property after you set the Type property. Each type supports different subtypes (for example, a column chart type can have clustered, stacked, or percent subtypes). The easiest way to obtain the number of the subtype is to record the subtype formatting using the macro recorder.

Subtotal   Method

Applies To: Range

Explanation: Creates subtotals for the range (or current region if the range is a single cell).

For help about using the Subtotal worksheet function in Visual Basic, see Using Worksheet Functions in Visual Basic.

Syntax: `object.Subtotal(groupBy, function, totalList, replace, pageBreaks, summaryBelowData)`

The Subtotal method has the following object qualifier and named arguments:

The *object* is the Range object and is required.

The *groupBy* argument is required, and is the field to group by, as a one-based integer offset.

The *function* argument is required, and is the subtotal function. Can be one of xlAverage, xlCount, xlCountNums, xlMax, xlMin, xlProduct, xlStDev, xlStDevP, xlSum, xlVar, or xlVarP.

The *totalList* argument is required, and is an array of one-based field offsets, indicating the fields to which the subtotals are added.

The *replace* argument is optional. If True, existing subtotals are replaced. If False or omitted, existing subtotals are not replaced.

The *pageBreaks* argument is optional. True to create page breaks after each group, False or omitted if no page breaks are created.

The *summaryBelowData* argument is optional. If xlBelow or omitted, the summary goes below detail. If xlAbove, the summary goes above detail.

Subtotals   Property

Applies To: PivotField

Explanation: Returns or sets an array of Boolean values corresponding to the subtotals showing with the specified field. This property is valid only for nondata fields. Read-write.

Syntax: `object.Subtotals`

The *object* is the PivotField object and is required.

Notes: This property returns an array of Boolean values, as shown in the following list.

Array Element	Meaning
1	Automatic
2	Sum
3	Count
4	Average
5	Max
6	Min
7	Product
8	Count Nums
9	StdDev
10	StdDevp
11	Var
12	Varp

If an array value is True, the field shows that subtotal. If automatic is True, all other values are set to False.

Summary   Property

Applies To: Range

Explanation: True if the range is an outlining summary row or column. The range should be a row or a column. Read-only.

Syntax: *object*.Summary

The *object* is the row or column, as a Range object and is required.

SummaryColumn   Property

Applies To: Outline

Explanation: Returns or sets the location of the summary columns in the outline, as shown in the following table. Read-write.

Value	Meaning
xlLeft	The summary column will be to the left of the detail columns in the outline.
xlRight	The summary column will be to the right of the detail columns in the outline.

Syntax: *object*.`SummaryColumn`

The *object* is the Outline object (ActiveSheet.Outline, for example) and is required.

SummaryRow   Property

Applies To: Outline

Explanation: Returns or sets the location of the summary rows in the outline, as shown in the following table. Read-write.

Value	Meaning
xlAbove	The summary row will be above the detail columns in the outline.
xlBelow	The summary row will be below the detail columns in the outline.

Syntax: *object*.`SummaryRow`

The *object* is the Outline object (ActiveSheet.Outline, for example) and is required.

Notes: Use `SummaryRow = xlAbove` for Word-style outlines, where category headers are above the detail. Use *SummaryRow = xlBelow* for accounting-style outlines, where summations are below the detailed information.

Superscript   Property

Applies To: Font

Explanation: True if the font is superscripted. Read-write.

Syntax: *object*.`Superscript`

The *object* is the Font object and is required.

Notes: This property is False by default.

SurfaceGroup   Property

Applies To: Chart

Explanation: Returns the surface ChartGroup of a 3D chart.

Syntax: *object*.`SurfaceGroup`

The *object* is the Chart object and is required.

Table   Method

Applies To: Range

Explanation: Creates a data table based on input values and formulas that you define on a worksheet.

Syntax: *object*.`Table`(*rowInput, columnInput*)

The Table method has the following object qualifier and named arguments:

The *object* is the object to which this method applies and is required.

The *rowInput* argument is optional, and is a single cell to use as the row input for your table.

The *columnInput* argument is optional, and is a single cell to use as the column input for your table.

Notes: Use data tables to perform a what-if analysis by changing certain constant values on your worksheet to see how values in other cells are affected.

TableRange1   Property

Applies To: PivotTable

Explanation: Returns the Range that contains the entire pivot table, but does not include page fields. Read-only.

Syntax: *object*.`TableRange1`

The *object* is the PivotTable object and is required.

Notes: The TableRange2 property includes page fields.

TableRange2   Property

Applies To: PivotTable

Explanation: Returns the Range that includes the entire pivot table, including page fields. Read-only.

Syntax: *object*.`TableRange2`

The *object* is the PivotTable object and is required.

Notes: The TableRange1 property does not include page fields.

TabRatio   Property

Applies To: Window

Explanation: Returns or sets the ratio of the width of the window workbook tabs to the width of the window horizontal scrollbar (as a number between zero and one; the default value is 0.75). Read-write.

Syntax: *object*.TabRatio

The *object* is the Window object and is required.

Notes: This property has no effect when DisplayWorkbookTabs is set to False (its value is retained, but it has no effect on the display).

Text   Property

Applies To: AxisTitle, Button, Buttons, Characters, ChartTitle, CheckBox, CheckBoxes, DataLabel, DataLabels, DialogFrame, DrawingObjects, DropDown, DropDowns, EditBox, EditBoxes, GroupBox, GroupBoxes, Label, Labels, OptionButton, OptionButtons, Range, TextBox, TextBoxes

Explanation: Returns or sets the text for the specified object, as shown in the following table. Read-write, except for the Range object, where this property is read-only.

Object	Text
AxisTitle, ChartTitle	The title text.
Button	The button text.
Characters	The text of this range of characters.
Controls	The control text (check box, dialog frame, drop down, edit box, group box, label, and option button).
DataLabel	The data label text.
Range	The actual text appearing in a cell, as a string. For example, if a cell is formatted to show dollar signs, returning the text of a cell will show the dollar sign. This can be used to create readable text representations of the values on a worksheet. Read-only.
TextBox	The text in the text box.

Syntax: `object.Text`

The **object** is the object to which this property applies and is required.

TextBoxes   Method

Applies To: Chart, DialogSheet, Worksheet

Explanation: Returns a single text box (a TextBox object, Syntax 1) or a collection of text boxes (a TextBoxes object, Syntax 2). Read-only.

Syntax 1: `object.TextBoxes(index)`

Syntax 2: `object.TextBoxes`

The TextBoxes method has the following object qualifier and named arguments:

The **object** is the object containing the text boxes and is required.

The **index** argument is required for Syntax 1, and is the name or number of the text box.

TextToColumns   Method

Applies To: Range

Explanation: Parses a column of cells containing text into several columns.

Syntax: `object.TextToColumns(destination, dataType, textQualifier, consecutiveDelimiter, tab, semicolon, comma, space, other, otherChar, fieldInfo)`

The TextToColumns method has the following object qualifier and named arguments:

The **object** is the Range object and is required.

The **destination** argument is optional, and is a range that specifies where Excel will place the results. If the range is larger than a single cell, the top left cell is used.

The **dataType** argument is optional, and specifies the format of the text to split into columns. Can be xlDelimited or xlFixedWidth. The default is xlDelimited.

The **textQualifier** argument is optional, and specifies the text qualifier. It can be one of xlDoubleQuote, xlSingleQuote, or xlNone. The default is xlDoubleQuote.

The **consecutiveDelimiter** argument is optional. True if consecutive delimiters should be considered as one delimiter. The default is False.

The **tab** argument is optional. True if dataType is xlDelimited and the tab character is a delimiter. The default is False.

The **semicolon** argument is optional. True if dataType is xlDelimited and the semicolon character is a delimiter. The default is False.

The **comma** argument is optional. True if dataType is xlDelimited and the comma character is a delimiter. The default is False.

The *space* argument is optional. True if dataType is xlDelimited and the space character is a delimiter. The default is False.

The *other* argument is optional. True if dataType is xlDelimited and the character specified by the otherChar argument is a delimiter. The default is False.

The *otherChar* argument is optional (required if other is True), and specifies the delimiter character when other is True. If more than one character is specified, only the first character of the string is used, remaining characters are ignored.

The *fieldInfo* argument is optional, and is an array containing parse information for the individual columns of data. The interpretation depends on the value of *dataType*.

When the data is delimited, this argument is an array of two-element arrays, with each two-element array specifying the conversion options for a particular column. The first element is the column number (one based), and the second element is one of the following numbers specifying how the column in parsed:

- ✔ General 2
- ✔ Text 3
- ✔ MDY date 4
- ✔ DMY date 5
- ✔ YMD date 6
- ✔ MYD date 7
- ✔ DYM date 8
- ✔ YDM date 9
- ✔ Skip the column

The column specifiers can be in any order. If a column specifier is not present for a particular column in the input data, the column is parsed using the General setting. This example causes the third column to be skipped, the first column to be parsed as text, and the remaining columns in the source data to be parsed with the General setting:

```
Array(Array(3, 9), Array(1, 2))
```

If the source data has fixed-width columns, the first element of each two-element array specifies the starting character position in the column (as an integer; character zero is the first character). The second element of the two-element array specifies the parse option for the column as a number from one through nine, as listed above.

The following example parses two columns from a fixed-width file, with the first column starting at the beginning of the line and extending for 10 characters. The second column starts at position 15 and goes to the end of the line. To avoid including the characters between position 10 and position 15, a skipped column entry is added.

```
Array(Array(0, 1), Array(10, 9), Array(15, 1))
```

ThisWorkbook   Property

Applies To: Application

Explanation: Returns the Workbook where the current macro code is running. Read-only.

Syntax: `ThisWorkbook`

Notes: This property cannot be used with an object qualifier. Do not type anything to the left of ThisWorkbook.

This property can be used only from inside Excel. You cannot use this property to access a workbook from another application.

When you want to refer to anything located in the same workbook as your macro, it is a good idea to use ThisWorkbook instead of the Workbooks(index) method. When you use ThisWorkbook, your macro will still work if you change the name of the workbook.

ThisWorkbook and ActiveWorkbook may or may not have the same value.

ThisWorkbook returns the workbook where the macro is stored.

TickLabelPosition   Property

Applies To: Axis

Explanation: Describes the position of tick labels on the specified axis (one of xlNone, xlLow, xlHigh, or xlNextToAxis). Read-write.

Syntax: *object*`.TickLabelPosition`

The *object* is the Axis object and is required.

TickLabelSpacing   Property

Applies To: Axis

Explanation: Returns or sets the number of categories or series between tick labels. Applies only to category and series axes. Read-write.

Syntax: *object*`.TickLabelSpacing`

The *object* is the Axis object and is required.

Notes: This property applies to the category and series axes only. Label spacing on the value axis is always calculated by Excel.

TickLabels   Property

Applies To: Axis

Explanation: Returns the TickLabels for the specified axis. Read-only.

Syntax: *object*.`TickLabels`

The *object* is the The Axis object and is required.

TickMarkSpacing   Property

Applies To: Axis

Explanation: Returns or sets the number of categories or series between tick marks. Applies only to category and series axes. Read-write.

Syntax: *object*.`TickMarkSpacing`

The *object* is the Axis object and is required.

Notes: This property applies to the category and series axes only. Use the MajorUnit and MinorUnit properties to set tick mark spacing on the value axis.

Title   Property

Applies To: AddIn, Workbook

Explanation: Returns or sets the long, descriptive title for the object, as a string. Read-only for AddIn, read-write for Workbook.

Syntax: *object*.`Title`

The *object* is the AddIn or Workbook object and is required.

ToolbarButtons   Method

Applies To: Toolbar

Explanation: Returns a single toolbar button (a ToolbarButton object, Syntax 1) or a collection of toolbar buttons (a ToolbarButtons object, Syntax 2) on the specified toolbar.

Syntax 1: *object*.`ToolbarButtons`(*index*)

Syntax 2: *object*.`ToolbarButtons`

The ToolbarButtons method has the following object qualifier and named arguments:

The *object* is the Toolbar object and is required.

The *index* argument is required for Syntax 1, and the name or number of the button.

Toolbars   Method

Applies To: Application

Explanation: Returns a single toolbar (a Toolbar object, Syntax 1) or a collection of toolbars (a Toolbars object, Syntax 2) in the current instance of Microsoft Excel. Read-only.

Syntax 1: *object*`.Toolbars(`*index*`)`

Syntax 2: *object*`.Toolbars`

The Toolbars method has the following object qualifier and named arguments:

The *object* is optional, and is the Application containing the toolbars.

The *index* is required for Syntax 1. The name or number of the toolbar.

Top   Property

Applies To: Application, Arc, Arcs, AxisTitle, Button, Buttons, ChartArea, ChartObject, ChartObjects, ChartTitle, CheckBox, CheckBoxes, DataLabel, DataLabels, DialogFrame, Drawing, DrawingObjects, Drawings, DropDown, DropDowns, EditBox, EditBoxes, GroupBox, GroupBoxes, GroupObject, GroupObjects, Label, Labels, Legend, Line, Lines, ListBox, ListBoxes, OLEObject, OLEObjects, OptionButton, OptionButtons, Oval, Ovals, Picture, Pictures, PlotArea, Range, Rectangle, Rectangles, ScrollBar, ScrollBars, Spinner, Spinners, TextBox, TextBoxes, Toolbar, Window

Explanation: Returns or sets the position of the specified object, in points (1/72 inch). Read-write, except for the Range object.

Syntax: *object*`.Top`

The *object* is the object to which this property applies and is required.

Notes: The Top property has several different meanings, depending on the object to which it is applied.

Object	Meaning
Application	The distance from the top edge of the physical screen to the top edge of the main Excel window, in points. With Windows, if the application window is minimized, this property controls the position of the icon (anywhere on the screen). On the Apple Macintosh the value is always zero; setting the value to something else will have no effect.
Button	The top position of the object, in points, measured from the top of row 1.

continues

Object	Meaning
Range	The distance from the top edge of row one to the top edge of the range, in points. If the range is discontinuous, the first area is used. If the range is more than one row high, the top (lowest numbered) row in the range is used. Read-only.
Toolbar	If the toolbar is docked (the Position property of the Toolbar object is not xlFloat), the number of points from the top edge of the toolbar to the top edge of the toolbar docking area.If the toolbar is floating, the number of points from the top edge of the toolbar to the top edge of the Excel workspace.
Window	The top position of the window, in points, measured from the top edge of the usable area (below the menus, top-docked toolbars, and/or the formula bar). You cannot set this property for a maximized window. Use the WindowState property to return or set the state of the window.
Arc, AxisTitle, ChartArea, ChartTitle, CheckBox, DataLabel, DialogFrame, Drawing, DrawingObjects, DropDown, EditBox, GroupBox, GroupObject, Label, Legend, Line, ListBox, OLEObject, OptionButton, Oval, Picture, PlotArea, Rectangle, ScrollBar, Spinner, TextBox, Title	The top position of the object, in points, measured from the top of row 1 (on a worksheet) or the top of the chart area (on a chart).

TopLeftCell   Property

Applies To: Arc, Button, ChartObject, CheckBox, Drawing, DropDown, EditBox, GroupBox, GroupObject, Label, Line, ListBox, OLEObject, OptionButton, Oval, Picture, Rectangle, ScrollBar, Spinner, TextBox

Explanation: Returns the cell that lies under the top left of this object. For drawing objects, this property applies only when the drawing object is on a worksheet. Read-only.

Syntax: `object.TopLeftCell`

The *object* is the object to which this property applies and is required.

TopMargin   Property

Applies To: PageSetup

Explanation: Returns or sets the size of the top margin, in points (1/72 inch). Read-write.

Syntax: `object.TopMargin`

The *object* is the PageSetup object (ActiveSheet.PageSetup, for example) and is required.

Notes: Margins are set or returned in points. Use the Application.InchesToPoints or Application.CentimetersToPoints function to convert.

ToRecipients   Property

Applies To: Mailer

Explanation: Returns or sets the direct recipients of the mailer. Read-write.

Syntax: `object.ToRecipients`

The *object* is the Mailer object and is required.

Notes: This property is an array of strings specifying the address, in one of the following formats:

- ✔ A record in the Preferred Personal Catalog. These names are one level deep ("Fred" or "June").

- ✔ A full path specifying either a record in a personal catalog ("HD:Excel Folder:My Catalog:Barney") or a plain record ("HD:Folder:Martin").

- ✔ A relative path from the current working directory specifying either a personal catalog record ("My Catalog:Barney") or a plain record ("Martin").

- ✔ A path in a PowerShare catalog tree of the form "CATALOG_NAME:<node>:RECORD_NAME" where <node> is a path to a PowerShare catalog. An example of a complete path is "AppleTalk:North Building Zone:George's Mac."

TotalLevels   Property

Applies To: PivotField

Explanation: Returns the total number of fields in the current field grouping. If the field is not grouped, TotalLevels returns the value 1. Read-only.

Syntax: *object*.`TotalLevels`

The *object* is the PivotField object and is required.

TrackStatus   Property

Applies To: RoutingSlip

Explanation: True if status tracking is enabled for the routing slip. Read-write before routing begins; read-only when routing is in progress.

Syntax: *object*.`TrackStatus`

The *object* is the RoutingSlip object and is required

TransitionExpEval   Property

Applies To: Worksheet

Explanation: True if Excel will use Lotus 1-2-3 expression evaluation rules for this worksheet. Read-write.

Syntax: *object*.`TransitionExpEval`

The *object* is the Worksheet object and is required

TransitionFormEntry   Property

Applies To: Worksheet

Explanation: True if Excel will use Lotus 1-2-3 formula entry rules for this worksheet. Read-write.

Syntax: *object*.`TransitionFormEntry`

The *object* is the Worksheet object and is required.

TransitionMenuKey   Property

Applies To: Application

Explanation: Returns or sets the alternate menu or help key, which is usually "/". Read-write.

Syntax: `object.TransitionMenuKey`

The **object** is the Worksheet object and is required

TransitionMenuKeyAction   Property

Applies To: Application

Explanation: Returns or sets the action taken when the alternate menu key is pressed (one of xlExcelMenus or xlLotusHelp). Read-write.

Syntax: `object.TransitionMenuKeyAction`

The **object** is the Application object and is required.

TransitionNavigKeys   Property

Applies To: Application

Explanation: True if alternate navigation keys are active. Read-write.

Syntax: `object.TransitionNavigKeys`

The **object** is the Application object and is required.

Trendlines   Method

Applies To: Series

Explanation: Returns a single trendline (a Trendline object, Syntax 1) or a collection of all the trendlines (a Trendline object, Syntax 2) for the series.

Syntax 1: `object.Trendlines(index)`

Syntax 2: `object.Trendlines`

The **object** is the Series object and is required.

The **index** argument is required for Syntax 1, and is the name or number of the trendline.

Underline   Property

Applies To: Font

Explanation: Returns or sets the type of underline applied to the font, as shown in the following table. Read-write.

Value	Meaning
xlNone	No underline.
xlSingle	Single underline.
xlDouble	Double underline.
xlSingleAccounting	Single accounting underline.
xlDoubleAccounting	Double accounting underline.

Syntax: `object.Underline`

The *object* is the Font object (ActiveCell.Font, for example) and is required.

Undo   Method

Applies To: Application

Explanation: Cancels the last user-interface action.

Syntax: `object.Undo`

The *object* is the Application object and is required.

Notes: This method can only be used to undo the last action taken by the user before running the macro, and it must be the first line in the macro. It cannot be used to undo Visual Basic commands.

Ungroup   Method

Applies To: DrawingObjects, GroupObject, GroupObjects, Range

Explanation: Range object: Promotes a range in an outline level (in other words, decreases its outline level). The specified range must be a row or column, or a range of rows or columns. If the range is in a pivot table, ungroups the items contained in the range.

GroupObject: Ungroups a group of drawing objects. Returns a DrawingObjects collection containing the objects in the group.

Syntax: `object.Ungroup`

The *object* is the object to which this method applies and is required.

Notes: If the active cell is in a field header of a parent field, all the groups in that field are ungrouped and the field is removed from the pivot table. When the last group in a parent field is ungrouped, the entire field is removed from the pivot table.

Union   Method

Applies To: Application

Explanation: Returns the union of two or more ranges.

Syntax: `object.Union(arg1, arg2,...)`

The Union method has the following object qualifier and named arguments:

The `object` is optional, and is the Application object.

The `arg1, arg2, ...` arguments are required and return the union of these ranges. At least two Range objects must be specified.

Unprotect   Method

Applies To: Chart, DialogSheet, Module, Workbook, Worksheet

Explanation: Removes protection from a sheet or workbook. This method has no effect if the sheet or workbook is not protected.

Syntax: `object.Unprotect(password)`

The Unprotect method has the following object qualifier and named arguments:

The `object` is the object to which this method applies and is required.

The `password` argument is optional, and is a string giving the case-sensitive password to use to unprotect the sheet or workbook. If the sheet or workbook is not protected with a password, this argument is ignored. If this argument is omitted and the sheet or workbook has a password, you will be prompted for the password.

Notes: If you forget the password, you cannot unprotect the sheet or workbook. It's a good idea to keep a list of your passwords and their corresponding document names in a safe place.

UpBars   Property

Applies To: ChartGroup

Explanation: Returns the UpBars on a line chart. Applies only to line charts. Read-only.

Syntax: `object.UpBars`

The `object` is the ChartGroup object and is required.

Update   Method

Applies To: OLEObject

Explanation: Updates the link.

Syntax: `object.Update`

The *object* is the OLEObject and is required.

UpdateFromFile   Method

Applies To: Workbook

Explanation: Updates a read-only workbook from the saved disk file version of the workbook if the disk version is more recent than the current copy of the workbook in memory. If the disk copy has not changed since the workbook was loaded, the in-memory copy of the workbook is not reloaded.

Syntax: `object.UpdateFromFile`

The *object* is the Workbook object and is required.

Notes: This method is useful when a workbook is opened as read-only by user A and read-write by user B. If user B saves a newer version of the workbook to disk while user A still has the workbook open, user A cannot get the updated copy without closing and reopening the workbook and losing view settings. The UpdateFromFile method updates the in-memory copy of the workbook from the disk file.

UpdateLink   Method

Applies To: Workbook

Explanation: Updates a Excel, DDE, or OLE link (or links).

Syntax: `object.UpdateLink(name, type)`

The UpdateLink method has the following object qualifier and named arguments:

The *object* is the Workbook object and is required.

The *name* argument is required, and specifies the name of the Excel or DDE/OLE link to update, as returned from the LinkSources method.

The *type* argument is optional, and specifies the link type. Can be either xlExcelLinks or xlOLELinks (also used for DDE links). xlExcelLinks if omitted.

UpdateRemoteReferences   Property

Applies To: Workbook

Explanation: True if remote references will be updated for the workbook. Read-write.

Syntax: `object.UpdateRemoteReferences`

The **object** is the Workbook object and is required.

UsableHeight   Property

Applies To: Application, Window

Explanation: Returns the height of the space that can be used by a window in the application window area (the window is not maximized). The height is returned in points (1/72 inch). Read-only.

Syntax: `object.UsableHeight`

The **object** is the Application or Window object and is required.

Notes: Adding a toolbar reduces the usable height.

UsableWidth   Property

Applies To: Application, Window

Explanation: Returns the width of the space that can be used by a window in the application window area (the window is not maximized). The width is returned in points (1/72 inch). Read-only.

Syntax: `object.UsableWidth`

The **object** is the Application or Window object and is required.

UsedRange   Property

Applies To: Worksheet

Explanation: Returns the Range of the worksheet that is used. Read-only.

Syntax: `object.UsedRange`

The **object** is the Worksheet object and is required.

UserName   Property

Applies To: Application

Explanation: Returns or sets the name of the current user (as a string). Read-write.

Syntax: `object.UserName`

The **object** is the Application object and is required.

UseStandardHeight   Property

Applies To: Range

Explanation: True if the row height of the Range object equals the standard height of the sheet. Read-write.

Syntax: `object.UseStandardHeight`

The **object** is the Range object and is required.

UseStandardWidth   Property

Applies To: Range

Explanation: True if the column width of the Range object equals the standard width of the sheet. Read-write.

Syntax: `object.UseStandardWidth`

The **object** is the Range object and is required.

Value   Property

Applies To: Application, Borders, CheckBox, CheckBoxes, DrawingObjects, DropDown, DropDowns, ListBox, ListBoxes, Name, OptionButton, OptionButtons, PivotField, PivotItem, PivotTable, Range, ScrollBar, ScrollBars, Spinner, Spinners, Style

Explanation: The meaning of the Value property depends on the object to which it is applied, as shown in the following table.

Object	Value
Application	Always returns "Microsoft Excel". Read-only.
Borders	Synonym for Borders.LineStyle.
CheckBox	Indicates check box status (xlOn, xlOff, or xlMixed).
DropDown, ListBox	Indicates the selected item in the list (the value is always between one and the number of items in the list). This method cannot be used with multi-select list boxes; use the Selected method instead.
Name	A string containing the formula that the name is defined to refer to, in A1-style notation, in the language of the macro, beginning with an equal sign. Read-write.
OptionButton	Indicates button status (one of xlOn, xlOff, or xlMixed).

Object	Value
PivotField	The name of the field in the pivot table.
PivotItem	The name of the item in the pivot table field.
PivotTable	The name of the pivot table.
Change the value of a cell	If the cell is empty, returns the value Empty. Use the IsEmpty function to test for this case. If the Range object contains more than one cell, returns an array of values. Use the IsArray function to test for this case.
ScrollBar	The position of the scroll box.
Spinner	A value between the minimum and maximum range limit.
Style	The name of the style.

Syntax: `object.Value`

The `object` is the object to which this property applies and is required.

Values   Property

Applies To: Scenario, Series

Explanation: Scenario object: Returns an array containing the current values for the scenario changing cells. Read-only.

Series object: Returns or sets a collection of all the values in the series. This can be a range on a worksheet or an array of constant values (but not a combination of both). See the examples for details. Read-write.

Syntax: `object.Values`

The `object` is the Scenario or Series object and is required.

VaryByCategories   Property

Applies To: ChartGroup

Explanation: If this property is True, Excel assigns a different color or pattern to each data marker. The chart must contain only one series. Read-write.

Syntax: `object.VaryByCategories`

The `object` is the ChartGroup object and is required.

continues

Verb   Method

Applies To: OLEObject

Explanation: Sends a verb to the server of the specified OLE object.

Syntax: `object.Verb(verb)`

The Verb method has the following object qualifier and named arguments:

The *object* is the OLEObject and is required.

The *verb* argument is optional, and is the verb that the server of the OLE Object should act upon. If this argument is omitted, the default verb is sent. The available verbs are determined by the object's source application. Typical verbs for an OLE 2 object are Open and Primary (represented by the xlOpen and xlPrimary constants).

Version   Property

Applies To: Application

Explanation: Returns the version number of Excel. Read-only.

Syntax: `object.Version`

The *object* is the Application object and is required.

VerticalAlignment   Property

Applies To: AxisTitle, Button, Buttons, ChartTitle, DataLabel, DataLabels, DrawingObjects, GroupObject, GroupObjects, Range, Style, TextBox, TextBoxes

Explanation: Returns or sets the vertical alignment of the object (can be one of xlBottom, xlCenter, xlDistributed, xlJustify, or xlTop). Read-write.

Syntax: `object.VerticalAlignment`

The *object* is the object to which this property applies and is required.

Notes: The xlDistributed alignment style works only in Asian versions of Excel.

Vertices   Property

Applies To: Drawing, DrawingObjects

Explanation: Returns or sets the vertices of a polygon or freehand drawing, as a two-dimensional array of vertex coordinates in points (1/72 inch) relative to the upper-left corner of cell A1. The x coordinate is in column one of the array, the y coordinate is in column two. Every drawing and polygon will have at least two vertices. Read-only.

Syntax: `object.Vertices`

The *object* is the object to which this property applies and is required.

Visible   Property

Applies To: Application, Arc, Arcs, Button, Buttons, Chart, ChartObject, ChartObjects, Charts, CheckBox, CheckBoxes, DialogSheet, DialogSheets, Drawing, DrawingObjects, Drawings, DropDown, DropDowns, EditBox, EditBoxes, GroupBox, GroupBoxes, GroupObject, GroupObjects, Label, Labels, Line, Lines, ListBox, ListBoxes, Module, Modules, Name, OLEObject, OLEObjects, OptionButton, OptionButtons, Oval, Ovals, Picture, Pictures, PivotItem, Rectangle, Rectangles, ScrollBar, ScrollBars, Sheets, Spinner, Spinners, TextBox, TextBoxes, Toolbar, Window, Worksheet, Worksheets

Explanation: True if the object is visible. For a chart, dialog sheet, module or worksheet, this property can be set to xlVeryHidden. This hides the object so that it can only be made visible by setting this property to True (the user cannot make the object visible). Read-write.

Syntax: *object*.`Visible`

The *object* is the object to which this property applies and is required.

Notes: The Visible property for a pivot item is True if the item is currently showing on the table.

If you set the Visible property for a name to False, the name will not appear in the Define Name dialog box.

VisibleFields   Method

Applies To: PivotTable

Explanation: Returns a single pivot field (a PivotField object, Syntax 1) or a collection of the visible pivot fields (a PivotFields object, Syntax 2). Visible pivot fields are showing as row, column, page or data fields. Read-only.

Syntax 1: *object*.`VisibleFields`(*index*)

Syntax 2: *object*.`VisibleFields`

The VisibleFields method has the following object qualifier and named arguments:

The *object* is the PivotTable object and is required.

The *index* argument is required for Syntax 1, and is the name or number of the pivot field to return (can be an array to specify more than one).

VisibleItems   Method

Applies To: PivotField

Explanation: Returns one visible pivot item (a PivotItem object, Syntax 1) or a collection of all the visible pivot items (a PivotItems object, Syntax 2) in the specified field. Read-only.

Syntax 1: *object*.`VisibleItems`(*index*)

Syntax 2: *object*.`VisibleItems`

The VisibleItems method has the following object qualifier and named arguments:

The *object* is the PivotField object and is required.

The *index* argument is required for Syntax 1, and is the number or name of the pivot item to return (can be an array to specify more than one).

VisibleRange   Property

Applies To: Pane, Window

Explanation: Returns the Range of cells that are visible in the window or pane. If a column or row is partially visible, it is included in the range. Read-only.

Syntax: *object*`.VisibleRange`

The *object* is the Pane or Window object and is required.

Volatile   Method

Applies To: Application

Explanation: Marks a user-defined function as volatile. A volatile function must be recalculated whenever calculation occurs in any cells of the worksheet. A non-volatile function is recalculated only when the input variables change. This method has no effect if it is not inside a user-defined function used to calculate a worksheet cell.

Syntax: *object*`.Volatile(`*volatile*`)`

The Volatile method has the following object qualifier and named arguments:

The *object* is the Application object and is required.

The *volatile* argument is optional. If True or omitted, the function is marked as volatile. If False, the function is marked as non-volatile.

Wait   Method

Applies To: Application

Explanation: Pauses a running macro until a specified time is reached.

Caution: The Wait method suspends all Microsoft Excel activity and may prevent you from performing other operations on your computer. Background processes, such as printing and recalculation, are continued.

Syntax: *object*`.Wait(`*time*`)`

The Wait method has the following object qualifier and named arguments:

The *object* is the Application object and is required.

The *time* argument is required, and is the time you want the macro to resume, in Excel date format.

Walls   Property

Applies To: Chart

Explanation: Returns the Walls of the 3D chart. Read-only.

Syntax: `object.Walls`

The *object* is the Chart object and is required.

WallsAndGridlines2D   Property

Applies To: Chart

Explanation: True if gridlines are drawn in 2D on a 3D chart. Read-write.

Syntax: `object.WallsAndGridlines2D`

The *object* is the Chart object and is required.

Weight   Property

Applies To: Border, Borders

Explanation: Returns or sets the the weight of the border (one of xlHairline, xlThin, xlMedium, or xlThick). Read-write.

Syntax: `object.Weight`

The *object* is the Border or Borders object and is required.

While…Wend   Statement

Explanation: Executes a series of statements as long as a given condition is True.

Syntax: `While (condition, statements) Wend`

The While…Wend statement syntax has these parts:

Part	Description
`condition`	Numeric or string expression that evaluates to True or False.
`statements`	One or more statements executed while condition is True.

Notes: If *condition* is True, all statements in **statements** are executed until the Wend statement is encountered. Control then returns to the While statement and condition is again checked. If *condition* is still True, the process is repeated. If it is not True, execution resumes with the statement following the Wend statement. While...Wend loops can be nested to any level. Each Wend matches the most recent While.

Caution: Do not branch into the body of a While...Wend loop without executing the While statement. Doing so may cause run-time errors or other problems that are difficult to locate.

Tip: The Do...Loop statement provides a more structured and flexible way to perform looping.

Width   Property

Applies To: Application, Arc, Arcs, Button, Buttons, ChartArea, ChartObject, ChartObjects, CheckBox, CheckBoxes, DialogFrame, Drawing, DrawingObjects, Drawings, DropDown, DropDowns, EditBox, EditBoxes, GroupBox, GroupBoxes, GroupObject, GroupObjects, Label, Labels, Legend, Line, Lines, ListBox, ListBoxes, OLEObject, OLEObjects, OptionButton, OptionButtons, Oval, Ovals, Picture, Pictures, PlotArea, Range, Rectangle, Rectangles, ScrollBar, ScrollBars, Spinner, Spinners, TextBox, TextBoxes, Toolbar, ToolbarButton, Window

Explanation: Returns or sets an object's width in points (1/72 inch). Read-write for all objects, except Range, which is read-only.

Syntax: *object*.Width

The *object* is the object this property applies to and is required.

Notes: The Width property has several different meanings, depending on the object to which it is applied.

Object	Description
Application	The distance from the left edge of the application window to the right edge of the application window.
Range	The width of the range.
Toolbar	The width of the toolbar. When you set the width, Microsoft Excel snaps both the width and the height to match the nearest allowable size.
Window	The width of the window. Use the UsableWidth property to determine the maximum size for the window. You cannot set this property if the window is maximized or minimized. Use the WindowState property to determine the window state.

Object	Description
Arc, Button, ChartArea, CheckBox, DialogFrame, Drawing, DrawingObjects, DropDown, EditBox, GroupBox, GroupObject, Label, Legend, Line, ListBox, OLEObject, OptionButton, Oval, Picture, PlotArea, Rectangle, ScrollBar, Spinner, TextBox, ToolbarButton, Window	The width of the object.

On the Macintosh, Application.Width is always equal to the total width of the screen, in points. Setting this value to any other value will have no effect.

In Windows, if the window is minimized, Application.Width is read-only and returns the width of the icon.

You can use negative numbers to set the Height and Width properties of the following drawing objects: Arc, Button, CheckBox, Drawing, DropDown, EditBox, GroupBox, GroupObject, Label, Line, ListBox, OLEObject, OptionButton, Oval, Picture, Rectangle, ScrollBar, Spinner, and TextBox. This causes the object to reflect or translate (the behavior depends on the object), after which the Top and Left properties change to describe the new position. The Height and Width properties always return positive numbers.

WindowNumber   Property

Applies To: Window

Explanation: Returns the window number. For example, a window entitled "BOOK1.XLS:2" has a window number of two. Most windows have a window number of one. Read-only.

Syntax: `object.WindowNumber`

The `object` is the Window object and is required.

Notes: The window number is not the same as the window Index, which is the position of the window within the Windows collection.

Windows   Method

Applies To: Application, Workbook

Explanation: Returns a single window (a Window object, Syntax 1) or a collection of windows (the Windows object, Syntax 2). Read-only.

Syntax 1: `object.Windows(index)`

Syntax 2: `object.Windows`

The Windows method has the following object qualifier and named arguments:

The `object` is optional, and is the Application or Workbook containing the windows.

The `index` argument is required for Syntax 1, and is the name or number of the window.

Notes: Syntax 2 returns a collection of both visible and hidden windows.

Windows   Object

Explanation: A collection of Window objects.

WindowState   Property

Applies To: Application, Window

Explanation: Returns or sets the state of the window, as shown in the following table. Read-write.

Value	Meaning
xlNormal	Window is not maximized or minimized.
lMaximized	Window is maximized (Windows only). Maximizing a window maximizes all windows on the Excel desktop.
xlMinimized	Window is minimized (Windows only).

Syntax: `object.WindowState`

The `object` is the Application or Window object and is required.

WindowsForPens   Property

Applies To: Application

Explanation: True if the computer is running under Windows for Pen Computing. Read-only.

Syntax: `object.WindowsForPens`

The **object** is the Application object and is required.

With   Statement

Explanation: Executes a series of statements on a single object or a user-defined type.

Syntax: `With object.statements End With`

The With statement syntax has these parts:

Part	Description
object	Name of an object or a user-defined type.
statements	One or more statements to be executed on object.

Notes: The With statement allows you to perform a series of statements on a specified object without requalifying the name of the object. For example, if you have a number of different properties to change on a single object, it is more convenient to place the property assignment statements within the With control structure, referring to the object once instead of referring to it with each property assignment. The following example illustrates use of the With statement to assign values to several properties of the same object.

```
With MyLabel
.Height = 2000
.Width = 2000
.Caption = "This is MyLabel"
End With
```

You can nest With statements by placing one With loop within another. Each object must be unique.

Related Topics: Do...Loop Statement, While...Wend Statement

Workbook   Object

Explanation: A workbook in Excel.

Workbooks   Method

Applies To: Application

Explanation: Returns a single workbook (a Workbook object, Syntax 1) or a collection of workbooks (the Workbooks object, Syntax 2). Read-only.

Syntax 1: `object.Workbooks(index)`

Syntax 2: `object.Workbooks`

The Workbooks method has the following object qualifier and named arguments:

The `object` is optional, and is the Application containing the workbooks.

The `index` is required for Syntax 1, and is the name or number of the workbook.

Notes: The collection returned by Syntax 2 of the Workbooks method does not include open add-ins, which are a special kind of hidden workbook.

You can, however, return a single open add-in if you know the file name.

Workbooks   Object

Explanation: A collection of Workbook objects.

Worksheet   Object

Explanation: A worksheet in a workbook. A worksheet can also be a Excel version 4 macro sheet, or Excel version 4 international.

Worksheet   Property

Applies To: Range

Explanation: Returns the Worksheet containing the specified range. Read-only.

Syntax: `object.Worksheet`

The `object` is the the worksheet containing this range and is required.

Worksheets   Method

Applies To: Application, Workbook

Explanation: Returns a worksheet (a Worksheet object, Syntax 1) or a collection of all worksheets (a Worksheets object, Syntax 2) in the workbook. Read-only.

Syntax 1: `object.Worksheets(index)`

Syntax 2: `object.Worksheets`

The Worksheets method has the following object qualifier and named arguments:

The `object` is optional for Application, required for Workbook; it is the object that contains worksheets.

The `index` argument is required for Syntax 1, and is the name or number of the worksheet to return.

Notes: This method returns worksheets with the Type property equal to xlWorksheet, not xlExcel4MacroSheet or xlExcel4IntlMacroSheet; use the Excel4MacroSheets method or the Excel4IntlMacroSheets method to return those types.

Using this method with no object qualifier is a shortcut for ActiveWorkbook.Worksheets.

Worksheets   Object

Explanation: A collection of Worksheet objects.

WrapText   Property

Applies To: Range, Style

Explanation: True if Excel wraps the text in the object. Read-write.

Syntax: *object*.WrapText

The *object* is the Range or Style object and is required.

Notes: Excel changes the row height of the range, if necessary, to display the text in the range.

Write #   Statement

Explanation: Writes raw data to a sequential file.

Syntax: Write #(*filenumber*,*outputlist*)

The Write statement syntax has these parts:

Part	Description
filenumber	Any valid file number.
outputlist	One or more comma-delimited numeric or string expressions to write to a file.

Notes: If you omit outputlist and include a comma after filenumber, a blank line prints to the file. Multiple expressions can be separated with a space, a semicolon, or a comma. A space has the same effect as a semicolon.

When Write # is used to output data to a file, several universal assumptions are followed so the data can always be read and correctly interpreted using Input #, regardless of locale:

✔ Numeric data is always output using the period (.) as the decimal separator.

✔ For Boolean data, either #TRUE# or #FALSE# is printed. The True and False keywords are not translated, regardless of locale.

✔ Date data is written to the file using the universal date format. When either the date or the time component is missing or zero, only the provided part gets written to the file.

✔ Nothing is written to the file if outputlist data is Empty. However, for Null data, #NULL# is output.

✔ For error data, the output appears as #ERROR errorcode#. The Error keyword is not translated, regardless of locale.

Unlike the Print # statement, the Write # statement inserts commas between items and quotation marks around strings as they are written to the file. You don't have to put explicit delimiters in the list. Write # inserts a newline character (carriage return or carriage return-linefeed) after it has written the final character in outputlist to the file.

Related Topics: Input # Statement, Open Statement, Print # Statement

WriteReserved   Property

Applies To: Workbook

Explanation: True if the workbook is write reserved. Read-only.

Syntax: `object.WriteReserved`

The `object` is the Workbook object and is required.

Notes: Use the SaveAs to set this property.

WriteReservedBy   Property

Applies To: Workbook

Explanation: Returns a string that names the user with current write permission for the workbook. Read-only.

Syntax: `object.WriteReservedBy`

The `object` is the Workbook object and is required.

XValues   Property

Applies To: Series

Explanation: Returns or sets an array of the x values of the series on an XY scatter chart. The XValues property can be set to a range on a worksheet or an array of values, but it may not be a combination of both. Read-write.

Syntax: `object.XValues`

The *object* is the Series object and is required.

XYGroups   Method

Applies To: Chart

Explanation: On a 2D chart, returns a single scatter chart group (a ChartGroup object, Syntax 1), or a collection of the scatter chart groups (a ChartGroups collection, Syntax 2).

Syntax 1: `object.XYGroups(index)`

Syntax 2: `object.XYGroups`

The XYGroups method has the following object qualifier and named arguments:

The *object* is the Chart object and is required.

The *index* argument is required for Syntax 1, and specifies the chart group.

Year   Function

Explanation: Returns a whole number representing the year.

Syntax: `Year(date)`

The *date* argument named argument is limited to a date or numbers and strings, in any combination, that can represent a date. If *date* contains no valid data, Null is returned.

Related Topics: Date Function, Date Statement, Day Function, Month Function, Now Function, Weekday Function,

Zoom   Property

Applies To: PageSetup, Window

Explanation: PageSetup object: Returns or sets a percentage to scale the worksheet for printing, between 10 and 400 percent. Read-write.

If this property is False, the FitToPagesWide and FitToPagesTall properties control how the worksheet is scaled.

Window object: Returns or sets the display size of the window, in percent (100 means show at normal size; 200 means the window is double size, etc.).

The property can also be set to True to set the window size to fit the current selection.

Syntax: `object.Zoom`

The *object* is the PageSetup or Window object and is required.

Notes: PageSetup object: This property applies only to worksheets.

All scaling retains the aspect ratio of the original document.

Window object: This function will only affect the sheet that is currently active in the window. To use this property on other sheets, you must first activate them.

ZOrder Property

Applies To: Arc, Arcs, Button, Buttons, ChartObject, ChartObjects, CheckBox, CheckBoxes, Drawing, DrawingObjects, Drawings, DropDown, DropDowns, EditBox, EditBoxes, GroupBox, GroupBoxes, GroupObject, GroupObjects, Label, Labels, Line, Lines, ListBox, ListBoxes, OLEObject, OLEObjects, OptionButton, OptionButtons, Oval, Ovals, Picture, Pictures, Rectangle, Rectangles, ScrollBar, ScrollBars, Spinner, Spinners, TextBox, TextBoxes

Explanation: Returns the z-order position of the object. Read-only.

Syntax: `object.ZOrder`

The **`object`** is the object to which this property applies and is required.

Notes: For any collection of objects, the object at the back of the z-order is collection(1), and the object at the front of the z-order is collection(collection.count). For example, if there are three ovals on the active sheet, the oval at the back of the z-order is ActiveSheet.Ovals(1), and the oval at the front of the z-order is ActiveSheet.Ovals(ActiveSheet.Ovals.Count).

Related Topics: BringToFront Method, SendToBack Method

INDEX

INDEX

INDEX

INDEX

INDEX

INDEX

INDEX

INDEX

INDEX

INDEX

INDEX

INDEX

INDEX

INDEX

INDEX

INDEX

INDEX

INDEX

INDEX

INDEX

INDEX

INDEX

INDEX

INDEX

INDEX

INDEX

INDEX

THE BAARNS UTILITIES™

Productivity Enhancements for Microsoft© Excel

Productivity is everything in today's business environment. The Baarns Utilities make your everyday Microsoft Excel activities easier and give you power user status without the power user learning curve. Included with this book is version 1 of The Baarns Utilities. Version 1 of the Utilities was written for Excel 4.0. To help you be more productive and organized, we have added even more tools to version 5 of The Baarns Utilities, which take advantage of the features in the new Excel 5.0. Upgrade to version 5 for just $19.95*.

Upgrade for just $19.95!

Here's what the experts say...

I found Baarns Utilities to be rock solid, providing fine error handling. The 13 tools are so tightly integrated into Excel that you might think you were actually using new features in Excel.

INFO WORLD

Excel is as loaded with features as Windows spreadsheets get, but The Baarns Utilities takes Excel to even greater heights. It's a must-have collection of Excel tools...this collection of utilities is a number cruncher's dream.

PC Computing

If you spend a lot of time working in Excel, you'll appreciate the nifty set of shortcut tools and gizmos provided by The Baarns Utilities.

PC WORLD

Version 5 Features include:

Baarns File Express allows you to create a file group and then add existing files to that group. These files can be found all over your hard drive or multiple drives, including network drives.

Baarns Path Manager will let you assign long names to custom "paths" for finding or saving files. Now FILE OPEN and FILE · SAVE can consistently and easily be directed to your desired destination.

Baarns Save Now works in conjunction with Baarns AutoSave, allowing you to have a tool to activate the AutoSave at any time you choose. Also, it will access your backup setting of the AutoSave even if AutoSave itself is turned off.

Baarns Case Master quickly and easily changes the text case on selected cells to UPPER, lower or Proper text in one easy step.

Baarns Paste Date & Time inserts the date and/or time into your Microsoft Excel document.

Baarns Text-O-Matic will help you add or delete text to the front or back of selected cells.

Baarns Startup will start Microsoft Excel the way you want to see it. Control how your first document is displayed and its size when opened.

Baarns Open allows you to open your files based on your starting document size preferences in Baarns Startup.

Baarns Phone Dialer will dial your phone for you when connected to your computer if you have a modem.

Hundreds of upgrades to the original thirteen utilities along with completely new on-line help.

Upgrade to version 5 for just $19.95 to experience the ultimate worksheet workout!

Coming to a VCR near you...

The Baarns Consulting Group, Inc. proudly presents...

Don Baarns on Excel 5.0

One of the world's leading Excel experts, Don Baarns will show you how to become more productive while working in Excel 5.0. These powerful fast-paced videos contain more bang for the buck than any other presentation on Excel. Get started on the road to becoming a true Excel power-user.

Save Over $10,000

Corporations all over the world pay tens of thousands of dollars to have the experts at Baarns Consulting Group, Inc. train everyone from secretaries to executives to developers. Find out what they learn from the expert at a fraction of the cost. Mr. Baarns has taught Excel classes to groups of 2 to 2000, and is the most qualified person to bring to you the hundreds of tips and tricks in Excel. ***Bring Don Baarns into your home or office to teach you about Excel 5.0.*** This Video series will be the best investment you will make to become super-productive quickly. Send for more information today on our complete video library, including Excel, Word, Access, Windows and more!

❑ Send me The Baarns Utilities upgrade for $19.95.*
❑ Send me information about the best Excel Videos ever.* *Available Spring 1994.*

Name _____ __ __

Address _____

_____

City _____ State _____ Zip _____

Telephone _____ FAX _____

Please bill my:

❑ VISA   Card Number _____

❑ MasterCard   Exp. Date _____

❑ American Express Signature _____

❑ Check enclosed*

* Please include $6.50 shipping and handling in the US and $1.65 tax in California. Videos to ship Spring 1994.
* Please include your FAX number for prompt service. Video pricing is per video, there are several in the series.

See reverse side for address and phone numbers.

About **Don Baarns** and **Baarns Consulting Group, Inc.**

Don Baarns has been a guest speaker at the MS Excel Developers Conference, the Windows & OS/2 Conference, the Microsoft Corporate Developer Tools Conference & Exposition, and many other industry events.

Mr. Baarns has taught the three-hour Advanced Macros training session at the Microsoft Developers' Tools Conference and has lectured on several Advanced Microsoft Excel subjects at the Microsoft Tech-Ed conferences. In addition, he teaches classes on advanced techniques for using Excel as a front-end to SQL Server and serves on a number of panels addressing advanced development issues.

Don Baarns has contributed to the advanced macro content in Ron Person's book, *Excel Tips, Tricks and Traps* (Que Corp., 1989), and has been quoted in *PC Magazine, PC Week, INFO World, Computer Network Reseller,* and featured on the television series "Computer Chronicles."

The Baarns Consulting Group develops worldwide and has extensive experience in LAN development projects using Microsoft Excel, Microsoft Word for Windows and Microsoft Visual Basic as front ends to SQL Server and other DBMs.

Baarns Consulting Group, Inc.
12807 Borden Avenue
Sylmar, CA 91342

Orders	1-800-377-9235
Orders	1-818-364-6148
FAX Orders	1-818-367-9673

Please mail this form to:

Baarns Consulting Group, Inc.
12807 Borden Avenue
Sylmar, CA 91342

WANT MORE INFORMATION?

CHECK OUT THESE RELATED TITLES:

	QTY	PRICE	TOTAL
Ultimate Windows 3.1. If you're looking for the most up-to-date and comprehensive reference on Windows 3.1, your search is over! Loaded with tips, features, bug-fixes—plus coverage of sound boards, CD-ROMs, and video—you'll find only the latest and most relevant information available. Includes a hypertext application with "2000 Windows Tips." ISBN: 1-56205-125-3.	____	$39.95	_____
Inside Windows NT. A complete tutorial and reference to organizing and managing multiple tasks and programs in Winows NT! This book focuses on integration capabilities and networking options of Windows NT—an inside look at the operating environment of the future! ISBN: 1-56205-124-5.	____	$39.95	_____
Maximizing Windows 3.1. *PC Magazine* quotes, "**Maximizing Windows 3.1** is among the best choices for serious users who need in-depth material." This complete guide provides expert tips, secrets and performance advice. Includes two disks with over six megabytes of Windows shareware. ISBN: 1-56205-044-3.	____	$39.95	_____
Integrating Windows Applications. This no-nonsense, practical guide to total application integration, for the intermediate and advanced user, provides business-oriented examples with emphasis on fast learning. Free disk includes examples, database files, and macros. ISBN: 1-56205-083-4.	____	$34.95	_____

Name _____

Company _____

Address _____

City _____ State ____ ZIP _____

Phone _____ Fax _____

☐ Check Enclosed ☐ VISA ☐ MasterCard

Card #_____Exp. Date _____

Signature _____

Prices are subject to change. Call for availability and pricing information on latest editions.

Subtotal _____

Shipping _____

$4.00 for the first book and $1.75 for each additional book.

Tax _____

Indiana residents add 5% sales tax.

Total _____

New Riders Publishing 201 West 103rd Street • Indianapolis, Indiana 46290 USA

Orders/Customer Service: 1-800-541-6789
Fax: 1-800-448-3804

Inside Excel 5
for Windows
REGISTRATION CARD

Fill out this card to receive information about future Excel books and other New Riders titles!

Name _____ **Title** _____

Company _____

Address _____

City/State/ZIP _____

I bought this book because: _____

_____

I purchased this book from:

☐ A bookstore (Name _____)

☐ A software or electronics store (Name _____)

☐ A mail order (Name of Catalog _____)

I purchase this many computer books each year:

☐ 1–5   ☐ 6 or more

I currently use these applications: _____

_____

_____

_____

I found these chapters to be the most informative: _____

_____

I found these chapters to be the least informative: _____

_____

Additional comments: _____

_____

☐ I would like to see my name in print! You may use my name and quote me in future New Riders products and promotions. My daytime phone number is:_____

New Riders Publishing 201 West 103rd Street • Indianapolis, Indiana 46290 USA

Fold Here
- -

New Riders Publishing
201 West 103rd Street
Indianapolis, Indiana 46290
USA

OPERATING SYSTEMS

INSIDE MS-DOS 6.2, SECOND EDITION

MARK MINASI

A complete tutorial and reference!

MS-DOS 6

ISBN: 1-56205-132-6

$39.95 USA

DOS FOR NON-NERDS

MICHAEL GROH

Understanding this popular operating system is easy with this humorous, step-by-step tutorial.

Through DOS 6.0

ISBN: 1-56205-151-2

$18.95 USA

INSIDE SCO UNIX

STEVE GLINES, PETER SPICER, BEN HUNSBERGER, & KAREN WHITE

Everything users need to know to use the UNIX operating system for everyday tasks.

SCO Xenix 286, SCO Xenix 386, SCO UNIX/System V 386

ISBN: 1-56205-028-1

$29.95 USA

INSIDE SOLARIS SunOS

KARLA SAARI KITALONG, STEVEN R. LEE, & PAUL MARZIN

Comprehensive tutorial and reference to SunOS!

SunOS, Sun's version of UNIX for the SPARC workstation, version 2.0

ISBN: 1-56205-032-X

$29.95 USA

GRAPHICS TITLES

INSIDE CORELDRAW! 4.0, SPECIAL EDITION

DANIEL GRAY

An updated version of the #1 best-selling tutorial on CorelDRAW!

CorelDRAW! 4.0
ISBN: 1-56205-164-4
$34.95 USA

CORELDRAW! SPECIAL EFFECTS

NEW RIDERS PUBLISHING

An inside look at award-winning techniques from professional CorelDRAW! designers.

CorelDRAW! 4.0
ISBN: 1-56205-123-7
$39.95 USA

CORELDRAW! NOW!

RICHARD FELDMAN

The hands-on tutorial for users who want practical information now!
CorelDRAW! 4.0
ISBN: 1-56205-131-8
$21.95 USA

INSIDE CORELDRAW! FOURTH EDITION

DANIEL GRAY

The popular tutorial approach to learning CorelDRAW!...with complete coverage of version 3.0!

CorelDRAW! 3.0
ISBN: 1-56205-106-7
$24.95 USA

GO AHEAD. PLUG YOURSELF INTO PRENTICE HALL COMPUTER PUBLISHING.

Introducing the PHCP Forum on CompuServe®

Yes, it's true. Now, you can have CompuServe access to the same professional, friendly folks who have made computers easier for years. On the PHCP Forum, you'll find additional information on the topics covered by every PHCP imprint—including Que, Sams Publishing, New Riders Publishing, Alpha Books, Brady Books, Hayden Books, and Adobe Press. In addition, you'll be able to receive technical support and disk updates for the software produced by Que Software and Paramount Interactive, a division of the Paramount Technology Group. It's a great way to supplement the best information in the business.

WHAT CAN YOU DO ON THE PHCP FORUM?

Play an important role in the publishing process—and make our books better while you make your work easier:

■ Leave messages and ask questions about PHCP books and software—you're guaranteed a response within 24 hours

■ Download helpful tips and software to help you get the most out of your computer

■ Contact authors of your favorite PHCP books through electronic mail

■ Present your own book ideas

■ Keep up to date on all the latest books available from each of PHCP's exciting imprints

JOIN NOW AND GET A FREE COMPUSERVE STARTER KIT!

To receive your free CompuServe Introductory Membership, call toll-free, **1-800-848-8199** and ask for representative **#K597**. The Starter Kit Includes:

■ Personal ID number and password

■ $15 credit on the system

■ Subscription to CompuServe Magazine

HERE'S HOW TO PLUG INTO PHCP:

Once on the CompuServe System, type any of these phrases to access the PHCP Forum:

GO PHCP   **GO BRADY**
GO QUEBOOKS   **GO HAYDEN**
GO SAMS   **GO QUESOFT**
GO NEWRIDERS   **GO PARAMOUNTINTER**
GO ALPHA

Once you're on the CompuServe Information Service, be sure to take advantage of all of CompuServe's resources. CompuServe is home to more than 1,700 products and services—plus it has over 1.5 million members worldwide. You'll find valuable online reference materials, travel and investor services, electronic mail, weather updates, leisure-time games and hassle-free shopping (no jam-packed parking lots or crowded stores).

Seek out the hundreds of other forums that populate CompuServe. Covering diverse topics such as pet care, rock music, cooking, and political issues, you're sure to find others with the same concerns as you—and expand your knowledge at the same time.